THE WORLD'S TOP
500
AIRPORTS

THE WORLD'S TOP
500
AIRPORTS

DAVID WRAGG

A catalogue record for this book is
available from the British Library

Published by Haynes Publishing,
Sparkford, Yeovil, Somerset BA22 7JJ, UK

Tel: 01963 442030 Fax: 01963 440001
Int. tel: +44 1963 442030
Int. fax: +44 1963 440001
E-mail: sales@haynes.co.uk
Website: www.haynes.co.uk

ISBN 978 184425 632 7

Library of Congress control no. 2009928024

Haynes North America, Inc.,
861 Lawrence Drive, Newbury Park,
California 91320, USA

Layout by G&M Designs Limited,
Raunds, Northamptonshire
Printed and bound in Great Britain

Contents

Preface   6

Introduction   7

Notes   10

THE WORLD'S TOP 500 AIRPORTS BY   11
COUNTRY AND PASSENGER NUMBERS

Colour plates section   225–256

Appendix I   The world's top 500 airports by passengers handled   433

Appendix II   The world's top 500 airports by cargo handled   439

Appendix III   The world's top 500 airports by aircraft movements   445

Glossary   451

Airports: listed alphabetically   453

IATA codes: listed alphabetically   459

Preface

Anyone attempting to list the world's airports in order of importance will find many statistics to choose from, but for dependable comparisons the most significant are the throughput of passengers, the tonnage of cargo handled, and the number of aircraft movements.

Subject to one's point of interest any one of these could be used, but for the purposes of this book the number of passengers handled has been selected as the main yardstick because this is closest to the travelling public's perception of an airport's status. The media will also tend to rate an airport by its number of passengers rather than the volume of cargo handled (which is largely of interest only to shippers), and there are cases where the number of aircraft movements can be misleading. For example Brighton, otherwise known as Shoreham and one of the first airports to have its own railway station in the late 1930s, has so many training flights and business and private aircraft movements that on this score alone it ranks 325 worldwide, yet by any other measure it does not make it into the top 500.

However, this is not to disparage Shoreham, which with the right train service could challenge Southampton for short distance flights to the Channel Islands and northern France, or even relieve the pressure on London Gatwick for flights to destinations such as Manchester, Birmingham or Cardiff.

Nevertheless, to allow quick comparisons, in the appendices you will find separate top-500 listings ranked in each case by one of the three main measures mentioned above. In the body of the book airports are grouped by country, and within each country they are listed in descending order of importance – that is the ones with the greatest annual throughput of passengers are shown first.

I am very grateful to Andrew Randall of Aerad for the airport charts and to Nancy Gautier of ACI for the use of their airport statistics for the year 2007. Without their help this would have been an even more difficult book to compile.

David Wragg, Edinburgh
November 2009

Introduction

Airports – love them or hate them?

It goes without saying that flying is a popular means of travel, and in some regions of the world it is really the only means. In Brazil and Colombia, for instance, large areas of dense jungle and mountain ranges can only be traversed by air, and in low population density countries such as Iceland, or the heavily-indented coastline of Norway, getting from one place to another fairly quickly would be impossible without air transport.

Yet, many people hate airports. From the passenger's point of view the congestion and delay born of anti-terrorist procedures (on top of the normal check-in process) have made the airport experience a less than happy one for almost everyone. There is hardly an airport terminal in the world that can comfortably accommodate the large backlogs of both people and baggage that so frequently build up while passengers wait to undergo security screening.

Add to this the high cost of buying even modest refreshments in many airports, and the proliferation of retail outlets taking up precious space, and there is little wonder that people find their time spent at airports is over-long, over-priced, and over-crowded.

Then there are those who live near airports and have to put up with the inevitable noise and the disruption caused by expansion. One theme that recurs throughout this book is that so many airports are regarded as bad neighbours and have restrictions placed on their operations, with either a curfew overnight, or a limitation of the number of aircraft movements or, as at Belfast City and Bournemouth, the number of passengers that can be carried annually.

Aircraft on approach are often so low that, as well as increased noise, their wake vortices can damage light structures or loosen roof tiles, not to mention the vexed question of environmental pollution. Despite this, housing around airports is never the cheapest to buy. Airport workers need them, and there is always a ready market. There are jobs for up to 100,000 people at a major airport such as London Heathrow, including those working off the airport and supplying its needs and those of the airlines. Indeed, when a major airport goes into decline, so too does the area around it.

Nevertheless, the arguments go on and they are no longer confined to Western Europe, North America, or the eastern side of Australia, but occur in many other parts of the world where there is sufficient prosperity for people to have concerns above those of just obtaining the basic necessities of life.

So, where should an airport go?

On shore or off shore?

The experience of trying to expand airports in Japan has been sufficiently traumatic for the authorities, and for those attempting to run airports, that the country is building its new airports on reclaimed land whenever possible. This is not the perfect solution as attempts to expand coastal airports on to reclaimed land elsewhere have run into objections over the impact on wildlife, while as the US Airways A320 Hudson River incident early in 2009 has shown, there is also concern about the impact *of* wildlife.

The truth is that airports offshore are not always the answer, and when they are, it is often one of desperation. Hong Kong had no choice, nor did Osaka. In the United Kingdom there were many who argued that Foulness, on the coast of Essex, the northern side of the Thames Estuary, would be an ideal site for what was then seen as London's third airport. Yet, this was an area that saw large numbers of migrating birds crossing it, and the same goes for the latest idea that instead of building a third runway at London's Heathrow Airport, there should be an estuary airport on the southern side of the Thames. Offshore airports also pose problems with the need for new roads and railways to link them to centres of population.

Some argue that making better use of provincial airports would solve the problem, but in fact it would ease it rather than solve it. There remains a need for an airport with as large a number of destinations as possible, and if it also allows as many connections as possible, so much the better. While London is surrounded by airports, with five that can justifiably claim to be a 'London airport' (Heathrow, Gatwick, Stansted, Luton, and City), Heathrow is the one with the most destinations and the best connections, but only for as long as it can cope. Already, many airports in the British Isles have lost their flights to Heathrow, forcing passengers to make long and tedious journeys by road or rail, or instead fly via Amsterdam or Paris. The fact that Heathrow has just two runways, and Gatwick, London's second airport, just one, is nothing to be proud of, especially when Atlanta has six, as has Amsterdam's Schiphol, while Paris Charles de Gaulle has four. There are also safety considerations, as mixing large and small airliners is inherently dangerous and requires careful monitoring of separation distances, which is counterproductive.

Having air services spread around five airports is a mixed blessing. It does provide flexibility if one airport is closed, but having more than one runway at the second, third, and fourth London airports would help to solve that problem. The main advantage with a large and heavily built-up metropolis is that the five airports may have overlapping markets, but many of them have their own segment of the Greater London area. For this reason, those who argued that, once Stansted opened, it should handle charter flights and Gatwick join Heathrow in being a scheduled service airport, were wrong. Clearly, they had never tried to cross from the south of London to the north with luggage and children or an elderly relative.

In Scotland, many believe that combining Edinburgh and Glasgow into one airport for central Scotland would ensure more flights and a broader spread of destinations. They are right, but at the cost of inconveniencing those living to the west of Glasgow and those living to the east of Edinburgh. On the other hand, developing Edinburgh as a hub for flights from Scandinavia and Northern Europe, with good onward transatlantic connections could be an opportunity waiting to be seized, and that would certainly increase the number of destinations served from Scotland.

The truth is that airports are a fact of life and cannot be 'un-invented'. It is a sad fact that they involve upheaval, especially when it affects people's homes, but the railways are not the panacea that many like to believe, and indeed railway history teaches us that they could be just as disruptive and unfriendly, especially when it came to building the major London termini. For example, even extending the line from Clapham Junction to Waterloo on arches still required more than 700 houses to be demolished in 1847–48 for a route with far fewer tracks than today. This was nothing compared to St Pancras, which saw 10,000 people lose their homes, while Liverpool Street required 7,000 people to move, despite approaching the City of London by tunnel. Even the dead were not immune, with more than 7,000 corpses having to be removed from a graveyard when the line was extended from London Bridge to Charing Cross, and St Pancras had also been reached through a graveyard.

There is nothing new, and nothing without some inconvenience. With a growing population and increasing mobility, to do nothing is not an option. Unfortunately, modern politicians shirk harsh decisions.

What's in a name?

If one lives near an airport, one usually hears people simply refer to 'the airport'. That, of course, is when one lives in a one-airport community. Many cities, and not just the capital cities, have more than one airport, and in some places, the airport for the next community might be more convenient for many travellers. The days when people talked about 'London Airport' or 'New York Airport' are gone. Today, one has to be more specific, or you might get off the airliner and find that your welcoming party is many miles away.

So, it makes sense to call an airport after the neighbourhood in which it is placed, or which is closest. Does it make sense to go beyond this? Adding 'international' to the name of an airport is usually superfluous in smaller countries, especially when it is the only airport and all flights are international. The habit may have started because of the practice in some countries, especially the United States, of designating airports as international once they have customs and immigration facilities. Elsewhere, there are airports of 'national standard' and 'international standard', which somehow suggests that the national runway may have a few potholes or the lighting be a few light bulbs short. In fact, appending 'international' to the title of an airport has become something of a status symbol and is indicative of an inferiority complex. Obviously it is important that would-be travellers, and others, such as schedulers, know the difference between Belfast City and Belfast International, but what was wrong with Aldergrove for the latter? One could have understood it if Nutts Corner were still the city's main airport – people can be so unkind sometimes.

Then there is the practice of naming an airport after a prominent figure. This is the current fashion, with one airport in the British Isles named after a pop star and another after a footballer. In the United States the same thing happens. In fact, it is not that new as many US military airfields were named not after the local community but after someone from the area killed in a flying accident, and not necessarily a war hero. The prob-

lem is that what happens when someone more deserving comes along? This is especially true of some airports that have changed their names two or even three times. Far too many of the names chosen for airports are transient, honouring personalities with fleeting fame either from politics or entertainment. One can understand an airport being named after, say, Alberto Santos-Dumont, the dapper Brazilian aeronaut who made the first powered heavier-than-air flight in Europe, as no one can take that achievement away and it cannot be surpassed. The same goes for Rome's Leonardo da Vinci, one of the great visionaries of flight. One can understand Belfast not wanting to name an airport after Sir James Martin, as passengers might not like to be reminded that they have not got an ejection seat, which would be impractical and a hazard in a transport aircraft anyway.

Of course, even with a fine name, there is always the risk that the airport itself might be downgraded when it cannot expand and a newer, roomier, busier, airport opens elsewhere, but serving the same city. This is what happened to Rio de Janiero Alberto Santos-Dumont. Poor Alberto!

Airport names should be chosen so that no one makes a mistake and chooses the wrong airport. Geographical names are usually permanent, with a few exceptions such as Wroclaw of course. There is also much to be said about brevity, and naming an airport after a long forgotten president or military figure is a mistake.

This also means that airports should be named honestly. The five main London airports are fine, and so too is Glasgow Prestwick as one can reach it from the centre of Glasgow far more quickly than one could reach any of the London airports, other than City, from the centre of London. That said, London City is not in the Square Mile but in Docklands. But is it right to describe Hahn as Frankfurt Hahn? There are some examples further north in Scandinavia and further south in Spain that also leave the arriving passengers with a fare to reach their destinations that makes their low-cost flight not so cheap. This is one that the competition authorities and those concerned about consumer rights seem to have overlooked, so far.

Notes

In compiling such a work, various sources have been used to find information on each airport, and not all airport operators provide information freely or willingly, and some not at all. Inevitably there are parts of the world with little information forthcoming, even for supposedly civil airports. Amongst the sources available to the researcher are those of the Aviation Safety Network, Wikipedia, and others, including some intended specifically for pilots or for tourists. Even these are dependent upon the information available to them, and it is not always possible to give precise details of incidents, for example.

I have tried to provide both metric and imperial measurements, vital for those of us who feel more comfortable with the latter, and when aircraft designations may be slightly confusing, as with the Fairchild FH-227, for example, explain that it is a licence-built F-27. Unless indicated otherwise, all runways are either paved or asphalt.

I have succumbed to the convention that when dealing with aircraft and their movements, 'port' is now left and 'starboard' is now right.

In an airport title, the rule in this book is that a name following an oblique stroke means an alternative name for the airport, while a name in brackets means an old name for an airport or the city that it serves.

IATA airport designators

Before the 1930s, existing airports used a two-letter abbreviation based on the weather station at the airports. So, at that time, for example, LA served as the designation for Los Angeles International Airport. But, with the rapid growth in the aviation industry, the designations expanded to three letters, and LA became LAX. The letter X does not otherwise have any specific meaning in this identifier. Many later airports were spared this problem, adapting easily to three letter designations, so that Edinburgh, as an example, is EDI.

THE WORLD'S TOP 500 AIRPORTS

by country and passenger numbers

ALBANIA

This small country has only one international airport, with civil aviation constrained by the country's isolation between the end of the Second World War and the 1990s. It missed out on post-war Europe's economic boom and the surge in tourism that lifted the economies of many of the poorer southern countries with scant natural resources or industry.

TIRANA INTERNATIONAL/ MOTHER TERESA: TIA

Rinas, Tirana, Albania

Owner and operator: Tirana International Airport SHPK
Runways: 18/36, 2,734m (8,971ft)
Terminals: One
Airlines using airport as base or hub: Albanian Airlines
Annual passengers: 1,107,325

Background

Albania's only international airport, Tirana International is 25km (almost 16 miles) north-west of the city and in the village of Rinas, by which name the airport is locally known.

It was opened in 1957 but was not busy, and its traffic potential became even more limited when the country passed from Soviet bloc to Chinese influence in 1960. It is only in recent years, since the collapse of communism, that the country has been opened up to foreign visitors, and traffic at the airport has begun to grow. In 2001 it was named after the missionary Mother Teresa. It was privatised in 2005 with a consortium, Tirana International Airport SHPK, being awarded a 20-year concession to operate and develop the airport. One of the first benefits of the concession was the opening of a new passenger terminal in March 2007, but this lacked airbridges and was almost immediately overcrowded as its designed capacity was surpassed in the first year of operation. The new terminal has now been extended.

ALGERIA

French colonial rule ensured that Algeria needed good communications across the Mediterranean with the mother country, but at first such communication was by flying boat. Many of the country's airports are a legacy from the colonial past and were originally built for military purposes, mainly for the French Air Force (the *Armée de l'Air*). Post-war development was hindered by the civil war, and in particular opposition to independence by settlers of French ancestry. The country has done less well in encouraging tourism than its neighbours, Morocco and Tunisia.

ALGIERS/HOUARI BOUMEDIENE: ALG

Dar el Beida, Algiers, Algeria

Owner and operator: EGSA
Runways: 05/23, 3,500m (11,482ft); 09/27, 3,500m (11,482ft)
Terminals: Two, designated New Terminal or Terminal 1 (for foreign airlines and with two halls) and Terminal 2 (reserved for Air Algérie)
Airlines using airport as base or hub: Air Algérie
Annual passengers: 3,804,731
Annual cargo: 20,926 tonnes
Annual aircraft movements: 49,724

Line L1 of the Algiers Metro is expected to be completed at the airport during 2010.

Background

Named after the country's first president, the airport is 17km (11 miles), south-east of Algiers. The airport dates from before the Second World War when it was built primarily as a military installation by the French, and known as *Maison Blanche*. It was used as the airport for Algiers after the Second World War, and while it was enlarged and developed, the violent war that preceded Algerian independence in 1962 inhibited tourism and commercial growth.

The airport has suffered from terrorist activity in recent years, despite the country having

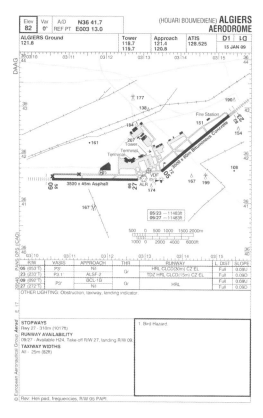

ARGENTINA

As one of the more prosperous Latin American countries during the first half of the 20th century, Argentina has a long history of air transport, dating from at least 1927, initially with French support. There were also flying-boat services across the broad estuary of the River Plate to Montevideo in Uruguay. Later, the pioneering US airlines reached down through South America to reach Buenos Aires, and prominent amongst these was the New York, Rio and Buenos Aires Airline, NYBRA, nicknamed 'near beer', and its rival Pan American Grace Airways, PANAGRA, a joint venture between Pan American Airways and a US shipping line.

BUENOS AIRES/MINISTRO PISTARINI INTERNATIONAL: EZE

Ezeiza, Buenos Aires, Argentina

Owner: Ministry of Planning and Public Services
Operator: Aeropuertos Argentina 2000
Runways: 11/29, 3,300m (10,827ft); 17/35, 3,105m (10,187ft); a third runway, 05/23, closed in 1997
Terminals: Three, designated A, B (Aerolineas Argentinas only), and C (charter flights and air cargo)
Airlines using airport as base or hub: Aerolineas Argentinas, Austral, LADE.
Annual passengers: 7,487,779
Annual cargo: 204,909 tonnes
Annual aircraft movements: 70,576

Background

Usually known by local inhabitants as 'Ezeiza International' because of its location, the airport is 22km (13¾ miles) from the city centre and was built between 1945 and 1949, when it was the largest airport in South America and the only one to have three runways. The name commemorates Juan Pistarini, a former general and government minister.

The first transatlantic flight into the still uncompleted airport was in 1946 by British

gained full independence so long ago. A bomb explosion in the terminal on 28 August 1992 killed 9 people and another 128 were wounded. The bomb was planted by Islamic extremists. Later, on 24 December 1994, an Air France Airbus A300, bound for Paris, was hijacked by Islamic terrorists before take-off, and on landing in Marseille French special operations personnel stormed the aircraft and killed the four terrorists, although 25 passengers were wounded.

In recent years the airport has been enlarged and developed, with a new terminal (known as Terminal 1) for foreign airlines opened in 2006, while Terminal 2 is the exclusive preserve of the state-owned Air Algérie. There is also a cargo terminal. For the future, another new terminal (Terminal 3) is being built for opening in 2012, and the runways will be strengthened and extended.

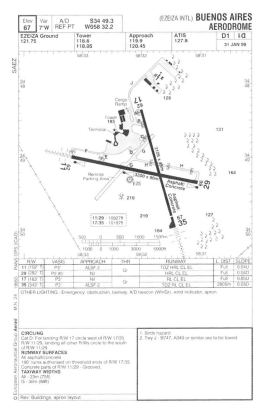

Elev 67	Var 7°W	A/D REF PT	S34 49.3 W058 32.2		(EZEIZA INTL)	**BUENOS AIRES AERODROME**
EZEIZA Ground 121.75		Tower 118.6 118.05		Approach 119.9 120.45	ATIS 127.8	D1 ⌐□ 31 JAN 08

R/W	VASIS	APPROACH	THR	RUNWAY	L. DIST	SLOPE
11 (102° T)	P3'	ALSF 2	Gr	TDZ HRL CL EL	Full	0.04U
29 (282° T)	P2.95'	Nil		HRL CL EL	Full	0.04D
17 (163° T)	P3'	Nil	Gr	RL CL EL	Full	0.05U
35 (343° T)	P3'	ALSF 2		TDZ RL CL EL	2805m	0.05D

OTHER LIGHTING : Emergency, obstruction, taxiway, A/D beacon (Wh/Gr), wind indicator, apron.

CIRCLING
Cat D: For landing R/W 17 circle west of R/W 17/35. R/W 11/29, landing all other R/Ws circle to the south of R/W 11/29.
RUNWAY SURFACES
All asphalt/concrete
180° turns authorised on threshold ends of R/W 17/35. Concrete parts of R/W 11/29 - Grooved.
TAXIWAY WIDTHS
All - 23m (75ft)
G - 30m (98ft)

Rev: Buildings, apron layout.

1. Birds hazard.
2. Twy J - B747, A340 or similar are to be towed.

South American Airways, which was later absorbed into BOAC (the British Overseas Airways Corporation).

In common with a number of airports in South America, the airport has had difficulty in raising funds for improvements, and its management and development has been let as a concession to Aeropuertos Argentina 2000. The first results of this have been a new terminal that opened in 2008, while in the near future there will be a new control tower and a new 3,000m runway.

BUENOS AIRES/JORGE NEWBERY: AEP

Buenos Aires, Argentina

Owner and operator: Aeropuertos Argentina 2000 S.A.
Runways: 13/31, 2,100m (6,890ft)
Terminals: One

Airlines using airport as base or hub: Austral; Aerolineas Argentina; LADE
Annual passengers: 5,665,808
Annual cargo: 14,076 tonnes
Annual aircraft movements: 81,340

Background

The original airport for Buenos Aires, it is just 2km (1¼ miles) north of the city centre and is by the River Plate. It was superseded by Buenos Aires Ministro Pistarini in 1949. Today, only flights from within Argentina or from Uruguay are handled. It is named after an Argentine pioneer of aviation.

On 31 August 1999, a flight by the domestic airline LAPA crashed on take-off, killing all 63 persons on board and another 2 on the ground.

ARMENIA

For many years part of the Soviet empire, Armenia is one of the poorer states, and after independence the national airline, Armenian International Airlines, struggled with the country's poor economic prospects, worsened by a civil war, before collapsing in 2001.

YEREVAN ZVARTNOTS INTERNATIONAL: EVN

Zvartnots, Yerevan, Armenia

Owner: General Department of Civil Aviation of Armenia
Operator: Armenia International Airports CJSC
Runways: 09/27, 3,849m (12,629ft)
Terminals: Two, designated Domestic and International
Airlines using airport as base or hub: Air Armenia; Armavia
Annual passengers: 1,382,685
Annual cargo: 9,999 tonnes

Background

The airport is at Zvartnots, and is some 10km (6¼ miles) west of Yerevan. It is owned by the Armenian government, but operated by Armenia International Airports, a subsidiary of Corporation America, a joint Armenian and United States enterprise.

The airport was completed in 1961 while Armenia was still part of the Soviet Union, and was extensively modernised in the 1980s, including a new terminal. After Armenia became independent of the former Soviet Union, a new cargo terminal was opened in 1998. The agreement with the current operator was signed in 2001 and is due to last for 30 years. One of the first benefits was the opening of a new terminal for international travellers in June 2007, with another terminal due to open by 2012. Despite the split from what is now the Russian Federation, the busiest route remains the one to Moscow, but a total of 34 foreign airlines now operate into Yerevan.

AUSTRALIA

As a prosperous and well-developed country, with vast distances separating the main centres of population, and also remote from the rest of the world, Australia was almost made for air transport, especially since the railways had developed piecemeal with different track gauges in many of the states. Post war, Australia had a two-airline policy on domestic services with a state-owned airline, Trans Australia Airways, and a private enterprise competitor, ANA Australian National Airways; while Qantas was restricted to international routes.

The early international routes were, of necessity, operated by flying boats, with Imperial Airways and Qantas cooperating on a service from Southampton to Sydney.

On domestic services, the vast distances and low population density of much of Australia meant that early progress was rapid. In 1937, services were introduced from Melbourne to Adelaide, Broken Hill and Sydney. Airliners were used to carry allied service personnel around Australia, and to evacuate civilians from Darwin and Broome after Japanese air raids on these towns.

SYDNEY/KINGSFORD SMITH INTERNATIONAL: SYD
Mascot, Sydney, New South Wales, Australia

Owner and operator: Sydney Airport Corporation

Runways: 16L/34R, 2,438m (7,998ft); 16R/34L, 3,968m (13,018ft); 07/25, 2,529m (8,297ft)

Terminals: Three, designated 1 (International), 2, and 3

Airlines using airport as base or hub: Qantas, Australian Air Express, Eastern Australia, Regional Express

Annual passengers: 32,323,380

Annual aircraft movements: 286,101

The airport is connected to the centre of Sydney by the Airport Link underground line.

Background

Opened as an aerodrome in 1920 when it was known as Sydney Airport, the first runways were

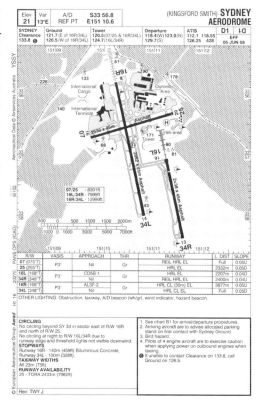

not built until 1933, largely from gravel, and a number of streams running across the airfield had to be diverted. Paved runways and a passenger terminal were built later. Before the end of the Second World War long-distance air travel to Australia was normally by flying boat, with a service started jointly by Imperial Airways and Qantas in the late 1930s, and these used Sydney Harbour. In 1953, the airport was renamed Sydney/Kingsford Smith International Airport to commemorate Charles Kingsford Smith, one of the Australian pioneers of civil aviation.

Traffic grew considerably after the introduction of jet aircraft shortened journey times and effectively ended Australia's relative isolation from North America and Europe. By the mid-1960s, it was clear that a new international terminal was needed and this opened officially in May 1970. Later that year, a Pan American flight saw the first Boeing 747 'jumbo jet' serve the airport. The main runway was extended during the 1970s, and an enlarged international terminal opened in 1992, but has been refurbished and expanded further since then. The rapid expansion of the airport, and especially of long-haul international traffic, prompted the question of either further expansion or of building a new airport, but the decision was taken to build a third runway on land reclaimed from Botany Bay. As elsewhere, increased air traffic created local opposition, and in response there are curfews restricting arrivals and departures at night, and runway operation is rotated.

In 2002, the airport was denationalised when it was sold to Southern Cross Airports Corporate Holdings, owned in part by a number of investment funds managed by Macquarie Bank, but the airport is leased and effectively remains on land owned by the Crown. The airport is undergoing a staged expansion which will take place over the period up to 2025. The expansions are controversial because the local authorities have no control over developments – a situation that is not unusual in some other types of transport infrastructure development, such as ports and harbours, which are considered to be on 'operational' land.

MELBOURNE/TULLAMARINE INTERNATIONAL: MEL
Melbourne, Victoria, Australia

Owner: Australia Pacific Airports Corporation
Operator: Australia Pacific Airports (Melbourne) Pty Ltd
Runways: 09/27, 2,286m (7,500ft); 16/34, 3,657m (11,998ft)
Terminals: Four, designated Terminal 1 (Qantas Domestic), Terminal 2 (International), Terminal 3 and Terminal 4 (low-cost airlines)
Annual passengers: 23,076,369
Annual aircraft movements: 184,052

Background
Tullamarine, or 'Tulla' as it is often called, was developed to replace Essendon Airport which was not only becoming increasingly congested during the 1960s, but also lacked sufficient runway length to comfortably handle jet aircraft

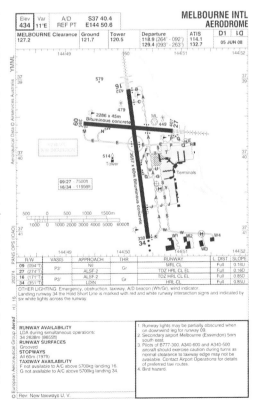

as sizes and weights increased. The airport was opened to international flights on 1 July 1970, and to domestic flights on 26 June 1971. In 1981, the Australian Federal Government established the Federal Airports Corporation and all 21 Australian airports were put under its control. At Melbourne the domestic terminals were upgraded in 1990 and the international terminals in 1991/1992. On 2 July 1997 the airport was privatised and ownership passed to the Australia Pacific Airports Corporation. Since privatisation, efforts have been made to have the airport simply referred to a Melbourne Airport to distinguish it from the other three airports in the Melbourne area.

The airport has not been without its incidents, although none of them has been an accident. On 29 May 2003 an attempted hijacking of a Qantas flight to Launceston, in Tasmania, was foiled by the cabin crew and passengers who restrained the would-be hijacker. More puzzling was the sudden illness that struck a number of people at what was then the South Terminal on 21 February 2005, causing its evacuation and closure. It began at 07.10 when a woman collapsed, and after several more people showed the same symptoms, the terminal was closed at 10.10. Altogether 57 people were affected, and of these ten were taken to hospital, but the true nature of the illness was never discovered.

In recent years, capacity has become a problem for Tullamarine and the airport has lost some of the European airlines that once served it, although in many cases Qantas services have replaced those lost. On the other hand, a reflection of Australia's greater links with the Asia-Pacific region has seen many airlines from the Far East commence operations, and in the future Virgin Atlantic may start services, although at present it code shares with Singapore Airlines. At one stage the other airport in the area, Avalon, was being used by low-cost airlines because Melbourne's fees were too high and the airport terminals were too congested, but they have been expanded in recent years and Terminal 4 is reserved for the growing number of flights by low-cost airlines, which have now switched to Tullamarine. For the future, a recurring issue is that of a direct railway link into the airport.

BRISBANE INTERNATIONAL: BNE
Brisbane, Queensland, Australia

Owner: Australian Federal Government
Operator: Brisbane Airport Corporation Pty Ltd
Runways: 01/19, 3,560m (11,680ft); 14/32, 1,700m (5,577ft); a third runway parallel to 01/19 should open around 2015
Terminals: Two, designated Domestic and International
Annual passengers: 18,374,667
Annual aircraft movements: 171,412

Background
Australia's third busiest airport, Brisbane International opened in 1988 to replace the original main airport for the city, which dated from 1925 and was situated on an area of flat agricultural land known locally as Eagle Farm. Qantas, then an acronym for Queensland & Northern Territories Aerial Service, started operations there the following year. At the time, there was another airport for the city, Archerfield Airport, with a far better runway and which became famous when Charles Kingsford Smith landed there on 9 June 1928 at the end of the first trans-Pacific flight in his Fokker FVII *Southern Cross*. Nevertheless, Eagle Farm benefited from being used as a base during the Second World War when the city became headquarters for the South Pacific Area and its supreme commander, General Douglas MacArthur. The USAAF upgraded the airport to the extent that post war it became the natural choice for a commercial airport.

Post war, traffic grew considerably, and by the 1970s the arrival of the jet age had shrunk distances to the extent that air travel became the natural choice for longer distances, and even emigrants to Australia went by air. The current airport, opened in 1988, was built on what had been the residential suburb of Cribb Island, and it needed large quantities of sand from Moreton Bay to stabilise the marshy ground and raise it above tide level.

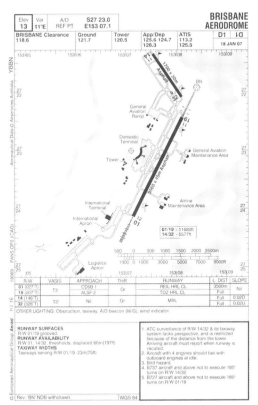

Terminals: Three, designated Terminal 1 (International), Terminal 2 (Qantas Domestic) and Terminal 3 (Domestic)

Airlines using airport as base or hub: Skywest

Annual passengers: 8,631,092

Annual aircraft movements: 102,857

Background

Perth's first airports were an airfield in the suburb of Maylands and another on the beach at Langley Park, but during the 1930s, as aircraft sizes increased, it became clear that neither had a long-term future. Eventually land was found and purchased in 1928 in an area known as Guildford. Although work had started, the outbreak of the Second World War saw the planned airport reconfigured as a temporary base for the Royal Australian Air Force, initially as a satellite of RAAF Pearce, and after the United States entered the war, the base was shared with the United States Navy. In 1944, while the base was

At the time it was built, all major Australian airports were in federal government ownership, but have since been privatised. Brisbane was bought on a 99-year lease by a consortium including Amsterdam's Schiphol Airport, and part of the future development involves building an 'Airport City' commercial area similar to that in the Netherlands. Other future development includes extending the domestic terminal, building a parallel runway (see above) and improving road access to the airport, as the current road network becomes extremely congested at peak periods.

PERTH INTERNATIONAL: PER

Guildford, Perth, Western Australia

Owner and operator: Westralia Airports Corporation

Runways: 03/21, 3,444m (11,299ft); 06/24, 2,163m (7,096ft)

still being used by the RAAF and USN, both Qantas Empire Airways and Australian National Airways began civil air services, using a hangar as a passenger terminal, as Maylands could no longer handle larger aircraft then entering service. Qantas was at this time using converted Liberator bombers on a service from Perth to Ceylon (now Sri Lanka). Despite this, Maylands remained in use on a limited basis until end-June 1963.

Post war, the airport became busier when first MacRobertson Miller moved from Maylands in 1948, and then the new state-owned domestic airline, Trans Australia Airlines (TAA). Poor road and railway links with the rest of Australia also meant that air cargo became very important at the new airport. In 1952, the airport was renamed Perth International Airport, even though a planned new passenger terminal, being built using steel and cladding from US buildings dismantled on Manus Island in the Pacific, was still not complete.

The new passenger terminal only lasted ten years until a new purpose-built terminal opened in 1962, just in time for that year's British Empire and Commonwealth Games being held in Perth. The new terminal handled both domestic and international flights, but within ten years it too had reached capacity, and had difficulty coping with the Boeing 747 'jumbo jet'. A new international terminal was built and opened in 1986, capable of handling up to five Boeing 747s at a time, and then was extended and refurbished in 2003 and 2004. Meanwhile, both Qantas and Ansett Airlines, its private enterprise rival, built new domestic terminals, and after the collapse of Ansett in 2001, the Ansett terminal became a general user facility.

The airport has an excellent safety record. The worst incident, in which no lives were lost, was when a Qantas Boeing 747 landing from Sydney on 2 September 1999 hit runway 06/24 with its number one engine. The cause was put down to a microburst or windshear due to the local terrain with the Darling Scarp creating rolling winds. The incident caused the airport to seek improvements in its weather monitoring.

For the future, the airport's management is guided by the '2024 Airport Masterplan' which aims to consolidate the existing domestic and international terminals into a single terminal on the south-eastern side of the airport, with the new airport having a railway link to the city centre. There is now some pressure to bring the dates for completion of the plan forward by more than ten years, while Qantas is upgrading its domestic terminal and Westralia Airports Corporation, the owner and operator of the airport, is upgrading road links between the terminals to make transfers easier. Work is also progressing on a new Terminal WA for flights within Western Australia.

ADELAIDE: ADL
West Beach, Adelaide, South Australia

Owner and operator: Adelaide Airport Ltd
Runways: 05/23, 3,100m (10,171ft); 12/30, 1,652m (5,420ft)
Terminals: One
Airlines using airport as base or hub: Alliance Airlines (operates as QantasLink), National Jet Systems, Regional Express Airlines, Tiger Airways Australia
Annual passengers: 6,498,169
Annual aircraft movements: 104,514

Background
Adelaide had an aerodrome as early as 1921 at the suburb of Hendon which was used by an air-mail service to Sydney. As a bigger site was needed, in 1927 a new airfield opened at Parafield, but after the Second World War this also proved to be too small and a site for a new airport was chosen at West Torrens, now West Beach, and the current airport opened in 1954. Initially there was no terminal, with passengers having to use an annex to one of the hangars until the Commonwealth government funded a temporary building. An international terminal was completed in 1982. It was not until 2005 that a new terminal replaced both the old 1950s-era temporary building and the international terminal. In 2007 it was announced that the new ter-

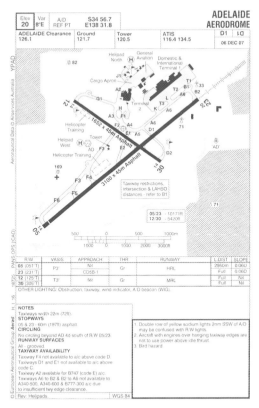

only by domestic air services and aircraft from Papua New Guinea, but also by Qantas flights from Europe.

The airport dates from 1928 when one Tom McDonald flew a de Havilland Gipsy Moth from a sand ridge close to the site of the airport. In 1934, the local population decided that an airport was necessary, especially for emergencies, and started a public subscription for its construction. The local council bought the site in 1936, and construction followed creating three runways out of sand, earth, and rock. During the Second World War the airport was purchased by the government for the Royal Australian Air Force, and a hard runway was opened in 1942. The airfield was also used by the United States Army Air Force for its transport squadrons. The runway was extended after the war, in 1949, and between 1962 and 1967 the entire airport was modernised and the runway strengthened to allow jet airliners to use it. During the early 1970s, the invest-

minal would be extended and the old international terminal demolished.

CAIRNS INTERNATIONAL: CNS

Aeroglen, Cairns, Queensland, Australia

Owner and operator: Cairns Airport Pty Ltd (CAPL)

Runways: 15/33, 3,196m (10,486ft); 12/30, 925m (3,035ft); there are also helipads

Terminals: Two, designated Domestic and International

Airlines using airport as base or hub: Australian Airlines

Annual passengers: 3,997,476

Annual aircraft movements: 98,538

Background

Situated in the appropriately-named suburb of Aeroglen, Cairns International is 7km (4¼ miles) from the centre of Cairns. It is served not

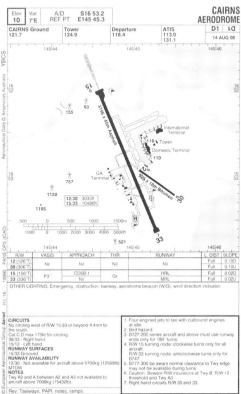

ment in the airport saw growing use by Trans Australia Airways and Ansett, while in 1975, Air New Guinea introduced flights to Port Moresby.

The growth in traffic at this time was in danger of outstripping the airport's facilities, and the Australian government handed over responsibility to what became the Port of Cairns Authority in 1981. The new owners extended the runway and built a new terminal building, with a dual international and domestic terminal opening in March 1984, and this was followed by a separate international terminal in 1990, with both built on reclaimed mangrove swamp. Currently, the domestic terminal is being redeveloped and this should finish in 2010.

The airport is home to a unit of the Royal Australian Flying Doctor Service and also the state helicopter emergency service.

The Cairns Port Authority sold the airport to a private consortium in December 2008.

GOLD COAST (COOLANGATTA): OOL
Bilinga, Gold Coast, Queensland, Australia

Owner and operator: Queensland Airports Ltd
Runways: 14/32, 2,342m (7,684ft); 17/35, 582m (1,909ft)
Terminals: One, known as the Eric Robinson Terminal, with international and domestic areas
Annual passengers: 3,916,326
Annual aircraft movements: 66,098

It is planned that the Gold Coast Railway will eventually operate into the airport.

Background
Some 100km (62½ miles) south of Brisbane on Australia's Gold Coast, the airport is one of Australia's fastest-growing.

It dates from 1936 when it was opened as a grass strip for emergency use, especially for aircraft flying airmail services between Brisbane and Sydney, and it was not until 1939 that it received its own regular passenger services. After the Second World War it was used as

Coolangatta Airport, hence the IATA designation OOL, by Butler Air Transport and Queensland Airlines. Ansett started to use the airport in 1950 with Douglas DC-3s and Trans Australia Airlines (TAA) followed in 1954. This growing use led to modernisation and improvements, so that by 1958 the runways and taxiways were paved and were later upgraded further to accommodate the Lockheed Electra turboprop and, later, the Douglas DC-9 short-haul jet airliner. The terminal in use today, the Eric Robinson Building, was opened in 1981.

After the war the airport was in state ownership, and in 1988 it was transferred to the Federal Airports Corporation, but it was not privatised until 29 May 1998 when it was acquired by Queensland Airports, which changed its name to Gold Coast Airport Pty Ltd in 1999. In 2003, this company was in turn taken over by Queensland Airports, which also owns and operates two other airports at Mount Isa and Townsville.

By this time the airport was handling international flights, starting with charters in 1990 and in 1998, the Air New Zealand subsidiary and low-cost airline, Freedom Air, started operations from Hamilton. In 2007, AirAsia started flights from Kuala Lumpur, followed by Air Pacific in 2008.

The terminal will have an extension completed in 2010 which will almost double its capacity and there will be facilities for low-cost carriers such as Tiger Airways, Virgin Blue and Pacific Blue, as well as Air New Zealand and Qantas.

TOWNSVILLE/GARBUTT: TSV
Garbutt, Townsville, Queensland, Australia

Owner: Department of Defence
Operator: Queensland Airports Ltd
Runways: 01/19, 2,438m (7,999ft); 07/25, 1,100m (3,609ft)
Terminals: One, with the southern part for international flights and the northern for domestic flights
Annual passengers: 1,487,580
Annual aircraft movements: 49,609

Background

Known variously as Townsville Airport, Townsville International Airport or Garbutt Airport in deference to the suburb in which it is located, it is also used by the Royal Australian Air Force which officially describes it as RAAF Base Townsville.

Townsville's first airport was built after the First World War and was in Thuringowa in what is now the suburb of Murray. Although it was licensed as a civil airport in 1930, it was already showing its limitations with only enough space for a single east-west runway, while much of the ground was boggy for most of the year. A new airport was built within the city itself using the Town Common, and the current airport opened on 1 February 1939 with two gravel runways.

On the outbreak of the Second World War the new airport was chosen for expansion as RAAF Base Townsville, with the intention of accommodating up to three fighter squadrons, although in fact only one was based there when the Royal Australian Air Force side of the airport became operational early in 1940. In 1941, the base was enlarged and the runways strengthened and lengthened to accommodate bombers and transport aircraft of the then United States Army Air Corps reinforcing the Philippines, with the work being finished just in time for the extension of the war to the Pacific. By this time, Townsville had three runways. With Japanese expansion across the Pacific and into New Guinea, additional bases had to be hastily built in the area, so that eventually five other military airfields were opened in the immediate vicinity of Townsville, and the base was renamed RAAF Base Garbutt to avoid confusion with another airfield, even though the commercial side of the airport continued as Townsville. The choice of name by the RAAF came from the base's proximity to a railway siding and stockyards owned by the Garbutt Brothers. The RAAF did not revert to the original name until 1951.

After the war the airport continued its dual existence as a civil airport and an air force base. Traffic grew steadily, with flights by Trans Australia Airlines, the state-owned domestic airline, and its private enterprise rival, Australian National Airways, and by the 1970s the airport was a regional hub for both airlines. Eventually Qantas, then restricted to international flights only, started to stage flights through Townsville, making it the first regional airport in Australia with international flights. On 18 April 1980, Ansett opened a route from Townsville to Singapore, one of the first international routes by the airline. The following year, a new international terminal was opened. A number of foreign airlines also started to fly into Townsville, including Garuda, Air New Zealand, Cathay Pacific, and Japan Airlines. Services reached Asia and the United States.

Further expansion followed, and in 1987 the international terminal was expanded to provide a domestic wing. This was just in time for the airline pilots' strike in 1989 which grounded most domestic flights, although a limited international service continued, but it was not until 1991 that domestic services returned to normal. The next crisis was the beginning of a programme of rationalising international flights, made more difficult as competition arose between Townsville and Cairns for the remaining flights, with the latter airport promising superior facilities. When a new international terminal opened at Cairns in 1993, only Qantas, Ansett, Cathay Pacific, and Garuda continued using Townsville, but by 1995 these had also moved. This was followed by a reduction in the frequency of domestic flights, made worse when Ansett ceased operations in late 2001, cutting the service between Townsville and Brisbane by 40 per cent. This was the nadir of the airport's fortunes, as the new low-fares airline, Virgin Blue, selected Townsville as its first regional destination, while Qantas, by this time also with a domestic network, introduced a service to Sydney. This was followed by modernisation of the domestic terminal which was completed in 2003.

AUSTRIA

Aviation in Austria has been inhibited by the difficult terrain and a well-established railway network. The country was absorbed by Germany in 1938, and after the war was initially occupied by the Allies. Austrian commercial aviation did not resume until 1957 with the formation of Austrian Airlines, although the airlines of other countries were already serving the country by this time.

VIENNA INTERNATIONAL: VIE

Schwechat, Vienna, Austria

Owner and operator: Flughafen Wien AG
Runways: 11/29, 3,500m (11,483ft); 16/34, 3,600m (11,811ft)
Terminals: Three, designated Terminal 1, Terminal 2, and low-cost Terminal 1A
Airlines using airport as base or hub: Austrian Airlines, Austrian Arrows

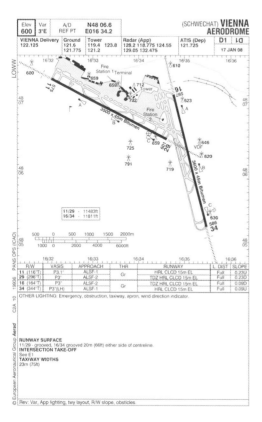

Annual passengers: 18,768,468
Annual cargo: 205,024 tonnes
Annual aircraft movements: 280,912

A City Airport Train (CAT) runs directly to Vienna Mitte, while the airport is also on the Vienna Stadt-Bahn.

Background

Vienna International was originally built as a military airfield for the Luftwaffe in 1938, and after the end of the Second World War, when Austria was occupied by the Allies, it became a base for the Royal Air Force. The airport replaced Vienna's airport at Aspern in 1954, but it was not until 1957 that Austrian commercial aviation was revived, after an interval of 20 years, with the formation of Austrian Airlines. Initially the airport had a single runway, which was extended to 3,000m in 1959, while work started on a new terminal the following year. A second runway was opened in 1972.

More recently, a new terminal has been opened and work will start soon on a third runway.

SALZBURG/W. A. MOZART: SZG

Salzburg, Austria

Owner and operator: Salzburger Flughafen GmbH
Runways: 16/34, 2,750m (9,022ft)
Terminals: Two, designated Terminal 1 and Terminal 2 (opened only during the winter skiing season)
Annual passengers: 1,946,422
Annual aircraft movements: 57,065

Background

Usually referred to simply as Salzburg Airport, it is just 2km (1¼ miles) south-west of the city centre, and is named after the famous composer Wolfgang Amadeus Mozart. It is owned 25 per cent by the city and 75 per cent by the regional government.

Salzburg's history of aviation dates from 1910 when aircraft used the racing circuit at Aigen.

Scheduled air services arrived much later, with the start of a Munich–Salzburg service in 1926 by the then new German airline, Deutsche Luft Hansa, predecessor of today's Lufthansa. A route linking Vienna, Salzburg, and Innsbruck followed in 1927, operated by Olag Osterre- ichische, which ceased operations after Ger- many annexed Austria in 1938. The airport was requisitioned by the Luftwaffe on the outbreak of the Second World War in Europe and all civil operations ended. It was one of the bases for the Messerschmitt Me262 jet fighter in 1944, and that year when the United States Army Air Force bombed the city 16 times, the airport escaped relatively unscathed.

After the war Salzburg was the first Austrian airport to return to operations, although Austria was occupied by the Allies at first and it was not until 1957 that the new Austrian Airlines began operations, although there were flights by for- eign airlines before this. A new control tower opened in August 1958 and a new passenger ter- minal was completed in 1966. Growth was steady at first, but the increasing popularity of winter sports holidays benefited the airport as the gateway to the main holiday areas, to the extent that a new, but very Spartan Terminal 2 was built for this traffic and only opens on winter Saturdays. In 2001, Salzburg was the first Austrian airport to be used by the Irish low-cost airline, Ryanair.

BAHRAIN

While airports in the Gulf were important stag- ing posts for longer-distance flights between the two world wars, it was not until after the Second World War that they began to become more important in their own right, either directly because of their position within oil-rich states, or because of their proximity to such states and their role as ports and business centres. Today, such small sultanates and their airports, and air- lines, have become important hubs and destina- tions rather than just landing fields.

BAHRAIN INTERNATIONAL: BAH
Al Muharraq, Bahrain, United Arab Emirates

Owner and operator: Department of Civil Aviation Affairs

Runways: 12L/30R, 3,956m (12,979ft); 12R/30L, 2,530m (8,302ft)

Terminals: One

Airlines using airport as base or hub: Bahrain Air, Gulf Air

Annual passengers: 7,320,039

Annual cargo: 385,278 tonnes

Annual aircraft movements: 87,417

Background

Located on the island of Al Muharraq, the air- port is 7km (just over 4 miles) from the centre.

Bahrain occupies a strategically important position in the Middle East and became the first international airport in the Gulf in 1932 when an Imperial Airways Handley Page HP42 airliner

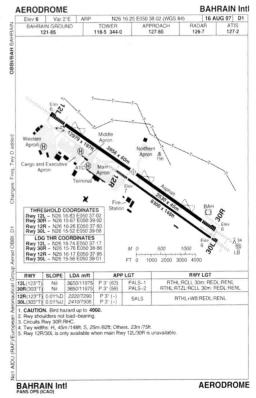

landed en route from London Croydon to Delhi. By 1936, this service had become twice-weekly, before it was superseded the following year by Short Empire 'C'-class flying boats operating from Hythe, near Southampton, to India and Australia. The flying boats used a stretch of water off Mina Salman.

After the war commercial aviation resumed and a local airline (Gulf Aviation) was established, which was the direct predecessor of today's Gulf Air, while the airport continued to be used by Imperial's successor, BOAC, but flying landplanes again. Other airlines from India and the Middle East also began using the airport. A new passenger terminal opened in 1961. The airport was one of the few to enjoy a regular supersonic air service when British Airways introduced Concorde flights between London Heathrow and Bahrain in 1976. For the rest of the 20th century the airport continued to grow and attract more international services while becoming both headquarters and hub for Gulf Air. A new terminal was opened in 1994, replacing earlier buildings, and an expansion programme started in 2006 involving renovation and enlargement of existing facilities.

BANGLADESH

DHAKA ZIA INTERNATIONAL: DAC

Dhaka, Bangladesh

Owner and operator: Civil Aviation Authority of
  Bangladesh
Runways: 14/32, 3,200m (10,500ft)
Terminals: One
Airlines using airport as base or hub: Biman
  Bangladesh Airlines, GMG Airlines, Best Air,
  United Airways (Bangladesh)
Annual passengers: 3,820,617
Annual cargo: 233,171 tonnes
Annual aircraft movements: 42,978

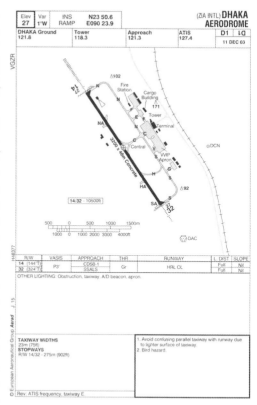

Background

Opened in 1981, the airport is named after a former president and is 20km (12½ miles) north of Dhaka. It is the country's most important airport. The national airline, Biman, dates from 1972 when it was founded to provide the country with international air services previously provided by Pakistan International before it gained independence in 1971.

The airport was the scene of a serious accident on 4 August 1984, when a Biman Bangladesh Fokker F-27 Friendship crashed into the swamps near the airport on its approach, with the loss of all 45 passengers and four crew.

BARBADOS

BRIDGETOWN/GRANTLEY ADAMS INTERNATIONAL: BGI

Seawell, Christchurch, Barbados

Owner and operator: Grantley Adams
    International Airport, GAIA, Inc.
Runways: 09/27, 3,353m (11,000ft)
Terminals: Two, built to appear as one and
    designated Departures and Arrivals
Airlines using airport as base or hub: LIAT
    (Leeward Islands Air Transport)
Annual passengers: 2,150,447

Background

Some 13km (8 miles) south of the centre of
Bridgetown, the airport was originally known as
Seawell after its locality, but the current name
was adopted in 1976 to commemorate the first
prime minister of Barbados.

The site of the airport was first used by an airline in 1939 when a KLM Royal Dutch Airlines
aircraft landed on what was no more than a grass
strip. The runway was paved during the Second
World War and a shed was used as a terminal
until a purpose-built structure opened in 1949.
The airport was used by British West Indies Airways, a regional affiliate of the then British
Overseas Airways Corporation (BOAC), and
from 1956 by Leeward Islands Air Transport
(LIAT). Development over the years included
assistance from the United States to strengthen
and extend the runway for use by military transports in support of the invasion of Grenada in
1983. The airport can handle aircraft up to and
including the Boeing 747, and was used by the
Concorde supersonic airliner on special charters
(a former British Airways Concorde is preserved at the airport in a special museum).

The terminal has been extended and is
described officially as two terminals, one for
departures and one for arrivals, but it has the
appearance of a single cohesive building. The
growth in tourism has prompted a rolling programme of expansion, although work was interrupted during the 2007 Cricket World Cup. With
the project complete, the airport is expected to
be able to handle the volume of traffic forecast
up to 2015.

There have been few accidents at the airport.
The worst was on 6 October 1976 when a
Cubana Douglas DC-8-40 caught fire after an
explosive device was detonated in the cabin
shortly after taking off for Jamaica. The pilots
were overcome by smoke or toxic gases and the
aircraft crashed into the sea killing all 73 passengers and crew.

BELGIUM

The history of air transport in Belgium is mainly
that of one airline, the national carrier Sabena,
and of one airport, Brussels. The country does
have other airports, including Antwerp and
Ostend, with the former having services to destinations such as London City Airport, while
Charleroi has established a niche for itself serving the booming low-cost (or budget) airline
sector. As with the other European colonial
powers, much emphasis was placed on links with
the colonies as well as services between European capitals. However, air transport grew less
quickly than in the United Kingdom and France,
due in part to the small size of the country and
the fact that the only colony of any importance
was the Belgian Congo, and there were no offshore islands to stimulate demand for air travel.
For many years little importance was attached to
either internal or external air services, and in
those pre-unification of Europe days no thought
was given to Brussels as a pivotal point in European air transport.

BRUSSELS NATIONAL: BRU

Zaventem, Brussels, Belgium

Owner and operator: The Brussels Airport
    Company.
Runways: 07L/25R, 3,638m (11,936ft); 07R/25L,
    3,211m (10,535ft); 02/20, 2,987m (9,800ft)
Terminals: One with two piers, A and B, while a
    low-cost airline pier is being completed

Airlines using airport as base or hub: EAT
(European Air Transport), Brussels Airlines, TUI
Airlines Belgium
Annual passengers: 17,838,214
Annual cargo: 747,434 tonnes
Annual aircraft movements: 264,366

Direct railway link from the airport station to
Brussels city centre, as well as to Liege and,
from 2010, Antwerp.

Background

The history of the airport, sometimes known locally as Zaventem, started in 1940 after the fall of Belgium when the Luftwaffe had an airfield built east of Brussels, although actually within the town of Melsbroek. There was a Belgian military airfield nearby and an airport for commercial flights at Haren. After the liberation of Belgium by Allied forces in September 1944, the RAF took over the airfield briefly for use by the Second Allied Tactical Air Force. However, it was soon to be used in the re-establishment of Belgian commercial air services. The airport at Haren was by this time too small, and Melsbroek became the new airport for the capital. During 1948, a new terminal building was opened and runways 02/20 and 07L/25R both extended. Over the next eight years, modernisation and expansion continued, with a new runway completed in 1956. Meanwhile, it was amongst the first major airports in mainland Europe to have a railway station built post war, with a line opened in 1955.

What amounted to a new airport followed in 1957 and 1958 with new terminal buildings completed on the Zaventem side of the airport. This meant that despite using the same runways, the airport had effectively moved from Melsbroek to Zaventem! Nevertheless, Melsbroek was not abandoned completely, and was handed over to the Belgian Air Force, which bases transport aircraft there. A new cargo terminal was completed in 1976.

The airport has suffered its share of serious accidents over the years. On 15 February 1961, a Sabena Boeing 707 crashed on approach, killing all 72 passengers and crew and one person on the ground. A Boeing 747-200F freighter of Kalitta Air overshot a runway on 25 May 2008, crashed into a field and split into three, although all five occupants survived and only needed treatment for minor injuries. An incident of a different kind was on 5 May 2006 when a maintenance hangar used by Sabena Technics caught fire, with the loss of a Belgian Air Force Lockheed C-130 Hercules and three Airbus A320 airliners belonging to three small airlines.

A completely new passenger terminal was completed in 1994 close to the 1958 building, which now has two piers, although a third is being built for the low-cost airlines which have been using another less convenient Brussels airport, Charleroi ('Brussels South Airport'), which is some 46km (28 miles) from the city. The airport has been privatised and is owned by the Brussels Airport Company, which itself is owned 75 per cent by the Australian Macquarie

AERODROME   BRUSSELS/National

| Elev 184 | Var 1°W | ARP | N50 54-08 E004 29-07 (WGS 84) | 12 APR 07 | D1 |

BRUSSELS DELIVERY	GROUND	TOWER	DEPARTURE
121·95	121·7 121·875 (S) 118·05 (N)	118·6 120·775 257·8	126·625
	MIL OPS	ATIS	
	398·025 140·575 ❷	132·475 (Arr) 121·75 (Dep)	

RWY DIMENSIONS IN FT
Rwy 02/20 — 9800 x 164ft
Rwy 07L/25R — 11935 x 148ft
Rwy 07R/25L — 10534 x 148ft

THRESHOLD COORDINATES
Rwy 02 — N50 53·24 E004 29·50
Rwy 20 — N50 54·66 E004 30·07
Rwy 07L — N50 54·02 E004 27·57
Rwy 25R — N50 54·69 E004 29·96
Rwy 07R — N50 53·37 E004 28·92
Rwy 25L — N50 53·94 E004 31·40

RWY	SLOPE	LDA m/ft	APP LGT		RWY LGT
02(014°T)	0·72%D	2941/9649	P 3° (49)	PALS-2	RTHL·RTDZ·REDL·RCLL 15m :RENL
20(194°T)	0·72%U	2767/9078	P 3° (56)	PALS-1	RTHL·REDL·RCLL 15m :RENL
07L(065°T)	0·15%D	3380/11089	P 3° (66)	—	RTHL·REDL·RCLL 15m :RENL
25R(245°T)	0·15%U	3338/10951	P 3° (61)	PALS-2	RTHL·RTDZ·REDL·RCLL 15m :RENL
07R(070°T)	0·15%D	3089/10135	P 3° (66)	—	RTHL·REDL·RCLL 15m :RENL
25L(250°T)	0·15%U	3211/10535	P 3° (63)	PALS-2	RTHL·RTDZ·REDL·RCLL 15m :RENL

1. Immediately after vacating the rwy after landing, acft are to contact GROUND:
  a. Landing Rwy 20, Rwy 25L: 121·875.
  b. Landing Rwy 02, Rwy 07L, Rwy 25R: 118·05.
This does not relieve the pilot from the need to obtain clearance to cross any rwy.
❷ Acft arriving/departing MELSBROEK (EBMB) to contact OPS 15min prior to ETA/ETD.

BRUSSELS/National   AERODROME
PANS OPS (ICAO)

No1 AIDU (RAF)/European Aeronautical Group Aerad EBBR D1   Changes: Buildings, frequencies

financial group, with the Belgian state retaining a 25 per cent share. The airport's traffic was badly affected by the collapse of the Belgian national airline, Sabena, in 2002 when the company's parent, Swissair, went into liquidation. Nevertheless, a new airline, SN Brussels emerged and has since linked with Virgin Express to form a new airline, Brussels Airlines.

CHARLEROI/BRUSSELS SOUTH: CRL

Gosselies, Charleroi, Belgium

Owner: Walloon Regional Government
Operator: Société Wallonne des Aéroports
Runways: 07/25, 2,550m (8,366ft)
Terminals: One
Annual passengers: 2,458,980
Annual aircraft movements: 70,734

There is a bus shuttle to Charleroi South Station with trains to Brussels and beyond.

Background

Commonly known as Charleroi Airport, it is actually more than 7km (about 5 miles) north of Charleroi and it is 46km (over 28 miles) from Brussels.

The Gosselies area has a long association with aviation, with a flying school founded there in 1919, and Fairey Aviation, one of the smaller British manufacturers, having established a subsidiary, Avions Fairey, at the site in 1931. While it became an airport after the Second World War, it remained in use for small-scale manufacturing. The Belgian airline, Sabena, launched a service to London during the 1970s, but this was short-lived and most of the activity involved private aircraft and flying lessons, although there were some holiday charter flights.

The growing pressure on the main airport at Brussels during the 1990s saw growing interest in the use of Charleroi for commercial air services as the 20th century drew to a close. The airport was relaunched as Brussels South Charleroi Airport and assistance was provided to encourage the Irish low-cost airline Ryanair to use the airport, although this arrangement had to end when the European Commission objected to the assistance as it could be counted as state aid, given the airport's public ownership. Ryanair dropped several of its routes from Charleroi, but other low-cost airlines started to use the airport, including Wizz Air, and at the time of writing the ban on assistance to new users of the airport appears to have been reversed.

BRAZIL

Vast distances, widely dispersed populations, and difficult terrain, with the country covered by dense tropical rain forests divided by wide and fast-flowing rivers, all result in air transport being the favoured way to travel. Added to this, Brazil is the largest, most prosperous and most technically advanced nation in South America. It is one of the leading producers of regional jet aircraft. Air transport has been deregulated in Brazil, and this may have contributed to the difficulties of some of the nation's airlines, including the national carrier, Varig, while the main domestic airline, VASP, which was also the country's second largest airline, has also collapsed. Such upheavals are certainly not unique to Brazil.

During the early days of aviation, Brazil's airline industry benefited from the support and involvement of Germany, that country being frustrated by the restrictions on aviation in their own country after the end of the First World War. During the Second World War, Brazil supported the Allies and made air bases available to the Americans, who did much to improve the infrastructure so that heavy bombers could fly maritime-reconnaissance patrols over the South Atlantic. Today, deregulation has spurred its air transport industry to greater growth, and even small communities, by international standards, have airports with significant flows of passengers and freight.

The country's airports are managed by the state-owned airport operator, INFRAERO, with many shared with the air force.

SÃO PAULO/GUARULHOS/ GOVERNOR ANDRÉ FRANCO MONTORO INTERNATIONAL: GRU

Cumbica, Guarulhos, São Paulo, Brazil

Owner and operator: INFRAERO
Runways: 09L/27R, 3,700m (12,140ft);
    09R/27L, 3,000m (9,843ft)
Terminals: Two, designated Terminal 1 and
    Terminal 2, each with two wings
Annual passengers: 19,560,963
Annual cargo: 488,485 tonnes
Annual aircraft movements: 187,960

Background

Known officially as São Paulo/Guarulhos – Governor André Franco Montoro International Airport, or locally simply as Cumbica International, because of its location, the airport is Brazil's busiest by passenger traffic and is situated 25km (just over 15 miles) from the centre of São Paulo. Despite the title, it is more of a domestic hub than an international one. André Franco Montoro was a governor of the state of São Paulo who died in 1999, and the name was changed officially in 2001, although the new name is hardly used by locals or travellers, probably because it is far too long.

The airport opened in 1985, before which long-haul jet airliners had to use Campinas, although many passengers transferred to smaller aircraft at Rio de Janeiro. The airport has grown rapidly with international flights to other Latin American nations and to the United States, Canada, and Europe, but airlines operating from the Far East and the Middle East have enjoyed less success.

Plans for expansion include building two additional terminals and a third runway.

SÃO PAULO/CONGONHAS: CGH

São Paulo, Brazil

Owner: City of São Paulo
Operator: INFRAERO
Runways: 17L/35R, 1,435m (4,708ft); 17R/35L,
    1,940m (6,365ft)
Terminals: One
Annual passengers: 15,250,058
Annual cargo: 34,905 tonnes
Annual aircraft movements: 205,264

Background

Often referred to simply as 'Congonhas' by the locals, the name came not from the locality, but from a plant that was common in the area. Although the airport was proposed as early as 1919, it was not built until much later and opened on 12 September 1936. From the early days, air cargo was important, and by the mid-1950s it was one of the world's leading air cargo airfields. Passenger services also developed, and by the 1980s there were direct international flights to airports in Argentina, Bolivia, Paraguay, and Uruguay, as well as international connections to transatlantic flights and services to North America at Rio de Janeiro.

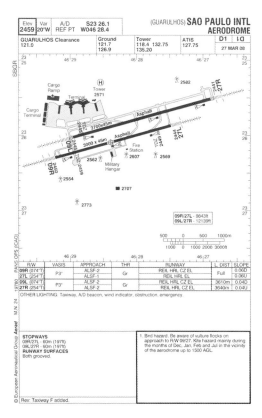

By this time, the airport was becoming over-crowded and congested. Its runways were not long enough for long-haul operations, and they also suffered from water lying on the surface. While another airport was available, Viracopas International, its location made it too remote for São Paulo residents, and the decision was taken to build a new airport, São Paulo-Guarulhos International, which opened in 1985. Neverthe-less, Congonhas remains important for short-haul and regional flights, which are an important part of Brazil's air traffic in the Central-South-ern Region where the airport is located.

There have been two serious accidents, both of which affected aircraft flown by one of the main domestic airlines, TAM. On 31 October 1996, a flight taking off from the airport struck a block of flats and crashed onto several houses, killing all 90 passengers and 6 crew, as well as 3 people on the ground. Another short-haul flight by TAM, flying from Salgado Filho, crashed on 17 July 2007 while attempting to land at Con-gonhas, with the loss of all 187 people on board. Less serious, on 24 October 2006, the airstair of a TAM Fokker 100 broke away from the aircraft after take-off, falling on to the roof of a super-market, but there were no casualties and the air-craft landed safely back at the airport shortly afterwards.

BRASÍLIA/PRESIDENT JUSCELINO KUBITSCHEK INTERNATIONAL: BSB

Brasília, Brazil

Owner and operator: INFRAERO
Runways: 11L/29R, 3,200m (10,499ft);
11R/29L, 3,300m (10,827ft)
Terminals: One
Annual passengers: 11,616,097
Annual cargo: 69,170 tonnes
Annual aircraft movements: 126,853

Background

Brazil's third busiest airport is named after a former president and serves the new federal cap-ital which was started in 1955 and had the legis-

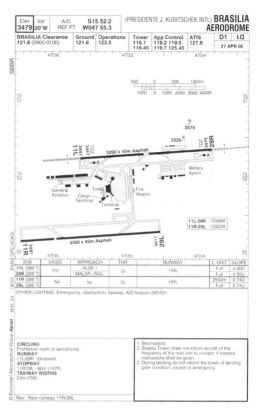

lature transferred in 1960. The airport was built at the same time, being essential not just for a capital city but also for communications within a large country with challenging topography and dense tropical jungle.

RIO DE JANEIRO (GALEÃO)/ANTONIO CARLOS JOBIM INTERNATIONAL: GIG

Rio de Janeiro, Brazil

Owner and operator: INFRAERO
Runways: 10/28, 4,000m (13,123ft); 15/33, 3,180m (10,433ft)
Terminals: Two, designated Terminal 1 and Terminal 2
Airlines using airport as base or hub: GOL, Varig Log, VRG Linhas
Annual passengers: 10,782,268
Annual cargo: 115,977 tonnes
Annual aircraft movements: 119,892

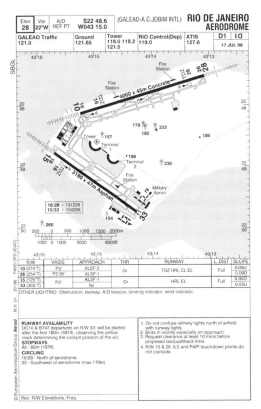

Elev 28	Var 22°W	A/D REF PT	S22 48.6 W043 15.0	(GALEAO-A.C.JOBIM INTL)	RIO DE JANEIRO AERODROME

GALEAO Traffic 121.0	Ground 121.65	Tower 118.0 118.2 121.5	RIO Control(Dep) 119.0	ATIS 127.6	D1	LG
					17 JUL 08	

R/W	VASIS	APPROACH	THR	RUNWAY	L DIST	SLOPE
10 (074°T)	P3°	ALSF-2				0.09U
28 (254°T)	P2.95°	ALSF-1	Gr	TDZ HRL CL EL	Full	0.09D
15 (125°T)	P3°	ALSF-1				0.05D
33 (305°T)		Nil	Gr	HRL EL	Full	0.05U

OTHER LIGHTING: Obstruction, taxiway, A/D beacon, landing indicator, wind indicator.

RUNWAY AVAILABILITY
DC10 & B747 departures on R/W 33: will be started after the first 180m (591ft), observing the yellow mark determining the cockpit position of the a/c.
STOPWAYS
All - 60m (197ft)
CIRCLING
10/28 - North of aerodrome.
33 - Southwest of aerodrome (max 170kt)

1. Do not confuse refinery lights north of airfield with runway lights.
2. Birds in vicinity especially on approach.
3. Request clearance at least 10 mins before proposed taxi/pushback time.
4. R/W 10 & 28: ILS and PAPI touchdown points do not coincide.

Rev: R/W Elevations, Freq.

© European Aeronautical Group Aerad

Background
Just 20km (about 12½ miles) from the centre of Rio de Janeiro, the airport was built on Governador Island and opened in 1952. From 1952 until 1985, it was the main international airport and hub for Brazil, but in that year it was overtaken by São Paulo Gaurulhos, largely due to a sharp fall in the number of visiting tourists. Despite this, INFRAERO, the government agency formed in 1970 to manage Brazil's airports, pressed ahead with the construction of a second terminal, but it was not until 2004 that passenger traffic began to grow again, and over the next three years more than doubled from 4.5 million to 10.4 million, helped by the diversion of flights from the congested city centre Rio de Janeiro Santos Dumont Airport to Galeão, reducing the former to regional airport status. Before this, the airport had been operating at around 24 per cent of its capacity.

The dual name for the airport is to commemorate the musician, Antonio Carlos Jobim.

SALVADOR/DEPUTADO LUÍS EDUARDO MAGALHÃES INTERNATIONAL: SSA
Salvador, Bahia, Brazil

Operator and owner: INFRAERO
Runways: 10/28, 3,005m (9,859ft); 17/35, 1,519m (4,985ft)
Terminals: One
Airlines using airport as base: GOL
Annual passengers: 6,629,990
Annual cargo: 71,136 tonnes
Annual aircraft movements: 90,989

Background
Some 20km (12½ miles) north of Salvador, the airport originally opened in 1925 as Santo Amaro do Ipitanga. It was rebuilt in 1941 so that

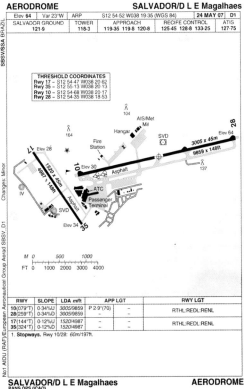

AERODROME				SALVADOR/D L E Magalhaes	
Elev 64	Var 23°W	ARP	S12 54 52 W038 19-35 (WGS 84)	24 MAY 07	D1
SALVADOR GROUND 121-9	TOWER 118-3	APPROACH 119-35 119-8 120-8	RECIFE CONTROL 125-45 128-8 133-25	ATIS 127-75	

THRESHOLD COORDINATES
Rwy 17 – S12 54-47 W038 20-62
Rwy 35 – S12 55-13 W038 20-13
Rwy 10 – S12 54-68 W038 20-17
Rwy 28 – S12 54-35 W038 18-53

RWY	SLOPE	LDA m/ft	APP LGT		RWY LGT
10(079°T)	0-34%U	3005/9859	P 2-9°(70)	–	RTHL:REDL:RENL
28(259°T)	0-34%D	3005/9859	–		
17(144°T)	0-12%U	1520/4987	–	–	RTHL:REDL:RENL
35(324°T)	0-12%D	1520/4987	–		

1. Stopways. Rwy 10/28: 60m/197ft.

No1 AIDU (RAF)/European Aeronautical Group Aerad SBSV_D1

Changes: Minor

SBSV/SSA BRAZIL

it would be available as an Allied air base during the Second World War. The wartime reconstruction stood the airport in good stead for many years. In 1955, the airport was renamed Dois de Julho, the name by which it is still known by many locally as it is the day the state became independent of Portugal, while the present name was adopted in 1998.

The airport was extensively renovated in 2000 and claims to be one of the most modern airports in Brazil. It is still used by the Forca Aerea Brasileira (Brazilian Air Force).

RECIFE – GUARARAPES/ GILBERTO FREYRE INTERNATIONAL: REC

Recife, Pernambuco, Brazil

Owner and operator: INFRAERO
Runways: 18/36, 3,315m (10,875ft)
Terminals: One

Annual passengers: 4,662,667
Annual cargo: 60,381 tonnes
Annual aircraft movements: 59,781

Background

A joint civil and military airport, Recife is, confusingly, also known as Guararapes or Gilberto Freyre International Airport.

PORTO ALEGRE/SALGADO FILHO INTERNATIONAL: POA

Porto Alegre, Rio Grande do Sul Province, Brazil

Owner and operator: INFRAERO
Runways: 11/29, 2,280m (7,481ft)
Terminals: One
Airlines using airport as base or hub: GOL, TAM
Annual passengers: 4,606,557
Annual cargo: 38,469 tonnes
Annual aircraft movements: 68,827

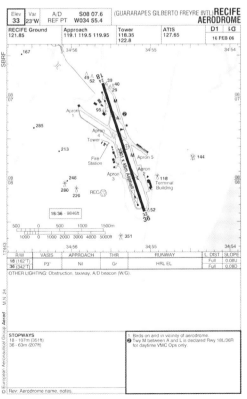

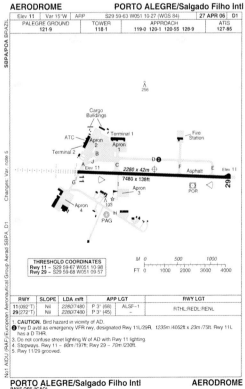

Background

One of the fastest-growing airports in Brazil, it is 6km (3¾ miles) from the centre of Porto Alegre. Recent expansion has been prompted by the emergence of low-cost airlines in Latin America, including the Brazilian airline GOL.

BELO HORIZONTE – TANCREDO NEVES/CONFINS: CNF

Belo Horizonte, Minas Gerais, Brazil

Owner and operator: INFRAERO
Runways: 16/34, 3,000m (9,843ft)
Terminals: One
Annual passengers: 4,521,711
Annual cargo: 19,702 tonnes
Annual aircraft movements: 55,491

Background

Named after a former president of Brazil, Tancredo Neves, but still more usually referred to as

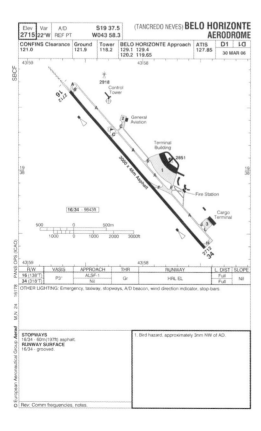

Confins, and in airline timetables as Belo Horizonte, the airport is 38km (24 miles) from the town centre of Belo Horizonte.

Opened in 1984, the airport was built by INFRAERO to reduce the congestion at Pampulha Regional Airport, and is now the largest and busiest airport in Minas Gerais. Until all flights at Pampulha were transferred to Tancredo Neves in 2005, the airport was under-used. Since the transfer, the airport has also attracted international services, with TAM Brazilian Airlines flying to Buenos Aires and TAP Air Portugal flying from Lisbon, while Copa flies from Panama City and American Airlines from Miami.

CURITIBA – AFONSO PENA INTERNATIONAL: CWB

São José dos Pinhais, Parana State, Brazil

Owner and operator: INFRAERO
Runways: 11/29, 1,800m (5,905ft); 15/33, 2,215m (7,267ft)
Terminals: One
Airlines using airport as base or hub: GOL, TAM Airlines
Annual passengers: 4,440,731
Annual cargo: 23,322 tonnes
Annual aircraft movements: 62,563

Background

Named after a former president of Brazil, Afonso Pena is 18km (11¼ miles) from the centre of Curitiba and is actually at São Jose dos Pinhais.

The airport dates from the Second World War when the United States Navy built an airfield for maritime-reconnaissance operations, and this became a mixed civil and military installation post war. In 1974, INFRAERO took over control and operation of the airport. A new passenger terminal opened in 1996 and the former terminal was rebuilt as a cargo terminal. The main runway was extended in 2008 and upgraded to Category III operation. Strong traffic growth continues, but the area suffers from morning mists and very unsettled weather, which up to the time of writing have not resulted in any accidents.

CONFINS/CONFREZA: CFO
Confreza, Mato Grosso, Brazil

Owner and operator: INFRAERO
Runways: N/A, 1,175m (3,855ft)
Terminals: One
Annual passengers: 4,340,129
Annual cargo: 25,602 tonnes
Annual aircraft movements: 55,491

Background
Relatively little information is freely available about this airport which has significant regional passenger traffic and is easily confused with Confins International (above).

FORTALEZA – PINTO MARTINS INTERNATIONAL: FOR
Fortaleza, Ceara State, Brazil

Owner and operator: INFRAERO/Forca Aerea
  Brasília
Runways: 13/31, 2,545m (8,350ft)
Terminals: One
Annual passengers: 3,919,820
Annual cargo: 38,172 tonnes
Annual aircraft movements: 47,226

Background
Opened in 1998, it is one of Brazil's newest airports and is shared with the air force.

RIO DE JANEIRO – SANTOS-DUMONT: SDU
Rio de Janeiro, Brazil

Owner and operator: INFRAERO
Runways: 02L/20R, 1,260m (4,134ft); 02R/20L, 1,323m (4,341ft)
Terminals: One
Airlines using airport as base or hub: Rio-Sul
Annual passengers: 3,214,415
Annual aircraft movements: 65,689

Background
Rio's second largest airport, it is just 2km (1¼ miles) from the city centre. It was superseded by Rio de Janeiro-Galeão because it had become too small and the runways were too short, having been built on reclaimed land which left no room for expansion. It suffered a major fire in 1999 that almost destroyed the terminal and was closed for six months for repairs. It is now limited to shorter domestic flights, having once handled international and even intercontinental flights.

The airport is named after Alberto Santos-Dumont, the pioneering Brazilian aviator and aeronaut, who was the first man to fly a heavier-than-air machine in Europe.

BELÉM/VAL DE CÃES INTERNATIONAL: BEL
Belém, Para State, Brazil

Owner and operator: INFRAERO
Runways: 06/24, 2,798m (9,180ft); 02/20, 1,830m (6,004ft)

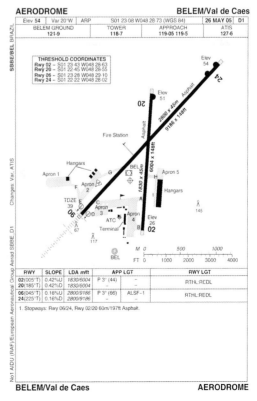

BELEM/Val de Caes   AERODROME

Terminals: One
Annual passengers: 2,377,348
Annual cargo: 19,444 tonnes
Annual aircraft movements: 40,124

Background

The larger of two airports serving Belém, Val-de-Cães is named after the locality and opened in 1934, for both civil and military use. During the Second World War it was upgraded and expanded with funds from the United States so that it could become a vital link in the ferrying of aircraft from factories in the United States and Canada to the operational theatres in North Africa and the Mediterranean. It was returned to civil use after the war, although the Forca Aerea Brasilia has continued to use it as a base up to the present.

Post war, it was used by Panair do Brasil and Pan American amongst other airlines, and in 1958 received its first purpose-built passenger terminal.

MANAUS – EDUARDO GOMES INTERNATIONAL: MAO

Manaus (Manaos), Amazonas State, Brazil.

Owner and operator: INFRAERO
Runways: 10/28, 2,700m (8,858ft)
Terminals: Two, designated Terminal 1
   (international and domestic) and Terminal 2,
   also known as Eduardinho, or 'Little Eduardo',
   (for regional flights and business aircraft)
Annual passengers: 2,251,256
Annual cargo: 170,132 tonnes
Annual aircraft movements: 44,303

Background

Opened in March 1976, when it was the first airport in Brazil to have airbridges, and was nicknamed 'The Supersonic Airport' after a visit by a Concorde airliner.

FLORIANÓPOLIS/HERCÍLIO LUZ INTERNATIONAL: FLN

Florianópolis (Desterro), Santa Carina, Brazil

Owner and operator: INFRAERO
Runways: 03/21, 1,500m (4,921ft); 14/32,
   2,300m (7,546ft)
Terminals: One
Annual passengers: 2,105,399
Annual cargo: 9,341 tonnes

Background

A joint military and civil airport, it dates from the Second World War and handles both domestic and international flights. The main operator is the Brazilian low-cost airline, GOL.

EURICO DE AGUIAR SALLES/ VITÓRIA/GOIABEIRAS: VIX

Goiabeiras, Brazil

Owner and operator: INFRAERO
Runways: 23/05, 1,750m (5,741ft)
Terminals: One
Annual passengers: 1,894,442
Annual cargo: 16,104 tonnes
Annual aircraft movements: 39,777

Background

Known variously as Eurico de Aguiar Salles Airport, Goiabeiras Airport (due to its location) or Vitória Airport, it is the busiest airport in Espirito Santo state, although only capable of handling aircraft of Boeing 737 or Airbus A320 size.

Developed as a commercial airport after the Second World War, it has failed to achieve its full potential as it needs to be expanded and modernised. Modernisation began in 2005, but has been delayed.

NATAL – AUGUSTO SEVERO INTERNATIONAL: NAT

Natal, Rio Grande do Norte, Brazil

Owner and operator: INFRAERO/Forca Aerea
   Brasilia

Runways: 16L/34R, 2,600m (8,530ft); 16R/34L,
   1,800m (5,905ft); 12/30, 1,825m (5,987ft)
Terminals: One
Annual passengers: 1,660,285
Annual cargo: 9,693 tonnes

Background

The airport for the state capital of Rio Grande
do Norte, it is mainly a regional airport with 12
airlines providing services to domestic destinations, but only TAP Air Portugal providing an
international service. It is also used by the
Brazilian Air Force.

GOIÂNIA/SANTA GENOVEVA: GYN

Goiânia, Goias State, Brazil.

Owner and operator: INFRAERO
Runways: 14/32, 2,501m (8,204ft)
Terminals: One
Annual passengers: 1,546,476
Annual cargo: 7,399 tonnes
Annual aircraft movements: 43,136

Background

A regional airport handling domestic flights. A
new terminal is currently under construction.

CUIABÁ – MARECHAL RONDON INTERNATIONAL: CGB

Cuiabá, Mato Grosso State, Brazil

Owner and operator: INFRAERO
Runways: 17/35, 2,300m (7,546ft)
Terminals: One
Airlines using airport as base or hub: GOL
Annual passengers: 1,280,002
Annual cargo: 7,561 tonnes
Annual aircraft movements: 39,443

Background

Very little information is publicly available
about this new airport, which serves domestic
services only. The most important operator is
the low-cost airline, GOL.

VIRACOPOS/CAMPINAS INTERNATIONAL: VCP

Campinas, São Paulo State, Brazil

Owner and operator: INFRAERO
Runways: 15/33, 3,240m (10,630ft)
Terminals: One
Annual passengers: 1,206,288
Annual cargo: 229,402 tonnes

Background

Brazil's second most important airport for cargo,
Campinas is 20km (12½ miles) from the centre
of Campinas.

The airport dates from 1960 when it was
opened to provide São Paulo with an airport
capable of handling the first generation of long-
haul jet airliners, such as the Boeing 707 and
Douglas DC-8. It is hard to regard this as *the* airport for São Paulo, however, as it is 99km (62
miles) from São Paulo city, but it remained the
main airport in the state until the opening of São
Paulo/Guarulhos in 1985. The opening of the
new airport effectively removed most of the
international flights from Campinas, but it still
has considerable regional air traffic.

While it was still new there was a serious accident at the airport on 23 November 1961 when a
de Havilland Comet 4 jet airliner of Aerolineas
Argentinas suffered an engine failure after take-
off and crashed into a forest, killing all 40 passengers and the crew.

BRUNEI

BRUNEI INTERNATIONAL/ BANDAR SERI BEGAWAN: BWN

Bandar Seri Begawan, Brunei

Owner and operator: Government of Brunei
Runways: 03/21, 3,658m (12,000ft)
Terminals: One
Airlines using airport as base or hub: Royal
   Brunei Airlines
Annual passengers: 1,447,580
Annual cargo: 21,150 tonnes

Background

The only international airport in the Sultanate of Brunei, it also doubles as the Royal Brunei Air Force's Rimba Air Base.

The original airport for Brunei was at Berakas using a former Second World War Japanese Army Air Force airfield, from which commercial operations began in 1953 with an internal air service, which was soon followed by flights into what is now Malaysia. By the 1970s, the airport was no longer adequate for the growth in traffic or the increase in aircraft sizes, and the current airport was built, opening in 1974. At the same time, a national airline, Royal Brunei Airlines, was established. The airport's traffic is mainly international, but there is a small domestic network of routes radiating out from it.

BULGARIA

Judging by the Bulgarian experience, the transition from a supply-led Communist economy to a market-led capitalist one is extremely difficult. New airlines have emerged, mainly serving the country's growing tourist trade, but Balkan Bulgarian Airlines, the national carrier, collapsed in 2002.

SOFIA INTERNATIONAL: SOF

Vrazhdebna, Sofia, Bulgaria

Owner and operator: Sofia Airport EAD
Runways: 09/27, 3,600m (11,811ft)
Terminals: Two, designated Terminal 1 and
   Terminal 2
Airlines using airport as base or hub: Air Via
   Bulgarian Airways, BH Air, Bulgaria Air,
   Bulgaria Air Charter, Hemus Air, Scorpion Air,
   Vega Airlines
Annual passengers: 2,746,330
Annual cargo: 17,389 tonnes
Annual aircraft movements: 43,076

Background

Often known locally as Vrazhdebna, after a village just to the north of the airport, Sofia Inter-

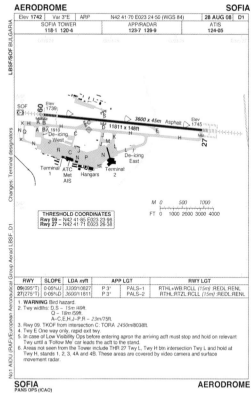

national is around 10km (6¼ miles) from the centre of the city.

The airport opened shortly before the outbreak of the Second World War to replace Sofia's original airport at Bozhurishte, which was no longer large enough to handle the growth in air traffic. During the Second World War it was used as a military air station by Bulgaria's own small air force, and then by the Luftwaffe, before being taken over by the Red Air Forces as the Soviet armies advanced towards Germany. While a new terminal was completed during the war years, built along the same lines as a contemporary railway terminus, it did not open until 1947, and remains as the current Terminal 1. One plan for the airport that was not realised was that it should have two intersecting runways.

The terminal was struggling to cope with the number of passengers by the late 1960s, and modernisation and extensions were made which were completed in 1975. At the same time, possible locations for a new airport were examined, but eventually it was decided to redevelop the existing site with a new runway parallel to the original one (which has become a taxiway), and a new terminal (the current Terminal 2), all of which opened on 27 December 2006. The new runway was intended for Category III operations because the airport, which is 531m (1,742ft) above sea level, has suffered from being unable to cope with bad weather, especially fog. Unfortunately, because of interference from security fencing and a new lorry park, the necessary navigational aids cannot be used. The one serious accident that can be attributed to bad weather was on 10 January 1984, when a Balkan Bulgarian Airlines Tupolev Tu-134 crashed on approach to the airport, with the loss of all 50 passengers and crew.

BOURGAS/BURGAS INTERNATIONAL: BOJ
Sarafovo, Bourgas, Bulgaria

Owner and operator: Burgas Airport
Runways: 04/22, 3,200m (10,499ft)
Terminals: One
Airlines using airport as base or hub: Balkan
    Bulgarian
Annual passengers: 1,949,197

Background
One of the first Bulgarian airports to open after the Second World War, the airport (known variously as Bourgas/Burgas International or locally as Sarafovo Airport because of its locality) has enjoyed strong growth since the collapse of Communism as the country has become a leading tourist destination. In 2006, Fraport, the operator of Frankfurt Airport, was awarded a 35-year concession by the Bulgarian government to develop Bourgas and Varna airports, both of which need to be modernised and enlarged. Most of the airport's aircraft movements are inclusive tour charter flights.

VARNA INTERNATIONAL: VAR
Varna, Bulgaria

Owner and operator: Varna Airport/Fraport
Runways: 09/27, 2,500m (8,202ft)
Terminals: One
Annual passengers: 1,493,267

Background
The airport for Bulgaria's main port, it dates from 1947 when it replaced the Tihina Airport which was no longer adequate for larger aircraft. For many years the airport mainly handled domestic flights and services to other Warsaw Pact countries, but the country was regarded as a prime tourist resort before the collapse of Communism and a new and larger terminal was opened in 1972, followed by a new runway in 1974. In 2006, Fraport, the operators of Frankfurt International Airport, were granted a 35-year concession to develop and manage both Varna and Bourgas. A new terminal opened in 2008.

CAMBODIA

Formerly a French colony, Cambodia was not directly involved in the 1959–75 Vietnam War but was eventually dragged into the conflict because Viet Cong guerrillas were using the country as a supply route. There was a violent civil war between 1970 and 1975, after which the country became isolated during the period of suppression under the Khmer Rouge regime. There followed invasion and occupation from Vietnam, with a further period of civil war, after which in the early 1990s a democratic government was re-established under a constitutional monarchy and the country began to return to stability and make the most of its potential as a tourist destination.

PHNOM PENH INTERNATIONAL: PNH

Phnom Penh, Cambodia

Owner and operator: Cambodia Airport
Management Services
Runways: 05/23, 3,000m (9,843ft)
Terminals: One
Airlines using airport as base or hub: Air
Cambodia
Annual passengers: 1,598,424
Annual cargo: 26,877 tonnes

Background

Built by the French before French Indo-China became independent in 1949, the airport was originally known as Pochentong International Airport. Air traffic growth was restricted when Cambodia became involved indirectly in the Vietnam War in the late 1960s and later during the suppressive Khmer Rouge regime. In 1995, following a return to democratic rule, the government signed an agreement to manage the airport with a French-Malaysian consortium which has been redeveloping and modernising it with a new runway and passenger terminal, a cargo terminal and a Category III instrument landing system. In recent years, passenger growth has been strong, fuelled by the return of tourists to the country, but this may now be affected by the world economic downturn.

SIEM REAP-ANGKOR INTERNATIONAL: REP

Siem Reap, Cambodia

Owner and operator: Government of Cambodia
Runways: 05/23, 2,550m (8,366ft)
Terminals: One
Airlines using airport as base or hub: Siem
Reap Airways
Annual passengers: 1,734,308

Background

Cambodia's largest airport is so named because of its proximity to the ancient temples at Angkor Wat. A new terminal was opened in 2006.

CANADA

Vast distances and isolated pockets of population, plus the heavy commuter traffic between major cities such as Montreal and Toronto, make Canada natural territory for air transport. For many years the country was served by two major nationwide airlines (both of which were founded by railway companies) – Trans Canada Airlines, the predecessor of today's Air Canada, and Canadian Pacific, which later became Canadian Airlines before being absorbed by its rival Air Canada in 2000.

The early days of Canadian aviation were those of small, pioneering, and under-funded bush operations, while travel between the large cities tended to be by railway, with the main cities grouped together in the east and east central area of the country, leaving just Vancouver, and to a lesser extent Calgary, to the west. Airports are generally either civil or military and only occasionally shared, with ownership usually vested in Transport Canada, but with local authorities usually operating the airports and levying an 'improvement fee' to pay for modernisation.

The proximity of Canada's airports to those of the United States meant that they were chosen as emergency landing sites for long-haul transatlantic and transpacific flights bound for the US when that country's airspace was closed after the terrorist attacks on New York and Washington on 11 September 2001. The exercise was known as 'Operation Yellow Ribbon', and largely passed without incident, although one aircraft had to be escorted to Vancouver by USAF fighters after a communications breakdown.

On an even more useful note, many Canadian airports offer pre-border clearance for passengers heading for US airports, saving time after landing as they avoid the usual queues for immigration control.

TORONTO/LESTER B. PEARSON INTERNATIONAL: YYZ

Toronto, Ontario, Canada

Owner: Transport Canada
Operator: Greater Toronto Airports Authority
Runways: 15L/33R, 3,368m (11,050ft);
   15R/33L, 2,770m (9,088ft); 06L/24R, 2,956m
   (9,697ft); 06R/24L, 2,743m (9,000ft); 05/23,
   3,389m (11,120ft)
Terminals: Two, designated 1 and 3, with an
   Infield Terminal as a temporary facility when
   major work is undertaken at 1 and 3
Airlines using airport as base or hub: Air
   Canada, Air Canada Jazz
Annual passengers: 31,452,848
Annual cargo: 504,608 tonnes
Annual aircraft movements: 425,500

Although a railway connection with Pearson from Toronto Union Station is planned, no completion date is available.

Background

Toronto's airport history started in 1937 when the Toronto Harbour Commission purchased a plot of land at Malton and built a terminal from a converted farmhouse, and two hard runways, an unusual feature at the time, especially as lighting was provided, and a grass runway. Malton Airport opened in 1939, but the following year it was sold to the City of Toronto. Throughout the Second World War it was used for the Empire Air Training Scheme, designed to train aircrew for the Royal Air Force and other British Empire air forces in the better weather and safer flying conditions of the dominions and colonies.

Post war, Malton was returned to the city and in 1949 the original terminal was replaced by a new terminal, capable of handling up to 400,000 passengers a year and with an observation area on the roof. The airport was renamed Toronto City Centre Airport, and continued expansion eventually resulted in most of the neighbouring town of Elmbank being demolished. One of the runways was extended to more than 11,000ft and used for test flights of jet fighters by Avro

Canada. The airport was taken over by Transport Canada in 1958, and in 1960 was renamed Toronto International Airport.

In the meantime, work had started on building a new terminal in 1957, and when this (known as T1) was completed in 1964, the earlier post-war terminal was demolished. T1 was also known as Aeroquay 1. Nevertheless, it was clear that with the arrival of the jet age, demand for air travel was growing more quickly than could be satisfied at what had been Malton Airport, and attention turned to building a completely new airport elsewhere. In 1972, the Canadian government made a compulsory purchase of land east of Toronto for what was conceived as Pickering Airport, but strong local objections caused delays, and in the meantime Toronto International was expanded with the addition of a second terminal (T2) similar in design to T1, and which opened in 1972. T2 supported Aeroquays 2 and 3. It was intended for

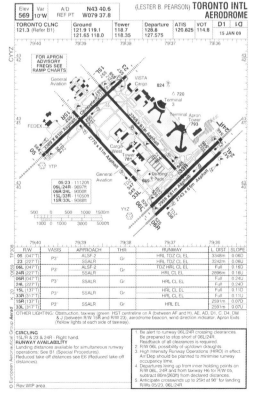

Canadian Pacific (later CP Air), American Airlines, and BOAC (later British Airways), but was unpopular with the airlines, who found it difficult to work and unsuitable for wide-bodied aircraft. It was also unpopular with passengers as it lacked windows. In the end, the state-owned Air Canada was forced to use it instead of the other airlines.

A busy airport, there have been some accidents. There was a major one at Toronto on 5 July 1970. An Air Canada Douglas DC-8 was flying from Montreal to Los Angeles via Toronto, but before landing the pilots accidentally deployed the spoilers, forcing them to go-around, but the aircraft was damaged in the attempted landing and broke-up during the go-around with the loss of all 100 passengers and 9 crew. On 26 June 1978, an Air Canada Douglas DC-9 on a flight to Winnipeg had take-off aborted, but overran the runway and crashed in the Etobicoke Creek, which is in a ravine, and 2 of the 107 passengers on board were killed. Much more fortunate was the Air France Airbus A340-300 landing from Paris on 2 August 2005, which was unable to stop on the runway during a severe thunderstorm and overran, again into the Etobicoke Creek, with the rear third of the aircraft bursting into flames. Despite this, there were no fatalities, although 43 passengers suffered minor injuries. Many in the air transport industry see this as a textbook example of a successful evacuation from a stricken aircraft in particularly difficult circumstances.

In 1984, the airport was renamed yet again as Lester B. Pearson International, after a former Canadian prime minister, but is more usually known simply as 'Toronto Pearson'.

Terminal 3 opened in 1991, although earlier the designation had been used for a temporary facility provided by CP Air. In 1996, operational control of the airport was passed from Transport Canada to the greater Toronto Airports Authority. Work began on a new Terminal 1 to replace the existing Terminals 1 and 2. A cargo terminal was also added to the centre of the airport between the two north-south parallel runways, and two new runways were added, with a new north-south runway (15R/33L) completed in 1997, and an east-west runway (06R/24L) opened in 2002. The new Terminal 1 opened in 2004, and has been built with expansion in mind. Meanwhile, Terminal 2 has been demolished. A LINK train provides a shuttle service between the two operational terminals.

A reduction in competition at the airport came when Air Canada acquired Canadian Airlines, the former CP Air, in 2000.

VANCOUVER INTERNATIONAL: YVR
Vancouver, British Columbia, Canada

Owner: Transport Canada
Operator: Vancouver International Airport
   Authority
Runways: 08L/26R, 3,029m (9,940ft); 08R/26L,
   3,505m (11,500ft); 12/30, 2,225m (7,300ft);
   26A, 1,066m (3,500ft)
Terminals: Four, designated Domestic,
   International, Trans-border pre-clearance (for
   flights to the United States only), and South
   Terminal (for regional airlines flying within
   British Columbia)
Airlines using airport as base or hub: Air
   Canada, Air Canada Jazz, Harmony Airways,
   Pacific Coastal Airlines
Annual passengers: 17,710,239
Annual cargo: 225,412 tonnes
Annual aircraft movements: 328,563

During 2009, the airport will be connected to the Canada Line rapid transit, linking it with Vancouver city centre.

Background
Allegedly stung by Charles Lindbergh's refusal to include the city on his post-transatlantic solo flight tour because of the lack of an airport in 1927, the city purchased land on Sea Island for the construction of an airport in 1929. Since then the airport has become Canada's main gateway for transpacific flights, handling more than any other Canadian airport, not just because of its position but also because of the large number of

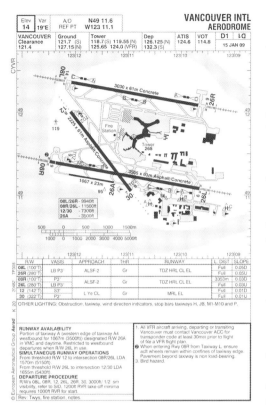

Canada Airbus A340 about to depart for Hong Kong collided with an Air Canada Jazz Dash 8 which was taxiing on the runway, but while both aircraft were damaged, there were no casualties. Less fortunate was the pilot of a light aircraft, a Piper Seneca, who took off on 19 October 2007, and crashed into an apartment building, killing the pilot and injuring two occupants of the flats.

MONTREAL/PIERRE ELLIOTT TRUDEAU INTERNATIONAL: YUL
Montreal, Quebec, Canada

Owner: Transport Canada
Operator: Aéroports de Montreal
Runways: 06L/24R, 3,353m (11,000ft);
   06R/24L, 2,926m (9,600ft); 10/28, 2,134m
   (7,000ft)
Terminals: One with three concourses:
   International, Trans-border pre-clearance, and
   Domestic
Airlines using airport as base or hub: Air
   Canada, Air Transat
Annual passengers: 12,407,934
Annual aircraft movements: 222,871

Canadians with Asian origins settled in the immediate area.

During the Second World War it was used as a Royal Canadian Air Force base, and its role became increasingly important after the entry of Japan into the war in December 1941.

The oldest of the four current terminals is the Domestic Terminal, opened in 1968 but completely renovated in recent years, while the most recent is the Transborder, opened in the late 1990s when the United States Customs and Immigration Departments introduced a policy of pre-clearance to ease entry into the USA. The South Terminal includes part of the original airport terminal.

There have been a number of accidents and incidents at Vancouver over the years. One of these was on 7 February 1968, when a Canadian Pacific Airlines Boeing 707 overran a runway when landing in heavy fog, killing one member of the crew. On 18 September 2008, an Air

While a direct railways link is planned, at present a shuttle bus operates between the terminal and Dorval railway station.

Background
Situated some 20km (12 miles) from the city centre by the town of Dorval on Montreal Island, Montreal-Pierre Elliott Trudeau International is more usually known as Dorval. It is shared by the large Bombardier aircraft factory which produces regional jet and turboprop airliners and business aircraft. It has the unusual history in that a replacement airport was built at Mirabel, and yet Dorval survived and remains the city's leading airport.

Montreal's first airport was Saint-Hubert, opened in 1927, but in a little more than ten years this was judged to be inadequate for the growth in traffic and aircraft sizes. Land at Dorval racecourse was purchased for the construction of an airport as the area rarely suffered from fog, but

should be constructed for Montreal at Sainte-Scholastique, which would become Montreal-Mirabel International Airport. The intention was to close Dorval to commercial traffic other than that from the aircraft factory, and as the start of a phased rundown, after Mirabel opened in 1975, it was planned that all international flights would be transferred. When Montreal-Mirabel opened on 29 November 1975, it was at the time the world's largest airport by land area, and no fewer than 23 international airlines operating into Montreal transferred their flights. Montreal-Dorval was defined as handling domestic flights and trans-border services to the United States.

Naturally, traffic at Dorval fell sharply, while the situation was made worse by economic decline in Montreal during the 1970s and 1980s which led many airlines to transfer their flights to Toronto, a larger city. This situation also affected Mirabel, because many airlines decided that they only needed to serve one destination in Eastern Canada. The better location of Dorval to the city centre also ensured that a steady drift of airlines away from Mirabel and back to Dorval started. Mirabel stopped handling scheduled passenger flights from 2004, and started to concentrate on air cargo and private and business aircraft.

With domestic, trans-border, and international flights back in the one airport, Dorval once again became a major hub airport, and Air Canada made it one of its two main hubs. In 2000, with a stated capacity of 7 million passengers annually, Dorval handled 9.4 million, and by 2007 the figure had risen to 12.4 million. In the meantime, the federal government gave the airport its present name in memory of a former prime minister, Pierre Elliott Trudeau, which many regarded as a strange decision as during his term of office Trudeau had been opposed to the airport. More important, in 2000 a programme of modernisation and expansion started, and this means that the capacity of the airport is around 20 million passengers a year.

Air safety has improved considerably over the years, and the introduction of jet aircraft was one

when it opened on 1 September 1941, Canada was at war and instead of an airport it opened as Royal Canadian Air Force Station Lachline. From the start it had three paved runways and post war it became Montreal-Dorval International Airport. In the early days, traffic was boosted by aircraft landing for refuelling after a transatlantic flight whilst en route to airports in the USA. During the 1950s, it became the busiest airport in Canada.

Montreal is in predominantly French-speaking Quebec, and in November 1960 the airport was renamed Aéroport International Dorval de Montreal. The following month a new terminal was opened, the largest in Canada at the time. A major expansion programme started in the late 1960s, but despite this and transatlantic flights no longer needing to use the airport for refuelling stops, the federal government decided that the airport would be heavily congested and overcrowded by 1985 and decided that a new airport

significant step forward. Nevertheless, there have been a number of accidents. One of these was on 29 November 1963, when a Trans-Canada Airlines Douglas DC-8 crashed shortly after taking off for Toronto, with the loss of all 118 people aboard. More fortunate were those aboard an Air Canada flight bound for Calgary on 23 September 2007, which had to return because of a failure of the undercarriage hydraulic system. The aircraft made a heavy landing and a hard stop, which started a fire in the undercarriage, but this was extinguished by the airport fire crews and all passengers and crew left the aircraft without injury. Almost a year later, on 26 August 2008, there was another lucky escape when an Air France Boeing 747 from Paris skidded off the runway on landing and got stuck in the grass, but again there were no casualties.

CALGARY INTERNATIONAL: YYC
Calgary, Alberta, Canada

Owner: Transport Canada
Operator: Calgary Airport Authority
Runways: 07/25, 1,890m (6,200ft); 10/28, 2,438m (8,000ft); 16/34, 3,863m (12,675ft); there are proposals to build a fourth runway
Terminals: One with four concourses, designated A (Domestic), B (Domestic), C (Domestic and US-bound) and D (includes International)
Airlines using airport as base or hub: Westjet
Annual passengers: 12,257,848
Annual cargo: 134,250 tonnes
Annual aircraft movements: 250,548

Background
Canada's fourth busiest airport, Calgary International is 17km (11 miles) north-east of the city centre. In common with many Canadian airports, it offers US border pre-clearance facilities.

Calgary's first airfield was opened at Bowness, 10km (6¼ miles) west of the city. It had a grass airstrip, which was usual at the time, and a small wooden hangar. Over the next 25 years, two other sites served as airfields for Calgary

until the present airport opened in 1939. Initially the airport was known as McCall Field, named after a local man who had been a fighter ace during the First World War. It was opened by the city, but the following year nationalised by the federal government for wartime use and did not revert to the local authority until 1949, after wartime use by the Royal Canadian Air Force, which left behind four surfaced runways and five hangars. Returned to civilian use, traffic grew steadily, and in 1956 a new air terminal replaced the 1939 building. The 1956 terminal was enlarged five times, but it was soon clear that it was not designed for the jet age and that a completely new terminal would be beyond local resources. So, in 1966, the airport was sold to the federal government for Canadian $2m on condition that the airport be modernised and a new terminal completed. Under federal ownership, the airport adopted its present title. The federal agency charged with the airport's development

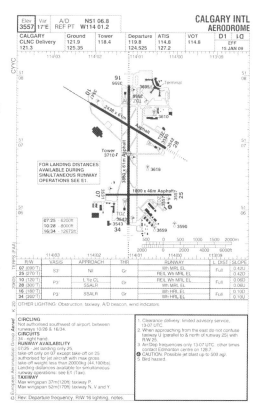

was Transport Canada, and they enlarged the entire airport and provided new road access as well as opening a new terminal in 1977.

In July 1992, the Calgary Authority, owned by the local authority, took over the operation of the airport and is responsible for any future development, while ownership remains with Transport Canada. In recent years, a new air traffic control tower has been opened.

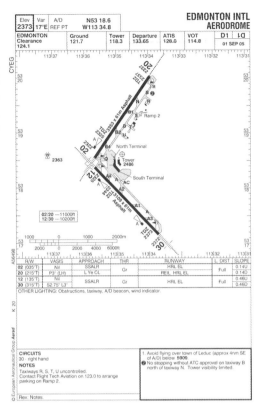

EDMONTON INTERNATIONAL: YEG

Edmonton, Alberta, Canada

Owner: Transport Canada
Operator: Edmonton Regional Airports Authority
Runways: 02/20, 3,353m (11,000ft); 12/30, 3,109m (10,200ft)
Terminals: Two, designated North Terminal and South Terminal
Airlines using airport as base or hub: Air Canada, Air Canada Jazz, Westjet
Annual passengers: 6,065,117
Annual cargo: 38,274 tonnes
Annual aircraft movements: 119,913

Background

Situated 26km (16 miles) south-west of Edmonton, it was opened in 1960 after it was realised that the then Edmonton Municipal Airport, now Edmonton City Centre Airport, could not handle the jet airliners entering service at that time. The airport opened before it was complete, and until 1963 passengers had to use a hangar as a terminal until the first permanent terminal, today's North Terminal, opened. The temporary hangar accommodation was enlivened by some works of art, but most of these have gone, other than a large mural 'Bush Pilot in Northern Sky', which has recently been renovated.

Initially, the new airport enjoyed rapid growth in passenger numbers, but this trend went into reverse during the 1980s and early 1990s, and the airport also suffered from strong competition from Edmonton City Centre Airport for short-haul traffic within both Alberta and British Columbia, and was also flying longer-distance passengers to other hub airports. The situation was restored by a local referendum in 1995 in which more than three quarters of the population voted in favour of all scheduled flights using Edmonton International, leaving Edmonton City Centre for general aviation and charter flights. As traffic grew again, the airport began to expand its facilities with the opening of a new terminal, the South Terminal, in 2005. Growth continued to be strong after this and in recent years topped 16 per cent in both 2006 and 2007. What might be described as a 'virtuous cycle' emerged with more passengers attracting more long-haul and non-stop flights and these in turn attracting more passengers.

For the future, the airport is extending the South Terminal in two phases, which should be completed during 2010, as well as making improvements to its de-icing facilities. Forecasts for passenger traffic in 2012 have been raised from 7.5 million to 9 million.

OTTAWA/MACDONALD-CARTIER INTERNATIONAL: YOW

Riverside South, Ottawa, Ontario, Canada

Owner: Transport Canada
Operator: Ottawa MacDonald-Cartier
    International Airport Authority
Runways: 04/22, 1,006m (3,300ft); 07/25,
    2,438m (8,000ft); 14/32, 3,050m (10,005ft)
Terminals: One
Airlines using airport as base or hub: Air
    Canada, Air Canada Jazz, First Air
Annual passengers: 4,088,528
Annual cargo: 22,670 tonnes
Annual aircraft movements: 73,342

There is a bus connection to a railway station, while in the longer term an extension of a rapid transit line into the airport terminal has been proposed.

Background

Just over 10km (6¼ miles) from the city centre, the airport is named after Sir John MacDonald and George-Etienne Cartier, although many still know it by its old name of Uplands. Despite being a port of entry with customs and immigration facilities, and having pre-clearance facilities for passengers heading for the United States, the immigration control limits international flights to aircraft of 165 seats or fewer.

The airport was originally an airfield for the Ottawa Flying Club during the 1930s, and the club still uses it. During the Second World War, Uplands became No. 2 Flying Training School under the British Empire Air Training Scheme which provided pilots and navigators for the Royal Air Force and the Fleet Air Arm. Post war, it remained a military airfield first for the Royal Canadian Air Force and then after reorganisation of the armed forces, the Canadian Armed Forces Air Command as CAFB Uplands. Joint civil and military use meant that during the 1950s it became Canada's busiest airport by aircraft movements. In addition to Trans-Canada Airlines, the processor of today's Air Canada, there were flights by Trans Air (the Canadian airline as opposed to the British and Swedish airlines of the same name), and Eastern Air Lines. New runways were built south of the original runways and a new terminal to handle jet aircraft, although the rehearsal for the opening ceremony in 1959 did not go to plan when a USAF Lockheed F-104 Starfighter went supersonic whilst making a low pass and shattered almost all of the glass in the terminal, and damaged door and window frames and ceiling tiles. The damage had to be repaired and the new airport did not open until April 1960.

Far more serious were some of the accidents at the airport, and amongst these was one to an Air Canada Douglas DC-8 training flight on 19 March 1967, which crashed on approach with the loss of all three crew (the only occupants). More than 20 years later a Bradley Air Services BAe748 crashed, again on approach, killing both pilots. More fortunate were the crew of a North American Airlines Fairchild Swearingen Metroliner which struck the runway with undercarriage retracted on 13 June 1997, causing serious damage and a fire, but the crew escaped without injury. There were also no injuries when a Miami Air International Boeing 727 landed on 15 September 2000 to pick up a hockey team, but ran off the runway. Another aircraft that ran off the runway was a WestJet Boeing 737 that landed from Calgary on 17 February 2008, possibly after freezing rain left the runway with a layer of ice, but the 94 passengers aboard the aircraft were unhurt.

The airport is now completely civil with commercial airlines and private flying. In recent years a new terminal has been built and it opened in October 2003, replacing the old terminal, although a section of it remained and was connected to the new terminal for peak period use and for turboprop aircraft until an extension to the new terminal opened in March 2008.

WINNIPEG JAMES ARMSTRONG RICHARDSON INTERNATIONAL: YWG

Winnipeg, Manitoba, Canada

Owner: Transport Canada

Operator: Winnipeg Airports Authority

Runways: 13/31, 2,652m (8,700ft); 18/36, 3,353m (11,000ft)

Terminals: Four, designated the Main Terminal (which most flights use), the Keewatin/Kivalliq and Perimeter/Calm Air Terminals (for local flights), and the Esso Avitat/Shell Aerocentre Terminal (for oil industry charters)

Airlines using airport as base or hub: Air Canada Jazz, WestJet

Annual passengers: 3,570,673

Annual cargo: 155,988 tonnes

Annual aircraft movements: 151,793

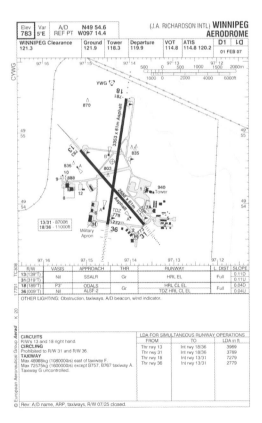

Background

Situated close to the city centre, near an aerospace-related industrial park, the airport dates from 1928 when it was opened as Stevenson Aerodrome, named after a local hero – the pioneer bush pilot Captain Fred Stevenson. It claims to be the first airport in Canada to handle international flights, and in 1958 was officially named as Winnipeg International Airport. It was renamed again in 2006, adopting the current title in memory of a local aviation entrepreneur.

The current terminal was opened in 1964 and was expanded and modernised in 1984. A new terminal is under construction and the first stage will be completed in 2010. Once it is open, the current terminal will be demolished and its place taken by an aviation museum. These and other changes to the airport have meant that a third runway, 07/25, has been closed, but future plans include either new runways or lengthening and strengthening the existing runways. The airport has only had to close once since 1986, and that was on 9 February 2009 when an ice storm hit the airport, but the runways were cleared and operational again later in the day. The following month, on 3 March, a Perimeter Airlines Metroliner suffered undercarriage failure and had to make a belly landing with 10 people aboard, but there were no casualties. Air cargo is also important to Winnipeg, and ambitious plans centre around a development known as CentrePort Canada complete with warehousing and distribution centres.

HALIFAX ROBERT L. STANFIELD/HALIFAX STANFIELD INTERNATIONAL: YHZ

Enfield, Nova Scotia, Canada

Owner: Transport Canada

Operator: Halifax International Airport Authority

Runways: 05/23, 2,682m (8,800ft); 14/32, 2,347m (7,700ft)

Terminals: One

Airlines using airport as base or hub: Headquarters for Air Canada Jazz and CanJet

Annual passengers: 3,469,062

Annual cargo: 29,753 tonnes
Annual aircraft movements: 80,965

Background

Halifax was originally served by an airport on the Halifax Peninsula, but this closed in 1942. After the Second World War and until 1960 the city used as its airport the Royal Canadian Air Force (later Canadian Armed Forces) base, RCAF Shearwater, constructed during the war for maritime reconnaissance operations. The present airport was then opened on a site at Kelly Lake, chosen because it was less affected by fog than other sites in the area.

The original 1960 passenger terminal was named in 2005 to commemorate Robert Stanfield, a former prime minister of the province of Nova Scotia, but in 2007 the name was given to the entire airport. Since 1998 the airport has been expanded and modernised, with the terminal extended and the runways strengthened. The only serious accident at Halifax was on 14 October 2004, when an MK Airlines Boeing 747-200F freighter crashed on take-off, killing all seven crew. In 2006 it started to provide US border pre-clearance for passengers bound for US destinations.

The airport includes production facilities for Pratt & Whitney Canada and Northrop Grumman.

VICTORIA INTERNATIONAL: YYJ

North Saanich, British Columbia, Canada

Owner: Transport Canada
Operator: Victoria International Airport Authority
Runways: 09/27, 2,134m (7,000ft); 02/20, 1,532m (5,026ft); 13/31, 1,525m (5,003ft)
Terminals: One
Annual passengers: 1,481,600
Annual aircraft movements: 163,936

Background

The airport is 22km (14 miles) north of Victoria and is close to the town of Sidney. It is beside Patricia Bay, and is known by many locals as Patricia Bay Airport, or even as 'Pat Airport'.

The airport dates from 1914, when it was simply a grass landing strip used for training by the Canadian Army. Between the wars its location beside Patricia Bay was an asset as it could handle seaplanes and flying boats as well as landplanes. Although used by commercial flights from 1943, when Trans Canada Airlines (predecessor of today's Air Canada) started services, the Royal Canadian Air Force retained control until 1948, when it passed to the Canadian Department of Transport, which named it Victoria (Patricia Bay) Airport. The RCAF remained at the airport until 1952, when it became a completely commercial operation. Nevertheless, the military connection resumed in 1980 when the Canadian Armed Forces Air Command based a squadron of Sea King anti-submarine helicopters at what the CAF call Patricia Bay.

The present name was adopted in 1959, and in 1997 the airport, while remaining in federal government ownership through Transport Canada, had operational control given to the Victoria Airport Authority, which is owned by the local authority. In 2000 a modernisation programme started, and this is due to continue in stages until 2020. An improvement levy is charged on all passengers, in common with other Canadian airports managed by a local authority, and one of the first results of the improvement programme will be the start of terminal expansion and US Customs and Immigration pre-clearance facilities for cross-border flights. There are also flights to Mexican resorts, so the airport justifies its 'international' appellation, but international flights are limited to aircraft with no more than 450 seats and, when disembarking, passengers leave the aircraft in groups of no more than 150 at a time.

KELOWNA INTERNATIONAL: YLW

Kelowna, British Columbia, Canada

Owner: Transport Canada
Operator: City of Kelowna
Runways: 16/34, 2,712m (8,896ft)
Terminals: One

Airlines using airport as base or hub: Kelowna
  Flightcraft Air Charter
Annual passengers: 1,363,391
Annual cargo: 90,544 tonnes

Background

Kelowna International is 11.5km (just over 7 miles) north-east of Kelowna.

The airport opened in 1947 as Ellison Field, after the local community, with a small terminal and a grass runway. The runway was covered with gravel during the following decade with assistance from the federal government, while the parking areas were paved. In 1958 the first regular air services to use the airport were introduced by Canadian Pacific Airlines using Douglas DC-3s, and prompted by this the city pressed the federal government for the funds for a longer paved runway, while also buying the land to expand the airport. In 1960 the new 1,630m (5,350ft) long paved runway opened, with an improved taxiway and apron. This was followed by a new passenger terminal and a new air traffic control tower, which replaced the original which used the chassis and platform of a lorry. Further improvements were made in the following three decades, upgrading the terminal, further extending the runways, and also improving operations during poor weather. A series of improvements starting in 1998 saw the terminal building doubled in size and additional parking space provided for aircraft. The airport is also the main base for Kelowna Flightcraft, a charter airline founded in 1974.

The airport has had a relatively untroubled existence, with the only accident being that on 14 July 1986 to a Pacific Western Airlines Boeing 737-200, calling at Kelowna during a flight from Calgary to Vancouver, which left the runway while landing. The 5 crew and 76 passengers suffered minor injuries.

CHINA, PEOPLE'S REPUBLIC OF

For many years the development of commercial aviation in China was inhibited by the internal divisions and unrest within the country, aggravated by Japanese intervention during the 1930s, even before the outbreak of the Second World War. Post war, and post Communist take-over, a new airline was established in cooperation with the Soviet Union, as well as another airline completely under Chinese control. Growing tension between China and the USSR resulted in the loss of the Soviet link, and the merging of the Soviet-backed Skoga and the Chinese Civil Aviation Corporation in 1964 to create a new airline, Civil Aviation Administration of China, CAAC, which was a typical bureaucratic all-embracing air transport organisation that included airports as well as an airline. The break-up of CAAC in 1988 led to the creation of first Air China, and then a large number of other airlines, some of which have survived and others of which have fallen by the wayside, while airports are now controlled by the provincial governments or the military.

The integration of the former British colony of Hong Kong and the former Portuguese colony of Macau into China, albeit with special administrative dispensations, means that to avoid confusion both territories are taken separately at the end of this section.

Despite the short period since the end of the CAAC, the Chinese air transport industry has matured quickly and airports have enjoyed rapid growth. Nevertheless, despite the prosperity of such places as Hong Kong and, within mainland China, Shanghai, and the regions bordering them, much of the country is still poor. Poverty, and strict political control, despite burgeoning private enterprise, mean that many of the other aspects of civil aviation well-established in the West such as inclusive tour charter airlines, are unlikely to emerge in the foreseeable future. The recent slowdown in the world economy may mean that recent growth will level out, at least for the near future.

One point to bear in mind: as with Russia, or at least the former Soviet Union, details of accidents can be difficult to find.

BEIJING CAPITAL INTERNATIONAL: PEK
Beijing, People's Republic of China

Runways: 18L/36R, 3,800m (12,468ft); 18R/36L, 3,200m (10,499ft); 01/19, 3,800m (12,468ft)
Terminals: Three, designated as Terminal 1, Terminal 2, and Terminal 3
Airlines using airport as base or hub: Air China, Air China Cargo, China Postal Airlines, China United Airlines, as well as regional hub for China Southern Airlines and Hainan Airlines
Annual passengers: 53,583,664
Annual cargo: 1,192,553 tonnes
Annual aircraft movements: 399,697

Terminals 2 and 3 are served by the Beijing Subway's Airport Express Line opened on 19 July 2008.

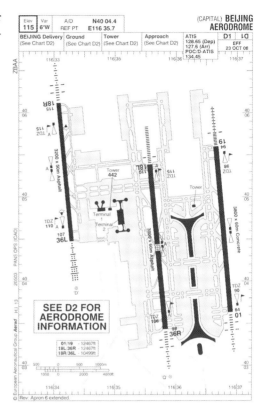

Background
Beijing Capital International Airport (or, in Pinyin, Běijīng Shǒudū Guójì Jīchǎng) is about 20 miles from the city centre and was opened on 2 March 1958 with just one small terminal, which survives to this day for the use of government VIPs. Despite the city changing its name from the European 'Peking' to the Chinese 'Beijing', it retains its old IATA code of PEK.

It has grown to become the country's largest and busiest airport. On 1 January 1980 a new and much larger terminal was opened, albeit with accommodation for just ten to twelve aircraft, and this too was outgrown by the rising volume of traffic, and a second larger terminal was built. But by the mid-1990s it was too small. The terminal was then closed for renovation after the opening of a second terminal.

Major expansion followed, and in 1999 a much enlarged airport opened to celebrate the 50th anniversary of the foundation of the People's Republic. The main terminal was designated Terminal 2, handling both domestic and international services and leaving the 1980 vintage Terminal 1 for the domestic services of China Southern Airlines. A third runway opened in October 2007 and a third terminal opened in February 2008, with a railway link to the city centre, ready for the Beijing Olympic Games that summer. Terminal 3 is the world's largest man-made structure. This expansion was funded by a 500 million Euro loan (US$625 million) by the European Investment Bank.

GUANGZHOU BAIYUN INTERNATIONAL: CAN
Guangzhou, People's Republic of China

Owner and operator: Guangzhou Baiyun International Airport Co.
Runways: 02L/20R, 3,600m (11,811ft); 02R/20L, 3,800m (12,467ft)

Terminals: One
Airlines using airport as base or hub: China
　Southern Airlines, FedEx Asia
Annual passengers: 30,958,374
Annual cargo: 694,923 tonnes
Annual aircraft movements: 260,835

Background

Guangzhou Baiyun International Airport (or, in Pinyin, Guǎngzhōu Báiyún Guójì Jīchǎng) opened on 5 August 2004, replacing an earlier airport of the same name, operational since 1932. The new airport is some five times larger than the earlier one. Apart from space and an end to the congestion of the original airport, the new airport is sited to allow round-the-clock operation without restrictions.

The name 'Baiyun' means 'white clouds', and refers to a mountain, Mt Baiyun, which was close to the old airport. Unofficially, the new airport is often called 'New Baiyun'.

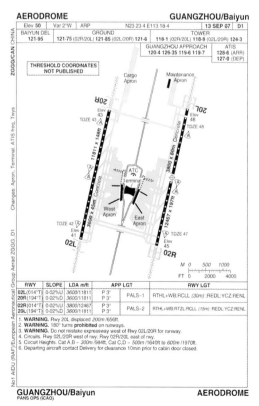

During 2008, Emirates, Qatar Airways, and Kenya Airways all started to operate flights to the airport, which is already a major cargo hub for Federal Express, which has established its largest hub outside the USA at Guangzhou, replacing that at Subic Bay in the Philippines.

Plans for the further development of the airport are already being implemented, including the construction of a third runway.

SHANGHAI PUDONG: PVG
Shanghai, People's Republic of China

Owner and operator: Shanghai Airport Authority
Runways: 17L/35R, 4,000m (13,123ft);
　17R/35L, 3,400m (11,154ft); 16/34, 3,800m
　(12,467ft)
Terminals: Two, designated 1 and 2
Airlines using airport as base or hub: China
　Eastern Airlines, Shanghai Airlines
Annual passengers: 29,083,510
Annual cargo: 2,559,310 tonnes
Annual aircraft movements: 253,535

The world's first commercial high-speed Maglev railway linking Pudong International with Longyang Road Metro station was opened in 2002. Shanghai Metro Line 2 will be extended into the airport during 2010 and link it with Shanghai Hongqiao Airport.

Background

Shanghai Pudong International Airport (or, in Pinyin, Shànghǎi Pǔdōng Guójì Jīchǎng) opened on 1 May 1999 to relieve Shanghai's other airport, Hongqiao (see below) of international flights as the older airport had become congested and expansion was not possible because of surrounding urban development. A second runway opened in 2005, and a third in 2008, on the same day that the second passenger terminal opened. The longer term plans call for five parallel runways and three terminals.

There have been the inevitable incidents at the airport, two of which seem to have come in early 2006. The first of these was the collapse of the nose gear of a Cargolux Boeing 747-400F

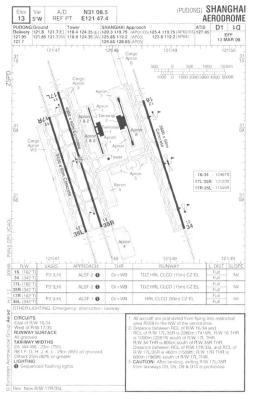

SHANGHAI HONGQIAO INTERNATIONAL: SHA

Shanghai, People's Republic of China

Owner and Operator: Shanghai Airports Authority
Runways: 18/36, 3,400m (11,154ft)
Terminals: One with separate domestic and international gates
Airlines using airport as base or hub: Air China, China Eastern, China Southern, Shanghai Airlines, Yangtze River Express
Annual passengers: 22,632,962
Annual cargo: 388,812 tonnes
Annual aircraft movements: 187,045

Shanghai Metro Line 2 is being extended into the airport.

Background

Shanghai's important position as a trading port meant that air transport was available before the

while parked outside the cargo terminal on 30 January. The second, also concerning the undercarriage, was on 13 May when a China Eastern Airbus A340-600 landing from Seoul burst all of its mainwheel tyres on landing – there were no casualties.

While Hongqiao was intended to concentrate solely on domestic flights, including those to the former Portuguese colony of Macau and the former British colony of Hong Kong, since 2007 it has also been served by flights from Seoul and Tokyo, largely because of its proximity to the centre of Shanghai, which means that it is still popular with business travellers as Pudong is almost 20 miles from the city centre.

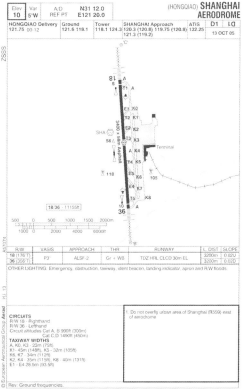

Japanese invasion, after which it was used for military purposes by the Japanese Army Air Force. Post war, Hongqiao became the city's airport, and was named Hongqiao International Airport (or, in Pinyin, Shànghǎi Hóngqiáo Guójì Jīchǎng) translating into English as Rainbow Bridge International Airport. Growing congestion and the lack of space for the necessary expansion meant that a new airport had to be built at Pudong, and this opened in 1999. The intention was that Hongqiao should then concentrate on domestic services plus flights to the former British colony of Hong Kong and the former Portuguese colony of Macau, but since 2007 international flights have been allowed once again to Tokyo Haneda and Seoul Gimpo, in each case providing city-pairs of airports close to city centres and therefore air services aimed mainly at business travellers.

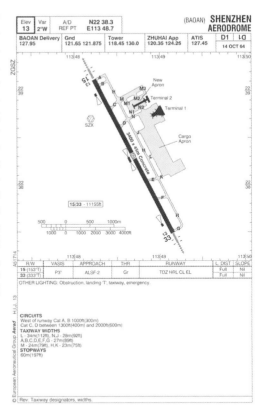

SHENZHEN BAO'AN INTERNATIONAL: SZX

Bao'an District, Shenzhen, Guangdong, People's Republic of China

Owner and operator: Shenzhen Airport
    Company Ltd
Runways: 15/33, 3,400m (11,155ft)
Terminals: Two, designated Terminal A (domestic
    only) and Terminal B
Airlines using airport as base or hub: Shenzhen
    Airlines, China Southern Airlines
Annual passengers: 20,619,164
Annual cargo: 616,046 tonnes
Annual aircraft movements: 181,450

No railway connection but apart from the usual buses and taxis, there are fast ferry services to Macau and Hong Kong.

Background
Shenzhen Bao'an International Airport (or, in Pinyin, Shēnzhèn Bǎo'ān Guójì Jīchǎng) was opened on 12 October 1991 and was originally known as Shenzhen Huangtian Airport, being situated between Huangtian and Fuyong villages.

CHENGDU SHUANGLIU INTERNATIONAL: CTU

Shuangliu, Chengdu, People's Republic of China

Owner and operator: The Civil Aviation
    Administration of the People's Republic of China
Runways: 02/20, 3,600m (11,811ft)
Terminals: One with domestic and international
    gates
Airlines using airport as base or hub: Air China,
    Sichuan Airlines
Annual passengers: 18,586,000
Annual cargo: 328,000 tonnes
Annual aircraft movements: 166,382

Metro railway link planned.

Background
Situated 16km (10 miles) from the centre of Chengdu, Chengdu Shuangliu International

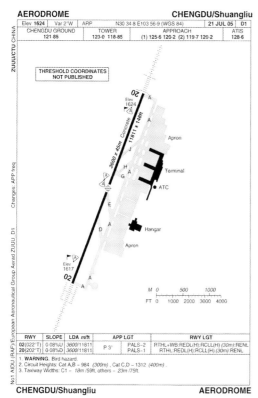

Background

Wujiaba was in use as an airfield before the First World War when a local warlord obtained some aircraft. While there is no record of its use during the years between the two world wars, it was used during the Second World War by the 'Flying Tiger' squadron of United States Army Air Force volunteers that flew in support of the Chinese led by Lt-Col (later General) Claire Lee Chennault.

Post war and post revolution, it became a commercial airport and has seen considerable expansion in passenger and cargo business in recent years as the Chinese economy has grown. In terms of both passengers and cargo, in 2007 it was China's seventh busiest airport, and eighth in terms of aircraft movements. The irony is that the success of Kunming Wujiaba International Airport has led to strong urban development in its vicinity, which will make future expansion extremely difficult and costly, and because of

Airport (or, in Pinyin, Chéngdū Shuāngliú Guójì Jīchǎng) is the major airport for its area. It was originally opened as a military base in 1938 at the height of the Sino-Japanese War, and remained in military hands throughout the war years. It enjoys busy cargo traffic and has passenger flights to more than 20 international destinations. A motorway and a Metro railway link are planned for the future.

KUNMING WUJIABA INTERNATIONAL: KMG

Kunming, Yunnan, People's Republic of China

Owner and operator: Yunnan Airport Group
Runways: 03/21, 3,400m (11,155ft)
Terminals: One
Annual passengers: 15,729,171
Annual cargo: 232,647 tonnes
Annual aircraft movements: 148,185

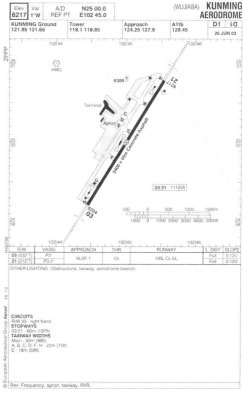

this the provincial government is planning a new airport.

HANGZHOU XIAOSHAN INTERNATIONAL: HGH

Hangzhou, People's Republic of China

Owner and operator: Hangzhou Xiaoshan
 International Airport Co. Ltd
Runways: 07/25, 3,600m (11,811ft)
Terminals: One
Airlines using airport as base or hub: Air China
Annual passengers: 11,729,983
Annual cargo: 195,711 tonnes
Annual aircraft movements: 148,128

Background

Hangzhou Xiaoshan International Airport (or, in Pinyin, Hángzhōu Xiāoshān Guójì Jīchǎng) serves the city of the same name, a major centre on the Yangtze River and the provincial capital

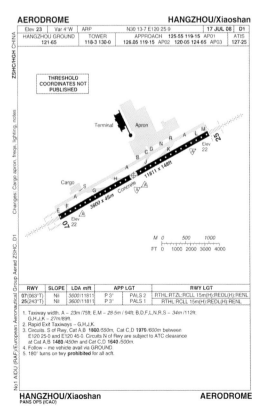

of Zhejiang. It is 27km (about 17 miles) from the city centre.

The airport is comparatively new, having been built to replace the old airport for the city which was shared with the military. After opening on 30 December 2000 the airport was designated an international airport by the Chinese government in late 2003, and customs and immigration facilities were provided from March 2004. The existing airport is regarded as being 'Phase 1', so further development can be expected once international trade recovers.

XI'AN XIANYANG INTERNATIONAL: XIY

Xi'an, Shaanxi, People's Republic of China

Owner and operator: Xi'an Xianyang
 International Airport
Runways: 05/23, 3,000m (9,842ft)
Terminals: Two, designated Domestic and
 International (which also includes flights to
 Hong Kong)
Airlines using airport as base or hub: China
 Eastern Airlines
Annual passengers: 11,383,782
Annual cargo: 112,048 tonnes
Annual aircraft movements: 119,404

Background

Xi'an Xianyang International Airport (or, in Pinyin, Xī'ān Xiányáng Guójì Jīchǎng) serves both the cities of Xi'an and Xianyang, but is much closer to the latter at 13km (around 8 miles) than Xi'an, which is 47km (almost 30 miles) away. It is the largest airport in the northwest of China and is used by tourists on the way to view the famous 'Terracotta Army'.

Originally, Xi'an was served by Xi'an Xiguan Airport, but the city already had a military airfield and it was decided in 1984 to convert this to commercial use and build a new international airport. The new airport opened on 1 September 1991 and Xi'an Xiguan Airport closed to commercial traffic at the same time. A third terminal and second runway are planned to be open by 2020.

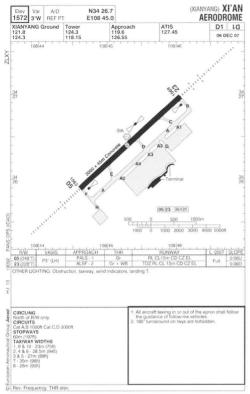

Elev	Var	A/D	N34 26.7		(XIANYANG) **XI'AN**
1572	3°W	REF PT	E108 45.0		**AERODROME**

XIANYANG Ground	Tower	Approach	ATIS	D1	LQ
121.8	124.3	119.6	127.45		
124.3	118.15	126.55			06 DEC 07

R/W	VASIS	APPROACH	THR	RUNWAY	L DIST	SLOPE
05 (048°T)	P3° (LH)	PALS - 1	Gr	RL CL15m CD CZ EL		0.06U
23 (228°T)		ALSF - 2	Gr + WB	TDZ RL CL 15m CD CZ EL	Full	0.06D

OTHER LIGHTING: Obstruction, taxiway, wind indicators, landing T.

CIRCLING
North of R/W only.
CIRCUITS
Cat A,B 1000ft Cat C,D 2000ft.
STOPWAYS
60m (197ft).
TAXIWAY WIDTHS
1, 9 & 10 - 23m (75ft)
2, 4 & 6 - 28.5m (94ft)
3 & 5 - 27m (89ft)
7 - 30m (98ft)
8 - 29m (95ft)

1. All aircraft taxiing in or out of the apron shall follow the guidance of follow-me vehicles.
2. 180° turnaround on twys are forbidden.

Rev: Frequency, THR elev.

On 6 June 1994, a China Northwest Airlines aircraft broke up shortly after taking off from Xi'an, possibly due to a maintenance problem, and all 160 passengers and crew were killed.

CHONGQING JIANGBEI INTERNATIONAL: CKG
Yubai, Chongqing, People's Republic of China

Owner and operator: Chongqing Airports Authority
Runways: 02/20, 3,200m (10,499ft)
Terminals: Two, with one handling domestic flights and the other international
Airlines using airport as base or hub: Air China
Annual passengers: 10,355,730
Annual cargo: 143,523 tonnes
Annual aircraft movements: 119,341

Background
Chongqing Jiangbei International Airport (or, in Pinyin, Chóngqìng Jiāngběi Guójì Jīchǎng) is 21km (about 13 miles) from the city centre.

XIAMEN GAOQI INTERNATIONAL: XMN
Xiamen, People's Republic of China

Owner and operator: Xiamen International Airport Group Company
Runways: 05/23, 3,400m (11,155ft)
Terminals: One
Airlines using airport as base or hub: Xiamen Airlines
Annual passengers: 8,684,665
Annual cargo: 193,625 tonnes
Annual aircraft movements: 85,251

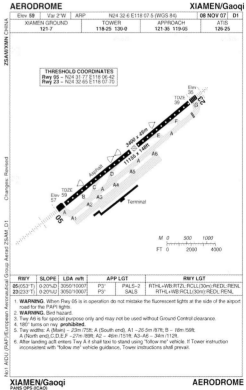

AERODROME   **XIAMEN/Gaoqi**

Elev 59	Var 2°W	ARP	N24 32·6 E118 07·5 (WGS 84)		08 NOV 07	D1
XIAMEN GROUND		TOWER	APPROACH	ATIS		
121·7		118·25 130·0	121·35 119·05	126·25		

THRESHOLD COORDINATES
Rwy 05 – N24 31·77 E118 06·42
Rwy 23 – N24 32·65 E118 07·70

RWY	SLOPE	LDA m/ft	APP LGT		RWY LGT
05(053°T)	0·20%D	3050/10007	P3°	PALS–2	RTHL+WB:RTZL:RCLL(30m):REDL:RENL
23(233°T)	0·20%U	3050/10007	P3°	SALS	RTHL+WB:RCLL(30m):REDL:RENL

1. **WARNING.** When Rwy 05 is in operation do not mistake the fluorescent lights at the side of the airport road for the PAPI lights.
2. **WARNING.** Bird hazard.
3. Twy A6 is for special purpose only and may not be used without Ground Control clearance.
4. 180° turns on rwy **prohibited.**
5. Twy widths: A (Main) – 23m /75ft; A (South end), A1 – 26.5m /87ft; B – 18m /59ft; A (North end),C,D,E,F – 27m /89ft; A2 – 46m /151ft; A3–A6 – 34m /112ft.
6. After landing acft enters Twy A it shall taxi to stand using 'follow me' vehicle. If Tower instruction inconsistent with 'follow me' vehicle guidance, Tower instructions shall prevail.

XIAMEN/Gaoqi   PANS OPS (ICAO)   **AERODROME**

Background

The primary airport in the province of Fujian, Xiamen Gaoqi International (or, in Pinyin, Xiàmén Gāoqí Guójì Jīchǎng) has developed rapidly in recent years, although growth may be inhibited by the current economic situation.

WUHAN TIANHE INTERNATIONAL: WUH

Wuhan, People's Republic of China

Owner and operator: Wuhan Tianhe
  International Airport Company
Runways: 04/22, 3,400m (11,155ft)
Terminals: Two, designated Terminal One and
  Terminal Two
Airlines using airport as base or hub: China
  Eastern Airlines, China Southern Airlines
Annual passengers: 8,356,340
Annual cargo: 89,596 tonnes
Annual aircraft movements: 85,251

Background

Located some 26km (16 miles) from the city centre, Wuhan Tianhe International Airport (or, in Pinyin, Wǔhàn Tiānhé Guójì Jīchǎng) opened on 15 April 1995. It has only one runway, but it is the busiest airport in the centre of China. A second terminal has been opened in recent years and a second runway is planned parallel to the existing one. Tianhe translated into English is Sky River.

NANJING LUKOU INTERNATIONAL: NKG

Nanjing, Jiangsu, People's Republic of China

Owner and operator: Jiangsu International
  Airports
Runways: 06/24, 3,600m (11,811ft)
Terminals: One
Annual passengers: 8,037,189
Annual cargo: 180,354 tonnes
Annual aircraft movements: 82,391

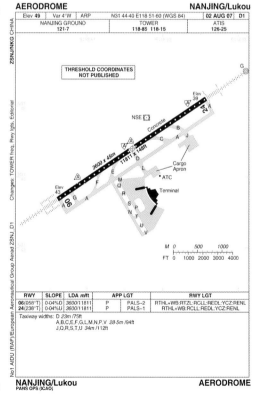

WUHAN/Tianhe

NANJING/Lukou

Background

Nanjing Lukou International Airport (or, in Pinyin, Nánjīng Lùkǒu Guójì Jīchǎng) serves the industrial city of Nanjing, a major centre for the Chinese motor industry, and is 35km (almost 25 miles) from Nanjing city centre.

CHANGSHA/DATUOPU: CSX

Changsha, Hunan Province, People's Republic of China

Owner and operator: Hunan Airport Authority
Runways: 18/36, 2,600m (8,502ft)
Terminals: One
Annual passengers: 8,069,989
Annual cargo: 68,630 tonnes
Annual aircraft movements: 82,041

Background

Little is known about Changsha/Datuopu International Airport, and it may be that there is some confusion with the newer airport at Changsha Huanghua, opened on 29 August 1989, given the traffic figures.

QINGDAO LIUTING INTERNATIONAL: TAO

Qing Dao, Shandong Province, People's Republic of China

Owner and operator: Shandong Province
Runways: 17/35, 3,400m (11,155ft)
Terminals: One
Annual passengers: 7,867,982
Annual cargo: 115,781 tonnes
Aircraft movements: 82,392

Background

Qingdao International Airport (or, in Pinyin, Qīngdǎo Liútíng Guójì Jīchǎng) is 31km (almost 20 miles) from the city centre. It has an extensive network of domestic and international routes and between the years 2004 and 2006 the passenger terminal was expanded and the runway lengthened.

HAIKOU MEILAN INTERNATIONAL: HAK

Haikou, Hainan, People's Republic of China

Owner and operator: Meilan Airport Company
Runways: 09/27, 3,600m (1,811ft)
Terminals: One
Airlines using airport as base or hub: Hainan Airlines
Annual passengers: 7,265,539
Annual cargo: 69,830 tonnes
Annual aircraft movements: 63,416

Background

Opened in 1999, Haikou Meilan International Airport is 25km (almost 16 miles) from Haikou on the island of Hainan. It is the largest airport on the island as well as the most modern.

DALIAN ZHOUSHUIZI INTERNATIONAL: DLC

Dalian, People's Republic of China

Owner: Air Force of the People's Liberation Army
Operator: Dalian Zhoushuizi International Airport Co. Ltd
Runways: 10/28, 3,300m (10,827ft)
Terminals: One
Airlines using airport as base or hub: China Southern Airlines
Annual passengers: 7,281,084
Annual cargo: 121,693 tonnes
Annual aircraft movements: 82,367

Background

Officially a military air station, Dalian Zhoushuizi International Airport (or, in Pinyin, Dàlián Zhōushuǐzǐ Guójì Jīchǎng) has been opened up to commercial flights since the 1980s, and is now a hub for China Southern Airlines. It is the busiest airport in north-east China.

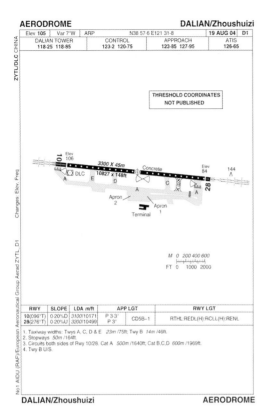

DALIAN/Zhoushuizi AERODROME

SANYA PHOENIX INTERNATIONAL: SYX
Sayan, Hainan, People's Republic of China

Owner and operator: Civil Aviation
  Administration of China
Runways: 08/26, 3,400m (11,155ft)
Terminals: One
Annual passengers: 5,311,622
Annual cargo: 28,634 tonnes
Annual aircraft movements: 59,284

Background
One of the newest and fastest-growing airports in China, Sanya Phoenix International Airport's growth is largely due to tourism.

LANZHOU: LHW
Lanzhou, Gansu, People's Republic of China

Runways: N/A
Terminals: One
Annual passengers: 2,510,903
Annual cargo: 20,492 tonnes

Background
Opened in 2001, the airport is sometimes known as Lanzhou Zhongchuan after the locality, and is 70km (43½ miles) north of Lanzhou.

LIJIANG: LJG
Lijiang Naxizu Zizhixia, Yunnan, People's Republic of China

Owner and operator: Yunnan Airport Group
Runways: N/A
Terminals: One
Annual passengers: 1,906,317

Background
A small regional airport that was built by the Allies late in the Second World War. After the war it became a civil airport. The main operator is China Eastern Airlines.

XISHUANGBANNA GASA: JHG
Jinghong, Xishuangbanna, Yunnan, People's Republic of China

Owner and operator: Yunnan Airport Group
Runways: 16/34, 2,200m (7,218ft)
Terminals: One
Annual passengers: 1,807,633
Annual cargo: 6,148 tonnes

Background
Little information is available about this regional airport.

ZHANG JIAJIE: DYG

Zhang Jiajie, Hunnan, People's Republic of China

Owner and operator: Hunnan Airport Group
Runways: No details are available regarding the runways
Terminals: One
Annual passengers: 1,516,721

Background

Little information is available about this airport, the name of which is spelt Zhang Jiajie or Zhangjiajie.

CHINA
(Hong Kong Special Administrative Region)

HONG KONG INTERNATIONAL/ CHEK LAP KOK: HKG

Chek Lap Kok, Hong Kong Autonomous Region, People's Republic of China

Runways: 07R/25L, 3,800m (12,467ft); 07L/25R, 3,800m (12,467ft)
Terminals: T1 and T2, plus China Business Aviation Centre

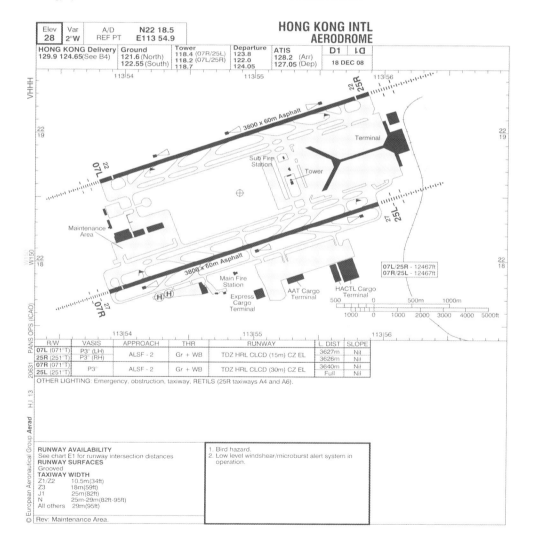

Elev 28	Var 2°W	A/D REF PT	N22 18.5 E113 54.9							HONG KONG INTL AERODROME

HONG KONG Delivery 129.9 124.65(See B4)	Ground 121.6 (North) 122.55 (South)	Tower 118.4 (07R/25L) 118.2 (07L/25R) 118.7	Departure 123.8 122.0 124.05	ATIS 128.2 (Arr) 127.05 (Dep)	D1 ⌐D 18 DEC 08

07L/25R - 12467ft
07R/25L - 12467ft

3800 x 60m Asphalt

Terminal
Sub Fire Station
Tower
Maintenance Area
Main Fire Station
AAT Cargo Terminal
HACTL Cargo Terminal
Express Cargo Terminal

500   0   500m   1000m
1000   0   1000   2000   3000   4000   5000ft

R/W	VASIS	APPROACH	THR	RUNWAY	L. DIST	SLOPE
07L (071°T)	P3° (LH)				3627m	Nil
25R (251°T)	P3° (RH)	ALSF - 2	Gr + WB	TDZ HRL CLCD (15m) CZ EL	3626m	Nil
07R (071°T)					3640m	Nil
25L (251°T)	P3°	ALSF - 2	Gr + WB	TDZ HRL CLCD (30m) CZ EL	Full	Nil

OTHER LIGHTING: Emergency, obstruction, taxiway, RETILS (25R taxiways A4 and A6).

RUNWAY AVAILABILITY
See chart E1 for runway intersection distances
RUNWAY SURFACES
Grooved
TAXIWAY WIDTH
Z1/Z2   10.5m(34ft)
Z3   18m(59ft)
J1   25m(82ft)
N   25m-29m(82ft-95ft)
All others   29m(95ft)

1. Bird hazard.
2. Low level windshear/microburst alert system in operation.

Rev: Maintenance Area.

Airlines using airport as base or hub: Air Hong
Kong, Cathay Pacific, Dragon Air, Hong Kong
Airlines, Hong Kong Express
Annual passengers: 47,042,419
Annual cargo: 3,777,964 tonnes
Annual aircraft movements: 305,010

Hong Kong Rapid Transit service to Hong Kong
and Kowloon.

Background

Opened on 6 July 1998, Chep Lap Kok (Hong
Kong International Airport) was built on land
reclaimed from the islands of Chek Lap Kok and
Lam Chau to replace the heavily congested Kai
Tak International with its single runway stretch-
ing out into Kowloon Bay and landward aircraft
approaching between tower blocks of flats. Chek
Lap Kok is connected to the northern side of
Lantau Island near the historic village of Tung
Chung, which has expanded into a new town.
Land reclamation for the airport added nearly
1% to the entirety of Hong Kong's surface area.

  According to *The Guinness Book of Records*,
the new airport is the most expensive airport to
date, and construction involved building new
road and rail links to the airport, with associated
bridges and tunnels, and major land reclamation
projects on both Hong Kong Island and in
Kowloon. Despite the cost, technical problems
at the new cargo terminal, called Super Terminal
One, or ST1, led to the cargo terminal at Kai
Tak being reopened briefly, and it took six
months for the new airport to function effectively. A second passenger terminal, T2, with
check-in facilities only, opened in July 2007.

  Rapid expansion has meant that this is the
third busiest airport in Asia, partly because of
the booming 'Tiger economy' of China and
partly due to a deliberate policy of liberalising
air services. Even so, a study ('HKIA 2030') is
underway to assess future growth and improved
access to the airport.

CHINA
(Macau Special Administrative Region)

MACAU INTERNATIONAL: MFM
**Taipa, Macau Special Administrative Region,
People's Republic of China**

Owner and operator: Sociedade do Aeroporto
Internacional de Macau S.A.R.L.
Runways: 16/34, 3,360m (11,024ft)
Terminals: One
Airlines using airport as base or hub: Air Macau
Annual passengers: 5,498,878
Annual cargo: 180,955 tonnes
Annual aircraft movements: 53,386

Background
Opened in 1995 towards the end of Portuguese
colonial rule, the airport is on the eastern end of

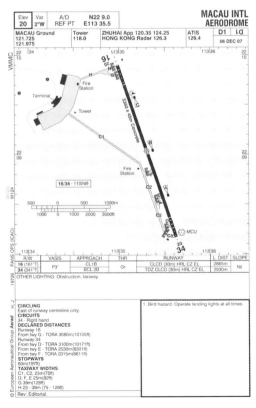

Taipa Island and on land reclaimed from the sea. Before the airport opened, Macau had heliports and a seaplane station, and a temporary airstrip at Coloane. The Hong Kong airline, Cathay Pacific, had operated a seaplane service between Macau and Hong Kong in the 1940s, but in more recent years such services were provided by helicopters. It could be argued that one reason why Macau failed to match the growth and prosperity of Hong Kong during the colonial period was the lack of an international airport.

Although now under Chinese control, passengers travelling to and from the People's Republic are still treated as international passengers for customs and immigration purposes.

COLOMBIA

No Latin American country can claim as long a history of air transport as Colombia, with the national flag carrier, Avianca, tracing its origins back to 1919, making it one of the oldest airlines in the world. As in many other South American countries, difficult surface conditions contributed to the appeal of air transport, despite Bogota, the capital, being 9,000ft above sea level. German interests were active in the country's air transport development during the early years, initially because they were frustrated by not being able to become involved in aviation in their home country because of the restrictions imposed by the Treaty of Versailles in 1919.

BOGOTÁ/EL NUEVO DORADO (EL DORADO) INTERNATIONAL: BOG

Bogotá, Colombia

Owner and operator: OPAIN SA
Runways: 13L/31R, 3,800m (12,467ft); 13R/31L, 3,800m (12,467ft)
Terminals: Two, the 'El Dorado' terminal with domestic and international concourses, and the *Punta Aereo* (Air Bridge) for Avianca and its subsidiary, SAM Colombia

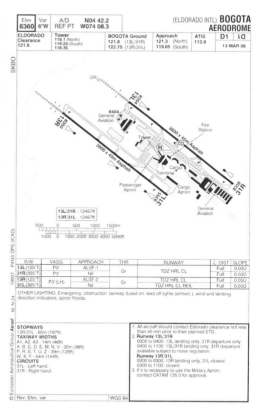

Airlines using airport as base or hub:
Aerorepublica, Aerosucre, Aires Colombia, Avianca, Lineas Aereas Suramericanas, SAM Colombia, SATENA

Annual passengers: 12,763,564
Annual cargo: 585,578 tonnes
Annual aircraft movements: 231,947

Background

One of the highest major airports in the world at an altitude of 2,628m (8,361ft), Bogotá's El Nuevo Dorado International dominates the Colombian air transport scene as the country's major airport and main international gateway. Colombia has a long history of air transport because of its difficult terrain, with mountains and dense forests that make surface transport difficult, slow, and costly.

The airport was built during the mid-1950s and opened with a temporary terminal – the 'El Dorado' terminal was not completed until 1959.

For many years this terminal served all flights with international and domestic concourses, but in 1981 the national airline, Avianca, and its subsidiary SAM Colombia, opened their own terminal for the high frequency domestic flights to Cali and Medellin, as well as international flights to Miami and New York. A second runway opened in 1998, parallel to the existing runway and of the same length. Despite the second terminal, the main terminal has continued to expand to keep pace with growing traffic.

A flight from Bogotá to Quito operated by TAME Linea Aerea del Ecuador crashed into a mountain shortly after taking off on 20 April 1998, with the loss of all 43 passengers and 10 crew. Another accident shortly after take-off was to a Kalitta Air Boeing 747-200 on 7 July 2008, carrying a consignment of flowers to Miami: a fire was reported in an engine, and when the aircraft attempted to return to the airport it crash-landed on a farm, killing three people on the ground, although the crew of eight survived.

CALI – ALFONSO BONILLA ARAGÓN/PALMASECA INTERNATIONAL: CLO
Palmira, Valle de Cauca, Colombia

Owner and operator: Aerocali
Runways: 01/19, 3,000m (9,842ft)
Terminals: One
Annual passengers: 2,406,823.
Annual cargo: 41,176 tonnes.
Annual aircraft movements: 55,013.

Background
Often known as Palmaseca International Airport, although it is near Palmira, Alfonso Bonilla Aragón International Airport is the second busiest airport in Colombia in terms of passengers, and, unusually for a secondary airport in South America, it is operational 24-hours a day. As with Madeira, it poses a stiff challenge to airline pilots, but in this case it is because it is in a long, but narrow, valley surrounded by mountains that reach up to 4,000m (14,000ft). Nevertheless, the airport can take aircraft as large as a Boeing 747.

Air transport is important in Colombia because of the difficult terrain that makes surface transport slow and costly. Cali's first airport was opened in September 1933 at El Guabito air station, a mixed civil and military facility. This was replaced in April 1943 by a new airport in the middle of the Cauca Valley, which in turn was replaced by the present airport on 24 July 1971, built as a result of Cali being awarded the 1972 Panamerican games. There has been little change to the airport since it opened.

Only one accident has occurred in recent years. On 20 December 1995 an American Airlines flight from Miami crashed into a mountain near the airport because of an error in programming the aircraft's computer guidance system.

MEDELLIN – JOSÉ MARÍA CÓRDOVA INTERNATIONAL: MDE
Medellin, Antioquia Department, Colombia

Owner and operator: Aerocivil
Runways: 18/36, 3,557m (11,483ft)
Terminals: One with separate international and domestic concourses
Annual passengers: 2,329,866
Annual cargo: 132,302 tonnes
Annual aircraft movements: 77,465

Background
José María Córdova International Airport is the more important of the two airports serving Medellin and is the country's third busiest airport. It handles both international and domestic traffic, having replaced the older airport of Olava Herrera, which handles regional flights only. The airport is being expanded with a new international terminal and a new cargo terminal. It is named after a local hero who rose to become an army general.

On 7 June 2006, a Boeing 747-200F freighter suffered an engine failure during take-off and, although the pilot aborted the take-off, the aircraft overran the runway, causing substantial damage to the aircraft, but without injury to the crew of six.

CARTAGENA DE INDIAS – RAFAEL NÚÑEZ INTERNATIONAL: CTG

Crespo, Cartagena, Colombia

Owner and operator: SACSA (Sociedad Aeroportuaria de la Costa S.A.)
Runways: 01/19, 2,600m (8,530ft)
Terminals: One
Annual passengers: 1,369,784
Annual cargo: 11,866 tonnes

Background

The busiest airport on Colombia's Caribbean coast in terms of passengers handled, it is the successor to two earlier airports in the area, one dating from 1920.

The first airport was at Bocagrande, which was able to handle both landplanes and hydro-aeroplanes (that is seaplanes and flying boats), with a service to Giradot. It was replaced in 1930 by a new airport on the island of Manzanillo, opened by an airline, SCADTA (Sociedad Colombo Alemana de Transporte Aereo), the predecessor of AVIANCA (Aerovias Nacionales de Colombia), which was formed in 1940. A new airline was formed in 1947, LANSA, which built two runways on the site of the present airport at Crespo, and which eventually sold out to AVIANCA, which transferred its operations from Manzanillo to Crespo. Eventually, AVIANCA sold the airport to the government. The airport was named after Rafael Núñez in 1986, a local who became president of Colombia three times.

The airport was privatised in 1996, and was taken over by the present owner and operator, SACSA, a Spanish-Colombian consortium. The airport has been modernised over the years, but is struggling to cope with increasing traffic. The two state governments in the area are considering building a new airport, most probably at Loma Arena, which if built could be used to develop international traffic but leaving domestic flights at Cartagena.

BARRANQUILLA – ERNESTO CORTISSOZ INTERNATIONAL: BAQ

Soledad, Barranquilla, Atlantico, Colombia

Owner and operator: Aeropuertos del Caribe S.A.
Runways: 05/23, 3,000m (9,842ft)
Terminals: Two, designated as International and Domestic
Airlines using airport as base or hub: AIRES Colombia; Avianca
Annual passengers: 1,157,576
Annual cargo: 31,123 tonnes

Background

Named after one of the pioneers of aviation in Colombia, Ernesto Cortissoz, the international airport is 7km (just over 4 miles) from the centre of the city.

There have been a number of incidents at the airport. On 17 March 1995, a DC-9 was destroyed by fire while parked (fortunately no one was on board at the time). There have also been three cases of aircraft overshooting when landing. The first of these was on 19 November 2006 when a Cielos Airlines Douglas DC-10 was landing in bad weather, and all six crew were injured. Just two days later, an Avianca airliner landing from Bogotá overran, but there appear to have been no casualties. On 23 August 2008, an AIRES Colombia flight from Curaçao overran because of an undercarriage problem, but again there seem to have been no casualties.

COSTA RICA

ALAJUELA/JUAN SANTAMARÍA INTERNATIONAL: SJO

Alajuela, Costa Rica

Owner: Government
Operator: HASDC, Houston Airport System Development Company
Runways: 07/25, 3,012m (9,881ft)
Terminals: Two, designated International and Regional

Airlines using airport as base or hub: TACA,
 LACSA, SANSA
Annual passengers: 3,031,954
Annual cargo: 79,758 tonnes
Annual aircraft movements: 70,532

Background

More usually referred to, especially in airline
timetables, as San José, Alajuela's Juan Santa-
maría International Airport is some 20km (12½
miles) from San José and is named after a
national hero who was killed in 1856. The airport has been modernised since 1997, including
a new terminal and air traffic control tower, and
in 2008, after some controversy, the management of the facility was handed over to Houston
Airport Development Company.

An unusual feature is that NASA has a small
hangar for high altitude research aircraft at
the airport.

CROATIA

Of all the different republics that have declared
independence since the collapse of the former
state of Yugoslavia, Croatia has the most major
airports, but traffic generally remains below pre-
civil war levels.

ZAGREB/PLESO: ZAG

Pleso, Croatia

Owner and operator: ZLZ
Runways: 05/23, 3,252m (10,669ft)
Terminals: One
Airlines using airport as base or hub: Croatia
 Airlines
Annual passengers: 1,992,455
Annual cargo: 10,781 tonnes
Annual aircraft movements: 43,258

Background

Sometimes referred to as Pleso because of the
suburb in which it is located, Zagreb Airport is
10km (6¼ miles) from the centre of Zagreb and
is Croatia's main international airport. It is

shared with the Croatian Air Force which uses
it as a fighter base.

Zagreb had a landing strip on the western side
of the city from as early as 1909 when a pioneering manufacturer, Slavoljub Penkala, needed
somewhere to test his aircraft. In 1927 there was
an airfield at Borongai to the east of the city, and
this started to be used by airlines from February
1928. After the Second World War, a former
military air station at Lucko, south-west of
Zagreb, became the city airport.

The present airport opened on 20 April 1962,
replacing Lucko. A new terminal was inaugurated in 1966, and in 1974 the runway was
extended to its present length and the terminal
was also expanded. Currently the airport is
undergoing a fresh round of development and
modernisation, and a new terminal with 11 airbridges is scheduled to open in 2011. A new parallel runway is also planned. Once the
modernisation is complete, the air force will
move to the southern end of the airport.

SPLIT: SPU

Split, Croatia

Owner and operator: Split Airport Authority
Runways: 05/23, 2,550m (8,366ft)
Terminals: One
Annual passengers: 1,182,387

Background

Sometimes known as Split Kaštela, as it serves
both towns, the area has had an airport since
before the Second World War, and at one time
enjoyed growing charter airline movements
carrying package holidaymakers. The fighting
and unrest that followed the break-up of the
former Yugoslavia badly affected traffic, even
though Split is well away from Bosnia, the
scene of most of the fighting. It is now served
by the new national carrier, Croatia Airlines,
and traffic has shown strong growth in recent
years.

Plans for the future include a three-phase
development plan spread over the period from
2009 to 2015, by which time the airport will have

a new terminal with airbridges, and a second runway.

DUBROVNIK/ČILIPI: DBV
Čilipi, Dubrovnik, Croatia

Owner and operator: Dubrovnik Airport Group
Runways: 12/30, 3,300m (10,827ft)
Terminals: One
Airlines using airport as base or hub: Air
    Adriatic, Dubrovnik Airlines
Annual passengers: 1,143,168

Background
Sometimes referred to locally as Čilipi Airport, after the location, the airport is almost 16km (10 miles) from the centre of Dubrovnik.

Dubrovnik's original airport was a grass strip at Gruda, which opened in 1936, but traffic was interrupted by the outbreak of the Second World War in Europe in September 1939 and the subsequent invasion of Yugoslavia the following year.

It was not until some time after the war ended that work began on the present airport, which opened in 1962. By 1971 the runway was extended, and in the years that followed the airport was expanded, with a domestic air traffic terminal opening in 1974, and a new international terminal in 1976. A cargo terminal opened in 1988. After the death of Yugoslavia's dictator, President Tito, the country broke up into its constituent states, and hostilities broke out, with the airport occupied in 1991 and 1992 by Serbian forces and its equipment destroyed. In 1993, operations resumed using temporary facilities, but traffic slumped from 1,460,354 passengers in 1987 to 395,458 in 2000. Traffic has since recovered, and a development plan is being implemented, with a new passenger terminal under construction and plans for a second runway.

During the immediate post-reopening period, a United States Air Force CT-43 VIP transport crashed into a hill on the approach to the airport, killing 35 people, including the then US Secretary for Commerce, Ron Brown.

CYPRUS
A country with a troubled past and which is now divided into Greek and Turkish zones. At one time Cyprus had just one airport at Nicosia (which was close to the dividing line between the two zones), but it is now closed and its IATA code is used by Paphos, one of the two new airports that have taken Nicosia's place. The island also has British Sovereign Base Areas, including a Royal Air Force station. There is just one airport in the Turkish zone, but because the Turkish area is not recognised by any country other than Turkey, it has few flights and does not qualify for inclusion in this book.

LARNACA INTERNATIONAL: LCA
Larnaca, Cyprus

Owner and operator: Department of Civil Aviation
Runways: 04/22, 2,980m (9,776ft)
Terminals: One
Airlines using airport as base or hub: Cyprus
    Airways
Annual passengers: 5,387,724
Annual cargo: 41,940 tonnes
Annual aircraft movements: 57,045

Background
Originally built during the 1930s and used as a Royal Air Force base in the Second World War and for many years afterwards, the site lay idle after the island became independent and the RAF moved into the UK Sovereign Base Areas of the island. It was reactivated as a civil airport in considerable haste in 1974 after the Turkish invasion of the island made Nicosia Airport untenable, and opened in February 1975 using prefabricated buildings. At first the runway was too short for jet aircraft and Cyprus Airways had to use Vickers Viscount turboprop aircraft leased from British Midland Airways.

The airport has developed since with a terminal and a much longer runway and, in addition to handling the substantial tourist traffic, is now being used as a hub by travellers to other destinations in the Near East. Under the first phase

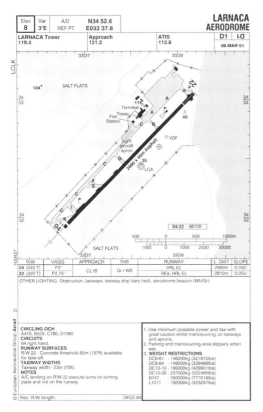

of a development programme, a new terminal opened in late 2009. Second phase plans are to extend this by 2013, and to lengthen the runway by 500m (about 1,650ft).

The airport's location in a troubled and divided island and close to the Middle East, especially Lebanon, has brought it into the various conflicts that have blighted the region. Perhaps the most dramatic event was on 19 February 1978. A Cyprus Airways airliner was hijacked by Palestinian terrorists who had murdered an Egyptian newspaper editor in Nicosia, but after touring airports in the Middle East and North Africa, it was forced to return to Larnaca where a 74-strong Egyptian anti-terrorist squad also arrived to deal with the hijacking, but without first obtaining the consent of the Greek Cypriot authorities, whose negotiators had already got the terrorists to surrender. A gun battle ensued between the Cypriot National Guard and the Egyptian anti-terrorist squad, who were even-

tually overpowered after 15 had been killed. On another occasion, on 5 April 1988, a hijacked Kuwait Airways Boeing 747 arrived at Larnaca to refuel, and two Kuwaiti hostages were killed and thrown out of the aircraft before it continued to Algeria. Much more happily, during the Israeli assault on Lebanon in 2006, Middle Eastern Airlines (MEA) evacuated much of its fleet to Larnaca for safety.

PAPHOS INTERNATIONAL: PFO

Paphos, Cyprus

Owner: Government of Cyprus
Operator: Hermes Airports Ltd
Runways: 11/29, 2,700m (8,858ft)
Terminals: One
Airlines using airport as base or hub: Cyprus Airways
Annual passengers: 1,819,182

Background

Paphos International is 16km (10 miles) from the town and serves the western end of the island. It is the second largest airport in Cyprus, after Larnaca.

It was built after the Turkish invasion of the island in 1974 led to partition and made the airport at Nicosia unusable. A modernised terminal opened in late 2008.

CZECH REPUBLIC

Czechoslovakia became an independent state after the collapse of the Austro-Hungarian Empire at the end of the First World War. The national airline, CSA, traces its history back to 1923, when Czechoslovak State Airlines (*Cesholsovenske Stani Aerolinie*) was formed, inaugurating a service linking Prague, Brno, and Bratislava on 1 March that year. Air services to neighbouring countries were established in the years before the first German invasion in 1938.

The collapse of the Soviet Union and of the Warsaw Pact was followed by a division of the country into the Czech Republic and Slovakia.

PRAGUE-RUZYNĚ: PRG

Prague, Czech Republic

Owner and operator: Airport Prague
Runways: 06/24 (06L/24R from 2010),
3,715m (12,191ft); 13/31, 3,250m
(10,665ft); 06R/24L, 3,500m (11,492ft) opens
in 2010
Terminals: Four, designated as North Terminals 1
and 2, and South Terminals 3 and 4 (Most
flights use the North Terminals)
Airlines using airport as base or hub: CSA
Czech Airlines, Smart Wings, Travel Service
Airlines
Annual passengers: 12,416,172
Annual cargo: 55,179 tonnes
Annual aircraft movements: 174,662

A Metro railway link between the city centre and
the airport is expected to be open by 2013.

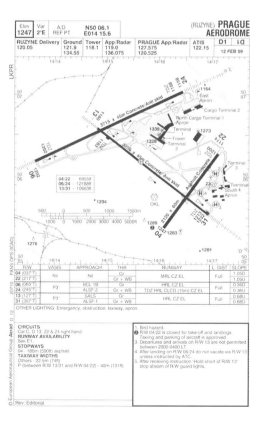

Background

Czech civil aviation started immediately after
the First World War, which resulted in the country's independence from the Austro-Hungarian
Empire, with flights from the military airfield at
Kbely, near Prague, in 1919. By the mid-1930s,
Kbely was having difficulty handling the growing traffic, and work started on the present airport at Ruzyně, which opened on 5 April 1937.
The design of the check-in building was sufficiently advanced to win a gold medal at that
year's International Art and Technical Exhibition in Paris. This building survives as the current Terminal 4, but is used mainly for business
and VIP flights.

The airport was used by the Luftwaffe after
the whole of Czechoslovakia was occupied in
1939, some months before the outbreak of the
Second World War in Europe. It was used by the
Allies at the end of the war. After the country
became a satellite of the Soviet Union, little was
done to develop the airport or its facilities, but
with the collapse of Communism and the end of
the Warsaw Pact in 1990, a major effort was
made to modernise and expand the airport,
which is in the almost unique position for an old
airport of having considerable room for expansion into the surrounding agricultural area. The
old terminals are on the south side of the airport,
with the new generation of terminals on the
north side, with the current Terminal 1 opened
in 1997 and Terminal 2 following in 2006. A new
runway, parallel to 06/24 and designated as
06R/24L will open in 2010.

DENMARK

Despite the small size of the country and its
small population, Denmark has a strategic location for air transport, and the capital's airport is
the main hub for the jointly-owned Danish-
Norwegian-Swedish airline, Scandinavian Airlines System (SAS). It was also home for one of
Europe's largest air charter airlines, Sterling,
which also moved into low-cost scheduled services, but collapsed in 2008.

COPENHAGEN: CPH

Copenhagen, Denmark

Owner and operator: Københavns Lufthavne
Runways: 04L/22R, 3,600m (11,811ft);
04R/22L, 3,300m (10,827ft); 12/30, 2,800m
(9,186ft)
Terminals: Three, designated Terminal 1,
Terminal 2, and Terminal 3, with a fourth,
designated Terminal A, opening in 2010
Airlines using airport as base or hub:
Scandinavian Airlines System (SAS), Cimber,
Jet Time, MyTravel Denmark, Star Air
Annual passengers: 21,356,134
Annual cargo: 395,506 tonnes
Annual aircraft movements: 257,591

Terminal 3 has a station on the Øresund Railway
Line and is served by the Öresundstågen
providing a direct service to the centre of
Copenhagen. Trains on the Copenhagen–
Stockholm high speed service also call but
cannot carry local passengers.

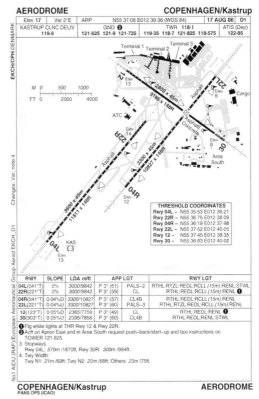

Background

The airport originally opened on 20 April 1925,
although with only a grass runway. A new passenger terminal opened in 1939, but it was not
until after the German invasion of April 1940
that the first hard runway was built, in 1941, with
the airport used as a Luftwaffe base throughout
the Second World War.

Post war, the airport returned to commercial
use, and in 1946 the formation of Scandinavian
Airlines System (SAS) by Denmark, Norway,
and Sweden, proved crucial to the airport's
future, as Copenhagen was chosen to be the
main base and the hub for long-haul flights. The
impact of this decision was that Copenhagen
soon became the third largest airport in Europe,
at least for a few years. One of the significant
results of the airport's position was that in 1954
it became one end of the world's first trans-polar
route, with SAS linking Copenhagen with Los
Angeles. Throughout this period the airport was
often referred to, especially in airline timetables,
by the name of the adjoining town of Kastrup.

The early post-war years were marred by an
accident to a KLM Douglas DC-3 that had
landed on 26 January 1947 on a flight from Amsterdam to Sweden. The aircraft took-off again
for Stockholm but, as it climbed to 50m (160ft),
it was seen to stall and then plunge earthwards,
exploding as it hit the ground and killing all 22
people on board. The cause was the captain's
failure to check that the rudder lock was
removed before take-off. Amongst those killed
was Prince Gustaf Adolf of Sweden and an
American singer and actress, Grace Moore.

In the late 1950s, the arrival of the jet age created a problem as it became clear that expansion
would be necessary to provide the longer runways needed, yet there were protests by the local
community. Nevertheless, Terminal 2 opened in
1960 along with a new air traffic control tower.
Once again plans for expansion arose at the end
of the decade with the introduction of the
Boeing 747 'jumbo jet', which added to the pres-

sure on space. A new cargo terminal opened in 1982, with the airport proving almost as important as a cargo hub as it had become for passengers. In 1991, the airport was partly privatised, and in 1998, Terminal 3 opened. Two years later the airport was linked to the Danish railway system, with trains not only to Copenhagen itself but also to Malmo in Sweden.

The Australian concern, Macquaire, bought a controlling interest in the airport in 2005.

For the future, a new terminal is being built, and a low-cost airline facility will open as Terminal A in 2010.

BILLUND: BLL
Billund, Denmark

Owner and operator: Billund Lufthavn A/S
Runways: 09/27, 3,100m (10,172ft)
Terminals: One
Annual passengers: 2,262,125
Annual aircraft movements: 52,725

Background
Billund Airport is Denmark's second busiest airport (although it is some way behind Copenhagen in terms of traffic) and has a significant number of charter flights. It is the airport nearest to the Legoland theme park. It is claimed to be important for cargo.

The airport was built as a cooperative venture when local people felt that the area needed an airport of its own. It opened on 1 November 1964, with Scandinavian Airlines System (SAS) operating a service to Copenhagen. Cargo flights followed during the 1970s with the airport being used as a refuelling point on routes between the United States and the Far East. Encouraged by this, the runway was extended in 1971. Plans for international flights were delayed while the then European Economic Community attempted to insist that Denmark should have just one international airport, but in 1984 the policy was reversed and Maersk Air started a service to Southend in England. Maersk developed a hub at Billund, but was acquired by Sterling Airways, which has since ceased operations. In 2002 a new passenger terminal was opened and the original terminal was converted for use as an air cargo centre.

DOMINICAN REPUBLIC

PUNTA CANA INTERNATIONAL: PUJ
Punta Cana, La Altagracia Province, Dominican Republic

Owner: City of Punta Cana
Operator: Grupo Punta Cana
Runways: 09/27, 3,100m (10,171ft)
Terminals: Basically one, as Terminal 2 and
    Terminal 3 (domestic) are offshoots of
    Terminal 1
Airlines using airport as base or hub: Caribair,
    Servicios Aereos Profesionales
Annual passengers: 3,615,609
Annual aircraft movements: 48,644

Background
Owned by the city of Punta Cana but privately-operated, Punta Cana International Airport is the busiest airport in the Dominican Republic, and its traffic consists mainly of holiday charter flights from North America and Europe, although there are also domestic and regional air services. The terminals are unusual in that they are largely open air with palm frond roofs. Plans for expansion include building a second runway, a new control tower, and improving the taxiways and aircraft parking areas.

There has been one serious accident at the airport in recent years. On 22 May 2005 a Skyservice Airlines Boeing 767-300 from Toronto landed heavily and suffered structural failure to the upper fuselage, although the aircraft was repairable and there were no reports of casualties amongst the 318 passengers and crew.

SANTO DOMINGO/LAS AMÉRICAS INTERNATIONAL: SDQ

Punta Caucedo, Santo Domingo, Dominican Republic

Owner: Government
Operator: Aeropuertos Dominicanos Siglo XXI
   S.A. (Aerodom), supported by Vancouver
   Airport Services (YVRAS)
Runways: 17/35, 3,355m (11,002ft)
Terminals: Three, designated Terminal A,
   Terminal B, and Domestic Terminal
Airlines using airport as base or hub: LAN
   Dominicana, Servicios Aereos Profesionales
Annual passengers: 2,752,531

Background
The international airport for the Dominican Republic, it is situated at Punta Caucedo just outside Santo Domingo.

The airport opened in 1959 and the name was changed in 2002 to Aeropuerto Internacional Las Américas-José Francisco Pena Gomez, but not surprisingly it is usually known simply as 'Santo Domingo' or 'Las Américas'. It has served as a hub for a number of airlines over the past half century, many of which have collapsed.

GREGORIO LUPERÓN/PUERTO PLATA INTERNATIONAL: POP

Puerto Plata, Dominican Republic

Owner and operator: Aeropuertos Dominicanos
   Siglo XXI S.A. (Aerodom)
Runways: 08/26, 3,081m (10,108ft)
Terminals: One
Annual passengers: 1,176,010

Background
The third airport of the Dominican Republic, it is named after General Gregorio Luperón, a former president. The airport's main traffic comes from the inclusive tour holiday market, mainly from North America and Western Europe, but a number of scheduled airlines also use the airport.

One of the worst accidents at the airport was when a Birgenair Boeing 757 took off for Frankfurt on 6 February 1996, and then crashed into the sea killing all 176 passengers and 13 crew. It was discovered in the post-accident investigation that an air speed pitot tube had been blocked, and after take-off the pilots would have no idea of the aircraft's airspeed. Much less serious, but it did close the airport for five hours, was an Air Turks and Caicos flight on 22 January 2009 which suffered a partial undercarriage collapse on landing.

ECUADOR

QUITO/MARISCAL SUCRE: UIO

Chaupicruz, Quito, Ecuador

Owner and operator: Quiport
Runways: 17/35, 3,120m (10,236ft)
Terminals: One with domestic and international
   concourses
Airlines using airport as base or hub: Aerogal,
   Icaro, LAN Ecuador, TAME
Annual passengers: 4,427,591
Annual cargo: 149,719 tonnes
Annual aircraft movements: 77,418

Background
Set in the Andes, so one of the highest of the world's major airports, Quito is 2,808m (9,214ft) above sea level and is situated in the city, which may be convenient but acts as a constraint as expansion is impossible. It is prone to high winds and low cloud, which makes operations difficult and dangerous. The airport opened in 1960 and is named after Antonio José de Sucre, one of the leaders of the movement for Ecuadorian independence from Spain. It should be replaced in 2010 by a new airport at Tababela, about 18km (11¼ miles) to the east of the city.

The airport has suffered a number of accidents over the years, possibly connected with the high altitude (which affects performance) and the weather conditions. Shortly after it opened in 1960, on 7 November an AREA Ecuador

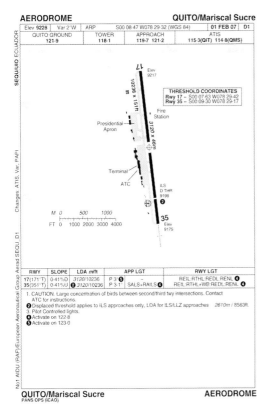

AERODROME

QUITO/Mariscal Sucre

| Elev 9228 | Var 2°W | ARP | S00 08·47 W078 29·32 (WGS 84) | 01 FEB 07 | D1 |

| QUITO GROUND 121·9 | TOWER 118·1 | APPROACH 119·7 121·2 | ATIS 115·3(QIT) 114·8(QMS) |

Elev 9217

THRESHOLD COORDINATES
Rwy 17 – S00 07·63 W078 29·42
Rwy 35 – S00 09·30 W078 29·17

Fire Station

Presidential Apron

10236 × 151ft

3120 × 46m

Terminal
ATC

ILS
D THR
9198

M 0   500   1000
FT 0 1000 2000 3000 4000

35 Elev
9175

RWY	SLOPE	LDA m/ft	APP LGT	RWY LGT
17(171°T)	0·41%D	3120/10236	P 3° ❶	–	REIL·RTHL·REDL·RENL ❶
35(351°T)	0·41%U	❷ 3120/10236	P 3·1°	SALS+RAILS ❶	REIL·RTHL+WB·REDL·RENL ❶

1. CAUTION. Large concentration of birds between second/third twy intersections. Contact ATC for instructions.
❷ Displaced threshold applies to ILS approaches only, LDA for ILS/LLZ approaches   2610m / 8563ft.
3. Pilot Controlled lights.
❶ Activate on 122·8
❺ Activate on 123·0

QUITO/Mariscal Sucre   **AERODROME**
PANS OPS (ICAO)

Fairchild FH-227 crashed into a mountain on approach, some 16km (10 miles) south of the airport, killing all 37 aboard. Another collision with a mountain came on 27 January 1980, when an Ecuadorian Air Force Lockheed C-130 Hercules was flying a missed approach, and all seven occupants were killed. On 18 September 1984 an Aeroservicios Ecuatorianos Douglas DC-8-50 cargo aircraft struggled to gain altitude at the end of the runway and crashed into a residential area, destroying 25 houses and killing 49 people on the ground as well as the crew of four. The surrounding mountains accounted for another aircraft on 3 June 1988 when an air force North American Sabreliner crashed killing all 11 on board. On 10 December 1992 another air force Sabreliner clipped a building 3km (2 miles) south of the airport and crashed into a residential area killing all ten occupants of the aircraft and three more on the ground. Another aircraft which flew into a mountain was a US-registered

Grumman Gulfstream II which selected the wrong VOR frequency while making a night approach to Quito, flew more than 16km (10 miles) further south than it should have and struck the Sincholagua volcano killing all seven occupants. Almost a year later, on 1 May 1996, a Fly Linhas Aereas Boeing 727-200 tried to abort a take-off in wet weather, but overshot the end of the runway and crossed a boundary road, but on this occasion there were no casualties; the subsequent investigation found the aircraft to be overloaded. A less happy outcome followed another runway overshoot on 29 August 1998, when a Cubana Tupolev Tu-154M crashed killing 56 of the 77 passengers. On 9 November 2007 an Iberia Airbus A340-600 slid off the runway, the undercarriage collapsed and two engines were damaged, but fortunately there were no serious injuries amongst the 333 passengers and crew.

There have been a number of other undercarriage collapses and tyre failures, again possibly due to the high altitude, but these have been without casualties.

GUAYAQUIL/JOSÉ JOAQUÍN DE OLMEDO (SIMÓN BOLÍVAR) INTERNATIONAL: GYE
Guayaquil, Ecuador

Owner and operator: Government
Runways: 03/21, 2,790m (9,154ft)
Terminals: One
Annual passengers: 2,996,424
Annual cargo: 73,473 tonnes
Annual aircraft movements: 71,271

Background
Originally called Simón Bolívar International Airport, Guayaquil adopted the current title in 2006 to commemorate a poet who was also at one time the local mayor. In 2006 a new terminal was opened and runway extensions completed. There have been plans for a new airport, but it was felt that traffic was not sufficient to justify the cost.

EGYPT

Egypt has one of the longest histories of air transport in the African continent, largely because it was not officially a European colony after the fall of the Ottoman Empire, even though the United Kingdom and France wielded considerable influence. It was a British-backed company, Misr Airwork, established in 1932, which was responsible for developing a domestic network, initially using de Havilland Dragon biplanes.

In recent years the growth in tourism to Egypt has seen the rising importance of a number of provincial airports, such as Luxor, close to the Valley of the Kings, and the Red Sea resort airport, Sharm el Sheikh.

CAIRO INTERNATIONAL: CAI

Cairo, Egypt

Owner and operator: Cairo Airport Authority
Runways: 05L/23R, 3,301m (10,830ft);
    05C/23C, 3,999m (13,120ft); 05R/23L,
    4,000m (13,124ft); 16/34, 3,178m (10,427ft)
Terminals: Three, designated Terminal 1 (for
    Egyptair and Middle Eastern airlines),
    Terminal 2 (for European and Far Eastern
    airlines), and Terminal 3 (opened in early
    2009 for Egyptair)
Airlines using airport as base or hub: Air Cairo,
    Air Memphis, Egyptair
Annual passengers: 12,577,451
Annual cargo: 275,312 tonnes
Annual aircraft movements: 121,845

The Cairo Metro will be extended to serve the airport, probably in 2010.

Background

The second most important airport in Africa after Johannesburg, Cairo International replaced the city's original airport at Heliopolis in 1963. The actual airfield was built by the United States as Payne Field Air Force Base during the Second World War and was handed over to the Egyptian authorities after the war.

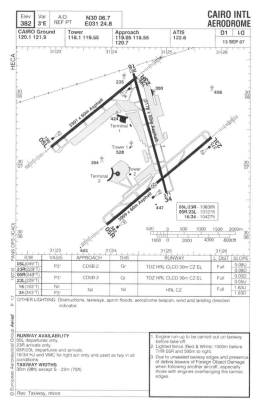

Commercial flights used the airport for many years until it became the official new airport for Cairo with the opening of what is now Terminal 1, known locally as the 'old airport', although modernisation and rearrangement of its halls as well as expansion, means that it is actually more up-to-date than Terminal 2. The new Terminal 3 was opened in 2009 for the exclusive use of Egyptair and is connected to Terminal 2 by a pedestrian walkway, while an automated 'Air Train' is planned to link all three terminals. The new runway, 05R/23L, is suitable for the Airbus A380. Construction of a new air traffic control tower is well advanced.

There has been one serious accident at the airport. On the inaugural flight of the Pakistan International Airlines service from Karachi to London via Cairo on 20 May 1965, the Boeing 720 was making a night approach, but the crew failed to monitor the rate of descent and the aircraft crashed killing 119 of the 125 aboard.

SHARM EL-SHEIKH INTERNATIONAL: SSH
Sharm el Sheikh, Egypt

Owner and operator: Egyptian Airport Holding
Company
Runways: 04L/22R, 3,081m (10,108ft);
04R/22L, 3,081m (10,108ft)
Terminals: Two, designated Terminal 1 and
Terminal 2
Airlines using airport as base or hub: Egyptair
Express
Annual passengers: 6,415,017
Annual aircraft movements: 47,699

Background
Originally opened on 14 May 1968 as Ophira
International Airport, it was initially mainly a
base for the Egyptian Air Force, but commercial
flights were allowed to serve the small town of
Ophira. The area has since become a popular

holiday destination, and the airport, now completely civil, has adopted the present name.
A second terminal was opened in May 2007,
mainly for international flights, many of which
are inclusive tour charters, but there are also two
domestic gates. In 2008, plans were unveiled for
a third terminal, but no completion date has been
given, or whether it may replace the older
terminal.

The one serious accident at the airport was on
3 January 2004, when a Boeing 737 operated by
Flash Airlines, an Egyptian air charter company,
crashed into the Red Sea after taking off. The
airline had a history of safety failures and had
been banned by several European countries.

HURGHADA INTERNATIONAL: HRG
Hurghada, Egypt

Owner and operator: Egyptian Airport Holding
Company
Runways: 16/34, 4,000m (13,123ft)
Terminals: One
Annual passengers: 5,945,254
Annual aircraft movements: 41,595

Background
Hurghada International is an Egyptian resort
airport served by many European charter airlines, it has a good safety record.

LUXOR INTERNATIONAL: LXR
Luxor, Egypt

Owner and operator: Egyptian Airport Holding
Company
Runways: 02/20, 3,000m (9,842ft)
Terminals: One
Annual passengers: 1,976,152
Annual cargo: 33,421 tonnes

Background
Situated 6km (almost 4 miles) east of the city,
Luxor International Airport is mainly used by
tourists visiting the Valley of the Kings. A serious
accident occurred at the airport on 20 February

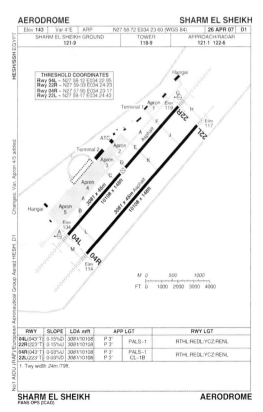

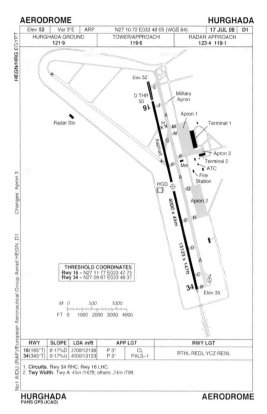

THRESHOLD COORDINATES
Rwy 16 – N27 11·77 E033 47·75
Rwy 34 – N27 09·67 E033 48·37

RWY	SLOPE	LDA m/ft	APP LGT		RWY LGT
16(165°T)	0·17%D	3700/12139	P 3°	CL	RTHL:REDL:YCZ:RENL
34(345°T)	0·17%U	4000/13123	P 3°	PALS–1	

1. Circuits. Rwy 34 RHC, Rwy 16 LHC.
2. **Twy Width.** Twy A *45m* /147ft; others *24m* /79ft

2009 when an Antonov An-12, operated by Aerolift, crashed when an engine caught fire during take-off, killing the crew of five.

EL SALVADOR

EL SALVADOR/COMALAPA INTERNATIONAL: SAL
Comalapa, San Salvador, El Salvador

Owner and operator: CEPA
Runways: 07/25, 3,200m (10,500ft); 18/36, 800m (2,625ft)
Terminals: One
Airlines using airport as base or hub: TACA
Annual passengers: 1,596,500
Annual cargo: 29,341 tonnes

Background
The airport is 50km (30¼ miles) from the centre of San Salvador, and is often known locally as Comalapa International Airport.

It dates from the late 1970s when it replaced Ilopango International Airport, which remains as an air force base. The airport terminal has been extended several times since it opened, with the number of gates increased from the original 7 to 17. In 2007, ADPI, a subsidiary of Paris Charles de Gaulle International Airport, was commissioned to study the future for the airport, which, unusually, actually has space in which to expand, and this has led to the current modernisation and expansion programme which will see the number of gates almost double to 30 by 2010, with a new terminal and a third runway parallel to the main one.

ESTONIA

LENNART MERI TALLINN (TALLINN) INTERNATIONAL: TLL
Tallin, Estonia

Owner and operator: Government of Estonia
Runways: 08/26, 3,070m (10,070ft)
Terminals: One
Airlines using airport as base or hub: Aero Airlines, Enimex, Estonian Air
Annual passengers: 1,722,653
Annual cargo: 22,639 tonnes
Annual aircraft movements: 38,844

Background
Just 4km (2½ miles) from the centre of Tallinn, the international airport adopted its present title in March 2009 in memory of a former president, Lennart Meri. Locally, it is often known as Ülemiste Airport because it sits on the shores of Lake Ülemiste.

Construction started in 1932, and although the airport was opened officially on 20 September 1936, it was in use for a year or so before the opening. Amongst the airlines using the airport before the Second World War were Aero (the predecessor of Finnair), Deutsche Luft Hansa (predecessor of Lufthansa), and the Polish airline, LOT. Although Estonia was neutral during the Second World War, the country was occupied by the Soviet Union. After the German invasion of Russia, the airport changed hands, and then back again as the Red Army advanced westwards. With the return of peace, Estonia became a Soviet republic, and between 1945 and 1989 the only airline using the airport was the Soviet state airline, Aeroflot. During this time the airport was also used by the military. A new passenger terminal was opened during the late 1970s and the runway was extended. In late 1989, SAS (Scandinavian Airlines System) introduced regular flights from Copenhagen. The terminal building was rebuilt in 1999 and enlarged in 2008.

ETHIOPIA

ADDIS ABABA BOLE (HAILE SELASSIE I) INTERNATIONAL: ADD
Bole, Addis Ababa, Ethiopia

Owner and operator: Ethiopian Government
Runways: 07L/25R, 3,700m (12,139ft); 07R/25L, 3,800m (12,467ft)
Terminals: Two, designated Terminal 1 (northbound flights) and Terminal 2 (Ethiopian Airlines and southbound flights)
Airlines using airport as base or hub: Ethiopian Airlines
Annual passengers: 2,832,449
Annual cargo: 46,877 tonnes
Annual aircraft movements: 44,811

Railway station at the airport with trains to Djibouti and Addis Ababa.

Background
Formerly known as Haile Selassi I International Airport, it is named after the local area and is 18km (just over 11 miles) east of Addis Ababa. It was built to replace the old Lideta Airport to the west of the city which is now limited to military

and general aviation use. Terminal 2 and the new runway, 07R/25L, opened in 2003.

The airport also includes one of the largest pilot training centres and aircraft maintenance facilities in Africa.

FIJI

NADI INTERNATIONAL: NAN
Nadi, Fiji

Owner and operator: Airports Fiji Ltd
Runways: 02/20, 3,273m (10,739ft); 09/27, 2,136m (7,007ft)
Terminals: One
Airlines using airport as base or hub: Air Pacific
Annual passengers: 1,395,165
Annual cargo: 72,755 tonnes

Background
Nadi was originally served entirely by sea, and then by flying boats, until the first airstrips were built and opened in 1939, paid for by the British colonial authorities but built by New Zealand. When the Second World War reached the Pacific in December 1941, the airstrips were taken over by the United States Army Air Force as USAAF Nadi, and used as heavy bomber bases to attack Japanese bases in the Philippines and the Solomons. When peace returned, the airport, which was much improved to cope with the heavy bombers, was handed over to New Zealand and the country's Civil Aviation Authority assumed control, with commercial flights returning in 1947, although at the time most airline timetables declared the airport as 'Nandi'.

When Fiji became independent in 1970, New Zealand assistance continued, but the airport was passed to Fijian control in 1979. Before this, the airport had become an important refuelling stop for transpacific flights, and passengers at the beginning of the jet age had to transfer from piston and turboprop airliners flying from Auckland to Douglas DC-8s and Boeing 707s for the rest of their flight to the United States. The airport was also at the time the centre of the world's largest flight information region, FIS, covering more than 4,000 square miles. Today, the size of the FIS is much reduced, but is still extensive and includes Tonga when the local air traffic control station is closed.

The development of the airport was helped by the post-war emergence of a local airline, Air Fiji, which initially served the smaller islands but which was renamed Air Pacific in 1972, and today has grown to connect Fiji with cities around the Pacific Rim, including Tokyo and Los Angeles, as well as Auckland and Sydney. Growth has been fuelled by the emergence of a tourist industry in the islands. Most aircraft movements are southbound due to the Sabeto mountain range being close to the airport's immediate north, but it is possible for aircraft up to Boeing 747 size to take off in a northerly direction if weather conditions dictate.

FINLAND

HELSINKI-VANTAA: HEL
Vantaa, Helsinki, Finland

Owner and operator: Finavia
Runways: 04L/22R, 3,060m (10,039ft); 04R/22L, 3,440m (11,286ft); 15/33, 2,901m (9,518ft)

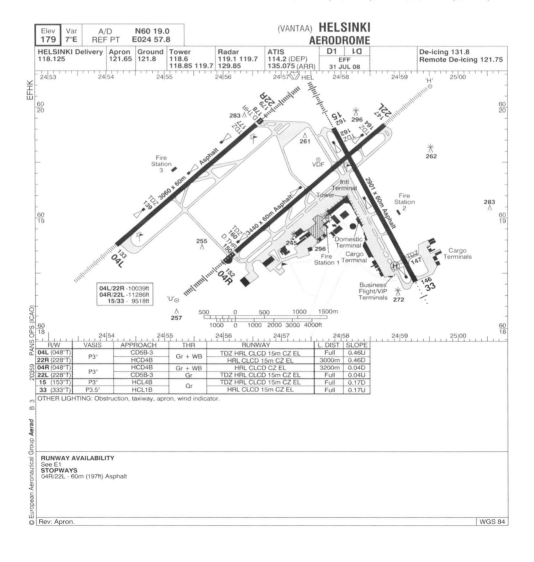

Terminals: Two, divided into Schengen and non-
Schengen areas (Schengen refers to the
European Union agreement on open borders
between member states)
Airlines using airport as base or hub: Air
Finland, Finnair, Finncomm Airlines
Annual passengers: 13,139,044
Annual cargo: 145,481 tonnes
Annual aircraft movements: 184,836

A railway link into the airport is expected to be
completed by 2013.

Background

Helsinki-Vantaa Airport was built in time for the
1952 Olympic Games and is the most important
airport in Finland. It is 20km (just over 12 miles)
from the centre of the city, and is operated by the
state-owned Finavia. Unlike many major airports, and especially those within such a short
distance from the city, there is room for expansion and the runways also allow some scope for
larger aircraft to be introduced.

FRANCE

France has one of the longest histories of air
transport. Indeed, it could even claim to have the
longest history as, during the siege of Paris by
Prussian forces in 1870, letters were sent from
the city using unmanned balloons. Perhaps more
to the point, the aircraft manufacturer, Farman,
started an air service between Paris and London
on 8 February 1919, using converted wartime
Farman Goliath bombers.

While the early flights were linking Paris and
London, the next priority became regular flying
boat services across the Mediterranean, linking
metropolitan France with her North African territories. During the 1920s and into the
early1930s, even travellers between the United
Kingdom and her colonial possessions would
make the journey across France by railway
rather than by air. Air France then embarked on
the task of linking France with her further flung
colonial possessions, initially in sub-Saharan

Africa and then in French Indo-China (now
Vietnam, Laos and Cambodia).

Today, the country has a large network of
regional airports, while in Paris, Charles de
Gaulle is the country's major airport and the one
usually used by international flights, while the
other large airport in the area, Orly, is mainly
used for domestic flights. One unusual feature is
that many of the airports outside Paris are
owned and operated by the local chambers of
commerce and industry. This a particularly
French feature as these organisations also run
some of the country's seaports.

NB: *Mulhouse Airport is listed as Basle/Mulhouse,
under Switzerland.*

PARIS CHARLES DE GAULLE: CDG
Paris, France

Runways: 08L/26R, 4,215m (13,829ft);
08R/26L, 2,700m (8,858ft); 09L/27R, 2,700m
(8,858ft); 09R/27L, 4,200m (13,780ft)
Terminals: Terminal 1, Terminal 2, Terminal 3
Airlines using airport as base or hub: Air France
Annual passengers: 59,922,177
Annual cargo: 2,297,896 tonnes
Annual aircraft movements: 552,721

Linked to the RER suburban Line B with two
stations inside the airport, although that for
Terminal 1 is distant from the terminal. Trains run
to the Gare du Nord. Terminal 2 has a TGV
station.

Background

Europe's busiest airport in terms of aircraft
movements, although second to London
Heathrow in passenger numbers, Paris Charles
de Gaulle is the main international gateway for
France. It was originally conceived as the *Aero-
port de Paris Nord*, although known locally as
Roissy, after the commune in which part of the
airport is located. It is 25km (just over 15 miles)
from the city centre. Conceived as a new airport
to ease the pressure on the overburdened Paris

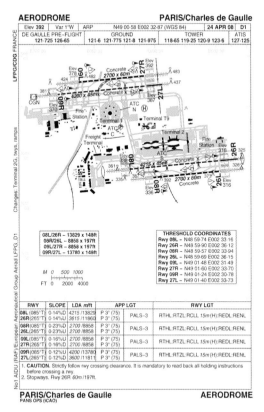

AERODROME   **PARIS/Charles de Gaulle**

Elev 392	Var 1°W	ARP	N49 00-58 E002 32-87 (WGS 84)	24 APR 08	D1

DE GAULLE PRE-FLIGHT	GROUND	TOWER	ATIS
121·725 126·65	121·6 121·775 121·8 121·975	118·65 119·25 120·9 123·6	127·125

LFPG/CDG FRANCE

Champas: Terminal 2G, twys, ramps

08L/26R – 13829 x 148ft
08R/26L – 8858 x 197ft
09L/27R – 8858 x 197ft
09R/27L – 13780 x 148ft

M 0   500 1000
FT 0   2000 4000

THRESHOLD COORDINATES

Rwy 08L – N48 59·74 E002 33·16
Rwy 26R – N48 59·90 E002 36·12
Rwy 08R – N48 59·57 E002 33·94
Rwy 26L – N48 59·69 E002 36·15
Rwy 09L – N49 01·48 E002 31·49
Rwy 27R – N49 01·60 E002 33·70
Rwy 09R – N49 01·24 E002 30·78
Rwy 27L – N49 01·40 E002 33·73

European Aeronautical Group Aead LFPG_D1

RWY	SLOPE	LDA m/ft	APP LGT	RWY LGT
08L (085°T)	0·14%D	4215 /13829	P 3° (75)	PALS–3	RTHL:RTZL:RCLL 15m (H):REDL:RENL
26R (265°T)	0·14%U	3615 /11860	P 3° (75)		RTHL:RTZL:RCLL 15m (H):REDL:RENL
08R (085°T)	0·23%D	2700 /8858	P 3° (75)	PALS–3	RTHL:RTZL:RCLL 15m (H):REDL:RENL
26L (265°T)	0·23%U	2700 /8858	P 3° (75)		RTHL:RTZL:RCLL 15m (H):REDL:RENL
09L (085°T)	0·16%U	2700 /8858	P 3° (75)	PALS–3	RTHL:RTZL:RCLL 15m (H):REDL:RENL
27R (265°T)	0·16%D	2700 /8858	P 3° (75)		RTHL:RTZL:RCLL 15m (H):REDL:RENL
09R (085°T)	0·12%U	4200 /13780	P 3° (75)	PALS–3	RTHL:RTZL:RCLL 15m (H):REDL:RENL
27L (265°T)	0·12%D	3600 /11811	P 3° (75)		RTHL:RTZL:RCLL 15m (H):REDL:RENL

1. **CAUTION.** Strictly follow rwy crossing clearance. It is mandatory to read back all holding instructions before crossing a rwy.
2. Stopways. Rwy 26R 60m /197ft.

No1 AIDU (RAF) European Aeronautical Group Aerad LFPG_D1

PARIS/Charles de Gaulle   **AERODROME**
PANS OPS (ICAO)

Orly, planning and construction began in 1966 and it opened on 8 March 1974 as Charles de Gaulle Airport, after the former president and wartime leader of the Free French forces. Initially there was just one terminal building of circular design and ten storeys high, and with seven satellite buildings, each with four gates. A similar design but with wide open spaces was adopted for Terminal 2, originally built for the exclusive use of Air France, again with seven satellite terminals. The modernisation and expansion of the airport has not been without its problems. On 23 May 2004, shortly after it had opened, the new Terminal 2E's roof collapsed killing four people and injuring three more. The terminal was designed by Paul Andreu, who had also designed Terminal 3 at Dubai, which had collapsed while under construction. A subsequent enquiry found that the daring design of the roof had left insufficient margin for safety, and had also been pierced by metal columns.

The terminal was rebuilt and eventually reopened in 2008.

Terminal 3 is reserved for low-cost airlines and charter flights. The rebuilt 2E is the airport's high security terminal for flights to areas regarded as being at risk of terrorist attack, and is used for flights to the USA and to Israel, for example. The airport is being further developed with the addition of two satellite terminals, one (Terminal 3E) of which will handle very large aircraft such as the Airbus A380.

The most significant serious accident at the airport was the crash of an Air France Concorde supersonic airliner taking-off for New York on a charter flight with German tourists on 25 July 2000. The aircraft was damaged by material that had dropped off an earlier flight and had been left on the runway. All those aboard the Concorde were killed, as well as four people on the ground when the aircraft crashed into a hotel.

PARIS ORLY: ORY

Paris, France

Owner and Operator: Aeroports de Paris
Runways: 02/20, 2,400m (7,874ft); 06/24, 3,650m (11,975ft); 08/26, 3,320m (10,892ft)
Terminals: Two, South and West
Airlines using airport as base or hub: A secondary hub for Air France, mainly domestic routes, and base for BA Open Skies
Annual passengers: 26,440,736
Annual cargo: 109,315 tonnes
Annual aircraft movements: 236,926

Orly is connected by the Orlyval automatic shuttle to the RER Line B at Antony Station, and a bus shuttle connects to the RER Line C at Rungis Station.

Background

Situated in the southern suburbs of Paris, it was originally used as an airship station from 1923. Orly became an airport in 1932 when it was opened as Villeneuve-Orly Airport to relieve the pressure on Le Bourget. During the Second World War, after the fall of France in June 1940, it was occupied by the Luftwaffe and used as a base, during which time it suffered repeated bombing raids by the RAF and USAAF. Following the liberation of Paris, the airfield was repaired by the USAAF and it became a Ninth Air Force base from which fighter-bomber missions were flown in September 1944 before the unit moved on, following the advancing Allied armies. The USAAF continued to use the airfield for communications and transport duties and even after it was returned to the French government on 1 January 1948, when it reverted to being a civil airport, then the USAF retained a presence there until 1967.

Orly has been eclipsed by the rise of Paris Charles de Gaulle as the French capital's premier airport, but remains important for domestic services and charter flights.

The airport's long history has not been uneventful. One of the worst accidents was on 3 June 1962 when an Air France Boeing 707, bound for Atlanta on a charter flight with that American city's civic leaders on board, crashed on take-off. There were 132 passengers and crew aboard the aircraft, and the only survivors were two female cabin attendants seated at the very back of the cabin. At the time, this was the world's worst air accident. Some time passed before the next accident, which was to a Varig flight from Rio de Janeiro which made an emergency landing 5km (some 3 miles) short of the runway on 11 July 1973 after reporting a fire in an aft lavatory. Of 134 passengers and crew aboard, only 10 crew and a passenger survived, with the fatalities being due mainly to smoke inhalation. This was followed by the loss of a THY Turkish Airlines McDonnell Douglas DC-10 on 3 March 1974, which crashed into the Ermenonville Forest shortly after take-off when an incorrectly closed cargo door burst open, causing a severe decompression which collapsed the floor of the passenger cabin severing the control cables. All of the 346 people aboard the aircraft were killed, again making it the worst air accident at the time.

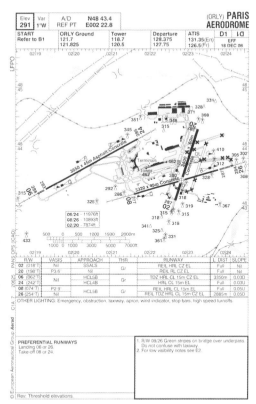

The airport has also suffered three terrorist attacks, the first two of which were unsuccessful. The first was on 13 January 1975 when several men, led by Ilich Sanchez, more usually known as Carlos the Jackal, attempted a mortar attack on an El Al airliner taking off for New York. They missed the Israeli aircraft but damaged a JAT Jugoslovenski Douglas DC-9 which had just disembarked its passengers. The same terrorist group tried again on 19 January, but came under fire from gendarmes armed with submachine guns. The Armenian terrorist organisation ASALA planted a bomb that exploded on 15 July 1983 by a counter used by THY Turkish Airlines, killing eight people and wounding more than fifty others.

NICE CÔTE D'AZUR: NCE
Nice, France

Owner: Nice Chamber of Commerce
Operator: Côte d'Azur Airports
Runways: 04L/22R, 2,570m (8,432ft); 04R/22L,
2,960m (9,711ft); there are also two helicopter
landing pads
Terminals: Two, designated Terminal 1 and
Terminal 2
Annual passengers: 10,399,513
Annual cargo: 11,546 tonnes
Annual aircraft movements: 190,078

Background
Nice has one of the longest associations with aviation as the site for the world's second aviation meeting in 1910. It is situated some 7km (4 miles) west of the town and is not only the main transfer airport for passengers for Monaco (with a helicopter air link from the airport) but is fre-

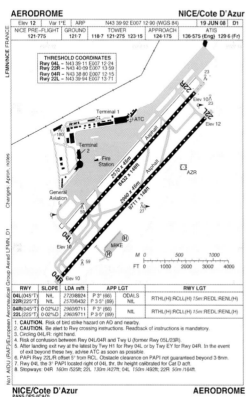

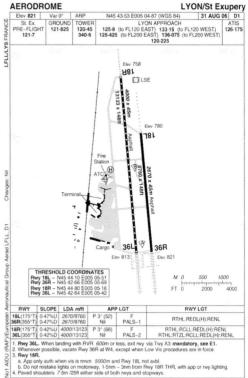

quently seen as a convenient route into northern
Italy.

LYON SAINT-EXUPÉRY: LYS
Colombier-Saugnieu, Lyons, France

Owner and operator: Aéroport de Lyon
Runways: 18L/36R, 2,670m (8,760ft); 18R/36L,
4,000m (13,124ft)
Terminals: Three, designated Terminal 1,
Terminal 2, and Terminal 3 (used mainly by
easyJet)
Annual passengers: 7,320,952
Annual cargo: 36,899 tonnes
Annual aircraft movements: 130,902

The airport has its own station for TGV (high-speed trains), Gare de Lyon Saint-Exupéry.

Background

Some 20km (12½ miles) from the centre of Lyon, the airport opened to traffic on 19 April 1975, although the formal opening was a week earlier, and replaced the former airport for the city at Bron, which was surrounded by urban development. When first opened, the airport was known as Lyon Satolas, but the name has been changed to commemorate the famous French pioneering aviator, Antoine de Saint-Exupéry, a local hero who had been an airmail pilot and died on a photo-reconnaissance mission during the Second World War.

MARSEILLE PROVENCE: MRS
Marignane, Marseilles, France

Owner and operator: Marseille Provence
Chamber of Commerce and Industry
Runways: 14L/32R, 3,500m (11,483ft);
14R/32L, 2,370m (7,778ft)

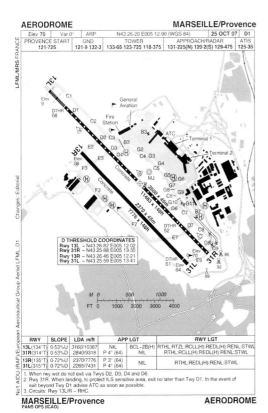

Terminals: Four, designated Terminal 1, Terminal 2, Terminal 3, and Terminal 4
Annual passengers: 6,962,773
Annual cargo: 51,384 tonnes
Annual aircraft movements: 120,615

Background

Originally known as Marseille Marignane Airport, it is 27km (17 miles) north-west of the city. It dates from 1934 but saw little use during the Second World War, as from the fall of France in 1940 until the German occupation of late 1942, it was Vichy Territory and the terms of the armistice with Germany banned military aviation.

It has not enjoyed the growth in traffic of the more fashionable destination of Nice. In addition to the normal commercial operations, it is also the base for the French Ministry of the Interior's aerial fire-fighting unit.

TOULOUSE BLAGNAC: TLS
Blagnac, Toulouse, France

Owner: Toulouse Chamber of Commerce and Industry
Operator: Aéroport Toulouse-Blagnac
Runways: 14L/32R, 3,000m (9,842ft); 14R/32L, 3,500m (11,482ft)
Terminals: Consist of four halls designated A, B, C, and D (opened in 2009)
Annual passengers: 6,161,522
Annual cargo: 55,225 tonnes
Annual aircraft movements: 95,116

Background

Situated 6.7km (just over 4 miles) north of Toulouse, the airport also serves as the flight testing ground for aircraft assembled at the nearby Airbus and ATR (Avions Transports Regional) plants.

The famous French aviation pioneer Clement Ader came from Muret, to the south-west of Toulouse, which leads some to claim that the city was the birthplace of aviation, but Ader was unsuccessful. Nevertheless, some years later Toulouse was home to flying displays before the

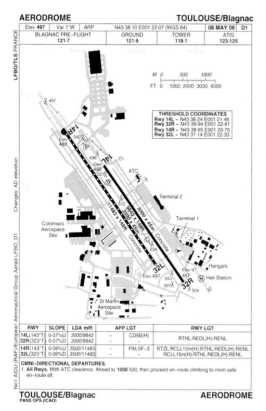

AERODROME TOULOUSE/Blagnac

| Elev **497** | Var 1°W | ARP | N43 38-10 E001 22-07 (WGS 84) | **08 MAY 08** | D1 |

| BLAGNAC PRE-FLIGHT 121·7 | GROUND 121·9 | TOWER 118·1 | ATIS 123·125 |

M 0   500   1000
FT 0 1000 2000 3000 4000

THRESHOLD COORDINATES
Rwy 14L – N43 38-24 E001 21-46
Rwy 32R – N43 36-94 E001 22-81
Rwy 14R – N43 38-65 E001 20-76
Rwy 32L – N43 37-14 E001 22-33

RWY	SLOPE	LDA m/ft	APP LGT	RWY LGT
14L(143°T)	0·07%U	3000/9842	–	CD5B(H)	RTHL:REDL(H):RENL
32R(323°T)	0·07%D	3000/9842	–		
14R(143°T)	0·08%U	3500/11483	–	PALSF–3	RTZL:RCLL15m(H):RTHL:REDL(H):RENL
32L(323°T)	0·08%D	3500/11483	–		RCLL15m(H):RTHL:REDL(H):RENL

OMNI-DIRECTIONAL DEPARTURES.
1. **All Rwys.** With ATC clearance. Ahead to 1000 500, then proceed en-route climbing to mnm safe en-route alt.

TOULOUSE/Blagnac
PANS OPS (ICAO)

AERODROME

First World War, and post war, on 1 September 1919, a Latecoere transport set up a mail service from Toulouse to Barcelona. Latecoere had established a factory at Toulouse in 1917, and was joined in 1920 by Dewoitine, who became France's leading manufacturer of fighters between the two world wars. The local chamber of commerce had set up an airfield at Francazal, which was used by both military and civil aircraft. In 1938 it was decided that the site at Blagnac should become a commercial airport, but the site also attracted aircraft factories and the workshops of the Armée de l'Air (French Air Force). Two runways and a hangar for commercial aircraft were also built.

After the fall of France in June 1940, Toulouse was left in the Vichy Zone, unoccupied until late 1942, after which the factories were used for the production of Heinkel and Junkers aircraft, and V1 and V2 missiles. The liberation in 1944 saw the airport taken over to provide barracks for

British troops. In 1945, all civil aviation was concentrated on Blagnac, including the activities that had remained at Francazal, and one of the temporary wooden barrack buildings used by the British troops became the terminal. The local chamber of commerce was given control of the airport in 1950, and immediately started to rebuild it. In the years that followed, runways were extended, and night lighting was installed, with the airport's first purpose-built terminal opening in 1953, while in 1954 the airport received its first instrument landing system. Aircraft manufacturing continued on the site, with factories for Sud Aviation (manufacturer of the Caravelle jet airliner), Breguet, and Potez-Fouga. A new control tower was completed in 1960 and the following year an air cargo terminal opened.

Throughout the 1960s, the airport was improved with the terminal building extended, and the runway lengthened and strengthened, before a second runway was commissioned in 1968 for the Anglo-French Concorde supersonic airliner. During this time, commercial use of the airport also grew, so that by 1977 the terminal building was becoming heavily congested, and a second terminal was opened the following year. This in turn had to be extended in 1993. The present terminals were opened from 2004 onwards.

In 2007, management of the airport was passed to a private company, Aéroport Toulouse-Blagnac.

BORDEAUX-MÉRIGNAC: BOD
Mérignac, Gironde, France

Owner and operator: Aéroport de Bordeaux
Runways: 05/23, 3,100m (10,171ft); 11/29, 2,415m (7,923ft)
Terminals: One, operated as two halls
Annual passengers: 3,463,205
Annual cargo: 12,487 tonnes
Annual aircraft movements: 68,687

There are plans to extend the Bordeaux tramway system to the airport.

Background

A joint civil and military airport, Bordeaux-Mérignac is some 10km (6¼ miles) from Bordeaux and is in the town of Mérignac.

The airport dates from 1917 when a military airfield was built on the site, and after the First World War it was shared with civil operators, with Air France operating from Mérignac to North Africa as well as to destinations in Europe. During the Second World War, the wartime leader of the Free French and future president, General Charles de Gaulle, was flown out of the airport to London, and after French surrender in 1940, it was taken over by the Luftwaffe and used for maritime-reconnaissance and anti-shipping sorties against Allied convoys crossing the Bay of Biscay. From 1943 until the liberation of France in 1944, it was attacked at intervals by the United States Army Air Force and the Royal Air Force.

Post war, the airport resumed commercial operations and was once again used by the *Armée de l'Air* (French Air Force) as a base, while in 1951 it became a NATO base and the United States Air Force took over, rebuilding Mérignac so that it could handle modern jet bombers and, coincidentally, also making it suitable for later use by jet airliners. United States Air Forces Europe moved out in 1958 and it returned to French control, although the US Army maintained a logistics centre there until 1961.

NANTES ATLANTIQUE: NTE
Bouguenais, Nantes, France

Owner and operator: CCI de Nantes
Runways: 03/21, 2,900m (9,514ft)
Terminals: One
Annual passengers: 2,589,890
Annual cargo: 11,692 tonnes
Annual aircraft movements: 55,356

Background

Nantes Atlantique is 8km (5 miles) south-west of Nantes near Bouguenais. It was originally known as Nantes Château Bougon. Like many French provincial airports, it is owned and managed by the local chamber of commerce. It is an international airport and has enjoyed strong growth in recent years, but cannot be expanded because of its proximity to the town. Permission has been given for the construction of a new airport for the area, which will be the Aéroport du Grand Ouest that is being built at Notre-Dame-des-Landes, some 30km (19 miles) north-west of Nantes, and which should be opened in 2015.

PARIS BEAUVAIS TILLÉ: BVA
Tille, Oise, France

Owner and operator: Chambre de Commerce et d'Industrie (CCI) de l'Oise
Runways: 13/31, 2,430m (7,972ft); 04/22, 1,105m (3,625ft)
Terminals: One
Airlines using airport as base or hub: Ryanair
Annual passengers: 2,155,633

Background

Originally meant to be a regional airport for the north of France, it is now associated with Paris for commercial reasons, even though it is 85km (just over 53 miles) north of the French capital. It is 3.5km (2 miles) north-east of Beauvais.

Built before the Second World War, the airport was taken over by the Luftwaffe after the fall of France in June 1940, and was not reopened for commercial use until 1956. It almost immediately established a link with low-cost air travel (even though regulation was still very tight, especially on international flights) when a British airline, Skyways, started low-cost coach-air services between London and Paris using flights between Lympe in Kent and Beauvais. Redevelopment for modern low-cost airlines began in 2005, during which passengers had to use a marquee as a terminal, and it is now a base for the Irish airline, Ryanair. The airport is limited both by restrictions on operating hours and also during poor weather when flights have to be diverted.

STRASBOURG: SXB
Entzheim, Bas-Rhin Departement, France

Owner and operator: CCI de Strasbourg et du
  Bas Rhin
Runways: 05/23, 2,400m (7,874ft)
Terminals: One
Annual passengers: 1,733,050
Annual aircraft movements: 45,046

The airport has a railway station but trains are
infrequent outside the peak periods.

Background
The airport is 10km (6¼ miles) from the city
centre. It occupies the site of a former Second
World War military air station. Improved high-
speed rail services have affected traffic at Strasbourg, despite the airport also serving the
European parliament which meets in the city at
intervals and requires members and officials to
travel to and from Brussels.

There have been two accidents at the airport
in recent years. The first was to an Air Inter
Fokker F-27 Friendship on 11 August 1973,
which crashed on landing after a cargo flight,
fortunately without casualties, and the aircraft
itself was later rebuilt. The second, far more
serious, was to an Air Inter (predecessor of Air
France Europe) Airbus A320 arriving from
Lyons on 20 January 1992, which flew into high
ground because the pilots incorrectly pro-
grammed the aircraft's flight control unit at the
start of the landing approach. Of the 96 people
aboard, 82 passengers and 5 crew were killed.

MONTPELLIER-MÉDITERRANÉE: MPL
Mauguio, Montpellier, Herault Departement,
France

Owner and operator: Chamber of Commerce
  and Industry of Montpellier
Runways: 13L/31R, 2,600m (8,530ft); 13R/31L,
  1,100m (3,609ft)
Terminals: One
Annual passengers: 1,286,877

Annual cargo: 5,797 tonnes
Annual aircraft movements: 80,583

Background
Often referred to locally as Fréjorgues Airport,
Montpellier is 7km (almost 5 miles) south-east
of Montpellier. The airport was the scene of
what could have been a serious accident on 12
February 1999, when an Air France Airbus A320
had a mid-air collision with a powered glider
that had just taken off, but fortunately the pilot
of the A320 was able to take evasive action and
neither aircraft was seriously damaged, and
there were no casualties.

Traffic has fallen slightly in recent years from
more than 1.5 million in 2003 to less than 1.3 million in 2007.

FRENCH OVERSEAS TERRITORIES

MARTINIQUE AIMÉ CÉSAIRE INTERNATIONAL/FORT-DE-FRANCE: FDF
Le Lamentin, Fort-de-France (Fort Royal),
Martinique, West Indies

Owner and operator: Aéroports Français
Runways: 09/27, 3,300m (10,826ft)
Terminals: One
Airlines using airport as base or hub: Air
  Caraibes
Annual passengers: 1,695,741
Annual cargo: 16,164 tonnes

Background
The largest airport in the French West Indies, it
is sited in a suburb of Fort-de-France. It was
opened in 1950 for both military and civil use,
and took its current title in 2007 to commemorate the author and local politician, Aimé
Césaire.

SAINT-DENIS – ROLAND GARROS: RUN
Saint-Denis, Reunion

Owner and operator: Reunion Chamber of
    Commerce and Industry
Runways: 12/30, 3,200m (10,499ft); 14/32,
    2,670m (8,760ft)
Terminals: One
Airlines using airport as base or hub: Air Austral
Annual passengers: 1,594,805
Annual cargo: 33,391 tonnes

There are tentative plans for a tram-train, which
will link the airport with Saint-Denis and Saint-
Paul.

Background
Opened after the Second World War, the airport
was originally known as Gillot Airport and is
7km (almost 4½ miles) east of Saint-Denis. It is
named after the pioneering French aviator,
Roland Garros, who was born in Saint-Denis.

FAA'A INTERNATIONAL/ PAPEETE: PPT
Faa'a, Papeete, Tahiti, French Polynesia

Owner and operator: Setil Aéroports
Runways: 04/22, 3,420m (11,220ft)
Terminals: One
Airlines using airport as base or hub: Air Tahiti
    Nui; Air Tahiti
Annual passengers: 1,511,340
Annual cargo: 18,173 tonnes
Annual aircraft movements: 55,300

Background
Faa'a Airport is 5km (just over 3 miles) southwest from the centre of Papeete and is the only
international airport in French Polynesia.

The airport is built on reclaimed land on a
coral reef, which has been extended in recent
years. Previously, the shortness of the runway
may have contributed to a number of accidents.
One of these was on 13 July 1973 when a Pan
Am Boeing 707 crashed into the sea just after
take-off, leaving just one survivor out of the 73
people on board. More fortunate were those
aboard two planes suffering landing accidents.
The first was on 12 September 1993 when an Air
France 747-400 ran off the runway after arrival
and ended up nose down in the sea, and the
second was on 24 December 2000 when a
Hawaiian Airlines Douglas DC-10 also overshot
the runway on landing. There was no loss of life
in either of these cases.

GERMANY

Germany is one of the few countries in which
the largest and busiest airport is not that of the
capital. Indeed, all of Berlin's airports combined
cannot match, let alone exceed, the total of the
busiest airport – Frankfurt. The background to
this is that post-war Germany was divided, so
the traditional capital since the state was created
in the 19th century, Berlin, was largely by-
passed, even though it remained the capital of
East Germany. Despite reunification and the
move of the federal capital from Bonn, which
shares an airport with Cologne, to Berlin, the
southern German airports reign supreme. While
Germany was divided, Lufthansa had its headquarters and main hub at Frankfurt, and the airport has remained the company's most
important airport and hub. The larger population and faster economic growth of West Germany helped, but the south of Germany was the
zone occupied by the United States, and Frankfurt became a financial centre of international
standing after the war. Today it has the European Central Bank. It also helped that Germany
recovered from the ruins of the Second World
War to become Europe's leading exporter of
manufactured goods.

One of the most environmentally conscious
countries in the world, Germany has seen considerable efforts made to cut short-haul domestic flights and instead encourage passengers to
use the railways, with Lufthansa even having
carriages painted in its colours and with its staff
on board, but despite this, the airline has had to

yield to pressure and reinstate short-haul flights. The relative proximity of Frankfurt to Munich has meant that the pressure on the former has been eased somewhat, with Munich becoming the second busiest airport by passengers. The same cannot be said for Hahn, a small airport almost 130km (80 miles) from Frankfurt, which is sold to the travelling public as Frankfurt Hahn by at least one low-cost carrier.

FRANKFURT: FRA

Frankfurt am Main, Germany

Runways: 07L/25R, 4,000m (13,123ft); 07R/25L, 4,000m (13,123ft); 18, 4,000m (13,123ft) [The opposite end of this runway, which would be designated 36, is not used.]; a fourth runway is approved and could be opened in 2010 or 2011.

Terminals: Two, with No. 1 having concourses A, B, and C, and No. 2 having concourses D and E. There are plans for a third terminal.

Airlines using airport as base or hub: Deutsche Lufthansa, Lufthansa Cargo

Annual passengers: 54,161,856

Annual cargo: 2,127,646 tonnes

Annual aircraft movements: 492,569

Terminal 1 has the airport regional railway station used by S-Bahn lines S8 and S9 which link the airport with Wiesbaden, Rüsselsheim, Mainz, and Hanau, as well as Frankfurt Central Station. The airport also has a long-distance station, opened in 1999, which is the terminus for the Cologne–Frankfurt high-speed railway.

Background

Although originally planned in 1930, construction was delayed by the Great Depression, and the airport did not open until 1936 when it was known officially as the Rhein-Main Airport and Airship Base. It was at the time second only to Berlin Templehof in importance in Germany. Regular airship services ceased in 1937 following the *Hindenburg* disaster. The airport was a major Luftwaffe base during the Second World War and was developed further using slave labour.

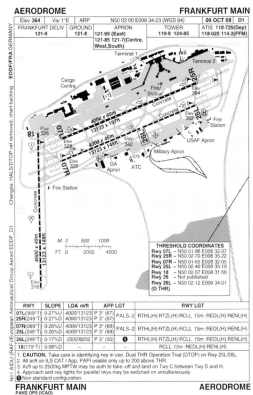

After the war, Frankfurt became a base for the United States Air Force and played an important part in the US contribution to the Berlin airlift which lasted from June 1948 to August 1949. The demands made on the airport led to the construction of a second runway. In 1955 the German airline Deutsche Lufthansa was re-established and began operations from Frankfurt. The two runways were extended to 3,000m in 1957, and in subsequent years were extended to 3,900m. Nevertheless, the airport did not resume its status as a major international hub until 1972, when the present Terminal 1 was completed. Planning for a third runway, 18 West, started in 1973, but led to strong protests by a burgeoning environmental movement, which continued even after it opened in 1984. A second terminal opened in 1994, and the airport was linked to the S-Bahn suburban railway network in 1999. Throughout this period, Frankfurt had also served as a

USAF base as Rhein-Main, but the USAF departed in 2005.

The sole serious accident at Frankfurt in recent years was during an air show at Rhein-Main AFB on 22 May 1983, when a Canadian Armed Forces Lockheed CF-104 Starfighter crashed, hitting a car being driven along a road near the airport, killing all five occupants. The pilot ejected safely.

Today, Terminal 1 is reserved for Lufthansa and the airline's partners in the Star Alliance. It is the airline's main base and most important hub, although the airline's second most important hub is at Munich, reasonably close by, to afford some relief for Frankfurt.

MUNICH 'FRANZ JOSEF STRAUSS': MUC

Munich, Bavaria, Germany

Owner and operator: Fughafen München GmbH
Runways: 08L/26R, 4,000m (13,123ft); 08R/26L, 4,000m (13,123ft); 09/27, 4,000m (13,123ft) under construction; there is also a helipad
Terminals: Two, designated 1 and 2
Airlines using airport as base or hub: Lufthansa
Annual passengers: 33,959,422
Annual cargo: 265,607 tonnes
Annual aircraft movements: 431,815

Connected to Munich city centre by Munich suburban services S1 and S8. Plans exist for a mainline railway station, and a tunnel already exists, but completion has been postponed because of cost increases.

Background

Situated 28km (17 miles) north-east of the city centre, Munich is second only to Frankfurt amongst German airports.

Munich 'Franz Josef Strauss' replaced the old airport for the city, Munich Reim, when it opened on 17 May 1992, perhaps best remembered for the air disaster to a BEA (British European Airways) Airspeed Ambassador (or 'Elizabethan') which killed many members of the Manchester United football team and for which the captain

of the aircraft was wrongly blamed. Construction of the new airport required the demolition of the village of Franzheim and the relocation of its population of 500. The need for the new airport lay not just in the growing congestion at Reim, but also the fact that Lufthansa's main base and hub at Frankfurt International was itself approaching saturation. The new airport was named after a former Bavarian prime minister, who was a keen private pilot and had been the driving force behind replacing the old airport at Reim. Nevertheless, as is often the case elsewhere, the airport is known simply by the city it serves, and it retained the Munich Reim IATA code. To start with there was a single terminal, but Terminal 2 opened in June 2003 and is reserved exclusively for Lufthansa and the airline's Star Alliance partners.

A third runway is planned, but, as elsewhere, this is proving controversial and a date for completion has yet to be finalised.

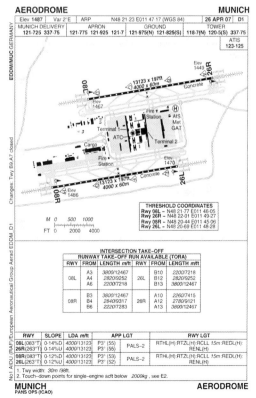

BERLIN TEGEL/OTTO LILIENTHAL: TXL

Berlin, Germany

Owner and operator: Berlin Airports
Runways: 08L/26R, 3,023m (9,918ft); 08R/26L, 2,428m (7,966ft)
Terminals: Three, designated Terminal A, Terminal C, and Terminal D.
Airlines using airport as base or hub: Air Berlin, Germania Express, Deutsche Lufthansa, Germania Fluggesellschaft
Annual passengers: 13,357,741
Annual cargo: 20,383 tonnes
Annual aircraft movements: 151,396

No railway connection, and the S-Bahn station 'Tegel' is not convenient for the airport.

Background

At one time one of four airports serving Berlin when the city was divided amongst the occupying powers after Germany's defeat in the Second World War, although in practice it was a case of 'East' and 'West' Berlin. Tegel is now one of the reunited city's two airports and is due to be closed around 2012, six months after the new Berlin-Brandenburg International Airport is due to open. It is named after the noted German gliding pioneer, Otto Lilienthal, despite the fact that he died when one of his hang gliders collapsed in mid-air.

Tegel was built between the two world wars after Germany was allowed to resume civil aviation, but came into prominence after the end of the Second World War. Initially, after the fall of Germany, Tegel was used as a Royal Air Force base, and was returned to civilian control in 1960. Meanwhile, post-war Berlin was divided, but so too was the country itself, leaving Berlin some distance inside what had become East Germany, or the German Democratic Republic. Three air corridors were designated for use by the three Western allies and only aircraft belonging to the military or to airlines registered in their countries and flown by their own nationals were allowed to use the corridors. This meant

that, after it was re-established in 1955, the German airline Lufthansa was not allowed to serve West Berlin. Domestic services from West Berlin to what was then West Germany could only be provided by the Allied airlines, and of these Air France soon reverted to simply flying to Paris, leaving the domestic market to Pan Am and the then BEA (British European Airways) while many other British and American airlines provided charter flights into and out of West Berlin. This situation persisted until 2 October 1990.

Tegel's importance to Berlin was amply demonstrated during the Berlin Airlift, when Allied military and civil aircraft had to keep the city functioning after the Soviet Union cut the road and rail links with West Germany. The result was that the runways were extended to take ever-heavier aircraft. As one of the airlines flying into Berlin, Pan Am operated a daily return cargo flight using a Boeing 727 between

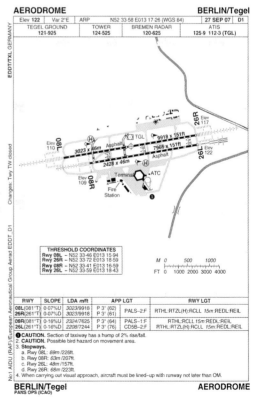

Templehof and Frankfurt. On 15 November 1966 the aircraft was diverted to Tegel because the runway at Templehof was being resurfaced, and on its approach, in snow with poor visibility, the aircraft crashed 16km (10 miles) from Tegel, killing the three-man crew. As the aircraft crashed on East German territory and the East Germans only returned half the wreckage, keeping the flight data recorder and cockpit voice recorder, the true cause of the accident has never been discovered.

While each zone of Berlin had its own airport, Air France moved its services from Tempelhof to Tegel in January 1960 as the former airport's runways were not long enough for jet aircraft. Pan Am operated a transatlantic service to and from New York JFK, which had to make refuelling stops at either Glasgow Prestwick or Shannon from May 1964 until October 1971. Eventually, all charter flights were also centred on Tegel, which at the time was under-utilised. One type of traffic that Berlin Tegel did attract between 1969 and 1982 was hijacked airliners belonging to the Polish airline, LOT, which landed at the airport where the French military authorities allowed them, and anyone else who did not want to return to Poland, to remain, while the aircraft, its crew and those passengers content to return to Communist Poland were allowed to take off again.

A distinguishing feature of the airport remains the main terminal (opened on 1 November 1974), a hexagonal building built around an open square on the south side of the airport. This can mean that an arriving passenger has just 30m (less than 100ft) to walk from an incoming aircraft to the street. Pan Am and British Airways (the successor to BEA) moved from Tempelhof to Tegel on 1 September 1975, confirming the airport's position as the main airport for Berlin.

On 3 October 1990, Germany was reunified and the restrictions on flights into Berlin were immediately removed. Lufthansa resumed services on 28 October, initially operating to Cologne (close to the then capital Bonn), Frankfurt, and London Gatwick. To ease the transition, Lufthansa bought Pan Am's Internal German Services Division, something which was more attractive than those of British Airways as Pan Am and Lufthansa both used Boeing aircraft. At the time, deregulation of air services within Europe was still distant, and the German government insisted that all charter flights entering and leaving Berlin should be by German-registered carriers. This meant the end of flights from Berlin to Amsterdam and Saarbrucken by airlines such as Britain's Dan-Air, although the airline could continue flying to British airports, and charter flights to holiday destinations by such airlines as Dan-Air and Britannia, but it also meant an influx of airlines such as Alitalia, Austrian, SAS, and Swissair, which had been long denied access to the city. The result of reunification and the liberalisation of the European air travel market was that traffic grew quickly and, far from being under-utilised as in the 1960s, Tegel became heavily used and congested. With little room for expansion, it will close six months after the new Berlin airport (Berlin-Brandenburg International) opens in 2012.

HAMBURG/HAMBURG-FUHLSBÜTTEL: HAM

Hamburg, Germany

Owner and operator: FHG, Flughafen Hamburg GmbH
Runways: 05/23, 3,250m (10,663ft); 15/33, 3,666m (12,028ft)
Terminals: Two, designated Terminals 1 and 2
Airlines using airport as base or hub: Hamburg International, Deutsche Lufthansa
Annual passengers: 12,780, 509
Annual cargo: 40,234 tonnes
Annual aircraft movements: 173,499

HVV S-Bahn Line 1 links the airport directly with the city centre at the Hauptbahnhof (main line station).

Background

Germany's oldest airport to remain in regular use, and originally opened for Zeppelin dirigi-

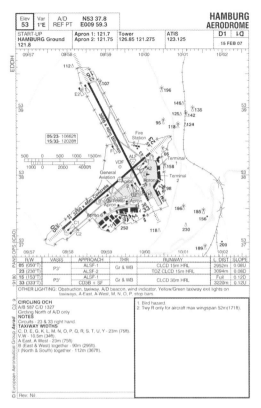

ble airships, Hamburg dates from 1911, and over the years has grown tenfold in size. It was used by the military in both world wars, and by the Allies after Germany surrendered in 1945. The majority shareholder is the local authority with 51 per cent.

In recent years, there have been plans to build a new airport for Hamburg at Kaltenkirchen, but these have been abandoned in favour of modernising the existing site with new terminal buildings.

There have been a number of accidents at the airport. On 27 July 1961 an Air France Boeing 707 flying from Paris to Anchorage and Tokyo via Hamburg, where it refuelled before flying over the North Pole, ran off the runway while taking off and was so badly damaged that it had to be scrapped, and four members of the crew and six passengers were badly injured. On 6 September 1970 a Paninternational BAC One-Eleven 500 was taking-off on a charter flight to

Malaga. Both engines failed shortly after take-off and the pilots tried to make a forced landing on the autobahn, but caught fire after both wings were sheered off by a bridge, killing 22 of the 121 people on board, including a crew member. Most recently, on 8 March 2001, a Cessna Citation jet suffered an undercarriage failure while landing, but there were no casualties.

COLOGNE BONN/KONRAD ADENAUER: CGN

Cologne/Bonn, Germany

Owner and operator: Flughafen Köln/Bonn GmbH

Runways: 14L/32R, 3,815m (12,516ft); 14R/32L, 1,863m (6,112ft); 06/24, 2,459m (8,068ft)

Terminals: Two, designated Terminal 1 and Terminal 2

Airlines using airport as base or hub: Federal Express, Germania, Germanwings, Lufthansa, Lufthansa CityLine, WDL Aviation, UPS (United Parcel Service)

Annual passengers: 10,471,660

Annual cargo: 710,244 tonnes

Annual aircraft movements: 151,029

The railway station, Bahnhof Köln/Bonn Flughafen, is on the InterCityExpress (ICE) Cologne–Frankfurt high-speed rail line with services direct to both city centres.

Background

Until German reunification saw the move of the German capital from Bonn to the old capital of Berlin, Cologne/Bonn was the airport for the capital of West Germany. Because of the capital connection, it is also the headquarters for the national airline, Deutsche Lufthansa, usually known simply as Lufthansa, although the airline's main operating base is at Frankfurt, Germany's most important airport. Cologne/Bonn is unusual in that it is set inside a nature reserve – the Wahner Heide.

The area can trace its history back to the early days of flying, to 1913 when Wahner Heide was

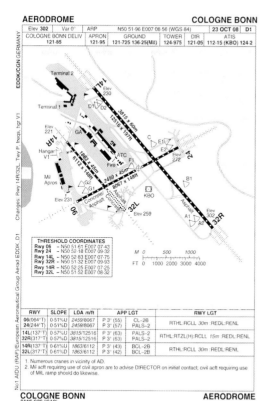

RWY	SLOPE	LDA *m/ft*	APP LGT		RWY LGT
06(064°T)	0·51%U	2459/8067	P 3° (55)	CL-2B	RTHL:RCLL *30m* :REDL:RENL
24(244°T)	0·51%D	2459/8067	P 3° (57)	PALS-2	
14L(137°T)	0·57%U	3815/12516	P 3° (63)	PALS-2	RTHL:RTZL(H):RCLL *15m* :REDL:RENL
32R(317°T)	0·57%D	3815/12516	P 3° (63)	PALS-2	
14R(137°T)	0·61%U	1863/6112	P 3° (43)	BCL-2B	RTHL:RCLL *30m* :REDL:RENL
32L(317°T)	0·61%D	1863/6112	P 3° (42)	BCL-2B	

1. Numerous cranes in vicinity of AD.
2. Mil acft requiring use of civil apron are to advise DIRECTOR on initial contact; civil acft requiring use of MIL ramp should do likewise.

COLOGNE BONN
PANS OPS (ICAO)   **AERODROME**

a military training area, and aircraft were used experimentally for artillery observation purposes. Little happened between the wars until, in 1939, an airfield was built for the Luftwaffe. Post war, with German surrender, the airport was taken over by the Royal Air Force and a 1,866m (6,127ft), runway was built. The airport was opened for commercial traffic in 1951, and in the years that followed grew rapidly as the airport for the German capital and for nearby Cologne. A new terminal was constructed and in 1986 it became the European hub for UPS (United Parcel Service).

The alternative name of the airport is in memory of the first post-war West German chancellor (the equivalent of a prime minister).

Despite the move of the German parliament back to Berlin following reunification, in the late 1990s an expansion programme began, including a second terminal and, in 2004, a new railway station with long-distance high-speed trains linking the airport not only with Cologne but also with Frankfurt. The airport was quick to cater for the new low-cost airlines that began operations at the start of the 21st century, with Germanwings and TUIfly starting in 2002, and passenger numbers rising by 43 per cent between 2002 and 2003. In 2006 easyJet and Wizz Air also began operations from the airport, whose management is now actively seeking to provide a base for a transatlantic low-cost carrier.

STUTTGART: STR

Stuttgart, Germany

Owner and operator: Flughafen Stuttgart GmbH
Runways: 07/25, 3,345m (10,974ft)
Terminals: Four, designated Terminal 1, Terminal 2, Terminal 3, and Terminal 4 (low-cost and charter airlines)
Annual passengers: 10,321,431
Annual cargo: 29,275 tonnes
Annual aircraft movements: 167,259

Stuttgart suburban railway lines S2 and S3 connect the airport with the city centre.

Background

Stuttgart was originally served by an airport at Boblingen, and the current airport was built to replace this, opening in 1938. During the Second World War it was a Luftwaffe fighter station and post war it was taken over by the then United States Army Air Force in 1945. In 1948 the United States Air Force handed the airport back to German civilian control, although the United States Army retained a presence and still has a helicopter base at the airport, as does the Baden-Wurttemberg State Police.

Redevelopment of the commercial airport began almost immediately in 1948 with the runway extended to 1,800m, then again to 2,250m in 1961, and finally to its current length of 3,345m in 1996, although the original 1930s terminal was not replaced until 2004, and there are now no fewer than four terminals. The airport still has just one runway, and contrary to experience elsewhere, many local people and

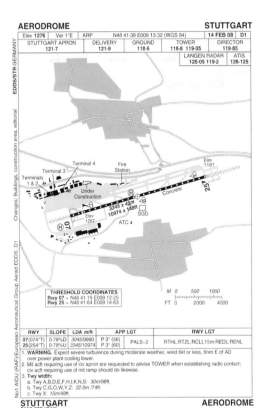

The airport has its own station with the passenger terminals connected to it by a monorail. Trains run directly from the airport station to the centre of Düsseldorf.

Background

Germany's third most important airport after Frankfurt and Munich, Düsseldorf has its own major airline, LTU, and is a secondary hub for Lufthansa, which introduced transatlantic operations to the airport in 2008.

Düsseldorf has a long connection with air travel as the Zeppelin LZ-III landed to the north of the city in 1909. Despite this, the present airport dates from its opening on 19 April 1927, some years after the end of the First World War because until then Germany had been banned from any kind of aeronautical activity. The airport was used during the 1930s for regular air services and was taken over by the Luftwaffe during the Second World War. Post-war, the businesses have been pressing for a second runway, but in 2008 it was announced that there will be no second runway until at least 2016.

DÜSSELDORF INTERNATIONAL: DUS

Düsseldorf, North Rhine-Westphalia, Germany

Owner and operator: Flughafen Düsseldorf GmbH

Runways: 05L/23R, 2,700m (8,858ft); 05R/27L, 3,000m (9,842ft)

Terminals: Three, designated Terminal A (Lufthansa and Star Alliance airlines), B, and C

Airlines using airport as base or hub: Headquarters and main base for LTU International and Privatair, and also used by Lufthansa

Annual passengers: 7,832,849

Annual cargo: 58,026 tonnes

Annual aircraft movements: 227,899

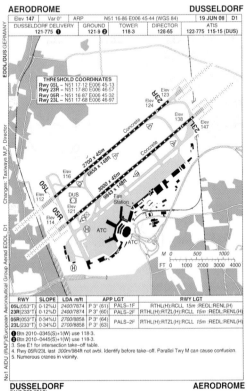

main runway was extended to 2,475m and reopened in 1950, although this was before the restoration of German commercial aviation, which followed in 1955 with the re-establishment of the national airline Lufthansa. Known post-war as Rhine-Ruhr Airport, a new terminal was completed in 1964, while the main runway was extended to 3,000m in 1969. The following year, complaints about noise saw night airmail flights abandoned, and in 1972, there was a ban on jet aircraft movements between 23.00 and 06.00 each night. Traffic continued to grow, however, and in 1973 a new central building and Terminal B opened, while in 1975 a railway connection between the airport and the centre of Düsseldorf opened, although until 2002, when a monorail link opened between the terminal and the station, passengers had to use a shuttle bus service. Terminal A opened later than Terminal B, in 1977, and in 1986 this was followed by Terminal C. A second runway opened in 1992.

By this time Düsseldorf was being used increasingly, especially by business travellers, as a major gateway for the lower Rhineland, home to much of Germany's heavy industry. A major blow to the airport's progress came in 1996 when fire broke out during work on the roof of Terminal A, killing 17 people in what was the biggest peacetime disaster in the state of North Rhine-Westphalia. The damage was so severe that afterwards passengers had to be accommodated in large tents until Terminal C could have a temporary extension, and Terminal A could reopen after rebuilding in 1998, the same year that the current title of Düsseldorf International was adopted.

Today, one of Europe's major airports, Düsseldorf is also a major centre for air cargo as well as passengers.

BERLIN SCHOENEFELD: SXF

Schoenefeld, Brandenburg, Germany

Owner and operator: Berlin Airports
Runways: 07R/25L, 3,000m (9,843ft)
Terminals: Three, designated Terminal A,
  Terminal B, and Terminal D

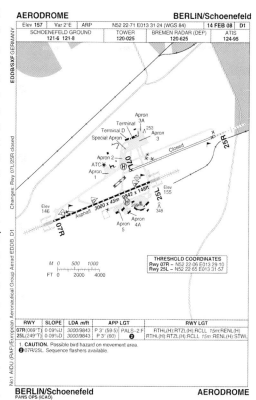

Airlines using airport as base or hub: Condor
  Berlin
Annual passengers: 6,331,191
Annual cargo: 8,255 tonnes
Annual aircraft movements: 66,392

Berlin Schoenefeld Flughafen Station is a short walk from the terminal and is on S-Bahn lines S9 and S45 running to the centre of Berlin. There is also a faster but less frequent regional railway service.

Background

The furthest from the city centre of Berlin's three airports, it is also the sole survivor, with Templehof already closed and Tegel set to close at some time in the future. Schoenefeld was the only airport for East Berlin during the years of Germany being divided, and it was both East Berlin's and East Germany's busiest airport throughout those years.

Opened on 15 October 1934 to serve the Henschel aircraft factory, it remained primarily a manufacturer's airfield until occupied by the advancing Red Army on 22 April 1945. The airfield was by this time suffering from considerable war damage, but this was repaired and in 1946 the Soviet air forces moved to Schönefeld from Johannisthal, while the Russian airline Aeroflot started a service from Moscow. The following year, the Soviet occupation authorities authorised the construction of a civilian airport on the site. The airport was handed over to the civilian authorities in 1954. During the next four decades, before German reunification, the airport was renamed several times by the authorities. Unlike the other Berlin airports, because it was outside the Berlin city boundaries, the restriction on only being used by aircraft belonging to airlines registered in the territories of the former wartime allies did not apply to Schönefeld, and the airport also became the main base of the East German airline Interflug as well as being used by Aeroflot.

During the years that the airport served East Berlin, there were a couple of serious accidents. One of these was on 12 December 1986 when an Aeroflot Tupolev Tu-134 crashed during its approach, killing 72 out of the 82 passengers and crew. The other was on 16 July 1989, when an Interflug Ilyushin Il-62 crashed into a field shortly after take-off, resulting in 21 deaths.

Once Germany and Berlin reunified, it became clear that three airports were no longer necessary and that a single airport would be more cost-effective, and as the one furthest from the city, Schönefeld had both the room for expansion and was least likely to cause disturbance from aircraft noise. Rather than incur the disruption of expanding and rebuilding Schönefeld, it was decided that a new Berlin-Brandenburg International Airport would be built on its southern boundary, and this is expected to open in 2011. The new airport will have the capacity for up to 50 million passengers annually.

HANNOVER: HAJ
Hannover, Lower Saxony, Germany

Owner and operator: Flughafen Hannover-Langenhagen GmbH

Runways: 09L/27R, 3,800m (12,467ft); 09C/27C, 780m (2,559ft); 09R/27L, 2,340m (7,677ft)

Terminals: Four, designated Terminal A, Terminal B, Terminal C, and Terminal D, with the latter used by charter airlines and by the Royal Air Force

Airlines using airport as base or hub: Air Berlin, TUIfly

Annual passengers: 5,644,746

Annual cargo: 16,318 tonnes

Annual aircraft movements: 88,352

The airport has an S-Bahn station, with trains to Hannover city centre, Hamelin, and Paderborn.

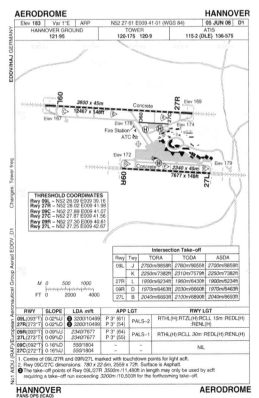

Background

Located 11km (almost 7 miles) north of the city centre, Hannover Airport was opened in 1952 after the city's original airport became too congested and had no room to expand. Two new terminals were opened in 1973, today's A and B, and at the time were renowned for their compact design. These were joined in 1998 by Terminal C, which is much larger. The present Terminal D is a converted hangar and is used to enable the Royal Air Force to move members of the British Army serving at bases in Germany.

The airport hosted the annual international air show, *Internationale Luft- und Raumfahrtausstellung*, between 1957 and 1990, but after a serious accident involving an RAF CH-47 Chinook helicopter in 1988, it was moved to Berlin in 1992 after German reunification.

NUREMBERG: NUE

Nuremberg, Bavaria, Germany

Owner and operator: Flughafen Nürnberg GmbH
Runways: 10/28, 2,700m (8,858ft)
Terminals: One
Airlines using airport as base or hub: Air Berlin
Annual passengers: 4,239,169
Annual cargo: 12,146 tonnes
Annual aircraft movements: 81,082

The U-Bahn has a station in the terminal with a direct service on Line U2 to the *Hauptbahnhof* (Central Station).

Background

The second busiest airport in Bavaria, it is 7km (4¾ miles) from the centre of Nuremberg. Despite the city's importance between the two world wars, the airport was actually opened in 1955. Its single runway, of limited length, confines it to the role of a regional airport, but both Frankfurt and Munich are within comfortable travelling distance.

FRANKFURT HAHN: HHN

Hahn, Rhein-Hunsrück, Rhineland-Palatinate, Germany

Owner and operator: Flughafen Frankfurt-Hahn GmbH
Runways: 03/21, 3,800m (12,467ft)
Terminals: One
Airlines using airport as base or hub: Ryanair
Annual passengers: 4,014,246
Annual cargo: 111,689 tonnes
Annual aircraft movements: 40,980

The railway connection is purely for freight.

Background

Despite being sold as 'Frankfurt Hahn', the airport is 130km (80 miles) to the west of Frankfurt – about the same distance as Southampton Eastleigh to London. Nevertheless, it has become an airport for the low-cost airline sector. Unusually, despite most flights being international, the name does not reflect this.

Built for the Luftwaffe, after the war it became Hahn AFB for the United States Air Forces in Europe (USAFE) and was used by fighter squadrons. After the collapse of the Warsaw Pact, the base was handed to the German authorities, although the USAF retained a communications section. The airport is still used by military charters for USAF and US Army personnel and their families, usually operated by Continental Airlines and United Airlines. It was decided that the airfield would make a suitable civil airport, and development was led by Fraport, owners of Frankfurt International Airport, which saw the airport as relieving the pressure on Frankfurt. Charges reflect the remote location and the basic facilities offered, with the main operator using the airport being the Irish low-cost airline Ryanair.

LEIPZIG/HALLE: LEJ
Leipzig, Saxony, Germany

Owner and operator: Flughaven Leipzig/Halle
   GmbH
Runways: 08L/26R, 3,600m (11,811ft);
   08R/26L, 3,600m (11,811ft)
Terminals: One
Airlines using airport as base or hub: DHL
Annual passengers: 2,719,256
Annual cargo: 85,446 tonnes
Annual aircraft movements: 50,972

The airport railway station is served by trains to
Leipzig and Halle, as well as to other destinations
in Germany.

Background
Sometimes known as Schkeuditz Airport, it
serves both Leipzig and Halle.

   The railway station at the airport is undoubtedly an asset, but the proximity of the railway
line means that aircraft have to taxi over a bridge
that crosses both the railway line and the main
access roads, which lie between the runways and
the terminal. The airport enjoyed considerable
investment in support of Leipzig's bid for the
2012 Olympic Games, but the event was
awarded to London. It has, nevertheless, benefited from DHL's transfer of its main European
freight hub from Brussels.

BREMEN: BRE
Bremen, Germany

Owner and operator: Flughafen Bremen GmbH
Runways: 09/27, 2,040m (6,693ft); 23, 700m
   (2,297ft)
Terminals: One, known as the Bremenhalle
Annual passengers: 2,232,018
Annual aircraft movements: 45,213

Background
Bremen Airport dates from 1913 when a flying
field was opened by the local flying club or aviation association, but it appears to have been
little used during the First World War. Post war,

with the start of regular air services in 1920 it
became a landing place for the KLM Royal
Dutch Airlines air service, linking Amsterdam
and Copenhagen via Bremen and Hamburg. It
became a Luftwaffe fighter station during the
Second World War. In 1945 it was seized by
Allied troops and was used as an air base, but
was returned to civilian control in 1949. When
the German national airline, Deutsche
Lufthansa, resumed operations in 1955, it
became an important part of the German domestic airline network, eventually operated by
DLT, the domestic airline, while international
services were also operated within Europe and
Scandinavia.

   The terminal, or *Bremenhalle*, has a small
aerospace museum with a Junkers W33 named
'Bremen', and a Spacelab module.

DORTMUND (WICKEDE): DTM
Dortmund, Germany

Owner and operator: Flughafen Dortmund
   GmbH
Runways: 06/24, 2,000m (6,560ft)
Terminals: One
Airlines using airport as base or hub: Eurowings
Annual passengers: 2,155,057
Annual cargo: 9,142 tonnes
Annual aircraft movements: 39,642

A shuttle bus connects the airport with
Holzwickede/Dortmund Flughafen railway
station.

Background
The airport is outside Dortmund and situated by
the small town of Wickede.

   Dortmund's first airport was in a suburb,
Brackel, which opened in 1925 and had a service
to Paris operated by Deutsche Aero-Lloyd,
which later merged with other airlines to form
Deutsche Luft Hansa, as it was known before the
Second World War. Traffic grew rapidly despite
the poor economic situation during the early
years. The airport was used by the Luftwaffe
during the Second World War, but after the

Allies invaded Germany it became a Royal Air Force base. When German commercial air services resumed in 1955, Dortmund was not served initially, and the airport was used by the British armed forces until the 1990s, and part of it is now used as a football training ground.

In 1960 the present airport was built on a new site at Wickede, but initially was little used as most traffic went through the main airports in the region, Cologne-Bonn and Düsseldorf, while there was also competition from Hannover and Münster. It was not until 1979 that commercial air services became significant, but at first they were mainly domestic scheduled routes, with Munich being the first, and inclusive tour charter flights during the summer months. A boost to the airport came with the creation of Eurowings in 1990, which used Dortmund as its base, and the pace of growth accelerated after 2000, helped by the opening of a new passenger terminal, and the emergence of the low-cost airlines, including easyJet, which established a hub in 2004, followed by Germanwings in 2007.

There are now plans to extend the terminal and lengthen the runway to 2,800m (9,193ft) while also extending operating hours from 22.00 to 23.00 at night.

DRESDEN: DRS
Klotzsche, Dresden, Germany

Owner and operator: Flughaven Dresden GmbH
Runways: 04/22, 2,850m (8,228ft)
Terminals: Two
Annual passengers: 1,849,836

Background
Still sometimes referred to as Dresden-Klotzsche, after the district in which it is located, the airport is located to the north of the city.

It opened on 11 July 1935, intended to be a commercial airport, but was almost immediately taken over by the Luftwaffe and played an important part in the invasion of Poland and, later, the Soviet Union, after which it became a fighter base. It was seized by the Russians in

their advance towards Berlin in 1945 and, after the war, was used by the occupying Soviet forces for training. It did not reopen for commercial flights until 16 June 1957, initially within East Germany and operated by the state airline Interflug, but international traffic to countries within the Warsaw Pact resumed in 1959. During the 1950s, it was also the scene of an abortive attempt to establish an East German aircraft industry.

The reunification of Germany in 1990 resulted in expansion of the airport to meet the increased number of flights, with many cities in Western Europe as well as the rest of Germany soon served from Dresden, which saw passenger traffic grow sevenfold between 1990 and 1995. A second terminal was opened in 1995, built on a former aircraft assembly plant, and a further terminal, opened in 2001, replaced the original terminal.

MÜNSTER OSNABRÜCK INTERNATIONAL: FMO
Greven, North Rhine-Westphalia, Germany

Owner and operator: Flughafen Münster/Osnabrück
Runways: 07/25, 3,600m (11,800ft)
Terminals: Two, designated as Terminal 1 and Terminal 2
Annual passengers: 1,581,458
Annual aircraft movements: 39,432

Background
Münster/Osnabrück is 25km (just over 15 miles) from Münster and 35km (almost 22 miles) from Osnabrück.

The airport is based on an airstrip near the village of Greven. The site was close to the Dortmund-Ems Canal, which was heavily bombed by the Royal Air Force during the Second World War and it was believed that the area contained many buried unexploded bombs. In 1967 the local authorities asked the British Army of the Rhine (BAOR), which had extensive bases in the area, for help in clearing the land of bombs and with drainage, as the area was badly drained.

The objective was to build an airport with a runway capable of handling Hawker Siddeley Trident and BAC One-Eleven airliners. The community presented BAOR with a glider and membership of the Greven gliding club as a gesture of gratitude for their work.

The new airport opened on 27 March 1972, and initially handled domestic flights and international charter flights, achieving official international airport status in 1986. The original terminal was replaced by a larger building in 1995, and this was joined by a second terminal in 2002. The runway was extended to its present length in 2008.

GHANA

In many African countries, the economic importance of an airport, or even the need for an airport for aid flights, is hampered by the lack of sufficient foreign currency to provide the advanced technology that makes an airport both efficient and safe. In Ghana, a new terminal opened without airbridges, while African airports lack railway connections to the nearest city centre. Tourism has come to the rescue in North Africa and in parts of East Africa, while South Africa has a stronger industrial base and a wealthier population.

KOTOKA INTERNATIONAL: ACC

Accra, Ghana

Owner and operator: Ghana Civil Aviation
    Authority
Runways: 03/21, 3,403m (11,165ft)
Terminals: One
Airlines using airport as base or hub: Ghana
    International Airlines, Antrak Air
Annual passengers: 1,179,990
Annual cargo: 59,507 tonnes

Background
Kotoka International is Ghana's most important airport. It was built before independence and is used today as a shared facility with the country's

air force. It is named after Colonel Emmanuel Kotoka who was shot near the airport during a *coup d'état* in 1967. New arrival and departure terminals opened in 2004, but without airbridges, and passengers (at the time of writing) are transferred between terminals and aircraft by bus.

GREECE

Even before mass tourism, the fact that the country has many offshore islands, and the importance of the shipping industry with the need to move ships' crews, meant that air transport was important for Greece. Nevertheless, the country has struggled financially since the Second World War, and has not always had the funding available for ambitious plans. Airports are state-owned, usually through the Hellenic Civil Aviation Authority, and many are shared with the armed forces.

Until relatively recently, all flights had to use mainland airports, and passengers for the islands had to change aircraft to complete their journey. Direct flights to the islands are now allowed, which should mean that these airports enjoy rapid growth in future, not least because direct flights will be less expensive and quicker.

ATHENS/ELEFTHÉRIOS VENIZÉLOS INTERNATIONAL: ATH

Spata, Athens, Greece

Owner: Hellenic Civil Aviation Authority
Operator: Athens International Airport S.A.
Runways: 03L/21R, 3,800m (12,467ft);
    03R/21L, 4,000m (13,123ft)
Terminals: Two, known as the Main Terminal and
    Satellite Terminal
Airlines using airport as base or hub: Aegean
    Airlines, Euroair, Olympic Airlines
Annual passengers: 16,518,851
Annual cargo: 118,237 tonnes
Annual aircraft movements: 205,295

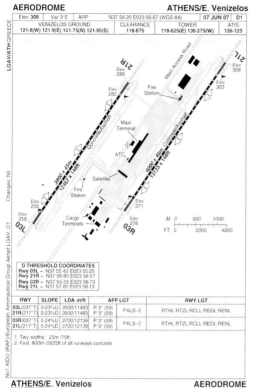

AERODROME   ATHENS/E. Venizelos

AERODROME				ATHENS/E. Venizelos	
Elev 308	Var 3°E	ARP	N37 56-20 E023 56-67 (WGS 84)	07 JUN 07	D1
VENIZELOS GROUND 121-8(W) 121-9(E) 121-75(N) 121-95(S)		CLEARANCE 118-675	TOWER 118-625(E) 136-275(W)	ATIS 136-125	

D THRESHOLD COORDINATES
Rwy 03L – N37 55-42 E023 55-25
Rwy 21R – N37 56-80 E023 56-57
Rwy 03R – N37 55-55 E023 56-73
Rwy 21L – N37 57-02 E023 58-13

RWY	SLOPE	LDA m/ft	APP LGT		RWY LGT
03L(037°T)	0-23%U	3500/11483	P 3° (59)		RTHL:RTZL:RCLL:REDL:RENL
21R(217°T)	0-23%D	3500/11483	P 3° (59)	PALS-2	
03R(037°T)	0-24%U	3700/12139	P 3° (59)		RTHL:RTZL:RCLL:REDL:RENL
21L(217°T)	0-24%D	3700/12139	P 3° (59)	PALS-2	

1. Twy widths: 23m /75ft.
2. First 800m /2625ft of all runways concrete.

ATHENS/E. Venizelos   AERODROME
PANS OPS (ICAO)

The airport has its own station, which is served by the Athens Metro Line 3 and by a suburban railway service to Proastiakos.

Background

A new airport built and opened in 2001 to replace the overcrowded and congested Athens (Ellinikon, or *Hellinikon*) International, which closed shortly afterwards enabling the IATA code to be transferred to the new airport. It is situated 20km (just over 12 miles) from the city centre, but the road journey is half as long again because of the terrain. It is named after a former prime minister of Greece, Elefthérios Venizélos, who was one of the ringleaders of the uprising against Ottoman rule in his native Crete in 1896.

Future development has been planned to take place in six phases that will treble its passenger capacity.

The one major accident was not actually at the airport, but on 14 August 2005 a Helios Air-

ways Boeing 737-300 crashed near Grammatikon, Attica, whilst flying from Larnaca in Cyprus. There were no survivors.

IRAKLION/NIKOS KAZANTZAKIS INTERNATIONAL: HER

Heraklion, Crete, Greece

Owner and operator: Greek Ministry of Defence
Runways: 09/27, 2,680m (8,793ft); 13/31, 1,574m (5,164ft)
Terminals: One
Annual passengers: 5,438,687
Annual aircraft movements: 43,852

Background

Iraklion is about 5km (3 miles) from the town. The airport dates from the 1930s, and during the German invasion of Crete in 1941 saw intense fighting for control between British and Greek

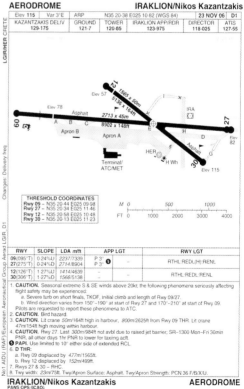

AERODROME				IRAKLION/Nikos Kazantzakis		
Elev 115	Var 3°E	ARP	N35 20-38 E025 10-82 (WGS 84)	23 NOV 06	D1	
KAZANTZAKIS DELIV 129-175	GROUND 121-7	TOWER 120-85	IRAKLION APP/RDR 123-975	DIRECTOR 118-025	ATIS 127-55	

THRESHOLD COORDINATES
Rwy 09 – N35 20-44 E025 09-98
Rwy 27 – N35 20-34 E025 11-46
Rwy 12 – N35 20-58 E025 10-48
Rwy 30 – N35 20-13 E025 11-23

RWY	SLOPE	LDA m/ft	APP LGT		RWY LGT
09(095°T)	0-24%U	2237/7339	P 3° ❶		RTHL:REDL(H):RENL
27(275°T)	0-24%D	2714/8904	P 3° ❶	–	
12(126°T)	1-27%U	1414/4639	–		RTHL:REDL:RENL
30(306°T)	1-27%D	1566/5138	–		

1. **CAUTION.** Seasonal extreme S & SE winds above 20kt; the following phenomena seriously affecting flight safety may be experienced:
   a. Severe turb on short finals, TKOF, initial climb and length of Rwy 09/27.
   b. Wind direction varies from 150°–190° at start of Rwy 27 and 170°–210° at start of Rwy 09. Pilots are requested to report these phenomena to ATC.
2. **CAUTION.** Bird hazard.
3. **CAUTION.** Lit crane 50m/164ft high in harbour, 800m/2625ft from Rwy 09 THR. Lit crane 47m/154ft high moving within harbour.
4. **CAUTION.** Rwy 27. Last 300m/984ft not avbl due to raised jet barrier; SR–1300 Mon–Fri 30min PNR, all other days 1hr PNR and 10min for taxiing acft.
❶ **PAPI.** Use limited to 10° either side of extended RCL.
6. **D THR:**
   a. Rwy 09 displaced by 477m/1565ft.
   b. Rwy 12 displaced by 152m/499ft.
7. Rwys 27 & 30 – RHC.
8. Twy width: 23m/75ft. Twy/Apron Surface: Asphalt. Twy/Apron Strength: PCN 36 F/B/X/U.

IRAKLION/Nikos Kazantzakis   AERODROME
PANS OPS (ICAO)

troops and German paratroops and air-landed troops. It remains as a military airfield for the Hellenic Air Force, but has also become the main point of entry for tourists visiting Crete, so that it is now the second busiest airport in Greece.

RHODES/DIAGORAS INTERNATIONAL: RHO
Paradisi, Rhodes, Greece

Owner and operator: Greek Civil Aviation
  Authority
Runways: 07/25, 3,306m (10,846ft)
Terminals: One
Annual passengers: 3,624,302

Background
The only airport on the Greek island of Rhodes, it is 14km (8¾ miles) from Rhodes town. It opened in 1977 to replace an earlier airport near Maritsa which could no longer cope efficiently with growing traffic, especially at the height of the summer tourist season. A new terminal opened in 2005, and over the next few years the airport is expected to expand, while it is already the fourth busiest airport in Greece in terms of passenger traffic.

CORFU/IOANNIS KAPODISTRIAS INTERNATIONAL: CFU
Kerkyra, Corfu, Greece

Owner and operator: Greek Civil Aviation
  Authority
Runways: 17/35, 2,375m (7,792ft)
Terminals: One
Annual passengers: 2,009,410

Background
The only airport on Corfu, a popular destination for holidaymakers from northern Europe. It is 3km (just under 2 miles) south of Corfu Town. Both Olympic Airways and Aegean Airlines serve the airport, but most traffic is international charter and low-cost airlines. It is named after Ioannis Kapodistrias, a local hero who became an important Greek diplomat.

CHANIA/IOANNIS DASKALOGIANNIS: CHQ
Chania, Crete, Greece

Owner and operator: Greek Ministry of Defence
  & Hellenic Civil Aviation Authority
Runways: 11/29, 3,347m (10,982ft)
Terminals: One
Annual passengers: 1,883,278

Background
Named after a Cretan rebel who fought against Ottoman rule, Chania is the second busiest airport on Crete and is also used by the Hellenic Air Force and NATO forces. It is close to Souda Bay, an anchorage used by the United States Navy during the Cold War.

KOS ISLAND INTERNATIONAL: KGS
Antimachia, Kos, Greece

Owner and operator: Hellenic Civil Aviation
  Authority.
Runways: 14/32, 2,390m (7,841ft)
Terminals: Two (Arrivals and Departures)
Annual passengers: 1,641,067

Background
Built after the Second World War, Kos, the only airport on the island, is 26km (16 miles) to the south-west of Kos Town and is close to Antimachia. For many years, the full potential of the airport could not be realised because of restrictions on airlines flying directly into the island, with passenger traffic directed via Athens. The two terminals are both modern.

THESSALONIKI MAKEDONIA INTERNATIONAL (MIKRA): SKG
Thessaloniki, Greece

Owner: Greek Government
Operator: Hellenic Civil Aviation Authority
Runways: 10/28, 2,440m (8,005ft); 16/34,
  2,400m (7,874ft)
Terminals: One

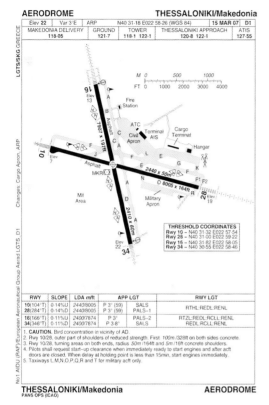

Aerosvit Airlines, flying from Odessa, lost contact with air traffic control and, during a second attempt at landing, crashed into the Pierian mountains, with the loss of all 70 people on board. Less serious, but dramatic, was the arrival of a Malév Tupolev Tu-154 on 4 July 2000. The pilots forgot to lower the undercarriage, and the plane skidded along the runway until they managed to take off and circle, lowering the undercarriage to make a safe landing at the second attempt. There were no casualties. The aircraft was only able to do this because the engines were mounted on either side of the tail rather than under the wings.

GUADELOUPE

POINT-À-PITRE (LE RAIZET) INTERNATIONAL: PTP
Abymes, Point-à-Pitre, Guadeloupe

Owner and operator: Government of
   Guadeloupe
Runways: 11/29, 3,505m (11,499ft)
Terminals: One
Airlines using airport as base or hub: Air
   Caribes
Annual passengers: 1,960,912
Annual cargo: 17,593 tonnes
Annual aircraft movements: 40,367

Background
Just 3km (less than 2 miles) from the centre of Point-à-Pitre, it is the largest airport in the French Caribbean. It opened in 1966. The runway is the longest in the Caribbean and can handle aircraft up to Airbus A380 size.

HUNGARY

Probably one of the stronger economies in Eastern Europe, since the fall of Communism the main state-owned industries have been privatised, including the main international airport at Budapest, while the main airline, Malév, has

---

Annual passengers: 4,168,557
Annual cargo: 5,759 tonnes
Annual aircraft movements: 46,399

Background
Originally known as Mikra Airport, because of its proximity to the village of that name, the airport is 15km (almost 10 miles) south-east of Thessaloniki. It is the oldest nationalised airport in Greece. It opened in 1930, and at the outset of the Second World War was used by the Hellenic Air Force before being taken over by the Luftwaffe following the German occupation of Greece.

Plans exist for the further development of the airport, starting with the extension of one runway on to land reclaimed from the sea, and in due course a much larger terminal building.

There has been one serious accident in recent years, and one near accident. On 17 December 1997 a Yakovlev Yak-42 of the Ukrainian

been quick to switch from Soviet equipment to Western.

BUDAPEST FERIHEGY INTERNATIONAL: BUD

Budapest, Hungary

Owner and operator: Budapest Ferihegy
  International Airport Operating
Runways: 13L/31R, 3,707m (12,162ft);
  13R/31L, 3,010m (9,875ft)
Terminals: Three, designated Terminal 1,
  Terminal 2A and Terminal 2B
Airlines using airport as base or hub: Farnair
  Hungary, Malév, Sky Europe Hungary, Travel
  Service Hungary, Wizz Air
Annual passengers: 8,581,071
Annual cargo: 68,144 tonnes
Annual aircraft movements: 124,298

The airport has its own station in Terminal 1, and Hungarian State Railways runs a direct service to Budapest Nyugati.

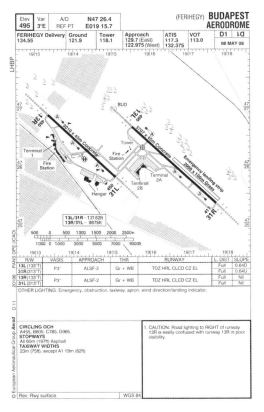

Background

Some 16km (10 miles) east of Budapest, Ferihegy was originally intended to be a joint civil and military airport when first planned in 1938, but work did not start until 1942, by which time the country was embroiled in the Second World War, and when it opened the following year it was as a military air base, with the civil terminal and other buildings only partially completed. During 1944, the airport suffered severe damage from the advancing Soviet armies which occupied Hungary.

After the war, the airport remained unused at first and it was not until 1947 that it was decided that it could be restored as a commercial airport. It opened on 7 May 1950 as the new base for the Hungarian-Soviet Civil Aviation Company (MASZOVLET), the predecessor of today's Hungarian flag carrier, Malév, to begin operations, which were initially international, linking Budapest with other Warsaw Pact countries. It was not until 1956 that Malév operated the first flight to the west with a service to Vienna, and

the following year KLM introduced a service from Amsterdam, by which time the passenger terminal was completed.

In the years that followed, a number of minor improvements were made as well as the main runway being lengthened, and it was not until 1977 that a new control tower was opened, and in 1983 a second runway, parallel to the existing one, became operational. The pace of development accelerated during the closing years of the 20th century, with Terminal 2 opened in November 1985, while the original terminal was designated Terminal 1. In 1993, transatlantic operations started with Malév flying to New York, and in 1998 a further terminal was opened designated 2B.

The airport was transferred from the Aviation and Airport Directorate of the Hungarian Government in 2002 to Budapest Airport Zrt, and in 2005 it was privatised with the state holding a minority share to the main British airport operator, BAA, although it was later sold to a consortium led by the German company HOCHTIEF.

Currently, the airport is undergoing further development, with a new building (BUD Skycourt) which will link Terminals 2A and 2B opening in late 2009, while Terminal 1 will be expanded with a new arrivals hall. A business park within the airport, similar to the 'Airport City' concept pioneered at Amsterdam Schiphol, and a new air cargo terminal, are all planned.

ICELAND

With a small population of fewer than 300,000 in an island roughly the same size as Ireland, and with no paved roads network outside the capital, Iceland lends itself to aviation, and every small community has its own airport – all of them too small to be included in this book, and many without IATA codes. The capital has two airports, one for international flights, with just one seasonal domestic route, and the other for domestic flights, much closer to the city centre, but with a considerable transfer time between the two. Only the country's sole international airport (Keflavik) is large enough to warrant a mention.

KEFLAVIK INTERNATIONAL: KEF
Keflavik, Iceland

Owner: Keflavik Airport Administration
Operator: Leifur Eiriksson Air Terminal Ltd
Runways: 02/20, 3,054m (10,020ft); 11/29, 3,065m (10,056ft)
Terminals: One
Airlines using airport as base or hub: Air Atlanta Iceland, Air Iceland, Iceland Express, Icelandair, Jet X
Annual passengers: 2,182,232
Annual cargo: 61,534 tonnes
Annual aircraft movements: 49,352

Background
Iceland's only international airport, and used as a mid-Atlantic hub by Icelandair, it is 50km (just over 31 miles) from the capital, Reykjavik. The airport only handles international flights, with the exception of one summer-only domestic route, which means that passengers transferring to the extensive network of domestic flights need to make a bus journey to Reykjavik Airport, 3km (just under 2 miles) from the city centre, and a transfer time of at least three hours is recommended. The airport and the terminal operator are both state-owned.

Formerly Danish territory, Iceland seized independence when Denmark was overrun by German forces in April 1940, and was itself invaded by British forces to prevent it falling into the hands of the Germans, as its position would have made it an ideal base for naval and air forces to attack transatlantic convoys. The United States used the country as a military base during the Second World War, and built the present airport for the United States Army Air Force, initially for fighters to defend Iceland and the convoys to Northern Russia assembling in the fjords, but a bomber station was also built. The fighter base was known as Patterson Field, and opened in January 1942, and the bomber base (Meeks Field) followed in March 1943. The airport also served as a staging post for transatlantic flights of military aircraft, including those being delivered to the European and Mediterranean theatres of war.

US forces withdrew in 1947, but with the start of the Cold War and Iceland becoming a member of the North Atlantic Treaty Organisation, the base reopened in 1951 and remained a NATO air station until 30 September 2006, when it was handed back to the Icelandic government. During its time as a military base, the airport established itself as Iceland's only international airport, but the civil terminal was in the middle of the base and travellers had to pass through military checkpoints until a new terminal, named after Leif Ericson, opened in 1987, and this has since been extended. The number of flights operating through the civil terminal grew rapidly in the period before deregulation of air services, as flying via Iceland became the cheapest way of crossing the Atlantic, and also meant that with a change of aircraft in Iceland, many more cities on both sides of the ocean could be linked. This established Iceland as a disproportionately large player in commercial aviation, even before its two main airlines, Loftleidir and Icelandic, merged.

INDIA

Indian Railways is one of the world's largest networks, and also one of the three largest employers, but the size of the country and the large population, combined with a poor infrastructure, has meant that India has a substantial number of airports and a vibrant air transport industry, helped in recent years by both the growth in tourism and also by the easing of restrictions on foreign investment and the payment of dividends to overseas investors. Another contribution to the development of India's air transport industry has been that the country has been an exporter of labour to the oil-rich countries of the Middle East, and especially the Gulf area, meaning that even fairly small airports are now handling international flights for Indian expatriate workers.

Until recently, India's airports were all state-owned, managed by the Airports Authority of India, but at Cochin a private enterprise airport project has opened, indicating that this may be the way forward, and that, when the world economic situation recovers, many state-owned airports may be privatised.

MUMBAI (BOMBAY)/ CHHATRAPATI SHIVAJI INTERNATIONAL: BOM
Mumbai, Maharashtra, India

Owner and operator: Mumbai International Airport Ltd (MIAL)
Runways: 14/32, 2,925m (9,596ft); 09/27, 3,445m (11,302ft)

Terminals: Six, designated 1A, 1B, 1C for domestic services, and 2A, 2B, 2C for international services
Airlines using airport as base or hub: Air India, Air Sahara, Indian Airlines, Indigo, Jet Airways, Kingfisher
Annual passengers: 25,236,400
Annual cargo: 536,432 tonnes
Annual aircraft movements: 236,585

Background
India's largest airport and most important airline hub was renamed Chhatrapati Shivaji in 1998 after the 17th-century emperor, Chhatrapati Shivaji Bhosle. Mumbai itself is still more usually known by its former name of Bombay, and this is reflected in the IATA code for the airport (BOM).

The airport has its origins in a military airfield, RAF Santa Cruz, built by the British before the Second World War, and which served in wartime as a fighter station for the Royal Air Force and Royal Indian Air Force. The original name was taken from the neighbouring community. After the war the airfield became a civilian airport, and control passed in 1950 to the Indian Ministry of Public Works and later to the Ministry of Civil Aviation. The airport continued to be known as Santa Cruz until it was expanded and a new international terminal, Terminal 2, was opened in 1981 at Sahar, but even today the domestic terminals are often referred to locally as Santa Cruz.

The airport has been the site of a number of serious accidents over the years, including one dating from its days as an RAF station. On 16 November 1947 an RAF Avro York transport attempted to make a three-engined landing, but the aircraft yawed and the pilots retracted the undercarriage to make a belly landing, which resulted in the aircraft being written off, but there were no casualties. Much later, on 16 March 1963, a CSA Czechoslovak Airlines Tupolev Tu-104 caught fire and was destroyed during refuelling at the airport – again there were no casualties. Far more serious was the accident on 27 July that year, when a United

Arab Airlines de Havilland Comet 4 flying from Tokyo to Cairo via Bangkok and Bombay encountered difficulties in making a landing approach, partly because the airport's instrument landing system was not fully functional, and for reasons that are still not clear, the aircraft plunged into the sea with the loss of all 8 crew and 55 passengers. The exact cause of the accident has never been discovered, as the wreckage was not recovered. Another very serious accident occurred to a Garuda Convair 990 which had called at Bombay while flying from Jakarta to Karachi, and which plunged to the ground within five minutes of taking off for the final leg of its journey, killing all 14 crew and 15 passengers. In June 1975 the airport had a succession of accidents, with an Air France Boeing 707 suffering an engine fire on the runway on the 12th; the runway had only just been repainted when, on the 17th, an Indian Airlines Sud Aviation Caravelle touched down too far down the runway and overran the end, with the aircraft being sufficiently badly damaged that it had to be written off, although there were no serious casualties amongst the 93 passengers and crew. On 12 October 1976, another Indian Airlines Caravelle took off for Madras, but the No. 2 engine caught fire and, while the aircraft was returning to land, it suddenly dived into the ground from a height of 300ft while just 1,000ft from the runway, killing all 95 people on board.

Today, Mumbai still has two terminals, but both have been extended, hence the designations 1A, 1B, etc. Terminal 1 (or Santa Cruz) is for domestic passengers, while Terminal 2 (or Sahar) is for international travellers. Both terminals use the same airside facilities but are physically separated landside, with a 10–15 minute drive between them. Terminal 1A is for Air India and Indian Airlines, which also has Terminal 2C, opened in October 1999, for its international services. A new control tower opened in 1996.

Mumbai has one of the world's poorest reputations for the punctuality of arriving flights, with 50.05 per cent late. The two runways are intersecting, and both are being extended.

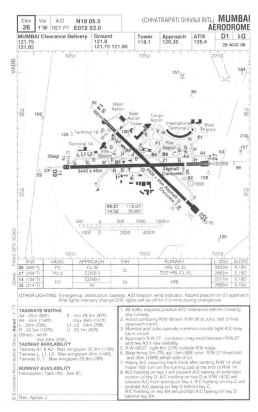

Expansion has been difficult, as urban development, often unplanned and unauthorised slum dwellings, has encroached on the boundaries. In February 2006, a business-led consortium created Mumbai International Airport Ltd (MIAL), charged with making improvements to the airport's existing facilities and preparing a long-term plan for its future development. MIAL unveiled its plans for the airport in October 2006, involving the rebuilding of Terminal 2 to create a new terminal and moving the control tower to provide a second parallel taxiway so that aircraft ground movements are clear of both runways. A link on the Mumbai Metro is also planned.

NEW DELHI/INDIRA GHANDI INTERNATIONAL: DEL

Delhi, India

Owner and operator: Delhi International Airport Ltd (DIAL)

Runways: 10/28, 3,810m (12,500ft); 09/27, 2,813m (9,229ft); 11R/29L, 4,430m (14,534ft)

Terminals: Two, designated Terminal 1 and Terminal 2, with a third under construction and

due to be opened in 2010, while there is a seasonal 'Hajj Terminal' for pilgrims to Mecca

Airlines using airport as base or hub: Air India, Air Sahara, Indigo, Jet, Kingfisher

Annual passengers: 23,346,895

Annual cargo: 431,623 tonnes

Annual aircraft movements: 225,510

The Delhi Metro will have a station at the airport from 2010.

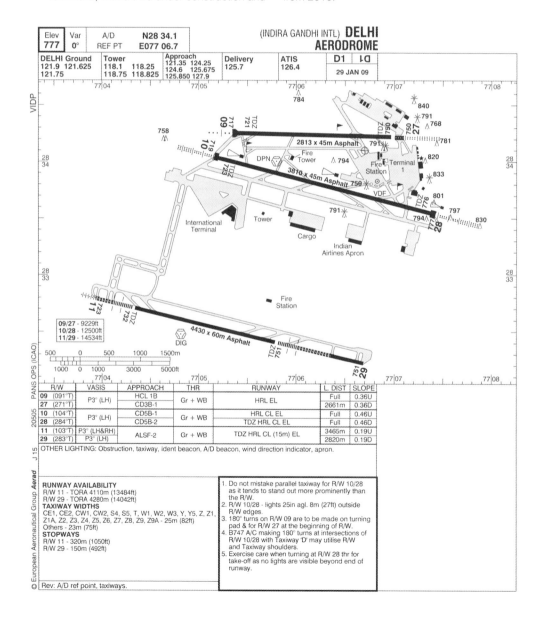

Background

Originally built during the Second World War as RAF Palam, it was handed over to the then Royal Indian Air Force before independence. The airfield continued its military role for many years after the war, but in 1962 commercial flights were switched to the airport from Safdarjung Airport, using a newly-built terminal. As air traffic continued to grow, a new terminal, four times the size of the existing building, was built. When this was opened on 2 May 1986 the current name was adopted after India's first woman prime minister, although many locals still refer to it as Palam. As a commercial operation, the airport was managed by the Airport Authority of India, but in 2008 management was handed over to a joint venture, Delhi International Airport Ltd, which will be responsible for financing future development. The planned expansion is intended to provide new runways and start with a new terminal, Terminal 3, which will be ready for the 2010 British Commonwealth Games. Between now and 2030, it is planned that passenger capacity should be increased fourfold.

There have been a couple of serious accidents since the airport opened. One of the first was to a Royal Nepal Airlines Fokker F-27 Friendship which arrived from Kathmandu in the middle of a severe thunderstorm, with turbulence and strong downdrafts causing the pilot to lose control and crash short of the runway. Incredibly, just one of the crew was killed; the other 4 crew and all 18 passengers survived. A far more serious accident occurred on 12 November 1996 when a Saudi Arabian Airlines Boeing 747 was climbing away after take-off and collided with an Air Kazakhstan aircraft which was about to land, killing all the occupants of both aircraft.

CHENNAI (MADRAS) INTERNATIONAL: MAA

Chennai (Madras), India

Owner: Government of India
Operator: Airports Authority of India

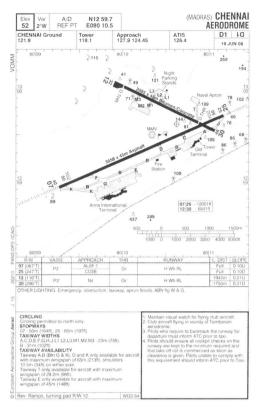

Runways: 07/25, 3,658m (12,001ft); 12/30, 2,045m (6,708ft)

Terminals: Two, with the Kamaraj Terminal for domestic flights and the Anna Terminal for international flights

Airlines using airport as base or hub: Air India, Jet Airways, Kingfisher Airways, Paramount Airways

Annual passengers: 10,424,213
Annual cargo: 267,696 tonnes
Annual aircraft movements: 121,224

There is an airport station at Tirusulam on the suburban railway network, with trains to the city centre, while the proposed Chennai Metro is planned to serve the airport.

Background

Opened between the two world wars when air services from Europe to India were usually operated by flying boats, the airport was first a

Royal Air Force base and then a Royal Indian Air Force base during the Second World War, before becoming a commercial airport post war. The national airline, Air India, operated its first flight between Mumbai (then known as Bombay) and Chennai (then known as Madras) in 1954. Because the original terminal was built on the north-east side of the airfield at Meenambakkam, the airport has often been referred to by this name, and sometimes as Anna Airport because of the more modern international passenger terminal. The original terminal survives as the air cargo centre. Both the Kamaraj domestic terminal and Anna international terminal were opened in 1988.

The airport has suffered a number of accidents over the years, although none of them has been fatal. The earliest of these was to an Indian Airlines Douglas C-54A, a converted military DC-4, which suffered an autopilot failure whilst en route to Madras on 8 September 1958, which also affected the hydraulic system. The pilots did not appreciate the nature of the problem and on landing the aircraft overshot the runway and crashed into an obstruction beyond the runway damaging the plane beyond repair. Another Indian Airlines aircraft was involved on 29 September 1986, when an Airbus A300 was taking off for Mumbai. The pilots spotted a large bird on the right side of the aircraft and another on the centre line, and as the aircraft started to rotate at 150 knots, there was a loud bang on the right side followed by vibration and they decided to abort the take-off, but the aircraft overshot the end of the runway and was damaged beyond repair. More fortunate was an Air Lanka Boeing 737 on 10 January 1992, landing at Madras from Colombo. On touchdown the right undercarriage collapsed and the No. 2 engine struck the runway, catching fire and causing the aircraft to swerve off the runway and suffer severe damage. Nevertheless, the fire was soon extinguished and, after substantial repairs, the aircraft returned to service. Finally, an Air France Boeing 747 freighter from Paris suffered a landing accident after flying a sector from Bangalore on 5 March 1999. The first approach was abandoned because of indications that the undercarriage was not down and locked, and on the second approach the pilots assumed that the undercarriage was down and locked, and that a red warning light for the nosewheel was a false indication, even though it remained after the undercarriage was recycled (that is, raised and lowered again). The nosewheel had, in fact, remained retracted and, on landing, the aircraft slid down the runway on its nose, causing it to catch fire. The crew of five managed to escape before the aircraft was completely burnt out, with its 66 tons of cargo.

The airport is currently being expanded and modernised with a new runway and plans for a new integrated terminal, while the Chennai Metro should reach the airport by 2013. For the longer term, there are also plans for a new airport to be built on a greenfield site.

BENGALŪRU (BANGALORE) INTERNATIONAL: BLR
Devanahalli, Karnataka, India

Owner and operator: Bangalore International Airport Limited
Runways: 09/27, 4,000m (13,123ft)
Terminals: One
Annual passengers: 9,929,717
Annual cargo: 176,252 tonnes
Annual aircraft movements: 123,141

A direct railway link, the Namma Metro, between the airport, with its own station, and the centre of Bengalūru (Bangalore) is expected to open during 2010.

Background
Built to replace the old Bangalore International Airport after being delayed for a decade, the new Bengalūru International opened on 23 May 2008. The city changed its name to Bengalūru in recent years.

Expansion of the airport is already planned, with a runway extension and even a second runway, and an extension of the passenger terminal.

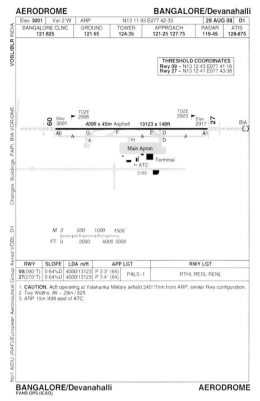

AERODROME   BANGALORE/Devanahalli

| Elev 3001 | Var 2°W | ARP | N13 11·93 E077 42·33 | 28 AUG 08 | D1 |

| BANGALORE CLNC | GROUND | TOWER | APPROACH | RADAR | ATIS |
| 121·825 | 121·65 | 124·35 | 121·25 127·75 | 119·45 | 128·675 |

THRESHOLD COORDINATES
Rwy 09 – N13 12·43 E077 41·16
Rwy 27 – N13 12·41 E077 43·38

RWY	SLOPE	LDA m/ft	APP LGT	RWY LGT
09(090°T)	0·64%D	4000/13123	P 3·3' (64)	PALS-1	RTHL·REDL·RENL
27(270°T)	0·64%U	4000/13123	P 3·4' (64)		RTHL·REDL·RENL

1. CAUTION. Acft operating at Yelahanka Military airfield 240°/7nm from ARP, similar Rwy configuration.
2. Twy Widths. All – 25m / 82ft.
3. ARP 15m /49ft east of ATC.

BANGALORE/Devanahalli   AERODROME
PANS OPS (ICAO)

KOLKATA (CALCUTTA) NETAJI SUBHASH CHANDRA BOSE INTERNATIONAL: CCU

Dum Dum, Kolkata (Calcutta), West Bengal, India

Owner and operator: Airports Authority of India
Runways: 01L/19R, 2,399m (7,871ft); 01R/19L, 3,627m (11,900ft)
Terminals: Two, designated Domestic Terminal and International Terminal
Airlines using airport as base or hub: Indian Airlines
Annual passengers: 7,223,537
Annual cargo: 93,718 tonnes
Annual aircraft movements: 78,623

There is an airport station on the Kolkata subway system.

Background

Originally known as Dum Dum Airport, after the locality in which it is set, some 17km (11 miles) from the city centre, the airport has been named after Subhash Chandra Bose, a leader in the Indian National Movement. Based on a former Second World War airfield, it has been extensively modernised, and a cargo terminal has been added in recent years, but the potential for further expansion and development is limited, not least because of a mosque within the airport, and current planning is that a new airport on a completely new site will be needed after 2016.

The airport has suffered a number of accidents, some of which date back to its days as an RAF station. The first of these, post war, was on 19 September 1945 when an engine of a Douglas C-47A Dakota caught fire while the plane was landing, causing it to overshoot the runway and collide with a water tank. It was a write-off. Just over a year later, on 20 October 1946, another

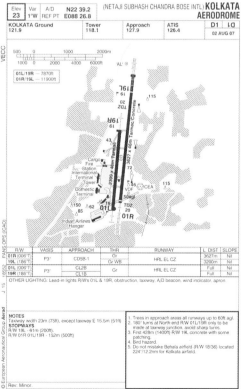

| Elev 23 | Var 1°W | A/D REF PT | N22 39.2 E088 26.8 | (NETAJI SUBHASH CHANDRA BOSE INTL) KOLKATA AERODROME |

| KOLKATA Ground 121.9 | Tower 118.1 | Approach 127.9 | ATIS 126.4 | D1 | LQ |
| | | | | 02 AUG 07 |

01L/19R — 7870ft
01R/19L — 11900ft

R/W	VASIS	APPROACH	THR	RUNWAY	L. DIST	SLOPE
01R (006°T)	P3'	CD5B-1	Gr	HRL EL CZ	3627m	Nil
19L (186°T)			Gr WB		3200m	Nil
01L (006°T)	P3'	CL2B	Gr	HRL EL CZ	Full	Nil
19R (186°T)		CL1B			Full	Nil

OTHER LIGHTING: Lead-in lights R/Ws 01L & 19R, obstruction, taxiway, A/D beacon, wind indicator, apron.

NOTES
Taxiway width 23m (75ft), except taxiway E 15.5m (51ft)
STOPWAYS
R/W 19L - 61m (200ft)
R/W 01R 01L/19R - 152m (500ft)

1. Trees in approach areas all runways up to 60ft agl.
2. 180° turns at North end R/W 01L/19R only to be made at taxiway junction, avoid sharp turns.
3. First 428m (1400ft) R/W 19L concrete with some patching.
4. Bird hazard.
5. Do not mistake Behala airfield (R/W 18/36) located 224°/12.2nm for Kolkata airfield.

Rev: Minor.

RAF transport, this time an Avro York, suffered an engine failure on take-off and could not gain height, and shortly afterwards crashed with the loss of all three crew.

Another C-47 was involved in an accident on 21 November 1951. The Deccan Airways aircraft was landing in poor visibility and struck a group of trees, killing all 4 crew and 16 passengers. Just over a month later, another C-47, this time an all-cargo aircraft belonging to Kalinga Airlines, was taking off in poor visibility when it also struck a group of trees and crashed, with the loss of the three crew. The next aircraft to be involved in an accident at the airport was a Handley Page Hermes belonging to Airwork (a predecessor of British Caledonian, an airline later taken over by British Airways) on a military charter or 'trooping by air' flight from Blackbushe to Singapore, which was landing on 1 September 1957 after flying a sector from New Delhi. Just before touchdown, a passing shower obscured the runway and the crew decided to go round, and were offered a radar-assisted approach. As he broke through the cloud, the captain turned down the radio, but instead of approaching runway 1R, he was approaching 1L, just as an Indian Airlines DC-3 was lining up on the runway and holding for take-off clearance. The Hermes struck the DC-3, killing all four occupants, although there were no fatalities aboard the larger aircraft. Another Indian Airlines aircraft, a C-47 or ex-military DC-3, was involved in an accident on 26 August 1961, when it took-off on a cargo flight at too low a speed and crashed, although the crew of three survived. An Indian Airlines Douglas C-54 was destroyed in a hangar fire on 3 May 1962. There seems to be something of a mystery about the loss of a Kalinga Airlines C-47 on 2 April 1964, which was damaged beyond repair, but there does not appear to have been any loss of life, although whether this was a landing or take-off accident is not clear.

The next accident was on 12 June 1968, when a Pan American Boeing 707 was on approach to the airport on the Bangkok to Calcutta leg of a round-the-world service, making a visual approach when it struck a tree a kilometre short of the runway and crashed. One of the 10 crew was amongst the fatalities, as were 5 of the 63 passengers. The crew had misunderstood the barometric pressure figures given to them by air traffic control and had incorrectly set the altimeter, which meant that they were flying 360ft lower than they should have been. On 23 September 1988, a Fokker F-27 Friendship of Vayudoot, an Indian airline now absorbed by Indian Airways, was taxiing ready to take off when a high-lift catering truck drove into the outer part of the port wing, damaging the wing and the port aileron. There were no casualties aboard the aircraft, but the three members of the catering truck crew were all seriously injured.

HYDERABAD/RAJIV GANDHI INTERNATIONAL: HYD
Shamshabad, Hyderabad, India

Owner: Government of Andhra Pradesh
Operator: GMR Hyderabad International Airport Ltd
Runways: 09/27, 4,263m (13,976ft)
Terminals: Two, designated Terminal 1 and Terminal 2
Annual passengers: 6,777,408
Annual cargo: 50,853 tonnes
Annual aircraft movements: 91,462

A rapid transit connection is planned for the future.

Background
Situated some 22km (14 miles) from Hyderabad at Shamshabad, the airport opened on 23 March 2008. It is named after a former prime minister of India, Rajiv Gandhi. It is being developed by a consortium that includes the government of the state of Andhra Pradesh, the Airports Authority of India, Malaysia Airports, and the GMR Group. Future plans call for the expansion of Terminal 1 and completion of Terminal 2, the completion of a second parallel runway, and possibly, once additional land is purchased, two further runways.

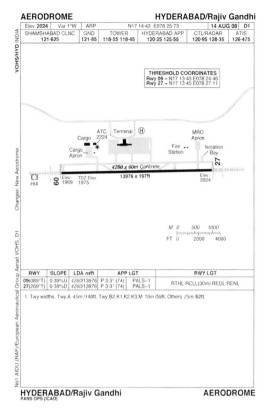

AERODROME					HYDERABAD/Rajiv Gandhi	
Elev 2024	Var 1°W	ARP		N17 14·43 E078 25·73		14 AUG 08	D1

SHAMSHABAD CLNC 121·625	GND 121·85	TOWER 118·55 118·45	HYDERABAD APP 120·25 125·55	CTL/RADAR 120·95 128·35	ATIS 126·475

THRESHOLD COORDINATES
Rwy 09 – N17 13·43 E078 24·46
Rwy 27 – N17 13·45 E078 27·11

ATC 2224 Terminal Ⓗ
Cargo
Cargo Apron
MRO Apron
Fire Station
Isolation Bay

4260 x 60m Concrete
HIA Elev 1969 TDZ Elev 1975 13976 x 197ft Elev 2024

M 0 500 1000
FT 0 2000 4000

RWY	SLOPE	LDA m/ft	APP LGT		RWY LGT
09(089°T)	0·39%U	4260/13976	P 3·3° (74)	PALS–1	RTHL:RCLL(30m):REDL:RENL
27(269°T)	0·39%D	4260/13976	P 3·3° (74)	PALS–1	

1. Twy widths. Twy A 45m /148ft; Twy B2,K1,K2,K3,M 18m /59ft, Others 25m /82ft.

HYDERABAD/Rajiv Gandhi   AERODROME
PANS OPS (ICAO)

COCHIN/KOCHI INTERNATIONAL AIRPORT: COK

Nedumbassery, Cochin, Kerala, India

Owner and operator: Cochin International
    Airport Ltd
Runways: 09/27, 3,400m (11,155ft)
Terminals: Two, designated as Domestic and
    International
Annual passengers: 3,162,227
Annual cargo: 25,287 tonnes

Background
India's first private enterprise airport, largely funded by investments from expatriate Indians, and the busiest in the south of India. It is 30km (almost 19 miles) from the centre of Cochin, or Kochi, and is sometimes known as Nedumbassery Airport after its location. The state government of Kerala has a 13 per cent stake, as has the central government.

Originally the area was served by airlines using an Indian Naval Service air station. By 1991 it was clear that rising traffic required a new airport, but this was not opened until May 1999, and the following month the domestic carrier, Indian Airlines, transferred its flights from the naval air station to the new airport. Before the new airport opened, there was a serious accident at Cochin. On 30 July 1998, an Indian-built Dornier 228-201 operated by Alliance Air, was taking off for Thiruvananthapuram when, at a height of 400ft, it was seen to pitch-up vertically and then stall, crashing onto a repair shop at the Indian Navy base, with the loss of all three crew and six passengers, as well as killing three workers in the repair shop and injuring another six. The accident was caused by poor maintenance of the aircraft.

A new terminal has since been opened, while rising tourist traffic and the growing prosperity of the country mean that future expansion is likely.

AHMEDABAD/SARDAR VALLABHBHAI PATEL INTERNATIONAL: AMD

Ahmedabad, Gujarat, India

Owner and operator: Airports Authority of India
Runways: 05/23, 3,599m (11,811ft)
Terminals: Two, designated as Domestic and
    International
Airlines using airport as base or hub: Indian
    Airlines, Jet Airways, Spice Jet
Annual passengers: 3,037,734
Annual cargo: 24,165 tonnes
Annual aircraft movements: 39,280

Background
Based on a former Royal Air Force station, it is 8km (5 miles) from the main railway station in Ahmedabad and is named after a former deputy prime minister. The international terminal is being extended at present, and once complete it will be double its present size. Nevertheless, the state government is considering a new airport for the future, possibly at Fedara, near Dholera on the Gulf of Khambhat.

GOA/DABOLIM: GOI

Dabolim, Goa, India

Owner and operator: Indian Naval
   Service/Airports Authority of India
Runways: 08/26, 3,458m (11,345ft)
Terminals: Two, designated International Terminal
   1 and Domestic Terminal 2.
Annual passengers: 2,528,358
Annual cargo: 5,186 tonnes

Although Indian Railways have a line that passes the airport, the nearest station is at Vasco da Gama, which is 4km (2½ miles) away.

Background

Goa was Portuguese territory until India seized it in 1961 and incorporated it into the Indian union as a separate state.

   The airport was built by the Portuguese colonial government during the early 1950s and it became the main base and hub for the airline TAIP, Transportes Aereos de India Portuguesa, which served destinations in India, Pakistan, and East Africa. After the Indian take-over, the airport was handed to the Indian Naval Service's Fleet Air Arm which occupies most of it, leaving the airport as a small corner of the air station. Commercial flights did not resume until 1966. Today, there are no commercial flights on weekdays between 08.30 and 13.00 as the base is used for naval flying training and even includes a ski-jump for training BAE Sea Harrier pilots. The growing number of charter flights carrying tourists are confined to a small period of the day, although plans have been made for night arrivals and departures to ease the pressure on the airport during its limited opening hours for civilian use. This has also led to a campaign locally for the return of the airport to full civilian use, with the INS units relocated to the new naval air station at Karwar, INS Kadamba, 70km (almost 44 miles) to the south, but senior naval officers have implied that the investment in Dabolim is too heavy for this. On the other hand, while a site for a new commercial airport for Goa at Mopa has been identified, this has been contro-versial and has been opposed by many who feel that it is not central enough. A proposed compromise has been that Mopa should handle international traffic, and Dabolim remain as a domestic airport. One thing is certain, there will be no early decision, as current plans call for Mopa to be open by 2020.

   Commercial operations at the airport seem to have been accident-free, with four of the five accidents since 2001 having been by INS Sea Harriers, one of which closed the airport to commercial operations for 90 minutes. Military aviation has far greater hazards than civil aviation, especially with aircraft such as the Sea Harrier which spend much time flying low and over water, and are vulnerable to bird strikes. The one accident that did not involve Sea Harriers was by two Indian Naval Service Ilyushin Il-18s, which collided in mid-air on 1 October 2002, with the loss of 12 naval personnel aboard the aircraft and 3 civilians on the ground.

THIRUVANANTHAPURAM (TRIVANDRUM) INTERNATIONAL: TRV

Thiruvananthapuram (Trivandrum), Kerala, India

Owner and operator: Airports Authority of India
Runways: 14/32, 3,398m (11,148ft)
Terminals: Three, designated Domestic,
   International, and 3 (mainly international)
Annual passengers: 2,054,501
Annual cargo: 32,091 tonnes

Background

The major airport in Kerala, it is 16km (10 miles) from the centre of Thiruvananthapuram, the new name for Trivandrum.

   The airport's history dates from 1932 when it was opened by the Kerala Flying Club. During the Second World War it was used by the Royal Air Force and Royal Indian Air Force. It returned to civil use after the war, and while mainly used for domestic flights, by the late 1970s Air India was operating international services to cities in the Gulf region, mainly carrying Indian expatriate workers. It was upgraded officially to an international airport in January 1991, making it the first in southern India. Since then the growth in international travellers, largely spurred by the region's growing tourist and information technology industries, meant that a third terminal opened in 2009 to handle international traffic.

There have been incidents involving two Indian Airlines airliners that flew out of Trivandrum. The first was on 9 December 1971, when an Indian-built BAe 748 airliner flying to Madurai, strayed off course and flew into a hillside. All 4 crew were killed, but 10 of the 27 passengers survived. In another incident on 26 April 1979 a bomb was planted in a forward lavatory of a Boeing 737-200, and as it descended towards its destination at Madras, it exploded, knocking out the instruments, but the aircraft landed and, although it overshot the runway (because anti-lock braking and reverse thrust were not available) and caught fire, all 6 crew and 61 passengers managed to escape.

GUWAHATI/LOKPRIYA GOPINATH BORDOLOI INTERNATIONAL: GAU
Guwahati, Assam, India

Owner and operator: Airports Authority of India
Runways: 02/20, 2,743m (9,000ft)
Terminals: One
Airlines using airport as base or hub: Pawan
    Hans (helicopter services); Air India Express
Annual passengers: 1,333,723

Background
Known variously as Lokpriya Gopinath Bordoloi International Airport or Guwahati International Airport, in the past it was also known as Borjhar Airport. It is named after a former chief minister of Assam, Gopinath Bordoloi.

Operated jointly by the Airports Authority of India and by the Indian Air Force, the airport was originally an RAF and Royal Indian Air Force base during the Second World War, mounting operations against Japanese forces in

Burma. It has also played its part post-independence in conflict between India and Pakistan until East Pakistan established independence as Bangladesh.

On 14 November 1951, an Airways (India) Douglas C-47 freighter crashed on take-off from Guwahati, but although the aircraft was written off, all three crew survived. Much less fortunate was the crew of another Airways (India) C-47 on 14 April 1953, which broke up in mid-air after taking-off from Guwahati because of being subjected to loads in excess of those for which it was designed. Inward bound to Guwahati on 21 January 1955, another cargo C-47 of Indian Airlines crashed into trees while making a premature descent in fog, with the loss of all three crew. Also inbound, but on a passenger flight on 19 October 1988, a Vayudoot Fokker F-27 Friendship flying from Silchar, undershot the runway with the loss of all 3 crew and 31 passengers.

KOZHIKODE (CALICUT): CCJ
Kozhikode (Calicut), Kerala, India

Owner and operator: Airports Authority of India
Runways: 10/28, 2,860m (9,383ft)
Terminals: Two, designated Domestic and
    International
Annual passengers: 1,284,813
Annual cargo: 9,701 tonnes

Background
Often known locally as Karipur Airport, it is 26km (16¼ miles) from the centre of Calicut and is one of three international airports serving the southern state of Kerala.

One of India's newest airports, pressure for its construction began in 1977, but it was not built for almost another 20 years, when it replaced an earlier airport of the same name. In recent years the runway has been extended and new terminal buildings opened. It became an international airport in 2006, with flights mainly to the Gulf region for expatriate Indian workers. The approach to the airport is through steep-sided valleys and special directional lighting is used to ensure a safe approach.

JAIPUR/SAWAI MAN SINGH INTERNATIONAL: JAI

Sanganer, Jaipur, Rajasthan, India

Owner and operator: Airports Authority of India
Runways: 09/27, 2,797m (9,177ft); 15/33,
   1,592m (5,223ft)
Annual passengers: 1,263,030

Background

Variously known as Jaipur or, after the locality, Sanganer Airport, it is officially known as Sawai Man Singh International Airport after being granted international status in December 2005. There are plans to extend the terminal and lengthen the runway to 3,658m (12,000ft).

The airport was the scene of an accident to an Indian Airlines Douglas DC-3 on 18 February 1969, which swung left just before lifting off the runway, and then struck the ground, becoming a complete write-off, because it was overloaded and the centre of gravity was too far aft. The 4 crew and 26 passengers all survived. The next accident was a landing accident when an Indian Airlines Vickers Viscount 700 landed downwind on a wet runway on 9 August 1971, overshot the runway and was again a complete write-off, but the 4 crew and 23 passengers survived. The third accident was on a training flight and, although the number of people on board has not been recorded, it is likely that there would have been at least two, possibly three, when an Indian Airlines Dornier 228-201 which skidded of the runway on 9 June 2002, and was scrapped as a result.

INDONESIA

Indonesia is one of a number of countries in Asia with a dynamic locally-owned air transport industry, with independent airlines blossoming despite the presence of a substantial state-owned airline, and a large number of airports, some of which only handle domestic flights, yet remain large enough to be included here. A combination of an island nation of considerable size (more than 4,800km/3,000 miles end-to-end) and difficult terrain once again means that air transport is the only feasible mode of transport for many journeys. As evidence of growing sophistication, Jakarta is one of the few airports in Asia outside of Japan or Hong Kong with a railway link between airport and city centre.

JAKARTA/SOEKARNO-HATTA INTERNATIONAL: CGK

Jakarta, Indonesia

Owner and operator: PT Angkasa Pura II
Runways: 07L/25R, 3,600m (11,811ft), planned
   to be extended to match 07C/25C; 07R/25L,
   3,660m (12,007ft); 07C/25C, 4,000m
   (13,122ft) planned
Terminals: Four, designated 1, 2, 3, and 4 (to be
   completed)
Airlines using airport as base or hub: Garuda
Annual passengers: 32,458,946
Annual cargo: 473,593 tonnes
Annual aircraft movements: 248,842

PT RaiLink connects Soekarno-Hatta International Airport to Jakarta Manggarai Station.

Background

Known locally as Cengkareng because of its proximity to the area, and it is this that gives the airport its IATA designation of CGK. Soekarno-Hatta International Airport, or *Bandar Udara Internasional Soekarno-Hatta* in Indonesian, is named after the country's first president, Soekarno, and his vice-president, Mohammed Hatta. It is just 20km (12½miles) from the city centre.

The airport opened in 1985, replacing two airports, Kemayoran, in central Jakarta, which handled domestic flights, and Halim Perdanakusuma International Airport to the east of the city. Kemayoran had been opened in 1928 by the Netherlands East Indies government, but during the post-independence period was regarded as being too small and too congested, while it also interfered with air traffic using

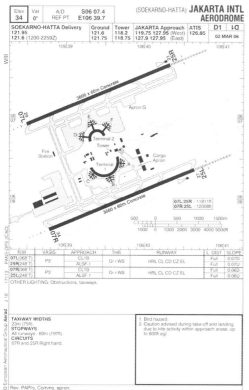

| Elev 34 | Var 0° | A/D REF PT | S06 07.4 E106 39.7 | (SOEKARNO-HATTA) **JAKARTA INTL AERODROME** | | |
| SOEKARNO-HATTA Delivery 121.95 121.6 (1200-2259Z) | | Ground 121.6 121.75 | Tower 118.2 118.75 | JAKARTA Approach 119.75 127.95 (West) 127.9 127.95 (East) | ATIS 126.85 | D1 ID 02 MAR 06 |

R/W	VASIS	APPROACH	THR	RUNWAY	L DIST	SLOPE
07L(068°T)	P3'	CL1B ALSF-1	Gr+WB	HRL CL CD CZ EL	Full	0.07D
25R(248°T)					Full	0.07U
07R(068°T)	P3'	CL1B ALSF-1	Gr+WB	HRL CL CD CZ EL	Full	0.06D
25L(248°T)					Full	0.06U

OTHER LIGHTING: Obstructions, taxiways.

TAXIWAY WIDTHS
23m (75ft).
STOPWAYS
All runways - 60m (197ft).
CIRCUITS
07R and 25R Right hand.

1. Bird hazard.
2. Caution advised during take-off and landing due to kite activity within approach areas, up to 600ft agl.

Rev: PAPI's, Comms, apron.

DENPASAR/NGURAH RAI INTERNATIONAL: DPS
Denpasar, Bali, Indonesia

Owner and operator: PT Angkasa Pura I
Runways: 09/27, 3,000m (9,842ft)
Terminals: Two, designated Domestic and International
Annual passengers: 5,888,265
Annual cargo: 44,861 tonnes
Annual aircraft movements: 62,689

Background
Ngurah Rai, also known as Denpasar International, dates from the Dutch colonial era and is named after an Indonesian freedom fighter. Using foreign aid, it was developed, starting in 1992, to handle the growing tourist traffic, which is now outgrowing the capacity of the airport so that a new one is being built in Jembrana in Western Bali.

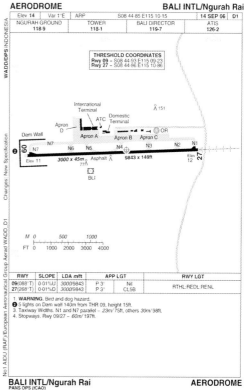

AERODROME			**BALI INTL/Ngurah Rai**	
Elev 14	Var 1°E	ARP	S08 44 85 E115 10-15	14 SEP 06 D1
NGURAH GROUND 118-9		TOWER 118-1	BALI DIRECTOR 119-7	ATIS 126-2

THRESHOLD COORDINATES
Rwy 09 – S08 44-93 E115 09-23
Rwy 27 – S08 44-86 E115 10-86

RWY	SLOPE	LDA m/ft	APP LGT		RWY LGT
09(068°T)	0-01%U	3000/9843	P 3'	Nil	RTHL:REDL:RENL
27(268°T)	0-01%D	3000/9843	P 3'	CL5B	

1. **WARNING.** Bird and dog hazard.
2. 5 lights on Dam wall 140m from THR 09, height 15ft.
3. Taxiway Widths. N1 and N7 parallel – 23m/ 75ft, others 30m/ 98ft.
4. Stopways. Rwy 09/27 – 60m/ 197ft.

Halim Perdanakusuma. The latter remains open for charters and for military use. A second terminal opened in 1992. Today, Terminal 1 is used for flights operated by the many Indonesian independent airlines, while Terminal 2 is used by the national airline (Garuda), and the domestic airline (Merpati), and for international flights. Both terminals are similar in that they are divided into three concourses. The airport was designed by the French architect, Paul Andreu, who also designed Paris Charles de Gaulle International Airport.

The new Terminal 3 is aimed at serving the growing number of low-cost carriers, while Terminal 4 is still to be completed.

The airport is busy, not simply because of its importance as a hub for domestic flights, or even as an Asian regional hub, but also because many travellers between Europe or the Middle East and Australia use it as a stop-over.

MEDAN/POLONIA INTERNATIONAL: MES

Medan, North Sumatra Province, Indonesia

Owner and operator: PT Angkasa Pura II
Runways: 05/23, 2,900m (9,514ft)
Terminals: Two, designated Domestic and
   International
Annual passengers: 5,004,398
Annual cargo: 33,649 tonnes
Annual aircraft movements: 53,795

Background

One of the few major airports to be within a city, Medan, known more usually locally as Polonia, or Banadara Polonia, is the fourth busiest airport in Indonesia. The name comes from the neighbourhood around the airport, which was formerly a 19th-century plantation owned by a Pole, which he named Polonia after the Latin name for his home country.

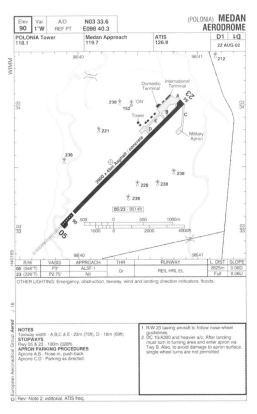

Plans were laid for an airstrip at Polonia after the First World War, but nothing was done, so when the first flight from Amsterdam reached what was then the Netherlands East Indies in 1924, it had to use the racecourse as a landing strip. This led the local representative of the colonial government to press the administration in Batavia to fund an airport at Medan. He was successful, and the airport opened in 1928 with a temporary dirt runway. Airline operations began almost immediately, with flights by KLM's East Indies subsidiary, KNILM. Traffic grew, and in 1936 a permanent paved runway was completed.

During the Second World War the airfield was used by the Royal Netherlands East Indies Air Force and by the other Allies after the fall of Malaya and Singapore, before the entire region was overrun by Japanese forces and used by the Japanese Army Air Force until Japan surrendered in 1945. Post war, it was used by Dutch forces against Indonesians fighting for independence, after which it became a base for the Indonesian Air Force, although it began to be used by commercial flights. In 1975 the government decreed that it would be run jointly by the air force and the civil aviation department. Ownership changed again in 1985 when it was handed over to Perum Angkasa Pura, now PT Angkasa Pura II.

The airport is difficult to operate and has suffered several serious accidents over the past 30 to 35 years as air traffic has increased. Aircraft have flown into mountains and into electricity pylons. In 2009 a new airport at Kuala Namu should open and most, if not all, of Polonia's traffic should be transferred.

The accidents have included a crash in 1979 of a Garuda Fokker F-28 Friendship that killed 64 people, and in 1987 32 people died aboard a Garuda McDonnell Douglas DC-9 which hit an electricity pylon on its approach to the airport. On 26 September 1997 a Garuda Airbus A300 crashed into a mountain near the city after an air traffic controller instructed the captain to turn right instead of left, killing all 234 people on board. The most recent accident was on 5 September 2005 to a Mandala Airlines Boeing 737-200, which crashed shortly after taking-off for Jakarta, killing at least 39 on the ground after crashing into a heavily populated area of the city. At least 104 of those aboard the aircraft also died, although 16 survived the accident but may have died later from their injuries.

SURABAYA/JUANDA INTERNATIONAL: SUB
Sidoarjo, Surabaya, East Java, Indonesia

Owner and operator: PT Angkasa Pura I
Runways: 10/28, 3,000m (9,843ft)
Terminals: One, with areas designated Terminal A (International) and Terminal B (Domestic)
Annual passengers: 3,488,320
Annual cargo: 32,475 tonnes
Annual aircraft movements: 87,587

Background
The airport opened in 1974 and is named after Djuanda Kartawidjaj, a former prime minister whose brainchild the airport was. It is second only to Jakarta Soekarno-Hatta in passenger numbers and aircraft movements.

There have been a number of accidents at Surabaya. On 17 November 1950 a Garuda C-47 landed and ran off the runway into a ditch, killing both pilots, but the cabin attendant and all 20 passengers survived. A training accident occurred on 26 March 2001when a Merpati Nusantara Airlines Fokker F-27 Friendship freighter crashed during a 'touch-and-go' manoeuvre, banking sharply to the left and crashing into shrimp ponds, killing the training captain and two others under instruction. Another accident occurred when a Lion Air McDonnell Douglas MD-82 landed after a flight from Bali with a defective thrust-reverser, a problem known to the pilots, and slid off the runway suffering considerable damage. On this occasion all 6 crew and 138 passengers survived. On 21Feburary 2007, an Adam Air Boeing 737 made a hard landing, after which it was noticed that the fuselage had buckled, although all aboard were unharmed.

The aircraft was withdrawn from service and scrapped.

A new terminal opened on 10 November 2006, and this includes both international and domestic areas. The original terminal building has been abandoned.

PEKANBARU/SULTAN SYARIF QASIM II INTERNATIONAL: PKU
Pekanbaru, Riau, Indonesia

Owner and operator: PT Angkasa Pura II
Runways: 18/36, 2,150m (7,053ft)
Terminals: One
Airlines using airport as base or hub: Riau Airlines
Annual passengers: 1,839,222
Annual cargo: 11,720 tonnes

Background
Built by the Dutch before independence, the airport is named after Sultan Syarif Qasim II, an important Indonesian historical figure. The airport handles a substantial number of local flights to the Riau Islands as well as domestic air services within Indonesia and international flights to other destinations in South-East Asia and Malaysia and Singapore. It is a major air station for the Indonesian Air Force, which operates Hawk light fighters and helicopters from the base.

Air traffic has outgrown the airport's facilities and there are plans to develop a replacement airport further away from the city of Pekanbaru, but no decision has been made over a location as yet.

PADANG/MINANGKABAU INTERNATIONAL: PDG
Kataping, Padang, West Sumatra, Indonesia

Owner and operator: PT Angkasa Pura II
Runways: 15/33, 2,749m (9,020ft)
Terminals: One
Annual passengers: 1,752,961
Annual cargo: 10,563 tonnes

Background

The main airport for West Sumatra, Minangkabau International is 23km (almost 15 miles) north-west of Padang. It opened in 2005, replacing the previous airport for the area at Tabing. There are ambitious plans for the future, including an extension of the terminal and lengthening of the runway to take aircraft up to Boeing 747 size, as well as building a railway to link the airport with Padang. The airport is named after a local tribal group.

PALEMBANG/SULTAN MAHMUD BADARUDDIN II: PLM
Palembang, South Sumatra, Indonesia

Owner and operator: PT Angkasa Pura II
Runways: 11/29, 2,500m (8,202ft)
Terminals: One
Annual passengers: 1,660,013
Annual cargo: 9,008 tonnes

Background

The airport for a major oil-producing area, it was used by the Japanese Army Air Force during the Second World War to defend the oilfields and refineries, and was attacked by the Royal Navy and the United States Navy. Post war, the airfield became a civil airport and has been modernised in recent years.

UJUNG PANDANG/SULTAN HASANUDDIN INTERNATIONAL: UPG
Ujung Pandang, Celebes, Indonesia

Owner: Government of Makassar
Operator: PT Angkasa Pura I
Runways: 13/31, 3,100m (10,171ft)
Terminals: One, but a second terminal is being built
Annual passengers: 1,600,083
Annual cargo: 17,181 tonnes
Annual aircraft movements: 51,698

Background

The airport is 17km (10½ miles) from Makassar and is the main airport for the eastern areas of Indonesia.

The airport was built in 1935 by the Netherlands East Indies government as Kadieng Airfield and with grass runways. It was used by both military and civil aviation from the start, but the first scheduled flights were by KNILM (Royal Netherlands East Indies Airways) to Singapore. During the Second World War, the Netherlands East Indies were occupied by Japanese forces in 1942, and the airport was taken over by the Japanese Army Air Force, which renamed it Mandai Field, and laid a 1,600m concrete runway. After the Japanese defeat, the airport runway was extended to 1,745m by the Dutch colonial authorities before the East Indies were granted independence.

After independence, the airport reverted to Mandai Airport, while a number of improvements were made, including lengthening the runway. The current title was adopted in 1985. After independence it was operated by the Directorate General of Air Transport, but control was handed to PT Angkasa Pura I in 1993. International flights returned in 1995 with a service to Kuala Lumpur by Malaysian Airlines System, with a Silk Air route to Singapore following later. The current terminal opened in August 2008, and is five times larger than the one it replaced, but the old terminal remains as accommodation for Indonesian Air Force units based at the airport, which operate Sukhoi Su-27 and Su-30 fighters. The airport also houses a regional air traffic control centre that stretches as far east as the Philippines. A runway extension was completed in March 2009.

The current title was adopted in August 2008 at the same time as the new terminal was commissioned.

PONTIANAK SUPADIO: PNK

Pontianak, West Kalimantan Province, Indonesia

Owner and operator: PT Angkasa Pura II
Runways: 15/33, 2,249m (7,380ft)
Terminals: One
Annual passengers: 1,378,529
Annual cargo: 9,024 tonnes

Background

Currently a regional airport served only by domestic flights. Over its history it had a couple of minor accidents. The earliest for which information is available was on 19 January 1973 when a Trans Nusantara Airways Douglas C-47 landed, struck the runway with its port wing, bounced twice and then crashed in flames, but fortunately the crew of four survived. The second was on 26 September 1994 when a Vickers Viscount 800 of Bouraq Indonesia Airlines was badly damaged on landing, but the two pilots, the only occupants, were unharmed and the aircraft was repairable.

IRAN

Despite what appear to be constant diplomatic difficulties with the West and with some at least of its neighbours in the Middle East, Iran has a substantial air transport industry with several airlines, including the state-owned national airline, Iran Air, and four of its airports are busy enough to be included in this book. International relationships, and air transport, were not helped by the shooting down of an Iran Air Airbus A300 en route from Tehran to Dubai on 3 July 1988 by the USS *Vincennes*, which cast a shadow over dealings between the two countries for many years.

TEHRAN/MEHRABAD: THR

Tehran, Iran

Owner and operator: Iranian Government
Runways: 11L/29R, 3,992m (13,048ft); 11R/29L, 4,038m (13,248ft); 09/27, 474m (1,556ft)
Terminals: Six, designated Terminal 1 (disused), Terminal 2 (international), Terminal 3 (Iranian Air Force), Terminal 4 (domestic), Terminal 5 or Hajj (pilgrimage), Terminal 6 (VIP)
Airlines using airport as base or hub: Iran Air
Annual passengers: 11,782,710
Annual cargo: 141,500 tonnes
Annual aircraft movements: 117,468

Background

Originally the main airport for Tehran, it lost most of its international traffic to the new Imam Khomeini International Airport when that opened in May 2004, but still retains domestic

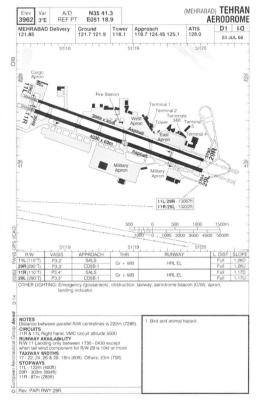

and regional traffic as it is closer to the centre of Tehran, and remains the busiest airport in the country by passenger numbers. The new airport was already planned before the 1979 Iranian Revolution, and would have been completed earlier but for work being delayed after the revolution.

There have been a number of serious accidents in recent years. On 20 April 2005 a Boeing 707-300 touched down and the undercarriage either failed or a tyre burst, but the aircraft slid off the runway and into the River Kan, with three passengers drowning in the river during the emergency evacuation from the aircraft. On 6 December 2005, an Iranian Air Force Lockheed C-130 Hercules crashed in Tehran shortly after taking off: no details of casualties are available. On 2 January 2008 an Iran Air Fokker 100 with 100 passengers on board skidded off the runway while taking off for Shiraz in a heavy snowstorm, losing part of its undercarriage, while a wing caught fire.

MASHHAD/SHAHID HASHEMI NEJAD INTERNATIONAL: MHD
Mashhad, Iran

Owner and operator: Islamic Republic of Iran Air
   Force
Runways: 14L/32R, 3,811m (12,503ft);
   14R/32L, 3,925m (12,877ft)
Terminals: One
Airlines using airport as base or hub: Iran Air
   Tours
Annual passengers: 4,089,282
Annual cargo: 42,907 tonnes

Background
An airfield built during the Second World War by the Allies, it has remained in military hands ever since, but also handles a substantial number of commercial flights. The terminal and associated facilities are currently being enlarged. The airport suffered a serious accident on 1 September 2006 when an Iran Air Tours Tupolev Tu-154 landing from Bandar Abbas burst a tyre and skidded off the runway, catching fire, resulting

in the deaths of 29 of the 147 passengers aboard the aircraft.

SHIRAZ INTERNATIONAL: SYZ
Shiraz, Fars Province, Iran

Owner and operator: Civil Aviation Authority of
   Iran
Runways: 11L/29R, 4,334m (14,334ft);
   11R/29L, 4,272m (14,272ft)
Terminals: Two, designated International and
   Domestic
Annual passengers: 2,154,894
Annual cargo: 8,705 tonnes
Annual aircraft movements: 45,424

Background
Shared with the Islamic Republic of Iran Air Force, Shiraz is reputed to be the most reliable airport in the country outside Tehran. It dates from the Second World War, when it was built as a base for the Imperial Iranian Air Force. It was extensively modernised and redeveloped in 2005, and has an extensive network of domestic flights as well as a number of international flights to destinations in the Gulf.

ISFAHAN INTERNATIONAL: IFN
Isfahan (Esfahan), Iran

Owner and operator: Iranian Islamic Air Force
Runways: 08L/26R, 4,397m (14,425ft);
   08R/26L, 4,397m (14,425ft)
Terminals: One
Annual passengers: 1,535,194
Annual cargo: 11,744 tonnes

Background
A military airfield that is open to commercial flights and is served by the main Iranian airlines.

IRELAND

For a country of some four million people, having three of the world's major airports is some achievement, but apart from the 'island effect' which gives air transport a boost, Ireland's strategic position has also meant that it was a vital refuelling point for transatlantic flights before aircraft ranges improved, and the country, as well as being a tourist area, has also in the past enjoyed the benefits of having much of its population working abroad. On the other hand, air transport was restricted for some years by the insistence that transatlantic flights into and out of the country should land at Shannon.

DUBLIN INTERNATIONAL: DUB

Dublin, Republic of Ireland

Owner and operator: Dublin Airport Authority

Runways: 10R/28L, 2,637m (8,652ft); 16/34, 2,072m (6,798ft); 10L/28R, 3,110m (10,200ft), due to open in 2014

Terminals: Two, designated Terminal One (with a Pier D extension), and Terminal Two (which should be open in 2010)

Airlines using airport as base or hub: Aer Lingus, Air Contractors, Cityjet, Ryanair

Annual passengers: 23,287,438

Annual cargo: 114,422 tonnes

Annual aircraft movements: 211,804

At present buses connect with railway stations and the Dublin tram network, but a new railway line, Metro North, is being built that should, by around 2014, provide a direct connection to the city centre.

Background

Although the site occupied by the airport dates from the First World War, when it was a base for the British Royal Flying Corps at Collinstown, to the north of Dublin, after Irish independence in 1922, it lay unused for many years until selected as a replacement for Dublin's first airport at Baldonnel, located to the south. Baldonnel had been opened in 1936 as a base for the

Irish government's new airline, Aer Lingus. The new airport opened at the end of 1939 and in January 1940 Aer Lingus operated the first flight, across the Irish Sea to Liverpool. Although Ireland remained neutral throughout the Second World War, the only air services operated during this period were to Liverpool and, occasionally, Manchester. A new terminal opened during 1940.

After the war expansion began, and increased pace during the 1950s with a growing number of British and European airlines using the airport. A paved runway was laid as aircraft weights grew. In 1958 Aer Lingus began transatlantic services, operating with a call at Shannon in the west of Ireland. In 1971 Aer Lingus took delivery of the first of two Boeing 747s, and a new terminal was built, opening the following year. At the other end of the scale, in 1983 a new subsidiary of the state airline was established, Aer Lingus Commuter, operating smaller aircraft on

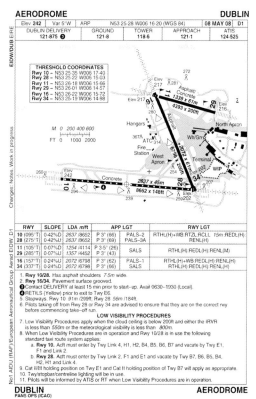

feeder routes from provincial centres in Ireland and also opening routes to new destinations across the Irish Sea. These operations were later reabsorbed into the parent company with the exception of some routes operated by Aer Arran, an independent regional airline. Dublin also became the headquarters for the pioneering Irish low-cost airline, Ryanair. To cope with growing demand, new piers were added and the terminal extended, with Pier D being a dedicated low-cost, quick turnround pier for airlines such as Ryanair.

While Shannon had been a major refuelling stop for transatlantic flights before the jet age, the practice of calling at the airport was an anachronism as aircraft ranges grew, but the importance of the airport to the economy of the west of Ireland meant that the Shannon stop continued. In 1993 a bilateral agreement allowed some flights to fly direct to Dublin, and a further agreement in 2006 increased this number, while the requirement for flights to call at Shannon ended completely in 2008. The importance of this is that transatlantic traffic through Dublin is set to increase and Aer Lingus, now flying a larger fleet of Airbus A330s, has identified a large number of US airports to which direct flights will now be viable. In the meantime, the Irish economy has transformed and this has led to rapid growth. There has also been an influx of migrant workers from Eastern Europe, which has also resulted in new destinations being served from Dublin. Direct services to the Gulf region have also been introduced in recent years by Arab airlines such as Gulf Air and Etihad Airways. During 2007 the US-EU 'Open Skies' agreement resulted in new transatlantic services being introduced from Dublin.

Since its opening, the airport had been operated by Aer Rianta, but control passed to the Dublin Airport Authority in 2004.

There has been one potentially serious accident at the airport since the Second World War. On 7 December 1985 an Aer Lingus Boeing 737-200 took off for London and flew into a flock of seagulls, with the left engine so badly damaged that it not only lost all power but was left hanging from the wing, forcing the crew to make an emergency landing back at the airport, which they did successfully, with all 6 crew and 117 passengers unharmed.

In common with many airports worldwide, Dublin has struggled to cope with traffic growth and has also encountered opposition to expansion, but a new runway and new terminal will both open in the next few years.

SHANNON INTERNATIONAL: SNN
Shannon, County Clare, Republic of Ireland

Owner: Irish Government
Operator: Dublin Airport Authority
Runways: 06/24, 3,200m (10,496ft)
Terminals: One
Airlines using airport as base or hub: Aer Lingus
Annual passengers: 3,620,623
Annual cargo: 27,842 tonnes
Annual aircraft movements: 48,122

Background
The airport exists alongside the town of the same name in the west of Ireland, and is 25km (almost 16 miles) from Limerick.

While the early experiments in transatlantic air travel used flying-boats and a terminal existed on the Shannon Estuary at Foynes, it was decided that an airport for landplanes would be needed, not just for transatlantic flights but also to open up the underdeveloped west of the Irish Republic. Shannon Airport opened in 1942, but it was not until 1945 that the runways were lengthened to handle transatlantic airliners. The delay was undoubtedly due to the fact that Ireland remained neutral during the Second World War and there was no military reason to develop an airport with substantial runways.

After the war, regular transatlantic air services grew rapidly, but at first the aircraft of the day needed to refuel at Shannon when flying west, and often also at Gander in Newfoundland, and again on the eastward flight. After a Pan American Douglas DC-4 had landed on a proving flight on 16 September 1945, American Overseas Airlines commenced a regular service on 24 October. The airport grew to meet the demand, and this was further boosted by Shannon becoming the first duty-free airport in the world in 1947, the same year that work on the airport was completed. One of the last airlines to start a transatlantic air service via Shannon was Ireland's own airline, Aer Lingus, which introduced a service to New York in 1958 using Lockheed Super Constellations. At this time, passengers had to fly from Dublin, stop at Shannon and then continue to New York as the air services agreement between Ireland and the USA stipulated flights from Shannon, not from Dublin, and US airlines wishing to operate to Ireland suffered the same restriction. Nevertheless, aircraft performance was improving and the last of the piston-engined airliners and the Bristol Britannia turboprop did not need to call at Shannon, and the new jet airliners introduced in the late 1950s also did not need to stop. The transit and refuelling business virtually disappeared within a couple of years.

As well as being a refuelling stop, Shannon's location has meant that it receives a substantial number of emergency landings as the last chance before an airliner starts to cross the Atlantic, or the first landfall for those heading east. It has also had a number of accidents over the years, with two of them involving KLM Royal Dutch Airlines. The first of these was on 5 September 1954 when a flight from Amsterdam to New York took off after refuelling, but crashed into a mudbank just outside the airport with the loss of 28 passengers. On 14 August 1958, another flight on the same route went down in the North Atlantic having earlier refuelled at Shannon.

It was not until 1971 that a new agreement allowed one American airline (Trans World Airways was selected) to operate to Dublin, but only on condition that it stopped at Shannon en route! Even this concession was obtained under duress as the US had first to threaten to ban Aer Lingus from using New York. It was not until 1993 that airlines were allowed to fly direct between the United States and Dublin, and even then half the flights had to land at Shannon. The restrictions ended in 2008, aided by the US-

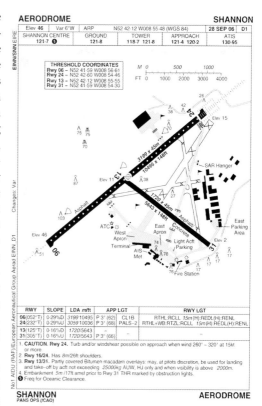

European Union 'Open Skies' agreement.

With the airport protected by the agreements between Ireland and the USA, traffic grew and in 1971 a new terminal opened. Nevertheless, some new traffic did appear, with Aeroflot using Shannon as a refuelling stop on routes to the Americas. The real resurgence of Shannon came as the 20th century drew to a close, with the Irish economy booming with EU subsidies, and American tourism growing as the political situation in Northern Ireland seemed to ease. The airport also began to develop its aircraft overhaul and maintenance business. Nevertheless, there have also been setbacks, with Aer Lingus dropping its four daily return flights to London Heathrow so that the slots could be used to provide a London Heathrow to Belfast service. CityJet, a subsidiary of Air France, introduced a twice-daily service to Paris Charles de Gaulle shortly afterwards.

CORK: ORK
Farmers Cross, Ballygarvan, Cork, Republic of Ireland

Owner and operator: Cork Airport Authority
Runways: 17/35, 2,133m (6,998ft); 07/25, 1,310m (4,298ft)
Terminals: One
Airlines using airport as base or hub: Aer Lingus, Aer Arran, Ryanair
Annual passengers: 3,178,365
Annual cargo: 5,546 tonnes
Annual aircraft movements: 70,961

Background
The third busiest airport in the Republic of Ireland, Cork is just 8km (5 miles) south of the city.

The decision to build an airport for Cork was taken in 1957 by the Irish government. The new airport opened on 16 October 1961, with the first airlines to use it being the national flag carrier, Aer Lingus, and Cambrian Airways, which operated to Bristol and Cardiff and later became part of British Airways. As traffic grew, the terminal was extended and this was completed in 1978. Initially the airport operated only flights to Great Britain, but during the early 1980s a subsidiary of the national airline, Aer Lingus Commuter, was formed to provide feeder flights into the airline's international and transatlantic flights from Dublin. The pioneering European low-cost carrier, Ryanair, started to serve the airport in 1987, while in 1988 the first stage of a terminal extension was completed, and the following year the main runway was extended by 310m (1,000ft). Further stages of the terminal extension were completed between 1991 and 1994. The original intention was that a new terminal should have airbridges, but the growing number of low-cost airlines using the airport made it clear that they did not want this costly facility, so when the new terminal opened in 2006, it had just one airbridge, although there is scope to add further airbridges in due course.

Originally the airport was owned and operated by Aer Rianta, which was renamed the Dublin Airports Authority, but local opinion wanted the airport controlled locally, and in 2003 the Cork Airport Authority was formed to own, manage and develop the airport. The main runway has been extended again, and the Irish Aviation Authority will shortly complete construction of a new air traffic control tower.

The airport is a vital link in communications in the far south of Ireland. However, it has its limitations, including being prone to fog and low cloud, yet the instrument landing system is just at Category II, and the runway length means that large wide-bodied aircraft cannot use the airport when fully laden or for long-haul flights.

ISRAEL

Despite frequent hostilities with neighbouring states over the past 60 years, and its small size and relatively small population, there are two major airports in Israel, and air traffic is generally buoyant, although sometimes affected by the limitations imposed on operations during the Jewish Sabbath, Saturday.

TEL-AVIV BEN GURION INTERNATIONAL: TLV
Tel-Aviv, Israel

Owner and operator: Israel Airports Authority
Runways: 03/21, 1,780m (5,840ft); 08/26, 3,657m (11,998ft); 12/30, 3,112m (10,210ft)
Terminals: Four, designated Terminals 1 (Domestic), 2 (Low-cost airlines and charter), 3 (International), and 4
Airlines using airport as base or hub: Arkia, El Al
Annual passengers: 10,526,445
Annual cargo: 350,351 tonnes
Annual aircraft movements: 84,568

Ben Gurion Airport Station is situated under Terminal 3 with trains direct to Tel Aviv and Haifa.

Background
Widely believed to be the most secure airport in the world, Ben Gurion International is some 15km (9 miles) south-east of Tel Aviv and is near

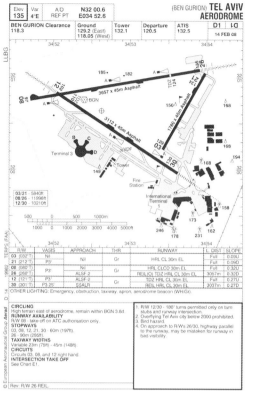

From 1948 the airport was known simply as Lod Airport, but in 1973 the name was changed to Tel-Aviv Ben Gurion International Airport in memory of Israel's first prime minister, David Ben Gurion. While throughout this time the airport facilities were expanded, during the 1980s mass immigration started from the Soviet Union and Ethiopia, and this continued into the 1990s. This led to plans being made to expand the passenger terminals, especially with the Millennium in mind when a large influx of tourists was expected, but the work was not finished, with the completion of Terminal 3, until 2004.

Throughout its history the airport has been seen as a target for extreme Palestinian terrorist groups and their sympathisers, but this has led to extensive security measures that have kept the airport safe, except that airliners hijacked elsewhere have been landed at Ben Gurion. Not all of the terrorist incidents have been by Palestinians. The worst incident was on 30 May 1972, known as the Lod Airport Massacre, when three members of the Japanese Red Army machine-gunned passengers in the international arrivals area, killing 24 and wounding another 80.

The airport is unusual in that when used east to west, when it becomes 26/08, the longest runway is known as the 'quiet' runway and is used to reduce the impact on residents of the surrounding area. The short runway is used mainly for private aircraft and for the Israeli Defence Force/Air Force, but in the future the IDF will be relocated away from the airport, and the runway will be extended so that it can handle normal commercial air traffic.

the ancient city of Lod, and at one time was named after Lod.

Originally built by the British, who held a League of Nations mandate to administer what was then known as Palestine, the airport was opened in 1936 as Lydda Airport because of its proximity to the Arab town of that name, and in 1943, during the Second World War, it became RAF Lydda, an important staging post for aircraft flying from Europe to the Middle East and Far East. The airfield had four concrete runways. Initially, most civilian flights were within Europe and the Middle East, but in 1946 Trans World Airlines started a service to New York. After the British withdrew in April 1948, it was occupied by Israeli forces on 10 July. Commercial flights did not resume until 24 November, but between 1948 and 1952, passenger traffic rose from 40,000 to 1.2 million annually. By the 1960s, domestic flights were being diverted to Sde Dov airport on the coast.

EILAT/J. HOZMAN: ETH
Eilat, Israel

Owner and operator: Israel Airports Authority
Runways: 03/21, 1,900m (6,234ft)
Terminals: One
Airlines using airport as base or hub: Arkia; Israir
Annual passengers: 1,109,472

Background

Eilat Airport, which is also known locally as J. Hozman Airport, is actually within the city with hotels and tourist centres to one side of the airport and the residential areas to the other.

The airport was opened in 1949 by the Israeli Defence Force/Air Force, but was used almost immediately for commercial air services because of the importance of providing good, fast, connections across the country. Once Lod Ben Gurion International and Haifa became fully operational, Israel's domestic airline, Arkia Israel Airlines, became the main operator at Eilat. In 1964 the runway was extended and a new passenger terminal opened, while there was a further runway extension in 1975, the same year that the airport received its first international flights, package holiday charters by the Danish airline, Sterling Airways.

More international routes opened in the years that followed, with development hindered by the small size of the airport, including the limited length of the runways and the size of the terminal, while aircraft parking areas are so cramped that two Boeing 757s cannot pass. The 1994 peace treaty between Israel and Jordan seemed to offer a way forward, with plans for joint use of the under-used airport across the border at Aqaba, which would become the Aqaba-Eilat Peace International Airport. Little action resulted, and in 1997 a new treaty stipulated that Eilat must continue to handle Israeli domestic services. As an alternative, a new airport is being built 20km (12½ miles) north of Eilat in an area near Be'er Ora, and this should open in 2010 or 2011, when all civilian flights will move from Eilat.

ITALY

Despite its popularity as a tourist destination, for many years the development of air transport in Italy was stifled by the presence of a single international airline and a single major domestic airline. This has now changed with deregulation and the country is now home to a number of independent airlines. The disposition of the new airlines clearly reflects the fact that the most prosperous part of the country is in the north, especially around Milan, while the south is much poorer, so that not all of the tourist traffic is inward. Milan has two airports officially, but Bergamo has become its third airport because of the marketing of the low-cost carriers who favour this airport, which is also popular with cargo airlines. Many of the regional airports are now opening up to international flights, although some, such as Florence, are limited because of space and restricted runway length.

Airport ownership and management is gradually changing, with state involvement reducing, while at Naples the airport is managed by the British-based BAA.

ROME (FIUMICINO)/LEONARDO DA VINCI: FCO
Rome, Italy

Owner and operator: Aeroporti di Roma
Runways: 16L/34R, 3,900m (12,795ft);
16C/34C, 3,600m (11,811ft); 16R/34L,
3,900m (12,795ft); 07/25, 3,309m (10,856ft)
Terminals: Five, designated A, AA, B, C, and Five
Airlines using airport as base or hub: Alitalia,
Meridiana
Annual passengers: 32,855,542
Annual cargo: 154,441 tonnes
Annual aircraft movements: 334,848

Trenitalia operates the Leonardo Express from the airport to Rome Termini Station, while there are also local trains to and from the airport.

Background

Originally opened on 15 January 1961 with two runways and named Fiumicino as the new international airport for the Italian capital, leaving Ciampino, much smaller, for domestic services and charter flights. It became and remains the sole hub for the national carrier, Alitalia, and during the 1960s the airline invested heavily so that by 1970 the airport had three runways. Domestic services appeared at the airport to ensure connec-

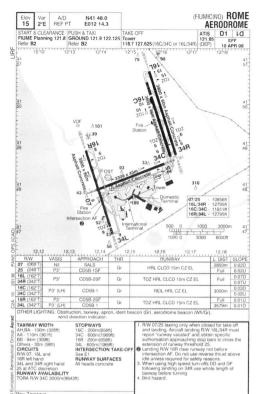

There has also been one accident, when a Uganda Airlines flight landing en route from London to Entebbe crashed short of the runway on 17 October 1988, after two missed approaches, killing 26 of the 45 passengers and all 7 crew.

MILAN MALPENSA: MXP
Milan, Italy

Owner and operator: SEA Aeroporti di Milano
Runways: 17L/35R, 3,915m (12,844ft);
17R/35L, 3,915m (12,844ft)
Terminals: Two, designated Terminal 1 (with two satellites, one for domestic and European Union traffic, and the other for traffic outside the European Union), and Terminal 2 (for charter and low-cost airlines). A third terminal is planned
Annual passengers: 23,885,391
Annual cargo: 486,667 tonnes
Annual aircraft movements: 267,941

tions to international flights. The name was changed to Leonardo da Vinci after opening. Between 1991 and 2000, the present terminal complex was completed, along with a new cargo terminal, Cargo City, which opened in 2004.

The airport has suffered from the conflicts in the Middle East, having twice been the scene of major terrorist attacks, which have seen it dragged unwillingly into the Israeli–Palestinian conflict. One of these occurred on 17 December 1973 when a Pan American flight was attacked with phosphorus bombs just as it was about to depart, with 30 passengers murdered. On 27 December 1985, during an attack timed to coincide with that in Vienna, terrorists shot and killed 16 people and wounded another 99. The following year, on 2 April, a TWA (Trans World Airlines) flight on a Rome–Athens sector had a bomb explode on board, blowing four passengers out of the aircraft in mid-air, but it managed to land safely.

The 'Malpensa Express' links the airport's Terminal 1 with Milan Cadona Station and the Milan underground systems Line M1 (Red) and Line M2 (Green).

Background

Italy's second most important airport after Rome/Leonardo da Vinci and the country's main air cargo airport, Milan serves the prosperous and industrialised north as well as some of the Italian lake resorts. The airport has replaced Linate as the main airport for Milan.

There have been a number of accidents at the airport. On 28 November 1951, a Douglas C-47 of Linee Aeree Italiane, one of the predecessors of Alitalia, overran the runway during take-off, damaging the aircraft beyond repair. Less than a month later, the same airline suffered a landing accident on 23 December to a Douglas DC-6, although the 4 crew and 24 passengers survived, but again the aircraft was a write-off. Far more serious was the accident to an Alitalia Douglas DC-8-43 on 2 August 1968 as it flew a sector from Rome to land at Malpensa, en route to Montreal. The aircraft came down more than 11km (almost 7 miles) north of the runway, and of the 85 passengers, 13 were killed, although all 10 crew survived. More fortunate were those aboard a TWA Boeing 707-320 arriving from New York on 22 December 1975, which also landed short of the runway, losing its undercarriage and all four engines as it slid to a halt, but the 8 crew and 117 passengers all survived. Another accident occurred during take-off on 2 July 1983 as an Altair Linee Aeree Sud Aviation Caravelle III took-off for London, with the number 2 (right) engine suffering an uncontained disc failure, with the crew managing to successfully abort the take-off. All 7 crew and 82 passengers survived.

MILAN/LINATE/ENRICCO FORLANINI: LIN

Milan, Italy

Owner and operator: SEA – Aeroporti di Milano
Runways: 18/36, 2,440m (8,005ft); 17/35, 601m (1,972ft)
Terminals: One
Annual passengers: 9,926,530
Annual cargo: 23,497 tonnes
Annual aircraft movements: 130,038

Background

The second largest airport for Milan, Linate was built during the early 1930s when the original airport for the city, Taliedo, became too small and overcrowded, a fate that also awaited Linate in the 1980s. It is named after Enrico Forlanini, a native of Milan and one of the early Italian pioneers of aviation. Despite being rebuilt and expanded during the 1960s and again during the

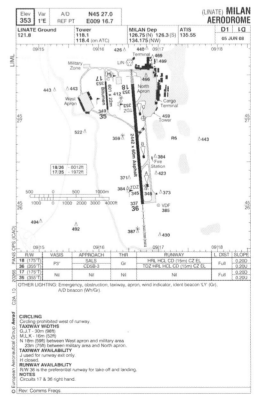

1980s, today it is used for domestic and European flights, mainly shorter routes but destinations are as far afield as Copenhagen and Stockholm. However, most of Milan's air traffic is now handled by Malpensa.

The airport was the scene of a serious accident on 8 October 2001, when an SAS (Scandinavian Airlines System) MD-80 taking-off for Copenhagen collided with a business jet that made a runway incursion in fog, with the loss of all aboard both aircraft and a number of workers in a hangar on the ground. After a light aircraft landed on taxiway 'T' on 15 June 2005, with the pilot mistaking it for runway 36R, the runways were renumbered with 18R/36L becoming 17/35.

VENICE MARCO POLO: VCE

Venice, Italy

Owner and operator: SAVE SpA
Runways: 04L/22R, 2,780m (9,121ft); 04R/22L, 3,300m (10,827ft)
Terminals: One
Annual passengers: 7,059,141
Annual cargo: 12,996 tonnes
Annual aircraft movements: 88,778

Bus connection to railway terminal, or water bus to the centre of Venice.

Background

One of two airports serving Venice, with the other being Treviso, mainly used by low-cost carriers, Venice Marco Polo is named after the Venetian explorer who established links with China. It was opened in the early 1960s to relieve the pressure on Treviso and has a modern terminal opened in 2002, but already close to capacity.

There have been a few accidents at the airport. One of these was on 6 March 1967 when an Aeralpi Short Skyvan crashed into the sea while attempting to land in bad weather, but all three aboard the aircraft survived. Bad weather also accounted for an accident on 14 September 1993, but with a much less fortunate outcome as all

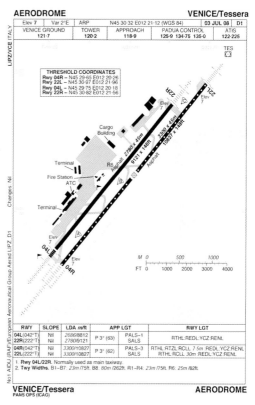

three aboard an Italian Air Force Piaggio PD.808 were killed when it crashed.

CATANIA FONTANAROSSA: CTA

Catania, Sicily, Italy

Owner and operator: Regional Government
Runways: 08/26, 2,438m (7,989ft)
Terminals: One
Annual passengers: 6,079,699
Annual cargo: 8,801 tonnes
Annual aircraft movements: 60,953

Background

Situated 5km (3 miles) south of Catania, Fontanarossa is the busiest airport in Sicily, although Catania is second in size to the regional capital, Palermo. While the fifth most important Italian airport in overall passenger traffic, it is third in domestic traffic after Rome/Leonardo da Vinci and Milan/Linate, doubtless because

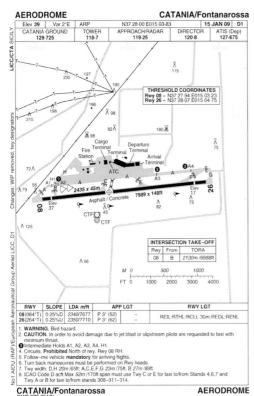

AERODROME — **CATANIA/Fontanarossa**

Elev 39	Var 2°E	ARP	N37 28·00 E015 03·83		15 JAN 09	D1
CATANIA GROUND 129·725	TOWER 118·7	APPROACH/RADAR 119·25		DIRECTOR 120·8	ATIS (Dep) 127·675	

THRESHOLD COORDINATES
Rwy 08 – N37 27·94 E015 03·23
Rwy 26 – N37 28·07 E015 04·75

INTERSECTION TAKE–OFF

Rwy	From	TORA
08	B	2130m /6988ft

RWY	SLOPE	LDA m/ft	APP LGT		RWY LGT
08 (084°T)	0·25%D	2340/7677	P 3' (52)	–	REIL:RTHL:RCLL 30m:REDL:RENL
26 (264°T)	0·25%U	2350/7710	P 3' (62)		

1. **WARNING.** Bird hazard.
2. **CAUTION.** In order to avoid damage due to jet blast or slipstream pilots are requested to taxi with minimum thrust.
❸ Intermediate Holds A1, A2, A3, A4, H1.
4. Circuits. **Prohibited** North of rwy. Rwy 06 RH.
5. Follow–me vehicle **mandatory** for arriving flights.
6. Turn back manoeuvres must be performed on Rwy heads.
7. Twy width: D,H 20m /65ft; A,C,E,F,G 23m /75ft; B 27m /89ft.
8. ICAO Code D acft Max 52m /170ft span must use Twy C or E for taxi to/from Stands 4,6,7 and Twy A or B for taxi to/from stands 308–311–314.

CATANIA/Fontanarossa
PANS OPS (ICAO) — **AERODROME**

Sicily is an island so road and rail competition is less.

The logistics of island life also explain why Catania had the first airport in the far south of Italy when it opened in 1924. The airport was overwhelmed by traffic by the late 1940s and a new airport was built, which opened in 1950. Growth in recent years has been far greater than expected, and in May 2007 a brand new terminal was opened, and this now appears to be in need of extension to cope with traffic.

There has been one serious accident at the airport, on 28 January 1999, when an Alitalia McDonnell Douglas MD-82 arrived on a flight from Naples. As the aircraft was about to touch down, it encountered a microburst or windshear, and the captain tried to go round, but the aircraft made a heavy landing and the left undercarriage collapsed, leaving the aircraft so badly damaged that it had to be scrapped, but all 6 crew and 78 passengers survived.

NAPLES INTERNATIONAL (CAPODICHINO): NAP

Naples, Italy

Owner and operator: BAA
Runways: 06/24, 2,628m (8,622ft)
Terminals: One
Annual passengers: 5,775,838
Annual cargo: 4,880 tonnes
Annual aircraft movements: 72,330

A station on Metro Line 1 and Metrocampania Nordest is planned for 2011.

Background

Located in an area known locally as 'Campo di Marte', the first connection with aviation was as early as 1910 when the first flying displays in Naples were performed. The site was taken over by the military during the First World War, primarily to provide air cover for Naples in the

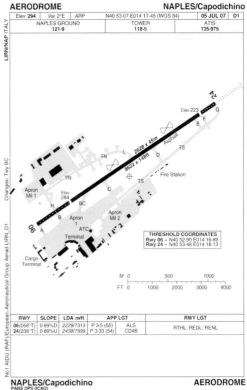

AERODROME — **NAPLES/Capodichino**

Elev 294	Var 2°E	ARP	N40 53·07 E014 17·45 (WGS 84)	05 JUL 07	D1
NAPLES GROUND 121·9		TOWER 118·5		ATIS 135·975	

THRESHOLD COORDINATES
Rwy 06 – N40 52·90 E014 16·89
Rwy 24 – N40 53·48 E014 18·13

RWY	SLOPE	LDA m/ft	APP LGT		RWY LGT
06 (058°T)	0·89%D	2229/7313	P 3·5 (55)	ALS	RTHL: REDL: RENL
24 (238°T)	0·89%U	2438/7999	P 3·33 (54)	CD4B	

NAPLES/Capodichino
PANS OPS (ICAO) — **AERODROME**

event of an Austro-Hungarian or German attack, which never materialised. Post war, the airport was dedicated to the Italian aviator, Ugo Niutta, and remained as a military base, and even today the airport is regarded officially as a military base open to commercial flights.

The first commercial air services started in 1950, initially with services to Rome, although it soon became a stop on the British European Airways services from London to Malta. In 1980 an organisation, Gestione Servizi Aeroporto Capodichino (GESAC) was created for the airport's administration, with the involvement of the city and the provincial government, and Alitalia. A 20-year development plan was initiated in 1995 with the assistance of the British Airports Authority, and in 1997 GESAC was privatised, with BAA acquiring a 70 per cent majority stake.

There have been some accidents to aircraft flying to Naples, of which the worst was on 22 October 1958, when a Vickers Viscount 700 of BEA (British European Airways) flying a Rome to Naples sector of a flight from London to Malta, was in a mid-air collision with a formation of Italian Air Force fighters; there were no survivors. As for accidents actually at Naples, the worst recorded was on 1 September 2001 when an Aero Lloyd Airbus A321 on a flight from Catania to Berlin was forced to divert. Explanations for the diversion vary, with some reports indicating an attempted hijacking by a Tunisian and others suggesting that a mentally ill man had a panic attack. What is known is that, in landing, the aircraft was badly damaged and had to be written off, although everyone aboard survived.

MILAN BERGAMO/ORIO AL SERIO INTERNATIONAL: BGY

Bergamo, Italy

Owner and operator: SACBO (Società
  Aeroporto Civile Bergamo Orio al Serio)
Runways: 10/28, 2,937m (9,636ft); 12/30, 778m
  (2,552ft)
Terminals: One

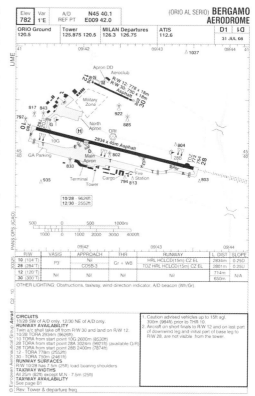

Annual passengers: 5,737,089
Annual cargo: 133,932 tonnes
Annual aircraft movements: 61,365

Background

Originally a small regional airport, despite being 45km (28 miles) from Milan, the airport is advertised by the many low-cost airlines that use it as 'Milan Bergamo'. The low-cost airlines and the growing use of the airport as a low-cost option for air freight operators together have ensured strong growth in recent years.

ROME CIAMPINO: CIA

Rome, Italy

Owner and operator: ADR
Runways: 15/33, 2,207m (7,242ft)
Terminals: One
Airlines using airport as base or hub: Mistral Air
Annual passengers: 5,351,910

Annual cargo: 22,999 tonnes
Annual aircraft movements: 65,633

Background

Some 15km (almost 10 miles) south-east of Rome, Ciampino dates from 1916 and has one of the longest records of continuous operation of any airport. It was the main airport for Rome until 1960, when Rome Fiumicino, now Rome/Leonardo da Vinci, opened. After its scheduled flights transferred to the new airport, Ciampino concentrated on charter flights, and especially those for business aircraft, but in recent years it has become the low-cost airport of choice for the growing number of low-cost or no-frills airlines.

It was one of the low-cost flights that suffered a serious accident at the airport on 10 November 2008, when a Ryanair Boeing 737-800, landing from Frankfurt, fell victim to bird strikes that damaged both engines. Unable to go round, the

aircraft made a heavy landing, closing the airport for more than 24 hours. Although the aircraft suffered damage to the undercarriage, engines and rear fuselage, the 6 crew and 166 passengers all survived without serious injury.

Before it lost its scheduled flights, Ciampino was handling around two million passengers annually, but due to the popularity of the low-cost carriers, the figure now is well in excess of five million. This success has meant that complaints about aircraft noise raised the question of a third airport for Rome, and in November 2007 Viterbo was chosen as the third airport for the city. Meanwhile, the terminal at Ciampino has been extended.

PALERMO/FALCONE-BORSELLINO INTERNATIONAL: PMO

Punta Raisi, Sicily, Italy

Owner: Regional Government
Operator: GESAP SpA
Runways: 07/25, 3,326m (10,912ft); 02/20, 2,074m (6,804ft)
Terminals: One
Annual passengers: 4,507,143
Annual aircraft movements: 52,152

Background

Named after two leading anti-Mafia judges who were murdered in 1992, the airport is 35km (22 miles) from Palermo, the capital of Sicily. The airport dates from 1960 when it was opened with two runways, but only basic terminal facilities until a new terminal was opened in the early 1990s. Since 1994 the airport has been managed by GESAP, a consortium of local authorities and the Palermo Chamber of Commerce.

There have been a number of serious accidents to aircraft at Palermo, especially to aircraft attempting to land at night or in bad weather. One of these was on 5 May 1972 when an Alitalia Douglas DC-8-40 from Rome crashed 5km (3 miles) from the airport because the pilots did not follow the established approach procedures. All 7 crew and 108 passengers died. On 22 February

AERODROME   **ROME/Ciampino**

| Elev 427 | Var 2°E | ARP | N41 47·97 E012 35·83 (WGS 84) | 06 JUL 06 | D1 |

| CIAMPINO DELIVERY 119·4 | GROUND 121·75 | TOWER 120·5 | ROME DIRECTOR 119·2 |

THRESHOLD COORDINATES
Rwy 15 – N41 48·48 E012 35·33
Rwy 33 – N41 47·43 E012 36·06

RWY	SLOPE	LDA m/ft	APP LGT		RWY LGT
15(152°T)	1.19%U	2207/7242	P 3° (65)	CD5B	RTHL:RTZL:RCLL 30m :REDL
33(332°T)	1.19%D	2207/7242	P 3·5° (49)	–	RTHL:RCLL 30m :REDL

1. Rwy 15 is the preferential and instrument runway.
2. Landing Rwy 33 not available in IMC, HN ±30.
3. PAPI mandatory HN and when visibility less than 5Km.

ROME/Ciampino   **AERODROME**
PANS OPS (ICAO)

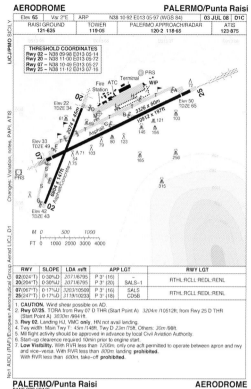

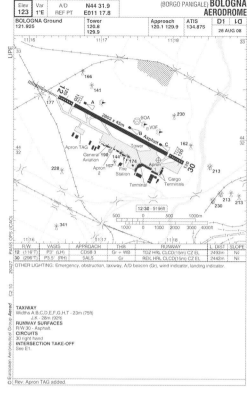

1978 all three persons aboard a Learjet 35A business jet died when it crashed into the sea on approach to Palermo. The death toll was far higher later that year on 23 December when an Alitalia McDonnell Douglas DC-9, landing from Rome, with an inexperienced first officer and a captain with limited experience on the DC-9, crashed into the sea 3km (just under 2 miles) from Palermo. All 5 crew died in the accident, but 21 out of 124 passengers survived. More recently, on 6 August 2005, a Tuninter ATR-72-200, flying a charter flight from Bari to Djerba, was forced to divert to Palermo short of fuel, but had to ditch in the sea, with the loss of 2 of the 4 crew and 14 out of 35 passengers.

BOLOGNA/GUGLIELMO MARCONI INTERNATIONAL: BLQ

Bologna, Emilia-Romagna, Italy

Owner and operator: Bologna City Council
Runways: 12/30, 2,800m (9,186ft)
Terminals: One
Annual passengers: 4,354,369
Annual cargo: 18,692 tonnes
Annual aircraft movements: 66,698

Background

Named after the famous electrical engineer and radio pioneer Guglielmo Marconi, the airport is 6km (3¾ miles) north-west of the city centre.

PISA/GALILEO GALILEI INTERNATIONAL: PSA

San Giusto, Pisa, Tuscany, Italy

Owner and operator: Tuscan Regional
  Government/Aeronautica Militare
Runways: 04L/22R, 2,792m (9,160ft); 04R/22L,
  2,993m (9,820ft)
Terminals: One
Annual passengers: 3,718,608
Annual cargo: 13,019 tonnes
Annual aircraft movements: 42,691

Airport railway station, with trains to both Pisa
and Florence.

Background

Pisa is the main airport in Tuscany, and it is
named after the famous scientist and
astronomer, Galileo Galilei, who was a native of
the city. It is just 2km (1¼ miles) from the city

centre and serves both Pisa and Florence, which
has the other airport for Tuscany but which
cannot handle large aircraft. The airport is used
extensively by low-cost airlines as well as the
more traditional or 'heritage' carriers.

In addition to commercial aviation, the airport is used by the Italian Air Force, the *Aeronautica Militare*, for its transport units using
Lockheed C-130J Hercules and the Alenia C-
27J Spartan.

VERONA/VALERIO CATULLO VILLAFRANCA INTERNATIONAL: VRN

Villafranca, Verona, Italy

Owner and operator: Aeroporto Valerio Catullo
  di Verona Villafranca SpA
Runways: 04/22, 3,067m (10,064ft)
Terminals: One
Annual passengers: 3,510,259
Annual aircraft movements: 43,023

Background

Known variously as Verona or Villafranca after
the district in which it is sited, the airport was
built as a military air station during the Second
World War and did not open to commercial traffic until the early 1960s, initially mainly for charter flights, although there was a regular service
to Rome. It was not until 1978 that it became
firmly established as a commercial airport with
a purpose-built terminal and other facilities, and
run by a consortium of local authorities and
provincial governments, including Trento and
Brescia.

Major redevelopment of the terminal was
completed in 1990 to cope with the growth in
passenger traffic, and in May 2006 an extension
of the terminal was opened, doubling the airport's passenger handling capacity.

A serious accident occurred on 13 December
1995 when the captain of a Banat Air Antonov
An-24B elected not to have the aircraft de-iced
during a turnround at Verona, despite falling
snow and a preceding Air France aircraft returning for further de-icing because of delays in

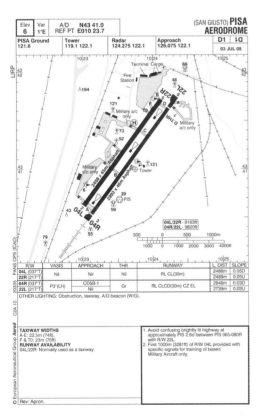

taking off, and once airborne the aircraft lost speed and stalled. All 8 crew and 41 out of 49 passengers died in the accident.

TURIN/CITTA DI TORINO INTERNATIONAL: TRN
Caselle, Turin, Italy

Owner and operator: Società Azionaria Gestione Aeroporto Torino SpA
Runways: 18/34, 3,300m (10,827ft)
Terminals: One
Airlines using airport as base or hub: Alitalia
Annual passengers: 3,500,728
Annual aircraft movements: 62,136

The airport terminal has a station for the Ferrovia Torino-Ceres, which is a railway link direct to the centre of the city.

Background
The airport is sometimes known as Caselle, after the neighbourhood.

Turin claims a long association with aviation, including the first flight by an aircraft built in Italy in 1909, and to be the home of the country's first aircraft factories. In 1926, Italy's first airline, SISA, operated a flying boat service between Turin and Trieste. The present airport opened in 1938, but initially was used for the Regia Aeronautica (the Italian Air Force) and the Luftwaffe during the Second World War, and did not open as a civil airport until 1953, when the terminal was completed. The first regular service was by Alitalia, linking Turin with Rome. A new terminal opened in 1993, and the railway station followed in 2001. The airport was completely remodelled and modernised in time for the Turin Winter Olympic Games in 2006.

CAGLIARI-ELMAS: CAG
Cagliari, Sardinia, Italy

Owner and operator: So.G.Aer. SpA
Runways: 14L/32R, 2,402m (7,877ft); 14R/32L, 2,805m (9,196ft)

Terminals: One
Annual passengers: 2,666,957
Annual cargo: 5,000 tonnes

Background
The airport is close to Cagliari on Sardinia and is named after Elmas as it is the nearest village. It is also known as Cagliari Mario Mameli, after a local notable. The main airport on Sardinia, it was originally opened on 3 May 1937, and was used first by the Regio Aeronautica and Luftwaffe during the Second World War and then by the Fleet Air Arm, RAF and USAAF to support the landings in the South of France in 1944. A new terminal was opened in 2003, and more recently the runways have been strengthened and resurfaced.

BARI/KAROL WOJTYLA INTERNATIONAL: BRI
Bari, Puglia, Italy

Owner and operator: Aeroporti di Puglia
Runways: 07/25, 2,440m (8,005ft); 12/30, 1,680m (5,512ft) currently closed
Terminals: One
Annual passengers: 2,385,427
Annual cargo: 4,040 tonnes

Background
Also known as Palese Macchie Airport after the village close to the airport, Bari International is 8km (5 miles) from the centre of Bari. The airport is named after Pope John Paul II.

Originally it was a base for the Regia Aeronautica (Italian Air Force) and dated from the Second World War. Commercial flights were allowed at the beginning of the 1960s and were initially operated by the state airline (Alitalia) before being taken over by its domestic counterpart, ATI (Aero Transporti Italiani) formed in 1964. At first, ATI used Fokker F27 Friendship twin-turboprop airliners, and when these were replaced by Douglas DC-9 jet airliners, a new runway had to be laid. Until 1981 the terminal was a building in the military zone, but a new terminal opened that year, although it had originally been intended as a cargo terminal. In 1990, preparing for the World Cup football matches, the runway was extended and the terminal modernised. Although the terminal was modernised again in 2000, a completely new terminal opened in 2005 and the following year the runway was lengthened again.

The airport was the scene of an accident to a Fokker F-27 Friendship of ATI on 30 October 1972. The aircraft crashed into a hill while en route from Naples, with the loss of all 3 crew and 24 passengers.

FLORENCE-PERETOLA/ AMERIGO VESPUCCI: FLR

Sesto Fiorentino, Tuscany, Italy

Owner and operator: Aeroporto di Firenze
Runways: 05/23, 1,716m (5,633ft)
Terminals: One
Annual passengers: 1,905,143

Background

Known variously as Florence Airport, Florence Peretola or simply Peretola, the airport was named in 1990 after the explorer Amerigo Vespucci, who was a merchant in Florence. Operations are limited by the length of the runway and the need for aircraft to backtrack along the runway. It is actually not in Florence but in the neighbouring area of Sesto Fiorentino.

Florence has a long history of aviation, with an airfield built in the Campo di Marte area as early as 1910, and this became the city's first airport after the First World War. Nevertheless, even at this early stage, encroaching urban development meant that it was soon too small as aircraft grew in size. The present airport was opened in the early 1930s as a simple grass field, and, at first, aircraft were able to take off in whichever direction suited the pilot. In 1938 the airport was enlarged and a 1,000m (3,283ft) asphalt runway opened in 1939. The Second World War prevented civil use of the airport and it was not until 1948 that commercial airline flights began, operated by Douglas DC-3s of Aerea Teseo, although this company soon col-

lapsed. Alitalia operated Rome–Florence–Milan and Rome–Florence–Venice services during the 1950s until these were taken over by its domestic affiliate, ATI (Aero Transporti Italiani).

In 1984 a runway extension to 1,400m (4,593ft) opened and the airport passed to Saf, which has since been renamed Aeroporto di Firenze, and the passenger terminal was rebuilt. Regular flights, which had dwindled away and were then suspended during reconstruction, returned in September 1986. In 1996 the runway was extended again to its current length and the terminal was also enlarged. For a period, Air UK operated from London Gatwick to Florence, a route later taken over by Meridiana, and today the airport has services to most of the main centres in Europe.

The airport suffers from its relatively short runway and also the fact that the much larger airport at Pisa has a direct railway service not only into Pisa itself, but to Florence as well, making Pisa a strong local competitor.

The airport was the scene of a serious accident on 30 July 1997, when an ATR-42 of Air Littoral arriving from Nice landed too fast and overshot the runway, coming to rest beside the perimeter road, with the death of a crew member, although the other 2 crew and 14 passengers survived. On 14 March 2004 a Cessna 525 business jet was written off after a take-off accident, although all seven occupants survived.

OLBIA COSTA SMERALDA: OLB

Olbia, Sardinia, Italy

Owner and operator: Geasar SpA
Runways: 06/24, 2,446m (8,025ft)
Terminals: One
Airlines using airport as base or hub: Meridiana
Annual passengers: 1,770,665

Background

One of two airports serving the Italian island of Sardinia, and built after the Second World War. Most of its passengers are tourists. The terminal was completely modernised in 2004.

ALGHERO/FERTILIA: AHO

Fertilia, Sardinia, Italy

Owner and operator: SOGEAAL (Societa di Gestione Aeroporto di Alghero) SpA
Runways: 02/20, 3,000m (9,843ft)
Terminals: One
Annual passengers: 1,298,950

Background

The smallest of the three airports in Sardinia, and locally known as Fertilia after the locality, it is 8km (5 miles) from Alghero. The airport opened in 1974 and at first was mainly used by flights from mainland Italy, but has shown strong growth in recent years as Sardinia has become increasingly popular with visitors from northern Europe, and has attracted the low-cost carriers, such as Ryanair.

GENOA CRISTOFORO COLOMBO: GOA

Genoa, Italy

Owner and operator: Aeroporto di Genova SpA
Runways: 11/29, 2,915m (9,564ft)
Terminals: One
Annual passengers: 1,116,211

Background

Built on reclaimed land, the airport is 6km (3¾ miles) from the centre of Genoa. Opened after the Second World War, modernisation of the terminal was completed in 2008.

JAMAICA

MONTEGO BAY/SANGSTER INTERNATIONAL: MBJ

Montego Bay, Jamaica

Owner and operator: Airports Authority of Jamaica
Runways: 07/25, 2,662m (8,735ft)
Terminals: Two, designated Domestic and International

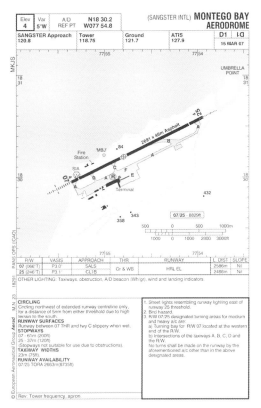

Airlines using airport as base or hub: Air Jamaica
Annual passengers: 3,136,601
Annual cargo: 5,457 tonnes
Annual aircraft movements: 44,762

Background

One of the largest and busiest airports in the Caribbean, the airport is named after a former prime minister of Jamaica.

The need for the airport was identified as long ago as 1936, but construction, which started in 1940, was not completed until 1947. Initially the airport was operated by its main user, Pan American Airways, until the government took it over in September 1949. The original terminal was on the north side of the runway, but a new terminal was built on the other side and opened in July 1959. The terminal was subsequently extended, and since 2000 a development programme has been in place for further extensions to the international terminal, and the runway will be extended in the near future to 3,046m (10,000ft).

The airport was the scene of a serious accident on 21 January 1960, when an Avianca Lockheed Super Constellation flying from New York to Bogota via Montego Bay crashed on landing. The aircraft had already had to divert to Miami because of engine trouble and, after resuming its flight, made a heavy landing at Montego Bay, which resulted in structural damage and caused the aircraft to slide down the runway in flames before coming to rest upside down. Two of the 7 crew and 35 out of 39 passengers died in the accident.

The airport's management is determined that it should remain the more important of Jamaica's airports, but industrial relations have been poor in recent years.

KINGSTON/NORMAN MANLEY INTERNATIONAL: KIN

Palisadoes, Jamaica

Owner and operator: NMIA Airports Ltd
Runways: 12/30, 2,713m (8,900ft)
Terminals: One
Airlines using airport as base or hub: Air
    Jamaica
Annual passengers: 1,735,659
Annual cargo: 17,313 tonnes

Background

Originally known as Palisadoes, after the district in which it is situated, the airport was originally built as a Royal Naval Air Station for the Fleet Air Arm, opening on 1 August 1941 as HMS *Buzzard*. After the Second World War it became the civil airport for Kingston and was used by British West Indies Airways, a regional affiliate of BOAC (British Overseas Airways Corporation).

The airport has been modernised and enlarged on several occasions, and most recently there have been extensions to the terminal so that it can handle projected traffic beyond 2020. It is the main base and hub for Air Jamaica.

The airport has suffered a number of accidents over the years. On 10 April 1953, a Lockheed Lodestar of Caribbean International Airways suffered an engine failure during take-off, was seen to bank and then crashed into the sea killing all 3 crew and all but one of the 14 passengers. There were later two accidents involving the same kind of aircraft, the Curtiss C-46 Commando. The first of these was on 26 November 1962, when a Lineas Aereas La Urraca was being ferried from Kingston to Bogota, and on taking-off was seen to crash into Port Henderson Hill, scraping across it and catching fire, with the deaths of the pilot and one of the two other occupants aboard. The aircraft would normally have had two pilots. The second accident involving a C-46 was on 13 September 1967, when a Capitol Airways aircraft was forced to ditch in the sea following an engine failure after taking-off. The two passengers and two crew survived.

An Air Jamaica McDonnell Douglas DC-9 bound for Detroit was hijacked and flown to Miami on 3 January 1974, but the hijacking ended peacefully without harm to passengers or crew.

JAPAN

Often regarded as an industrial powerhouse, Japan was slow to embrace deregulation and greater competiveness in air transport, with three large airlines dominating the market. Nevertheless, between deregulation in 1998 and 2006 four new airlines were created.

The country's rapid economic and industrial growth since the end of the Second World War has seen it become home to some of the world's busiest airports, despite the strong competition from high speed railway lines. This is partly because the country is spread across a group of islands. Because of the high population density and the fact that much of the country is mountainous, Japan has also become a leader in the construction of offshore airports built on reclaimed land, finding the engineering challenges less onerous than the political ones of building onshore in the face of militant environmentalists.

TOKYO/HANEDA: HND

Ota, Tokyo, Japan

Owner: Tokyo Aviation Bureau, Ministry of Land, Infrastructure and Transport

Operator: Japan Airport Terminal Co. Ltd

Runways: 16R/34L, 3,000m (9,843ft); 16L/34R, 3,000m (9,843ft); 4/22, 2,500m (8,202ft); a fourth runway is planned

Terminals: Two, with a third for international flights under construction

Airlines using airport as base or hub: JAL (Japan Airlines), ANA (All Nippon Airways)

Annual passengers: 66,823,414

Annual cargo: 852,454 tonnes

Annual aircraft movements: 331,818

Both the Tokyo Monorail and the Keikyū Airport Line serve the airport.

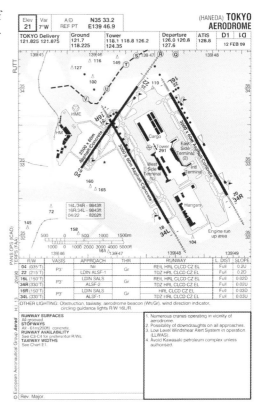

Background

Japan's largest civil airport when it opened as Haneda Airfield (*Haneda Hikojo*) in 1931, the original airport was beside Tokyo Bay at the southern end of today's airport complex. It replaced a Japanese Army Air Force air station at Tachikawa as the main hub and base for the then national airline, Japan Air Transport. Throughout the 1930s, the airport handled flights to destinations in Japan, Korea and Manchuria, which at the time were Japanese colonies. In 1939, the original runway was extended to 800 metres and a second 800 metre runway was completed.

Haneda was used by the military during the Second World War and after Japanese surrender in 1945, the United States Army Air Force took it over as Haneda Army Air Base. The USAAF evicted many nearby residents to make room for extending one runway to 1,650m and the other to 2,100m.

While still a military air station, Haneda received its first international flights in 1947 when Northwest Orient Airlines (now Northwest Airlines) introduced scheduled services from the USA, and used the airport as a hub to serve China, South Korea and the Philippines. Japan Airlines began its first domestic operations from Haneda in 1951. The United States Air Force gave part of the base back to Japan in 1952, providing the space for the new Tokyo International Airport. The remainder was returned to Japan in 1958, and the Japan Airport Terminal Company was established to ensure its development and management using private capital. Meanwhile, several European carriers had introduced services to Haneda, with BOAC operating de Havilland Comet flights to London via the southern route in 1952, and SAS operating DC-7 flights to Copenhagen via Anchorage beginning in 1957.

JAL and Aeroflot began a joint service from Haneda to Moscow in 1967. Other airlines at Haneda during this period included Pan Am,

Sabena, Swissair, Canadian Pacific Airlines, Cathay Pacific Airways and Air Siam. Both Pan Am and Northwest Orient used Haneda as an Asian regional hub. The airport's instrument landing system became operational in 1961.

Earlier, a new terminal building was opened in May 1955, and this was followed by a second terminal exclusively for domestic traffic in September 1964, in time for the Tokyo Olympic Games. In 1970, a new international arrivals terminal was opened. JATC was given responsibility for developing Tokyo's second airport at Narita (see page 143), where work commenced in February 1973, to ease the growing pressure at Haneda. When Narita opened in 1978, it was intended to take all international flights, but while most international flights moved, Taiwanese airlines remained at Haneda Airport to avoid Japan becoming embroiled in the political conflict between Taiwan and the People's Republic of China. China Airlines (the main Taiwanese carrier) served Taipei and Honolulu from Haneda; Taiwan's second major airline, Eva Air, joined CAL at Haneda in 1989.

In recent years, the lack of spare capacity at Narita has meant that Haneda has been handling a growing number of international flights. As the Tokyo Metropolitan Government used the adjacent area of Tokyo Bay as a waste dumping site, creating a large amount of landfill, space was provided for renewed expansion and in July 1988, a new runway opened on the landfill area. In September 1993, the old airport terminal was replaced by a new West Passenger Terminal, nicknamed 'Big Bird', which was built farther out on the landfill. Two new runways were completed in March 1997 and March 2000. In 2004, Terminal 2 opened at Haneda, largely for ANA, while the 1993 terminal was redesignated as Terminal 1, and became the base for JAL, Skymark and Skynet Asia Airways.

The opening of a new domestic airport, known as Ibaraki or Hyakuri, in 2009 should ease the pressure on Haneda.

There have been a number of accidents at or near the airport. Of the more recent, one occurred on 9 February 1982 when a Japan Airlines flight crashed near the airport, supposedly because of a deliberate action by the pilot, killing 24 of the 174 occupants of the aircraft. The worst single airliner accident to-date was on 12 August 1985 when a flight bound for Osaka lost control and crashed into a mountain, with the loss of 520 out of the 524 passengers after the aircraft's tailplane was lost making control impossible. One flight also suffered a hijacking shortly after take-off. This was an All Nippon Airways flight on 23 July 1999, with the hijacker killing the aircraft's captain before he could be subdued, but the co-pilot managed to land the aircraft safely without further loss of life.

TOKYO/NARITA INTERNATIONAL: NRT
Narita, Chiba, Tokyo, Japan

Owner and operator: Narita International Airport Corporation
Runways: 16R/34L, 4,000m (13,123ft); 16L/34R; 2,180m (7,152ft) being extended to 2,500m (8,202ft)
Terminals: Two, designated Terminal One and Terminal Two
Airlines using airport as base or hub: JAL Japan Airlines, ANA (All Nippon Airways)
Annual passengers: 35,478,146
Annual cargo: 2,254,421 tonnes
Annual aircraft movements: 195,074

Originally intended to be connected to a Shinkansen high-speed line, this was abandoned because of land acquisition issues. There are separate stations for the two terminals, and these are served by the Keisei Electric Railway and Japan Railways. There will be a third line, the Narita Rapid Railway, from 2010.

Background
Japan's second busiest airport and the country's international airport and leading air cargo centre, Narita International Airport, or *Narita Kokusai Kūkō*, is almost 40 miles from the city centre. For several years it was known officially as the New Tokyo International Airport, and the

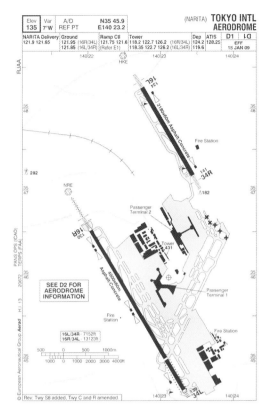

| Elev | Var | A/D | N35 45.9 | (NARITA) | **TOKYO INTL** |
| 135 | 7°W | REF PT | E140 23.2 | | **AERODROME** |

NARITA Delivery	Ground	Ramp Ctl	Tower	Dep	ATIS	D1	LD
121.9 121.65	121.95 (16R/34L)	121.75 121.6	118.2 122.7 126.2 (16R/34L)	124.2	128.25		EFF
	121.85 (16L/34R)	(Refer E1)	118.35 122.7 126.2 (16L/34R)	119.6			15 JAN 09

constructed two steel towers to obstruct aircraft using the airport, but these were forcibly dismantled.

Initially, the airport was without a direct railway connection and passengers had to use a transfer bus, but a railway service to Terminal One was opened in March 1991 by Japan Railways and the Keisei Railway. Narita was privatised on 1 April 2004.

For the future, runway extensions are planned, and the Narita Rapid Railway is due to open in 2010, reducing the travelling time to central Tokyo from around an hour to forty minutes or less. The original plan to restrict international flights to Narita no longer holds good, and Haneda has been handling a growing number of international flights, a process that is set to continue as Narita has itself become congested, and a new runway is planned for Haneda.

Amongst the accidents and incidents at the airport, there was one on 22 June 1985, resulting from terrorist activity, when an item of luggage that had come from Vancouver, exploded while being loaded aboard an Air India flight, killing two baggage handlers. In 1997 a departing United Airlines flight encountered such severe turbulence that many passengers were badly injured and the aircraft had to return to the airport, with one woman passenger later dying from her injuries. Most recently, on 23 March 2009, a FedEx (Federal Express) cargo flight landing from Guangzhou in China crashed on Runway 16R/34L, killing both pilots and closing the runway for the day.

current title was not adopted until 2004.

The need for a second airport to relieve the pressure on Tokyo/Haneda was apparent as early as 1962, when it was proposed that a new airport be built to take all international flights, leaving Haneda for Japan's substantial domestic air traffic. The location was dictated by the shortage of suitable land closer to the city, and also to avoid air traffic congestion from Haneda and the many US air bases. As has become common in many parts of the world, the decision was controversial and the protests were a factor in the later new airports at Osaka and Nagoya being built offshore. An edge was given to the protests by fears that the airport was in reality to be another US air base, so although the 1966 plan was for opening in 1971, the airport was not completed until 1978. Even so, it opened with just one of the planned three runways, and a second runway was not opened until 2002. At one time, in the 1980s, the airport's opponents

NEW CHITOSE AIRPORT/SAPPORO: CTS

Sapporo, Chitose, Hokkaidō, Japan

Owner and airfield operator: Ministry of Transport

Terminal operator: Hokkaidō Airport Terminal Co. Ltd

Runways: 1L/19R, 2,999m (9,839ft); 1R/19L, 2,999m (9,839ft)

Terminals: One, divided into domestic and international sections

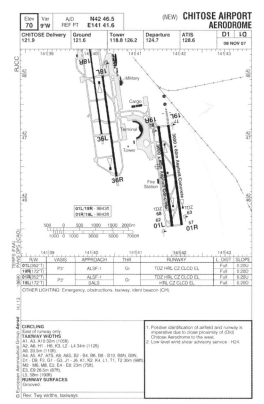

Airlines using airport as base or hub: Japan
    Airlines and All Nippon Airways are the main
    users
Annual passengers: 18,361,366
Annual cargo: 274,269 tonnes
Annual aircraft movements: 98,827

The airport has a railway station on a spur off the
Hokkaidō Railway Company with trains direct to
Sapporo.

Background

Opened in 1991 to replace the original airport
for Chitose, which was shared with the Japanese
Air Self-Defence Force and which remains as a
military air station. Its original airport code,
SPK, is now used by the small Okadama Airport
in central Sapporo. The original plans for the
airport were that it should become another
major international gateway for Japan, and initially there were services to Europe as well as to

China, Australia, and New Zealand, but the
European services have since been discontinued
because of poor loadings, and the runways are
not suitable for long non-stop services by wide-
bodied aircraft. The main market today consists
of tourists arriving for winter sports.

Before being developed as the new airport for
Chitose, the old Sapporo airport suffered from a
number of serious accidents, but there have been
none in the past 20 years.

FUKUOKA: FUK

Fukuoka, Japan

Owner and operator: Japanese Ministry of
    Transport
Runways: 16/34, 2,800m (9,186ft)
Terminals: Two, designated Domestic and
    International
Annual passengers: 17,902,563
Annual cargo: 292,694 tonnes
Annual aircraft movements: 71,456

Background

Previously known as Itazuke Air Base, and
despite having just one runway it is the fourth
busiest airport in Japan. It occupies the site of the
USAF air base at Itazuke, built in 1952 and
which was handed back to Japan in 1972. It is still
used by the Japanese Air Self-Defence Force.

Despite its importance, the airport only
briefly had a transpacific service during the
1990s when Delta Air Lines provided a service
with Portland on the US west coast. There is no
room to expand the airport, which many have
compared to the former airport for Hong Kong,
Kai Tek, and it means that in the future the airport will have to be moved to a new site, either
further inland or to an offshore island (both of
which have proved to be controversial), or be
built on reclaimed land. While the mayor has
declared that he wants Fukuoka to be the venue
for the Olympic Games, it is now too late to do
anything in time for 2016. The result of the present situation is that the airport is classified as
second class, and flights are banned from 22.00
to 07.00.

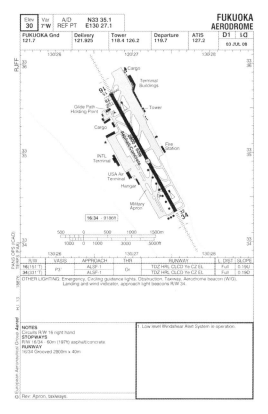

Elev	Var	A/D	N33 35.1					FUKUOKA
30	7°W	REF PT	E130 27.1					AERODROME

FUKUOKA Gnd 121.7	Delivery 121.925	Tower 118.4 126.2	Departure 119.7	ATIS 127.2	D1	⌐ロ

03 JUL 08

16/34 · 9186ft

R/W	VASIS	APPROACH	THR	RUNWAY	L DIST	SLOPE
16(151'T)	P3'	ALSF-1	Gr	TDZ HRL CLCD Ye CZ EL	Full	0.19U
34(331'T)		ALSF-1		TDZ HRL CLCD Ye CZ EL	Full	0.19D

OTHER LIGHTING: Emergency, Circling guidance lights, Obstruction, Taxiway, Aerodrome beacon (W/G), Landing and wind indicator, approach light beacons R/W 34.

NOTES
Circuits R/W 16 right hand
STOPWAYS
R/W 16/34 - 60m (197ft) asphalt/concrete.
RUNWAY
16/34 Grooved 2800m x 40m

1. Low level Windshear Alert System in operation.

Rev: Apron, taxiways.

The airport saw the end of a hijacking on 16 December 1989. A CAAC Boeing 747 was hijacked shortly after taking off from Shanghai for San Francisco by a man wanting to be flown to South Korea, which refused to accept the aircraft, and it diverted to Fukuoka instead, where the hijacker was simply pushed out of the cabin door by a member of the crew. Another hijacking occurred on an All Nippon flight from Osaka on 20 January 1997, with the hijackers demanding to be flown to the United States, but the Boeing 777 landed at Fukuoka where the hijacking ended after a day, with everyone aboard the aircraft safe. There have also been a number of accidents since the airport opened. On 13 June 1996 a McDonnell Douglas DC-10 of Garuda took off for Jakarta via Bali, but suffered a failure of the No. 3 engine as it accelerated down the runway and the take-off was aborted, but the aircraft had little runway left and overshot it breaking through a fence, and

then crossing a ditch and a road. Out of the 15 crew and 260 passengers, 3 passengers died, and another 18 were seriously injured. More recently, on 12 August 2005, an engine caught fire on a Japan Airlines aircraft that had just taken off for Honolulu. While the fire was extinguished, metal fragments fell into a residential area injuring two people on the ground.

OSAKA: ITM
Osaka, Japan

Owner: Ministry of Land, Infrastructure and Transport
Operator (terminal only): Osaka International Airport Terminal Co. Ltd
Runways: 14L/32R, 1,828m (5,997ft); 14R/32L, 2,999m (9,840ft)
Terminals: Two, designated North Terminal and South Terminal
Airlines using airport as base or hub: Japan Commuter
Annual passengers: 16,622,853
Annual cargo: 845,976 tonnes
Annual aircraft movements: 125,637

Served by the Osaka Monorail, which links the airport with the city's northern suburbs and provides connections to the city centre.

Background
Originally, Osaka's air transport connections were by seaplanes and flying boats which used a seaplane station in the estuary of the Kizu River. Eventually the local government planned to build a new airport, known as the 'No. 1 Osaka Airport', but also for seaplanes and flying boats, in the Yamato River estuary. Nevertheless, local business protested and there were also concerns about the sea mists for which the area was notorious, and this led to the decision to build an airfield for landplanes at Itami, which was known as the 'No. 2 Osaka Airport' when it opened in 1939. The timing was completely wrong for civil aviation, but right for the military, and for its first few years, the airport became a base for the Japanese Army Air Force during the Second

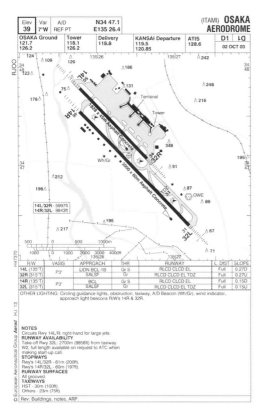

World War. After Japan surrendered, the airport was taken over by the then United States Army Air Force as Itami Air Base.

In 1958 Itami was handed back to the Japanese, and was renamed Osaka Airport. The following year it became an international airport. Over the next few years, many of the world's major long-haul airlines used the airport, although the Northwest Airlines route between New York and Sydney via Osaka became controversial when it was discovered that less than 30 per cent of the passengers on the Osaka-Sydney leg were either from or bound for the United States.

The 1960s and 1970s were a difficult period for the airport as the area surrounding it had become a dormitory town for workers commuting to Osaka, who objected to the noise of the new jet airliners, and the use of the airport by the USAF for refuelling and maintenance (even though this provided work for the Shin Meiwa aircraft fac-

tory) was unpopular with those Japanese who opposed the US involvement in the Vietnam War. When, in 1966, the Japanese government bought land on to which the airport could expand, with traffic for Expo 70 in mind, the protesters forced the government to impose restrictions on operations at the airport, including a night curfew on aircraft movements that began as early as 9pm. Faced with these difficulties, attention turned to developing an alternative to meet Osaka's air transport needs, and the end result was the opening of Kansai International Airport offshore on reclaimed land in Osaka Bay in 1994.

Perversely, having objected to the operations at Osaka International, the local population then objected to plans to close the airport and transfer all flights to Kansai for economic reasons. The compromise that was eventually reached was that Osaka International would continue as a domestic airport, although it has remained as an airport for VIP visits, and All Nippon still maintains a maintenance base to which large aircraft are often ferried, and there is some international cargo traffic. To enforce its will on the airport and the airline using it, the Japanese government imposed further restrictions in April 2006, limiting the airport to twin-engined aircraft only. A proposal to ban wide-bodied aircraft was derided as impractical given the volume of traffic, while a further proposal to reduce the airport to second-class status was opposed because it would mean that the surrounding communities would become liable to meet a third of its operating costs.

OSAKA/KANSAI INTERNATIONAL: KIX
Osaka, Japan

Owner and operator: Kansai International Airport Co.

Runways: 6L/24R, 4,000m (13,123ft); 6R/24L, 3,500m (11,483ft)

Terminals: One

Airlines using airport as base or hub: Japan Airlines, Japan Commuter, All Nippon Airways, Nippon Cargo Airlines

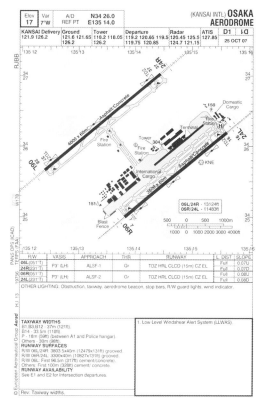

Elev 17	Var 7°W	A/D REF PT	N34 26.0 E135 14.0					(KANSAI INTL) **OSAKA**
								AERODROME

KANSAI Delivery	Ground	Tower	Departure	Radar	ATIS	D1	I-Q
121.9 126.2	121.6 121.65	118.2 118.05	119.2 120.85 119.5	120.45 125.5	127.85		25 OCT 07
	126.2	126.2	119.75 120.85	124.7 121.15			

R/W	VASIS	APPROACH	THR	RUNWAY	L DIST	SLOPE
06L(051°T)	P3° (LH)	ALSF-1	Gr	TDZ HRL CLCD (15m) CZ EL	Full	0.07U
24R(231°T)					Full	0.07D
06R(051°T)	P3° (LH)	ALSF-2	Gr	TDZ HRL CLCD (15m) CZ EL	Full	0.08U
24L(231°T)					Full	0.08D

OTHER LIGHTING: Obstruction, taxiway, aerodrome beacon, stop bars, R/W guard lights, wind indicator.

TAXIWAY WIDTHS
B1,B3,B12 - 37m (121ft).
B14 - 33.5m (110ft).
P - 18m (59ft) (between A1 and Police hangar).
Others - 30m (98ft).
RUNWAY SURFACES
R/W 06L/24R: 3803.5x40m (12479x131ft) grooved.
R/W 06R/24L: 3300x40m (10827x131ft) grooved.
R/W 06L: First 96.5m (317ft) cement/concrete.
Others: First 100m (328ft) cement/ concrete.
RUNWAY AVAILABILITY
See E1 and E2 for intersection departures.

Rev: Taxiway widths.

1. Low Level Windshear Alert System (LLWAS).

06L/24R - 13124ft
06R/24L - 11483ft

Annual passengers: 15,937,314
Annual cargo: 154,710 tonnes
Annual aircraft movements: 128,628

Japan Railways West operates an express service to Shin-Oska and Kyoto, while the Nankai Railway runs to Namba Station.

Background

The airport was built as it became impossible to extend Osaka International at Itami or increase the number of aircraft movements, especially late in the day or at night. Kansai opened in 1994 on an artificial island created by land reclaimed from Osaka Bay. The choice of position was influenced by the experience of airport planners in Tokyo, and while it was originally proposed to build the new airport closer to Kobe, this had also drawn protests. The airport had to be able to withstand earthquakes and tidal waves, but during construction the reclaimed land settled

far more than had been foreseen, requiring further materials to be added. Nevertheless, the integrity of the construction was proved when, on 17 January 1995, the Kobe earthquake (with its epicentre just 20km, less than 13 miles, away from the airport), which killed almost 6,500 people on Honshu, left the airport almost untouched.

The heavy construction costs resulted in the airport having some of the highest landing fees in the world, and at first this discouraged many airlines, but a policy of discounting rates has allowed traffic to recover and it has shown strong growth in recent years. It is also the case that there is strong competition between many of the major international airports in Japan, and in the case of Kansai, this includes the new airport at Kobe.

Since opening, the airport has continued to expand, with the second runway opened in 2007, and plans are for a third runway and another terminal.

The airport includes a Japanese Maritime Self-Defence Force base.

NAHA: OKA

Naha, Okinawa, Japan

Owner and operator: Ministry of Land, Infrastructure and Transport
Runways: 18/36, 3,000m (9,843ft)
Terminals: Two, designated Main Terminal and International Terminal
Annual passengers: 14,950,970
Annual cargo: 244,631 tonnes
Annual aircraft movements: 123,596

Background

Not to be confused with the much smaller airport of the same name in Indonesia, Naha in Okinawa was established during the Second World War as a base for the Japanese Army Air Force. It was captured by the Americans during the fierce fighting of the Battle of Okinawa in April 1945, and subsequently became a base for the United States Army Air Force for heavy bombing raids on the Japanese Home Islands.

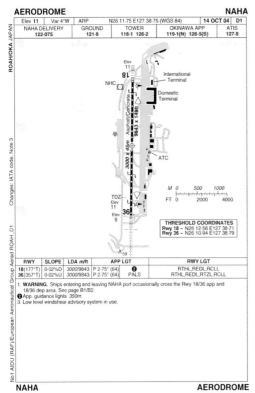

NAHA   AERODROME

flights to Taiwan, Hong Kong, and mainland China.

NAGOYA/CHŪBU CENTRAIR INTERNATIONAL AIRPORT: NGO

Nagoya, Japan

Owner and operator: Central Japan International Airport Co. Ltd, CJIAC

Runways: 18/36, 3,500m (11,483ft)

Terminals: One, usually referred to as the 'Main Terminal'

Annual passengers: 11,862,895

Annual cargo: 276,377 tonnes

Annual aircraft movements: 104,033

The airport is on the Nagoya Railroad's Meitetsu Airport Line, which runs to a city centre terminus alongside that for Japanese Railways. There are also high speed ferry links between the mainland and the airport.

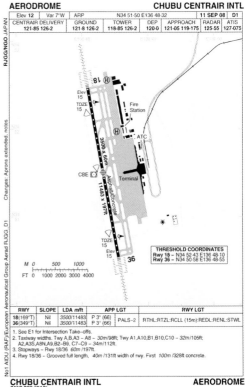

Post-war, Okinawa remained occupied by US forces for longer than the rest of Japan, and the based was not handed back to the Japanese until 31 May 1971. In 1979 it became a Japanese Air Self-Defence Force base and remains a joint military and civil base to this day, JASDF units have been joined by those of the Japanese Maritime Self-Defence Force, as well as the Coast Guard and police.

The airport has had one serious accident, but was also the emergency landing site for a Philippine Airlines Boeing 747-200 on which a bomb had exploded, killing a passenger, during its flight from Cebu to Tokyo. The one accident was on 20 August 2007, when a China Airlines Boeing 737-800 suffered an engine explosion shortly after landing, which gutted the aircraft, although all of the passengers and crew escaped to safety.

Civil operations at the airport are dominated by services to Japan, but there are international

Background

Variously known locally as 'Chūbu' or 'Centrair', the airport opened on 17 February 2005, and the existing Nagoya Airport was closed to scheduled air services and renamed Nagoya Airfield. It was built offshore in Ise Bay on reclaimed land, partly to overcome environmental objections and partly because industry demanded round-the-clock cargo flights. Construction took less than five years. The airport has been built in a 'D' shape to allow sea currents to flow properly, and benefits from experience at Nagasaki and Kansai. It brings Japan's total of offshore airports to five. Chūbu has relieved both Kobe Airport and New Kitakyūshū Airport of much of the pressure on their air cargo operations.

The terminal is being expanded with additional parking ramps for aircraft and this is due to be completed in 2010, and a second 4,000m (13,133ft) runway is also planned.

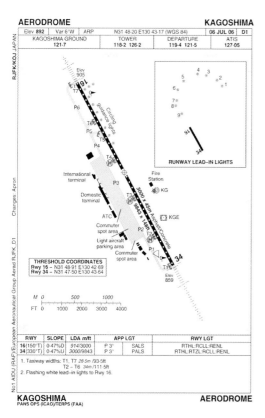

KAGOSHIMA: KOJ

Kirishima, Kagoshima, Japan

Owner and operator (airport): Ministry of Land, Infrastructure and Transport
Operator (terminal): Kagoshima Airport Building Co. Ltd
Runways: 16/34, 2,999m (9,840ft)
Terminals: One
Annual passengers: 5,591,176
Annual cargo: 48,805 tonnes

Background

Opened in 1944 as a military airfield for the Japanese Army Air Force, it was used post war by the USAF and did not open as a commercial airport until 1962.

JORDAN

While not one of the wealthy oil-producing states of the Middle East, Jordan has also suffered from the loss of a substantial area of its territory first to the Israelis and then to Palestinians. There is just one international airport.

AMMAN/QUEEN ALIA INTERNATIONAL: AMM

Zizya, Jordan

Owner and operator: Civil Aviation Authority of Jordan
Runways: 08L/26R, 3,660m (12,008ft); 08R/26L, 3,660m (12,008ft)
Terminals: Two
Airlines using airport as base or hub: Air Universal, Jordanian Aviation, Royal Jordanian Airlines, Sky Gate International
Annual passengers: 3,850,347
Annual cargo: 84,900 tonnes
Annual aircraft movements: 44,346

Background

Opened in 1983, the airport is 32km (20 miles) south of the Jordanian capital, Amman. It is

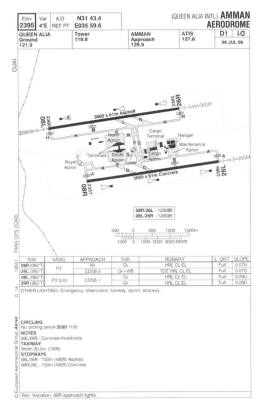

named after Queen Alia, killed in an air accident in 1977.

There are two passenger terminals and a cargo terminal. A consortium was assembled and in 2007 awarded responsibility for the renovation and modernisation of the airport for 25 years, with one of the first results being the opening of a new terminal in 2011. The consortium includes Aéroports de Paris Ingénierie, and Abu Dhabi and Jordanian interests.

Despite its location, the airport has suffered few terrorist incidents.

KAZAKHSTAN

ASTANA: TSE

Astana, Kazakhstan

Owner: Republic of Kazakhstan
Operator: Malaysia Airports Holdings Bhd

Runways: 04/22, 3,500m (11,484ft)
Terminals: Two, designated Domestic and International
Airlines using airport as base: Air Astana
Annual passengers: 1,170,919
Annual cargo: 4,677 tonnes

Background

The main airport for Kazakhstan, it is 14km (almost 9 miles) from the centre of the capital.

The first airfield for Astana was opened in 1931. The present airport was a Soviet-era creation which was completely rebuilt and opened in 2005. It is managed and developed by a Malaysian company. In recent years it has enjoyed very strong growth, which reached 40.4 per cent between 2006 and 2007.

KENYA

In common with many British colonies, after the Second World War air transport in Kenya was provided by an offshoot of the British Overseas Airways Corporation (BOAC), East African Airways Corporation (EAAC). East African had been formed in 1946 by BOAC and the colonial administrations of Kenya, Uganda, Tanganyika, and Zanzibar. At first the airline provided feeder services within East Africa for BOAC's trunk routes, but EAAC broke out of the regional role in 1957, when international services were started to London, Karachi, Aden, and Salisbury (now Harare). When, in 1977, the participating nations opted to disband the airline and establish their own national operations, only Kenya had the potential to do so.

The growth of tourism in Kenya has also seen the country establish a diverse air transport sector, mainly to tourist centres, which has meant that it is one of the few countries in Africa, outside of Egypt, Morocco, and South Africa, to have more than one major airport handling international flights.

NAIROBI/JOMO KENYATTA INTERNATIONAL: NBO

Embakasi, Nairobi, Kenya

Owner and operator: Kenya Airports Authority
Runways: 06/24, 4,117m (13,507ft)
Terminals: One
Airlines using airport as base or hub: Blue Bird
    Aviation, Kenya Airways
Annual passengers: 4,861,706
Annual cargo: 276,881 tonnes
Annual aircraft movements: 72,692

Background

The busiest airport in Central Africa, and named after the country's first prime minister and president, it is 15km (almost 10 miles) from the centre of Nairobi.

The airport opened in May 1958, and during the early 1970s the current terminal was opened, leaving the original terminal, on the other side

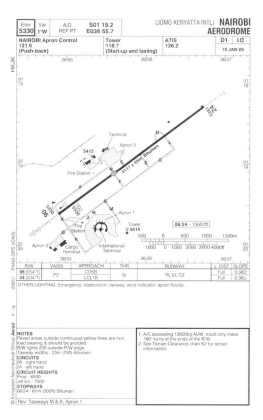

of the airport, to be used by the Kenya Air Force, which has a flying school at the airport.

Amongst the accidents at the airport, the worst involved a Lufthansa Boeing 747-100 on 20 November 1974, as the aircraft crashed on taking off for Johannesburg having earlier landed from Frankfurt, with the loss of 59 out of the total of 157 passengers and crew aboard the aircraft. A Canadair CL-44 freighter of Tradewinds Airways diverted to Nairobi on 6 July 1978 after its right main gear failed to lock-up after taking off from Mombasa for Kigali in Rwanda with a cargo of 20 tons of cement. The affected undercarriage leg collapsed on landing and the aircraft was damaged beyond repair, although all four crew survived. In May 1989 a Somali Airlines Boeing 707-320 overshot the runway and came to rest in a field, but all 70 people aboard survived. Much less fortunate were those aboard a Boeing 707-320 of Sudania Air Cargo which crashed on landing from Khartoum on 4 December 1990, killing all 10 of those aboard.

MOMBASA/MOI INTERNATIONAL AIRPORT: MBA

Port Reitz, Mombasa, Kenya

Owner and operator: Kenya Airports Authority
Runways: 03/21, 3,350m (10,991ft); 15/33,
    1,363m (4,473ft)
Terminals: One
Annual passengers: 1,345,786
Annual cargo: 9,296 tonnes

Background

Mombasa International is Kenya's second busiest airport after Nairobi and is named after a former president, Daniel Arap Moi.

The airport was built during the Second World War and opened in 1942 as Port Reitz Airport, or HMS *Kipanga*, as a shore station for the Royal Navy's Fleet Air Arm so that aircraft from ships of the British Eastern Fleet could be landed ashore while the aircraft carriers were in port at Kilindini Harbour. It was also used by the Royal Air Force and by the South African Air Force in operations against Italian forces in Abyssinia, today's Ethiopia.

While the airfield became a civil airport at the end of the war, it was not until 1979 that it became an international airport, with direct flights from Europe and the Middle East as Mombasa became an important tourist destination. The runways were extended between 1994 and 1995, and ILS equipment added to improve operations during poor weather.

There have been a number of accidents at or near to the airport. One of these was a Malawi Police Force Short Skyvan that ran out of fuel on 24 April 1986, and crash-landed 18km (just over 11 miles) short of the runway, using a road until it hit a tree, writing the aircraft off, but with all four occupants surviving. Such a lucky escape was not available to the six crew of an Air Memphis Boeing 707-320 that took off for Cairo with 34 tons of fish on 10 March 1998, but struck the runway lights and then hit a small hill before breaking up and catching fire. Terrorists attempted to shoot down a chartered Arkia Boeing 757 which had just taken off from Mombasa for Tel Aviv on 28 November 2002, using two SA-7 Strela surface-to-air guided missiles, but failed and the captain decided to continue his flight.

KOREA, SOUTH
(Republic of Korea)

Korea's own history of civil aviation is relatively short as it was a Japanese colony for many years, and after gaining independence after the Second World War, was soon embroiled in the Korean War. Nevertheless, since the mid-1950s it has become one of the rapid growing 'Tiger' economies of the Far East and its airports have been part of this, not least because of the tremendous volumes of air freight shipped through them. Most airports are owned by the state working through the Korea Airports Corporation.

SEOUL/INCHEON AIRPORT: ICN
Seoul, Republic of Korea

Owner: Republic of Korea (South Korea)
Operator: Incheon International Airport
   Corporation (IIAC)
Runways: 15L/33R, 3,750m (12,303ft);
   15R/33L, 3,750m (12,303ft); 16/34, 4,000m
   (13,123ft)
There is also a helipad
Terminals: One major passenger terminal
Airlines using airport as base or hub: Korean
   Air, Asiana
Annual passengers: 31,421,801
Annual cargo: 2,555,580 tonnes
Annual aircraft movements: 213,914

The Incheon International Airport Railroad, A'REX, opened on 23 March 2007, linking the airport with Gimpo Airport, where there is a connection to the Seoul Subway, and A'REX will

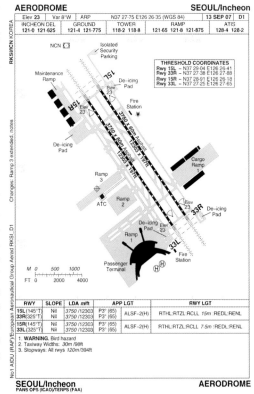

be extended into the centre of Seoul in 2010. The airport itself also has a commuter railway station and another one at the cargo terminal.

Background

The airport is west of Incheon, occupying the two islands of Yeongjong and Yongyu and land reclaimed from the sea that once lay between them. The airport is one of the most modern in the world, having been constructed after the Seoul Olympics of 1988 had shown the original airport at Gimpo to be inadequate for rapidly growing traffic, with South Korea also being amongst the world's fastest growing economies in the late 20th century and early 21st. Construction started in 1992 and took eight years, and after six months of trial operations, it opened in March 2001. Designed to be developed in a series of phases, the second phase was initiated in February 2002 and completed in 2008. No decision has been made on the third phase, although the fourth phase is due to be completed by 2020. The passenger terminal is claimed to be the fifth largest in the world, while there are three cargo terminals, designated A, B, and C.

Gimpo continues to handle both domestic and international traffic, and there are good road and railway connections between the two to ease transfers. To-date there have been no serious accidents at the airport.

SEOUL/GIMPO INTERNATIONAL: GMP

Seoul, Republic of Korea

Owner and operator: Korea Airports Corporation
Runways: 14L/32R, 3,600m (11,811ft);
    14R/32L, 3,200m (10,499ft)
Terminals: Two, designated Domestic and
    International
Airlines using airport as base or hub: Korean Air
Annual passengers: 13,811,294
Annual cargo: 186,622 tonnes
Annual aircraft movements: 112,199

Airport passenger terminal served by the Seoul Subway system's Line 5.

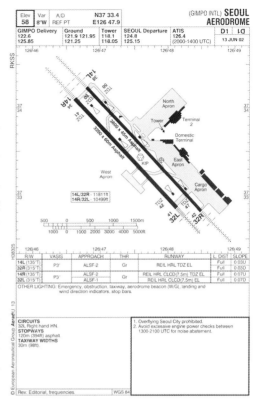

Background

Seoul Gimpo International had its origins as an airfield built by the Japanese, who had colonised Korea early in the 20th century, and opened in 1939 during the period of the Sino-Japanese War. After the Second World War it was taken over by the Allies, and as Korea had only limited air power, mainly for training purposes, it was used by the Allies during the Korean War. It was not until 1958 that it reverted to civilian use and became the main airport for Seoul, named Gimpo after a nearby community. Rapid growth in the years that followed saw it expand until at one time it had a domestic terminal and two international terminals, but the Seoul Olympics of 1988 showed that the airport was already heavily congested and a new airport, Seoul Incheon International, was opened in 2001, relieving Gimpo of much of its international traffic. A railway connection to the airport was withdrawn, but during the

1990s the Seoul Subway Line 5 was extended to the airport.

There have been no serious air accidents at the airport at the time of writing, but no fewer than four aircraft either bound for Seoul or flying from it have met with en route problems, including one being shot down by a Soviet fighter.

Today the airport has two terminals, one for domestic traffic and the other for the remaining international traffic, as well as a cargo terminal.

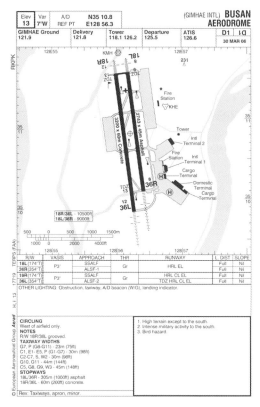

JEJU (CHEJU): CJU
Jeju City, Republic of Korea

Owner and operator: Korea Airports
  Corporation
Runways: 06/24, 3,000m (9,843ft); 13/31,
  1,910m (6,268ft)
Terminals: One, with international and domestic
  gates
Annual passengers: 12,297,159
Annual cargo: 223,057 tonnes
Annual aircraft movements: 93,285

Background
Opened in 1968, Jeju is now the third most important airport in the Republic of Korea (South Korea), and serves the city of the same name, formerly known as Cheju. The fact that the area is an island may well account for the heavy traffic.

BUSAN (PUSAN)/GIMHAE INTERNATIONAL: PUS
Busan, South Korea

Owner and operator: Korea Airports Corporation
Runways: 18L/36R, 2,745m (9,007ft); 18R/36L,
  3,200m (10,499ft)
Terminals: Two, designated International and
  Domestic
Airlines using airport as base or hub: Korean Air
Annual passengers: 7,410,502
Annual cargo: 74,946 tonnes
Annual aircraft movements: 63,776

The Busan-Gimhae light rapid transit line opens in 2010 and will link into the Busan subway system.

Background
The airport opened in 1976 as Kimhae International Airport and is now Gimhae International Airport, reflecting local name changes, while Busan itself was known earlier as Pusan, hence the designation PUS. For most of its existence it has managed with one terminal, but international flights have been moved to a new terminal that opened in late 2007.

Alone amongst major airports in South Korea, there have been two serious accidents at Busan. The first of these was on 15 April 2002 when an Air China Boeing 767-200ER, approaching from Beijing in bad weather, crashed into a hill, killing 128 of the 166 passengers and crew. The second was on 12 August 2007, when a Jeju Air Bombardier Dash 8 Q400 skidded off the runway, damaging the aircraft and injuring six of its occupants.

KOSOVO

PRISTINA INTERNATIONAL: PRN
Slatina, Pristina, Kosovo (former Republic of Yugoslavia)

Owner and operator: Pristina International
    Airport J.S.C.
Runways: 17/35, 2,510m (8,210ft)
Terminals: One
Annual passengers: 1,093,812
Annual cargo: 17,614 tonnes

Background
Pristina International is 16km (10 miles) outside the capital of Kosovo and is shared with Slatina Air Base.

The airport was opened in 1965, but for several years only handled flights to and from Belgrade, the then federal capital of Yugoslavia. It was not until the 1990s that it was served from Germany and Switzerland. Operations ceased during the war in Kosovo, at the end of which, in June 1999, there was confrontation between Russian troops and those deployed by the North Atlantic Treaty Organisation (NATO) under United Nations auspices. After the two groups agreed to cooperate, the airport reopened on 15 October 1999 as a military airport, largely to keep the UN forces supplied, but the restoration of civilian flights within the former Yugoslavia and beyond was also encouraged. The apron and passenger terminal were renovated and opened in 2002, and traffic soon approached the million passengers mark. The terminal and aprons have since been further overhauled and expanded, and control is now back with the government of Kosovo, which manages the airport through a state-owned company, Pristina International Airport.

KUWAIT

A small but prosperous oil-producing state on a pivotal position on routes between the East and Europe, air transport in Kuwait has suffered mixed fortunes due to the aggressive posture adopted towards it by Iraq. A threatened invasion during the early 1960s was prevented by prompt action by British forces, but the country was overrun by Iraq in August 1990, and the airport was stripped of much of its equipment. It took some years after the small country recovered its independence before operations could return to normal.

KUWAIT INTERNATIONAL: KWI
Kuwait City, Kuwait

Owner and operator: Directorate General of Civil
    Aviation.
Runways: 15L/33R, 3,500m (11,483ft);
    15R/33L, 3,400m (11,155ft)
Terminals: One, but a second (to be designated
    Terminal 2) opens in 2010
Airlines using airport as base or hub: Jazeera
    Airways, Kuwait Airways
Annual passengers: 6,956,550
Annual cargo: 177,413 tonnes
Annual aircraft movements: 83,561

Background
Situated some 16km (10 miles) south of Kuwait City, the airport has a dual civil and military role as part of it is occupied by Al Mubarak Air Base and the headquarters of the Kuwait Air Force.

Kuwait's first airport was on the outskirts of Kuwait City at Dasma, which opened in 1927 and was used by aircraft of Imperial Airways on the long route from London Croydon to India. The airport's own first commercial flights followed in 1932, and in 1934 the discovery of oil brought prosperity and the need to transport foreign workers, making air transport more important. It was decided that a new airport was necessary, but planning was abandoned on the outbreak of the Second World War in Europe in September 1939. After the war a new airport was

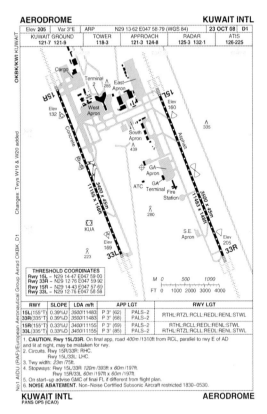

during their seven month occupation the airport was looted of anything that could be useful, and much of its infrastructure was damaged. Kuwait was liberated on 26 February 1991, and on 2 March the airport opened for limited operations, becoming fully operational again by December. A new departure hall was added to the main terminal in 2003, and a second terminal opens in 2010.

LATVIA

RIGA INTERNATIONAL: RIX
Riga, Latvia

Owner and operator: Republic of Latvia
Runways: 18/36, 3,200m (10,500ft)
Terminals: One, but with areas designated as A, B, and C, with B handling the Schengen area passengers
Airlines using airport as base or hub: airBaltic, LatCharter, RAF-Avia
Annual passengers: 3,160,945
Annual cargo: 8,130 tonnes
Annual aircraft movements: 47,347

Background
The busiest airport in the Baltic States, Riga International is 13km (8 miles) south-west of the capital city. It was opened in 1973 when the previous airport, Spilve, had become congested and was too small for modern aircraft. After Latvia broke free from the Soviet Union in 1990, a programme of modernisation began and this was completed in 2001, with an extension to the terminals opened in 2006. Future plans are for a completely new terminal. Although state-owned, the airport is structured as a company, which could ease the way for private investment in the future.

There was one serious accident at Riga on 13 August 1961 when an Aeroflot Ilyushin Il-18 landed from Moscow in thick fog, but overshot the runway and crashed. Details of the numbers aboard the aircraft or of casualties are not available.

opened in 1947 at Al-Nugra near Nuzha, but for daylight flying only at first. As air traffic grew, new buildings and hangars were erected.

It was not until 1954 that a new national airline was established for Kuwait (Kuwait National Airways) although the name was changed to Kuwait Airways the following year when the government took a half share in the airline. Kuwait became independent in 1961 and operations started that year at a new airport at Mugwa, served by BOAC (British Overseas Airways Corporation), Lufthansa, KLM Royal Dutch Airlines, United Arab Airlines, Air India, and several Lebanese carriers. The second phase of Mugwa's development followed in 1965 with a new runway and air traffic control tower. A new passenger terminal and a cargo terminal followed in 1980, while in 1986 a new runway and a new air traffic control tower opened.

This steady progress was rudely interrupted in 1990 when Iraqi forces invaded Kuwait, and

LEBANON

BEIRUT RAFIC HARIRI INTERNATIONAL: BEY

Khalde, Beirut, Lebanon

Owner and operator: Middle East Airports
  Services
Runways: 03/21, 3,800m (12,467ft); 16/34,
  3,395m (11,138ft); 17/35, 3,250m (10,663ft)
Terminals: One
Airlines using airport as base or hub: MEA
  (Middle East Airlines), MenaJet
Annual passengers: 3,408,834
Annual cargo: 63,845 tonnes
Annual aircraft movements: 49,964

Background

Probably the most famous and troubled airport
in the world over the past half century, Beirut
International is 9km (about 5 miles) from the
city centre and is the Lebanon's only commercial airport.

The airport opened in the years following
Lebanese independence on 23 April 1954, when
it replaced the former airport for Beirut, Bir
Hassan, which could no longer handle the
growth in traffic volumes. At the start it had a
modern terminal and two runways. During the
1950s and 1960s it grew to become the major hub
for the Middle East as Lebanon prospered and
became an important business and tourist centre.
It had several airlines based at the airport,
including MEA (Middle East Airlines) and Air
Liban, which later merged, the cargo airline
Trans Mediterranean Airways (TMA), and
Lebanese International Airways. This steady
progress was arrested on the night of 28/29
December 1968 when Israeli commandos
mounted an attack in retaliation for an attack on
an El Al airliner at Athens. Thirteen Lebanese
airliners were destroyed, and the resulting loss
of traffic saw Lebanese International collapse,
although MEA recovered in the years that
followed.

A further blow followed in 1975 when a civil
war started in the Lebanon, which continued for
15 years. Both MEA and TMA managed to continue operations for most of this time, but the
airport was largely avoided by foreign airlines.
In the midst of the conflict, the terminal was
modernised in 1977, only to be almost destroyed
in 1982 when Israeli forces invaded Lebanon and
the terminal was shelled. A barracks was built on
part of the airport, and used by US servicemen,
but this was bombed by terrorists in 1983 with
the loss of 241 lives. Meanwhile, the runways
had been upgraded in 1982 and 1984.

The civil war ended in 1990, leaving the airport badly damaged and outdated, and in 1994 a
ten-year reconstruction programme started,
including the building of a new terminal and two
new runways, as well as other facilities, such as
a general aviation terminal. The first phase of
the new terminal was opened in 1998 and the old
terminal demolished. The remainder of the terminal was completed in 2000, but not opened
until 2002. It was renamed Beirut Rafik Hariri
International Airport in June 2005 in memory of
an assassinated former prime minister.

Once again, recovery was doomed. Hezbol-
lah terrorists were using the country as a base
and this led to war with Israel in 2006. On 13
July, all three runways were damaged by Israeli
air-to-ground missiles, but after the attack MEA
managed to evacuate four Airbus A321s and an
A330 using a taxiway for take-off. The airport
reopened on 17 August, and while limited air
services resumed, mainly by MEA and Royal
Jordanian, Israel maintained an air blockade
until 7 September. After it was lifted, other airlines returned over the following few days. It
was not until June 2007 that the United States
lifted a ban on air traffic between the USA and
Lebanon that had been in force since the hijacking of a TWA flight in 1985.

Since then, the airport has been closed once
again, albeit briefly, due to unrest. Plans are
already in hand to restore the airport and
develop its facilities, including a new air cargo
terminal.

LITHUANIA

VILNIUS INTERNATIONAL: VNO

Vilnius, Lithuania

Owner and operator: Vilnius International Airport
Runways: 02/20, 2,515m (8,251ft)
Terminals: One
Airlines using airport as base or hub: FlyLal,
Aurela
Annual passengers: 1,717,222
Annual cargo: 5,780 tonnes

The airport has its own railway station with a
direct service to the centre of the city.

Background

The largest of the four civil airports in Lithuania, Vilnius International is just 7km (less than
4½ miles) from the city centre.

The airport was built as a military base by the
Soviet Union and opened in 1944. Passenger
flights started after the Second World War and a
passenger terminal was opened in 1954. After
the break-up of the Soviet Union, management
and development of the airport was given to a
new state-owned concern, Vilnius International
Airport. Unusually, the carrier with the largest
share of the market is airBaltic, from Estonia.
The original 1950s Soviet-era arrival building
has been joined by a new terminal, opened in
November 2007, which segregates Schengen and
non-Schengen passengers.

There has been one serious accident at the airport in recent years. On 12 September 2007, an
SAS (Scandinavian Airlines System) Bombardier Dash 8 Q400 en route from Copenhagen
to Palanga in Lithuania was diverted to Vilnius
when undercarriage problems were detected by
the pilots. On landing, the right main undercarriage leg collapsed. All 4 crew and 48 passengers
were unharmed. Later, SAS grounded all aircraft of this type, and then disposed of them.

LUXEMBOURG

LUXEMBOURG/FINDEL INTERNATIONAL: LUX

Sandweiler, Luxembourg

Owner and operator: Lux-Airport: Société de
l'Aéroport de Luxembourg SA
Runways: 06/24, 4,000m (13,123ft)
Terminals: Two, both international
Airlines using airport as base or hub: Cargolux,
Luxair
Annual passengers: 1,642,848
Annual cargo: 856,741 tonnes
Annual aircraft movements: 82,060

Background

Opened after the Second World War, the airport
is 6km (almost 4 miles) from Luxembourg City.
It is the only international airport in the Grand
Duchy.

The airport was used by Luxembourg Airlines from 1948, a company supported by a
British company, Scottish Airways, and then by
Seaboard World Airlines of the United States.
The present national airline, Luxair, was
founded in 1962 and is today the main operator,
although the airport also handles a substantial
volume of cargo and is the main base for Cargolux, the all-cargo airline. It has been modernised and expanded over the years, but
development is inhibited by the small size of the
country and the ease with which passengers can
reach airports in Germany and France.

MALAYSIA

KUALA LUMPUR INTERNATIONAL: KUL

Subang, Kuala Lumpur, Malaysia

Owner and Operator: Malaysian Airports
Runways: 14L/32R, 4,124m (13,530ft);
14R/32L, 4,056m (13,288ft)
Terminals: One main terminal, with a satellite
terminal A and a low-cost carrier terminal

Airlines using airport as base or hub: AirAsia,
   Malaysian Airlines

Annual passengers: 26,453,379

Annual cargo: 652,895 tonnes

Annual aircraft movements: 193,688

The KLIA Express provides a non-stop link with
the KL City Centre Air Terminal, and the KLIA
Transit provides a commuter-standard service on
the same route with intermediate stops. The KL
City Centre Air Terminus has passenger and
baggage check-in facilities for a small number
of airlines.

Background

The present Kuala Lumpur International was
built to replace Subang, the original airport for
Kuala Lumpur, because it was decided that
Subang could not handle projected traffic
growth. One consideration was that Malaysia
was due to host the 1998 Commonwealth
Games, so an influx of visitors was expected.
The decision was controversial because of the
new airport's distance from the city centre, more
than 51km (some 32 miles), and because many
also believed that the then existing airport still
had room for expansion. This latter concern was
underlined by continued work on improvements
at Subang even while the new airport was being
built, with Terminal 3 opened in 1993 and Terminal 2 reopening after refurbishment in 1995.

The new airport was opened on 27 June 1998,
although flights were not transferred until 30
June, when Subang was renamed as Sultan
Abdul Aziz Shah Airport to avoid confusion.

Traffic has not always grown as expected
with the Asian economic crisis, the SARs and
Bird Flu scares, and more recently the rapid rise
in the price of fuel and a worldwide economic
downturn. Nevertheless, the airport is planned
to continue developing until 2020, with an additional terminal and eventually capacity for up to
130 million passengers annually, almost five
times the number for 2007. In the meantime, it
has followed many other airports by having a
special terminal for low-cost carriers and their
passengers.

There have been a couple of minor accidents
at Kuala Lumpur in recent years. A Saudi Arabian Airlines Boeing 747 slipped into a drainage
ditch as it taxied from the hangar to the terminal
for a return flight to Saudi Arabia in 2001, but
none of the six crew aboard at the time was hurt.
On 14 July 2007 an airbridge suddenly moved
downwards damaging the door of a Malaysia
Airlines Airbus A330 ready to depart for Beijing,
but no one on the aircraft was injured and there
was no one on the airbridge at the time.

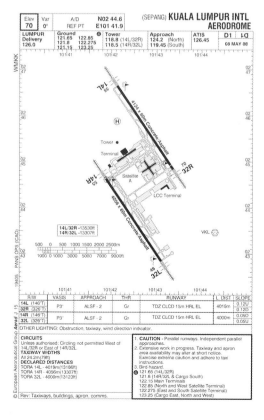

KOTA KINABALU INTERNATIONAL: BKI

Kota Kinabalu, Sabah, Malaysia

Owner and operator: Malaysia Airport Holdings
   Berhad

Runways: 02/20, 3,780m (12,402ft)

Terminals: Two, designated Terminal 1 and
   Terminal 2

Airlines using airport as base or hub: AirAsia
Annual passengers: 4,536,835
Annual cargo: 39,682 tonnes
Annual aircraft movements: 52,047

Background

The main airport for Sabah and also serving Borneo, Kota Kinabalu is the second busiest airport in Malaysia and is 8km (5 miles) south-west of the city centre.

Originally built for the Japanese Army Air Force during the Second World War, it was heavily bombed by Allied forces until the surrender of Japan in 1945. It was known post war by the Allies as Jesselton Airfield, Jesselton being the name for Kota Kinabalu during the colonial era. After the war it was used as a civil airport, but it was not until 1957 that a new terminal and hard runway were completed. The runway was extended in 1959 for Malayan Airways Vickers Viscount turboprop airliners, and

then again in 1963 for de Havilland Comet 4 jet airliners. An unusual incident occurred on 18 September 1993 when a 13.5 square metre area of subsidence occurred at the edge of the runway, which had to be closed for more than an hour. A larger terminal building was opened during the 1970s, and in the years that followed the runway was extended again for Boeing 747 operations. The original terminal was known as the 'old airport'. In 2006 both terminals were enlarged, and in 2007 the original terminal became Terminal 2 while the more modern became Terminal 1. The older building is being used increasingly for low-cost carriers. During 2009 a further runway extension was opened. AirAsia is making the airport its main hub for flights between Malaysia and China, as the airport is the closest Malaysian airport to mainland China.

One of the first accidents at the airport was on 16 November 1991 when three policemen flying in a Royal Malaysian Police Pilatus Porter died when the aircraft crashed at the airport. An AirAsia Boeing 737 skidded while landing on 8 November 2004, and of the 5 crew and 111 passengers, 3 passengers were slightly injured evacuating the aircraft.

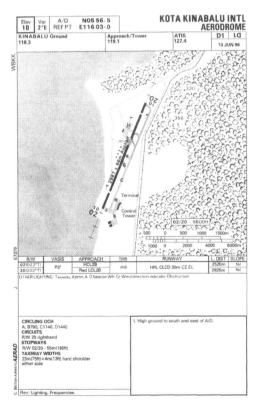

KUCHING INTERNATIONAL: KCH

Kuching, Sarawak, Malaysia

Owner and operator: Malaysia Airports Holdings Berhad
Runways: 07/25, 3,780m (12,402ft)
Terminals: One
Airlines using airport as base or hub: AirAsia, MAS Malaysian Airlines
Annual passengers: 3,236,468
Annual cargo: 26,955 tonnes

Background

The main airport for Sarawak, it is 11km (almost 7 miles) south of Kuching and is a base for the Royal Malaysian Air Force.

The airport was built by the British while Sarawak was still a colony in the years after the Second World War, opening on 26 September

1950. From the start it had the necessary requirements for a passenger airport, including terminal, hard runway, direction-finding equipment, and radio. It soon became the airport for not just Sarawak but also for Brunei and North Borneo, although air services were sparse to begin with and consisted simply of a weekly Douglas DC-3 flight to Singapore. Nevertheless, within a few years, traffic grew significantly and in 1959 the runway was extended to allow Vickers Viscount turboprop aircraft to use the airport. It was extended again in 1962 so that de Havilland Comet 4 jet airliners could be handled, and the terminal was extended at the same time.

Sarawak became part of the Federation of Malaysia in November 1963. In 1971, the federal government started to prepare a master plan for the airport's development, one result of which was the extension of the runway, and this was completed in 1976. In 1983 a new terminal complex on the north side of the airport was opened. The runway was strengthened in 1982 to handle Airbus A300 aircraft.

In addition to a couple of bomb hoaxes in 2006, there have been a small number of accidents at Kuching in recent years. One of these involved a Royal Malaysian Air Force de Havilland Canada DHC-4 Caribou transport on a training flight in 1999, which crashed at the end of the runway killing all five personnel on board. In February 2006 a Malaysia Airlines Airbus A330 slipped off the runway while taxiing before take-off, but there were no casualties. Nevertheless, the accident closed the airport for some hours. On 13 January 2007 a Boeing 737-200 of Gading Sari Aviation crash-landed, badly damaging the fuselage and undercarriage while the right engine was torn off. The accident closed the airport for six hours, but the four crew were unhurt.

Traffic growth has remained strong and the early years of the present century saw further improvements, with a new terminal opened in 2006 and the runway extended in 2008. The airport is now able to handle any aircraft, up to and including the Airbus A380.

PENANG INTERNATIONAL: PEN
Bayan Lepas, Penang, Malaysia

Owner and operator: Malaysia Airports Holdings Berhad
Runways: 04/22, 3,352m (10,997ft)
Terminals: One, but a basic budget or 'community' terminal may be added
Airlines using airport as base or hub: AirAsia, Firefly
Annual passengers: 3,174,195
Annual cargo: 208,584 tonnes
Annual aircraft movements: 39,265

Background
Originally known as Bayan Lepas International Airport, after the locality, the airport is 16km (10 miles) south of Georgetown, Penang's capital city. It has a new passenger terminal, and a cargo terminal was completed in 2000. It has become a hub for the Malaysian Airways' low-cost subsidiary, Firefly, and is a major route point for AirAsia.

The sole incident at Penang occurred on 9 January 2000 when a Korean Air Boeing 747-200F, on a cargo flight from Seoul, lost a section of flap on its approach, with the flap tearing a metre-wide hole in the fuselage. The aircraft landed safely, and the crew of three were unharmed, but it was grounded following the accident.

MIRI: MYY
Miri, Sarawak, Malaysia

Owner and operator: Malaysia Airports Holdings Berhad
Runways: 02/20, 2,745m (9,006ft)
Terminals: One
Airlines using airport as base or hub: MASWings
Annual passengers: 1,454,167
Annual cargo: 5,370 tonnes

Background
The airport not only serves the town of Miri, but is the main gateway for the state of Sarawak and

is a hub for rural air services. These were formerly provided by FlyAsianXpress, but are now operated by MASWings. The airport is close to the border with Brunei. It dates from the period of British colonial rule but has been extensively modernised.

There have been a couple of accidents near Miri in the past 20 years. One of these was on 30 July 1993 when a Short Skyvan of Hornbill Skyways had to make an emergency landing in the jungle some 13km (just over 8 miles) from the airport, with one of the 15 passengers being killed. On 6 September 1997 a Dornier 228-212 of Merpati, the Indonesian Airline, operating a service for Royal Brunei from Bandar Seri Beggawan, crashed into a hill some 14km (almost 9 miles) from Miri, killing the crew of 2 and all 8 passengers.

JOHOR BAHRU/SENAI INTERNATIONAL/SULTAN ISMAIL INTERNATIONAL: JHB
Senai, Johor Bahru, Malaysia

Owner: Malaysian Airports
Operator: Senai Airport Terminal Services Sdn Bhd
Runways: 16/34, 3,354m (11,004ft)
Terminals: One
Airlines using airport as base or hub: Air Asia, Firefly
Annual passengers: 1,324,952
Annual cargo: 5,508 tonnes

Background
The main airport for both Johor and the surrounding southern states in the Malaysian peninsula, it is known officially as Sultan Ismail International Airport, but more usually locally as Senai or Johor Bahru.

The airport opened in 1974, its construction prompted by the tendency of travellers to use Singapore Airport as more convenient than Kuala Lumpur. It has failed to make the most of its potential, largely due to the limited number of destinations served, and in recent years has attempted to attract passengers from Singapore.

Moves to stimulate passenger growth have been limited by the airport being dropped from the Malaysian Airlines network during a period of retrenchment, but is served by the low-cost carriers Air Asia and Firefly. In 2003 it became the first airport in Malaysia to be managed by a private concern, Senai Airport Terminal Services. Plans exist to lengthen the runway, build a parallel taxiway to increase the number of aircraft movements, and develop a major air cargo terminal.

LANGKAWI INTERNATIONAL: LGK
Langkawi, Kedah, Malaysia

Owner and operator: Malaysia Airports Holdings Berhad
Runways: 03/21, 3,810m (12,500ft)
Terminals: One
Annual passengers: 1,122,911

Background
This modern airport is on the island of Langkawi, a duty-free zone which also hosts the Langkawi International Maritime and Aerospace Exhibition (LIMA) which was responsible for the one serious accident at the airport, when in December 2007 three paratroopers were killed when their parachutes didn't open. It handles both domestic and international flights.

MALDIVES

MALÉ INTERNATIONAL: MLE
Hulhulé Island, Maldive Islands

Owner and operator: Maldives Airports Company
Runways: 18/36, 3,200m (10,499ft); there is also a base for seaplanes adjacent to the airport
Terminals: One
Airlines using airport as base or hub: Air Maldives, Trans Maldivian
Annual passengers: 2,591,094
Annual cargo: 37,089 tonnes
Annual aircraft movements: 88,308

Background

Sometimes still referred to by its old name of Hulhulé Airport, after the island on which it stands, Malé is the main international airport for the Maldives, although Gan, predominantly used over the years as a technical stop for both the RAF and USAF, has now been upgraded to international standards, but has still to receive regular services.

The airport dates from 12 April 1966 and adopted its current name in November 1981. The terminal, used predominantly by international flights (although there are local feeder services to the other islands in the atoll), is recent, while there are plans for a second runway and extra space will be obtained by reclaiming land from the sea and joining Hulhulé Island to Hulhumalé Island. Non-connecting domestic flights can now use a small airport and there is also a seaplane station adjacent to Malé International.

There have been a number of accidents in recent years. On 18 October 1995 an Air Maldives Dornier 228 left the runway and struck a seawall before ending up in a lagoon while landing, damaging the aircraft beyond repair, although there are no reports of fatalities. A Hummingbird Helicopters Mil Mi-8 lost control after taking-off due to the loss of hydraulic pressure, with four of the occupants slightly injured. Another collision with the seawall occurred on 17 May 2004 when a Trans Maldivian Airways de Havilland Canada Twin Otter floatplane attempted to take off, with both pilots and 1 of the 18 passengers seriously injured and the aircraft destroyed. A Maldivian Dornier 228 with 13 passengers taking-off for Hanimaadhoo experienced undercarriage problems soon afterwards and returned to Malé safely without further incident.

MALTA

Situated in the middle of the Mediterranean and almost halfway between Gibraltar and Suez, and also roughly halfway between Sicily and Libya, Malta has long had an important strategic role. It was initially served by flying boat services from first France and then direct from the United Kingdom, and before the Second World War Imperial Airways had identified Ta'Kali as a future civil airport, but this became a Royal Air Force fighter station during the war and remained as a military airfield afterwards. The civil airport used another RAF station at Luqa. At one time the RAF had three bases on the island, plus an emergency landing strip between Luqa and Hal Far at Safi.

LUQA/MALTA INTERNATIONAL: MLA
Luqa, Malta GC

Owner and operator: Malta International Airport plc
Runways: 06/24, 2,377m (7,799ft); 14/32, 3,544m (11,627ft)
Terminals: One
Airlines using airport as base or hub: Air Malta
Annual passengers: 2,980,257
Annual cargo: 18,052 tonnes

Background

Malta's only airport and serving all three populated islands, Luqa was originally a Royal Air Force station built before the Second World War. At that time, Imperial Airways was planning to build a new airport for civil use at Ta'Kali, which became a wartime fighter station and remained as such for many years after the war before closing. After the war, Luqa continued as an RAF base, occupied by maritime-reconnaissance and bomber squadrons, but also became the island's civil airport, initially using converted Nissan huts as terminals. A new purpose-built terminal opened in 1957 and was used by scheduled services, mainly provided by BEA (British European Airways), which also oper-

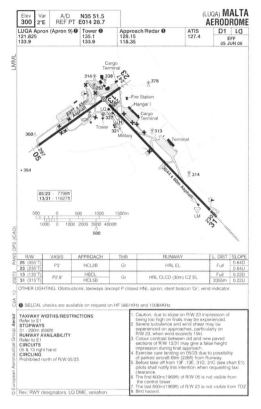

ated as the Malta Airlines, and charter flights, mainly for British servicemen and their families.

Because of its use for many years as a Royal Air Force base, and in addition to having maritime-reconnaissance and bomber aircraft stationed there, it was also an important staging post for transport aircraft en route to the Middle East and India.

Luqa has had a number of accidents and incidents since the Second World War, and there have also been instances of aircraft hijackings. On 17 May 1953 an RAF Vickers Valetta (the military version of the Viking airliner) suffered jammed ailerons shortly after taking off, landed back on the grass next to the runway and then hit the runway caravan before bursting into flames, with the death of 2 crew and 22 others aboard the aircraft. Another Vickers Valetta, which took off on 16 December 1953, had problems with the propeller of its No. 2 engine, and while the pilots tried to return to the airport, the

aircraft crashed just outside and was burnt out with the loss of one of the five people aboard.

Not all of the accidents involved military aircraft, as 'trooping by air' became the standard for Britain's armed forces and it was common for aircraft to be chartered from commercial airlines. On 13 April 1954, an Avro York of Scottish Airlines had difficulty starting one of the four engines because of starter-motor failure, so the captain tried windmilling the propeller during a high speed taxi in the hope of starting it, which worked, but he couldn't stop the aircraft on the runway, which it overran and was damaged beyond repair, albeit without any fatalities. In an attempt to avoid overshooting the runway on landing on 20 May 1958, the captain of a Dan-Air York retracted the undercarriage, but the aircraft struck a wall and was written off, but without any fatalities. Before this, the worst accident at Luqa occurred on 18 February 1956, when another Scottish Airlines York, taking off on a military charter to London, suffered an engine fire as it climbed out, but the propeller was not feathered and the aircraft started to yaw, before stalling and diving to the ground with the loss of all 5 crew and 45 passengers.

Engine fires were an all too common weakness with piston-engined aircraft, and the arrival of the turboprop and later the jet marked a reduction in such events, and a step change in reliability. In any case, engine problems were just one aspect of aircraft safety. On 5 January 1960, a Vickers Viscount 700 of BEA (British European Airways) landed from London and suffered a hydraulic failure while taxiing, losing nosewheel steering and wheel brakes. The pilots tried to raise the undercarriage, but this was also inoperative, and the aircraft eventually ran out of control until it was finally stopped by the control tower. Fortunately, all 5 crew and 46 passengers survived.

Before the terrorist attacks on New York and Washington on 11 September 2001, one of the worst hijackings for loss of life occurred on 24 November 1985, when an Egyptair Boeing 737-200 was seized while flying from Athens to Cairo, with the hijackers demanding to be taken to Libya or Tunisia. The aircraft landed at Luqa to refuel, during which time 2 wounded cabin attendants and 11 women were released. The request for fuel was refused and negotiations followed, lasting for 22 hours before the hijackers then shot one of their hostages and threatened to shoot another every five minutes unless the aircraft was refuelled and released. After five hostages had been killed, it was stormed by Egyptian security forces, and in the fighting that ensued, further deaths followed, and out of 98 passengers and crew, 60 died.

After independence, the British presence was run down and Malta's own armed forces used the former Royal Naval Air Station at Hal Far as a base, while Luqa also became the base for Malta's own airline, Air Malta. The runways were lengthened and a major redevelopment programme culminated in 1992 with the opening of a new terminal, while the former terminal, which had been extended, was converted as a cargo terminal. At one stage, a helicopter service linked the airport with the second Maltese island of Gozo, using Mil Mi-8 helicopters.

The airport also hosts the annual Malta Air Show, visited by military and civil aircraft each summer.

MAURITIUS

PLAINE MAGNIEN/SIR SEEWOOSAGUR RAMGOOLAM INTERNATIONAL: MRU

Plaine Magnien, Plaisance, Mauritius

Owner and operator: Airports of Mauritius
    Company
Runways: 14/32, 3,370m (11,056ft)
Terminals: One
Airlines using airport as base or hub: Air
    Mauritius
Annual passengers: 2,562,830

Background
The main international airport for the island republic of Mauritius, it is 48km (30 miles) from Port Louis, the capital.

It was originally known as Plaisance Airport, after the locality, and was first built in 1945, when it was used mainly as a Royal Air Force station. The current name was adopted in 1987. It has been upgraded extensively on several occasions since opened and can accommodate wide-bodied aircraft, but still has a simple single-storey terminal. It is the home base for Air Mauritius.

The one serious accident at the airport in the past half-century was to a Qantas Lockheed Super Constellation taking-off for the Cocos Islands on 24 August 1960. Its No. 3 engine lost power just before the nose wheel lifted and efforts to stop the aircraft using reverse pitch were unsuccessful. It overshot the runway, dived into a gulley and caught fire. The aircraft was destroyed, but the 12 crew and 38 passengers survived.

MEXICO

The past 30 years have seen a substantial number of new airlines started in Mexico, including the country's first low-cost carrier, while more recently free trade with the United States and Canada has fuelled the expansion of air transport in Mexico and made Mexican airports much busier.

MEXICO CITY/BENITO JUÁREZ INTERNATIONAL: MEX

Mexico City, Mexico

Owner and operator: Grupo Aeroportuario de la
    Ciudad de México
Runways: 05L/23R, 3,952m (12,966ft);
    05R/23L, 3,900m (12,795ft)
Terminals: Two, numbered 1 and 2
Airlines using airport as base or hub: Aeronaves
    de Mexico, Click Mexicana, Mexicana
Annual passengers: 25,881,662
Annual cargo: 411,383 tonnes
Annual aircraft movements: 378,161

There is a Metro station immediately outside Terminal 1.

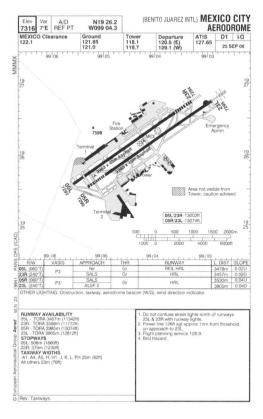

Background

The busiest airport in Latin America, it was named after a 19th-century president in 2006. The airport is 'hot and high' at 2,230m (7,316ft) above sea level, which places range or payload restrictions on departing flights, but despite this the growth in tourism and business travel has meant that there are flights to more than a hundred destinations across the globe.

In common with many older airports, there are severe constraints on growth, hence it suffers considerable congestion, and some estimate that current passenger numbers could be as much as 60 per cent higher were it not for the restrictions imposed by having just two runways. Pressure has been constant for more than 50 years, with Terminal 1 (opened in 1958) enlarged in 1970, 1989, 1998, 2000, and again in 2004. Terminal 2 (only completed in 2001) was torn down and replaced by a new Terminal 2 in 2007, with an internal monorail system linking the two.

There have been a number of accidents at the airport, many of them serious. One of these was on 21 September 1969, when a Mexicana Boeing 727 was approaching from Chicago, bounced some 1,500m (4,925ft) from the runway, and then hit a railway embankment. 5 out of 7 crew and 22 out of 111 passengers were killed. On 16 August 1976 an Avianca Boeing 720 was landing in a heavy rainstorm. It touched down, lifted off, and then landed on the nosewheel, wrecking the aircraft, but there appear to have been no fatalities. Another very serious accident occurred on 31 October 1979, when a Western Airlines McDonnell Douglas DC-10 landed on the wrong runway and ran into construction vehicles. In the resulting accident 78 people died out of 88 aboard the aircraft, including one on the ground. A Douglas DC-8-43F cargo aircraft of Aeronaves del Peru crashed into a mountain while descending towards the airport on 1 August 1980, killing all three crew. A Convair CV880 belonging to Groth Air was burnt out on 11 May 1983 while waiting on the ground. Mexico's Secretary of the Interior was killed on 4 November 2008 when his Learjet 45 executive aircraft crashed on the approach to the airport on a flight from San Luis Potosi.

CANCÚN INTERNATIONAL: CUN
Cancún, Mexico

Owner and operator: Aeropuertos del Sureste (ASUR)
Runways: 12L/30R, 3,500m (11,483ft); 12R/30L, 2,400m (7,875ft)
Terminals: Three, designated Terminal 1 (closed), Terminal 2 (with a satellite), and Terminal 3
Annual passengers: 11,483,741
Annual cargo: 17,585 tonnes
Annual aircraft movements: 114,067

Background
One of the fastest-growing airports in the Americas, and second only to Mexico City in traffic volume, Cancún serves the Caribbean coast of the Yucatán Peninsula and is a major tourist des-

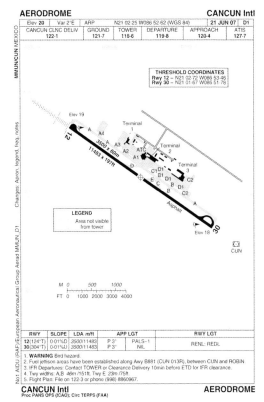

Airlines using airport as base or hub:
    Aeromexico, Aeromexico Connect, Mexicana
Annual passengers: 7,784,286
Annual cargo: 124,318 tonnes
Annual aircraft movements: 164,244

Background

Guadalajara International Airport is 16km (10 miles) from the city, and is also known as Don Miguel Hidalgo y Costilla International Airport after the 'father of Mexican independence'. The airport opened in 1966 and has since become a hub for several Mexican airlines. It is owned by Grupo Aeroportuario del Pacifico, a Spanish company with interests in several Mexican airports. In recent years extensive work has doubled the capacity, ending the situation under which an aircraft had just a one in three chance of actually parking at a terminal gate. Both Aeromexico and Mexicana have extensive aircraft maintenance facilities at the airport.

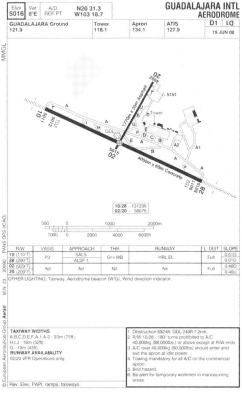

tination, including a growing number of transatlantic flights.

There have been a couple of accidents at the airport, including one on 26 December 1980 when a BAe 125 business jet hit trees after take-off and crashed killing all three occupants. Little is known about another accident on 15 March 1984 that saw an Aero Cozumel Convair 240 written off after an engine failed during take-off.

GUADALAJARA/DON MIGUEL HIDALGO Y COSTILLA INTERNATIONAL: GDL

Guadalajara, Jalisco, Mexico

Owner and operator: Grupo Aeroportuario del Pacifico
Runways: 10/28, 4,000m (13,123ft); 02/20, 1,818m (5,964ft)
Terminals: Two, designated Terminal 1 (with two concourses, A and C) and Terminal 2

A Continental Airlines Boeing 737-500 was written off during a landing accident on 16 September 1998. The pilots were making their second attempt at landing from Houston after a missed approach, and after touchdown the aircraft slipped off the runway, possibly because of meteorological factors, as the aircraft landing before them had experienced something similar. The Boeing's nosewheel collapsed and the aircraft was badly damaged, but there were no fatalities amongst the 6 crew and 108 passengers. On 14 September 2007 a Boeing 737-200 of Magnicharters suffered a collapsed undercarriage on landing, which badly damaged both engines (the aircraft having to be destroyed as a result), but none of the 6 crew or 103 passengers was killed.

MÉRIDA – MANUEL CRESCENCIO REJÓN INTERNATIONAL: MID

Mérida, Yutacán, Mexico

Owner and operator: ASUR (Aeropuertos de Sureste)
Runways: 10/28, 3,200m (10,499ft); 17/35, 2,300m (7,546ft)
Terminals: One, with two concourses designated A (domestic only) and B (domestic and USA)
Annual passengers: 1,291,575
Annual cargo: 16,080 tonnes

Background
Situated on the southern edge of Mérida, the airport is capable of handling aircraft up to Boeing 747 size, but usually the largest aircraft are Boeing 737 or Airbus A320 size. It was completely rebuilt between 1999 and 2001.

MONTERREY/GENERAL MARIANO ESCOBEDO INTERNATIONAL: MTY

Monterrey, Apodaca, Nuevo León, Mexico

Owner and operator: Grupo Aeroportuario Centro Norte (OMA)
Runways: 11/29, 3,000m (9,843ft); 16/34, 1,801m (5,909ft)

Terminals: Three, designated Terminal A (with North Concourse domestic flights and South Concourse international flights), Terminal B, and Terminal C
Annual passengers: 6,856,100
Annual cargo: 41,396 tonnes
Annual aircraft movements: 116,752

Background
The larger of two airports serving Monterrey, the other being Del Norte International, it is the most modern in Mexico and has seen major expansion in 2003 and 2007, with Terminal B opening in early 2009.

A Mexicana Boeing 727 approaching from Mexico City on 4 June 1969 was directed to fly a holding pattern, but the captain turned the aircraft to the left instead of the right and flew it into rising terrain, killing all 7 crew and 72 passengers. On 31 October 2002, an Aeromexico Douglas DC-9 landing from Guadalajara was

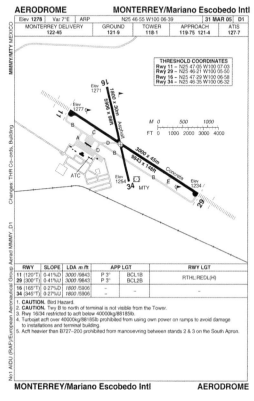

written off after a missed approach led to a second approach, in which the aircraft overshot the runway and the nosewheel collapsed. There were no fatalities amongst the 4 crew and 86 passengers.

TIJUANA/GENERAL ABELARDO L. RODRÍGUEZ INTERNATIONAL AIRPORT: TIJ
Tijuana, Baja California, Mexico

Owner and operator: Grupo Aeroportuario del
    Pacifico
Runways: 09/27, 2,960m (9,711ft)
Terminals: One commercial terminal with two
    concourses, and a military terminal known as
    the 'Old Airport Terminal'
Airlines using airport as base or hub:
    Aeromexico, Aeromexico Connect
Annual passengers: 4,760,531
Annual cargo: 17,104 tonnes
Annual aircraft movements: 65,460

Background
Just 100m from the border with the United States, Tijuana shares an airfield with the Mexican air force, and it was originally a purely military installation which started to accept commercial flights in 1965. As traffic grew rapidly, a new terminal was opened in 1970 and the original terminal became the armed forces base. The airport is named after a former governor of the state of Baja California who became president of Mexico from 1932 to 1934.

The airport terminal was extended in 2002 when Concourse A and Concourse B were added, doubling its capacity. The airport has become the only one in Latin America with flights to Asia, with Aeromexico now serving Shanghai and Tokyo from the airport.

The first commercial aircraft accident at the airport was shortly after it started to take civil flights. On 9 July 1965 a Bristol Britannia of Aeronaves de Mexico approaching from Mexico City was forced to make an emergency landing when the main landing gear would not lock, and collapsed on the runway. The 9 crew and 73 pas-

sengers were unharmed. On 6 September 2001 an Aeroliteral Saab 340B suffered a double engine failure while on approach from Ciudad Juarez, and crash landed on farmland 24km (15 miles) from the airport, writing the aircraft off, but without harm to the passengers and crew.

TOLUCA/LIC. ADOLFO LÓPEZ MATEOS INTERNATIONAL: TLC
Toluca de Lerdo, Mexico

Owner and operator: Administradora
    Mexiqueuse del Aeropuerti Internacional de
    Toluca (AMAIT)
Runways: 15/33, 4,200m (13,780ft)
Terminals: Two, designated Terminal 1
    (domestic) and Terminal 2 (international)
Annual passengers: 3,295,092
Annual cargo: 31,823 tonnes
Annual aircraft movements: 87,806

Background
Named after a former president, Toluca is encouraged to handle traffic for Toluca itself, but it is also being developed as an alternative to Mexico City for low-cost carriers. It also serves as the first alternate should Mexico City International be closed, as Toluca has the longest runway in Mexico. Like Mexico City International, it is high at 2,580m (8,466ft) above sea level. Until 2007 the airport had four terminals with the low-cost carriers Interjet and Volaris each having their own, but all traffic has now been concentrated on two terminals. Due in part to the low-cost airlines, passenger traffic has soared from 145,000 in 2002 to 3.3 million in 2007.

The sole accident at the airport appears to be to a BAe 125 on 9 July 1999, when the aircraft, carrying cargo for DHL, hit a wall as it approached the airport in poor visibility, killing all four occupants.

PUERTO VALLARTA/LIC. GUSTAVO DÍAZ ORDAZ INTERNATIONAL: PVR

Puerto Vallarta, Mexico

Owner and operator: Grupo Aeroportuario del Pacífico
Runways: 04/22, 3,100m (10,171ft)
Terminals: Essentially two terminal buildings, with a Main Terminal or Hall A, and a satellite or Hall B
Annual passengers: 3,134,221
Annual aircraft movements: 50,501

Background

A Mexican town and resort on the Pacific Ocean, the airport is named after a former president. It opened in 1962 with an international service to Los Angeles via Mazatlan, while package holidays were offered by the Mexican Aviation Company. Today, traffic volumes during the summer holiday season are twice those of the winter months.

There have been two serious accidents at the airport in recent years. The first was on 20 June 1973 when a Douglas DC-9 of Aeromexico crashed as it approached from Houston, with the loss of all 5 crew and 22 passengers. More serious, on 31 January 2000, an Alaska Airlines McDonnell Douglas MD-83 took-off for Seattle via San Francisco and the elevators jammed, leaving the aircraft to crash into the Pacific with the loss of all 88 passengers and crew.

SAN JOSÉ DEL CABO/LOS CABOS INTERNATIONAL: SJD

San José del Cabo, Baja California Sur, Mexico

Owner and operator: Grupo Aeroportuario del Pacífico
Runways: 16/34, 3,000m (9,843ft)
Terminals: Three, with four concourses between them, with Terminal 1 and Terminal 3 handling airline traffic and Terminal 2 being for general aviation

Annual passengers: 2,932,345
Annual cargo: 3,518 tonnes
Annual aircraft movements: 44,485

Background

Los Cabos is the second largest airport in Baja California. It has three terminals, although Terminal 2 is really a general aviation terminal, but Terminal 1 is the main terminal for both domestic and international flights, while Terminal 3 is mainly used to relieve Terminal 1. A fourth terminal is under construction and is much needed as the airport's existing facilities are under considerable pressure.

HERMOSILLO/GENERAL IGNACIO PESQUEIRA GARCIA INTERNATIONAL: HMO

Hermosillo, Sonara State, Mexico

Runways: 05/23, 2,300m (7,546ft); 11/29, 1,100m (3,609ft)
Terminals: One, with two gates for international passengers
Airlines using airport as base or hub: Aeromexico Connect
Annual passengers: 1,478,057
Annual cargo: 6,793 tonnes
Annual aircraft movements: 48,297

Background

Hermosillo Airport, or General Ignacio Pesqueira Garcia International Airport, sometimes even known as General Ignacio L. Pesqueira International Airport, is a joint civil and military installation dating from before the Second World War. It is named after a 19th century general who led the Mexican army against the French when they invaded. The airport is close to the US border and has flights to a number of US cities, including Las Vegas, Los Angeles, and Phoenix. In addition to its own flights, the airport serves as the first alternative for Tijuana, and can handle aircraft up to Boeing 777 size.

CULIACÁN/FEDERAL BACHIGUALATO INTERNATIONAL: CUL
Culiacan, Sinaloa State, Mexico

Owner and operator: Grupo Aeroportuario
   Centro Norte
Runways: 07/20, 2,300m (7,546ft)
Terminals: One
Airlines using airport as base or hub:
   Aeromexico Connect
Annual passengers: 1,305,255
Annual cargo: 4,379 tonnes
Annual aircraft movements: 61,675

Background
A joint military and civil airport, Culiacán has a range of domestic and international air services, as well as being an active base for the Mexican Air Force.

A number of accidents have occurred in recent years. Two of these were cargo flights using North American Sabreliners. The first was on 30 December 2006, when the aircraft crashed after hitting some poles and finally hit a building, killing both pilots, the sole occupants. On 5 July 2007, another Sabreliner suffered a burst tyre as it was taking-off, and skidded off the runway on to a road, with the deaths of all three people aboard the aircraft and another seven on the ground, while five more were seriously injured. A third accident, on 5 November 2007, was to a Cessna Grand Caravan of Aero Calafia, with a single pilot and 14 passengers, which had just taken off for Cabo San Lucas when it lost height while making a sharp turn and crash-landed in a field, coming to rest inverted, but without serious casualties amongst those aboard.

LEÓN/GUANAJUATO/DEL BAJÍO INTERNATIONAL: BJX
Silao, Guanajuato State, Mexico

Owner and operator: Grupo Aeroportuario del
   Pacifico
Runways: 13/31, 3,499m (11,480ft)

Terminals: One
Annual passengers: 1,285,859

Background
Officially, the airport is known as Guanajuato International, but it serves both León and the city of Guanajuato, the capital of the state of the same name. It has good cross-border links with the United States, including direct flights as far afield as Atlanta, although most cross-border flights are to cities in the southern USA.

A take-off accident destroyed a Curtis C-46 of Tigres Voladoreson on 18 June 1955 as the aircraft crashed into trees following an engine failure, causing the death of one of the 39 passengers. The next serious accident was to a Douglas DC-9 of Aeromexico as it landed on 2 September 1976 and overshot the runway, happily without casualties aboard or on the ground.

ACAPULCO/GENERAL JUAN N. ÁLVAREZ INTERNATIONAL: ACA
Acapulco, Guerrero, Mexico

Owner and operator: Grupo Aeroportuario
   Centro Norte
Runways: 06/24, 1,700m (5,579ft); 10/28,
   3,302m (10,832ft)
Terminals: One
Annual passengers: 1,090,963

Background
Variously known as General Juan N. Álvarez International or simply as Acapulco International, the airport is 26km (16 miles) from the city centre.

The airport dates from the late 1940s and is the largest in the southern Pacific coastal region of Mexico. It can handle aircraft up to and including the Boeing 747, and there are several airbridges. The busiest route is to Mexico City, but there are flights to other cities in Mexico, and to the United States and Canada.

Accidents at Acapulco in recent years include one on 13 August 1966 an Aeronaves de Mexico Douglas DC-8-51, on a training flight, crashed while turning and killed all six people aboard. A Convair CV990 of Modern Air Transport landing from New York on 8 August 1970 on a positioning flight, undershot the runway and collided with the approach lights and caught fire, killing one of the eight crew aboard (there were no passengers). Little is known about an accident to a Hawker Siddeley HS748 on 27 July 1973, except that the aircraft was operated by SAESA (Servicios Aereos Especiales SA) and appears to have had just three occupants, all crew, who were unharmed as it crashed on landing.

VERACRUZ/GENERAL HERIBERTO JARA INTERNATIONAL: VER
Veracruz, Jalapa State, Mexico

Owner and operator: Aeropuertos del Sureste (ASUR)
Runways: 09/27, 1,523m (4,997ft); 18/36, 2,400m (7,874ft)
Terminals: One
Annual passengers: 1,054,803

Background
Named after a former president, the airport handles both domestic and international traffic. There has been just one accident, on 31 March 1975, to a Lockheed Lodestar which crashed after hitting trees following take-off, killing both occupants.

MOROCCO

The country's history of French and Spanish colonial rule meant that its early air transport links were largely provided by the former colonial powers, especially the French. Both Air France and Iberia played a part in setting up the national airline, Royal Air Maroc, which superseded two struggling independent airlines. In recent years, a thriving independent sector has emerged. The airports are state-owned and date from colonial days. Rabat, the capital city, is not one of the country's major airports, which are situated in tourist areas.

CASABLANCA/ MOHAMMED V: CMN
Nouasseur, Casablanca, Morocco

Owner and operator: ONDA (National Airports Office)
Runways: 17L/35R, 3,720m (12,205ft); 17R/35L, 3,720m (12,205ft)
Terminals: Three, designated Terminal 1 (currently closed for renovation), Terminal 2, and Terminal 3
Airlines using airport as base or hub: Jet4you, Royal Air Maroc, Regional Air Lines
Annual passengers: 5,858,192
Annual cargo: 60,934 tonnes
Annual aircraft movements: 72,742

There is a railway service from the station under Terminal 1 to the centre of Casablanca operated by ONCF.

Background
Situated 30km (19 miles) south-east of Casablanca and named after King Mohammed V, it is Morocco's busiest airport. It is known locally simply as Nouasseur, after the neighbouring town.

The airport occupies the site of a former United States Air Force Strategic Air Command base, known as Nouasseur AFB, in what was then French Morocco, and developed from a wartime facility to accommodate Cold War nuclear-armed bombers during the early and mid-1950s. Morocco became independent in 1956, and after US intervention in the Lebanon in 1958, the government demanded that America withdrew its forces, and by early 1963 they had done so.

The airport then became completely commercial and expanded rapidly with the growth in Morocco's tourist traffic, and it also became an important air cargo centre. The original terminal, now Terminal 1, is being renovated, and all traffic uses the other two terminals. It is one

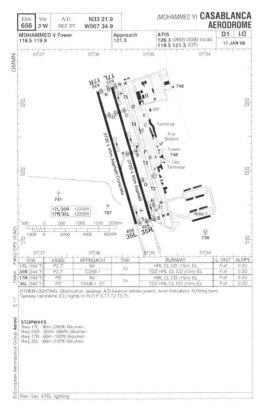

Elev	Var	A/D	N33 21.9	(MOHAMMED V) **CASABLANCA**
656	3°W	REF PT	W007 34.9	**AERODROME**

GMMN

PANS OPS (ICAO)

© European Aeronautical Group. Aerad E.17 1994

© Rev: Var, ATIS, lighting.

Airlines using airport as base or hub: RAM
(Royal Air Maroc)

Annual passengers: 3,050,916

Background

Built by the French before Moroccan independence, Marrakech has enjoyed considerable traffic growth based on a buoyant tourist trade. It is the most southerly of the main Moroccan airports.

AGADIR AL MASSIRA: AGA

Agadir, Morroco

Owner and operator: ONDA
Runways: 10/28, 3,200m (10,498ft)
Terminals: One
Annual passengers: 1,496,875

Background

The airport dates from pre-independence when it was opened for military use. Traffic has been boosted by Morocco's growing popularity as a tourist destination. A new terminal has been opened, replacing the older building. The airport can handle Category II instrument landings.

No serious accidents near the airport have been recorded in recent years.

of the few airports in Africa to have a railway link.

There seem to have been just a couple of serious accidents since the airport became completely commercial. The first of these was on 1 July 1967 to a CSA Czech Airlines Ilyushin Il-18, diverted to Casablanca because of fog at Rabat, which crashed 13km (8 miles) from the runway on its second attempt at landing. On 1 April 1970 a Sud Aviation Caravelle of Royal Air Maroc crashed on approach as control was lost at 500ft, and on impact the fuselage broke in two killing 61 of the 82 passengers and crew.

MARRAKECH-MENARA INTERNATIONAL: RAK

Marrakech, Morocco

Owner and Operator: ONDA
Runways: 10/28, 3,100m (10,170ft)
Terminals: One

MUSCAT AND OMAN

MUSCAT INTERNATIONAL (SEEB INTERNATIONAL): MCT

Muscat, Muscat and Oman

Owner and operator: Oman Airports
Management Company
Runways: 08/26, 3,589m (11,775ft); 02/20,
750m (2,461ft) this is an unpaved dirt strip
Terminals: One
Airlines using airport as base or hub: Oman Air
Annual passengers: 4,218,498
Annual cargo: 77,392 tonnes
Annual aircraft movements: 41,383

Background

Formerly Seeb International Airport, Muscat International is 30km (about 19 miles) from the old town and about half that from the main residential district.

Muscat's original airport was opened in 1929, and was Bait Al Falaj Airport, which was basically a dirt landing strip mainly intended for Royal Air Force use, but also used by the Oman Petroleum Development Company. In 1950 the Gulf Aviation Company was formed in Bahrain, and as its operations spread it started flying into Muscat using Douglas DC-3 airliners. Later, both British Airways and Pakistan International Airways started to fly into Muscat, while the light aircraft division of Gulf Air gave rise to the founding of Oman Air, which now uses Muscat as its base.

Bait Al Falaj was by this time proving unsatisfactory for larger and heavier aircraft, and there was little room to expand. A new airport was needed, and work started in 1970 on Seeb Airport, which opened on 23 December 1973. The opening coincided with the start of a period of rapid economic growth in the Gulf, and ten years after opening, the terminal had to be enlarged, while in 1991 a new cargo terminal was opened. In 2002, management of the airport passed to a consortium that included BAA, but reverted to the government of the sultanate in 2004 after disagreements on future development. The current name was officially adopted on 1 February 2008 to link the airport more closely with the city of Muscat.

For the future, further expansion and modernisation is in progress and will include a new terminal and a new runway capable of handling the new Airbus A380. The first stage of this programme should be completed during 2011.

NEPAL

KATHMANDU/TRIBHUVAN INTERNATIONAL: KTM
Kathmandu, Nepal

Owner and operator: Civil Aviation Authority of Nepal

Runways: 02/20, 3,050m (10,007ft)

Terminals: Two, designated Domestic and International

Airlines using airport as base or hub: Buddha Airlines, Cosmic Air, Royal Nepal Airlines, Yeti Airlines

Annual passengers: 2,539,488

Annual cargo: 18,051 tonnes

Annual aircraft movements: 77,282

Background

The airport dates from the early 1950s, and for many years all flights were operated by Indian

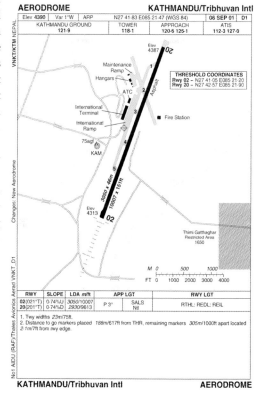

Airlines. It is the country's only international airport and is about 6km (just under 4 miles) from the centre of Kathmandu.

The airport's high location, at 1,338m (4,390ft) surrounded by mountains, makes operations difficult, although the number of accidents has fallen in recent years. The worst year was 1992 with two very serious accidents. The first was on 31 July when a Thai Airways International Airbus A310 crashed into a mountain while on approach, with the loss of all 113 passengers and crew. This was followed on 28 September by a Pakistan International Airways Airbus A300 which crashed with the loss of all 167 passengers and crew. On 17 January 1995 a Royal Nepal Airlines de Havilland Canada Twin Otter, flying to Rumjatar, had difficulty climbing and struck the perimeter fence before plunging into fields, killing one of the 3 crew and one of the 21 passengers. There was a similar accident when a Nepal Airlines Twin Otter went off the runway on 24 December 2008. Before this, on 5 September 1999, a Necon Air BAe 748 approaching from Pokhara collided with a communications mast and crashed into woods 25km (just over 15 miles) west of Kathmandu killing all five crew and all ten passengers. Growing Communist Chinese pressure on the country has also had an impact, with an Indian Airlines airliner hijacked on 26 December 2000, and on 27 December 2008, a bomb was detonated near the main entrance to the airport.

NETHERLANDS

The Netherlands has one of the longest histories of commercial aviation in Europe, with the national flag carrier KLM tracing its history back to 1919. While colonial air links were as much a driving force with the Dutch as with the British and French, the Dutch were mainly advocates of landplane operation rather than the flying boats favoured by Imperial Airways and Air France. Despite being a small country with a dense railway network and new high-speed links to Belgium, France, and Germany, there are three substantial airports, and the main airport at Amsterdam Schiphol is the fifth busiest by passenger numbers in Europe, and is a major international hub. The operator, Schiphol Group, not only also operates the airport at Rotterdam, but is involved heavily in airport development around the world.

AMSTERDAM SCHIPHOL: AMS
Amsterdam, Netherlands

Owner and operator: Schiphol Group
Runways: 18R/36L, 3,800m (12,467ft); 18L/36R, 3,453m (11,155ft); 18C/36C, 3,300m (10,826ft); 06/24, 3,500m (11,483ft); 09/27, 3,453m (11,329ft); 04/22, 2,014m (6,608ft); the shortest runway is mainly used for general aviation movements, while a seventh runway is planned.
Terminals: A single large terminal divided into three separate departure halls, with a new development, known as Terminal 4 but indistinguishable from the main terminal, and a new low-cost pier, H
Airlines using airport as base or hub: Arkefly, KLM Cityhopper, KLM Royal Dutch Airlines, Martinair, Transavia
Annual passengers: 47,794,994
Annual cargo: 1,651,385 tonnes
Annual aircraft movements: 454,360

There is a railway link to Amsterdam and other major cities in the Netherlands by Netherlands Railways, NS, including Thalys high-speed international trains.

Background
The airport is one of the largest in Europe and is just over 9km (5½ miles) south-west of Amsterdam. It is unusual in that it is 3km (10ft) below sea level.

Although the Netherlands was neutral, Schiphol was originally built during the First World War as a military air station and opened on 16 September 1916. In addition to a barracks, an open field served as a runway and aircraft standing area. The area had a long connection

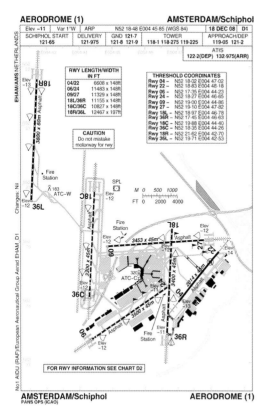

AERODROME (1) — **AMSTERDAM/Schiphol**

Elev –11	Var 1°W	ARP	N52 18·48 E004 45·85 (WGS 84)		18 DEC 08	D1
SCHIPHOL START 121·65	DELIVERY 121·975	GND 121·7 121·8 121·9	TOWER 118·1 118·275 119·225	APPROACH/DEP 119·05 121·2		
				ATIS 122·2(DEP) 132·975(ARR)		

RWY LENGTH/WIDTH IN FT

04/22	6608 x 148ft
06/24	11483 x 148ft
09/27	11329 x 148ft
18L/36R	11155 x 148ft
18C/36C	10827 x 148ft
18R/36L	12467 x 197ft

THRESHOLD COORDINATES

Rwy 04 –	N52 18·02 E004 47·02
Rwy 22 –	N52 18·83 E004 48·18
Rwy 06 –	N52 17·35 E004 44·23
Rwy 24 –	N52 18·27 E004 46·65
Rwy 09 –	N52 19·00 E004 44·86
Rwy 27 –	N52 19·10 E004 47·82
Rwy 18L –	N52 18·97 E004 46·78
Rwy 36R –	N52 17·45 E004 46·63
Rwy 18C –	N52 19·88 E004 44·40
Rwy 36C –	N52 18·35 E004 44·26
Rwy 18R –	N52 21·62 E004 42·70
Rwy 36L –	N52 19·71 E004 42·53

CAUTION
Do not mistake
motorway for rwy

FOR RWY INFORMATION SEE CHART D2

AMSTERDAM/Schiphol
PANS OPS (ICAO)

AERODROME (1)

with the military, having originally been part of Fort Schiphol, which had been built on the Haarlemmermeer polder, a low-lying large lake across which many ships were lost in violent storms before it was drained in 1852 and reclaimed. In English, Schiphol translates as 'ship hole', a reflection of the many ships lost there.

Although scheduled air services between Amsterdam and London started in 1919, commercial use of the airfield did not come until 17 December 1920, when it was known as *Schiphol-les-bains*. Between the wars, expansion was helped by the fact that the Dutch, unlike the British, French, and Americans, concentrated on developing long-haul air services with landplanes rather than flying boats.

The country was swiftly overrun by German forces in May 1940 at the start of the Second World War, and the airport was used as a Luftwaffe base until liberation in late 1944. It

returned to civilian use post war. Considerable effort has been put into developing Schiphol's role as a major hub. KLM acquired an interest in the British airline, Air UK, to use it to develop connecting flights from regional centres in the UK, and eventually absorbed the airline. KLM operates a 'seven wave' system of arrivals and departures to facilitate international connections. Despite this, many airlines have found the airport to be too costly and have moved their base of operations to Rotterdam and Eindhoven, but the creation of a low-cost pier (H) is intended to overcome this problem.

The Dutch aircraft manufacturer, Fokker, moved its factory to a site near the airport in 1951, but the company has since collapsed after producing a series of successful feeder and short-haul aircraft, starting with the F27 Friendship and ending with the F100. Schiphol is one of the most welcoming airports for visitors and aviation enthusiasts, with a large open roof area (the Panoramaterras), but this is not accessible to passengers using the airport as an interchange. It is unusual in that the Rijksmuseum has an annex at the airport providing passengers with a taste of its collections.

The airport has suffered a number of serious accidents since the Second World War. The first of these was on 14 November 1946, when a Douglas C-47 of KLM Royal Dutch Airlines flying from London attempted to land in thick fog. The captain opted to go around on the first two attempts, and on the third attempt he realised that he wasn't lined up with the runway, and made a sharp turn to the left at low speed, which made the aircraft stall and the left wing hit the ground, causing the aircraft to crash and catch fire, killing all 5 crew and 21 passengers. In more recent years, one major accident with most of the victims on the ground was on 4 October 1992 to an El Al Boeing 747 freighter. The aircraft lost its No. 3 engine, which in turn knocked the No. 4, right-outer, engine off its pylon, making it very difficult to handle and it crashed into a block of flats in the Bijlmer district, killing not just the crew of 3 and an airline employee travelling in the aircraft, but also 43 people on the ground, and injuring many others. On 4 April 1994 a KLM Cityhopper Saab 340 flying to Cardiff returned to Amsterdam with engine trouble, putting the No. 2 engine to flight idle, but at the last minute decided to execute a go-around and put only the No. 1 engine to full power, causing the aircraft to roll to the right, stall, and then hit the ground. Three of the 24 occupants, including the captain, were killed, and 9 others were seriously injured.

The most recent accident was on 25 February 2009 to a THY Turkish Airlines Boeing 737-800 landing from Istanbul. The aircraft's radio altimeter gave an incorrect height reading and the autothrottle closed the throttle levers to middle, while the crew failed to monitor airspeed, so that the aircraft stalled 1km (just over half a mile) short of the runway. Nine occupants, including the 2 pilots, were killed and a further 86 injured out of a total of 7 crew and 128 passengers.

In addition to these accidents, the airport also suffered a fire at its detention centre on 27 October 2005, killing 11 and injuring another 15 out of 350 occupants.

EINDHOVEN (WELSCHAP): EIN
Eindhoven, Netherlands

Owner and operator: Eindhoven Airport
    NV/Royal Netherlands Air Force
Runways: 04/22, 3,000m (9,842ft)
Terminals: One
Annual passengers: 1,544,098
Annual cargo: 33,858 tonnes

Background
Originally known as Welschap, the airport is 7.5km (4½ miles) west of Eindhoven. It is the second busiest airport in the Netherlands.

The airport was opened before the Second World War and was bombed by the advancing German forces in May 1940, and by the Allies in the years that followed. It was reopened as an airport and as a base for the RNAF after the war, and it is still a base for the air force's transport units. It is also a NATO base with the alliance's Movement Coordination Centre Europe. There have been proposals to move the Dutch air force units from Eindhoven to Enschede, which is a military air station that is little used at present, to allow Eindhoven to increase the number of commercial flights handled.

ROTTERDAM: RTM
Rotterdam, South Holland, Netherlands

Owner and operator: Schiphol Group
Runways: 06/24, 2,200m (7,218ft)
Terminals: One
Annual passengers: 1,146,144
Annual cargo: 65,529 tonnes

Background
The third busiest airport in the Netherlands by passenger numbers, it is almost 6km (3½ miles) north-west from the centre of Rotterdam. It is even lower than Schiphol at 4m (around 14ft) below sea level.

Rotterdam had an airport before the Second World War, but this was destroyed to ensure that it could not be used by the Germans in 1940 and, instead of rebuilding it, it was decided to build a completely new airport on reclaimed land, the *Zestienhoven* polder. The new airport opened in October 1956 and soon attracted the major European airlines, including Air France, Lufthansa, and Swissair. Speculation in the 1970s over whether the airport should be closed or relocated to allow for housing development stifled the airport's development, and traffic slumped as carriers switched their flights elsewhere. It was not until the 1990s that growth returned, and in 2001 it was decided that the airport would remain open on its present site for up to 100 years. Nevertheless, KLM has ended its flights to London Heathrow, and most flights using the airport use regional aircraft, although there are some Boeing 737 and Airbus A320 flights, mainly on charters to holiday destinations.

NETHERLANDS ANTILLES

ARUBA/QUEEN BEATRIX INTERNATIONAL: AUA
Aruba, Netherlands Antilles

Owner and operator: Aruba Airport Authority NV
Runways: 11/29, 2,814m (9,232ft)
Terminals: One
Airlines using airport as base or hub: Aruba
   Airlines, Tiara Air
Annual passengers: 1,837,413

Background
The airfield was built before the Second World War for the Dutch armed forces based in the Netherlands Antilles. After the occupation of the Netherlands in 1940, it was used by the United States Army Air Force's Sixth Air Force for anti-submarine operations, protecting the approaches to the Panama Canal, and was also used by fighter units. After the war it returned to Dutch control and was also used by commercial aircraft, being served by KLM Royal Dutch Airlines and the Dutch Caribbean airline (Air ALM), which used Aruba as a hub until the island withdrew from the Netherlands Antilles in 1986. It is named after Queen Beatrix of the Netherlands.

The airport is now heavily used by US airlines, including Continental and US Airways, and has US border pre-clearance facilities. It has flights to many cities in North America and also to Western Europe, especially the Netherlands, but many of these are package holiday charter flights rather than scheduled services.

There have been few serious accidents at or near the airport. On 14 July 1990 a TPI International Airways Lockheed Electra suffered a failure of its No. 3 engine propeller gearbox, with the propeller breaking off and damaging the No. 4 propeller, which also separated and passed under the aircraft damaging the No. 2 propeller and also severing the hydraulics and power lines, as well as puncturing the pressurised fuselage.

The aircraft returned to Aruba on just one engine and made an emergency landing. The aircraft was damaged beyond repair but the 3 crew of this cargo plane survived. Little has been recorded about the loss of a Dassault Falcon of JetSul Taxi Aero on 13 February 2005 other than that it was written off in a wheels-up landing accident and was later donated to a flight simulator club.

ST MAARTEN/PRINCESS JULIANA INTERNATIONAL: SXM
St Martin, Leeward Islands

Owner and operator: Princess Juliana
   International Airport Holding Company NV
Runways: 10/28, 2,433m (7,980ft)
Terminals: One
Airlines using airport as base or hub: Windward
   Islands Airways
Annual passengers: 1,651,826
Annual cargo: 4,895 tonnes
Annual aircraft movements: 75,055

Background
The airport for the Netherlands end of the island of Saint Martin (or St Maarten), it is one of the busiest airports in the Eastern Caribbean, and is the main gateway for the smaller Leeward Islands, including Anguilla. The airport is notorious for its short runway, and pilots have to make a low approach over the tourist beach to make use of as much of the runway as possible. In 2007 KLM Royal Dutch Airlines replaced the Boeing 747 used on flights from Amsterdam with a McDonnell Douglas MD-11.

The airport was built as a military airstrip in 1942, but started handling commercial flights in 1943. It became an important airport for the Eastern Caribbean after the war, and by 1964 had to be remodelled and upgraded, with a new control tower and passenger terminal. Further modernisation followed in 1985, and again in 2001, once again with a new terminal building and control tower. It is named after Juliana of the Netherlands, who was crown princess at the time the airport opened.

There have been no serious accidents at the airport.

CURAÇAO/HATO INTERNATIONAL: CUR
Curaçao, Netherlands Antilles

Owner and operator: Curaçao Airport Partners
Runways: 11/29, 3,410m (11,187ft)
Terminals: One
Airlines using airport as base or hub:
Headquarters for Dutch Antilles Express; Insel Air
Annual passengers: 1,274,046
Annual cargo: 17,124 tonnes

Background
Curaçao is sometimes known as Hato International Airport, but the closest city is Willemstad. It has the second longest runway in the Caribbean.

The airport was built during the 1930s and opened as Dr Albert Piesman International Airport. During the Second World War, after the German occupation of the Netherlands, it became a US base, used by the United States Army Sixth Air Force for anti-submarine patrols over the Caribbean. After the war the airport reverted to civil use and was the hub of Air ALM and its successor, Dutch Caribbean Airlines, until it suspended operations in 2004. A new passenger terminal opened in 2006.

An AVENSA Douglas DC-6B on a domestic flight within Venezuela on 27 November 1961 was hijacked, as was an Avianca Boeing 727 on a domestic flight within Colombia on 11 May 1978, but in both cases the hijackers were overpowered quickly and no lives were lost. An Air Jamaica Boeing 727 suffered a partial undercarriage collapse on landing from Kingston on 16 November 1990, but all 8 crew and 59 passengers survived, and the aircraft was later repaired.

NEW ZEALAND
The remote position of New Zealand, its long-standing links with the United Kingdom, a relatively small and scattered population, and the division of the country into two islands all point to air transport being important. While internal services were operated by landplanes, during the early days of long-haul air transport, flying boats were used. Because of its small population, New Zealand did not rank as highly as Australia when the Empire Air Mail Scheme was inaugurated in 1937, and when the governments of the two countries and the United Kingdom founded Tasman Empire Airways (TEAL) in 1940, it was largely as a feeder into the Imperial Airways and Qantas joint service linking Sydney and Southampton. TEAL (the predecessor of Air New Zealand) remained an operator of flying boats until the 1950s, and they were replaced by Lockheed Electra turboprop landplanes in 1959.

AUCKLAND INTERNATIONAL: AKL
Auckland, North Island, New Zealand

Owner and operator: Auckland International Airport Ltd (AIAL)
Runways: 05L/23R, 3,108m (10,197ft); 05R/23L, 3,635m (11,926ft)
Terminals: Two, designated Domestic and International
Airlines using airport as base or hub: Air Freight NZ, Air New Zealand, Freedom Air
Annual passengers: 12,222,096
Annual cargo: 224,774 tonnes
Annual aircraft movements: 155,662

Background
Auckland is New Zealand's most important airport and the main point for international arrivals and departures. It was first used by the Auckland Aero Club which leased the land in 1928. The first commercial airport for Auckland, used initially mainly by domestic air services, was at Whenaupai, to the north-west of the city, and it was not until 1960 that work began on the cur-

rent airport, which opened for traffic in November 1965, although the official opening was in late January 1966.

A new international terminal opened in 1977, named after the pioneering aviatrix Jean Batten, and this was extensively renovated in 2005, separating arriving and departing international passengers as a result of the terrorist attacks in New York and Washington on 11 September 2001, and has since been extended again for the Airbus A380. A third runway is being built ready for the Rugby World Cup in 2011.

The airport has suffered three serious accidents, although in recent years. The first was on 4 July 1966 when an Air New Zealand Douglas DC-8 on a crew training flight crashed back on to the runway after take-off, killing two of the five crew members. On 17 February 1979 an Air New Zealand Fokker F-27 Friendship crashed into Manukua Harbour while on approach, killing one of the crew and a passenger. A Convair 580 (a turboprop conversion of the 340), operated by Mainfreight, crashed shortly after take-off at night on 31 July 1989, with the loss of the crew of three.

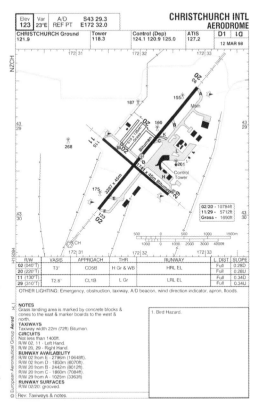

CHRISTCHURCH INTERNATIONAL: CHC

Harewood, Christchurch, New Zealand

Owner and operator: Christchurch International Airport Ltd
Runways: 02/20, 3,288m (10,785ft); 11/29, 1,741m (5,712ft); 02/20, 515m (1,690ft) grass, used for general aviation; there is a helicopter terminal with landing pads adjacent to the airport
Terminals: One
Annual passengers: 5,635,166
Annual cargo: 25,625 tonnes
Annual aircraft movements: 134,058

Background

The busiest airport in New Zealand's South Island, it is 12km (7½ miles) north-west of the city centre and dates from 1953. An unusual feature is that Christchurch is prone to a strong north-westerly wind, so the secondary runway (11/29) is at right angles to the main runway and is used when the wind is north-westerly.

Although a civil airport, since the closure of RNZAF Wigram, Royal New Zealand Air Force aircraft use the airport when needed, and it is also used for 'Operation Deep Freeze' by RNZAF, USAF, USN, and US Air National Guard units operating into Antarctica.

Major expansion of the airport started in 2006, and one of the first results of this has been a new control tower, while there will be a new domestic and international terminal that is planned to be completed in 2011, after which the existing terminal will be demolished.

WELLINGTON INTERNATIONAL: WLG

Wellington, New Zealand

Owner: Infratil/Wellington City Council
Operator: Wellington International Airport Ltd
Runways: 16/34, 2,026m (6,647ft)
Terminals: Two, designated Domestic and
   International
Annual passengers: 4,784,294
Annual aircraft movements: 109,512

Background

The airport is situated 7km (more than 4 miles) south of the New Zealand capital and there had been private flying there since 1929. When it opened for commercial business in 1935 it was known as Rongotai Airport, because of its location on the Rongotai isthmus. It was closed on 27 September 1947 on grounds of safety as it still used a grass runway that became slippery and unsafe during the winter. Air traffic was transferred to Paraparaumu Airport, 56km (35 miles) north of Wellington, which became the country's busiest airport, but Paraparaumu was not suitable for further development as a major gateway to New Zealand because of the surrounding terrain. At this time flying boats were used for long-haul operations by Tasman Empire Airways (predecessor of today's Air New Zealand), and the country's airports handled short-haul, mainly domestic, traffic.

After complete rebuilding of the site, the current airport was opened on 25 October 1959, initially with a runway of 1,630m, which was extended later to 1,936m for Air New Zealand's Douglas DC-8 airliners. The opening day was marred by two incidents at the air show being held to mark the event. Flying in turbulent conditions, a Royal New Zealand Air Force Short Sunderland flying boat managed to scrape its keel on the runway, while a Royal Air Force Avro Vulcan bomber damaged its undercarriage and a wing. Although a new international terminal was opened in 1979, the domestic terminal at the new airport used a corrugated iron hangar for many years, and it was not until

Ansett New Zealand began competing with Air New Zealand on domestic services in 1986 that a completely new domestic terminal was provided as an extension to the international terminal. Later plans to widen the taxiways had to be abandoned because of protests by local residents.

No less than six sites for a new airport have been considered over the past 20 years, but instead it has been decided to remain at Rongotai. In 1998 the city council sold a two-thirds stake in the airport to Infratil. A new terminal was opened in 1999 and linked with the international terminal, and safety zones have been provided at both ends of the runway.

The airport suffers from having just two long-haul airlines, Air New Zealand and Qantas, and even these have proposed a code-share to increase load factors, but the New Zealand authorities have rejected this. The shortness of the runway remains a problem, and extension

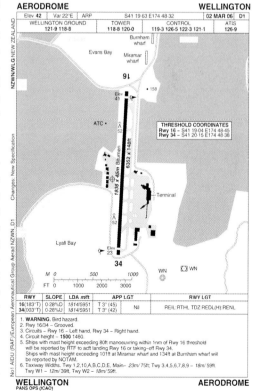

into the bay would be costly and difficult, while neither airline has shown any interest in providing long-haul services to the United States or beyond, especially as Air New Zealand found load factors on its service from Christchurch to Los Angeles so poor that it abandoned the service in 2006. Local business leaders have argued that Christchurch provided a poor comparison because it had a predominately agricultural local economy, while Wellington has more industry and commerce, as well as being the capital.

The airport also suffers from a combination of a short runway and high winds, yet there have been relatively few accidents. One of these was to a United Airlines Boeing 747 diverted from first Auckland and then Christchurch because of fog in 1991. The aircraft landed safely, but had to offload its passengers and freight before it could take off again.

NIGERIA

While Nigeria was served by Imperial Airways, and then by its successor the British Overseas Airways Corporation (BOAC), services and airfields within the region had been developed by the Royal Air Force during the Second World War. The former RAF services were taken over by the West African Airways Corporation (WAAC) which had been formed in 1946 by the governments of Nigeria, the Gold Coast (now Ghana), Sierra Leone, and Gambia, when these were all British colonies, with investment by BOAC. In 1958, following independence, WAAC's services were taken over by Nigeria Airways, which also took over the Lagos–Kano service of Nigeria Air Services, and then added extensions from Lagos to Freetown, Bathurst, and Dakar. Despite the booming economy from oil exports, Nigeria Airways ceased operations in 2003, and since that time intercontinental airline operations have been largely provided by Virgin Nigeria, although locally-owned airlines are also developing.

LAGOS/MURTALA MUHAMMED INTERNATIONAL: LOS
Ikeja, Lagos, Nigeria

Owner and operator: FAAN (Federal Airports
    Authority of Nigeria)
Runways: 18L/36R, 2,743m (8,999ft); 18R/36L,
    3,900m (12,794ft)
Terminals: Two, designated Terminal 1
    International, and Murtala Muhammed
    Terminal 2 Domestic
Airlines using airport as base or hub: ADC
    Airlines, Aerocontractors, Arik Air, Virgin
    Nigeria
Annual passengers: 4,450,726
Annual cargo: 130,076 tonnes
Annual aircraft movements: 79,082

Background
Named after a former military head of state, the airport opened on 15 March 1979. It is the busiest airport in Nigeria, but during the final decades of the 20th century achieved an unenviable reputation for criminal activity both inside and outside the passenger terminals, and with gangs even raiding the cargo holds of aircraft, while customs and immigration officials solicited bribes. The US at one stage banned direct flights, and some travel guides advised passengers to travel via Kano instead, taking a domestic flight to Lagos, itself a doubtful piece of advice given the country's air safety record. Following democratic elections in 1999 the security situation improved and the airport terminals have been cleaned, and baggage handling and air-conditioning equipment repaired. The US Federal Aviation Administration revoked its suspension of direct flights in 2001.

The airport is shared with the Nigerian Air Force.

The original terminal was replaced by new terminals for domestic and international flights, but the domestic terminal was destroyed by a fire in 2000 and the old terminal brought back into service as a domestic terminal until a new one could be built, and this was opened in April 2007. The two current terminals are about 1km

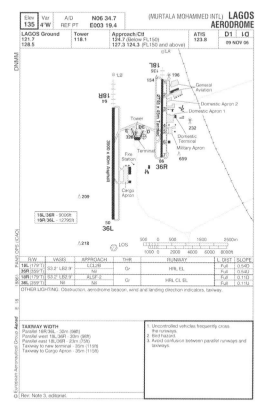

Elev 135	Var 4°W	A/D REF PT	N06 34.7 E003 19.4	(MURTALA MOHAMMED INTL) **LAGOS AERODROME**		
LAGOS Ground 121.7 128.5		Tower 118.1	Approach/Ctl 124.7 (Below FL150) 127.3 124.3 (FL150 and above)		ATIS 123.8	D1 |.O 09 NOV 06

R/W	VASIS	APPROACH	THR	RUNWAY	L DIST	SLOPE
18L (179°T)	S3.2° LB2.9°	LCL2B	Gr	HRL EL	Full	0.54D
36R (359°T)		Nil			Full	0.54U
18R (179°T)	S3.2° LB2.9°	ALSF-2	Gr	HRL CL EL	Full	0.11D
36L (359°T)	Nil	Nil			Full	0.11U

OTHER LIGHTING: Obstruction, aerodrome beacon, wind and landing direction indicators, taxiway.

TAXIWAY WIDTH
Parallel 18R/36L - 30m (98ft)
Parallel west 18L/36R - 30m (98ft)
Parallel east 18L/36R - 23m (75ft)
Taxiway to new terminal - 35m (115ft)
Taxiway to Cargo Apron - 35m (115ft)

1. Uncontrolled vehicles frequently cross the runways.
2. Bird hazard.
3. Avoid confusion between parallel runways and taxiways.

Rev: Note 3, editorial.

apart, and both are likely to be expanded in the future. The country has been renewing bilateral agreements with other nations and signing new agreements, so air traffic is likely to continue to increase.

According to the Aviation Safety Network, the airport has had 16 accidents since 1968, although not all of them resulted in fatalities. The first of these, on 13 July 1968, was to a Sabena Boeing 707-320 on a cargo flight from Brussels, which crashed into trees 14km (almost 9 miles) north of the airport as it approached, with the loss of all seven occupants. Another Boeing 707-320 cargo flight, operated by Angola Air Charter, crashed on 21 July 1988, again on approach and 10km (just over 8 miles) north of the airport. By far the most serious accident was to a Nigerian Air Force Lockheed C-130H Hercules which is believed to have taken off with 158 people, including the crew, on board, on 26 September 1992, and after take-

off first one engine failed, than a second, and finally a third, and despite an attempt to ditch in a canal, the aircraft crashed nose first into a swamp. The number of casualties is still unknown. A de Havilland Canada DHC-6 Twin Otter operated by Bristow Helicopters crashed on 23 April 1995 while trying to land in strong winds and heavy rain, when it encountered a microburst (a phenomenon also known as windshear) and struck the runway nosewheel first, and while a go-around was attempted, the aircraft narrowly avoided a deep ditch and two Hercules transports before colliding with a Fokker F-27 Troopship of the Nigerian Air Force. One of the pilots was killed, but the other pilot and seven passengers survived. On 24 June 1995 a Tupolev Tu-134 of Harka Air Services landed from Kaduna and overshot the runway, hitting a concrete culvert some distance beyond the end of the runway. Out of the 74 passengers, 16 were killed, although the 6 crew appear to have survived.

ABUJA/NNAMDI AZIKIWE INTERNATIONAL: ABV
Abuja, Nigeria

Owner and operator: Federal Airports Authority of Nigeria
Runways: 04/22, 3,609m (11,842ft)
Terminals: Two, designated International and Domestic
Annual passengers: 2,198,674
Annual cargo: 3,737 tonnes

Background
Named after Nigeria's first president, it is the main airport for the country's capital city. It is currently under a five-year development programme to improve its passenger and air cargo facilities by 2011.

NORWAY

Norway, with its long and heavily indented coastline, is ideal territory for internal air transport, otherwise anyone travelling any distance is either compelled to change between road or rail transport and ferries, or take a slow coastal steamer. Given the sheltered landing places available in the fjords, the early air services were mainly operated by seaplanes or small flying boats, and it was not until after the Second World War that many of today's airports were built.

OSLO/GARDERMOEN: OSL

Gardermoen, Oslo, Norway

Owner and operator: Oslo Lufthavn AS
Runways: 01L/19R, 3,600m (11,811ft);
  01R/19L, 2,950m (9,678ft)
Terminals: One, with domestic and international
  halls
Airlines using airport as base or hub: SAS
  Braathens
Annual passengers: 19,043,800
Annual cargo: 97,311 tonnes
Annual aircraft movements: 226,303

The Gardermobanen railway link departs from a railway built into the airport terminal, and trains run to Oslo Central Station.

Background
Gardermoen was used as an airfield as early as 1912 when, as Fredericksfeldt, it was the site of early experiments with aircraft by the Norwegian Army. Within a few years a substantial airfield had developed, with hangars and barracks. It was still in use when the Germans invaded in 1940, and after seizing the airfield, they rebuilt it with two 2,000m runways. After the war the airfield continued as a military installation while also being used for commercial flights, including the long-distance flights by the original Norwegian long-haul airline, Braathens. Nevertheless, the main airport for post-war Oslo was Fornebu, even though for many years that airport's run-

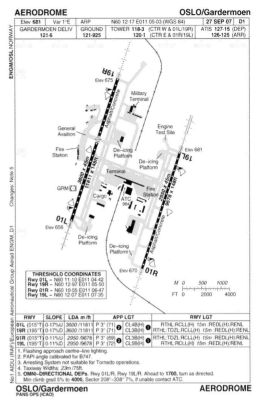

ways were too short, and it was not until the 1990s that SAS was able to move its Oslo–New York service to Fornebu. Once this happened, Gardermoen reverted to being primarily a military base.

Nevertheless, all was not well at Fornebu, which dated from 1939 and by this time was suffering from capacity problems and still had just one runway. Constructed on a peninsula, expansion posed severe physical problems and there was little possibility of a railway link to the airport. In October 1992 the Norwegian parliament decided that Oslo needed a new airport and chose Gardermoen as the site. The decision was also taken that the new airport should be self-financing, with a new company formed for its development and operation, Oslo Lufthavn AS, although this was managed as a subsidiary of Avinor, the Norwegian civil airports authority, and also took over operation of Forbeu.

Gardermoen opened and became the main Oslo airport on 8 October 1998, leaving Fornebu as a seaplane station only. The opening was just in time for deregulation, and traffic grew rapidly as there was a price war amongst airlines, including a new low-cost Norwegian arrival, Color Air, but this did not last long as Color Air suspended operations in 1999. That same year, Northwest Airline introduced a service between Oslo and Minneapolis, but this was abandoned because of poor load factors. The SAS service to New York was abandoned in October 2001, but in 2004 Continental Airlines began operations on this route. By this time, Norwegian Air Shuttle had introduced services to some 50 international and 10 internal destinations. In 2006, the airport opened Europe's first infrared de-icing hangar at the airport.

Scandinavian airports have a good safety record, despite the often-extreme weather conditions encountered. One of the worst days was 14 December 1998, when a combination of freezing fog and freezing rain created an icy glaze at Gardermoen. Around 20 aircraft engines were damaged by ice during take-off, and five aircraft had to make emergency landings with just one engine working. The event was not unique, as Denver International suffered the same problems in 2002. The risks bad weather brings led to an accident to a Cessna Grand Caravan operated by Air Team flying a cargo charter of newspapers on 4 December 1994. As the aircraft prepared to take off in sub-zero temperatures, the rain turned to snow, and as it climbed out the aircraft stalled and crashed into woods, killing the only occupant, the pilot. The only other accident at the airport was on 14 February 2006, when an SAS Commuter Fokker 50 suffered an undercarriage collapse while it was waiting for passengers to board.

BERGEN/FLESLAND: BGO

Bergen, Norway

Owner and operator: Avinor

Runways: 17/35, 2,990m (9,810ft); there is also a helipad

Terminals: Two, designated International and Domestic

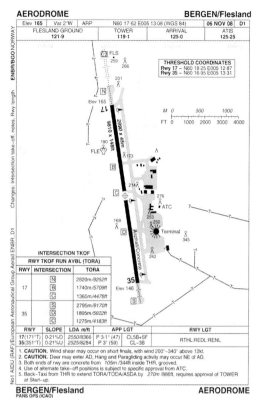

Airlines using airport as base or hub: Bergen Air Transport

Annual passengers: 4,852,740

Annual cargo: 6,103 tonnes

Annual aircraft movements: 99,172

The Bergen Light Rail is expected to run into the airport at some point in the future.

Background

While land was bought by the local authority for an airport in 1937, it was not built until after the Second World War and did not open until 1955, primarily funded by NATO for possible military use. With the discovery of North Sea oil, traffic grew considerably, while, because of the heavily-indented coastline of Norway, air transport is important for domestic journeys. A new terminal was opened in 1988 and a new air traffic control tower in 1991. Future plans include extending the international terminal, better aircraft parking, a de-icing platform, and ground and secondary radar, as well as extending a light railway line into the terminal.

STAVANGER/SOLA: SVG

Sola, Stavanger, Norway

Owner and operator: Avianor
Runways: 18/36, 2,556m (8,385ft); 11/29, 2,449m (8,035ft); there is also a helipad
Terminals: One for fixed-wing aircraft, plus a helicopter terminal for offshore oil platforms
Airlines using airport as base or hub: CHC Helicopter Service, Norsk Helikopter
Annual passengers: 3,528,426
Annual cargo: 9,862 tonnes
Annual aircraft movements: 79,904

Background

Just outside Stavanger at the small town of Sola, Stavanger Sola is Norway's third largest airport

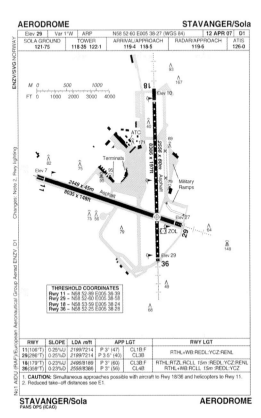

and also a busy helicopter base serving the offshore oil industry.

The airport was opened on 29 May 1937 and boasts being only the second in Europe to have a concrete runway. On 9 April 1940, the airport was attacked by German forces and seized by paratroops, becoming a Luftwaffe base for the remainder of the Second World War. Strategically placed, especially after the Allies started sending convoys to Russian ports in the Arctic, the Germans enlarged the airfield considerably.

After the war the Royal Norwegian Air Force started to use Sola until commercial air traffic built up, and for some years a fighter squadron was based at the airport. The Norwegian airline, Det Norske Luftartsselskap (DNL), which later became the Norwegian contribution to the Scandinavian Airlines System (SAS), started operations from Oslo in 1946, as did the privately-owned Braathens South American & Far East Air Transport (Braathens SAFE) with flights to Europe, the Far East, and South America carrying mainly ships' crews for the parent company's shipping interests. When Braathens' long-haul services were taken over by SAS, the airline became Norway's domestic airline and operated from Stavanger to Oslo, Kristiansand, Bergen, and a number of other coastal towns. SAS operated the international routes as well as to Bergen and northern Norway, but this division ended when air transport in Norway was deregulated in 1994, even though the country is not a member of the European Union. Widerøe opened a base at Sola in the late 1980s. A number of foreign airlines also started to operate into Sola, some of them immediately after the war, such as British European Airways (BEA), and others later, including Dan-Air and Air UK, both of which have since been taken over, and more recently, City Star and Eastern Airways.

The airport was well-placed to benefit from the start of North Sea oil exploration in 1971, and several helicopter operators started to use Sola as their base, while a couple of airlines also attempted to enter the helicopter business before rationalisation started and Sola now has two resident helicopter operators. In 1987 the current terminal opened and the old one was converted for use by helicopters. The new terminal had nine skybridges, the first in Norway, when it opened. One effect of the oil industry involvement is that Stavanger–Aberdeen is now an important route, but the busiest schedule remains that to Oslo with 25 flights a day.

In recent years the terminal has been modernised and extended, and much has been done to extend operations when visibility is poor. The airport also has an aviation museum, *Flyhistorisk*.

While the fixed-wing squadrons have gone, the Royal Norwegian Air Force still has a presence at Sola, with Westland Sea King helicopters based there for search and rescue operations. From time to time other military aircraft visit, as Norway is a member of NATO.

There was just one serious accident to an aircraft approaching the airport. On 9 August 1961 a chartered Eagle Airways Vickers Viking was flying from London to Stavanger, but the aircraft deviated from its course and crashed into a steep hill, killing all 3 crew and 36 passengers.

TRONDHEIM/VAERNES: TRD
Stjørdal, Trondheim, Norway

Owner and operator: Avinor/Royal Norwegian
   Air Force
Runways: 09/27, 2,759m (9,052ft); 14/32,
   1,454m (4,771ft) currently closed
Terminals: Two, designated Terminal A for
   domestic flights, and Terminal B for
   international flights
Annual passengers: 3,406,281
Annual cargo: 6,672 tonnes
Annual aircraft movements: 54,954

The airport has its own railway station, Trondheim Airport Station at Vaernes, on the Norlandsbanen with trains running to Trondheim and Nordland, and also to Hell.

Background
Norway's fourth largest airport, Trondheim, on an area known as Vaernes, is 36km (22½ miles)

east of Trondheim and is a hub for the southern part of the Nordland region.

A former farm, Vaernes was purchased by the Norwegian Army in 1887 to build an army camp. On 26 March 1914 it was first used for aviation when the army's new Maurice Farman Longhorn took off. By 1919, three aircraft were stationed at Vaernes and a hangar was built the following year. The site remained a military airfield, and after the German invasion in April 1940 it was taken over by the Luftwaffe, and three new runways were built for attacks against Allied shipping. It played an important part in the offensive against Allied convoys carrying war materiel to the Soviet Union. At the end of the war, the base was occupied by the Royal Air Force, which withdrew shortly afterwards handing the base back to Norwegian control, and it became a Royal Norwegian Air Force base and was its main flying school in 1952.

Between the wars, seaplane and flying boat services had operated along the coast of Norway, and these resumed after the war with Det Norske Luftfartsselskap (DNL), which later became the Norwegian contribution to Scandinavian Airways System (SAS) flying floatplane variants of the Junkers Ju52. The decision to convert the airfield to a civil airport was taken in 1951, with NATO contributing towards the construction of the military side, which ensured that overall the airport was large given the size of the communities served. The new airport opened on 21 October 1961, although SAS had been operating between Vaernes and Oslo since 1952, and were joined by Braathens SAFE in 1956. The airport received a new terminal in 1965, but capacity problems were already apparent with the growth in charter flights to the resorts of southern Europe. Another new terminal opened in 1982, and this was converted for international flights and designated Terminal B in 1994 when a new domestic terminal opened, designated Terminal A. A railway station was opened at the airport that same year.

Following deregulation of air services in 1998 a low-cost airline started to operate on the route to Oslo – Color Air competing with Braathens and SAS – and intense competition resulted, with Color Air eventually collapsing and Braathens being purchased by SAS to become SAS Braathens.

The airport also accommodates the Norwegian Home Guard and continues to have a NATO role, although this is much reduced following the collapse of the Warsaw Pact.

There was one serious accident at Trondheim on 23 February 1987 as an SAS, Scandinavian Airlines System McDonnell Douglas DC-9-41 was on approach having flown from Bodo. The captain, contrary to company regulations, contacted his head office and forgot to deploy the spoilers, which he deployed and then retracted at the last minute as he realised his mistake. The aircraft hit the runway hard and, although the aircraft was able to go around again and land, it was badly damaged and had to be scrapped. The 4 crew and 103 passengers were unhurt.

TROMSØ: TOS
Tromsoe, Norway

Owner and operator: Avinor
Runways: 01/19, 2,392m (7,848ft)
Terminals: One
Airlines using airport as base or hub: Widerøe
Annual passengers: 1,606,226
Annual aircraft movements: 40,063

Background
Northern Norway's largest airport, Tromsø is just 3.1km (less than 2 miles) from the centre of the town. While it is an important hub for flights into many smaller airports in Finnmark, many passengers fly to these directly from Oslo.

While Tromsø town had enjoyed regular air services since the 1930s, these were operated by seaplanes and flying boats until the airport opened on 14 September 1964. The airport became a hub for regional flights using short take-off and landing (STOL) aircraft such as the de Havilland Twin Otter in 1974. The original terminal was replaced in 1977, while the present terminal only dates from 1998 when it was built during modernisation of the airport, which also

included a new control tower. The terminal includes a number of airbridges for jet airliners. During the modernisation of the late 1990s, the runway was extended over the road leading to the airport, with the road now in a tunnel.

The airport has been the scene of two accidents. The first was on 12 September 1972 when a Royal Air Force Lockheed C-130K Hercules veered off the runway into a ditch while landing and was so badly damaged that it had to be scrapped. There appear to have been no casualties. The second was on 17 July 1973 when a chartered Convair CV640 (a turboprop conversion of a CV240-440 series) operated by SATA, a Swiss airline, made a heavy landing and the undercarriage collapsed, but the 4 crew and 56 passengers survived.

BODØ: BOO
Bodo, Norway

Owner and operator: Avinor
Runways: 07/25, 3,394m (11,136ft)
Terminals: One
Airlines using airport as base or hub: Widerøe
Annual passengers: 1,519,837
Annual aircraft movements: 44,149

Background
A joint civil and military airport, it is the largest base for the Royal Norwegian Air Force and is just south of the town of Bodø itself.

Bodø has a long history of aviation, having been served first by postal flights and then by passenger air services since 1921, but all these were operated by seaplanes or small flying boats. A temporary airstrip was built at Bodø during the Anglo-French intervention in Norway after the German invasion in 1940. The runway consisted of wooden planks laid over the swampland to allow the RAF to put Gloster Gladiator fighters into the air for the defence of the town. It was not until the Germans took over the area that a permanent airfield with a concrete runway was built.

The present airfield and airport was built on a new site by NATO during the Cold War to deter a Soviet invasion of Western Europe through Scandinavia. The plans were prepared in 1950 during the Korean War, and the facility was due to be completed the following year, but while the civil side of the airfield opened in 1952, the military area didn't open until 1956. In 1988, the military area was substantially enlarged and modernised by NATO so that it could handle large numbers of aircraft in a crisis. Meanwhile, Bodø developed into a regional airport and as a hub for flights to smaller airfields in the region, with a new terminal opened in recent years. One feature of the airport is the Norwegian Aviation Museum, built next to the airport and funded by the Norwegian government.

The military side of the airport is occupied by a Royal Norwegian Air Force fighter squadron, operating Lockheed F-16 Fighting Falcons, and a flight of Westland Sea King search-and-rescue helicopters.

The airport has had two incidents in recent years, both to Dornier 228-200 aircraft operated by Kato Airline. On 4 December 2003 an aircraft approaching to land from Rost was struck by lightning, which damaged the tailplane so badly that the rudder could not be used. The first attempt at landing was abandoned, and on the second attempt the aircraft landed heavily and the undercarriage collapsed, resulting in heavy damage to the fuselage. Although the aircraft was written off, both pilots and the two passengers survived. The second occurred when an asylum-seeker, whose application had been rejected, ran amok in an aircraft with an axe, possibly one carried on the aircraft for emergencies, causing the aircraft to divert to Brodø while the man was restrained by passengers. It landed safely.

SANDEFJORD/TORP: TRF

Stokke, Norway

Owner and operator: Sandefjord Lufthavn AS
Runways: 18/36, 2,950m (9,675ft)
Terminals: One
Airlines using airport as base or hub: Widerøe; Helifly

Annual passengers: 1,519,305
Annual aircraft movements: 39,076

Background

Sandefjord or Sandefjord Torp, is situated in the south-east of the country, between the towns of Sandefjord and Stokke, the airport is often referred to as Oslo-Torp by the low-cost airlines that use it as a cheaper alternative to Oslo Gardermoen, turning it from a Norwegian regional airport to an airport with two-thirds of its traffic international. It is the largest airport not run by the Norwegian state airport holding company, Avinor, but instead Sandefjord Lufthavn AS is owned by the two municipalities and a private investment group.

The airport dates from the Cold War era when it was built during the early 1960s by NATO as a military air station. It was opened to commercial air traffic, and Norsk Air began services to Bergen, Stavanger, and Trondheim using Embraer Bandeirante two-turboprops before the airline was acquired by Widerøe, which now has a hub and a maintenance base at the airport. Helifly also has a maintenance base and operates from the airport in support of the offshore energy industry. The airport came close to closure when Oslo's new airport at Gardermoen opened, as the government decided that the east of the country only needed one airport, but the local authorities took the airport over and operations continued. The Irish low-cost airline, Ryanair, started operations from London Stansted in 1997, and since then the airport has become Norway's leading low-cost airport, with Ryanair joined by Wizz Air. The airport was bought from the Royal Norwegian Air Force in 2006.

The terminal is being enlarged and the taxiways widened to cope with the steady rise in traffic, but there is a threat from Rygge's Moss Airport, which has been given approval for development as a commercial airport and is expected to compete for the low-cost market.

PAKISTAN

Pakistan emerged as an independent nation with the partition of India in 1947. Initially, the country was divided in two, separated by India, and with the national airline operating out of both West and East Pakistan, with the former being the larger, more populous and prosperous. For many years the Pakistan Air Force, using Bristol 170 Freighters, maintained a regular air transport operation between the two halves of the country, as air transport was much quicker than going by sea round the Indian subcontinent. When East Pakistan gained its independence, all operations were concentrated on what had been West Pakistan. Pakistan was the first non-Communist country to be able to operate air services into Communist China.

While air transport was originally in the hands of Pakistan International Airlines, in recent years a healthy private airline sector has developed, but airports remain in state ownership. Although it was decided to build a new capital at Islamabad, the old capital, Karachi, remains the most important airport in the country as old established commercial links take far longer to change than a simple move of the seat of government.

KARACHI/JINNAH (QUAID-E-AZAM) INTERNATIONAL: KHI

Karachi, Sind, Pakistan

Owner and operator: Civil Aviation Authority of Pakistan

Runways: 07L/25R, 3,200m (10,500ft); 07R/25L, 3,400m (11,155ft)

Terminals: One, with a West Satellite Concourse for domestic flights and an East Satellite Concourse for international flights

Airlines using airport as base or hub: Aero Asia International, Airblue, PIA Pakistan, Shaheen Air International

Annual passengers: 6,081,448

Annual cargo: 171,330 tonnes

Annual aircraft movements: 52,990

Background

Until recently known as Quaid-e-Azam (translating as 'Great Leader') in honour of the founder of Pakistan, Muhammad Ali Jinnah, the airport is now known as Jinnah International. It is the main hub for three airlines, including Pakistan International, Shaheen International, and Airblue.

The first airport in what was then British India, Karachi opened in 1929 and one of the early structures was a large black hangar intended for use by the giant British airship *R101*. This was just one of three hangars built for the *R101*, but it was never used as it crashed in France on its outward flight from the UK. The hangar was demolished in the 1960s, but far more enduring was the original terminal from the days of British rule that served as the airport's sole passenger facility for many years and survives today as office accommodation. Two further terminals were added during the 1980s,

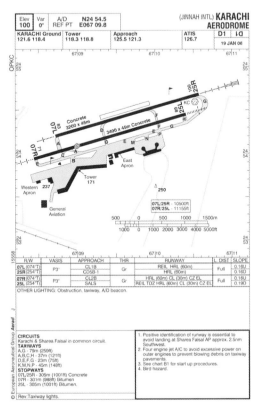

becoming 2 and 3, but were replaced by the Jinnah Terminal which opened in 1992 and today brings together all of the airport's traffic.

The airport prospered after independence in 1947, partly because Karachi was the first capital and partly because of the greater need for en route refuelling facilities at the time. The move of the seat of government to Islamabad, the longer ranges of modern aircraft and the emergence of Dubai as a major hub airport in the Middle East, all combined to make Karachi less important, a situation not helped by the uncertain political situation. Nevertheless, since 2000, traffic started to grow again and a wider range of airlines have begun serving the airport, although passenger numbers fell 1.2 per cent between 2006 and 2007.

The airport has been the scene of a number of accidents since the Second World War. One of these was the first accident to a jet-powered airliner when, on 3 March 1953, a de Havilland Comet 1A of Canadian Pacific Airlines (which later became Canadian Airlines before being taken over by Air Canada) was being delivered to the airline and failed to take off because the nose was lifted too high by an inexperienced pilot. The aircraft crashed into a river bed with the loss of all on board – five crew and six non-revenue passengers. A flight landing from Goa, when it was still a Portuguese colony, crashed into the airport's fire brigade building on 2 November 1957, although the 27 occupants of the TAIP (Transportes Aereos da India Portuguesa) Vickers Viking all survived. Far less fortunate were those aboard a Pakistan International Airlines (PIA) Vickers Viscount 800 on a post-delivery training flight on 14 August 1959, which had to abandon a landing attempt as the aircraft was not aligned with the runway and executed a go-around, but was next seen approaching with engines Nos. 3 and 4 inoperative, and as it landed yawed to the right and the wing hit a wall before the aircraft burst into flames. Two of the three crew members aboard the aircraft were killed. A PIA Boeing 720 on a domestic flight to Quetta on 8 January 1981 returned to Karachi when the pilots found that the nosewheel would not lower, and made a nosewheel-up landing which damaged the aircraft beyond repair, but the 7 crew and 79 passengers survived. A Pan Am Boeing 747 was also damaged beyond repair on 4 August 1983 when it landed from New Delhi on a wet runway with the thrust reverser deactivated on the No. 4 engine, but on landing the engine powered up with the aircraft yawing off the runway – the 16 crew members and 227 passengers were unharmed. On 21 January 1995 a Kazakhstan Airlines Tupolev Tu-154 failed to lift off because it was overloaded by six tons. The captain aborted the take-off, but the aircraft overshot the runway and was damaged beyond repair. The 12 crew and 105 passengers survived.

Another nosewheel incident on 15 August 2002 resulted in substantial damage to an Antonov An-12 of Intercity Airways as it landed on a cargo flight, although the seven crew members were unharmed.

One incident occurred to a Boeing 707-320 of Ethiopian Airlines on 18 June 1969 while it was parked at the airport and two bombs were thrown at it, but the aircraft was repaired and returned to service.

LAHORE/ALLAMA IQBAL INTERNATIONAL: LHE
Lahore, Pakistan

Owner and operator: Pakistan Civil Aviation
  Authority
Runways: 18L/36R, 3,310m (11,024ft);
  18R/36L, 2,900m (9,514ft)
Terminals: Two, designated the Allama Iqbal
  Terminal and the Hajj Terminal
Airlines using airport as base or hub: PIA
  (Pakistan International Airlines)
Annual passengers: 3,091,590
Annual cargo: 76,348 tonnes
Annual aircraft movements: 39,534

Background
Pakistan's second largest airport after Karachi's Jinnah International, Allama Iqbal is named after a poet and philosopher who advocated

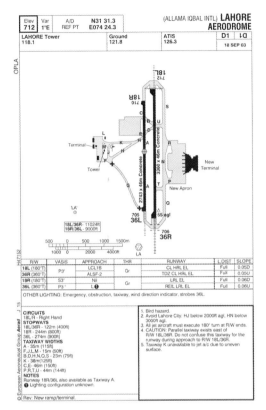

ating the air bridge between West and East Pakistan, and crashed shortly after take-off due to unknown causes, killing the crew of two. Almost a decade later, an Avro York leased from TMA (Trans Mediterranean Airways) by Kuwait Airways suffered an undercarriage failure as it landed at Lahore on a cargo flight, although the three crew members survived.

Two Pakistan Air Force Lockheed Hercules were both written off in a ground collision on 1 February 1979, but no details are available about occupants or casualties.

Weather also intervened on one occasion when the Beechjet 400A owned by the Punjab Government was wrecked when a hangar collapsed on the aircraft during a storm on 6 June 2004. No one was aboard at the time.

A number of aircraft were lost or damaged during hijackings. One of these was an Indian Airlines Fokker F-27 Friendship which had been flying between Srinagar and Jammu-Satwari when it was hijacked and diverted to Lahore on 30 January 1971 and was set alight and destroyed by the three hijackers on 2 February. The passengers and crew had been released by this time. Another aircraft that was hijacked and flown to Lahore was also an Indian Airlines plane, but on this occasion a Boeing 737-200 that had been flying from New Delhi to Bombay (now Mumbai), but on this occasion the aircraft survived, as did the 6 crew and 77 passengers. Yet another Indian Airlines Boeing 737-200 was hijacked and flown to Lahore on 29 September 1981 by a gang of five Sikh terrorists while it was flying from New Delhi to Amritsar. They released 46 of the 177 people on board after landing, and the aircraft was stormed and the hijackers arrested the following day, apparently without any fatalities amongst the remaining passengers and crew. An almost identical hijacking followed on 4 August 1982, same route and same type of airliner from the same airline, except that the plane was recovered within the day. A larger Indian Airlines aircraft, an Airbus A300, was seized by hijackers on 5 July 1984, although this time with nine Sikhs, and diverted from its Srinagar to New Delhi flight to Lahore,

independence for the country. It is 15km (almost 10 miles) from the city centre.

When Pakistan became independent in 1947, Lahore was served by Walton Airport, but this was unable to handle jet aircraft as the runways were too short and there was no room for expansion. The present airport was opened in 1962, and for many years was more usually known as Lahore International Airport. From the outset, it could handle aircraft of Boeing 747 size.

A major reconstruction programme ended in 2003 with what amounted to almost a completely new airport, which adopted the current title. The remains of the original airport are now used by the Pakistani Air Force, although the old terminal is used by airlines carrying Hajj pilgrims to Mecca. Further expansion is now in hand with the extension of the main terminal.

Amongst the accidents at Lahore was one on 25 September 1952 when a Bristol 170 of what was then the Royal Pakistan Air Force was oper-

where the hijackers surrendered and the 10 crew and 254 passengers were released.

ISLAMABAD/BENAZIR BHUTTO INTERNATIONAL/CHAKLALA: ISB
Rawalpindi, Punjab, Pakistan

Owner and operator: Pakistan Civil Aviation Authority
Runways: 12/30, 3,287m (10,785ft)
Terminals: One
Airlines using airport as base or hub: Pakistan International Airlines (PIA), Shaheen Air International, Airblue
Annual passengers: 3,035,966
Annual cargo: 54,530 tonnes
Annual aircraft movements: 48,110

Background
Islamabad is the third largest airport in Pakistan, and is also known as Chaklala Airbase as it is shared with the Pakistan Air Force, which uses it for transport and communications units. It is actually located near to Rawalpindi. It was built to provide an airport for the post-independence capital of Pakistan, which became the seat of government in 1967. It was originally known officially as Islamabad International Airport, but the present title was adopted in June 2008 to commemorate the assassinated party leader and ex-prime minister.

The airport has been modernised and extended since it opened, but a new airport is being built and should open in 2010.

Amongst the accidents at the airport was one to an almost new Vickers Viscount 800 on 18 May 1959, as the pilot tried to turn the aircraft at the end of the runway after landing, but instead the aircraft skidded, the undercarriage collapsed and one wing was broken as it slipped into a monsoon ditch. The next recorded accident was on 15 September 1985 when two de Havilland Canada Twin Otters were involved in a ground collision, but both aircraft were repaired and there were no injuries. The occupants were also lucky to escape on 4 February 1986 when a PIA Boeing 747-200 from Karachi, with 17 crew and 247 passengers aboard, belly landed on the runway at Islamabad after the pilots forgot to lower the undercarriage.

PANAMA

PANAMA CITY/TOCUMEN INTERNATIONAL: PTY
Tocumen, Panama

Owner and operator: Tocumen SA
Runways: 03L/21R, 2,682m (8,800ft); 03R/21L, 3,050m (10,006ft)
Terminals: One
Airlines using airport as base or hub: Aeroperlas, Copa Airlines
Annual passengers: 3,805,312
Annual cargo: 82,462 tonnes
Annual aircraft movements: 74,438

Background
Panama's main airport, Tocumen, is 24km (15 miles) from Panama City and is named after the nearest town.

The airport was built as Patilla Point Airfield by the United States Army Air Force during the Second World War and used by the US Sixth Air Force to defend the Panama Canal. After the war it was opened as the country's international airport on 1 June 1947. A hangar was used as a terminal until a terminal building was completed in 1954, and today this is used as the cargo terminal. A new passenger terminal was opened in 1978. Briefly, during the 1980s, the airport was known as Omar Torrijos International Airport after a former president, but the name reverted to Tocumen after the US invaded in 1989.

The airport is owned and operated by the state-owned Tocumen SA. In 2006 a modernisation and expansion programme began, which has resulted in the expansion of the passenger terminal.

There have been a number of accidents at the airport, many of which have involved cargo flights. One of these was on 27 March 1953 when a Curtis C-46 of AREA Ecuador, landing from

Miami, suffered an undercarriage failure and veered off the runway into a ravine, but the two crew members survived. Another cargo flight was involved in an accident on 4 August 1965 when a RIPSA (Rutas Internacionales Peruanes SA) Douglas C-54, flying from Peru to Miami, crashed after take-off when an engine caught fire, killing all seven people aboard. Before the end of the year, on 7 December, another C-46, belonging to Aerolineas Carreras Transportes Aereos, crashed 40km (25 miles) from the airport with the loss of all seven occupants. A much more modern aircraft than any of these was a civil Lockheed Hercules of TAB (Transportes Aereos Bolivianos), which crashed on 28 September 1979 as it climbed out of Panama, killing the only occupants, the four crew members.

There have also been some accidents to passenger flights, including a McDonnell Douglas DC-10 of KLM Royal Dutch Airlines, which skidded off the runway on landing on 3 June 1983, followed by a nosewheel collapse, but the aircraft was repairable and the 10 crew and 17 passengers survived. Another landing accident was to the local airline, COPA (Compania Panama de Aviacion) on 19 November 1993, when a Boeing 737-100 landed from Miami although not properly aligned with the runway and in wet weather veered off the runway and across a taxiway with the nose gear collapsing and the aircraft suffering considerable damage, but again the 6 crew and 86 passengers survived. Unfortunately, no such good fortune was available for the two crew and four passengers aboard an IAI Westwind executive jet on an air ambulance flight as it took-off for Washington on 2 July 2004 having flown in earlier from Quito. As it took-off, the nose pitched upwards and the aircraft veered sharply before hitting the ground and finally ending up inverted in an empty hangar, killing all on board and one person on the ground.

PERU

LIMA/JORGE CHÁVEZ INTERNATIONAL: LIM
Callao, Lima, Peru

Owner and operator: Lima Airport Partners
Runways: 15/33, 3,507m (11,506ft)
Terminals: One
Airlines using airport as base or hub: Aero Condor, Cielos del Peru, LAN Peru, Star Peru, TACA Peru
Annual passengers: 7,505,832
Annual cargo: 225,370 tonnes
Annual aircraft movements: 92,880

Background
Situated some 11km (7 miles) from the city centre, the airport was opened in 1960 as Lima-Callao International Airport after the area in which it was located. The current title of Jorge

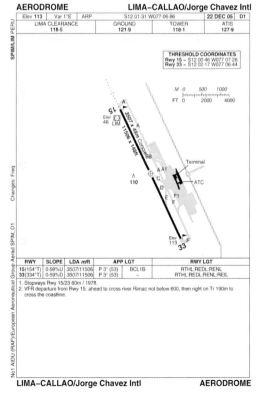

LIMA–CALLAO/Jorge Chavez Intl   AERODROME

Chávez International was adopted in June 1965 in memory of the Franco-Peruvian aviator, Jorge Chávez Dartnell, who in 1910 was the first man to fly across the Alps, although his flight ended in a fatal accident. The airport replaced the original one for the country, the Limatambo Airport at San Isidro, which could no longer cope with the growth in traffic. The current terminal building opened in 1965.

The new airport failed to keep pace with change, and in 2001 the Peruvian government, although retaining ownership, granted a concession for its management and development to Lima Airport Partners, a consortium which includes Fraport, operator of Frankfurt International Airport. In February 2005 a renovation and expansion project was completed with the opening of a new concourse with seven boarding bridges, but construction of the second runway has been delayed.

An accident occurred at the airport on 15 April 1995, when a Tupolev Tu-134 of Imperial Air landed from Cuzco-Velazco on a domestic flight after suffering a tyre failure during take-off. The left main undercarriage would not extend and the aircraft was damaged beyond repair on landing, although the 5 crew and 68 passengers survived. Another landing accident was to an Aero Contente Boeing 737-200 on 13 December 2003, arriving from Caracas, when the crew were distracted by a warning that the flaps were deployed asymmetrically and forgot to lower the undercarriage, leaving the aircraft to skid along the runway, again being damaged beyond repair, although the 6 crew and 94 passengers survived. Another accident occurred on 15 March 2005 as an ATSA (Aero Transporte SA) Antonov An-26 was taking-off for Loreto in Mexico, on a cargo flight. It left the ground, but after the undercarriage was raised, dropped down again and struck the runway, skidding to a halt, having taken-off without any flap and while overweight. The crew of four survived this incident.

PHILIPPINES

Like Japan, the Philippines is an island nation, but the comparison stops there, unless one counts the many airfields constructed by the Japanese during the Second World War. The population is much smaller and such manufacturing industry as there is operates on a much smaller scale, with agriculture and fisheries being far more important. The country has also failed to make the most of tourism in the way that Indonesia has managed. As a result there is just one major airport in the islands, serving the capital, Manila.

MANILA/NINOY AQUINO INTERNATIONAL: MNL
Manila, Philippines

Owner and operator: Manila International Airport Authority
Runways: 06/24, 3,737m (12,261ft); 13/31, 2,258m (7,408ft)
Terminals: Four, designated Terminal 1, Terminal 2 (Centennial Terminal), Terminal 3, and Manila Domestic Passenger Terminal
Airlines using airport as base or hub: Air Philippines, Cebu Pacific, Philippine Airlines, SEAIR, ZestAir
Annual passengers: 20,467,627
Annual cargo: 388,551 tonnes
Annual aircraft movements: 188,797

A taxi is necessary to reach the railway, but there are plans to extend the Manila Light Rail Transit System's Yellow Line to an airport station.

Background
Originally, Manila was served by an airport at Nielson Field, opened in 1937 and known as the Manila International Air Terminal. This was used as a base by the Japanese Army Air Force during the Second World War, but today little remains as it has been turned over to urban development as Makati City. After the Second World War, in 1948, a new airport was built on the present location next to Nichols Field, later

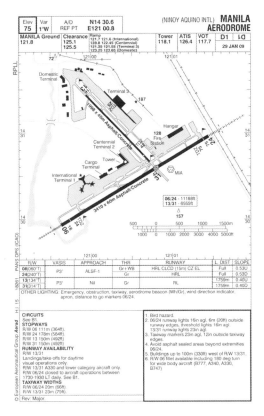

Elev 75	Var 1°W	A/D REF PT	N14 30.6 E121 00.8		(NINOY AQUINO INTL) **MANILA** **AERODROME**

| MANILA Ground 121.8 | Clearance 125.1 125.5 | Ramp 121.7 121.6 (International) 128.8 122.45 (Centennial) 121.35 121.55 (Terminal 3) 123.25 123.65 (Domestic) | Tower 118.1 | ATIS 126.4 | VOT 117.7 | D1 | LO 29 JAN 09 |

R/W	VASIS	APPROACH	THR	RUNWAY	L. DIST	SLOPE
06(060°T)	P3°	ALSF-1	Gr+WB	HRL CLCD (15m) CZ EL	Full	0.53U
24(240°T)			Gr	HRL	Full	0.53D
13(134°T)	P3°	Nil	Gr	RL	1759m	0.40U
31(314°T)					1759m	0.40D

OTHER LIGHTING: Emergency, obstruction, taxiway, aerodrome beacon (Wh/Gr), wind direction indicator, apron, distance to go markers 06/24.

CIRCUITS
See B1.
STOPWAYS
R/W 06 111m (364ft).
R/W 24 178m (584ft).
R/W 13 150m (492ft).
R/W 31 150m (492ft).
RUNWAY AVAILABILITY
R/W 13/31
Landings/take-offs for daytime visual operations only.
R/W 13/31 A330 and lower category aircraft only.
R/W 06/24 closed to aircraft operations between 1730-1930 LT daily. See B1.
TAXIWAY WIDTHS
R/W 06/24 20m (66ft)
R/W 13/31 23m (75ft).
Rev: Major.

1. Bird hazard.
2. 06/24 runway lights 16in agl. 6m (20ft) outside runway edges, threshold lights 16in agl. 13/31 runway lights 23in agl.
3. Taxiway markers 23in agl, 12in outside taxiway edges.
4. Avoid asphalt sealed areas beyond extremities 06/24.
5. Buildings up to 100m (330ft) west of R/W 13/31.
6. R/W 06 fillet available including 180 deg turn for wide body aircraft (B777, A340, A330, B747)

nal' as completion coincided with the centenary of Philippine independence from Spain. Terminal 3 was scheduled to be completed in 2002, but in the end opened in 2008. The opening of the new terminal is seen as essential for renewed growth and it is hoped that it will attract many airlines that abandoned calls at Manila because of congestion at the airport.

There have been a number of accidents and incidents at the airport. One of the worst was the loss of three aircraft on one day, 19 November 1970, when three Douglas C-47s belonging to different airlines were written off in a typhoon. On 20 May 1964, another C-47 was destroyed in a hangar fire.

Inevitably, some of the accidents date from the time when the airport was a United States Army Air Force base. On 27 August 1945 a Douglas C-54 (the military variant of the DC-4) crashed due to a mechanical failure, although neither the number on board nor their fate has been recorded.

A Pan American Boeing Stratocruiser, flying from San Francisco to Singapore, stopped to refuel at Manila on 2 June 1958, but as the aircraft touched down the undercarriage collapsed and a passenger was killed as a propeller fragment penetrated the cabin. The crew of 8 and the other 48 passengers survived. On 12 September 1969 a PAL (Philippine Air Lines) BAC One-Eleven 400, on approach from Cebu on a domestic flight, flew into a hillside causing the deaths of 4 out of the 5 crew and all but one of the 42 passengers. A similar fate awaited a Pan American Boeing 707-320 cargo flight as it approached Manila from Guam on 25 July 1971, with the loss of the crew of four. A PAL (Philippine Air Lines) BAe 748 suffered a burst tyre during take-off on 10 May 1975, and in the resulting accident the aircraft was so badly damaged that it was written off, but all 43 occupants survived. A landing accident occurred on 27 February 1980 when a China Airlines Boeing 707-320 from Taipei overshot the runway and caught fire, with the loss of 2 of the 135 passengers and crew. In another landing accident on 21 July 1989, a PAL BAC One-Eleven 500 overshot the runway

known as the Villamor Air Base. A new international standard runway and terminal were built and opened in 1954, and were followed by a new control tower and a terminal for international passengers which opened in 1961. The original terminal was destroyed by fire in 1972 and a slightly smaller terminal was built and opened in 1973, acting as the international terminal until 1981 when a new international Terminal, (designated Terminal 1) opened, and the second terminal was used for domestic services until it too was destroyed by fire in 1985.

The airport was renamed on 17 August 1987 in celebration of Begnino 'Ninoy' Aquino, Jr., who was assassinated at the airport after returning from the United States on 21 August 1983.

The airport underwent considerable expansion during the 1980s, with Aéroports de Paris acting as consultants, which resulted in the building of two new terminals (2 and 3), the former being known as the 'Centennial Termi-

in poor visibility and hit some cars on a road. While the 98 occupants of the plane survived, there were 8 fatalities on the ground.

A charter flight using a MATS Manila Aero Transport System Douglas C-47 on 26 April 1990 suffered an engine failure during take-off, hit a telegraph pole and then crashed into a rice paddy, causing the deaths of 7 of the 21 passengers. The 3 crew members survived. One unusual accident was on 11 May 1990 to a PAL Boeing 737, which burst into flames on pushback, possibly due to faulty wiring igniting fuel vapour, and of the 120 people aboard, 8 passengers died. All 21 passengers and crew aboard an Aerolift Philippines Beechcraft 1900C and another 4 people on the ground were killed when the aircraft crashed into a residential area after taking-off, possibly due to an engine failure. A de Havilland Canada Twin Otter was destroyed as it taxied across a runway and was struck by a Boeing 737 taking off on 2 April 1996. An Asian Spirit DHC-7, with 45 passengers and a crew of four, was written off after a landing accident on 4 September 2002 when it returned to Manila with undercarriage problems, but all aboard survived. A cargo flight operated by an Aboitz Air NAMC YS-11 crashed on landing when the aircraft veered off the runway on 16 November 2006, but there were no casualties amongst the nine people aboard the aircraft.

The airport has suffered at least one hijacking, to a PAL Philippine Air Lines Fokker F-27 Friendship on 6 November 1968, when four hijackers took over the aircraft and demanded money, but the incident lasted less than a day.

POLAND

WARSAW FREDERIC CHOPIN: WAW
Warsaw, Poland

Owner and operator: Polish Airports State Enterprise
Runways: 11/29, 2,800m (9,186ft); 15/33, 3,690m (12,106ft)

Terminals: Three, designated Terminal 1, Terminal 2, and the Etiuda Terminal
Airlines using airport as base or hub: Central Wings, Eurolot, LOT Polish Airlines, Sky Express, White Eagle Aviation
Annual passengers: 9,268,476
Annual cargo: 48,095 tonnes
Annual aircraft movements: 153,480

A railway station has been built under Terminal 2 and a direct line to Warsaw Śródmieście Station is being constructed.

Background
Warsaw already had an airport at Mokotow Field, but by 1924 encroaching urban development was affecting air traffic and inhibiting expansion, and the Ministry of Railways bought land near the village of Okęcie to build a new Central Airport. When the Central Airport opened in 1933, Mokotow closed. Usually

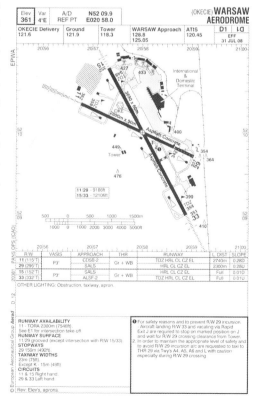

known in Poland as Okęcie, the airport was used briefly by Polish forces during the German invasion of Poland in September 1939, but during the war the airport was almost destroyed, first in resistance against the invading German armies, and then as the Germans retreated in the face of the Red Army in 1944.

Post war, with Poland firmly part of the Soviet Bloc, the new Polish airline, LOT, made the airport usable, and operations restarted. In 1956 responsibility for the airport was transferred from the airline to the state. A new international terminal opened in 1969, but domestic flights had to continue using the pre-war terminal until it was replaced by a new terminal in 1992, known as the Etiuda Terminal. The airport received its present name in March 2001 to commemorate the Polish pianist and composer, Frederic Chopin. The Etiuda terminal remains in use for low-cost carriers, while a new Terminal 2 was opened in 2008, and at some stage in the future this will have a direct railway link to Warsaw.

Deregulation of air transport in Europe, and the European Union-United States 'Open Skies' agreement, mean that there is still considerable potential for growth, and plans have been mooted to convert a disused military airfield north of Warsaw into a second airport for the city, possibly for low-cost and charter carriers only. This same market is also causing local authorities with suitable ex-military airports in their area to consider conversion and reopening for commercial use with the assistance of private investors.

The airport was the scene of an accident on 19 December 1962 when a LOT Polish Airlines Vickers Viscount 804, attempting a go-around, crashed with the loss of all 33 passengers and 5 crew. Another accident while attempting a go-around occurred on 14 March 1980 when a LOT Ilyushin Il-62, arriving from New York, crashed with the loss of all 87 passengers and 7 crew. A LOT Il-62 was also lost on 9 May 1989 when, due to an engine failure, it was returning to the airport shortly after taking-off, but on approach the aircraft crashed into woodland with the loss of 187 passengers and the crew of 10. On 14 Sep-

tember 1993 a Lufthansa Airbus A320, landing from Frankfurt, overshot the end of the runway and crashed into the embankment killing the co-pilot and a passenger, and another 68 passengers and crew were injured.

KRAKÓW/JOHN PAUL II INTERNATIONAL: KRK
Balice, Krakow, Poland

Owner and operator: MPL Balice
Runways: 07/25, 2,550m (8,366ft)
Terminals: Two, designated as International Terminal 1 and Domestic Terminal 2.
Annual passengers: 3,068,199
Annual aircraft movements: 40,269

The *Balice Ekspres* links the airport directly to Kraków Główny railway station.

Background
Named after the first Pole to become Pope, Kraków-Balice is near the village of Balice 11km (almost 7 miles) west of the centre of Kraków. It was opened in 1964 and has since become Poland's second busiest airport, although it has strong competition from Katowice International, which is not far away. Originally known as Kraków-Balice Airport, the name was changed to John Paul II International Airport Kraków-Balice in 1995, as the then Pope had spent much of his life there. This was rather long and cumbersome, so the name was shortened to *Kraków Airport im. Jana Pawla II* in September 2007.

Initially, the airport resisted low-cost airlines, such as Ryanair when it attempted to launch a service in 2003, but the regional government of Kraków threatened to build a new airport close by, using the infrastructure of an old military air station, and this encouraged the airport to accommodate Ryanair and other low-cost airlines.

In March 2007, a separate domestic terminal, the present Terminal 2, was opened, and a substantial expansion of the international terminal is now in hand.

There have been two minor incidents at the airport, both without casualties. On 24 April 1977, an attempted hijacking of a LOT Polish Airlines Tupolev Tu-134 was cut short by the aircraft being stormed and the hijacker arrested. More recently, on 28 August 2007 a Ryanair Boeing 737-800, landing from Shannon, blew a front tyre and an emergency evacuation of passengers followed, and the airport was closed for a short time.

KATOWICE INTERNATIONAL: KTW

Pyrzowice, Katowice, Poland

Owner and operator: Górnośląskie Towarzystwo Lotnicze (GTL)
Runways: 09/27, 2,799m (9,183ft)
Terminals: Two, designated Terminal A and Terminal B
Annual passengers: 1,985,216
Annual cargo: 7,772 tonnes

Background

The airport is situated 30km (almost 19 miles) north of the centre of Katowice. Terminal B was opened in 2007.

There has been one significant, and somewhat unusual, incident in recent years. On 27 October 2007 a Boeing 737-800 chartered by the United Nations destroyed dozens of approach and landing lights whilst landing at Katowice. There were no reports of passengers or crew being injured, or of the extent of damage to the aircraft, but the approach lights were out of service for three weeks while new lights were installed.

WROCLAW/COPERNICUS: WRO

Wroclaw, Poland

Owner and operator: Wroclaw Airport Company
Runways: 11/29, 2,500m (8,202ft)
Terminals: One passenger terminal with separate domestic and international areas
Annual passengers: 1,271,195

Background

The airport is 10km (6¼ miles) south-west of the centre of Wroclaw.

Before the Second World War, Wroclaw and the surrounding area was part of Germany, with the city known as Breslau. The airport dates from 1938 when it was built as a Luftwaffe station, and was used for aircraft covering the invasion of Poland that started the Second World War in Europe in September 1939. It was too far west to help the invasion of the Soviet Union in 1941, but was used first by the Germans and then by the Red Air Forces as the Red Army advanced westwards towards Germany in 1944 and 1945. The Russians continued to use the airport as a military base after the war ended, but soon transferred it to the Polish authorities, when it became a commercial airport. Until the overthrow of Communism and the break-up of the Warsaw Pact, airline services at the airport were almost entirely domestic flights.

The present operator was formed in 1992 and the assets at the airport owned by the Polish Airports Authority were transferred to it in 1993. That was the same year that the airport received its first international flights, with a service to Frankfurt starting in January. The period since has seen the airport modernised with a new international area for the passenger terminal opened in 1997, and a new domestic area followed in 1998. A cargo terminal was opened in 1999, and a new air traffic control tower started operations in 2001. The arrivals area of the terminal was enlarged in 2008 to separate Schengen and non-Schengen travellers. A new passenger terminal is planned, and the first stage should be open in 2010.

In December 2005 the airport was named after the famous astronomer, Nicolaus Copernicus, a Pole.

PORTUGAL

Although one of the colonial powers, the relative poverty of Portugal until recent years meant that air transport did not assume the importance in communications with the empire as it did in the case of the United Kingdom and France. Indeed, for many years communication with Madeira was by flying boat.

LISBON PORTELA: LIS

Lisbon, Portugal

Owner and operator: ANA Aeroportos de
     Portugal
Runways: 03/21, 3,805m (12,484ft); 17/35,
     2,400m (7,874ft)
Terminals: Two, designated Terminal 1
     (International) and Terminal 2 (Domestic)
Airlines using airport as base or hub: TAP Air
     Portugal
Annual passengers: 13,392,059
Annual cargo: 94,515 tonnes
Annual aircraft movements: 144,800

Background

Probably the closest to the city centre of any airport serving a European capital, Lisbon Portela, often referred to locally simply as 'Portela' because of its proximity to the suburb, or more usually simply as 'Lisbon', dates from 15 October 1942. Portugal was neutral during the Second World War and the city was important to both sides as a route into and out of occupied Europe. When it opened, the airport had four 1,000m (3,250ft) runways, but now has two much longer runways. It has enjoyed its share of the boom in tourist traffic since the end of the Second World War, but further expansion is almost impossible as the city's growth has spread itself around the airport. The intention is to build a new airport at Alcochete, which is already a training base for the air force, but this facility will be relocated long before the airport opens in around 2017.

The current Terminal 2 is the first of a series of measures intended to help the airport manage

traffic growth until the new airport opens, and it may also be opened up to charter flights and low-cost carriers, while it is also intended to further expand Terminal 1.

Unusually, two of the accidents at the airport involved training flights. The first of these was on 12 January 1949 when a TAP Air Portugal Douglas DC-4 made a heavy landing and was written off because of the damage, but there were no casualties. The second was to a Morane Saulnir Paris trainer of the Aeronavale (the French Navy's air arm) on 25 May 1958, which undershot the runway and caught fire, but again with no serious injuries to the crew of two. The next accident was to a Force Aerea Brasileira (Brazilian Air Force) Douglas C-54, taking the bodies of Brazilian service personnel, killed in action during the Second World War Italian campaign, from Rome back to Rio de Janeiro for burial, which crashed on landing and caught fire, but the nine crew members escaped. Finally, a

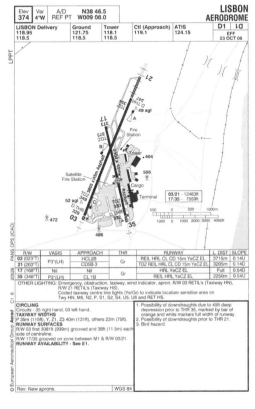

positioning flight from Paris to Lisbon for an Air Enterprise Learjet 23 ended with the aircraft making a belly landing, and while both pilots escaped, the aircraft did not and was damaged beyond repair.

FARO: FAO

Faro, Algarve, Portugal

Owner and operator: ANA Aeroportos de
 Portugal
Runways: 10/28, 2,610m (8,169ft)
Terminals: One
Annual passengers: 5,470,472
Annual aircraft movements: 45,428

Background
The airport is 7km (4½ miles) west of Faro and has grown substantially with the region's increasing popularity as a holiday destination. It has largely catered for charter and low-cost air-

lines, but is now attracting business traffic from the region and across the border in Spain.

The airport has seen two accidents, the first of which was extremely serious. On 21 December 1992, a McDonnell Douglas DC-10-30 of Martinair Holland was hit by windshear as it landed from Amsterdam in heavy rain, and struck the runway, with the undercarriage collapsing and the aircraft skidding along the runway, losing a wing and catching fire. Two of the 13 crew were killed as well as 54 of the 327 passengers. The next accident was far less serious, but could have been a disaster as the aircraft was overweight and the pilots decided not to reduce fuel, which would have meant making a refuelling stop, or off-loading passengers. The Avialinii 400 Tupolev Tu-154 took-off for Moscow on 1 August 2003, and as it left the runway struck trees and was damaged, but the pilots opted to continue their flight to Moscow, and would appear to have landed safely.

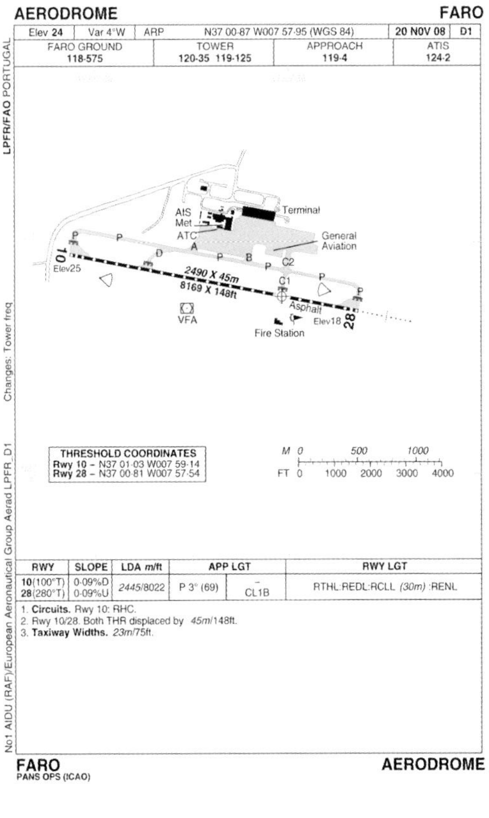

AERODROME FARO — LPFR/FAO PORTUGAL — Changes: Tower freq — No1 AIDU (RAF)/European Aeronautical Group Aerad LPFR_D1

FARO PANS OPS (ICAO) AERODROME

OPORTO/PORTO DR. FRANCISCO DE SÁ CARNEIRO INTERNATIONAL: OPO

Oporto, Portugal

Owner and operator: ANA Aeroportos de
 Portugal SA
Runways: 17/35, 3,479m (11,417ft)
Terminals: One
Annual passengers: 3,986,748
Annual cargo: 32,585 tonnes
Annual aircraft movements: 53,410

The terminal is served by the Porto Metro's Line E with a direct service to the city centre.

Background
Some 10km (6 miles) north-west of the city, it is named after a Portuguese politician, Francisco de sá Carneiro, who was killed when his aircraft crashed en route to the airport. It is Portugal's third busiest airport.

On 14 May 1997 a Saab 340 of Regional Aereas Lineas landed from Madrid without the crew being aware that the runway was under repair and the threshold was displaced. The aircraft touched down, ran across a trench and the undercarriage was sheered off, damaging the aircraft beyond repair. The 3 crew and 35 passengers survived the experience.

MADEIRA/FUNCHAL: FNC
Santa Caterina, Santa Cruz, Madeira, Portugal

Owner and operator: Aeroportos da Madeira
Runways: 05/23, 2,777m (9,110ft)
Terminals: One
Annual passengers: 2,418,489
Annual cargo: 8,711 tonnes

Background
Known variously as Madeira Airport, Funchal Airport or, due to the locality, Santa Caterina Airport, it is the only airport on the island.

Originally, air travel to Madeira was by flying boat, but an airport was opened on 18 July 1964, with a runway of 1,600m (5,253ft) which was built at the bottom of a hillside and sloping, with approach over the sea. It was demanding, even for experienced pilots, and aircraft taking off for destinations in northern Europe had to land at Lisbon to refuel as they could not carry a full load of fuel out of the island, and passenger weight had to be spread evenly throughout the aircraft for take-off and landing. The runway was extended by 200m (656ft) in 1985, but this was eight years after a TAP Air Portugal Boeing 727 had overshot the runway, hit a bridge and split into three, with the loss of many lives. In 2000 a massive runway extension, that almost doubled its length, was opened, and this has been built on a series of 180 columns, each almost 70m (230ft) high, rather than reclaiming land from the sea, and has been compared to landing on an aircraft carrier. It won an international award for outstanding structures.

The accident to the TAP Boeing 727-200 on 19 November 1977 was one of two that year at the airport. The aircraft landed on a scheduled service from Brussels with a stop at Lisbon in poor weather with a low cloud base and heavy rain, and the first approach was aborted. On the second approach the aircraft touched down too far down the runway, in this case landing in the 'downhill' direction, and aquaplaned down the runway, overshot, plunged down a steep slope, hit a bridge, sheering off a wing and splitting the fuselage in three, before plunging vertically over a cliff and on to a beach. Six of the 8 crew were killed, as well as 125 of the 156 passengers. Within a month (18 December 1977) this was followed by a Sud Aviation Caravelle 10R of SATA (SA de Transport Aerien) landing from Zurich and Geneva on a charter flight, with a new captain at the controls being monitored by an experienced captain. The difficult landing for a new captain was intended to be made by day, but departure had been delayed by a mechanical problem. The aircraft approached too low and the radio altimeter settings were not checked, leaving the aircraft to ditch with the loss of one of the 5 crew and 35 of the 52 passengers.

QATAR

DOHA INTERNATIONAL: DOH
Doha, Qatar, United Arab Emirates

Owner and operator: Qatar Civil Aviation Authority
Runways: 16/34, 4,572m (15,000ft)
Terminals: One
Airlines using airport as base or hub: Qatar Airways
Annual passengers: 13,903,320
Annual cargo: 365,265 tonnes
Annual aircraft movements: 116,666

Background
Despite having just a single runway, Doha has over-capacity and is competing with Dubai for international transit traffic as well as its core business of foreign workers for the energy industries. It is the home base and hub for Qatar Airways and, in that sense, is in direct competition with Dubai as an intercontinental hub, and has been extended several times. The runway is

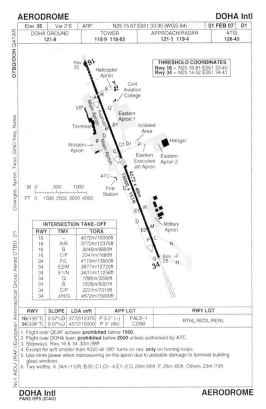

then slid tail first into the airport fire station, with the fuselage breaking into three sections and killing 45 of the 64 occupants, including 4 members of the crew.

ROMANIA

BUCHAREST/HENRI COANDĂ INTERNATIONAL: OTP

Otopeni, Bucharest, Romania

Owner and operator: Compania Naţională Aeroporturi Bucureşti SA

Runways: 08L/26R, 3,500m (11,484ft); 08R/26L, 3,500m (11,484ft)

Terminals: One, divided into three halls for international arrivals, international departures and domestic flights

Airlines using airport as base or hub: Blue Air, Romavia, Tarom

Annual passengers: 4,978,587

Annual cargo: 17,423 tonnes

Annual aircraft movements: 70,588

A shuttle bus runs to the airport station with trains direct to Bucharest Gara de Nord.

Background

Some 18km (11 miles) north of the centre of Bucharest, Henri Coandă Airport is the main international airport in Romania.

It is on the site of a Second World War air station at Otopeni used by the Romanian Air Force and the Luftwaffe, and post war it continued as a military air base. Initially, commercial flights into and out of Bucharest used Baneasa Airport, but by 1965 this was too small for growing air traffic, and the airfield at Otopeni was developed as a new airport for the capital, and was later named after the Romanian aircraft designer, Henri Coandă. The existing runway was extended and a passenger terminal opened. The passenger terminal was extended in 1970 and a second runway was laid parallel to the original.

Romania was outside the Warsaw Pact but effectively a closed society for many years, and

amongst the longest in the world. It will be replaced by 2010 by the 'New Doha International Airport'.

On 29 June 1977 the airport saw the conclusion of a hijacking attempt by a Lebanese man who seized a Gulf Air Vickers VC10 in flight between London and Muscat and Dubai, but which landed at Doha where he was overpowered by the army. There was also a serious accident involving an Alia Royal Jordanian Airlines Boeing 727-200 landing from Amman in a thunderstorm and heavy rain on 14 March 1979. The aircraft made a missed approach and a go-around was performed, but on the second attempt at landing the wind veered and the pilots found that they had an increasing tailwind, and they decided to overshoot and fly on to land at Dahran, for which the air traffic controller gave clearance, but as the aircraft was overshooting the runway and started to climb, it encountered windshear and struck the runway, bounced, and

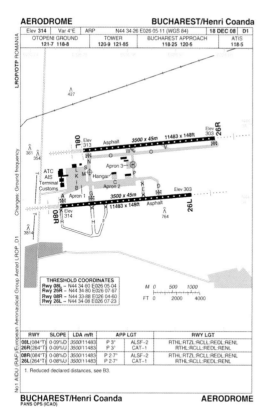

AERODROME				BUCHAREST/Henri Coanda	

written off in a post-maintenance test flight as it landed heavily with the left wing down, and both the No. 1 and No. 2 engines broke-off, but the 13 company personnel aboard seem to have survived. Finally, on 30 December 2007, a Tarom Boeing 737-300, taking-off for Sharm el Sheikh, collided with maintenance vehicles on the runway in fog, damaging the left wing, No. 1 engine, and the left main landing gear, but while the aircraft was written off, all 6 crew and 117 passengers appear to have survived.

RUSSIAN FEDERATION

One can either be very optimistic or very pessimistic about the state of commercial aviation in the Russian Federation, which, with the Ukraine, really is the rump of the former Soviet Union. The real point is, of course, that so much of aviation in these countries is commercial in name only, with operators having to learn how to operate in a market economy and forget all that they ever learnt about the old Soviet-style command economy. For much of its history, Aeroflot was operated on military lines and was almost indistinguishable from the Soviet Air Force's transport elements.

In the Russian Federation, aviation is not a luxury but a necessity because of the vast distances, the harsh climate, and difficult terrain – all of which puts aviation at a distinct advantage over other forms of transport. In the far northern wastes, road and railway construction is often simply not an option, with marshland in summer and extreme cold Arctic temperatures in winter. The failure of the attempt to construct the so-called 'Stalin Railway' in northern Siberia proves the point.

One oddity is that so many of the post-Aeroflot Russian airlines take the name of their home airport for their own title that there is sometimes difficulty in distinguishing between operators at the same base. There are few examples in the West of airlines adopting airport

it is only recently that the country has begun to attract visitors. Although easyJet flies into Henri Coandă, as a rule low-fare airlines have not been encouraged and are usually handled at Baneasa instead.

The airport has suffered a number of accidents. Two in 1977 both featured Ilyushin Il-18 aircraft. The first was on 21 April when a Tarom aircraft crashed during a touch-and-go operation, presumably a training flight, but there are few further details other than that the aircraft was destroyed. On 23 November a Malév Hungarian Airlines Il-18 was taxiing in heavy rain after landing from Istanbul, en route to Budapest, when it collided with two lorries in an area where they were prohibited, and the aircraft was written off – again, there are no details of any casualties. A Tarom Tupolev Tu-154 crashed while taking-off on a training flight on 9 February 1989, killing all five personnel on the flight deck. A Romavia Boeing 707-320 was

names. As for the airports themselves, many are still struggling to evolve from the Soviet-era grim terminals that doubled as monuments to the Revolution and to Soviet labour, but for those with a substantial amount of tourist and business traffic, things are changing for the better.

There are two points to make. The first is that several city names have been changed since the collapse of Communism, with many pre-revolution names restored. The other is that, as with the People's Republic of China, details of accidents can be difficult to find, or at least in full, especially pre-1990. The harsh climate and the poor reputation for reliability of Soviet-era commercial aircraft have contributed to an accident record that is far from the best in the world.

MOSCOW DOMODEDOVO INTERNATIONAL: DME

Moscow, Russian Federation

Owner: Russian Ministry for Civil Aviation
Operator: The East Line Group
Runways: 14L/32R, 3,800m (12,467ft); 14R/32L, 3,500m (11,483ft); 14C/32C, 2,600m (8,531ft) currently closed
Terminals: Two, designated Terminal 1 for domestic and Terminal 2 for international flights
Airlines using airport as base or hub: Aeroflot
Annual passengers: 18,755,098
Annual cargo: 133,662 tonnes
Annual aircraft movements: 181,141

'Aeroexpress' trains run non-stop from the airport to Moscow Paveletsky railway terminus.

Background

Russia's largest and busiest airport, Domodedovo is one of three major airports serving the Moscow area along with Sheremetyevo International Airport and Vnukovo Airport. It was originally built for long-haul domestic services within the then Soviet Union, and although services had started the previous year, was opened officially in May 1965. In late 1966, a

second runway parallel to the original was opened. The airport was the first to operate supersonic flights when the Tupolev Tu-144 'Concordski' started a short-lived service to Alma Ata.

Management of the airport was transferred to the East Line Group in 1996 on a 75-year lease, although the airport continues to be owned by the state. Heavy investment has been made in the airport to bring it up to modern standards and has attracted a number of airlines away from Sheremetyevo, including British Airways, Lufthansa, Swiss, Qatar, and Japan Airlines, and the main Russian airline, Aeroflot, has moved its cargo operations to Domodedovo. As a result, the airport has enjoyed rapid growth in traffic, including an increase of 52.8 per cent in international passengers between 2003 and 2004. A substantial area of land has been reserved for expansion around the airport which could more than double the number of runways.

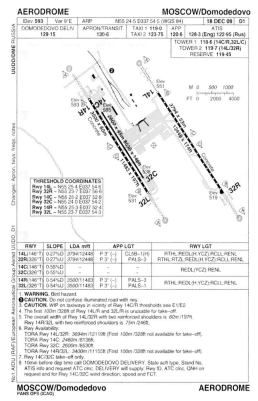

Originally, one terminal served with two piers, one for domestic flights and the other for international, but in 2006 Terminal 2 was brought into use for international passengers, and a second stage of its development will be completed in 2012, when there will also be a new domestic Terminal 3.

The airport has had an eventful history. One of the worst events was in August 2004 when two female Chechen suicide bombers penetrated security and destroyed two aircraft belonging to Volga-Avia Express and to Siberia Airlines, and killed 90 passengers. A mysterious attempt, or perhaps non-attempt, at hijacking a Tupolev Tu-154 occurred on 9 August 1998 when a cabin attendant aboard an East Line flight from Tyumen found a random note demanding money and fuel to fly the aircraft to another country. After landing, the aircraft was taken to a remote corner of the airport, but no hijacker appeared. The women and children were taken off the aircraft, after which the male passengers followed, but were searched by security personnel, as was the aircraft, but no weapons were found. Earlier, an Aeroflot Ilyushin Il-62M was destroyed on 1 October 1992 by a fire started when a cigarette end was dropped during refuelling.

There have also been many accidents in recent years. One of these was to an Antonov An-8 on 9 August 1979 on landing, when its undercarriage collapsed and fire broke out, with two passengers who survived the initial impact running into a propeller and being killed. No details are available of the numbers aboard the aircraft or any other casualties. On 5 December 1999, an Ilyushin Il-114T operated by Tashkent Aircraft Production was getting ready to take off for Tashkent on a cargo flight when a gust of wind locked the rudder to the left, and instead of returning to the stand, as advised by the flight engineer, the captain opted to take off using the main undercarriage brakes to maintain direction, but the aircraft yawed to the left immediately it left the ground and hit a wall, bursting into flames and killing all but two of the seven crew members. A positioning flight to Moscow by a Community of Sahel-Saharan States Ilyushin Il-62M on 29 March 2006 saw the aircraft suffer an unspecified landing accident, break into three, and finally stop some distance from the runway, but the six crew members all survived. While an ATRAN-Aviatrans Cargo Airlines Antonov An-12 climbed away from Domodedovo on 29 July 2007, heading for Omsk, both right engine propellers autofeathered and the aircraft banked before stalling and falling out of the sky into a forest 4km (2½ miles) from the end of the runway, killing all seven crew members.

MOSCOW SHEREMETYEVO INTERNATIONAL: SVO
Moscow, Russian Federation

Owner and operator: International Airport Sheremetyevo
Runways: 07L/25R, 3,550m (11,647ft); 07R/25L, 3,700m (12,139ft)
Terminals: Three, designated Terminal 1, Terminal 2 (being renamed Terminal B), and Terminal C
Airlines using airport as base or hub: Aeroflot, Aeroflot-Don, Atlant Soyuz, Avianergo, RusAir
Annual passengers: 14,039,843
Annual cargo: 128,152 tonnes
Annual aircraft movements: 164,664

Aeroexpress operates from a station at Terminal 2, with a shuttle bus from Terminal 1 direct to Moscow Savyolovsky and Belorussky.

Background
Moscow's second airport, Sheremetyevo, was opened on 11 August 1959, initially for international flights. On 3 September 1964 Sheremetyevo-1 was opened for domestic flights, and on 1 January 1980 a new terminal, Sheremetyevo-2, opened in time for the Moscow Olympics. Sheremetyevo-2 is the larger of the two older terminals and is now known simply as Terminal 2. Unusually, there is no connection between the two terminals other than the railway station shuttle from Terminal 1, and they have been described as two separate airports using the same set of runways. Terminal 2 is used for interna-

tional flights, leaving Terminal 1 for domestic flights. A new terminal for short-haul international flights is designated C, and a new Terminal B will replace Terminal 2 in the near future.

Amongst the accidents at the airport was that on 7 May 1958 to a Soviet Air Force Ilyushin Il-18A being operated for a government agency, which suffered an engine fire while on a test flight and then crashed before the crew could make an emergency landing, killing all ten occupants. Much more fortunate were those aboard an Antonov An-24 of MSAP Kiev on 29 July 1962 which also suffered an engine fire, but during take-off so that the aircraft overshot the end of the runway before catching fire. All aboard appear to have survived. Failure to clear the snow from the edges of the runway was a primary cause for the accident to a Tupolev Tu-114 on 17 February 1966 as it took off on Aeroflot's inaugural flight to Conakry and Brazzaville in West Africa, for not only could the pilots not see the lights at the edge of the runway, the aircraft hit a snowdrift on its left, and the pilot, in attempting to correct by turning right, caused a propeller to strike the runway and the aircraft then crashed and burst into flames. Out of the 48 occupants, 35 were killed. Engine failure was behind the approach accident to a Tupolev Tu-134 landing at the airport on 17 July 1972, when both engines flamed out because the pilots had forgotten to switch on a fuel transfer pump. There are no details of casualties, but the aircraft was written off. Certainly, no one survived the third attempt at landing from Leningrad (now St Petersburg) by an Aeroflot Ilyushin Il-62 on 13 October 1972. The airport's instrument landing system was switched off, and the aircraft crashed into a lake killing all 10 crew and 164 passengers.

Not all of the accidents at the airport involved Russian aircraft. On 28 November 1972, a JAL (Japan Air Lines) Douglas DC-8, bound for Tokyo, made a steep take-off and either because a spoiler was inadvertently deployed or an engine failed due to icing, the aircraft crashed shortly after leaving the runway, killing 9 of the 14 crew and all but 10 of the 62 passengers. A Russian-built aircraft, an Ilyushin Il-18 of

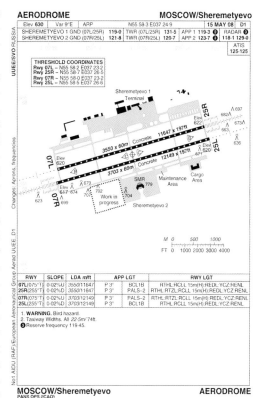

Balkan Bulgarian Airlines, crashed on approaching from Sofia on 3 March 1973, having aborted one approach, possibly due to icing of the tailplane, killing all 25 occupants. Icing was also behind an accident on 21 May 1986 when the crew of an Aeroflot Tupolev Tu-154B taking-off from Chelyabinsk forgot to switch on the heating for the air speed pitot tube, which froze as the aircraft flew through heavy snow on the approach, giving a zero reading and causing the crew to believe that the aircraft was about to stall, they dived the aircraft and applied full engine power, creating loads in excess of 3G which caused substantial damage to the airframe before the aircraft landed safely at Mosow. Weather was also a factor in an accident on 9 March 2000 when a chartered Yakovlev Yak-40D of Vologodskiye Airlines took off for Kiev. The departure was hurried as the aircraft had been de-iced, but the 30-minute period before the work had to be repeated was almost up because the passengers were late arriving. The pilots taxied out, ignoring warnings that the taxiways were slippery, and in their haste set insufficient flap for take-off. The aircraft climbed out and stalled, rolled left and struck the ground, killing all 4 crew and the 5 passengers.

A German-registered Learjet 35A of Air Charter crashed on take-off on 14 December 1994 after the pilot lost control, killing one of the two pilots, but the four passengers survived. Another business aircraft accident on 20 May 2005 was to a Dassault Falcon 20, which landed because of engine problems and was damaged beyond repair after it came off the runway; there are no details about the fate of the occupants or their number.

A hijacking ended at the airport on 10 December 1997 when an Ilyushin Il-62 of Magma Airlines landed from Magadan, with the hijacker demanding money and to be flown to Switzerland, but the aircraft was stormed, apparently without harm to the passengers or crew, of whom there were believed to be 155 in total.

An Ilyushin Il-86 of Pulkovo Aviation Enterprise on a positioning flight to St Petersburg crashed on take-off on 28 July 2002 after the pilot lost control, killing 14 of the 16 company employees aboard.

MOSCOW VNUKOVO INTERNATIONAL: VKO

Moscow, Russian Federation

Owner and operator: JSC 'Vnukovo Airport'
Runways: 06/24, 3,000m (9,842ft); 02/20, 3,060m (10,039ft) is closed
Terminals: Two, designated Terminal A and Terminal B
Airlines using airport as main base or hub: Aeroflot-Don, Gazpromavia, Karat Air, Rossiya Airlines, VIM Airlines
Annual passengers: 6,799,678
Annual cargo: 24,402 tonnes
Annual aircraft movements: 121,977

The Vnukovo Express runs directly from the terminals to Moscow Kiyevsky station.

Background

One of three major airports serving the Russian capital, with Moscow Domodedovo and Sheremetyevo, Vnukovo is 28km (27½ miles) from the city centre. It is the smallest and oldest of the three Moscow airports.

The original airport for Moscow, Khodynka, was congested by the late 1930s, and the decision was taken to build a new airport at Vnukovo, which opened on 1 July 1941, a little more than a week after the German invasion of the Soviet Union. Throughout the remainder of the Second World War the airport was used by the military and did not become a civil airport until peace returned. Post-war air traffic rose steadily, although flights outside the Soviet Union were restricted to those of the Warsaw Pact countries. In September 1956 the airport had its first jet airliner depart, when a Tupolev Tu-104 took off for Omsk and Irkutsk. The airport was expanded ready for the 1980 Summer Olympic Games.

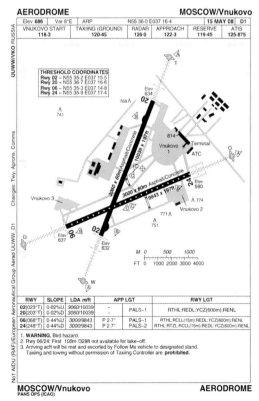

With the end of the Soviet Union, the airport became a public company in 1993, although for a period the Russian federal government held a controlling share, which it has since transferred to the city authorities in Moscow. At present it is in the middle of a major programme of redevelopment which will continue until 2013. Part of the redevelopment has been the rebuilding of the terminals, while the Vnukovo Express, a direct line to the centre of Moscow, opened in 2005.

It remains the VIP airport for Moscow, and Tupolev, the Russian aircraft manufacturer, has a maintenance facility at Vnukovo.

Amongst the accidents at the airport was that on 14 June 1957 when a LOT Polish Airlines Ilyushin Il-14P arrived from Warsaw, made a lower approach than instructed by air traffic control below a low cloud base and in poor weather with turbulence and heavy rain, crashing short of the runway and killing four of the five crew, and five of the eight passengers. A Romanian Ilyushin Il-14P also crashed later that year, on 4 November, killing all four occupants, but no other details have been released for this accident. By contrast, the authorities were surprisingly open about an accident on 26 August 1969 when an Aeroflot Ilyushin Il-18B landed from Noril'sk, but the crew forgot to lower the undercarriage, leaving the aircraft skidding along the runway before the cabin caught fire, and while the 8 crew members survived, 16 of the 94 passengers did not. On 7 May 1973 another Aeroflot aircraft, a Tupolev Tu-154, had its spoilers deployed during take-off and crashed after stalling, with the aircraft a complete wreck, but there are no details of numbers of passengers or crew, or of any casualties. A much older aircraft, an Aeroflot Tupolev Tu-104 (the first generation of Soviet jet airliners) took-off on 17 March 1979 but an engine caught fire shortly afterwards and the aircraft returned, dropping below the recommended approach in poor visibility so that the aircraft struck an electricity pylon, recovered, and then crashed into a frozen field, losing both wings and the cockpit. The aircraft was almost 11 tonnes overweight and the captain had just 32 hours in command of the aircraft type. Surprisingly, only one of the 6 crew was killed, but so too were 85 out of the 100 passengers aboard the aircraft.

A Russian military Antonov An-22A crashed on 2 June 1980 as it was returning to the airport with an engine fire, but failed to reach the runway, killing the three occupants, all crew members. Another military aircraft, on this occasion an Italian Air Force Douglas DC-9-32, was damaged beyond repair on 8 February 1999 when it was in a ground collision with an Ilyushin Il-96. A US registered Canadair CRJ100SE, a VIP modification of a Canadair regional jet, was written off on 13 February 2007 as it took off on a positioning flight to Berlin, but the three crew members survived. Another Russian military aircraft, a Tupolev Tu-134AK, ran off the runway after a night landing on 10 August 2007, but there appear to have been no casualties amongst the 11 occupants, and the aircraft was later repaired.

ST PETERSBURG (LENINGRAD) PULKOVO: LED
St Petersburg, Russian Federation

Owner and operator: City of St Petersburg
Runways: 10L/28R, 3,397m (11,145ft); 10R/28L, 3,780m (12,401ft)
Terminals: Two, designated as Pulkovo-1 (mainly for domestic flights), and Pulkovo-2 (for international flights)
Airlines using airport as base or hub: Rossiya
Annual passengers: 6,138,823
Annual cargo: 29,372 tonnes
Annual aircraft movements: 86,878

Background
Situated to the south of the city, with Pulkovo-1 some 20km (12½ miles) from the centre and Pulkovo-2 around 11km (11½ miles) from the centre, the airport was originally known as Shosseynaya Airport after the name of the nearest railway station, while the city itself had been renamed Leningrad after the Russian revolution. The airport opened on 24 June 1932. In the years that followed, air traffic grew slowly with

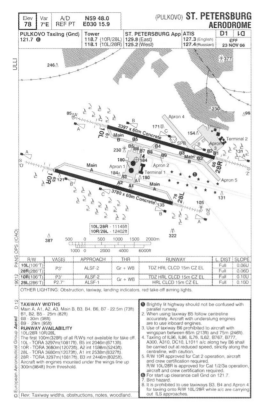

Elev 78	Var 7°E	A/D REF PT	N59 48.0 E030 15.9		(PULKOVO) **ST. PETERSBURG** AERODROME		
PULKOVO Taxiing (Gnd) 121.7 @		Tower 118.7 (10R/28L) 118.1 (10L/28R)		ST. PETERSBURG App 129.8 (East) 125.2 (West)	ATIS 127.3 (English) 127.4 (Russian)	D1	D	EFF 23 NOV 06

R/W	VASIS	APPROACH	THR	RUNWAY	L. DIST	SLOPE
10L(106°T)	P3°	ALSF-2	Gr + WB	TDZ HRL CLCD 15m CZ EL	Full	0.06U
28R(286°T)					Full	0.06D
10R(106°T)	P3°	ALSF-2	Gr + WB	TDZ HRL CLCD 15m CZ EL	Full	0.10U
28L(286°T)	P2.7°	ALSF-1		HRL CLCD 15m CZ EL	Full	0.10D

OTHER LIGHTING: Obstruction, taxiway, landing indicators, red take-off aiming lights.

TAXIWAY WIDTHS
Main A, A1, A2, A3, Main B, B3, B4, B6, B7 - 22.5m (73ft)
B1, B2, B5 - 25m (82ft)
B8 - 30m (98ft)
B9 - 29m (95ft)
RUNWAY AVAILABILITY
10L/28R 10R/28L
The first 100m(328ft) of all R/W's not available for take off.
10L - TORA 3297m(10817ft), B5 int 2046m(6713ft).
10R - TORA 3680m(12073ft), A2 int 1598m(5243ft).
28L - TORA 3680m(12073ft), A1 int 2538m(8327ft).
28R - TORA 3297m(10817ft), B3 int 2446m(8025ft).
Aircraft with engines mounted under the wings line up 300m(984ft) from threshold.

❶ Brightly lit highway should not be confused with parallel runway.
2. When using taxiway B5 follow centreline accurately. Aircraft with underslung engines are to use inboard engines.
3. Use of taxiway B6 prohibited to aircraft with wingspan between 65m (213ft) and 75m (246ft).
4. Taxiing of IL96, IL86, IL76, IL62, B767, B777, A300, A310, DC10, L1011 a/c along twy B6 shall be carried out at reduced speed, strictly along the centreline, with caution.
5. R/W 10R approved for Cat 2 operation, aircraft and crew certification required.
R/W 10L/28R is approved for Cat 1/2/3a operation, aircraft and crew certification required.
❻ For start up clearance call Gnd on 121.7.
❼ Bird hazard.
8. It is prohibited to use taxiways B3, B4 and Apron 4 for taxiing onto R/W 10L/28R while a/c are carrying out ILS approaches.

Rev: Taxiway widths, obstructions, notes, woodland.

© European Aeronautical Group Aerad D.12 PANS OPS (ICAO) ULLI 1902

air transport normally only available for senior members of the government, the military and the Communist Party.

After the German invasion of the Soviet Union in June 1941, Leningrad was soon surrounded and a long siege began. The airport came under attack not just from the air, but also from German artillery positioned in the Pulkovo Hills. The Germans withdrew in January 1944, but the airport could not be returned to use immediately as the runways were very badly damaged, and it was not until 1945 that mail and cargo flights could resume. Passenger services did not restart until February 1948, but by the following year some 30 destinations, all inside Russia, were being served.

The airport terminal was extended in 1951 to handle larger aircraft, and in 1955–6, the runway was extended for the new Tupolov Tu-104 jet airliner. International operations started in 1965 after International Civil Aviation Organisation

standards were implemented. The current name was adopted on 24 April 1973, when the new Pulkovo-1 terminal was opened to handle domestic traffic. Pulkovo-2, dating from the 1950s, was rebuilt and reopened in 2003.

Currently, the airport is being extensively rebuilt and modernised in a programme that extends to 2025, but one of the first results will be a new terminal that will open in 2011.

The airport saw the end of a hijacking when an Aeroflot Tupolev Tu-154B landed from Irkutsk after being seized by a family of 11 who demanded to be flown to London. The aircraft was stormed by KGB troops and, in the fighting, five hijackers were killed, as well as three passengers and a cabin attendant, while explosions destroyed the tail of the aircraft.

There have also been accidents, such as that on 23 May 1991 when An Aeroflot Tupolev Tu-154B landed heavily from Sukhumi in heavy rain and undershot the runway. The undercarriage collapsed and the aircraft started to break up. The crew of 6 survived, but 13 of the 172 passengers were killed, as well as another two people on the ground. Little has been revealed about an accident to a Tupolev Tu-134A of Pulkovo Aviation Enterprise (the former Leningrad division of Aeroflot) except that it was written-off on 8 January 2002, and that there were no recorded casualties. Much less badly damaged was the Aeroflot Russian International Airlines Tupolev Tu-154M that suffered an uncontained engine failure on taking-off on 30 June 2008, with take-off aborted and only minor damage to the aircraft.

YEKATERINBURG/ EKATERINBURG (SVERDLOVSK) KOLTSOVO: SVX

Koltsovo, Russian Federation

Owner and operator: Koltsovo International Airport
Runways: 08L/26R, 2,497m (8,192ft); 08R/26L, 3,025m (9,925ft)
Terminals: Two, designated International and Domestic

Airlines using airport as base or hub: Ural
   Airlines, Aviacom Zitotrans
Annual passengers: 2,345,535
Annual cargo: 16,965 tonnes

Background

Known locally as Koltsovo after the locality, the
airport is 16km (10 miles) south-east of Yekaterinburg (or Ekaterinburg), the city was known as
Sverdlovsk after the Bolshevik revolution and has
only reverted to its original name in recent years.

The airport was originally opened as a military air station in 1928 and, in addition to combat
aircraft, was also used by transport aircraft from
1943 onwards. It started commercial operations
after the war, but did not become an international airport until 1993. A new international
terminal was opened in December 2005 and a
new terminal for domestic flights in October
2007. A large cargo terminal and distribution
centre is being built, along with a third runway,
all of which should open during 2009.

There was a serious accident at the airport on
16 November 1967 when an Aeroflot Ilyushin Il-
18 crashed after take-off when an engine caught
fire and the propeller could not be feathered.
Becoming uncontrollable the aircraft dropped
out of the sky, inverted. There were no survivors
amongst the 8 crew and 122 passengers. Another
Aeroflot aircraft, a Tupolev Tu-104B bound for
Khabarovsk, crashed on 30 September 1973 after
losing its artificial horizon as it climbed away and
entering a left spin, again leaving no survivors
amongst the 8 crew and 100 passengers. An
engine failure to a Yakovlev Yak-40 after take-
off on 7 October 1978 for Kostanay saw the aircraft unable to maintain height with the two
remaining engines and it flew into a hill, killing
the crew of 4 and 34 passengers. Little is known
about the loss of an Aeroflot Antonov An-12 on
7 February 1987 other than that the aircraft was a
complete write-off. Another Aeroflot Antonov
An-12 was lost on 13 January 1989 when the No.
3 and No. 4 engines both jammed on full power
because of damaged control cables, and although
the crew tried to land the aircraft, it ground-
looped on touchdown and was destroyed.

NOVOSIBIRSK TOLMACHEVO: OVB
Novosibirsk, Siberia, Russian Federation

Owner and operator: Novosibirsk Joint Stock
   Company
Runways: 07L/25R, 2,995m (9,825ft) grass
   runway; 07R/25L, 3,600m (11,811ft); 16/34,
   3,605m (11,826ft)
Terminals: Two, designated Domestic and
   International
Airlines using airport as base or hub: S7 Airlines
Annual passengers: 1,873,498
Annual cargo: 19,001 tonnes

Background

Novosibirsk Tolmachevo Airport is 16km (10
miles) from the city centre of the third largest
city in Russia.

The airport opened in 1957 and was operated
by the United Tolmachevo Aviation Enterprise
and the Soviet Union's Ministry of Civil Aviation until 1992 when it became a publicly-quoted
company, albeit with the state retaining a 51 per
cent controlling interest. Runway 16/34
recently opened.

Since it opened, the airport has had a number
of accidents. On 12 August 1969 an Aeroflot
Antonov An-12, believed to be on a cargo flight,
crashed on approach after two engines had
failed, with the death of all aboard, a crew of
four. A Tupolev Tu-104, also of Aeroflot, was
written off in a heavy landing on 30 August 1975.
There are no details of the number of people
aboard the aircraft or of their fate. A Cessna
Citation V air ambulance of Tyrol Air Ambulance flying from Innsbruck to Siberia diverted
to the airport on 27 January 2009 when the
undercarriage failed, and the crew did three fly-
bys so that those on the ground could confirm
that the undercarriage was indeed still up before
the pilots made a forced landing, seemingly
without casualties amongst the four people
aboard.

SAMARA (KUIBYSHEV) KURUMOCH INTERNATIONAL: KUF

Samara, Russian Federation

Owner and operator: Kurumoch International
  Airport Authority
Runways: 05/23, 2,548m (8,360ft); 15/33,
  3,001m (9,846ft)
Terminals: One
Annual passengers: 1,393,828
Annual cargo: 4,565 tonnes

Background

Situated 35km (almost 22 miles) from the centre of Samara, which was known as Kuibyshev until recently, Kurumoch dates from the immediate post-Second World War period when it was developed as a joint military and civil facility.

The airport has suffered a number of accidents. Little is known about that on 10 November 1963 other than that it involved an Aeroflot Il-18, which was damaged beyond repair, possibly after landing from Moscow. At least two of the occupants of an Aeroflot Tupolev Tu-124 were killed after it force-landed with engine problems on 9 July 1973, but surprisingly the aircraft is reported as having been repaired. There was a substantial death toll on 20 October 1986 when an Aeroflot Tupolev 134A arriving from Yekaterinburg made a blind landing but came in too low and touched down so heavily that the aircraft broke up as it left the runway, with the deaths of 4 of the 7 crew and 66 of the 85 passengers. A cargo Polyot Antonov An-26 landed heavily on 24 June 1993 damaging the nose gear before leaving the runway, but the crew of five survived and, after repair, the aircraft was sold to an operator in the Democratic Republic of the Congo. Less fortunate were those aboard an UTAir Tupolev 134A passenger flight from Surgut on 17 March 2007, which landed in poor visibility short of the runway, damaging the undercarriage, losing a wing, and rolling over. The 7 crew survived, but there were 6 fatalities amongst the 50 passengers.

SAUDI ARABIA

Air transport in Saudi Arabia has been boosted by the growing importance of the country as the world's leading producer and exporter of oil, an industry which has attracted investment and expatriate workers, and has also given a substantial number of Saudis the means to travel. The country is also the home of the holy city of Mecca which attracts massive numbers of Moslem pilgrims, especially during the annual Hajj. With scant resources other than oil, the country needs to import much of its food and almost all manufactured goods requirements, with the more valuable items arriving by air. The substantial financial resources available to the state have meant that money has never been an obstacle in airport construction.

JEDDAH – KING ABDULAZIZ INTERNATIONAL: JED

Jeddah, Saudi Arabia

Owner and operator: GACA (General Authority
  of Civil Aviation of Saudi Arabia)
Runways: 16L/34R, 3,690m (12,106ft);
  16C/34C, 3,299m (10,825ft); 16R/34L,
  3,800m (12,467ft)
Terminals: Three, designated North Terminal and
  South Terminal, and a special Hajj Terminal for
  pilgrims to Mecca
Airlines using airport as base or hub: Saudi
  Arabian Airlines, NAS Air, Sama Airlines
Annual passengers: 14,432,426
Annual cargo: 209,118 tonnes
Annual aircraft movements: 115,819

A railway connection is planned for the future
'New Jeddah International Airport'.

Background

Opened on 31 May 1981, Jeddah King Abdulaziz International Airport, often known as KAAI, reflects the country's great prosperity from its vast oil reserves. It also enjoys a special location in that it is the airport closest to Mecca, and it has a special terminal to handle the annual surge of

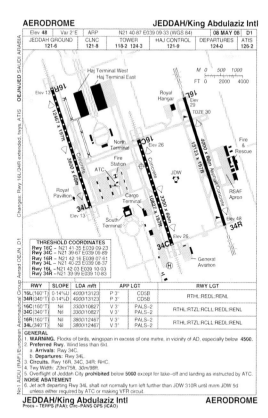

AERODROME				JEDDAH/King Abdulaziz Intl	
Elev 48	Var 2°E	ARP	N21 40.87 E039 09-33 (WGS 84)		08 MAY 08	D1
JEDDAH GROUND	CLNC	TOWER	HAJ CONTROL	DEPARTURES	ATIS
121-6	121-8	118-2 124-3	121-9	124-0	126-2

THRESHOLD COORDINATES
Rwy 16C – N21 41·35 E039 09-23
Rwy 34C – N21 39·67 E039 09-89
Rwy 16R – N21 42.16 E039 07-61
Rwy 34L – N21 40·23 E039 08-37
Rwy 16L –N21 42.03 E039 10-03
Rwy 34R –N21 39.99 E039 10-83

RWY	SLOPE	LDA m/ft	APP LGT		RWY LGT
16L(160°T)	0-14%U	4000/13123	P 3°	CD5B	
34R(340°T)	0-14%D	4000/13123	P 3°	CD5B	RTHL:REDL:RENL
16C(160°T)	Nil	3300/10827	V 3°	PALS-2	
34C(340°T)	Nil	3300/10827	V 3°	PALS-2	RTHL:RTZL:RCLL:REDL:RENL
16R(160°T)	Nil	3800/12467	V 3°	PALS-2	
34L(340°T)	Nil	3800/12467	V 3°	PALS-2	RTHL:RTZL:RCLL:REDL:RENL

GENERAL
1. WARNING. Flocks of birds, wingspan in excess of one metre, in vicinity of AD, especially below **4500**.
2. Preferred Rwy. Wind less than 6kt.
  a. Arrivals: Rwy 34C.
  b. Departures: Rwy 34L.
3. Circuits. Rwy 16R, 34C, 34R: RHC.
4. Twy Width: 23m/75ft, 30m/98ft.
5. Overflight of Jeddah City **prohibited** below **5000** except for take-off and landing as instructed by ATC.
NOISE ABATEMENT
6. Jet acft departing Rwy 34L shall not normally turn left further than JDW 310R until mnm JDW 5d unless either required by ATC or making VFR circuit.

JEDDAH/King Abdulaziz Intl   AERODROME
Procs – TERPS (FAA); Circ–PANS OPS (ICAO)

pilgrimage flights. The North Terminal is for all airlines, while the South Terminal was originally reserved for Saudi Arabian Airlines, but is now used also by the new private enterprise Saudi carriers, NAS Air and SAMA Airlines. Extensive development is planned for the future, which will result in the 'New Jeddah Airport' with four terminals and enhanced runways and aircraft parking, as well as a railway link.

The airport has suffered just two serious accidents. The first of these was on 30 November 1979, before the formal opening, when a Boeing 707-320 of Saudi Arabian Airlines suffered such extensive damage during a heavy landing that it was scrapped and used for spares. No details are available of the number of occupants or whether they were injured. The second was a Hajj charter flown by a McDonnell Douglas DC-8-61 of the Canadian airline Nationair (but chartered by Nigeria Airways) destined for Sokoto in Nigeria on 11 July 1991. On taking off, two tyres

burst, and once airborne there were problems with cabin pressurisation, followed by a hydraulics failure, and as the pilots attempted to return to the airport, the aircraft crashed killing all 14 crew and 247 passengers. Burst tyres were also a problem with an Airbus A300 of PIA (Pakistan International Airlines) as the aircraft began its take-off run on 1 March 2004, while the control tower warned the crew of a wheel on fire. The take-off was aborted, during which pieces of tyre entered the engines and caused substantial damage, but the aircraft managed to stop and the 12 crew and 261 passengers were all safely evacuated. The aircraft was a write-off.

RIYADH KING KHALID INTERNATIONAL: RUH

Riyadh, Saudi Arabia

Owner: GACA (General Authority of Civil Aviation of Saudi Arabia)
Operator: Fraport
Runways: 15L/33R, 4,205m (13,796ft); 15R/33L, 4,205m (13,796ft)
Terminals: Four, designated Terminal 1 (international flights), Terminal 2 (Saudi Arabian international flights), Terminal 3 (Saudi Arabian domestic flights), and Terminal 4 (unused)
Airlines using airport as base or hub: Saudi Arabian Airlines
Annual passengers: 12,134,112
Annual cargo: 216,469 tonnes
Annual aircraft movements: 112,210

Background

Situated 35km (almost 22 miles) north of Riyadh, the airport has its own private terminal for the Saudi Royal Family and a mosque. It has expanded from a military airfield into an airport to meet the country's rapidly growing demand for air travel, and during the 1990–1 Gulf War was used by the USAF for its in-flight refuelling units.

The airport suffered a fatal accident on 19 August 1980, when a Saudi Arabian Lockheed TriStar made a scheduled stop on its way to Jeddah from Karachi. Within a few minutes of

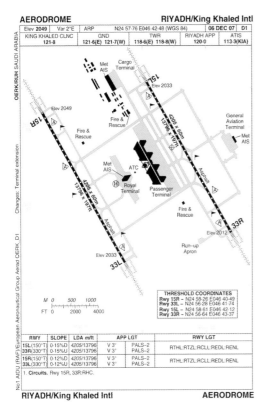

AERODROME				RIYADH/King Khaled Intl	
Elev 2049	Var 2°E	ARP	N24 57·76 E046 42·48 (WGS 84)	06 DEC 07	D1
KING KHALED CLNC 121·8		GND 121·6(E) 121·7(W)	TWR 118·6(E) 118·8(W)	RIYADH APP 120·0	ATIS 113·3(KIA)

THRESHOLD COORDINATES	
Rwy 15R –	N24 58·26 E046 40·49
Rwy 33L –	N24 56·26 E046 41·74
Rwy 15L –	N24 58·61 E046 42·12
Rwy 33R –	N24 56·64 E046 43·37

RWY	SLOPE	LDA m/ft	APP LGT		RWY LGT
15L (150°T)	0·15%D	4205/13796	V 3°	PALS-2	RTHL:RTZL:RCLL:REDL:RENL
33R (330°T)	0·15%U	4205/13796	V 3°	PALS-2	
15R (150°T)	0·12%D	4205/13796	V 3°	PALS-2	RTHL:RTZL:RCLL:REDL:RENL
33L (330°T)	0·12%U	4205/13796	V 3°	PALS-2	

1. Circuits. Rwy 15R, 33R:RHC.

RIYADH/King Khaled Intl   AERODROME

taking off from Riyadh there were warnings of a fire in a cargo hold and the captain decided to return to Riyadh. Even before it landed there was smoke in the cabin and the throttle for the No. 2 engine, located in the tail, stuck. Although passengers were fighting to get to the emergency exits, on landing the captain told the cabin crew not to evacuate, and he advised the control tower that he would taxi the aircraft on to a taxiway and then evacuate. The engines were shut down but the expected evacuation did not follow, leaving the rescue crews to fight to open the cabin doors from outside. When opened they found piles of dead bodies behind the doors, and the interior of the cabin burst into flames. All 14 crew and 287 passengers were dead.

DAMMAM/KING FAHD INTERNATIONAL: DMM
Dammam, Saudi Arabia

Owner and operator: GACA (General Authority of Civil Aviation of Saudi Arabia)
Runways: 16L/34R, 4,000m (13,124ft); 16R/34L, 4,000m (13,124ft)
Terminals: One for general passengers, plus a Royal terminal for VIPs
Airlines using airport as base or hub: Sama Airlines, Saudi Arabian Airlines
Annual passengers: 4,158,261
Annual cargo: 66,622 tonnes
Annual aircraft movements: 48,653

Background
The world's largest airport by land area, and larger than the neighbouring territory of Bahrain. It is the main airport in the east of Saudi Arabia, from which originally most people found Bahrain to be the most convenient airport. It was opened in 1999 behind schedule and over budget, and initially it was badly under-used as poor roads left many local people continuing to use Bahrain. The roads have been improved since the airport opened, but it is still performing at far below its designed capacity.

MADINAH/PRINCE MOHAMMAD BIN ABDULAZIZ INTERNATIONAL: MED
Madinah, Saudi Arabia

Owner and operator: GACA (General Authority of Civil Aviation of Saudi Arabia)
Runways: 17/35, 4,008m (13,149ft); 18/36, 3,060m (10,039ft)
Terminals: One
Annual passengers: 2,009,790
Annual cargo: 4,806 tonnes

Background
Often known simply as Prince Mohammad Airport, or even more simply as 'Mohammad', Madinah is a regional airport and serves the city of Medina. Most flights are domestic, but it does

handle some international flights, and these become more numerous during the Hajj season, when almost a quarter of the annual traffic is handled. The airport opened in 1974, and plans for expansion include upgrading to full international standards.

ABHA: AHB
Abha, Saudi Arabia

Owner and operator: GACA (General Authority of Civil Aviation of Saudi Arabia)
Runways: 13/31, 3,350m (10,991ft)
Terminals: One
Annual passengers: 1,525,118
Annual cargo: 4,326 tonnes

Background
Situated between the cities of Abha and Khamis Mushayt, the airport is a new regional airport and is served by Saudi Arabian Airlines and the new Saudi low-fares carrier, Sama Airlines.

SENEGAL

DAKAR-YOFF/LÉOPOLD SÉDAR SENGHOR INTERNATIONAL: DKR
Dakar, Senegal

Owner and operator: Government of Senegal
Runways: 03/21, 1,500m (4,921ft); 18/36, 3,490m (11,450ft)
Terminals: One
Airlines using airport as base or hub: Air Senegal International
Annual passengers: 1,875,000

Background
Developed before the Second World War, while Senegal was still a French colony, as a military air station, it is the main airport in Senegal and was once one of the five hubs of the French-backed airline, Air Afrique. Originally known as Dakar-Yoff, it was renamed after the first post-independence president, Léopold Sédar Senghor, who governed from 1960 to 1980. For some years it was one of a number of airports around the world supported by NASA to provide an emergency landing site for the space shuttle programme, until a dip in the main runway that could damage a shuttle was noted.

The airport's accident history can be traced back to the years immediately following the Second World War. On 13 April 1947 an Avro York of BSAA (British South American Airways, later absorbed by BOAC, which in turn became British Airways) made three attempts to land in bad weather after flying a sector from Lisbon, and on the fourth attempt the undercarriage failed and the aircraft landed on its belly, with the loss of the lives of six of the nine passengers, although the three crew survived. Amongst the causes were primitive facilities at the airport at the time, and the York with its high wing and low-slung fuselage offered passengers little protection. Within a couple of months, another vintage aircraft, an Amoit AAC.1, a licence-built Junkers Ju52/3M, of Air France was damaged beyond repair on 7 June, although there are no other details available about this flight.

The airport was amongst the first to experience the jet age, with the French airline, UTA (Union Transportes Aeriens) amongst the few operators of the de Havilland Comet 1A, having Dakar on its network. On 25 June 1953 a Comet landed and overshot the runway, coming to rest on its belly in one of the few survivable accidents with this ill-fated aircraft, which had seven crew and ten passengers on board. Less fortunate were those aboard a de Havilland Canada Twin Otter on 9 December 1993, which was approaching when, at between 2,500ft and 2,700ft, it collided with an NAMC YS-11 which had just taken-off, and while the larger aircraft managed to return to Dakar, the Twin Otter plunged into the sea killing the pilot and both passengers. It seems that everyone aboard an ATR-42 of TACV, Cabo Verde Airlines, survived an undercarriage collapse on 24 October 2005. The aircraft is reported as having been repaired, but there are accounts of it being at Dakar as late as January 2007.

SERBIA-MONTENEGRO

BELGRADE NIKOLA TESLA: BEG

Surčin, Belgrade, Serbia (former Republic of Yugoslavia)

Owner and operator: Aerodrom 'Beograd-Nikola Tesla' PE

Runways: 12/30, 3,400m (11,155ft)

Terminals: Two, designated as Terminal 1 and Terminal 2

Airlines using airport as base or hub: Aviogenex, JatAirways

Annual passengers: 2,515,968

Annual cargo: 8,806 tonnes

Annual aircraft movements: 45,770

Background

Also known as Surčin, after the locality, Nikola Tesla is 12km (7½ miles) west of the centre of Belgrade. It is Serbia's busiest airport.

Belgrade's first international airport, Dojno Polje, opened on 25 March 1927 on the site of what later became Novi Beograd. The following year, the local airline, *Aeroput*, began operations. There were four grass runways initially and a modern terminal building was opened in 1931. By 1939 the airport was being used by airlines from as far afield as the UK, France, the Netherlands, and Poland. It was taken by German forces after the invasion of what was then Yugoslavia in 1941, and during the war it became a base for the Luftwaffe and the Italian Regia Aeronautica. It was bombed by Allied forces based in Italy during 1944, and then the German forces destroyed what was left as they withdrew. The advancing Soviet forces rebuilt the airport as a forward base, and it was also used by transport aircraft during 1945.

It was not until 1947 that commercial aircraft returned to the airport. Initially it became a major hub for Jugoslovenski Aerotransport, or JAT, and the first western aircraft to use it after the war appeared the following year. The airport continued to be used throughout the 1950s, but it soon became clear that it was unable to handle the traffic and was also unsuitable for jet airliners. The current airport was built and opened on 28 April 1962. Early in 1964 the old airport was closed and the site cleared for urban development. It was given its current name on 10 July 2006 to celebrate the 150th anniversary of the birth of the scientist Nikola Tesla, while a month earlier a much-modernised and extended Terminal 2 was reopened.

Since the civil war that followed the break up of Yugoslavia, traffic has been increasing, and future plans call for new terminals and possibly a second runway.

There has been one serious accident at the airport in recent years. An Ilyushin Il-76, that had taken off for Malta with a cargo of military equipment on 19 August 1996, suffered an electrical fault and circled for three hours to burn off fuel before landing back at Belgrade, but on its approach it crashed into a field and caught fire, killing all 12 occupants.

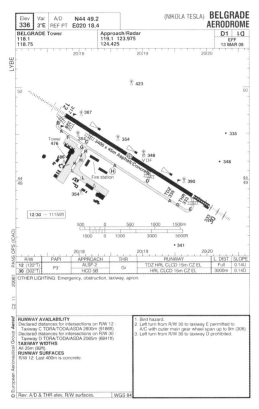

SINGAPORE

SINGAPORE CHANGI INTERNATIONAL: SIN

Singapore Changi International (Pinyin: Xīnjiāpō Zhāngyí Jīchǎng), Changi Island, Singapore

Owner: Government of Singapore

Operator: Civil Aviation Authority of Singapore/Republic of Singapore Air Force

Runways: 02L/20R, 4,000m (13,123ft); 02C/20C, 4,000m (13,123ft); 02R/20L, 2,750m (9,022ft)

Terminals: Five, Nos. 1 to 4, and Budget Terminal

Airlines using airport as base or hub: Singapore Airlines, Singapore Airlines Cargo, SilkAir, Tiger Airways, Jetstar Asia Airways, Valuair, Jett8 Airlines Cargo

Annual passengers: 36,701,556

Annual cargo: 1,918,159 tonnes

Annual aircraft movements: 223,488

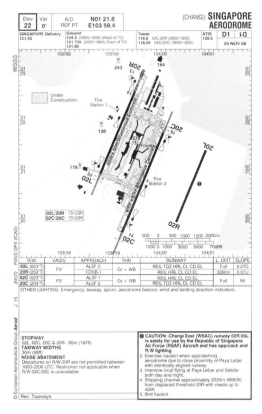

The inter-terminal Changi Airport Skytrain operates between Terminals 1, 2 and 3, with a total of seven stations, and designated cars for transit passengers and visitors.

Changi Airport Station on the Singapore Mass Rapid Transit System is located underground between Terminals 2 and 3 with a shuttle service between Changi Airport Station and Tanah Merah Station.

Background

Singapore's main airport from 1930 to 1937 was at Seletar. This was replaced in 1937 by a new airport at Kallang, while Seletar continued to be used for general aviation. Kallang remained in use until 1955 when it too was replaced by a new airport at Paya Lebar, known officially as Singapore International, which opened in 1955 with just a single runway and a small passenger terminal. The Changi site had been used as a prison and then, during the Japanese occupation from 1942 onwards, it was the notorious prisoner-of-

war camp. After the Second World War it became a base for the Royal Air Force as RAF Changi. By the 1970s, Paya Lebar was clearly inadequate for the rapidly rising traffic, which soared over a relatively short time from 300,000 passengers annually to 1.7 million.

The initial results of a study into the future of air transport for Singapore was that the existing airport should receive a second runway and new terminal facilities, but action was delayed because of the oil crisis during the early 1970s. It became apparent that the site at Paya Lebar was ideal for commercial development and was, in any case, liable to be surrounded by urban development that would restrict future growth. As a result, it was decided in 1975 to build a completely new airport at Changi, on the eastern side of the island, where approaches and take-offs could be over the sea, avoiding problems with aircraft noise, and the airport could easily be expanded by land reclamation. Even so, some expansion at the existing airport was necessary to relieve congestion in the intervening period until the new airport could be opened.

The airport, usually referred to simply as 'Changi', opened in 1981. Over the next two years, much of the airport was completed, including a main runway and a hangar for large aircraft. Terminal 2 opened in 1990, and Terminal 3 in 2008, after being delayed over fears of the impact of terrorism on air traffic growth. In the meantime, both the earlier terminals were upgraded and expanded. Rapid traffic growth, encouraged in recent years by the Air Hub Development Fund, launched in 2003 to encourage airlines to use Changi. While a Commercially Important Persons terminal has been established, Changi has joined other Asian airports in catering for the budget traveller using low-cost airlines, and a Budget Terminal was opened in 2006.

Changi has consistently received awards for the quality of its service, and continued expansion is envisaged that may see the airport doubling in size. The main resident airline, Singapore Airlines, is the first to put the new Airbus A380 'Super Jumbo' into service, and the airport has become a major stopping point for airlines operating between Europe and Australia.

Inevitably, there were some accidents and incidents at the old airport for Singapore, and at Changi while still an RAF base, but there have also been problems at the new airport. The first of these was the hijacking of a Singapore Airlines Airbus A310 en route from Kuala Lumpur on 25 March 1991 by four Pakistani hijackers whose demands included being flown on to Australia. After landing at Changi the aircraft was stormed by special forces and all 4 hijackers were killed, leaving the 9 crew and the other 114 passengers unharmed. On 13 December 2002, an Arrow Air Douglas DC-8-62F on a cargo flight landing from Tokyo overshot the runway in wet weather after there was confusion over who was the handling pilot and the aircraft touched down too far along the runway to stop. The aircraft was written off, but the four crew escaped.

SLOVAKIA

BRATISLAVA/MILAN RASTISLAV ŠTEFÁNIK: BTS
Bratislava, Slovakia

Owner and operator: Airport Bratislava a.s.
Runways: 04/22, 2,900m (9,515ft); 13/31, 3,190m (10,466ft)
Terminals, Three, designated Terminal A, Terminal B, and Terminal C
Airlines using airport as base or hub:
  SkyEurope Airlines
Annual passengers: 2,004,541

Background
The main Slovakian international airport, it is 9km (just over 5½ miles) from the city centre.

Bratislava's first airport was at Vajnory, which opened in 1923 when Czechoslovak State Airlines (CSA) started trial flights between Prague and Bratislava. The present airport dates from after the Second World War, when it was constructed between 1947 and 1951. In 1993 it was named after Milan Rastislav Štefánik, a Slovakian diplomat and one of the founders of Czechoslovakia, killed when his aircraft crashed near the city in 1919. A new terminal opened in 1971 and today this is used for departures, while Terminal B, opened in 1994, is used for arrivals from outside the Schengen area, while the newest terminal, C, is reserved for arrivals from within the Schengen area. The airport was privatised in 2004.

Over the years there have been a number of accidents at the airport. One of these was on 24 November 1966 when a TABSO Ilyushin Il-18, diverted from Prague because of bad weather, crashed into the foothills of the Liuttyle Carpathians shortly after taking-off, with the loss of all 74 passengers and 8 crew. Another Il-18 operated by CSA Czechoslovak Airlines landing from Prague on 28 July 1976 crashed into a lake while flying a go-around, with the loss of 6 crew and 69 out of the 73 passengers, although another 2 died later from their injuries. A Mil Mi-8 helicopter, carrying the wife of the then president of Czechoslovakia, crashed in fog into a field on the approach to the airport on 20 October 1977, killing all aboard.

SLOVENIA

LJUBLJANA/JOŽE PUČNIK (BRNIK AIRPORT): LJU

Ljubljana, Slovenia (former Republic of Yugoslavia)

Owner and operator: Aerodrom Ljubljana, d.d.
Runways: 13/31, 3,300m (10,827ft)
Terminals: Two, designated Terminal 1 (or the 'old' terminal), and Terminal 2 (the newer terminal, not fully completed)
Airlines using airport as base or hub: Adria Airways
Annual passengers: 1,515,839
Annual cargo: 13,989 tonnes
Annual aircraft movements: 46,517

Background

At one time one of the main airports used by visitors to the former Yugoslavia, Ljubljana is often known locally as Brnik Airport because of its proximity to the village of that name. It has been named after Jože Pučnik, who died in 2003, and was an intellectual and politician. It is 26km (just over 16 miles) from Ljubljana itself.

The airport dates from 24 December 1963, and before the break-up of Yugoslavia was a major tourist airport. Traffic fell dramatically during the civil war that affected many parts of the country, and has only started to recover over the past two years. It has its own airline, Adria Airways, the national airline of Slovenia, which has its origins as the former Yugoslavia's main charter airline but is now a scheduled carrier. A new passenger terminal is being built, with the first phase already in use, so that the airport can divide arriving passengers into Schengen and non-Schengen streams for immigration and customs control. Work on the second phase of the terminal should be completed by 2011. A new air cargo and logistics centre is also planned.

The airport was the scene of a serious accident on 1 September 1966 when a Bristol Britannia of Britannia Airways (later Thomsonfly, and now part of TUI), landing from London at night, crashed into a wood after the handling pilot failed to set the altimeter using local information given to him by the controller, so that the aircraft was more than 1,000ft too low. Of the crew, 6 out of the 7 died, along with 92 out of the 110 passengers.

SOUTH AFRICA

JOHANNESBURG INTERNATIONAL/OR TAMBO INTERNATIONAL (JAN SMUTS): JNB

Johannesburg, South Africa

Owner and operator: Airports Company of South Africa
Runways: 03L/31R, 4,418m (14,495ft); 03R/31L, 3,400m (11,155ft)
Terminals: Three, divided into three areas designated Domestic, Transit, and International
Airlines using airport as base or hub: 1Time Airline, Comair, Inter Air South Africa, Mango, Safair, Solenta Aviation, South African Airlink, South African Airways, South African Express, Vulkanair
Annual passengers: 17,787,673
Annual cargo: 360,831 tonnes
Annual aircraft movements: 226,992

Work is proceeding on a terminal for the 'Gautrain', which will run from the airport to Sandton, Johannesburg's main business district.

Background

Originally known as 'Jan Smuts Airport', after the South African soldier and statesman (who was instrumental in the formation of the RAF in 1918), Johannesburg was opened in 1952, two years after Smuts' death. Before this, Johannesburg had been served by Palmietfontein Inter-

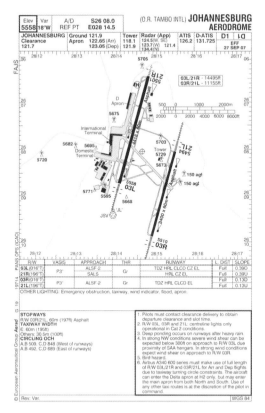

to refuel meant that the national airline, South African Airways, had to adopt special versions of the Boeing 747, the 747-SP, with extended range. At the end of the policy of apartheid (translated strictly as separate development) the airport's name was changed to the politically neutral Johannesburg International, even though Smuts was never associated with the earlier policy.

In 1996 the airport overtook Cairo as the busiest in Africa, and remains South Africa's busiest airport and main international gateway because of the city's status as the country's main business centre.

The current name was adopted in 2006 after a former president of the African National Congress and anti-apartheid activist, Oliver Tambo. The change has been criticised within the country because of the cost and its political nature, and the fact that the name means little or nothing to most outsiders.

Accidents at the airport in the past 50 years or so have included one to a Vickers Viscount 800 undergoing 'hot and high' trials at the airport. On 20 October 1957, during some circuits of the airport, the aircraft approached too steeply and made a heavy landing, wrecking the undercarriage. Although no one was killed, the aircraft was written off, but at least one report indicates that the fuselage was salvaged and used for a new aircraft built for BEA (British European Airways). Overloading by 5 tons and poor weight distribution ensured that a Ramaer Cargo Ilyushin Il-18 failed to take off for Burundi on 17 December 1997. The captain aborted the attempt and the aircraft overshot the end of the runway. Fortunately, the four crew survived the experience.

One unusual accident occurred on 20 May 1998. Iberia had resumed flights to Johannesburg after an interval of ten years, and the Airbus A340 that had arrived from Madrid had been parked after the passengers had disembarked. A BAe 748 belonging to Intensive Air arrived later and a hydraulic failure after landing meant that the aircraft ran out of control, and first damaged the Airbus with the propeller of

national Airport, while originally most flights between Europe and South Africa had been by flying boats to Cape Town and Durban. From the start, Jo'burg's new airport was ready for the jet age being at the end of the British Overseas Airways Corporation's route from London Heathrow flying the ill-starred de Havilland Comet I jet airliner. Much later, it was to be used for trials of the Anglo-French Concorde supersonic airliner to assess how the aircraft would perform from an airport that has become renowned for being 'hot and high' being almost 1,700m or (5,500ft) above sea level.

For much of the airport's history, South Africa was ostracised by other countries because of its opposition to black majority rule and its support for neighbouring Rhodesia (now Zimbabwe), which declared unilateral independence from the United Kingdom. Even so, the airport continued to grow, but the reluctance of most black African countries to allow landing rights

its No. 1 engine, and then jammed itself under the larger aircraft when its fin caught on the underside of its fuselage. No one was hurt in the accident, but both aircraft needed repairs, and the inaugural return flight to Madrid was cancelled. Another A340, this time belonging to Emirates Airlines, had a narrow escape during a take-off incident on 9 April 2004, when the aircraft failed to respond to the controls and only became airborne when the captain selected emergency 'go around' power, but the lights at the end of the runway were wrecked and the aircraft suffered damage. It returned to the airport and landed safely with all 14 crew and 216 passengers unharmed.

CAPE TOWN (D. F. MALAN) INTERNATIONAL: CPT

Cape Town, South Africa

Owner and operator: Airports Company of
    South Africa
Runways: 01/19, 3,195m (10,483ft); 16/34,
    1,699m (5,574ft)
Terminals: Five, designated International Arrivals,
    International Departures, Domestic Arrivals,
    Domestic Departures, South African Airways
    Domestic Departures
Airlines using airport as hub: South African
    Airways
Annual passengers: 7,548,735
Annual aircraft movements: 93,232

Background

For many years named after a former prime minister of South Africa (not to be confused with the fighter ace of the same surname) and often still known as D. F. Malan, the airport grew with the post-war change from flying boats to landplanes for long-haul air services. It is still South Africa's busiest airport. It is currently being developed so that it can handle double the present traffic by 2015.

A South African Airways Boeing 737-800 taking off from Cape Town was nearly hijacked by a Zimbabwean student armed with a hyperdermic syringe on 17 June 2006, but he was over-

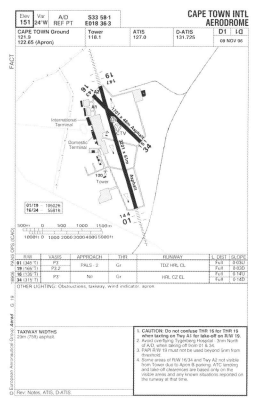

powered by passengers and later arrested. A Boeing 737-200 of Nationwide Airlines lost its right (or No. 2) engine climbing out from the airport on a flight to Johannesburg on 7 November 2007, but returned to land safely.

DURBAN INTERNATIONAL (LOUIS BOTHA): DUR

Durban, South Africa

Owner and operator: Airports Company of
    South Africa
Runways: 06/24, 2,439m (8,000ft)
Terminals: One
Airlines using airport as base or hub: Executive
    Aerospace
Annual passengers: 4,799,702
Annual cargo: 8,126 tonnes
Annual aircraft movements: 55,743

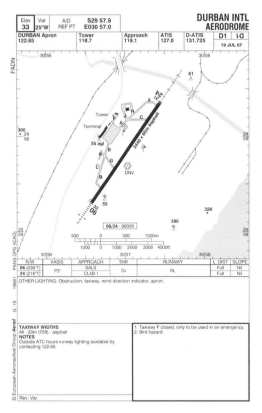

Elev	Var	A/D	S29 57.9					DURBAN INTL
33	25"W	REF PT	E030 57.0					AERODROME

DURBAN Apron 122.65		Tower 118.7		Approach 119.1	ATIS 127.0	D-ATIS 131.725	D1	LO
							19 JUL 07	

R/W	VASIS	APPROACH	THR	RUNWAY	L. DIST	SLOPE
06 (036°T)	P3'	SALS	Gr	RL	Full	Nil
24 (216°T)		CL4B-1			Full	Nil

OTHER LIGHTING: Obstruction, taxiway, wind direction indicator, apron.

TAXIWAY WIDTHS
All - 23m (75ft) - asphalt
NOTES
Outside ATC hours runway lighting available by contacting 122.65.

1. Taxiway F closed, only to be used in an emergency.
2. Bird hazard.

Background

Unusually, Durban International, known earlier as Louis Botha, after the South African statesman, has a canal, the Umlazi, at the northern end of its runway. The airport has seen a decline in international traffic in recent years, not helped by the shortness of the runway, which would be costly to extend.

Over the past 30 years there have been a number of proposals to build a new airport, but work did not start until 2007 on what will be the King Shaka International Airport, and it is intended that it should be open for the 2010 Football World Cup, after which Durban International will be closed and the land used for industrial development.

A cargo flight operated by a Southern Gateway Antonov An-32 heading for Bulawayo on 7 May 1998 suffered an electrical fire on the flight deck and managed to make an emergency landing at a small airstrip, and although a wing hit a

tree and the undercarriage collapsed, the crew of four were unharmed.

PORT ELIZABETH (H. F. VERWOERD): PLZ

Port Elizabeth, Eastern Cape, South Africa

Owner and operator: Airports Company South Africa
Runways: 08/26, 1,980m (6,496ft); 17/35, 1,677m (5,501ft); 10/28, 1,160m (3,805ft) grass
Terminals: One
Annual passengers: 1,491,800
Annual cargo: 7,716 tonnes
Annual aircraft movements: 64,593

Background

Port Elizabeth Airport is just 3.2km (2 miles) south of the city centre, and boasts that it is the 'Ten Minute Airport', as most areas of the city can be reached within ten minutes.

The airport was opened in 1936 with a single runway, a hangar, and a concrete apron, although the site had been used by an airmail service from Cape Town since the late 1920s. The airport was enlarged during the Second World War when it was used by No. 42 Air School of the Royal Air Force, part of the British Empire Air Training Scheme, and by the South African Air Force, although commercial operations continued using the north side of the airport. It remained in SAAF hands after the war, and in 1954 its first jet aircraft were five de Havilland Vampires. Meanwhile, the commercial operations had been moved to a temporary airport at St Albans, some 25km (just over 15 miles) from the city centre, while the airport was rebuilt with new runways, passenger terminal, and an air traffic control building. The new airport opened in 1955.

The apron was extended to take larger aircraft in 1973, and in 1980 a new departures terminal opened. A major upgrade of the airport, including combining arrivals and departures in a single terminal building, was completed in 2004. The airport cannot handle long-haul flights because of the limited length of the runways, although a lightly-loaded Boeing 747 has used the airport. There are plans to extend the main runway for direct long-haul flights.

There was a serious accident near the airport on 15 October 1951 when an SAA (South African Airways) Douglas C-47, which had taken off for Durban, hit a mountain, killing all 13 passengers and 4 crew.

SPAIN

Once one of the most backward nations in Western Europe, the development of civil air transport in Spain was different from that of France and the United Kingdom. It would be wrong to suggest that the Spanish were indifferent to air transport, however, as a fleet of military Junkers Ju52/3 trimotor transports was used to ferry troops of the Spanish Foreign Legion from Ceuta and Melilla in North Africa to Spain at the outset of the Spanish Civil War.

Much of the history of Spanish commercial aviation has been that of the national airline, Iberia, largely because the Spanish economy was tightly regulated. The airline was originally founded in 1927 as Iberia Air Transport. These manoeuvres failed to establish a solid footing for air transport in Spain, largely because of the impact of the Spanish Civil War, which saw many routes suspended and aircraft requisitioned for the war effort by both sides. During the Second World War, despite Spanish neutrality, air services were limited to links with Portugal, Spanish Morocco and Spain's offshore islands.

An unusual feature of Spanish airline operations during the 1960s was the vehicle ferry services from Barcelona to Palma de Mallorca on the largest of the Balearic Islands, using Aviation Traders Carvairs, converted Douglas DC-4s. By this time the country had become a major tourist destination. Most of the foreign visitors arrived in aircraft owned by foreign airlines because there were few independent Spanish airlines before Spain became a member of the European Union, and deregulation encouraged the growth of new airlines. As elsewhere, there is a tendency for the new low-cost airlines to use different terminals or even different airports from their well-established rivals. Most of the nation's airports are operated by the state-owned AENA (Aeropuertos Españoles y Navegación Aérea).

MADRID-BARAJAS: MAD
Madrid, Spain

Owner and operator: AENA
Runways: 15R/33L, 4,100m (13,451ft); 15L/33R, 3,500m (11,483ft); 18L/36R, 3,500m (11,483ft); 18R/36L, 4,350m (14,272ft)
Terminals: 1, 2, and 3, with 4 reserved for Iberia and its subsidiaries or franchisees
Airlines using airport as base or hub: Air Comet, Audelia Air, Cygnus Air, Iberia, Pan Air, Swiftair, with Air Nostrum and Spanair using the airport as a secondary base or regional hub
Annual passengers: 52,122,702
Annual cargo: 356,427 tonnes
Annual aircraft movements: 483,284

Madrid Metro Line 8 runs to terminals 4 and 2, with the latter providing access to terminals 1 and 3.

Background
Work on an airport for Madrid originally started in 1927, and it opened to both international and domestic flights on 22 April 1931, although it was another two years before these flights were established on a regular basis, initially with Lineas Aéreas Postales Españolas (LAPE) operating between Madrid and Barcelona. To begin with there was a single small terminal capable of handling up to 30,000 passengers a year. Regular international flights followed. It was not until 1944 that the first paved runway, just 1,400m long, opened, but by 1950 another two paved runways had been built.

Capacity had increased to 500,000 passengers annually by the time the first transatlantic serv-

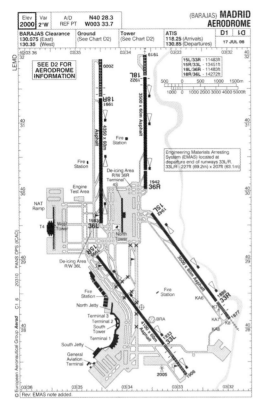

terminal, and in 1998 a new control tower was completed. Between 1998 and 2006, new runways and terminals were completed and the existing designations were adopted. The runways are amongst the longest in Europe, with the main problem at the airport being that it is prone to fog.

Today, the terminals at Madrid have the largest area of any in Europe and the airport is the major gateway between Europe and Latin America.

The airport has suffered from a number of accidents in its history. One of these was on 27 November 1983 when an Avianca Boeing 747 approaching from Bogota hit a hill and lost its right wing, after which the aircraft cartwheeled and broke into five pieces before stopping inverted. Just 11 of the 169 passengers survived, and all 23 members of the crew were killed. The following month, on 7 December, an Iberia Boeing 727 collided as it took off with an Aviaco Douglas DC-9 that had entered the runway, killing a total of 135 people, 93 of them on the Iberia flight and 42 on the Aviaco DC-9. On 20 August 2008, a Spanair McDonnell Douglas MD-82 taking-off for Las Palmas on Gran Canaria veered after lifting off, hit the ground and broke into several parts, catching fire, with the loss of 154 lives and leaving 14 passengers injured.

One problem with transport and communications in Spain has been the recurring danger of terrorism, initially from ETA (the Basque separatist organisation) but more recently there has also been an attack by extreme Islamic groups. The main terrorist incident at the airport was on 30 December 2006, when a bomb went off in a car park, levelling it and killing two men who had been sleeping in their car. In this case ETA claimed responsibility.

ices were introduced in the 1950s, linking Madrid with New York, by which time there were five runways and a second terminal opened in 1957. The following decade saw both the increasing use of jet aircraft and rapid growth due to Spain's fast-expanding tourist industry. A new international terminal was opened, which remains as today's Terminal 1. In 1974, Iberia began a high frequency 'no booking' shuttle service linking Madrid with Barcelona, known as the *Puente Aéreo* (Air Bridge) or *Pont Aeri* in Catalan, and this became the world's busiest air service, with no fewer than 971 flights a week in 2007, with departures every 30 minutes, until the construction of a high speed railway line between Spain's two largest cities.

Meanwhile, the airport continued to grow, with expansion boosted by Madrid hosting the football World Cup in 1982, which involved enlarging what had become two terminal complexes. In 1994 the airport opened its first cargo

Above: The busiest Australian airport is Sydney. This is an interior view of the main terminal. *(Sydney Airport Corporation)*

Overleaf: Brussels is the main base for European Air Transport, now part of DHL and whose livery their aircraft carry. This is part of their fleet of Boeing 757s. *(DHL)*

Below: A clear view of the approach over the sea to Adelaide in South Australia. The intersecting runways can be clearly seen. *(Adelaide Airport Ltd)*

Above: An interior view of the busy main terminal at Edmonton in Western Canada. *(Edmonton Regional Airports Authority)*

Above left: An important regional hub in the Far East, Brunei International is home to Royal Brunei Airlines, one of whose Boeing 767-300ERs is seen here in the sunset. *(Royal Brunei)*

Below left: The most important airport in the west of Canada, Vancouver is also the nation's second busiest by passengers and has a substantial regional traffic as well as domestic and international flights. *(Vancouver International Airport Authority)*

Below: An Air Canada Airbus is de-iced at Montreal prior to taking-off in mid-winter. *(Air Canada)*

Hong Kong is one of the busiest air cargo hubs. Here a Cathay Pacific Boeing 747 is loaded. *(Cathay Pacific)*

The busiest airport in Scandinavia and the main base for SAS (Scandinavian Airlines System), this panorama of Copenhagen gives a clear idea of the size of the airport. *(Københavns Lufthavne)*

The second most important airport in Denmark, Billund's traffic is mainly within northern Europe and Scandinavia. *(Billund Lufthavn A/S)*

Business jet movements at Paris CDG with a Dassault Falcon nearest the camera and a Gulfstream taking-off in the background. *(Aéroports de Paris)*

Above: Regional aircraft are mainly in evidence in this night photograph of Dresden airport, Germany. *(Flughaven Dresden GmbH)*

Left: One of Europe's busiest airports and in this overview, intercontinental aircraft dominate the foreground, Frankfurt is the main base for Lufthansa and is an important air cargo centre as well as a passenger hub. The parent company, Fraport, is involved in airport consultancy services worldwide. *(Fraport)*

Left: Cologne-Bonn was the airport for the capital Bonn before German reunification and although well-placed, is looking for 'Open Skies' transatlantic services to assure its future. *(Flughafen Köln/Bonn GmbH)*

Below: Air Berlin is one of the major operators at Dresden. *(Flughaven Dresden GmbH)*

Left: One of Germany's busiest airports, especially for business travellers, Dusseldorf is also the main base for PrivatAir, as well as a Lufthansa hub. *(Flughafen Dusseldorf)*

Above: An Aer Lingus Airbus A320 departs from the passenger terminal at Dublin. A second passenger terminal opens soon. *(Dublin Airport Authority)*

Below: Once a major refuelling point for transatlantic flights, Shannon in the Irish Republic still sees many long-haul aircraft despite increased ranges. *(Dublin Airport Authority)*

Above left: Milan Malpensa is also a major handler of air cargo as Italy's main manufacturing areas are in the north of the country. This is the cargo terminal. *(SEA Aeroporti di Milano)*

Above right: The largest Luxembourg airline is the all-cargo operator Cargolux, one of whose Boeing 747-400Fs is seen loading in this scene. *(Cargolux)*

Below: A KLM Royal Dutch Airlines McDonnell Douglas MD-11 takes-off from Amsterdam Schiphol. The name means 'ship hole' owing to the many wrecks that could be seen before the land was reclaimed, but it has been far more successful as an airport! *(KLM Royal Dutch Airlines)*

Above: New Zealand's busiest airport, Auckland is served by many airlines and is seen here with a Qantas Airbus A380. *(Auckland International Airport Ltd, AIAL.)*

Right: An aerial panorama of Oslo Gardermoen, Norway. *(Oslo Lufthavn)*

Overleaf: The landside view of the terminal at Ljubljana, Slovenia, doubtless as seen by many tourists as they start their homeward journey. *(Aerodrom Ljubljana, d.d.)*

Below: Aukland's passenger terminal with aircraft from Singapore and Dubai. *(Auckland International Airport Ltd, AIAL.)*

Above: A Philippines Airlines Airbus A319 takes-off from Manila. *(PAL Philippines Airlines)*

Right: An aerial view showing all of Barcelona Airport with the runways and terminals. *(AENA)*

Below: An Embraer E-170 regional jet of LOT Polish Airlines takes-off from Warsaw. *(LOT Polish Airlines)*

Above left: Terminal 4 is the most recently opened terminal at Madrid, a major hub especially for travellers between Europe and Latin America. *(AENA)*

Above: This is a view of the airport from inside the terminal, or 'Sky City' at Stockholm-Arlanda. *(LFV)*

Left: A busy scene at Madrid showing two of the terminals and the control tower. Many of the aircraft in the foreground belong to Spanair, which at the time of writing is owned by SAS Scandinavian Airlines System. *(AENA)*

Right: The control tower at Izmir, a resort airport but still the third busiest in Turkey. *(Turkish State Airport Management)*

Overleaf: Keeping airports open in areas with a heavy winter snowfall is no light task – this is a snow-blower at Stockholm-Arlanda. *(LFV)*

A dispatcher waits while an easyJet Airbus A319 leaves the stand at East Midlands Airport. *(Manchester Airports Group)*

Airside at the terminal at Edinburgh International, Scotland's busiest airport.

A distant view of Edinburgh International, with the aircraft on the right at the freight terminal and beyond them is the passenger terminal. The runway is the shorter of the two.

A landside view of the modern passenger terminal at Jersey. (*States of Jersey*)

Above: The shape of things to come: the Airbus A380 prototype at London-Heathrow. Plans for a much needed third runway are proving controversial, but airport expansion is an issue worldwide. *(Ian Black)*

Left: An aerial view of London City Airport, built on reclaimed land in disused docks, with the River Thames and former Millennium Dome in the background. Movements are limited by the lack of a taxiway. *(London City Airport Ltd)*

Below: A line up of Jet2 aircraft at one of Manchester's two terminals on a wet day. The airport is the busiest in the UK outside the London area. *(Jet2.com)*

Above left: An aerial view of the terminals at Chicago Midway, and while the city's second largest airport, it is clearly still very busy. *(City of Chicago – Chicago Airport System)*

Above right: An artist's impression of the Skylink train that connects the terminals at Dallas/Fort Worth. *(DFW Airport Board)*

Right: A Frontier Airbus passes under a footbridge at Denver International's Jeppersen Terminal. *(Frontier)*

Below: A night-time aerial view of the control tower and one of the terminals at Chicago O'Hare, which has been the world's busiest passenger airport in the past and is still a close second. The aircraft closest to the camera are regional feeder aircraft, but in the distance long-haul aircraft can be seen. *(City of Chicago – Chicago Airport System)*

Above: A night view of the Jeppersen Terminal at Denver. *(City and County of Denver Department of Aviation)*

Left: An aerial view of the novel Jeppersen International Terminal at Denver, with the airfield in the background. *(City and County of Denver Department of Aviation)*

Below: The landside of the passenger terminal at Des Moines airport, Iowa, USA. *(City of Des Moines Aviation Department)*

Above: Kansas City International is a major maintenance base for American Airlines, shown here. *(Kansas City)*

Left: An aerial view of Kansas City International, showing the runways and, in between, the terminals and apron areas. *(Kansas City)*

Above right: The departure terminal at Las Vegas with the apron and airbridges beyond, clearly in use by US Airways. *(Clark County)*

Right: Low-cost airlines have transformed the fortunes of many airports, especially when, as at Oakland in California, they can provide a lower-cost alternative to larger airports. Here are Southwest Airlines Boeing 737s at Oakland. *(Port of Oakland)*

The end carriages of the 'SkyTrain' at San Francisco Airport provide a good view of the airport. *(San Francisco Airport Commission)*

Tulsa is home to a major FedEx Federal Express freight terminal, seen here with a McDonnell Douglas MD-11 and two Airbus A300s. *(Federal Express)*

BARCELONA: BCN

Barcelona, Catalonia, Spain

Owner and operator: AENA
Runways: 07L/25R, 3,352m (10,997ft);
    07R/25L, 2,660m (8,727ft); 02/20, 2,540m
    (8,335ft)
Terminals: Three, designated A, B, and C
Airlines using airport as base or hub: Iberia,
    Aviaco, Vueling Airlines, Clickair
Annual passengers: 32,794,575
Annual cargo: 100,360 tonnes
Annual aircraft movements: 352,489

The Spanish railway operator, RENFE, serves the airport on its R10 line, which links the airport with Barcelona Estació de França, with stops at connecting stations for the Barcelona Metro en route. In the near future, it will have a new railway station for the Spanish high speed AVE network and to Lines 2 and 9 of the Barcelona Metro.

Background

Barcelona has had an airfield since 1916, at El Remolar, but this suffered from severe limitations, so a new airfield was opened at El Prat in 1918. This was while scheduled air services were yet to start, and the initial use of the airfield was by the Spanish Navy for its small fleet of dirigible airships. It was not until 1927 that scheduled air services began with the launch of a service by Iberia to Madrid, which later became the world's busiest air route.

Spain underwent a damaging civil war during the late 1930s, and afterwards was too weakened to take part in the Second World War. It was not until 1948 that the first transatlantic service was operated into Barcelona, by Pan American World Airways flying the then new Lockheed Constellation. Nevertheless, during the 1960s passenger traffic began to grow rapidly with the inclusive tour package holiday business bringing large numbers of people from northern Europe to Spain. A new control tower was built in 1965 and a rebuilt terminal opened in 1968.

In 1974, Iberia began a high-frequency 'no-booking' shuttle service linking Madrid with

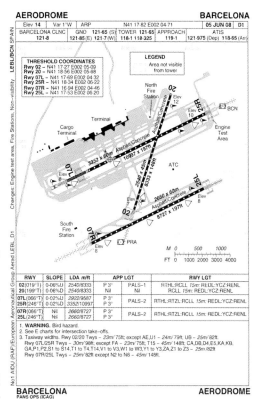

Barcelona, known as the *Puente Aéreo* (Air Bridge) or *Pont Aeri* in Catalan, and this became the world's busiest air service, with no less than 971 flights a week in 2007, operating every half hour, until the construction of a high speed railway line between Spain's two largest cities provided strong competition.

As elsewhere, the Olympic Games proved a major stimulus to the airport's modernisation and development, and the 1992 Summer Olympics resulted in the construction of a second terminal, while an additional runway has been built more recently. Further expansion with a third terminal and a new control tower has followed. The airport is busy as the city is Spain's main industrial centre and one of the two main business centres, and the airport also serves some of the major holiday resorts. For the future, the airport has further expansion planned, with a new satellite terminal due to be open by 2012. Despite this growth, Iberia is withdrawing its domestic services to Barcelona, transferring them to Clickair, the low-cost airline in which Iberia has a stake, with the exception of the Puente Aéreo which will remain with Iberia, and instead is developing transatlantic services from the airport as well as from Madrid, and will use it as its main station for services to Asian destinations.

Given the pressure at peak holiday season, the airport has had relatively few serious aircraft accidents, and one of these was to a small cargo aircraft. On 18 February 1998 an Ibertrans Aérea Swearingen Metro took off for Brussels, and once airborne the captain asked to be allowed to return, but on approach the aircraft strayed from its course and crashed in flames killing both pilots, the only occupants.

PALMA DE MALLORCA (SON SANT JOAN): PMI

Palma de Mallorca, Islas Baleares, Spain

Owner and operator: Aena (Aeropuertos Españoles y Navegación Aérea)
Runways: 06L/24R, 3,270m (10,728ft); 06C/24C, 2,500m (8,202ft); 06R/24L, 3,000m (9,842ft)
Terminals: Two, designated Terminal A and Terminal B
Airlines using airport as base or hub: Aerolíneas de Baleares
Annual passengers: 23,223,970
Annual cargo: 26,408 tonnes
Annual aircraft movements: 197,354

Background

Although the third busiest airport in Spain after Madrid and Barcelona, during the summer months the tourist traffic ensures that this is one of the busiest airports in Europe. The airport grew largely with the demand for inclusive tour package holiday flights during the 1950s, 1960s, and 1970s, and a new Terminal A was opened in 1965 followed by a Terminal B in 1972, which was originally reserved for charter flights. The old Terminal B has now been closed, and Terminal A has four main gate areas – A, B, C, and D,

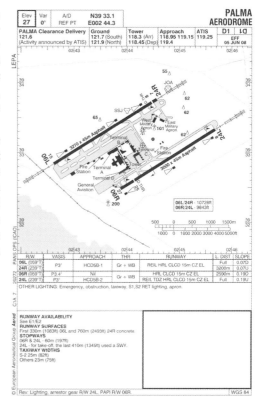

while a new Terminal B, or *Modulo B*, is used for flights within the Balearic Islands.

Given that the airport is used by many inclusive tour charters, it is interesting that the two most serious accidents in recent years have been to cargo flights. The first was on 8 March 1993 when a Douglas C-47 of an airline called ARM was taking-off, but an engine failed almost immediately the aircraft lifted off the runway and the aircraft crashed killing both pilots. The second was on 12 April 2002 when a Tadair Swearingen Merlin III was landing from Madrid and slid off the runway, colliding with a structure, and again both pilots were killed.

MÁLAGA: AGP

Málaga, Spain

Owner and operator: Aena (Aeropuertos Españoles y Navegación Aérea)

Runways: 13/31, 3,200m (10,500ft); a second runway will open in 2010

Terminals: Three, designated Terminal 1 and Terminal 2, with Terminal 3 opened in 2009

Annual passengers: 13,577,585

Annual cargo: 6,906 tonnes

Annual aircraft movements: 129,693

The Cercanías Málaga railway directly links the airport with Málaga city centre and Fuengirola.

Background

Ideally situated both for the upmarket resort of Málaga and for the more popular Torremolinos, regular air services using Málaga date from as early as 1919 when the city was connected with Barcelona, Alicante, Casablanca, Tangier, and Toulouse. In 1937 the airport became a flying school for the Spanish air force, and international commercial flights did not return until 1946.

The airport's single runway was extended in the 1960s to accommodate jet aircraft at the start of the boom in holidays in Spain for people from the northern European countries, and a new passenger terminal was also opened in 1968. This was joined by a second terminal in 1972 for charter flights, which by this time comprised the majority of aircraft movements. A new terminal, the *Pablo Ruiz Picasso*, opened in 1991 and became the new Terminal 2, with domestic passengers and those for the European mainland using Pier B, and passengers for the British Isles using Pier C. The old Terminal 1 then became a general aviation terminal. A cargo terminal opened later.

A second runway is due to open in 2010.

The worst accident at the airport was on 13 September 1982 when a Spantax Douglas DC-10 was taking-off on a charter flight to New York when the nose wheel started to lose the tread on a tyre followed by vibration and the nose wheel beginning to break up, as the vibration continued after rotation, the captain assumed that he could not control the aircraft in the air and aborted the take-off, but the aircraft veered off the runway, hit a building, lost the No. 3 (right) engine and burst into flames, killing 3 of the 13 crew and 47 of the 381 passengers. Another serious accident was on 29 August 2001 when a Binter Mediterraneo CASA 235 approached from Melilla, one of the Spanish enclaves in Morocco, but before landing a fire warning was noted on the No. 1 (left) engine. An emergency landing was made with both engines shut down, but the plane collided with approach lights before landing short of the runway, skidding, and hitting structures before coming to rest by an embankment. One of the 3 crew died along with 3 of the 44 passengers, some of whom were trapped in the aircraft for ten minutes before rescue teams could force open a rear door.

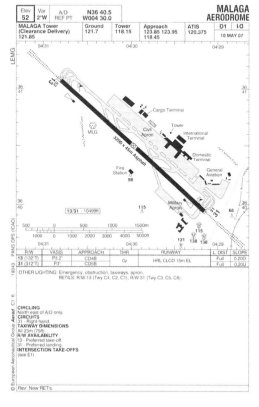

GRAN CANARIA/
LAS PALMAS: LPA

Gran Canaria, Canary Islands, Spain

Owner and operator: Aena (Aeropuertos Españoles y Navegación Aérea)
Runways: 03L/21R, 3,100m (10,200ft); 03R/21L, 3,100m (10,200ft)
Terminals: Two, designated Terminal A and Terminal B/C
Airlines using airport as base or hub: Binter Canarias
Annual passengers: 10,348,997
Annual cargo: 40,312 tonnes
Annual aircraft movements: 114,351

Background

Originally opened as a military air base, commercial operations began on 7 April 1930 after a royal decree declared that it would become a civil airport. While major development took some time, awaiting the growth in tourism, the airport has seen rapid expansion in recent years as the Canary Islands have become a major holiday area for people from northern Europe, not least because of the warm winter weather. Nevertheless, this growth was delayed and much later than in mainland Spain and the Balearic Islands because of the great distances involved.

It remains as an air force base with an *Ejército del Aire* fighter squadron stationed near to the southern end of the eastern runway.

ALICANTE: ALC

Alicante, Spain

Owner and operator: Aena (Aeropuertos Españoles y Navegación Aérea)
Runways: 10/28, 3,000m (9,842ft)
Terminals: Two, designated Terminal 1 and Terminal 2
Airlines using airport as base or hub: Ryanair
Annual passengers: 9,109,926
Annual cargo: 4,540 tonnes
Annual aircraft movements: 79,750

A station within a new terminal, due to be completed in 2009, will eventually handle AVE Spanish high-speed trains.

Background

Some 9km (just under 6 miles) south-west of the port and resort of Alicante, the airport was to begin with known as El Altet and is the main airport for the Murcia Region.

Originally Alicante had been served by an airport at La Rabassa, which had opened in 1936, and the present airport replaced it when it opened on 4 May 1967. A second passenger terminal was opened during the early 1970s, and before the end of the decade, the runway was extended to 3,000m. It became a base for the low-cost airline, Ryanair in 2007. The airport has one of the best safety records of any in Spain.

A new terminal will have been completed in 2009, while a railway station for the Spanish AVE high-speed railway network is planned.

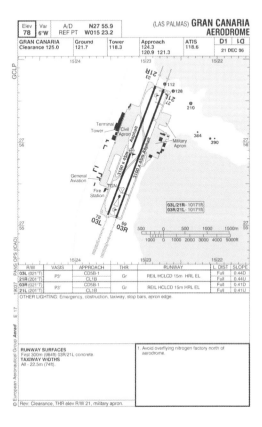

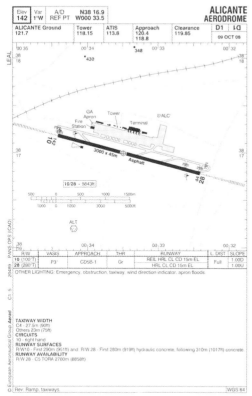

Elev	Var	A/D	N38 16.9					ALICANTE
142	1°W	REF PT	W000 33.5					AERODROME

ALICANTE Ground	Tower	ATIS	Approach	Clearance	D1	I.O
121.7	118.15	113.8	120.4	119.85		
			118.8		09 OCT 08	

R/W	VASIS	APPROACH	THR	RUNWAY	L. DIST	SLOPE
10 (100°T)	P3°	CD5B-1	Gr	REIL HRL CL CD 15m EL	Full	1.00D
28 (280°T)				HRL CL CD 15m EL		1.00U

OTHER LIGHTING: Emergency, obstruction, taxiway, wind direction indicator, apron floods.

TAXIWAY WIDTH
C4 - 27.5m (90ft)
Others 23m (75ft)
CIRCUITS
10 - right hand
RUNWAY SURFACES
R/W10 - First 290m (951ft) and R/W 28 - First 280m (919ft) hydraulic concrete, following 310m (1017ft) concrete.
RUNWAY AVAILABILITY
R/W 28 - C5 TORA 2700m (8858ft)

Rev: Ramp, taxiways.   WGS 84

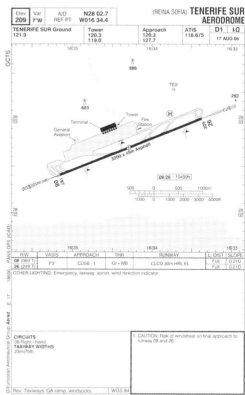

Elev	Var	A/D	N28 02.7		(REINA SOFIA) TENERIFE SUR
209	7°W	REF PT	W016 34.4		AERODROME

TENERIFE SUR Ground	Tower	Approach	ATIS	D1	I.O
121.9	120.3	120.3	118.675		
	119.0	127.7		17 AUG 06	

R/W	VASIS	APPROACH	THR	RUNWAY	L. DIST	SLOPE
08 (069°T)	P3°	CD5B - 1	Gr+WB	CLCD 30m HRL EL	Full	0.21U
26 (249°T)					Full	0.21D

OTHER LIGHTING: Emergency, taxiway, apron, wind direction indicator

CIRCUITS
08 Right - hand
26 (249°T)
TAXIWAY WIDTHS
23m (75ft)

1. CAUTION: Risk of windshear on final approach to runway 08 and 26.

Rev: Taxiways, GA ramp, windsocks.   WGS 84

TENERIFE SOUTH (TENERIFE SOUTH-REINA SOFIA): TFS

Tenerife, Canary Islands, Spain

Owner and operator: Acna (Aeropuertos Españoles y Navegación Aérea)
Runways: 08/26, 3,200m (10,498ft)
Terminals: One
Annual passengers: 8,615,757
Annual cargo: 27,765 tonnes
Annual aircraft movements: 65,836

Background

The airport was opened on 6 November 1978 as a fog-free airport and to relieve Tenerife North, which had suffered the worst accident in aviation history the previous year when two Boeing 747s collided on its runway in drifting fog. It was originally named after Queen Sofia but is now known simply as Tenerife South.

VALENCIA: VLC

Malises, Valencia, Spain

Owner and operator: Aena (Aeropuertos Españoles y Navegación Aérea)
Runways: 04/22, 1,130m (3,707ft); 12/30, 3,200m (10,499ft); there is also a helipad
Terminals: One
Airlines using airport as base or hub: Air Nostrum
Annual passengers: 5,924,386
Annual cargo: 13,382 tonnes
Annual aircraft movements: 96,591

Lines 3 and 5 of the Valencia metro network link the airport to the centre of Valencia.

Background

Situated some 9km (almost 6 miles) west of the city, Valencia was until recently also used by the Spanish Air Force. A new terminal was opened in

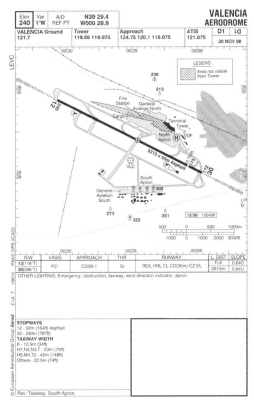

Elev 240	Var 1°W	A/D REF PT	N39 29.4 W000 28.9		VALENCIA AERODROME	
VALENCIA Ground 121.7		Tower 118.55 119.075		Approach 124.75 120.1 119.075	ATIS 121.075	D1 ↳Ω
						20 NOV 08

R/W	VASIS	APPROACH	THR	RUNWAY	L DIST	SLOPE
12(116°T)	P3'	CD5B-1	Gr	REIL HRL CL CD(30m) CZ EL	Full	0.64D
30(296°T)					2915m	0.64U
OTHER LIGHTING: Emergency, obstruction, taxiway, wind direction indicator, apron.						

STOPWAYS
12 - 50m (164ft) Asphalt
30 - 240m (787ft)
TAXIWAY WIDTH
K - 10.5m (34ft)
H7,N2,N3,T - 23m (75ft)
H5,M4,T2 - 45m (148ft)
Others - 22.5m (74ft)

© Rev: Taxiway, South Apron.

LANZAROTE: ACE
Arrecife, Lanzarote, Canary Islands, Spain

Owner and operator: Aena (Aeropuertos Españoles y Navegación Aérea)
Runways: 03/21, 2,400m (7,874ft)
Terminals: Two, with the main terminal used for both international and domestic flights and the older terminal for inter-island flights
Airlines using airport as base or hub: Binter Canarias
Annual passengers: 5,625,242
Annual cargo: 6,020 tonnes
Annual aircraft movements: 52,968

Background
The need for an airfield arose during the 1930s for communications between the Canary Islands and with mainland Spain, but completion was delayed by the Spanish Civil War and it was not until 24 July 1941 that an airport opened. It was

2007 in time for the America's Cup yacht race.

It was decided to build an airport near Valencia in 1927, and the harbour was soon able to handle seaplanes and flying boats, but it took some time to settle on a suitable location for an airport and it did not open until March 1933. The first regular scheduled air services started in September 1934, linking Valencia with Madrid, and today this is still the airport's busiest route. It was not until 1946 that work started on hard surfaces for the runways, which was completed in 1949. The main runway was extended in 1958, and a new passenger terminal opened in 1983, replacing one that had been opened just some ten years' earlier. This was replaced in turn by another new terminal in 2007. The airport has had very few accidents since it opened.

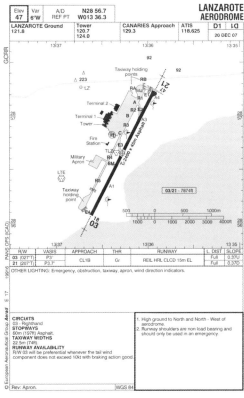

Elev 47	Var 6°W	A/D REF PT	N28 56.7 W013 36.3			LANZAROTE AERODROME	
LANZAROTE Ground 121.8		Tower 120.7 124.0		CANARIES Approach 129.3	ATIS 118.625	D1 ↳Ω	
						20 DEC 07	

R/W	VASIS	APPROACH	THR	RUNWAY	L DIST	SLOPE
03 (027°T)	P3'	CL1B	Gr	REIL HRL CLCD 15m EL	Full	0.37U
21 (207°T)	P3.7'				Full	0.37D
OTHER LIGHTING: Emergency, obstruction, taxiway, apron, wind direction indicators.						

CIRCUITS
03 - Righthand
STOPWAYS
60m (197ft) Asphalt.
TAXIWAY WIDTHS
22.5m (74ft).
RUNWAY AVAILABILITY
R/W 03 will be preferential whenever the tail wind component does not exceed 10kt with braking action good.

1. High ground to North and North - West of aerodrome.
2. Runway shoulders are non load bearing and should only be used in an emergency.

© Rev: Apron. WGS 84

decided that the *Ejército del Aire* (Spanish Air Force) also needed a base in the islands, and this was constructed at Arrecife, and from 1946 was also available for civil use, but this did not become significant until March 1970 after a passenger terminal and air traffic control centre opened. There have been a number of improvements over the years, including the present passenger terminal which opened in 1999, but the original terminal is still used for inter-island flights by Binter Canarias, and is also an aviation museum.

GERONA-COSTA BRAVA: GRO
Gerona, Catalonia, Spain

Owner and operator: Aena (Aeropuertos Españoles y Navegación Aérea)
Runways: 02/20, 2,400m (7,874ft)
Terminals: One
Airlines using airport as base or hub: Ryanair

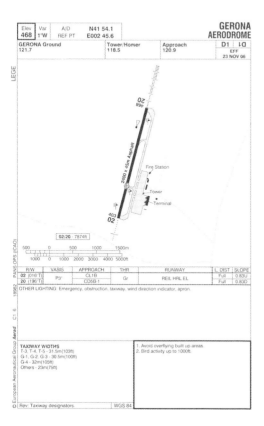

Annual passengers: 4,839,047
Annual aircraft movements: 45,282

Background
Opened in 1965, passenger traffic grew slowly for the next 20 years, and in 1997 the airport still only handled 533,445 passengers per year. Sitting 12km (7½ miles) south of Gerona, the airport is sometimes referred to as Barcelona-Gerona by the low-cost airlines, who are now its main users, even though it is 92km (57½ miles) from Barcelona. Despite this, since 1997, passenger traffic has grown more than tenfold because of the low-cost airlines, and it is now a hub for Ryanair.

IBIZA: IBZ
Ibiza, Balearic Islands, Spain

Owner and operator: Aena (Aeropuertos Españoles y Navegación Aérea)
Runways: 06/24, 2,800m (9,186ft)
Terminals: One
Annual passengers: 4,750,785
Annual cargo: 4,377 tonnes
Annual aircraft movements: 57,853

Background
Ibiza is the airport for the island of the same name and also the airport used by those travelling to and from the neighbouring island of Formentara. It is, by its very nature, highly seasonal, with 85 per cent of passengers travelling during just six months of the year.

The airport dates from the Spanish Civil War (1936–9) when it was used by the military and remained open in the years that followed for emergency use. Some commercial flights were handled between 1949 and 1951, but the airport closed in the latter year, and did not reopen again until 1958 to handle the traffic expected with the emergence of Spain's tourist industry. During the first year, most of the destinations served were in Spain, but rapid growth followed, with charter flights coming mainly from Northern Europe, and in more recent years the airport has seen an influx of low-cost airlines.

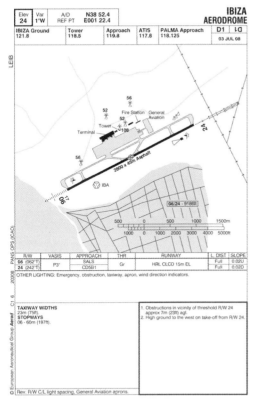

Elev 24	Var 1°W	A/D REF PT	N38 52.4 E001 22.4		IBIZA AERODROME

IBIZA Ground 121.8	Tower 118.5	Approach 119.8	ATIS 117.8	PALMA Approach 118.125	D1 LD

03 JUL 08

R/W	VASIS	APPROACH	THR	RUNWAY	L DIST	SLOPE
06 (062°T)	P3°	SALS	Gr	HRL CLCO 15m EL	Full	0.02U
24 (242°T)		CD5B1			Full	0.02D

OTHER LIGHTING: Emergency, obstruction, taxiway, apron, wind direction indicators.

TAXIWAY WIDTHS 23m (75ft).
STOPWAYS 06 - 60m (197ft).

1. Obstructions in vicinity of threshold R/W 24 approx 7m (23ft) agl.
2. High ground to the west on take-off from R/W 24.

Rev: R/W C/L light spacing, General Aviation aprons.

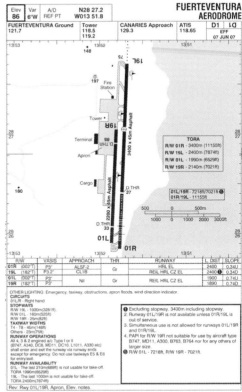

Elev 86	Var 6°W	A/D REF PT	N28 27.2 W013 51.8		FUERTEVENTURA AERODROME

FUERTEVENTURA Ground 121.7	Tower 118.5 119.2	CANARIES Approach 129.3	ATIS 118.65	D1 LD EFF

07 JUN 07

TORA
R/W 01R - 3400m (11155ft)
R/W 19L - 2400m (7874ft)
R/W 01L - 1990m (6529ft)
R/W 19R - 2140m (7021ft)

01L/19R - 7218ft/7021ft
01R/19L - 11155ft

R/W	VASIS	APPROACH	THR	RUNWAY	L DIST	SLOPE
01R (002°T)	P3°	ALSF-2	Gr	HRL EL	2400	0.34U
19L (182°T)	P3.2°	CL1B		REIL HRL CZ EL	2400	0.34D
01L (002°T)	P3°		Gr	HRL EL	1900	0.74U
19R (182°T)	P3°	Nil	Gr	REIL HRL CZ EL	1890	0.74D

OTHER LIGHTING: Emergency, taxiway, obstructions, apron floods, wind direction indicator.
CIRCUITS
01L/R - Right hand
STOPWAYS
R/W 19L - 1000m(3281ft).
R/W 01L - 160m(525ft)
R/W 19R - 25m(82ft)
TAXIWAY WIDTHS
T4 - T8 - 45m(148ft)
Others - 23m(75ft)
RUNWAY OPERATIONS
All 4, 3 & 2 engined a/c Type I or II (B747, A340, DC8, MD11, DC10, L1011, A330 etc) shall enter and exit the runway via runway ends except for emergency. Do not use taxiways E5 & E6 for entry/exit.
RUNWAY AVAILABILITY
01L - The last 210m(689ft) is not usable for take-off.
TORA 1990m(6529ft)
19L - The last 1000m is not usable for take-off.
TORA 2400m(7874ft)

❶ Excluding stopway. 3400m including stopway.
2. Runway 01L/19R is not available unless 01R/19L is out of service.
3. Simultaneous use is not allowed for runways 01L/19R and 01R/19L.
4. PAPI for R/W 19R not suitable for use by aircraft type B747, MD11, A300, B763, B764 nor for any others of larger size.
❺ R/W 01L - 7218ft, R/W 19R - 7021ft.

Rev: Rwy 01L/19R, Apron, Elev, notes.

FUERTEVENTURA: FUE

El Matorral, Fuerteventura, Canary Islands, Spain

Owner and operator: Aena (Aeropuertos Españoles y Navegación Aérea)
Runways: 01/19, 3,400m (11,155ft)
Terminals: One
Annual passengers: 4,604,219
Annual aircraft movements: 44,871

Background

Some 6km (3¾ miles) from Puerto del Rosario (the capital of Fuerteventura), the airport was built during the mid-1960s to encourage tourism to one of the least developed of the Canary Islands. The airport suffered the loss of low-cost airline Ryanair early in 2009 when it cut its services to the island, blaming the local tourist authority for not promoting the island sufficiently.

SEVILLE/SAN PABLO: SVQ

Seville, Spain

Owner and operator: Aena (Aeropuertos Españoles y Navegación Aérea)
Runways: 09/27, 3,360m (11,024ft)
Terminals: One
Annual passengers: 4,501,932
Annual cargo: 8,056 tonnes
Annual aircraft movements: 65,087

Background

Seville's main airport and the second busiest in Andalusia after Málaga, San Pablo is 9km (5½ miles) east of Seville. It competes to some extent with the airport at Faro, over the border in Portugal.

The airport was built between 1915 and 1919, and commercial air services used it from 1919. In 1936, at the start of the Spanish Civil War, it was the landing place for troops of the Spanish

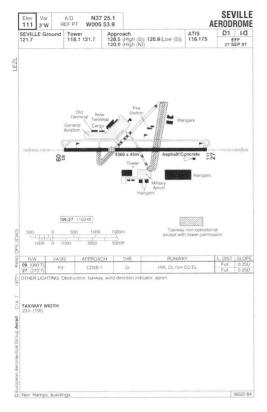

Elev	Var	A/D	N37 25.1			SEVILLE
111	3°W	REF PT	W005 53.9			AERODROME

SEVILLE Ground	Tower	Approach		ATIS	D1	LG
121.7	118.1 121.7	128.5 (High (S)) 120.8(Low (S)) 120.0 (High (N))		118.175	EFF 27 SEP 07	

Old Terminal New Terminal Fire Station General Aviation Cargo Hangars

3360 x 45m Asphalt/Concrete
Tower
Military Apron
Hangars
Hangars

09/27 11024ft

Taxiway non-operational except with tower permission

500   0   500   1000   1500m
1000   0   1000   3000   5000ft

R/W	VASIS	APPROACH	THR	RUNWAY	L. DIST	SLOPE
09 (090°T)	P3	CD5B-1	Gr	HRL CL15m CD EL	Full	0.25U
27 (270°T)					Full	0.25D

OTHER LIGHTING: Obstruction, taxiway, wind direction indicator, apron.

TAXIWAY WIDTH
23m (75ft)

Rev: Ramps, buildings.   WGS 84

Legion, brought from North Africa to bolster the Nationalist forces. After the Second World War it underwent extensive reconstruction and became the main departure point for flights to South America from Spain, but most of this traffic eventually passed to Madrid and Barcelona. The next major stimulus for the airport was Expo '92, for which it was rebuilt and modernised.

BILBAO: BIO
Loiu, Bilbao, Spain

Owner and operator: Aena (Aeropuertos Españoles y Navegación Aérea)
Runways: 10/28, 2,000m (6,562ft); 12/30, 2,600m (8,530ft)
Terminals: One, with two wings
Annual passengers: 4,260,406
Annual aircraft movements: 63,079

There are plans to extend the railway into the terminal in the future.

Background
The main airport in northern Spain and especially for the surrounding Basque country, it is 5km (just over 3 miles) north of the city.

The idea of an airport in northern Spain dates from 1927, but it took another nine years before work was authorised on an airport at Sondika, and eventually work began in 1937. By this time Spain was embroiled in the Spanish Civil War (1936–9), and throughout this period the airport was used mainly by the military. It was not until 1940 that work on the commercial side of the airport started, and the airport did not open to commercial traffic until 19 September 1948, and even then it was another two years before the terminal opened. The original terminal was named Carlos Haya, after a Bilbao airman. At first the airport had hard-packed earth runways, but it also included a flying club hangar and refuelling facilities for Campsa, the state fuel monopoly.

An instrument landing system was installed in 1965 and, during the years that followed, the runways were surfaced, the passenger terminal was enlarged, and a cargo terminal was completed.

More recently, a new taxiway and aircraft parking apron were completed in 1996, and a new air traffic control tower opened in 1999, while on 19 November 2000 a new terminal opened on the north side of the airport. The terminal is now being extended – a difficult task as the building was originally designed in the shape of a flying dove, and doesn't easily lend itself to enlargement without spoiling the visual effect.

Bilbao is an important industrial and commercial centre, but the north of Spain has been largely by-passed during the massive tourist development of the Costas, so the airport is much less busy than those in the main tourist areas. Nevertheless, the area does attract visitors from elsewhere in Spain as well as business traffic.

There has been one serious accident at the airport. On 19 February 1985 an Iberia Boeing

727-200, approaching from Madrid, dropped below the minimum safe height and struck the base of aerials on a mountain top, with the left wing breaking off and the fuselage hitting the mountain side, killing the 7 crew and 141 passengers.

TENERIFE NORTH (LOS RODEOS): TFN

Santa Cruz de Tenerife, Tenerife, Canary Islands, Spain

Owner and operator: Aena (Aeropuertos Españoles y Navegación Aérea)
Runways: 12/30, 3,400m (11,155ft)
Terminals: One
Airlines using airport as base or hub: Binter Canarias
Annual passengers: 4,123,554
Annual cargo: 27,765 tonnes
Annual aircraft movements: 65,836

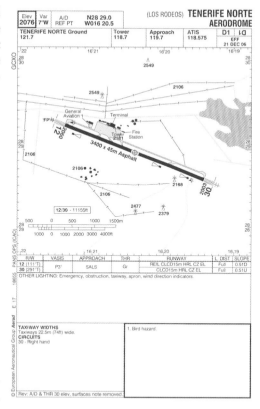

Background

Formerly known as Los Rodeos Airport, Tenerife North is one of two airports on the island, and today has become an inter-island hub with flights to the other six Canary Islands, as well as mainland Spain, the rest of Europe, Caracas (Venezuela) and the United States. Its busiest route is that to Gran Canaria, with around 40 flights daily.

The use of the site for aviation pre-dates the airport when, during the late 1920s, it was selected as a landing place for an Arado VI flown from Berlin by the then Deutsche Luft Hansa, the predecessor of today's Lufthansa. A regular air service began in May 1930 when CLASSA (Compañía de Líneas Aéreas Subvencionadas SA), started the first air link between Madrid and Los Rodeos, although this had to fly via Casablanca, Cap Juby, and Gando in Gran Canaria. Even so, it was not until the late 1930s that the airstrip was expanded and a small hangar built, taking from 1935 to 1939 because of the shortage of funds, but General Franco flew from the airport in July 1936 to take part in the Spanish Civil War. It was not until the Spanish Civil

War ended and the Second World War had begun, that flights started on a permanent basis, with an Iberia de Havilland Dragon Rapide operating between Los Rodeos and Gando from late January 1941.

By 1946 the airport had a paved runway, hangars, and a passenger terminal, with the runway extended several times during the late 1940s and 1950s, as well as being equipped with lighting. The runway had been extended to 3,000m (9,840ft) by 1964 so that Douglas DC-8 jet airliners could use the airport. The runway was strengthened later so that Boeing 747s could use it, and in 1971 an instrument landing system was installed.

Despite this steady improvement, the airport has always been known for bad fog, and in 1977 was the site of the worst accident in aviation history, when a Pan Am Boeing 747 which, having missed a turning was taxiing along the runway to turn off at the next exit, was hit by a KLM

Royal Dutch Airlines Boeing 747 as it took off, with the loss of 583 lives on both aircraft, leaving just over 60 survivors. This accident and the weather conditions were factors in the decision to build an airport closer to sea level at what is now Tenerife South, and this opened in November 1978.

There had been a number of serious accidents at the airport before this. On 5 May 1965 the pilots of an Iberia Lockheed Super Constellation, on approach from Madrid, were warned that visibility had fallen below the minima, and they executed a go-around. On the second approach they decided to go-around again, but hit equipment on the ground, and the aircraft crashed and broke up in farmland. The accident killed 6 of the 9 crew members and 24 out of the 40 passengers. All 7 crew and 148 passengers aboard a Spantax Convair CV-990 were killed on 3 December 1972 when it crashed just after taking off for Munich in very poor visibility.

One accident that followed was on 25 April 1980 to a Dan-Air Boeing 727 on approach from Manchester, which was told to fly a holding pattern, but it entered at the wrong point putting the aircraft off course and flying too low for the surrounding terrain. Towards the end, the aircraft was flying in the wrong direction and turned towards a mountain range into which it crashed, killing all 8 crew and 138 passengers.

Despite the new airport, Tenerife North continues to play an important part in air transport in the Canary Islands. A new terminal opened in 2002, and this was augmented by an inter-island section opened in 2005.

MENORCA/MAHÓN: MAH

Menorca, Balearic Islands, Spain

Owner and operator: Aena (Aeropuertos Españoles y Navegación Aérea)
Runways: 01L/19R, 2,350m (7,710ft); 01R/19L, 2,100m (6,890ft)
Terminals: One
Annual passengers: 2,771,997
Annual cargo: 3,721 tonnes

Background

Sometimes known as Mahon Airport, after the capital of Minorca, the airport serves the whole island and was opened on 24 March 1969 when the neighbouring San Luis Airport closed. It suffered from a partial roof collapse during work on an extension to the terminal in September 2006, but the terminal extension was completed in early 2008.

SANTIAGO DE COMPOSTELA/ LAVACOLLA: SCQ

Santiago de Compostela, Galicia, Spain

Owner and operator: Aena (Aeropuertos Españoles y Navegación Aérea)
Runways: 17/35, 3,200m (10,499ft)
Terminals: One
Annual passengers: 2,048,706
Annual cargo: 4,580 tonnes

Background

Also known locally as Lavacolla, the airport is on the outskirts of the city, the most important centre in Galicia, the north-west corner of Spain.

The airport dates from 1932 when a local flying club was formed and opened an airfield. It was taken over by the military in 1937 during the Spanish Civil War, although it was used by an airline operating a regular service from Santiago to Salamanca, Valladolid, and Zaragoza. Although Spain was neutral during the Second World War, there was little development until the 1950s when the airport began to expand as the area became popular with tourists from central Spain and also for pilgrims to the shrine of St James in Santiago. The passenger terminal, opened in 1969, has been expanded on several occasions and the airport gained Category III ILS (instrument landing system) status in 1993.

MURCIA-SAN JAVIER: MJV

San Javier, Spain

Owner and operator: Aena (Aeropuertos
  Españoles y Navegación Aérea)
Runways: 05R/23L, 2,300m (7,546ft); 05L/23R,
  874m (2,869ft) unsurfaced earth runway;
  14/32, 800m (2,625ft) unsurfaced earth
  runway
Terminals: One
Annual passengers: 1,994,582

Background

Shared with the Spanish Air Force or *Ejército del Aire*, the airport is actually at San Javier and is 27km (nearly 17 miles) south of Murcia.

The airport was built before the Second World War and for most of its existence it has handled relatively little traffic, but the emergence of the low-cost carriers has brought strong growth, more than 20 per cent between 2006 and 2007, after growing tenfold between 1995 and 2004, with the airport serving the southern part of the Costa Brava as well as the resorts of the Costa Calida.

ASTURIAS INTERNATIONAL: OVD

Santiago del Monte, Spain

Owner and operator: Aena (Aeropuertos
  Españoles y Navegación Aérea)
Runways: 11/29, 2,200m 7,218ft
Terminals: One
Annual passengers: 1,554,318

Background

The airport is 15km (almost 10 miles) from Aviles, 40km (25 miles) from Gijon, and 47km (almost 30 miles) from Oviedo. It is basically a small regional airport, built on the site of a former military airfield, and most of the traffic consists of domestic scheduled flights to Madrid and Barcelona, as well as to the Canary and Balearic Islands. There are some international flights, mainly to London Stansted, Paris-Orly and Brussels.

JEREZ: XRY

Jerez de la Frontera, Spain

Owner and operator: Aena (Aeropuertos
  Españoles y Navegación Aérea)
Runways: 02/20, 2,300m (7,546ft)
Terminals: One
Annual passengers: 1,537,533
Annual aircraft movements: 50,364

Background

The airport is 10km (6¼ miles) north of Jerez de la Frontera in the south of Spain. The airport is on the site of a former *Ejército del Aire* (Spanish Air Force) base, but has a new terminal and control tower. Domestic flights account for just over a third of the passenger activity, and international traffic is mostly from Britain and Germany, the airport having enjoyed rapid growth since being chosen by the Irish low-cost airline, Ryanair.

GRANADA INTERNATIONAL/ FEDERICO GARCÍA LORCA GRANADA-JAÉN: GRX

Sante Fe/Chauchina, Granada, Spain

Owner and operator: Aena (Aeropuertos
  Españoles y Navegación Aérea)
Runways: 09/27, 2,900m (9,514ft)
Terminals: One
Annual passengers: 1,448,017

Background

Usually referred to in airline timetables simply as Granada, the airport is 15km (less than 10 miles) from the city, and has been named after a local poet.

The airport was built as a base for the Spanish Air Force between the two world wars and became an important regional airport after the war. Overwhelmingly, passenger traffic is Spanish domestic, with just a few international flights to major European destinations.

VIGO-PEINADOR INTERNATIONAL: VGO
Vigo, Spain

Owner and operator: Aena (Aeropuertos
   Españoles y Navegación Aérea)
Runways: 02/20, 2,400m (7,874ft)
Terminals: One
Annual passengers: 1,405,786

Background
A regional airport serving the north of Spain.
The only international service at the time of
writing is to Paris-Charles de Gaulle, but the relative isolation of the area means that air transport is the most attractive option.

REUS: REU
Reus, Tarragona, Catalonia, Spain

Owner and operator: Aena (Aeropuertos
   Españoles y Navegación Aérea)
Runways: 07/25, 2,455m (8,060ft); 12/30, 950m
   (3,119ft)
Terminals: One
Airlines using airport as base or hub: Ryanair
Annual passengers: 1,295,612

Background
The main centre served by Reus is Tarragona,
almost 8km (5 miles) away, but many low-cost
carriers are promoting the city to passengers
bound for Barcelona, which is 75km (almost 47
miles) away. One result has been that passengers
using the airport rose from 500,000 in 1995 to 1.4
million in 2005, although the numbers have since
fallen. A new arrivals hall has been opened at
the terminal.

LA CORUÑA: LCG
Alvedro, La Coruña, Coruña Province, Spain

Owner and operator: Aena (Aeropuertos
   Españoles y Navegación Aérea)
Runways: 04/22, 1,940m (6,365ft)
Terminals: One
Annual passengers: 1,251,606

Background
Known locally as Alvedro Airport, La Coruña
is primarily a regional airport handling domestic flights.

LA PALMA: SPC
La Palma, Canary Islands

Owner and operator: Aena (Aeropuertos
   Españoles y Navegación Aérea)
Runways: 01/19, 2,200m (7,218ft)
Terminals: One
Airlines using airport as base or hub: Binter
   Canarias; Islas Airways
Annual passengers: 1,207,177

Background
A small airport on the Canary Island of La
Palma, served by both inter-island flights and
flights to mainland Spain and the northern European cities which provide many of the charter
flights using the airport. Little is known about
its history.

ALMERÍA: LEI
Almería, Spain

Owner and operator: Aena (Aeropuertos
   Españoles y Navegación Aérea)
Runways: 08/26, 3,200m (10,499ft)
Terminals: One
Annual passengers: 1,202,763

Background

Serving both the province of Almería and the city of the same name, this modern airport is about 10km (6¼ miles) from the provincial capital. It has both domestic and international flights, with many of the latter being by charter airlines with inclusive tour passengers, or by the new low-cost airlines such as easyJet and Ryanair.

SRI LANKA

As with many countries, the history of air transport in Sri Lanka has been essentially that of one airline, Sri Lankan Airlines, the name adopted for Air Lanka in 1999, and its colonial predecessor, Air Ceylon. The airport has had a difficult history, with Sri Lanka stricken by civil war and guerrilla activities by the self-styled Tamil Tigers, although the fleet is stronger today than ever before.

COLOMBO – BANDARANAIKE INTERNATIONAL: CMB

Katunavake, Colombo, Sri Lanka

Owner and operator: Airport and Aviation Services (Sri Lanka) Ltd
Runways: 04/22, 3,350m (10,991ft)
Terminals: One
Airlines using airport as base or hub: Sri Lankan Airlines
Annual passengers: 4,898,891
Annual cargo: 164,792 tonnes
Annual aircraft movements: 42,878

Background

Sri Lanka's only international airport, it is 35km (22 miles) north of Colombo. It was built for the Royal Air Force during the Second World War as RAF Negombo, and after independence it became a Royal Ceylon Air Force base in 1957. The airport is still shared with what is now the Sri Lankan Air Force.

The airport for Colombo had been at Ratmalana, but after the war the former RAF

Negombo was chosen as a replacement. It was upgraded, and terminals and aprons were built with aid from Canada. It opened in 1967 and became the new home for Air Ceylon. The airport adopted its present name in 1970 after a former prime minister, but in 1977 it was renamed Katunayake International Airport before reverting to its previous name in 1995. Since then, the name Katunayake has been reserved for the Sri Lankan Air Force base which occupies part of the airport site. Growth has been difficult because tourism has been discouraged by continuing terrorist activity, which at one time saw Sri Lankan Airlines lose most of its fleet in a terrorist attack. Nevertheless, the terminal has been expanded and modernised, with eight jet-bridges opened in 2005, and in 2007 the military presence was reduced to provide more space for passenger traffic. Plans for the future include the construction of a second runway and a separate domestic terminal.

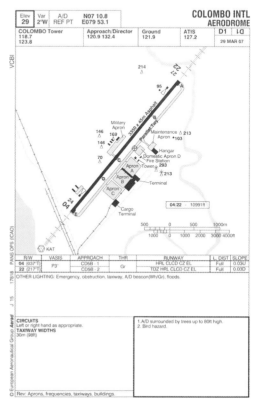

While there have been a number of accidents at the airport, these have been eclipsed by the terrorist attacks on the airport and on aircraft parked at the airport, especially those of Air Lanka and its successor Sri Lankan Airlines. One of the first of these was on 3 May 1986 when a bomb exploded aboard an Air Lanka Lockheed TriStar as passengers were boarding for a flight to the Maldives, killing 14 passengers and destroying the aircraft. The most devastating attack was on 24 July 2001 when a 14-strong 'Black Tiger' suicide squad penetrated Katunayake air station and destroyed eight military aircraft, killing seven personnel, and then turned their attentions to the civil side of the airfield, destroying two Airbus A330s, an A340, and an A320. Another attack on the air station on 25 March 2007 led to passengers aboard aircraft being evacuated and led to safety, but an evacuation of a Saudi Arabian Airlines Boeing 747 as it taxied ready to take off for Jeddah resulted in 62 injuries amongst the 420 passengers and 22 crew aboard: the evacuation was prompted by a telephone call claiming that there was a bomb aboard the aircraft, but a search showed this to have been a hoax.

Accidents have included an Antonov An-12 of Sky Cabs on a cargo flight which crashed on approach when it ran out of fuel, killing six of the eight crew and four people in the two houses into which it crashed on 24 March 2000. On 4 February 2004 an Ilyushin Il-18D belonging to Phoenix Aviation and carrying cargo landed enroute to Dubai, but the altimeter was incorrectly set and the aircraft touched the sea more than 10km (almost 7 miles) short of the runway before eventually making a belly landing alongside the runway.

SUDAN

KHARTOUM INTERNATIONAL: KRT
Khartoum, Sudan

Owner and operator: Government of Sudan
Runways: 18/36, 2,980m (9,777ft)
Terminals: One
Airlines using airport as base or hub: Azza Transport, Badr Airlines, Sudan Airways, Trans Attico
Annual passengers: 2,190,377
Annual cargo: 135,479 tonnes
Annual aircraft movements: 139,426

Background
Opened after the Second World War, the airport is due to be replaced during 2010–1 by a new international airport with two runways, each 4,000m (13,133ft) in length. The current airport is shared with the Sudanese Air Force, and it is not clear whether this arrangement will continue with the new airport or whether the current airport will become simply a military base.

The airport has been the site of a number of hijackings and accidents. One of the former ended on 30 March 2007 when a Sudan Airways aircraft landed, and while accounts vary, the hijacker was eventually detained without harm to anyone aboard the aircraft. June 2008 proved to be a bad month for air safety at the airport. On 10 June a Sudan Airways aircraft landed from Amman and, while taxiing to the terminal, the right engine caught fire and 81 people were killed, leaving 123 survivors. At the end of the month, on 30 June, an Ilyushin Il-76 took off and exploded into a fireball, killing the four crew members.

SWEDEN

STOCKHOLM-ARLANDA: ARN

Stockholm, Uppland, Sweden

Owner and operator: LFV
Runways: 01L/19R, 3,301m (10,830ft)
01R/19L, 2,500m (8,201ft)
08/26, 2,500m (8,201ft)
Terminals: Four, designated 2, 3, 4, and 5
   (charter flights)
Airlines using airport as base or hub: FlyNordic,
   Nordic Airways, SAS, Skyways Express
Annual passengers: 17,968,023
Annual cargo: 122,922 tonnes
Annual aircraft movements: 218,549

The Arlanda Express operates direct to
Stockholm Central Station.

Background

Sweden's largest airport and the third largest in
the Scandinavian countries, Arlanda was completed in 1959 and opened to traffic the following
year. The first flights from 1960 were transatlantic as Stockholm-Bromma airport's runways
were too short for larger long-haul aircraft.
Even so, Arlanda did not open officially until
1962. Strangely, the name 'Arlanda' is contrived,
having been selected in a competition and
derived from Arland, the old name for the area,
now known as Husby-Arlinghundra, while the
'a' was added to comply with other Swedish
names ending as 'land' and as a pun on the verb
'landa', meaning to land. Oddly, the present Terminal 5, used for charter flights, was the original
terminal.

   Domestic traffic was not transferred from
Bromma until 1983, using the newly-opened
Terminal 4, although later two new terminals (2
and 3) were opened for domestic traffic, until 2
was reallocated to international traffic. The
third runway was ready in 2002, but remained
unused until the following year.

   The airport has seen a number of accidents.
One of the first was on 1 November 1969 when
a Linjeflyg Convair 440 on a training flight had

a simulated engine failure on take-off, but the
left wing struck the ground and the aircraft
veered off the runway as the undercarriage collapsed. The crew of four survived, but the aircraft was a write-off. The following year, on 5
January, a Spantax Convair 990 was being ferried from Stockholm to Zurich on three engines
as engine No. 4 was unserviceable, but on taking
off the aircraft hit trees and five of the ten occupants were killed. On 14 July 1973 a Sterling Airways Sud Aviation Caravelle taxied into an
obstruction and was damaged beyond repair.
Another Caravelle, belonging to SAS (Scandinavian Airlines System) was also damaged
beyond repair on 25 January 1974. An Aeroflot
Tupolev Tu-154, taking off for Moscow, aborted
the take-off and overshot the runway, damaging
the aircraft, although none of the 74 passengers
or the crew was harmed. A landing accident
occurred on 16 August 1980 when a JAT
(Jugoslav Air Transport) Boeing 707 arrived

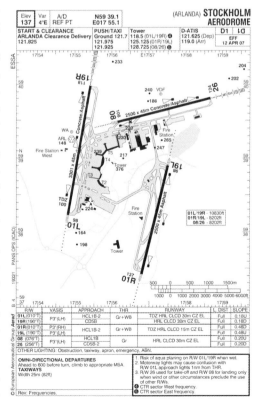

during a thunderstorm and with a strong tail-wind, overshot the runway and punctured several tyres before stopping, but all aboard survived. A chartered Transwede Caravelle, taking off for Alicante on 6 January 1987, was badly affected by ice at lift-off and fell back on the runway so heavily that the undercarriage collapsed and the aircraft slid off the runway before catching fire. All 27 people aboard survived, but the aircraft was a write-off. Ice also caused another accident on 27 December 1991 when an SAS McDonnell Douglas MD-81, taking off for Copenhagen, ingested ice into both engines and crashed shortly after take-off, although none of the 129 aboard was killed. A heavy landing by a Tarom Rombac One-Eleven on 7 October 1997 led to a nose wheel steering failure and the aircraft ran off the runway on to grass, with the passengers and crew able to alight normally, but the aircraft was declared a write-off and taken to be used as a fire trainer. Two engineers taxiing an SAS Commuter Saab 2000 on 8 October 1999 lost control and ran the aircraft into a closed hangar door, injuring them and writing-off the aircraft.

A number of aircraft hijack attempts have also ended at the airport. On 26 May 1977 an Aeroflot Antonov An-24, that had been flying from Donetsk to Riga, landed at Stockholm, where the hijacker surrendered to police. Another Aeroflot flight, a Tupolev Tu-154, calling at Stockholm on an Oslo–Moscow service, was hijacked by three men who were arrested at Stockholm. The most recent hijacking was on 20 February 1993 when an Aeroflot Tu-134, flying between Tyumen and St Petersburg, was taken over and the pilots forced to fly to Stockholm after first making a refuelling stop at Tallin, where 30 passengers were released. On landing, the hijacker demanded an aircraft capable of flying to the United States, but eventually surrendered and released the remaining 40 passengers and the crew.

GOTHENBURG-LANDVETTER: GOT
Landvetter, Sweden

Owner and operator: Luftfartsverket
Runways: 03/21, 3,299m (10,823ft)
Terminals: Two, designated International and Domestic
Annual passengers: 4,385,910
Annual cargo: 61,790 tonnes
Annual aircraft movements: 64,336

Background

The second busiest airport in Sweden and the main airport for Gothenburg, it is at Landvetter, a small town 20km (12½ miles) to the east of Gothenburg.

The airport opened in 1977 to replace Torslanda Airport, which had become too congested, and all flights were transferred from Torslanda at the time. While traffic has grown steadily,

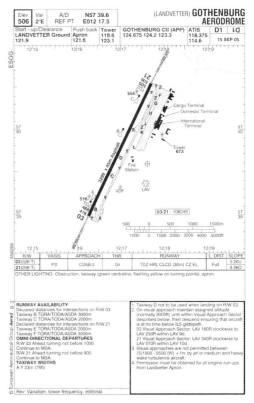

Landvetter is one of two airports serving Gothenburg, with the other being Gothenburg City Airport, originally Säve Flygplats, a disused military air base, which is used by many low-cost airlines.

STOCKHOLM-SKAVSTA: NYO
Nyköping, Sweden

Owner and operator: Abertis A/S
Runways: 08/26, 2,878m (9,442ft); 16/34,
  2,039m (6,690ft)
Terminals: One
Airlines using airport as base or hub: Avitrans,
  Ryanair
Annual passengers: 1,994,512

Background
Despite its name, Stockholm-Skavsta is 100km (62 miles) south of the Swedish capital.

The airport dates from the mid-1940s when it was opened as a base for the Swedish Air Force, and did not become a commercial airport until 1984. Little used at first, the appearance of low-cost airlines provided rapid growth after Ryanair opened a route to London-Stansted in 1997, and in 2006 the airline established a hub at the airport. The previous year, Finnair's service between Helsinki and Boston called at Skavsta, but this has now been transferred to Stockholm-Arlanda.

MALMÖ (MALMÖ-STURUP): MMX
Malmö, Sweden

Owner and operator: Swedish Civil Aviation
  Administration
Runways: 11/29, 797m (2,615ft); 17/35, 2,800m
  (9,186ft)
Terminals: One
Annual passengers: 1,911,722
Annual cargo: 47,529 tonnes
Annual aircraft movements: 40,091

Background
Until recently, known as Malmö-Sturup Airport, it is 28km (17½ miles) from Malmö, but is also convenient for Copenhagen, which is 55km (34¼ miles) away across the Oresund Bridge, and is used as a diversionary airport for the Danish capital.

Malmö was originally served by Bulltofta Airport, which opened in 1923, but it could not expand as urban development encircled it. The present airport opened in 1972, costing twice as much as the original estimates, and Bulltofta closed, although air traffic control remained there until 1983. In October 2007, Sterling Airlines announced plans to use the airport as one of its bases, with three aircraft stationed there and new low-cost routes from Malmö to London-Gatwick and five Mediterranean holiday destinations, so the airport was badly affected when Sterling ceased operations a year later.

STOCKHOLM-BROMMA: BMA
Stockholm, Sweden

Owner and operator: Luftfartsverket A/S
Runways: 12/30, 1,668m (5,742ft)
Terminals: One
Airlines using airport as base or hub: Malmö
  Aviation
Annual passengers: 1,835,349
Annual aircraft movements: 62,137

Background
The closest airport to the centre of Stockholm, at just 8km (5 miles), Bromma was opened in 1936 to fulfil a need for a purpose-built airport for the Swedish capital. It claims to be the first European airport to have opened with paved runways. While Sweden was neutral during the Second World War, the airport was used by BOAC (British Overseas Airways Corporation), flying converted military aircraft, including the de Havilland Mosquito, to carry ball bearings and diplomats from Sweden to Scotland.

After the war, with the return of peace to Europe, the airport's traffic grew rapidly, and it became an important base and hub for ABA (Aktiebolaget Aerotransport), the Swedish contribution to SAS (Scandinavian Airlines System) and the domestic carrier Linjeflyg, itself later absorbed by SAS. The airport, nevertheless, could not expand as traffic grew because of urban encroachment, and was unable to handle large jet transports such as the Douglas DC-8. A new airport, Stockholm-Arlanda, was built and opened to long-haul traffic in 1960, with European air services following during 1961 and 1962, and finally domestic services in 1983. Bromma did not close, but instead was used by business aircraft and flying schools. Revival for Bromma came after the opening of London-City Airport with flights by Malmö Aviation to London-City as well as Gothenburg and Malmö. A new control tower opened in 2002 and other extensive improvements were completed in 2005, but future development is restricted by lack of room and opposition to aircraft noise. A new runway at Arlanda and a fast railway link have raised the question of whether Bromma would be better closed with its traffic transferred to Arlanda and the land given over to residential and commercial development, but Bromma remains popular with its users.

Sadly, but inevitably, given its long history, the airport has had a number of accidents. The first of these post war was to a Vickers Valetta (military version of the Viking airliner) of the Royal Air Force on 18 February 1951, which made an emergency landing in poor weather with the No. 2 engine shut down and problems with the radio, while smoke was entering the cabin. As the aircraft was not properly aligned with the runway, because of the problems of flying with just one engine, the captain attempted an overshoot, but icing led to a belly landing in a clearing, with 1 out of the 22 occupants killed. Not long afterwards, on 1 April 1951, a Douglas C-47 of SAS (Scandinavian Airlines System), arriving from Copenhagen, crash-landed into a field, although the 4 crew and 18 passengers survived. There was a long interval before the next accident, which was on 15 January 1977 when a Vickers Viscount 800 of Skyline Sweden, but leased by Linjeflyg, arriving from Jonkoping, stalled when the stabilisers became covered in ice and crashed 4.5km (just under 3 miles) from the airport, killing all aboard, 3 crew and 19 passengers.

SWITZERLAND

In addition to Switzerland's place as a major business centre and a holiday destination, the country has become a hub for many international flights. The small size of the country means that one airport popularly recognised as 'Swiss', is in fact in France, while one of the approaches to Zurich is over Germany.

ZÜRICH: ZRH
Kloten, Zürich, Switzerland

Owner and operator: Flughafen Zürich
Runways: 10/28, 2,500m (8,202ft); 14/32, 3,300m (10,827ft); 16/34, 3,700m (12,139ft)
Terminals: Two
Airlines using airport as base or hub: Swiss International, Edelweiss Air
Annual passengers: 20,682,092
Annual cargo: 289,958 tonnes
Annual aircraft movements: 268,476

Zurich Flughafen Station is under the airport and has trains not only to the centre of Zurich but also to many other Swiss towns and cities.

Background
The airport is 12km (7 miles) north of Zürich, the main financial and business centre in Switzerland, and is the country's main international airport.

Air transport came to Zürich in 1919 with the foundation of an airline, Ad Astra Aero, which later became part of the Swiss Air Transport Company, Swissair. Rapid expansion occurred during the 1930s, with routes from Zürich to most of the capital cities of Europe, although there were few long-haul flights before the Second World War as Switzerland lacked colonies. Although Switzerland was neutral during the war, most operations were suspended

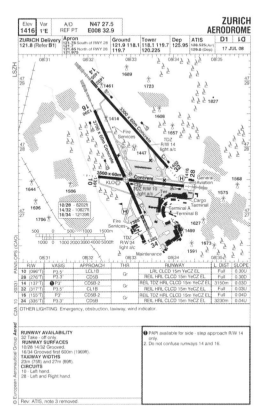

The airport has an excellent safety record and many of the accidents have not involved fatalities. Those seeking political asylum have tended to see it as a haven. An example of this was one of the early flights by JAT (Jugoslovenski Air Transport) when the pilots of a Douglas DC-3, with their families amongst the passengers, and flying a domestic service from Ljubljana to Belgrade, diverted to Zürich seeking asylum. An accident occurred on 18 August 1970 to a CSA (Ceskoslovenské Aerolinie) Tupolev Tu-124 landing from Prague, as the flight engineer was preoccupied with a pressurisation problem and forgot to lower the undercarriage, leaving the aircraft to make a belly landing, and while the 6 crew and 14 passengers were unharmed, the aircraft was damaged beyond repair. More embarrassing than serious, on 21 February 1990 a Crossair Saab 340A, being used for a training session, had the undercarriage retracted while the aircraft was stationary on the ground.

One accident that could have been serious in 1992 was to an Aeroflot Tupolev Tu-154M flying from Milan to Moscow via Zürich. Landing in heavy rain and severe turbulence, the pilots executed a go-around, but on the second attempt the aircraft hit some high antennae which damaged the flaps and prevented them from turning the aircraft to the left, but it nevertheless made a safe flapless landing, no doubt to the relief of the 9 crew and 136 passengers. Bad weather also affected a Korean Air Boeing 747 on a flight to Zürich, with hailstones causing severe damage to the cockpit windows, radar dome, and engines, but the aircraft managed to land safely on 14 September 1994. After repairs, it departed on 22 September 1994 without passengers and cabin crew, but failure to observe the operating instructions for a hail-damaged aircraft meant that it cleared some buildings by around 50m (163ft). After this shaky start, it reached Pusan safely. Far less fortunate were those aboard a Crossair Avro RJ100 as it approached on 24 November 2001, but dropped below the minimum height, struck trees and crashed. Three of out of the crew of 5 were killed, as were 21 of the 28 passengers. To ease

on the grounds of safety and also to conserve precious fuel, which had to come through neighbouring countries.

With operations resuming in 1945, after the war, Zürich rapidly became one of Europe's major airline hubs. The first transatlantic routes linking Switzerland with New York were from Geneva because of the number of international organisations based there, but Zürich rapidly became the more important airport. This led to some friction with Swissair at one time planning to concentrate all long-haul flights on Zürich, to the dismay of Francophone Geneva. The airport suffered a major blow when Swissair collapsed in 2002, but the carrier's feeder subsidiary, Crossair, was saved and provided the basis for a new airline, Swiss International, and the airport has recovered its standing with 7.8 per cent passenger growth in 2007. Even without Swissair, around a hundred airlines use Zürich on a regular basis.

approaches at Zürich, an agreement was signed between Switzerland and Germany on 18 October 2001 allowing aircraft to use German airspace at certain times.

GENEVA COINTRIN INTERNATIONAL: GVA

Geneva, Switzerland

Owner and operator: Aeroporte Internationale de Geneva

Runways: 05/23, 3,900m (12,795ft); 05/23, 823m (2,700ft) a grass landing strip for light aircraft

Terminals: One

Airlines using airport as base or hub: easyJet Switzerland, Baboo, PrivatAir, Swiss International

Annual passengers: 10,791,466

Annual cargo: 36,599 tonnes

Annual aircraft movements: 190,006

Railway station with trains to Geneva and to other Swiss cities.

Background

The second most important airport in Switzerland and with the longest runway in Europe, Geneva Cointrin, named after a nearby village, has a long history having opened on 23 September 1920. The first scheduled air services followed in 1922, from Geneva to Paris via Lausanne, to Lyon, and a service via Zurich and Munich to Nuremberg. At this time the airport consisted of a grass runway, a small administrative building with a café, which doubled as a passenger terminal, and two wooden hangars, but it did have radio communications and radio-direction finding to guide aircraft to the airport. Over the next few years, the number of routes radiating out from the airport increased to six, and in 1931, the first brick-built hangars were completed.

The local canton (the basis of Swiss communities) decided on a major development programme in 1935, as a result of which the airport had it first concrete runway open in 1937, 405m

long, and asphalt taxiways. The runway was extended to 1,065m in 1940 and work started on a new terminal building, as well as a lighting system. Further growth was inhibited by the Second World War for, although Switzerland remained neutral, it was surrounded by territory engaged in the conflict, apart from Vichy France, which was itself occupied by German forces in late 1943.

After the war the runway was almost doubled in length to 2,000m and opened in 1946. On 2 May 1947, Swissair, the Swiss Air Transport Company, introduced a transatlantic service to New York. The new terminal opened in 1949. Between 1956 and 1958 the Swiss and French governments agreed an exchange of territory to allow the runway to be extended to 3,900m and the new airport terminal to have a 'French sector' with a road link to France regarded as part of French territory. The airport was by this time receiving Vickers Viscount turboprop services

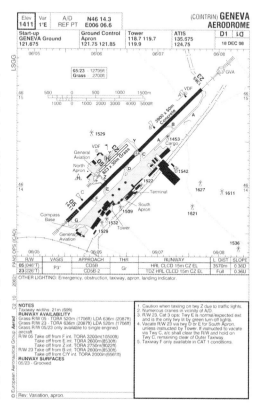

operated by British European Airways, but in 1959 jet aircraft began with a Scandinavian Airlines System Sud Aviation Caravelle operating from Copenhagen. A new passenger terminal opened in 1968, and this received a railway station in May 1987, which in effect became the terminus for all Swiss Railways trains operating to Geneva. The following year a new freight terminal opened, while the old passenger terminal, considerably renovated, was reopened as a weekend 'charter terminal' for holiday flights. The main passenger terminal was later extended in 1995.

Despite this progress, a major blow fell in 1996 when Swissair announced that most of its long-haul flights would be based on Zürich, with Geneva only retaining transatlantic services to New York and Washington. This gave rise to the local canton committing to the end of the Swissair monopoly, albeit with a transitional period. On the other side of the balance sheet, Swiss control moved its headquarters to Geneva in 1998. Development of the airport continued throughout this period, with the terminal extended by the opening of a west wing in June 2000, while a business aviation terminal opened in 2002. A new east wing for the main terminal opened in 2009.

The airport has had a relatively uneventful existence. Nevertheless, on 5 March 1989 a two-month old Fokker 100 of KLM Royal Dutch Airlines suffered a partial undercarriage collapse on landing, causing substantial damage to the aircraft, although the 5 crew and 95 passengers were unharmed. An Air Inter Airbus A300 flying from Palma de Mallorca was hijacked en route and landed at Geneva so that the hijacker could make a political statement, but he was arrested after the plane was stormed.

EUROAIRPORT BASEL-MULHOUSE-FREIBURG: BSL

Mulhouse, Saint-Louise, France

Owner and operator: Euroairport SA
Runways: 16/34, 3,900m (12,795ft); 08/26, 1,820m (5,971ft)

Terminals: One, divided into Swiss and French areas
Airlines using airport as base or hub: easyJet Switzerland
Annual passengers: 4,262,277
Annual cargo: 44,036 tonnes
Annual aircraft movements: 82,025

Background

Generally regarded as a Swiss airport and almost certainly the most international airport in the world, shared by France and Switzerland and with easy access to Germany, serving the towns of Basel in Switzerland, Mulhouse in France and Freiburg in Germany. It is actually in France, but under a 1946 treaty citizens of both countries can access the airport without any restrictions, but there is a customs and immigration station in the middle of the terminal. The French half of the terminal is the Schengen area with free access to all inhabitants of European Union countries,

and is used by passengers travelling to and from Germany as a result. Air Berlin has its check-in desks on the French side, and easyJet has its check-in desks on the Swiss side. The airport's board has eight representatives of France and another eight for Switzerland. The road linking the airport with Switzerland, the *Zollfreistrasse*, has no junctions with any French highway.

The airport has three IATA airport codes, with MLH for France and EAP as an international code, but it is generally referred to by the Swiss code of BSL. Nevertheless, this can lead to some complications when buying tickets with differences in fares for the same journey!

The idea of a joint airport for the two countries first surfaced before the Second World War, but the occupation of France meant that no action could be taken until after the war. An agreement in 1946 provided for an airport to be constructed at Blotzheim, with France providing the land and the Swiss canton of Basel meeting the building costs. The money was voted for the work before the treaty was signed in 1949 and, in fact, the airport was already open by this time with a 1,200m (3,900ft) runway, and a temporary terminal which opened on 8 May 1946. During the next few years the runway was extended and the *Zollfreistrasse* was built, with completion by 1953.

Development of the airport has required a referendum in the Basel Canton, and the first major expansion was in the 1960s, and in the years that followed the terminal and the runways were extended. Throughout this period the airport was known as Basel/Mulhouse, or more usually at the time Basle/Mulhouse. In 1987 the name of EuroAirport Basel-Mulhouse-Freiburg was adopted, although still not widely used after more than 20 years. It was decided that the terminal should be enlarged in 1998, with a new Y-finger dock, and this was completed between 2002 and 2005.

While the work was still under way, a blow to Swiss confidence was the collapse of the national airline, Swissair, in 2001. Its regional subsidiary, Crossair, had established its base at Basel, but when this was transformed into Swiss International Airlines as a successor to Swissair, it moved its base to Zürich. This meant that as the first phase of the new terminal opened in 2002, it was under-utilised and the number of flights and passengers at the airport actually dropped. In 2004, the low-cost airline, easyJet Switzerland established a base at the airport, and traffic has risen since then. The airline, in fact, relocated from Geneva to Basel because the former airport was too expensive for its low-cost model.

A serious accident occurred as an Invicta Airlines Vickers Vanguard approached the airport from Bristol on 10 April 1973 in poor weather. The crew became disorientated and allowed the aircraft to drop below the prescribed minimum height and it brushed against a wooded hillside and disintegrated, except for the tailplane where some survivors were found. Out of the crew of 6, just 2 survived, and 104 of the 139 passengers died.

Much less serious was an accident to a German-registered Shorts 360 operated by Express Airways. On a training flight, the aircraft returned to Basel with a hydraulic problem, and after landing the brakes failed, leaving the aircraft to collide with a hangar, but there were no serious injuries and the aircraft was repaired.

TAIWAN

TAIPEI TAOYUAN (CHIANG KAI-SHEK) INTERNATIONAL: TPE
Taoyuan, Taipei, Taiwan

Owner and operator: Civil Aviation Administration of Taiwan
Runways: 6/24, 3,350m (10,991ft); 5/23, 3,660m (12,008ft)
Terminals: Two, designated Terminal 1 and Terminal 2
Airlines using airport as base or hub: China Airlines, EVA Air, TransAsia
Annual passengers: 23,425,794
Annual cargo: 1,605,681 tonnes
Annual aircraft movements: 169,120

Taipei Rapid Transit System will be linking the two terminals and providing a direct line to the city centre in the near future.

Background

Taipei Taoyuan is another example of an airport being built to relieve the overcrowding and congestion at an earlier airport, in this case Taipei Songshan Airport, which came under growing pressure during the 1960s. In 1970, the decision was taken to build a new airport, which opened on 21 February 1979 with a single terminal and was one of ten major construction projects approved by the Nationalist Chinese government earlier in the decade. The original intention was it should be called Taoyuan International Airport, but it was named after Generalissimo Chiang Kai-shek, the first president and founder of Nationalist China, until the current title was adopted in 2006.

Strong air traffic growth led to the building of Terminal 2, which was opened, although not fully completed, in late July 2000, and finally opened completely in January 2005. There are plans for a Terminal 3, which, once opened, will allow the original terminal to be demolished.

The airport has been the scene of a couple of serious accidents. One of these was on 16 February 1998 when a China Airlines flight landing from Denpasar-Bali crashed into a residential area killing all 196 passengers and crew and another 6 people on the ground. A Singapore Airlines flight taking-off for Singapore after dark on 31 October 2000 used a closed runway with construction equipment parked on it, and rammed into the equipment after lifting off, killing 82 of those aboard.

KAOHSIUNG/SIAOGANG INTERNATIONAL: KHH

Siaogang, Kaohsiung, Taiwan

Owner and operator: Civil Aeronautics Administration
Runways: 09/27, 3,150m (10,335ft)
Terminals: Two, designated Domestic and International
Annual passengers: 5,717,242
Annual cargo: 70,241 tonnes
Annual aircraft movements: 67,149

MRT Kaohsiung Red Line rapid transit links Kaohsiung International Airport Station with the city centre.

Background

Sometimes known as Siaogang International Airport, because of the locality, it was originally built as a Japanese military airfield when Taiwan was occupied by Japanese forces between 1895 and Japan's surrender in 1945. On the creation of Nationalist China after the revolution on the mainland, the airport retained its military role for another 20 years. The pressing need for improved air transport links persuaded the authorities to convert the airfield into a commercial airport, which opened in 1965, and in 1969 it

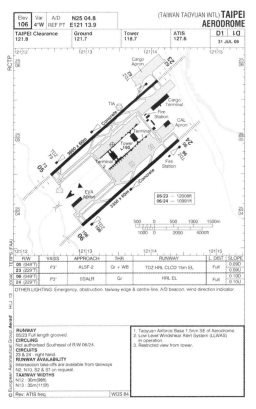

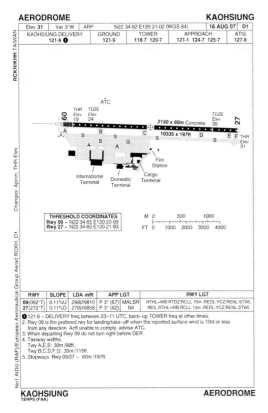

AERODROME   KAOHSIUNG

Elev 31	Var 3°W	ARP	N22 34·62 E120 21·02 (WGS 84)	16 AUG 07	D1

KAOHSIUNG DELIVERY 121·8 ❶	GROUND 121·9	TOWER 118·7 120·7	APPROACH 121·1 124·7 125·7	ATIS 127·8

RCKH/KHH TAIWAN · Changes: Apron, THR Elev · No1 AIDU/RAF/European Aeronautical Group Aerad RCKH_D1

3150 x 60m Concrete · 10335 x 197ft

THRESHOLD COORDINATES
Rwy 09 – N22 34·65 E120 20·09
Rwy 27 – N22 34·60 E120 21·93

RWY	SLOPE	LDA m/ft	APP LGT	RWY LGT
09(092°T)	0·11%U	2990/9810	P 3°(67) MALSR	RTHL+WB.RTDZ.RCLL 15m.REDL.YCZ.RENL.STWL
27(272°T)	0·11%D	2700/8858	P 3°(62) Nil	REIL.RTHL+WB.RCLL 15m.REDL.YCZ.RENL.STWL

❶ 121·8 – DELIVERY freq between 23–11 UTC, back-up TOWER freq at other times.
2. Rwy 09 is the prefered rwy for landing/take-off when the reported surface wind is 10kt or less from any direction. Acft unable to comply, advise ATC.
3. When departing Rwy 09 do not turn right before DER.
4. Taxiway widths.
   Twy A,E,S: 30m /98ft.
   Twy B,C,D,F,G: 35m /115ft.
5. Stopways. Rwy 09/27 – 60m /197ft.

KAOHSIUNG   AERODROME
TERPS (FAA)

was allowed to handle international flights, initially as charters, but regular scheduled flights followed in 1972, although for many years only Hong Kong and Tokyo were served. Early in the 1990s, connecting flights to Taiwan Taoyuan International were introduced, while at the same time more services were introduced to destinations throughout South-East Asia, and in 1997 a separate international terminal opened. Longer-haul services to the United States were introduced, once by EVA Air in 1998 and later by Northwest Airlines, but neither survived long due to poor load factors.

More recently, domestic air traffic has slumped following the launch of the Taiwan High Speed Railway in January 2007. For future growth the airport is placing its hopes on direct scheduled and charter flights to mainland China.

TANZANIA

DAR-ES-SALAAM JULIUS NYERERE INTERNATIONAL: DAR

Dar-es-Salaam, Tanzania

Owner and operator: Tanzania Airports Authority
Runways: 05/23, 3,000m (9,842ft); 14/32, 1,000m (3,280ft)
Terminals: Two, designated Terminal I and Terminal II
Airlines using airport as base or hub: Air Tanzania, Coastal Aviation, Precision Air
Annual passengers: 1,450,558
Annual cargo: 18,449 tonnes
Annual aircraft movements: 55,938

Background

The main airport for Tanzania's largest city, it is named after the country's first president.

The first airport for what was, then, Tanganyika (a German colony at the time), was opened at Kurasini in 1918 and named Mkeja Airport. The country passed to British administration after German defeat in the First World War. After the Second World War, with rapid growth in air traffic, the original airport was unable to cope with the rise in demand or the increase in aircraft sizes, so a new airport was opened, known as Dar-es-Salaam Airport, with a single terminal, but a second terminal was opened in 1985. The current title was adopted in 2006.

THAILAND

BANGKOK – SUVARNABHUMI INTERNATIONAL: BKK

Bangkok, Thailand

Owner and operator: Airports of Thailand
Runways: 01R/19L, 4,000m (13,123ft); 01L/19R, 3,700m (12,139ft)
Terminals: One
Airlines using airport as base or hub: Thai Airways International, Bangkok Airways, Orient Thai Airlines, PBair and Thai AirAsia

Annual passengers: 41,210,081
Annual cargo: 1,220,001 tonnes
Annual aircraft movements: 87,064

The 'Pink Line' high-speed link to the centre of Bangkok opens in 2009.

Background

Built to replace Bangkok Don Muang International Airport (see below) whose designation it adopted apart from a two-week period during which both airports were operational, with Suvarnabhumi handling domestic flights from 15 September 2006 before taking all flights from 28 September. The name was chosen by the Thai King, and means 'The Golden Land', a traditional name for the area running from Burma through Thailand to Cambodia and Laos. The airport has the world's highest air traffic control tower and the third largest terminal building.

The airport project suffered from controversy during planning and construction, notably from those who claimed that the area was supposed to be inhabited by evil spirits. After opening, problems were discovered with water seepage into the runways, leading to tarmac separation and cracking. In January 2007, Thai Airways announced a plan to move some of its domestic operations back to Don Muang International Airport because of overcrowding. Three days later the Ministry of Transport recommended temporarily reopening Don Muang while repair work on the runways at Suvarnabhumi proceeded. Thai Airways said it would shift most of its domestic flights back, keeping flights with high international passenger connections.

Unusually for a modern airport, it was opened before the planned high-speed link, known as the 'Pink Line', linking the centre of Bangkok, and the suburban railway system, was ready, but this was scheduled to open in late 2009.

Inevitably the airport has been affected by the continuing political instability of Thailand. The most extreme case was when People's Alliance for Democracy protestors occupied the departure lounge on 26 November 2008, stranding 3,000 passengers in the airport while all flights were suspended until the protestors left the airport on 2 December and operations were able to resume on 5 December once clearing up and security checks were completed.

Plans for future development include building up to four additional runways and two additional terminal buildings.

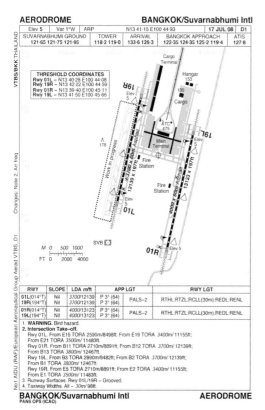

PHUKET INTERNATIONAL: HKT
Phuket, Thailand

Owner and operator: Airports of Thailand
Runways: 09/27, 3,000m (9,843ft)
Terminals: Two, designated Terminal 1 (for domestic flights) and Terminal 2 (for international flights)
Annual passengers: 5,704,365
Annual cargo: 18,005 tonnes
Annual aircraft movements: 41,719

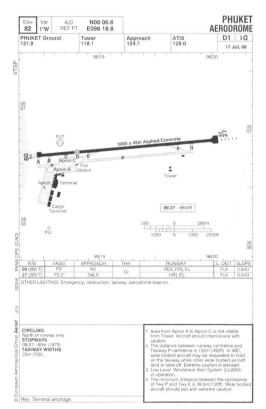

Elev 82	Var 1°W	A/D REF PT	N08 06.6 E098 18.8				PHUKET AERODROME
PHUKET Ground 121.9		Tower 118.1		Approach 124.7	ATIS 128.0	D1	iᏟ
						17 JUL 08	

VTSP

3000 x 45m Asphalt/Concrete

PUT

Apron C
Apron B — Fire Station
Apron A
Terminal

Cargo Terminal

Tower

09/27 - 9843ft

500   0   500m
1000   0   1000   2000ft

R/W	VASIS	APPROACH	THR		RUNWAY	L. DIST	SLOPE
09 (085°T)	P3°	Nil			REIL HRL EL	Full	0.64U
27 (265°T)	P3.2°	SALS	Gr		HRL EL	Full	0.64D

OTHER LIGHTING: Emergency, obstruction, taxiway, aerodrome beacon.

CIRCLING
North of runway only.
STOPWAYS
09/27 - 60m (197ft)
TAXIWAY WIDTHS
23m (75ft).

1. Area from Apron A to Apron C is not visible from Tower. Aircraft should manoeuvre with caution.
2. The distance between runway centreline and Taxiway P centreline is 150m (492ft). In IMC, wide bodied aircraft may be requested to hold on the taxiway while other wide bodied aircraft land or take-off. Extreme caution is advised.
3. Low Level Windshear Alert System (LLWAS) in operation.
4. The minimum distance between the centrelines of Twy P and Twy E is 39.5m (130ft). Wide bodied aircraft should taxi with extreme caution.

Rev: Terminal airbridge.

© European Aeronautical Group Aerad J15 2003/6 PANS OPS (ICAO)

Background

Situated some 32km (20 miles) from Phuket itself, the airport was originally opened as a small regional airstrip following the Second World War, but has grown significantly, initially on the back of domestic traffic but, in more recent years, with the massive growth in tourism.

There have been a number of accidents and incidents at the airport. One of these was on 15 April 1985 when a Thai Airways Boeing 737-200 crashed after both engines flamed out, and all 11 occupants died. Pilot error is believed to have been behind an accident on 31 August 1987 when a Thai Airways aircraft crashed into the sea on final approach, killing all 83 people aboard. More recently, on 16 September 2007, a One-Two-GO Airlines McDonnell Douglas MD-82 landing from Bangkok landed heavily in driving rain after experiencing severe windshear, with the aircraft splitting in two and bursting into flames, and of the 7 crew and 123 passengers, 89 died and another 41 were injured.

BANGKOK – DON MUEANG INTERNATIONAL: DMK
Bangkok, Thailand

Owner and operator: Airports of Thailand
Runways: 03L/21R, 3,700m (12,139ft); 03R/21L, 3,500m (11,482ft)
Terminals: One, designated Terminal 3 (Terminal 1 and Terminal 2 are currently unused)
Airlines using airport as base or hub: One-Two-GO Airlines
Annual passengers: 4,805,240
Annual cargo: 22,753 tonnes
Annual aircraft movements: 87,064

Trains run from the airport to Bangkok Hua Lamphong station.

Background

Don Mueang occupies the site of a Thai Army air base opened on 27 March 1914, although it may have been used earlier, as the first aircraft were received as early as 1913 when a small group of Thai army officers returned from France. It did not become a civil airport until 1924, when KLM Royal Dutch Airlines started using the airport as a staging post on its long-haul service from Amsterdam to Batavia in the Netherlands East Indies (now Indonesia). Between the two world wars there was heavy fighting between royalists and government forces at the airport during the Boworadet Rebellion in 1933. During the Second World War, Thailand was occupied by Japan and used by the Japanese Army Air Force, which resulted in a number of attacks by Allied aircraft.

After the war, as Don Muang, it became one of the main hubs in Asia, as well as Thailand's leading airport for both international and domestic flights, while during the Vietnam War it was used by the United States Air Force as a secure airport for transport flights. It was, and remains, a Royal Thai Air Force base. The airport became increasingly busy and congested,

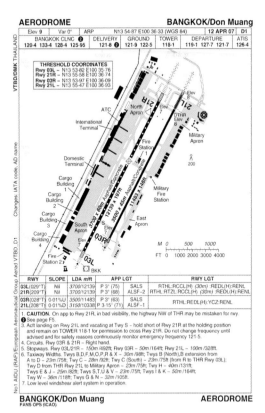

AERODROME   **BANGKOK/Don Muang**

Elev 9	Var 0°	ARP	N13 54·87 E100 36·33 (WGS 84)		12 APR 07	D1

BANGKOK CLNC ❷	DELIVERY	GROUND	TOWER	DEPARTURE	ATIS
120·4 133·4 128·4 125·95	121·8 ❷	121·9 122·5	118·1	119·1 127·7 121·7	125·4

THRESHOLD COORDINATES
Rwy 03L – N13 53·82 E100 35·76
Rwy 21R – N13 55·58 E100 36·74
Rwy 03R – N13 53·97 E100 36·09
Rwy 21L – N13 55·47 E100 36·93

RWY	SLOPE	LDA m/ft	APP LGT		RWY LGT
03L(029°T)	Nil	3700/12139	P 3° (75)	SALS	RTHL:RCCL(H) (30m) :REDL(H):RENL
21R(209°T)	Nil	3700/12139	P 3° (68)	ALSF–2	RTHL:RTZL:RCCL(H) (30m) :REDL(H):RENL
03R(028°T)	0·01%U	3500/11483	P 3° (63)	SALS	RTHL:REDL(H):YCZ:RENL
21L(208°T)	0·01%D	3150/10338	P 3·15° (71)	ALSF–1	

1. **CAUTION:** On app to Rwy 21R, in bad visibility, the highway NW of THR may be mistaken for rwy.
❷ See page F5.
3. Acft landing on Rwy 21L and vacating at Twy S - hold short of Rwy 21R at the holding position and remain on TOWER 118·1 for permission to cross Rwy 21R. Do not change frequency until advised and for safety reasons continuously monitor emergency frequency 121·5.
4. Circuits. Rwy 03R & 21R – Right hand.
5. Stopways. Rwy 03L/21R – 150m /492ft; Rwy 03R – 50m /164ft; Rwy 21L – 100m /328ft.
6. Taxiway Widths. Twys B,D,F,M,O,P,R & X – 30m /98ft; Twys B (North),B extension from A to D – 23m /75ft; Twy C – 28m /92ft; Twy C (South) – 23m /75ft (from R to THR Rwy 03L); Twy D from THR Rwy 21L to Military Apron – 23m /75ft; Twy H – 40m /131ft; Twys E & J – 25m /82ft; Twys S,T,U & V – 23m /75ft; Twys I & K – 50m /164ft; Twy W – 36m /118ft; Twys G & N – 32m /105ft.
7. Low level windshear alert system in operation.

BANGKOK/Don Muang   **AERODROME**
PANS OPS (ICAO)

prompting the construction of a major new airport for Bangkok at Suvarnabhumi (see above), which opened on 27 September 2006 and the BKK code for Bangkok was transferred to the new airport. The opening of Suvarnabhumi was fraught with problems, including runway cracking, and many domestic flights resumed at what was by this time known as Don Mueang on 24 March 2007, with only those for passengers wishing to connect with an international flight remaining at Suvarnabhumi. Initially, Don Mueang was also used by charter flights because of the high landing fees at Suvarnabhumi, but to discourage this traffic and the low-cost airlines from switching from the new airport, the same landing fees are now being charged at Don Mueang. Nevertheless, Terminal 2 may reopen as a low-cost airline terminal.

Over the past 35 years, the airport has suffered a number of accidents. On 25 December 1976, an Egyptair Boeing 707-320, approaching

from Cairo, crashed into an industrial estate near the airport killing all 53 aboard. This was followed on 27 April 1980 by a Thai Airways BAe.748, approaching from Khon Kaen, crashing in a thunderstorm 13km (8 miles) from the airport with the loss of all 4 members of the crew and 40 of the 49 passengers. After taking off from Don Mueang for Vienna on 26 May 1991, a Lauda Air Boeing 767 suffered an uncommanded deployment of the thrust reverser for the No. 1 engine, killing all 10 crew and 213 passengers. A Qantas Boeing 747-400 suffered considerable damage on 23 September 1999 when it overshot the runway on landing. On 3 March 2001 a Thai Airways Boeing 737-400, preparing for a flight to Chiang Mai, was destroyed in an explosion, killing one of the five cabin crew aboard the aircraft, which was waiting for a former Thai prime minister, and 150 passengers. It is believed that fuel vapour may have caused the explosion. There were no injuries when a Singapore Airlines Boeing 777-200ER stopped beyond a painted stop line and its left-wing tip was clipped by a Thai Airways Airbus A330-300 taxiing before take-off on 19 April 2005.

The final act of the hijacking of a Garuda Douglas DC-9 was played out at the airport on 31 March 1981, which had been taken over flying between Palembang and Medan. The hijackers ordered the captain to fly to Colombo, but as the aircraft didn't have enough fuel, it refuelled first at Penang and then landed at Don Mueang on 28 March. The hijacking ended when the aircraft was stormed by Thai special forces, with the death of two hijackers and of the aircraft's captain, but the passengers and the rest of the crew were released.

The airport remains an RTAF base, and an unusual feature is the golf course between the two parallel runways.

CHIANG MAI INTERNATIONAL: CNX
Chiang Mai, Thailand

Owner and operator: Airports of Thailand
Runways: 18/36, 3,100m (10,171ft)

Terminals: One
Annual passengers: 3,290,856
Annual cargo: 22,869 tonnes

Background
The main airport in the north of Thailand, it became much better known to many travellers when Bangkok's Suvarnabhumi Airport was closed by protesters in 2008, when several airlines diverted their flights via Chiang Mai, and it also handled the evacuation of Filipino workers trapped in Bangkok.

HAT YAI INTERNATIONAL: HDY
Hat Yai, Thailand

Owner and operator: Airports of Thailand
Runways: 08/26, 3,050m (10,007ft)
Terminals: One
Annual passengers: 1,390,145
Annual cargo: 9,786 tonnes

Background
The airport is 9km (just over 5½ miles) from the centre of Hat Yai. It enjoys a seasonal surge of pilgrims travelling on the annual Hajj pilgrimage to Mecca. It was targeted by terrorists in April 2005 when a bomb placed in the departure lounge by Pattani separatists exploded killing one passenger and wounding another ten.

TRINIDAD AND TOBAGO

PORT OF SPAIN – PIARCO INTERNATIONAL: POS
Piarco, Trinidad, Trinidad and Tobago

Owner and operator: Airports Authority of
    Trinidad and Tobago
Runways: 10/28, 3,200m (10,500ft); there are
    also two helipads
Terminals: One
Airlines using airport as base or hub: Caribbean
    Airlines

Annual passengers: 2,388,444
Annual cargo: 32,828 tonnes
Annual aircraft movements: 66,309

Background
Set in northern Trinidad, Piarco is 25km (almost 16 miles) east of Port of Spain and is the main airport in Trinidad and Tobago.

The airport originally opened on 8 January 1931, replacing two landing strips at the Queen's Park and the Mucarapo Field, while the Cocorite Docks handled flying boats and seaplanes. An early user was the *Compagnie Générale Aéropostale*. During the Second World War it became a Fleet Air Arm training base as RNAS Piarco (HMS *Goshawk*) before being made available to the United States Army Air Force and the United States Navy in return for Lend-Lease military aid to the United Kingdom. The US forces mounted anti-submarine patrols over the Caribbean, even before formally entering the

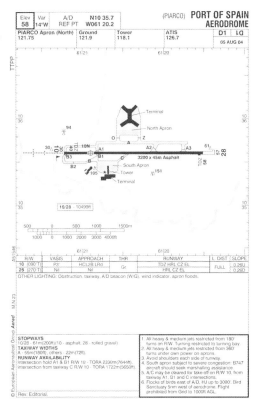

war in December 1941 and also used the airport for transport flights. During the war, a hard runway was laid, along with taxiways and aircraft parking areas, and a number of hangars were built.

The airport returned to civil use after the war and became a major airport in the services of British West Indies Airways, in which BOAC (the British Overseas Airways Corporation) was a major shareholder. The airport continued to grow and develop after Trinidad and Tobago became independent, and in more recent years a new terminal building with airbridges and taxiways, was completed in 2001. The former terminal building is now used for air cargo. A new control tower is planned and, while at present the airport is shared with the Air Guard of Trinidad and Tobago, there are plans to build a new military airfield nearby. The airport is the base and main hub for Caribbean Airways and also houses a flying school.

The airport has suffered a number of minor accidents, although none fatal, in recent years. An Aéropostale McDonnell Douglas MD-80 broke a nose wheel after running into an open trench on the taxiway in 2001, while in 2005 a Tobago Express Bombardier Dash 8 Q300 had to make an emergency landing after the nose wheel hung up. The previous year three aircraft, two belonging to BWIA and one to Continental, were damaged in a case of poor ground handling.

TUNISIA

Unlike neighbouring Algeria to the west and Libya to the east, Tunisia has succeeded in developing substantial tourist traffic and this has meant that the country's main airports have developed over the past forty years or so. It has also meant that Monastir, a resort, has a busier airport than the capital, Tunis.

MONASTIR – HABIB BOURGUIBA INTERNATIONAL: MIR
Monastir, Tunisia

Owner and operator: TAV (Tepe Akfen Ventures)
Runways: 07/25, 2,903m (9,678ft)
Terminals: One
Airlines using airport as base or hub: Nouvelair Tunisie
Annual passengers: 4,282,055

Background
The airport has been developed for the tourist trade, and most of the traffic is carried by charter airlines.

TUNIS CARTHAGE INTERNATIONAL: TUN
Tunis, Tunisia

Owner and operator: Tunisian Civil Aviation & Airports Authority
Runways: 01/19, 3,200m (10,499ft)
11/29, 2,840m (9,318ft)
Terminals: One
Airlines using airport as base or hub: Tunisair, Nouvelair Tunisia, Sevenair, Tunisavia
Annual passengers: 3,946,765
Annual cargo: 17,703 tonnes
Annual aircraft movements: 51,944

Background
The airport for Tunis, it is also busy with large numbers of holiday charter flights, in addition to the commercial traffic of a capital city. The historic ruins of Carthage are just to the north of the airport.

There has been one serious accident at the airport in recent years. On 7 May 2002 a Boeing 737-500 of Egyptair was approaching from Cairo, but crash-landed 6km (almost 4 miles) short of the runway, killing 3 of the 6 crew and 14 out of 62 passengers.

DJERBA-ZARZIS: DJE

Djerba Island, Tunisia

Owner and operator: Tunisian Civil Aviation and
    Airports Authority.
Runways: 09/27, 3,043m (10,171ft)
Terminals: One
Annual passengers: 2,449,471

Background

A small airport, which has grown since Tunisia
became independent of France, largely because
of tourist traffic.

TURKEY

ISTANBUL – ATATÜRK
INTERNATIONAL: IST

Yeşilköy, Istanbul, Turkey

Owner: General Directorate of State Airports
Operator: TAV Airport Management
Runways: 18L/36R, 3,000m (9,843ft); 18R/36L,
    3,000m (9,843ft); 06/24, 2,300m (7,546ft)
Terminals: Three, designated A, B, and C (cargo)
Airlines using airport as base or hub: THY
    Turkish Airlines
Annual passengers: 25,561,435
Annual cargo: 341,454 tonnes
Annual aircraft movements: 262,248

There is a light railway running from the airport to
Aksaray, which also serves some parts of the
European side of the city.

Background

Turkey's busiest and most important airport,
Istanbul Ataturk is named after the founder of
the modern secular Turkish state and is on the
European side of Istanbul, while there is another
airport, Sabiha Gökçen International Airport,
on the Anatolian or Asian side of the city,
although this currently handles around 3.7 million passengers and is more likely to be affected
by the new high-speed railway line between
Istanbul and the capital, Ankara, than Istanbul

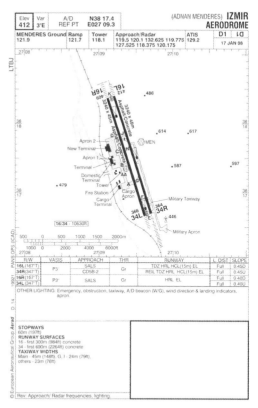

Ataturk. In the five years leading up to 2007,
passenger traffic almost doubled, and while
tourism and international business travel
accounted for much of this, domestic traffic virtually quadrupled because of the booming Turkish economy. Plans for the future include a
fourth runway, but a new airport is also planned
north of the city, convenient for the Levant business district, making four airports in all, but the
current third airport, Hezarfen, is too small to
make a significant impact.

The airport has had some 14 accidents and
incidents over the past half-century, but none of
these has resulted in any fatalities.

ANTALYA INTERNATIONAL: AYT

Antalya, Turkey

Owner and operator: DHMI-Antalya-Turkey-Havalimani

Runways: 18L/36R, 3,400m (11,154ft); 18C/36C, 3,400m (11,154ft); 18R/36L, 2,990m (9,809ft)

Terminals: Two, designated Terminal 1 and Terminal 2

Annual passengers: 17,795,523

Annual aircraft movements: 115,002

Background

The existing regional airport was developed specifically to boost Turkey's growing tourist industry, with Antalya's international Terminal 1 completed in 1998, and then joined later by a second terminal. By 2005, of all Mediterranean tourist airports, Antalya came second only to Majorca, and today handles 40 per cent of all international passenger traffic in Turkey.

IZMIR ADNAN MENDERES: ADB

Izmir, Turkey

Owner and operator: Turkish State Airport Management

Runways: 16L/34R, 3,240m (10,630ft); 16R/34L, 3,240m (10,630ft)

Terminals: One

Annual passengers: 5,297,986

Annual cargo: 15,716 tonnes

Annual aircraft movements: 51,774

There is a railway station with trains to the centre of Izmir, but service is very infrequent.

Background

One of Turkey's most important airports because of its proximity to the main tourist

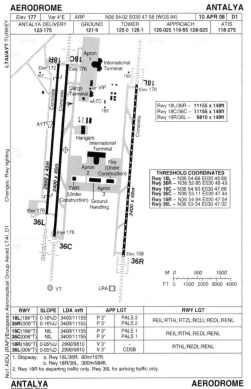

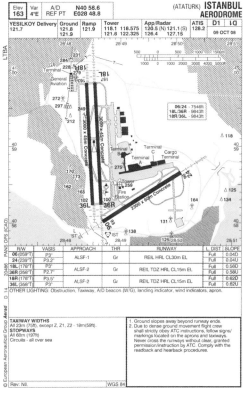

resorts, it is 18km (11 miles) south of the city. It is named after the first democratically-elected Turkish prime minister, Adnan Menderes. Formerly a military airfield, it has had to expand rapidly to cope with the country's fast-growing tourist traffic, and in 2006 a new terminal was opened.

The airport has suffered one serious accident, which occurred on 26 January 1974, a THY Turk Hava Yollari Fokker F-28 Fellowship taking-off for Istanbul crashed after stalling because of ice on the wings, killing 4 of the 5 crew aboard the aircraft and 62 of the 68 passengers.

ANKARA ESENBOĞA: ESB

Esenboga, Ankara, Turkey

Owner and operator: TAV Airport Management
Runways: 03L/21R, 3,750m (12,303ft);
03R/21L, 3,750m (12,303ft)
Terminals: One
Airlines using airport as base or hub: THY
Turkish Airlines, THY Express
Annual passengers: 5,062,971
Annual cargo: 19,589 tonnes
Annual aircraft movements: 63,909

Background
The airport for the capital city of Turkey, it is 28km (17½ miles) from the city centre, and 953m (3,125ft) above sea level. The name Esenboğa is taken from a nearby village and means 'healthy bull'!

The airport opened in 1955 and has grown gradually as Ankara is not a major tourist destination, unlike Istanbul and Izmir, but development has taken place, including the opening of a new passenger terminal in October 2006.

Partly because of its altitude, the airport has been the scene of a number of serious accidents over the past half century or so. Bad weather was a factor in the loss of a United States Air Force Douglas C-124C Globemaster on 28 November 1957, as the aircraft hit the ground during its approach, killing the crew of three, the only occupants. Some accidents in the past have also

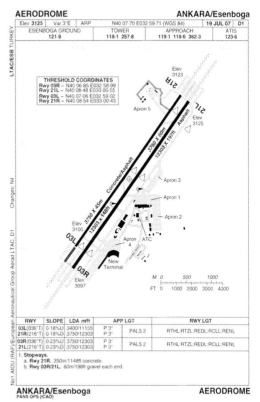

provided few clues to investigators as to the cause, and one of these was on 19 January 1960 when an SAS (Scandinavian Airlines System) Sud Aviation Caravelle approached at the end of a sector from Istanbul and struck the ground short of the runway, killing all 7 crew and the 35 passengers. While it was snowing at the time of the next accident, with a light covering of snow on the wings, a problem with the artificial horizon was regarded as the cause . On 21 December 1961, a BEA (British European Airways) de Havilland Comet 4B, flying from London to Nicosia via Ankara, climbed away too steeply after take-off and stalled, killing all 7 crew and 20 of the 27 passengers. Heavy snow as a Boeing 727-200 of THY Turkish Airlines landed from Istanbul on 16 January 1983 may have been a factor in the aircraft landing just short of the runway, breaking up and catching fire, killing 47 of the 60 passengers, although all 7 crew survived. Far more fortunate were those aboard another 727-200, operated by Torosair, which took-off for Maastricht on 25 August 1989, hit an aerial and returned to the airport without injury to the 8 crew or 157 passengers, but the aircraft was too badly damaged to be repaired.

Despite the airport's location, there seems to have been just one hijacking, which was on 10 April 2007, when a Pegasus Airlines Boeing 737-800 which was diverted to land at Ankara while on a domestic flight. The hijacker claimed to have a bomb, but surrendered after 40 minutes on the ground.

ISTANBUL SABIHA GÖKÇEN INTERNATIONAL: SAW
Istanbul, Turkey

Owner and operator: Limak-GMR-MAHB Consortium
Runways: 06/24, 3,000m (9,842ft)

AERODROME   ISTANBUL/Sabiha Gokcen

RWY	SLOPE	LDA m/ft	APP LGT	RWY LGT
06(064°T)	0·11%U	3000/9843	P 3·5° PALS-2	RTHL:RTZL:RCLL(15m):REDL:YCZ:RENL
24(244°T)	0·11%D	3000/9843	P 3·5° CL1B(H)	RTHL:RCLL(15m):REDL:RENL

1. Taxiway Widths: Main 45m/148ft others 25m/82ft
2. Stopways: Rwy 06 & 24 – 60m/197ft
3. Seagulls in vicinity of AD.

ISTANBUL/Sabiha Gokcen   AERODROME

Terminals: Two, designated Domestic and International
Airlines using airport as base or hub: Pegasus, Sun Express
Annual passengers: 3,791,625
Annual cargo: 10,802 tonnes
Annual aircraft movements: 44,451

Background
Istanbul's second airport after Ataturk International, which is on the European side of the Bosphorus, it is named after the first Turkish woman fighter pilot. Serving the Asian side of the city, the airport was built to relieve the pressure on Ataturk International, and in 2007 a consortium of Turkish and Indian interests, with Malaysia Airport Holdings, was awarded the contract for developing and maintaining the airport. Currently, the international terminal is being enlarged to handle up to 10 million passengers annually, more than three times the current number.

DALAMAN (MUĞLA): DLM
Muğla, Turkey

Owner and operator: Turkish Government Airport Management
Runways: 01/19, 3,000m (9,842ft)
Terminals: One
Annual passengers: 2,959,036

Background
The airport mainly serves the tourist trade and most of its traffic is international, for which a new terminal on four levels was opened in 2008.

MILAS-BODRUM: BJV
Bodrum, Turkey

Owner and operator: Turkish Government Airport Management
Runways: 11/29, 3,000m (9,482ft)
Terminals: Two, designated International and Domestic
Annual passengers: 2,592,852

Background

Normally referred to simply as Bodrum, the airport is 36km (22½ miles) north-east of Bodrum and 16km (10 miles) south of Milas.

The airport only dates from the late 1990s and received a new terminal in 2000, which has been designated for international traffic, while the old terminal is now reserved for domestic flights. The two terminals are a kilometre apart and without easy interchange.

ADANA ŞAKIRPAŞA: ADA

Adana, Adana Province, Turkey

Owner and operator: State Airport Authority (DHMI)
Runways: 05/23, 2,750m (9,022ft)
Terminals: One
Annual passengers: 2,302,535
Annual cargo: 7,501 tonnes

Background

Usually referred to as Adana Airport, but sometimes by the full title of Adana Şakirpaşa Airport, it is 3.5km (2 miles) from the centre of Adana. It was completed as a military airport in 1937 and became solely a commercial airport in 1956. It is mainly used by charter and low-cost airlines carrying tourists, but also has direct flights to Turkish Northern Cyprus.

TRABZON: TZX

Trabzon, Turkey

Owner and operator: Turkish Government Airport Management
Runways: 11/29, 2,640m (8,661ft)
Terminals: One
Annual passengers: 1,484,522

Background

Primarily used by domestic flights, with 94 per cent of passengers being domestic, making it a regional airport. Future growth will depend on whether Turkish Black Sea resorts can emulate the success of those on the Mediterranean.

UKRAINE

KIEV – BORYSPIL INTERNATIONAL: KBP

Kiev, Ukraine

Owner and operator: Ukrainian Department of Aviation
Runways: 18L/36R, 4,000m (13,123ft); 18R/36L, 3,500m (11,483ft)
Terminals: Three, designated Terminal A (for domestic flights), B (for international flights), and Terminal C (for VIP use), while a fourth terminal D is being built, and a Terminal E will be added by 2015
Airlines using airport as base or hub: ARP 410 Airlines, Business Aviation Center, Ukraine Air Alliance, Ukraine Air Enterprise, Ukraine International Airlines, UM Air
Annual passengers: 5,674,548
Annual cargo: 33,541 tonnes
Annual aircraft movements: 83,726

Background

Some 29km (18 miles) east of Kiev, the airport is named after the neighbouring town of Boryspil, and is one three airports serving Kiev and the surrounding area, but handles 60 per cent of the country's commercial air traffic and is the leading international gateway for the country.

Originally, Boryspil was a military airfield within what was then the Ukrainian Soviet Socialist Republic, but the republic's government ordered that it be converted to civil use, and it opened as a commercial airport on 7 July 1959. The first regular routes were to Moscow and Leningrad (now St Petersburg). The following year, the Soviet airline, Aeroflot, started to base aircraft and aircrew at the airport. A new passenger terminal opened in 1965. During this time the Soviet Air Force continued to use the airport for its air transport regiments.

Ukraine seized independence on the break-up of the Warsaw Pact and the Soviet Union, and the local division of Aeroflot provided the foundation for Air Ukraine, so that by the turn of the century Boryspil had become a hub airport, and

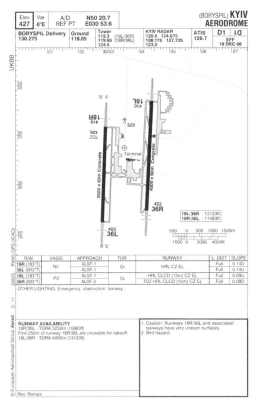

UNITED ARAB EMIRATES

DUBAI INTERNATIONAL: DXB
Dubai, United Arab Emirates

Owner: Government of Dubai
Operator: Department of Civil Aviation
Runways: 12L/30R, 4,000m (13,124ft);
12R/30L, 4,000m (13,124ft)
Terminals: Three, designated 1, 2 and 3, with a
fourth under construction
Airlines using airport as base or hub: Emirates,
Emirates SkyCargo and flyDubai
Annual passengers: 34,348,110
Annual cargo: 1,668,505 tonnes
Annual aircraft movements: 260,530

In 2009 the Dubai Metro Red Line should have
stations completed in Terminals 1 and 3.

Background
The largest city in the United Arab Emirates,
without oil wealth, Dubai depends on trade and
acting as a major focal point for communications
in order to prosper. The small sheikdom has a
long tradition of civil aviation, and during the
Second World War flying boats operated by
BOAC (British Overseas Airways Corporation), itself newly-created from the forced
merger of Imperial Airways with its rival,
British Airways, operated an inverted horseshoe
service from South Africa via Dubai and India
to Australia.

It was not until 1959 that the then ruler,
Sheikh Rashid bin Saeed Al Maktoum, ordered
the construction of an airport for landplanes.
The airport opened for traffic the following year
with a single 1,800m (5,906ft) runway of com-
pacted sand, capable of handling aircraft such as
the Douglas DC-3, Vickers Viking, or Bristol
170. There were also parking and aircraft turning areas and a small passenger terminal. In May
1965 an asphalt runway 2,804m (9,200ft) long
was opened, while the terminal was also
enlarged. This was followed during the year by

it is now amongst the busiest airports in Eastern
Europe.

There have been a couple of serious accidents
in recent years, although without fatalities. The
first of these was to an Air Ukraine Tupolev Tu-
154B on 5 September 1992, when the crew found
that the undercarriage would not retract fully
and returned to land, but on touchdown the
undercarriage collapsed and the aircraft was sufficiently damaged to be a write-off. Another
undercarriage collapse occurred on 5 September
2004 when one of the Antonov Design Bureau's
own An-12s landed on a cargo flight and the aircraft was a complete write-off.

the installation of runway lighting, and modern navigational aids were added in the years that followed. The runway was further extended to 3,810m (12,500ft) during the 1970s, and Dubai became an important refuelling point for airliners operating between Europe and the Far East and Australia. A second runway was opened in April 1984 and the terminal facilities were further improved. Nevertheless, by this time an increasing number of aircraft were able to fly non-stop from Europe to Singapore and even Hong Kong, especially as airspace over the then Soviet Union was made available. Much more needed to be done to keep Dubai on the airline schedules.

A programme of improvements, including runway lengthening and the construction of additional terminals, 2 and 3, opened in 2008. The development had not been without its problems, with part of Terminal 3 collapsing on 28 September 2004. In the meantime, another major boost to the airport's traffic had come earlier with the creation of a Dubai airline, Emirates, in 1985. Intended to be the national airline for the UAE, Emirates developed a route network that embraced other cities in the UAE and the Middle East, and then developed into one of the world's largest airlines with a route network that covers Europe and the Far East, and has more recently crossed the Atlantic to the United States. By using Dubai as a hub for passengers between Europe and the Far East and Australia, the airline has done much to boost both the airport's traffic and Dubai's place as a resort, and encouraged the development of other businesses in the sheikdom.

Expansion and upgrading at Dubai continues, while the government has revealed plans for a new airport, Al Maktoum International. It is expected upon completion to be the fourth largest airport in the world by physical size, and with up to six parallel runways. Construction is expected to finish by the year 2017, and to underline that this will be additional capacity and not a replacement for the existing airport, a plan exists for the Dubai Metro to build a new line, the Purple Line, linking the two airports.

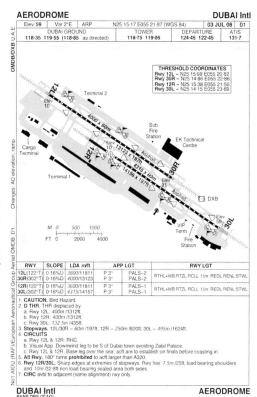

Meanwhile, Terminal 4 is under construction at Dubai and extensions are in hand for Terminal 3.

Given the airport's location, it is not surprising that it was the scene of a hijacking of a British Airways Vickers VC10 in November 1974. The aircraft landed at Tripoli and then flew on to Tunis, where a passenger was murdered before the hijackers finally surrendered after 48 hours.

The one serious accident at the airport in recent years has been the collapse of the nose gear of a Biman Bangladesh Airlines Airbus A310 taking-off for Dhaka on 12 March 2007, with 14 passengers suffering minor injuries. The accident closed the only active runway for eight hours.

ABU DHABI INTERNATIONAL: AUH

Abu Dhabi, United Arab Emirates

Owner and operator: Abu Dhabi Airports Company

Runways: 13/31, 4,100m (13,452ft)

Terminals: Three, designated Terminal 1, Terminal 2, and Terminal 3

Airlines using airport as base or hub: Etihad Airways

Annual passengers: 6,926,000 (Airport authority figures)

Annual cargo: 317,207 tonnes

Annual aircraft movements: 82,287

Background

Abu Dhabi is the second busiest airport by passengers in the United Arab Emirates. Its growth in recent years has been stimulated by the founding of Etihad Airways in 2004. The airport has recently opened its third terminal, which gives it a capacity of 12 million passengers, about twice the 2007 traffic figures. A new terminal should open in 2012, and work is progressing on a new cargo terminal and a new 4,000m (13,133ft) runway parallel to the existing runway.

Abu Dhabi's aviation history dates from 1929 when the Royal Air Force opened a flying-boat station, and this was also available to Imperial Airways. The land airport was first opened in the city as Al Bateen in the 1960s. It was later moved to its present site 32km (nearly 20 miles) south-east of the city, and reopened in 1982.

SHARJAH INTERNATIONAL: SHJ

Sharjah, Sharja and Kelba, United Arab Emirates

Owner and operator: Sharjah International Airport

Runways: 12/30, 4,060m (13,320ft)

Terminals: One

Airlines using airport as base or hub: Air Arabia, AVE.com, British Gulf International Airlines, Click Airways

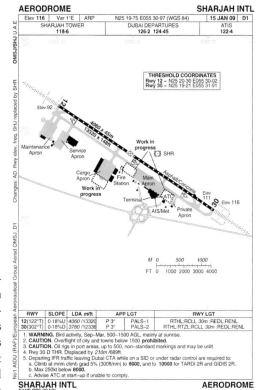

Annual passengers: 4,324,313

Annual cargo: 312,285 tonnes

Annual aircraft movements: 54,006

Background

Formerly a staging post for military aircraft en route to India and the Far East, Sharjah is still a joint military and civil airport. It is the base for the low-cost airline, Air Arabia.

The airport has had a couple of serious accidents. On 15 December 1997 a Tajikistan Airlines Tupolev Tu-154B, landing from Dushanbe, was too low when it made its final turn and crashed, killing 6 of the 7 crew and all 79 passengers. More recently, on 10 February 2004, a Kish Air Fokker F-50 crashed as it approached, killing 43 of the 46 people aboard.

UNITED KINGDOM
(And Associated Territories)

The United Kingdom was one of the first countries to use air transport, initially for international services from London to Paris and Amsterdam, and then to link the mother country with the countries of the British Empire. The links with empire relied heavily on flying boats, culminating in the Empire Air Mail Scheme, which started in 1935. At home, a number of independent operators developed domestic air services, spurred on by the four mainline railway companies, which together formed Railway Air Services.

The airport scene in the British Isles is vastly different today from that between the wars, or even in the immediate post-Second World War years. It is still possible to land on the beach at Barra in the Hebrides, when the tide is out, and this is used by a scheduled air service; and the country also has the shortest air service in the world between Westray and Papa Westray, just two minutes in the timetable but shown by a television news programme to be just 100 seconds from start to finish: island-hopping doesn't become more literal than that!

As for the airports themselves, most of those that existed before the war are no longer in use today. Croydon was once the main landplane terminal for London, but is now closed. Many other airports that once featured in the nation's airport network no longer handle scheduled flights, if they handle anything at all, and these include Portsmouth, Rochester, and Swansea. Others have survived, such as the so-frequently renamed East Midlands, London-Gatwick, and Birmingham International, but poor little Shoreham, one of the first to have its own railway station, and now renamed Brighton, no longer handles regular air services. The country was left a rich legacy of airport sites by the rapid expansion of the Royal Air Force and the Royal Navy's Fleet Air Arm during the Second World War, but today the main airports are under mounting pressure both from the growth in traffic and in aircraft sizes on the one hand, and from opponents to expansion on the other. In this the country is not unique. The pressure and need to expand is not confined to London and the southeast, but now includes airports in Scotland and in the north of England.

Airports in the United Kingdom are in diverse ownership, but few are owned by the state, and these are mainly those required by and shared with the armed forces, as well as airports in the Scottish Highlands and Islands. Some are in local authority ownership and others in private hands.

LONDON HEATHROW: LHR
Hounslow, Middlesex, UK

Owner and operator: BAA
Runways: Northern 09L/27R, 3,901m x 45m (12,799ft x 148ft); Southern 09R/27L, 3,660m x 45m (12,008ft x 148ft); a third runway is planned for after 2015
Terminals: Five, designated Terminals 1, 2, 3, 4, and 5 (rebuilding planned for Terminals 1 and 2)
Airlines using airport as base or hub: British Airways, Virgin Atlantic, bmi
Annual passengers: 68,068,304
Annual cargo: 1,395,905 tonnes
Annual aircraft movements: 481,479

Heathrow Express railway connection to London Paddington. Also served by Piccadilly underground line, linking airport with central London and Kings Cross/St Pancras railway termini.

Background

Between the two world wars, Croydon (south of London) was the main airport for London and the south of England, and had the distinction of providing the world's first commercial airline terminal, which opened in 1928, but by the late 1930s the site at Heathrow had already been identified as the future airport for London, although a final decision was not reached until 1943 after a total of 52 sites had been considered.

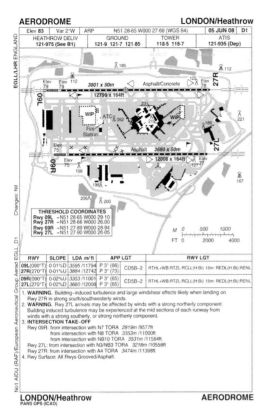

No1 AIDU (RAF) /European Aeronautical Group /Aerad EGLL_D1   Changes: Nil   EGLL/LHR ENGLAND

AERODROME   **LONDON/Heathrow**

| Elev 83 | Var 2°W | ARP | N51 28·65 W000 27·68 (WGS 84) | | 05 JUN 08 | D1 |

| HEATHROW DELIV 121·975 (See B1) | GROUND 121·9 121·7 121·85 | TOWER 118·5 118·7 | ATIS 121·935 (Dep) |

THRESHOLD COORDINATES
Rwy 09L –N51 28·65 W000 29·10
Rwy 27R –N51 28·66 W000 26·00
Rwy 09R –N51 27·89 W000 28·94
Rwy 27L –N51 27·90 W000 26·05

M 0   500   1000
FT 0   2000   4000

RWY	SLOPE	LDA m/ft	APP LGT		RWY LGT
09L(090°T)	0·01%D	3595 /11794	P 3° (66)	CD5B-2	RTHL+WB·RTZL·RCLL(H·Bi) 15m· REDL(H·Bi)·RENL
27R(270°T)	0·01%U	3884 /12742	P 3° (73)		
09R(090°T)	0·02%U	3353 /11001	P 3° (65)	CD5B-2	RTHL+WB·RTZL·RCLL(H·Bi) 15m· REDL(H·Bi)·RENL
27L(270°T)	0·02%D	3660 /12008	P 3° (65)		

1. **WARNING.** Building–induced turbulence and large windshear effects likely when landing on Rwy 27R in strong south/southwesterly winds.
2. **WARNING.** Rwy 27L arrivals may be affected by winds with a strong northerly component. Building induced turbulence may be experienced at the mid sections of each runway from winds with a strong southerly, or strong northerly component.
3. **INTERSECTION TAKE–OFF**
   Rwy 09R: from intersection with N7 TORA 2919m /9577ft
            from intersection with N8 TORA 3353m /11000ft
            from intersection with N810 TORA 3531m /11584ft.
   Rwy 27L: from intersection with N3/NB3 TORA 3218m /10558ft
   Rwy 27R: from intersection with A4 TORA 3474m /11398ft
4. Rwy Surface: All Rwys Grooved/Asphalt.

LONDON/Heathrow   **AERODROME**
PANS OPS (ICAO)

The location had been a military airfield during the First World War as Hounslow Heath and had seen the first international commercial flights by Air Transport & Travel in 1919. Work on the first runway started in 1944, while the airport was under military control, not being transferred to the then Ministry of Civil Aviation until January 1946. Officially opened on 31 May 1946, the first arrival was an Avro Lancastrian (a converted Lancaster bomber) of the state-owned long-haul airline, British Overseas Airways Corporation (BOAC), which had flown from Australia. The first terminal building had still to be completed, and instead a 'village' of tents was used on the north side of the airfield. The first terminal buildings were built of prefabricated concrete.

It was not until April 1955 that the Europa Building (the current Terminal 2) was opened for short-haul flights, while facilities for pilots, offices, restaurants, and a viewing area were housed in the Queens Building. The London Air Traffic Control Centre transferred from Uxbridge to the new Heathrow tower. In the meantime, in 1952 Heathrow had become the first airport to handle jet airliners when a de Havilland Comet I arrived on a scheduled flight from Johannesburg. In 1954, Heathrow also started to be used by the state-owned British European Airways (BEA) and several European national carriers. Traffic grew quickly, and in 1968 a dedicated short-haul terminal (the current Terminal 1) – at the time Europe's largest airport terminal – was opened. A cargo depot was also opened, linked by a road tunnel to the Central Terminal Area. During the decade that followed, a new central bus station was opened, and the airport was linked to the London Underground system when the Piccadilly Line, a tube line, was extended to the airport. By this time Heathrow was being operated by a nationalised company, the British Airports Authority, formed in 1966, which was eventually privatised in July 1987. Long-haul flights were using Terminal 3, which was extended, with airbridges added, ready for the introduction of the Boeing 747 'jumbo jet'. From 1976 to 1993 the airport was the British terminal for the Concorde supersonic airliner.

Despite, first, a second London airport being opened at Gatwick during the late 1950s and, later, a third at Stansted (while Luton also became an airport for London, and a new airport, London City, was built in the Docklands), Heathrow continued to grow, becoming the world's leading airport for international traffic and one of the top five airports in the world overall. By the 1970s the value of the cargo shipped through the airport was second only to the London Docks. A new terminal, Terminal 4, was opened in 1986 and the Piccadilly Line was extended to serve it, while in 1998 the Heathrow Express was inaugurated, with trains running non-stop to London Paddington. The Heathrow Express was followed in 2005 by Heathrow Connect, a stopping service to Paddington, mainly intended for those working at the airport. A new air-traffic control tower had opened the previous year.

The Spanish consortium, Ferrovial, purchased BAA airports in 2006, operating them through a subsidiary, Airport Development and Investment Limited (ADI).

Terminal 5 was opened in March 2008, being reserved exclusively for British Airways, the largest airline based at Heathrow. That same month, Singapore Airlines began commercial services at Heathrow with its new Airbus A380 'super jumbo'. No fewer than four US airlines operate into Heathrow – Continental, Delta, North West and US Airways, replacing Pan American and Trans World, which had used the airport in the 1950s and 1960s.

Although Heathrow had a third runway at one time, mainly for use when crosswinds closed the main runways, this was taken over by other developments, and a new third runway, to the north of and parallel to the existing two runways, is planned. This has caused controversy, and many opponents are calling for a completely new airport for London in the Thames Estuary. The third runway is not expected to open before 2017, and in the meantime the airport is competing for traffic with major airports in Europe, sometimes with as many as six runways, and has lost many services from the less busy UK airports, with some of their transfer traffic being routed via Amsterdam or Paris.

There have been more than 30 accidents at or around Heathrow since the Second World War. Many of the earlier accidents were because of fog, a persistent menace that frequently interrupted operations until Category III 'blind landing' became standard. One accident in poor visibility involved a Sabena Douglas DC-3 on 2 March 1948, landing at night from Brussels, which crashed killing all 3 members of the crew and 17 of the 19 passengers. Although the weather was much better, on 2 September 1958 a Vickers Viking of Independent Air Travel which took-off on a cargo flight to Nice suffered engine failure and was forced to return, but on approach the aircraft could not maintain height and crashed into houses, killing the crew of three and four people on the ground. Not all crashes in fog resulted in fatalities, and one of the more for-

tunate was to a BEA (British European Airways) Vickers Viscount on 7 January 1960, approaching from Dublin, with the captain not warned of worsening visibility. The aircraft landed on its nose wheel, which collapsed followed by fire which destroyed the aircraft, although all 5 crew and 54 passengers escaped. On 27 October 1965 a BEA Vickers Vanguard from Edinburgh made two attempts to land before deciding to use one of the airport's holding stacks to see if visibility improved, but after half an hour decided to try again as another aircraft had landed safely (but followed by one which decided to go-around). On the third approach, at the last minute the pilots decided to overshoot again, but selected the wrong flap setting and while the instruments showed the aircraft to be climbing, it was still descending and struck the runway, bursting into flames and killing all aboard; 6 crew and 30 passengers.

One accident in which the weather played no part was on 8 April 1968 to a BOAC (British Overseas Airways Corporation) Boeing 707-420 which suffered problems with the No. 2 engine shortly after taking off for Sydney with a first stop at Zürich. The crew followed the procedure for an engine failure, but then discovered that it was on fire, and as they made a turn back towards the airport, the engine fell off into a reservoir. On landing, the fire spread and an explosion of the left hand side of the aircraft scattered debris widely and a pool of burning fuel spread under the aircraft closing off the over-wing emergency exits and also burning an escape shoot on the right hand side of the aircraft. In the circumstances, it was amazing that 10 of the 11 crew and 112 of the 116 passengers survived.

At the time, Heathrow was considerably less busy than today, and traffic was more varied. On 3 July 1968, a BKS Air Transport (later absorbed into British Airways) Airspeed Ambassador landed from Deauville with a cargo of eight racehorses, but suffered a hydraulic failure just before touchdown and banked sharply. The crew tried to initiate a go-around but the aircraft continued to bank sharply and struck two

Hawker Siddeley Trident airliners of BEA, one of which had to be written off, before catching fire and rolling over on to its back, killing six of the crew of eight (which would have included the grooms for the horses).

A number of aircraft hijackings have ended at British airports. One of these was on 6 September 1970 when an El Al Boeing 707-420, flying from Tel Aviv to New York via Amsterdam, was seized in mid-air. One of the hijackers threw a hand grenade down the cabin aisle, which failed to explode, before being seized by an Israeli sky marshal. The captain requested an emergency landing at Heathrow. One of the hijackers was shot dead, but there were no other casualties aboard.

One of the worst accidents at the airport was to a BEA Trident which took-off for Brussels on 18 June 1972. At the time, jet aircraft leaving Heathrow had to follow noise abatement procedures before climbing away, and on this occasion the co-pilot was distracted from monitoring the flaps by the captain suffering a heart attack, and there was an abrupt loss of altitude resulting in the aircraft crashing into a field near Staines, killing all 9 crew and all 109 passengers. Potentially far more serious was the failure of the engines of a British Airways Boeing 777-200ER coming in from Beijing on 17 January 2008, when the engines wound down and the aircraft landed just short of the runway, narrowly missing a perimeter road and damaging a fence. The undercarriage collapsed and fuel tanks ruptured, but there was no fire. While the aircraft was a write-off, all 16 crew and 136 passengers survived. The cause is believed to have been ice in the fuel, and the engine manufacturer has been ordered to redesign its fuel pumps, but the decision remains controversial.

The airport has also suffered a number of terrorist incidents. In one of these the Irish Republican Army planted several bombs in a car park, which exploded and injured two people. The IRA also fired mortars into the airport between 8 and 13 March 1994. The worst terrorist incident was the planting of a bomb on a Pan American Boeing 747 leaving for New York on 21 December 1988, which exploded in mid-air over the town of Lockerbie in southern Scotland, killing all 259 occupants of the aircraft and another 11 on the ground. There was also a theft of gold bullion on 26 November 1983, and an attempted theft on 17 May 2004.

LONDON GATWICK: LGW
Horley, Surrey, UK

Runways: 08R/26L, 3,316m (10,879ft)
Terminals: Two, North and South
Airlines using airport as base or hub: Astreus, Monarch, easyJet
Annual passengers: 35,218,374
Annual cargo: 176,822 tonnes
Annual aircraft movements: 266,552

Railway station with fast services to London Victoria, as well as to London Blackfriars, London Bridge, Brighton, Guildford, Reading and Thameslink services to Bedford.

Background

Gatwick was originally a small flying club, the Surrey Aero Club, founded in 1930, but in 1934 the then Air Ministry gave the aerodrome a licence to allow it to be used by commercial aircraft. The first airline to operate out of Gatwick was Hillman's Airways, flying to Belfast and Paris, and the following year this merged with Spartan Airways and United Airways to create Allied British Airways (known as British Airways) which became a rival for Imperial Airways on European routes. That year, 1935, also saw the Southern Railway open one of the first airport railway stations with two trains an hour on the London Victoria to Brighton service. The world's first circular airport terminal ('The Beehive') opened in 1936 and included a subway from the railway station, allowing passengers to remain under cover from the time they boarded a train at Victoria or Brighton until they boarded an aircraft.

The main airline at Gatwick, British Airways, was merged with Imperial Airways in 1939 to form a new airline, the British Overseas Airways

Corporation (BOAC). Civil operations were suspended on the outbreak of the Second World War and the airport was taken over by the Royal Air Force, but after the war they resumed. In 1952 the then government approved Gatwick's development as a second airport for London, and the airport closed in March 1956 for complete rebuilding. It officially reopened on 9 June 1958. Initially it was mainly used by charter flights, but in 1962 work began on expansion, with the terminal building doubled in size and two piers added. The famous 'Gatwick Express' non-stop dedicated train from London Victoria was launched in 1984, the same year that the airport opened a new air traffic control tower, which remains one of the highest in Europe. A new terminal, the North Terminal, opened in 1988.

By this time, Gatwick had been used by many British and foreign airlines, including many charter operators, but was also the home base for first British United Airways and then its successor, British Caledonian Airways, officially designated to be the 'second force' in British air transport competing with British Airways, then state-owned. A network of scheduled services had developed, and included services to South America and Africa as well as within Europe, which included the 'Silver Arrow' low-cost rail-air-rail service from London to Paris. While the airport was constrained by an agreement with the local community to a single runway, a taxiway was developed as a second runway whenever the main runway had to be out of use. Gatwick also began to be used increasingly by British Airways (which was later privatised) as an alternative to London Heathrow, and eventually BA acquired the two main operators at Gatwick, British Caledonian and Dan-Air. The airport continued to be popular with charter airlines, and was also home to Britain's first low-cost airline, Laker Airways, which launched its 'Skytrain' (low-cost, no-frills) service between Gatwick and New York. A helicopter service was introduced for transfer passengers between Gatwick and Heathrow, but this ceased when

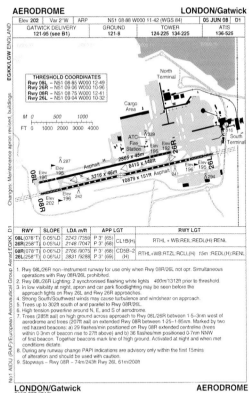

the new M25 London Orbital Motorway opened, and express coaches were used instead.

BAA was privatised in July 1987, and in June 2006 the Spanish consortium, Ferrovial, purchased the BAA airports, operating them through a subsidiary, Airport Development and Investment Limited (ADI). During this period, expansion continued with both the North and South terminals expanded so that, today, Gatwick is the world's busiest single-runway airport. A second runway is desperately needed at peak periods, but future growth is inhibited until well into the next decade by the single-runway agreement. Nevertheless, despite London now having five airports, Gatwick remains No. 2. The airport is likely to be sold in the near future as the government has decided to end BAA's near monopoly on London's airports, and Gatwick is one that BAA is expected to sell.

There have been relatively few accidents at the airport, but two of these were in poor visibility as Gatwick is prone to fog, especially early in the morning. On 17 February 1959 a THY Turkish Airlines Vickers Viscount crashed in heavy fog near Horley on its approach, with 14 of the 24 occupants killed. Almost a decade later, on 5 January 1969, an Ariana Afghan Airlines Boeing 727-100, flying from Kabul via Frankfurt, crashed into a house while landing in poor visibility with the flaps not correctly set, killing 50 of the 66 aboard the aircraft and another 2 on the ground. Much less serious was the accident to a BIA (British Island Airways) Handley Page Dart Herald on 20 July 1975, which took off, retracted the undercarriage, but then settled back on to the runway – the 45 passengers and crew were unhurt.

LONDON STANSTED: STN

Stansted, Essex, UK

Owner and operator: BAA
Runways: 05/23, 3,048m (10,000ft)
Terminals: One
Airlines using airport as base or hub: Ryanair, easyJet
Annual passengers: 23,777,277
Annual cargo: 228,747 tonnes
Annual aircraft movements: 208,423

Railway station with Stansted Express services to London Liverpool Street and cross-country services to Cambridge and Peterborough.

Background

London's third airport, and the third busiest in the British Isles, Stansted was originally built as a Second World War bomber base for the USAAF in 1942 and known as Stansted Mountfichet. After the war it became an RAF storage and maintenance depot, and between March 1946 and August 1947 it was also used to accommodate German prisoners of war before they could be repatriated. It was taken over by the Ministry of Civil Aviation in 1949, but in 1954 it passed again to what was by this time the United States Air Force, which extended the runway in anticipation of the airfield becoming a NATO

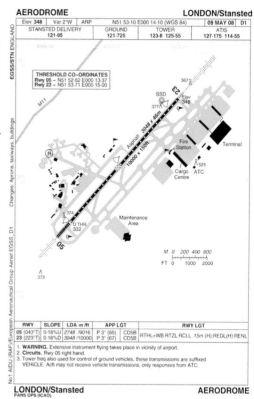

base, but this did not happen and the airfield returned to the Ministry of Civil Aviation in 1959. Afterwards, it was little used other than as an airfield fire-fighting school until the British Airports Authority took it over in 1966, and opened a small passenger terminal in 1969. With both Heathrow and Gatwick under pressure, plans were laid for a third London airport and, after much controversy and a public inquiry, Stansted was chosen, with an initial limit on the number of aircraft movements. The new airport opened in 1991 and initially was used mainly by Air UK (since absorbed by KLM) and by the pioneering Irish low-cost airline, Ryanair, as well as by air freight airlines. It later attracted the new low-cost carriers, including BA's subsidiary, Go, which was later sold to easyJet, and it also acted as a diversionary airport for London's main airport at Heathrow.

Long-haul scheduled routes were provided first by American Airlines and then later by

Continental, but neither operation was viable and were soon withdrawn.

Stansted currently operates only domestic and European scheduled flights, as well as charters, but has been identified as needing a second runway to allow continued expansion, while the terminal is also to be expanded. At the time of writing, the sale to the owners of London City Airport has been agreed.

There have been just a few accidents at Stansted since it became London's third airport, and it also saw the end of a hijacking. One accident was to a BAe.748 chartered from Emerald Airways by the Leeds United football team, which suffered an engine explosion on take-off followed by an emergency landing and evacuation, but there were only a few minor injuries amongst the passengers. A much more serious accident was when a Korean Air Cargo Boeing 747 crashed shortly after take-off because of pilot error, killing all four crew members. Most recent was the emergency landing on 27 February 2002 of a Ryanair Boeing 737-800 from Dublin after ground staff saw smoke coming from an engine. The aircraft was evacuated within 90 seconds on coming to a stop, but the cabin crew had difficulty opening the emergency exits, which led to an Air Accidents Investigation Branch recommendation that cabin crew training be improved. Investigation also showed that the smoke came from a broken bearing and there was no fire damage to the engine.

The hijacking occurred when an Ariana Afghan Airlines Boeing 727 was taken over and directed to Stansted with 156 passengers and crew. The aircraft remained at the airport for four days before the hostages were freed and the hijackers surrendered. The hijackers and many of the passengers immediately applied for political asylum.

The airport is one of two UK airports designated to receive flights 'at risk', meaning flights that have been hijacked. The other airport is Glasgow Prestwick.

MANCHESTER INTERNATIONAL: MAN

Greater Manchester, UK

Owner: Manchester Airports Group
Operator: Manchester Airport plc
Runways: 05L/23R, 3,048m (10,000ft); 05R/23L, 3,050m (10,007ft)
Terminals: Three, designated Terminal 1, Terminal 2, and Terminal 3
Airlines using airport as base or hub: bmi, bmibaby, Flybe, Jet2, Monarch, Thomas Cook, Virgin Atlantic
Annual passengers: 22,362,106
Annual cargo: 166,546 tonnes
Annual aircraft movements: 222,778

Railway station with trains to Manchester, reached by travelator, known as the 'Skylink', and also served by trains from the north of England and Scotland.

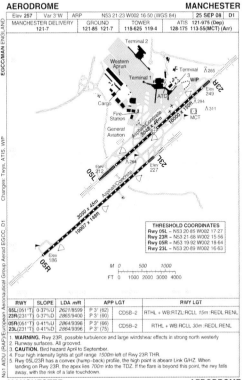

Background

The largest British airport outside the London area, it is owned by a consortium of ten local authorities, and is the largest airport in the UK in public ownership. The airport was originally built by the City of Manchester and was known as Ringway, after the community near where it was located in Cheshire. It opened on 25 June 1938 with a flying display and the arrival of a KLM flight from Amsterdam. Other operators included the railway-owned Great Western and Southern Airlines, but KLM remained the only international operator from the airport until it was closed on the outbreak of the Second World War on 3 September 1939. During the war years it was taken over by the Royal Air Force as RAF Ringway, and it became a major training station for British paratroopers. The war years also saw the hangars on the north-west side of the airport used for the production of aircraft by Fairey and Avro, while the runways were used for flight testing aircraft such as the Avro Manchester and Lancaster heavy bombers, and the York transport. Between June and December 1941 two asphalt runways of 3,000ft were laid, and later extended to 4,300ft.

After the war the airport was handed back to Manchester and it started to grow rapidly. Its first transatlantic service began on 28 October 1953 when Sabena, the Belgian airline, had its service to New York call regularly at the airport. A further runway extension, completed in 1958, enabled airliners to fly non-stop across the Atlantic from Manchester. In late 1962, the first purpose-built post-war passenger terminal was opened, and it was the first in Europe to have aircraft piers.

The current title was adopted in 1972. While a recasting of local government boundaries in 1974 brought the entire airport into Manchester, further expansion soon saw the airport spread back into neighbouring Cheshire in the early 1980s. By this time the airport had one full-length runway of 10,000ft, but when a second runway was built, despite a large number of objections, it lay entirely within Cheshire. The second runway cannot be used between 10pm and 6am unless the first runway is closed for maintenance. An important development in recent years has been the construction of an air-freight terminal.

While Manchester is set to continue expansion, with an extension of its terminals and additional taxiways as older buildings are demolished, it remains to be seen whether further runways will be built. Many see Liverpool Airport expanding further to ease the pressure on Manchester.

The failure of a wing bolt led to an accident when, on 14 March 1957, a BEA (British European Airways) Vickers Viscount 700, coming in from Amsterdam, crashed into houses on approach to Manchester, killing all 20 passengers and crew and 2 people on the ground. This was followed by the airport's worst disaster to date, on 4 June 1967, when a British Midland Airways Canadair DC-4M Argonaut (a licence-built DC-4), landing from Palma de Mallorca, crashed near the centre of Stockport following an aborted approach to Manchester and the failure of all four engines because of fuel problems, killing 72 people. A take-off accident followed on 22 August 1985 when a British Airtours Boeing 737-200 suffered an engine failure and fire, with the captain aborting the take-off and swerving the aircraft towards the fire station, but 55 people died, many from smoke inhalation, and the accident resulted in aircraft having floor level illuminated guides to make evacuation in poor visibility easier. Much less serious was the landing by a PIA (Pakistan International Airlines) Boeing 777-200ER from Karachi on 1 March 2005, which had a fire around the left landing gear on landing, leading to the evacuation of all aboard, with minor injuries to some passengers and some slight damage to the aircraft.

Although no one was hurt, on 16 July 2003 an Excel Airways Boeing 737-800 with 7 crew and 190 passengers took-off while vehicles were working at the end of the runway without allowing for the reduced length, clearing them by just 17m (56ft).

LONDON LUTON: LTN
Luton, Bedfordshire, UK

Owner: Luton Borough Council
Operator: London Luton Airport Operations Ltd
Runways: 08/26, 2,160m (7,087ft)
Terminals: One
Airlines using airport as base or hub: easyJet,
    Monarch, Thomson
Annual passengers: 9,948,959
Annual cargo: 38,652 tonnes
Annual aircraft movements: 120,243

Railway connection: Shuttle bus to Luton Airport
Parkway airport station, trains to London St
Pancras, Nottingham, and Leicester.

Background

What was originally known as Luton Airport
opened on 16 July 1938, and during the Second
World War it was a Royal Air Force fighter station. After the war, control of the airport
returned to the local authority, and a number of
small airlines and business aircraft charter companies operated from it. One company, Autair,
developed a small network of routes serving
minor destinations in the English regions before
changing its name to Court Line and becoming
an inclusive tour air charter company, before its
collapse in 1974. Meanwhile, another charter airline, Euravia, became Britannia Airways, at one
time Europe's largest air charter airline, before
more recently changing its name to Thomson
Airways, and Monarch Airlines (which dates
from 1968) continues to use the airport as its base
to the present time.

A missile testing base was established just outside the airport by English Electric in 1949, but
this closed almost 20 years later, by which time it
was part of the then British Aircraft Corporation.

The airport grew quickly with the increasing
popularity of inclusive tour package holidays,
and a new terminal opened in 1985. To stress the
airport's proximity to London, the name was
changed to London Luton Airport in 1990, but
the following year it suffered a major reverse

when Ryanair, an Irish airline that had flown
into the airport for some years, transferred its
UK base to the new third London airport at
Stansted. Nevertheless, this problem was soon
overcome when other charter airlines, and the
budget airline Debonair, started to operate
flights from London Luton, and, most important
of all, the airport became the base and first hub
for a new low-cost carrier, easyJet.

To fund further expansion, in 1997 the management of the airport was contracted to London
Luton Airport Operations Limited, a company
backed by Barclays Bank, who later sold it to TBI
plc. As demand continued to grow, a new terminal was opened in late 1999 and, within this, space
was left for further expansion, which enabled a
new departure hall to be opened in July 2005.
The airport's growth throughout these years was
boosted by deregulation of air services within the
European Union. While most of this growth lay
with low-cost airlines operating within Europe,

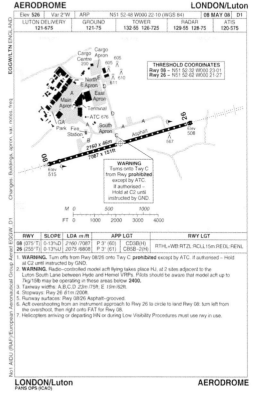

an all-business class airline, Silverjet, started flights to New York Newark and Dubai in 2006 using its own business-class terminal, but the airline ceased operations when fuel prices peaked during summer 2008.

The growth of London Stansted has not eclipsed London Luton, which has its niche in the airline market and has continued to grow in its own right. There has long been a need for a full-length runway, though, although the existing runway proved capable of handling Court Line's Lockheed TriStar wide-bodied airliners and the wide-bodied Airbuses of Monarch. Nevertheless, there has been local opposition to a planned runway extension and a new terminal, as there was to an earlier plan to extend the runway, and the plans were abandoned in July 2007. Some rationalisation of flights may follow the merger of Thomson Airways and Thomsonfly, formerly Britannia Airways, with First Choice in mid-2009.

On 14 September 1967 an Autair Airspeed Ambassador, sometimes also known as an Elizabethan after the fleet names given by BEA (British European Airways) to its aircraft, was landing from Luxembourg in poor visibility and in darkness, when the pilots retracted the flaps to the take-off position and the aircraft overran the runway and its undercarriage collapsed. The aircraft was a complete write-off but the 5 crew and 64 passengers were unharmed. Another Autair aircraft, a Hawker Siddeley HS125 business jet on a training flight, was much less fortunate on 23 December 1967, with a simulated engine failure on take-off causing the aircraft to descend, hit a factory and kill both pilots. Another landing accident with a runway overshoot occurred when an Aer Turas Douglas DC-7CF arrived from Dublin on 3 March 1974 on a cargo flight, but with six grooms as passengers as the return flight would be carrying horses. Problems in selecting reverse pitch on the engines, and then in handling the emergency braking, saw all main wheel tyres burst and the aircraft plunged down an embankment before coming to rest. All four crew and six passengers made an emergency evacuation, but the flight engineer returned to the aircraft when he saw a fire under one of the engines and activated the fire extinguishers on all four engines.

Prompt action by the pilots of a Court Line BAC One-Eleven 500 taking-off for Munich on 18 April 1974 meant that a serious accident was less severe than it might have been after a Piper Aztec twin-engined light aircraft strayed on to the runway as the One-Eleven was accelerating along it. The captain of the airliner managed to raise the port wing and steer the aircraft to the right, clipping the top of the light aircraft, which killed the pilot and injured a passenger who had the sense to duck, before making a full emergency stop and evacuating all 5 crew and 86 passengers safely. The wing tanks of the airliner were found to be leaking fuel as a result of the accident. Another take-off accident that year was on 21 June when a Dan-Air Boeing 727-100 was departing for Kerkyra in Greece. After making a 180° turn on the runway before starting the take-off roll, rotation was delayed and the aircraft hit lights at the end of the runway, before climbing away and landing at London Gatwick. The 8 crew and 126 passengers were unharmed, and the aircraft was later repaired.

BIRMINGHAM INTERNATIONAL (ELMDON): BHX
Elmdon, Birmingham, West Midlands, UK

Owner and operator: Birmingham International Airport Ltd
Runways: 15/33, 2,599m (8,527ft)
Terminals: Two, designated Terminal 1 (scheduled and charter flights), and Terminal 2 (low-cost carriers)
Airlines using airport as base or hub: bmiBaby, Flybe
Annual passengers: 9,232,776
Annual cargo: 13,533 tonnes
Annual aircraft movements: 114,717

AirRail Link cable-driven people mover links terminals with Birmingham International Railway Station with services to Birmingham New Street and London Euston.

Background

Still often referred to as Elmdon, the airport was opened on 8 July 1939 by the owner and operator, Birmingham City Council. The original airport had an 'art deco' terminal and a grass runway. During the Second World War it was requisitioned and used by the Royal Air Force as a flying school for RAF and Fleet Air Arm pilots, as well as by Short Stirling and Avro Lancaster heavy bombers manufactured at the Austin Motor Company's factory that had been changed over to aircraft production under the 'shadow factory' scheme. The aircraft were transported by road minus their wings, which were attached before test and delivery flights from Elmdon. Wartime usage required the construction of two hard runways, with 06/24 at 753m (2,469ft) and 15/33, which survives to this day, at 1,271m (4,170ft).

Elmdon was released to civilian use in mid-1946, although the state retained control, and commercial use must have been limited as it was used for air displays. It was not handed back to the City of Birmingham until April 1960. Under new ownership, the main runway was extended to allow its use by jet airliners. Under local government reorganisation, ownership passed to the West Midlands County Council in 1974. In 1984 a new terminal was opened, which was followed in 1991 by a second terminal, initially known as the 'Eurohub', combining both domestic and international passengers. The airport had been privatised in 1983, although a 49 per cent stake was held by seven local authorities in the West Midlands, including Birmingham. In 1987 ownership passed to Birmingham International Airport, a public company owned by the seven local authorities. The airport was amongst the first to use the Maglev Airport Rapid Transit System to connect the terminals with Birmingham International, a main line railway station, but this had to be abandoned in 1995 because of high operating costs and the difficulty in obtaining spare parts. It was replaced by a cable-driven people mover, the AirRail Link, which opened in 2003.

The shorter of the two runways, 06/24, which had not been extended, was closed in Jan-

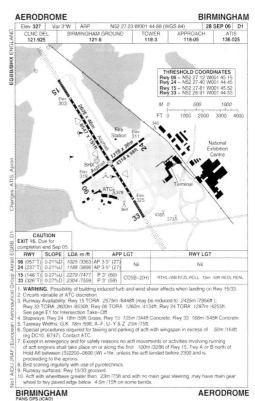

uary 2008, largely because of its inconvenient position. A master plan for the future covers the period to 2030, but is proving controversial as it envisages a parallel runway. In the meantime, the remaining runway is being extended to 3,000m (9,843ft), and with a starter strip will have an additional 150m in time for the London Olympic Games in 2012, when the airport's management believes it can attract extra traffic and larger aircraft. The terminals are also to be enlarged.

Serious accidents at the airport included the crash on taking-off for Bangor, Maine, of a Bombardier CL604 business jet on 4 January 2002. The aircraft had been parked overnight, but the pilots did not request de-icing, and as the aircraft took-off, ice on the wings caused one wing to dip, the aircraft rolled over and crashed on to the grass at the side of the runway, catching fire. The three crew and two passengers were killed. More fortunate were the crew of a

TNT Airways Boeing 737-300 on a cargo flight, which was flying from Liege to London Stansted, but diverted to East Midlands because of poor visibility at Stansted. As it landed at East Midlands, the autopilot disengaged briefly and the aircraft touched down off the runway losing its right main landing gear, and the crew opted to overshoot and divert to Birmingham, where they landed safely but blocked the runway and closed the airport for some hours. As the autopilot had been disconnected by one of the pilots while attempting to react to a message from air traffic control, their employer decided that the accident was a case of human error, and dismissed both of them.

EDINBURGH (TURNHOUSE): EDI
Edinburgh, Scotland, UK

Owner and operator: Scottish Airports (part of BAA)
Runways: 06/24, 2,557m (8,389ft); 12/30, 1,798m (5,899ft)
Terminals: One
Airlines using airport as base or hub:
Flyglobespan, easyJet, Ryanair
Annual passengers: 9,049,103
Annual cargo: 46,747 tonnes
Annual aircraft movements: 128,158

Tramway link to city centre under construction, due to open in 2012.

Background
Today one of Britain's fastest-growing airports, originally it was a First World War aerodrome for the Royal Flying Corps, and after the RAF was created in 1918, it became RAF Turnhouse. An unusual feature is that the airfield bordered the railway line from Edinburgh to Aberdeen (part of the East Coast Main Line) and for many years aircraft arrived by train, broken down into crates. An airfield railway station was closed during the late 1930s. At this time, the airfield was a base for a Royal Auxiliary Air Force fighter squadron (manned by part-time reservists) and during the Second World War it

provided fighter protection both for the nearby city of Edinburgh and for the major naval base and dockyard on the other side of the Firth of Forth at Rosyth.

After the war, commercial services started with the introduction of flights to London by the then British European Airways. Nevertheless, what was still known as Turnhouse remained in RAF hands until responsibility passed to the Ministry of Aviation in 1960. The RAF maintained a small presence at the airport for the next 30 years and later its area was used to develop air freight operations. Although the British Airports Authority was created in 1966, it did not take over the airfield until 1971. Major development followed, and in 1977 what was effectively a new airport opened. It became one of the three destinations served by what were known as the domestic trunk routes from London, and was served from both London Heathrow and London Gatwick. While services were pio-

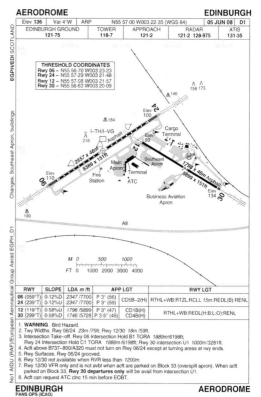

neered by BEA, and developed by its successor, British Airways, Edinburgh also saw competition on these routes, first from British Eagle and then British United (later British Caledonian), British Midland, and Air UK. BA introduced and operated Europe's first no-booking shuttle services on its domestic trunk routes, including the Heathrow-Edinburgh service.

BAA was privatised in 1987, and in 2006 the Spanish consortium, Ferrovial, took over the company through a UK-based subsidiary. Later that year, a major new terminal extension was opened. In the meantime, Edinburgh had also attracted the new low-cost airlines such as Ryanair and easyJet, and scheduled transatlantic services were introduced by Continental. The airport's resident low-cost airline, with services to North America and Europe, is Flyglobespan. Today, services are operated to all five London airports and to a growing range of destinations in Europe and North America.

There have been relatively few accidents at the airport. The most recent was to a Loganair Short 360 on 27 February 2001, operating a mail flight to Belfast, which crashed into the Firth of Forth when both engines flamed out because of slush resulting from the air intakes not having been protected while the aircraft was parked at the airport in heavy snow. Both pilots were killed.

GLASGOW (RENFREW): GLA

Paisley, Renfrewshire, Scotland, UK

Owner and operator: Scottish Airports (part of BAA)

Runways: 05/23, 2,658m (8,720ft); 09/27, 1,104m (3,622ft)

Terminals: One

Airlines using airport as base or hub: Loganair, FlyBe

Annual passengers: 8,798,381

Annual cargo: 4,350 tonnes

Annual aircraft movements: 107,959

Railway connection to centre of Glasgow planned.

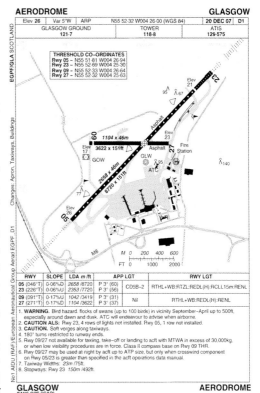

Background

Glasgow Airport was officially opened in June 1966, replacing an earlier airport at Abbotsinch, and initially services were operated to and from London Heathrow and also to airports in the Scottish Highlands and the Western Isles. Until 1975 it was owned by Glasgow Corporation, but ownership was transferred to the British Airports Authority in 1975. Amongst the developments since the airport opened have been Europe's first no-booking shuttle services on BA's domestic trunk routes, including the Heathrow-Glasgow service. Nevertheless, the full potential for Glasgow was inhibited for many years by the direction of all transatlantic services to Prestwick, which effectively split the traffic between the two airports, and in more recent years Prestwick has become more important for low-cost operations. Nevertheless, Glasgow was chosen by Emirates for a daily service to Dubai.

The airport terminal has been progressively developed in recent years and Glasgow continues to serve both charter and scheduled services, as well as being the main base for Scotland's main internal airline, Loganair, for many years a franchisee for British Airways and now for FlyBe.

The airport has not been without its moments of drama, of which the most recent was a terrorist attack on the passenger terminal on 30 June 2007. Two Islamic terrorists drove a flaming Jeep Cherokee into the landside part of the terminal, with one of them later dying from his injuries, but serious damage to the terminal did not occur and police and civilians apprehended the terrorists. Well before this, on 8 February 1999, a Jersey European Airways, predecessor of Flybe, Fokker F-27 Friendship made an emergency landing with nose wheel problem, and although the undercarriage dropped perfectly, the nose wheel collapsed on landing and the aircraft overshot the runway, stopping just short of the busy M8 motorway. The airport's most serious accident followed on 3 September 1999, when a Cessna 404 with 11 people aboard, including 9 aircrew for Airtours took-off for Aberdeen, but crashed shortly after take-off following engine trouble, with the captain shutting down the wrong engine as he returned to the airport. The aircraft crashed with the loss of eight of the occupants, and the other 3 were seriously injured.

BRISTOL INTERNATIONAL (LULSGATE): BRS

Lulsgate, Bristol, England, UK

Owner and operator: South West Airports Ltd
Runways: 09/27, 2,011m (6,598ft)
Terminals: One
Airlines using airport as base or hub: easyJet
Annual passengers: 5,926,774
Annual aircraft movements: 76,428

Background

For many years there was competition between Bristol's two airports, the one in Somerset at Lulsgate Bottom and the other the manufac-

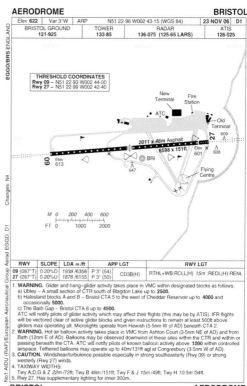

turer's airfield for the Bristol Aeroplane concern, manufacturer of the Britannia turboprop airliner and later the British assembly line for the Concorde supersonic airliner. It was at the latter that, in 1927, a group of local people started a flying club, which became so successful it moved to its own premises built on farmland at Whitchurch, to the south of the city. In 1930, Bristol (Whitchurch) Airport opened. During the Second World War, Whitchurch was one of the few civil airports still operating in the UK, with the British Overseas Airways Corporation (BOAC) operating flights for government personnel.

Meanwhile, in September 1940 the Royal Air Force flying school at Weston-super-Mare built a relief landing ground on Broadfield Down at Lulsgate Bottom, although the location suffered from fog, so Filton and Cardiff had to be used as alternatives. In 1941, Fighter Command began using the airfield for experimental purposes and it underwent considerable expansion with a hard runway 3,900ft long. The new runway was ready in January 1942, but overall the airfield lacked many of the amenities of an air station and the resident units moved to RAF Zeals, and Flying Training Command regained use of the airfield.

Lulsgate Bottom was abandoned by the RAF in 1946, although it retained an aviation connection for the Bristol Gliding Club and was also used for motor cycle and car racing. Whitchurch remained in use, but as aircraft sizes and weights rose, it needed a runway extension, which was difficult because of urban development. It was decided to make Lulsgate Bottom the new airport for Bristol, and the gliding club found new facilities elsewhere.

Bristol Lulsgate Airport opened in 1957. In 1963 the runway was lengthened, and the terminal was extended in 1965, although in 1968 a new terminal opened. It was owned and operated by Bristol City Council, and while used by up to 17 charter airlines by 1980, earlier it had also been used by Cambrian Airways, later absorbed into British Airways. In 1987 the operations, assets, and personnel were transferred from the City of Bristol to a company owned by the City of Bristol until First Group, a bus and train operator, bought a controlling interest in 1997. A new terminal building opened in March 2000.

The airport was chosen as a hub by the fast-expanding low-cost carrier easyJet, and passenger numbers began to grow rapidly. In January 2001, Macquarie, the Australian finance group, and Cintra bought the airport, which they operate through a company called South West Airports Ltd. Despite the progress over the years, Bristol is one of the largest airports in the British Isles not to have jet ports or airbridges, so that passengers either walk or are taken by bus between terminal and aircraft. The limited length of the runway also means that large aircraft seldom use the airport, while in January 2007, after resurfacing, many airlines abandoned the airport temporarily because of concerns about poor braking on the runway in wet conditions.

Plans for expansion are proving to be controversial, but the same controversy prevented the development of Filton as an airport for Bristol, despite it being close to the junction of the M4 and M5 motorways and to the main railway line from London to Cardiff. Filton cannot be closed, and remains as an airport as wings for the European Airbus are built there and are moved to final assembly in Hamburg and Toulouse by air.

There have been just two serious accidents at the airport, both to Vickers Viscount aircraft. The first of these was on 21 September 1967, when an Aer Lingus Viscount 800 landing from Dublin was not aligned correctly with the runway, and while the captain tried to correct this just before touchdown, the right wingtip and the propeller of No. 4 engine were both damaged. An overshoot was attempted, but because of obstructions ahead, the pilot retracted the undercarriage and made a wheels-up landing, writing off the aircraft, but there were no fatalities amongst the 4 crew and 17 passengers. On 19 January 1970, a Viscount 700 of Cambrian Airways, later absorbed into British Airways, was damaged beyond repair after a heavy landing, but all 4 crew and 59 passengers survived.

NEWCASTLE INTERNATIONAL: NCL
Newcastle-upon-Tyne, England, UK

Owner and operator: Newcastle International Airport Ltd
Runways: 07/25, 2,329m (7,641ft)
Terminals: One
Annual passengers: 5,701,395
Annual cargo: 8,728 tonnes
Annual aircraft movements: 79,484

The Tyne & Wear Metro has a station at the terminal with trains running directly to Newcastle city centre and to Sunderland.

Background
Situated more than 9km (almost six miles) north-west of the city centre, the airport is cur-

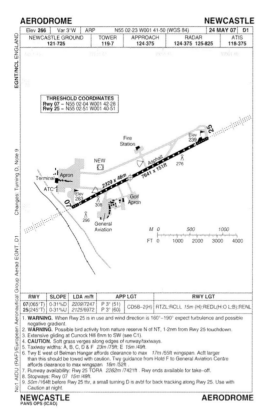

AERODROME   **NEWCASTLE**

Elev 266	Var 3°W	ARP	N55 02-23 W001 41-50 (WGS 84)		24 MAY 07	D1
NEWCASTLE GROUND 121·725		TOWER 119·7	APPROACH 124·375	RADAR 124·375 125·825		ATIS 118·375

THRESHOLD COORDINATES
Rwy 07 – N55 02·04 W001 42·28
Rwy 25 – N55 02·51 W001 40·51

RWY	SLOPE	LDA m/ft	APP LGT		RWY LGT
07(065°T)	0·31%D	2209/7247	P 3° (51)		RTZL:RCLL 15m (H):REDL(H:O L:B):RENL
25(245°T)	0·31%U	2125/6972	P 3° (60)	CD5B–2(H)	

1. **WARNING.** When Rwy 25 is in use and wind direction is 160°–190° expect turbulence and possible negative gradient.
2. **WARNING.** Possible bird activity from nature reserve N of NT, 1·2nm from Rwy 25 touchdown.
3. Extensive gliding at Currock Hill 8nm to SW (see C1).
4. **CAUTION.** Soft grass verges along edges of runway/taxiways.
5. Taxiway widths: A, B, C, D & F 23m /75ft; E 15m /49ft.
6. Twy E west of Belman Hangar affords clearance to max 17m /55ft wingspan. Acft larger than this should be towed with caution. Twy guidance from Hold F to General Aviation Centre affords clearance to max wingspan 16m /52ft .
7. Runway availability: Rwy 25 TORA 2262m /7421ft . Rwy ends available for take–off.
8. Stopways: Rwy 07 15m /49ft.
9. 50m /164ft before Rwy 25 thr, a small turning D is avbl for back tracking along Rwy 25. Use with Caution at night.

NEWCASTLE   **AERODROME**
PANS OPS (ICAO)

rently owned by seven local authorities, with 51 per cent, and Copenhagen Airport. It was opened on 26 July 1935, when it had a grass runway, hangar and workshops, and a clubhouse for a flying club. It was little used during the Second World War, with most activity at other airfields nearby, but in the 1950s a serious effort was made to attract commercial air services, with flights to the Channel Islands. By the end of the decade, the north-east's own airline, BKS (later absorbed into British Airways), was operating services to London Heathrow and later to destinations in Ireland and to Paris and Bergen.

The rate of growth accelerated during the 1960s with the rise in popularity of foreign holidays, which saw the airport become an important point for inclusive tour charter flights. A new runway was opened, with a new parking apron and air traffic control tower. In the following decade, the airport was classed as Category B, a regional international airport.

Towards the end of the century, the airport once again had its own airline, Gill Air, while the Norwegian airline, Braathens, operated flights to several destinations in Norway. The terminal was extended to cope with the rising traffic, and when Gill Air collapsed in the wake of the terrorist attacks in New York and Washington, its place was taken by the low-cost airline, Go, with a service to London Stansted. In 2001 Copenhagen Airport took a 49 per cent stake in the airport.

In August 2004 extensions to the departure area of the terminal opened, while the airport became the UK's first regional airport to have self-service check-in kiosks. In 2007 Emirates started the airport's first long-haul service with flights to Dubai. The continued growth in traffic has, nevertheless, made it more difficult for light aircraft to obtain slots to use the airport.

Currently the airport is in the middle of a master plan that runs to 2016 and which will see a runway extension and improved access, with the possibility of a heavy railway link. A new control tower, known as the 'Emirates Tower' has been opened. The overall objective is to almost double the present capacity to 10 million by 2015 and treble it to 15 million by 2030.

There have been few serious accidents at the airport in recent years, and of these two concerned light aircraft, one of which crashed en route some distance from Newcastle, and the other was because of an undercarriage problem. On 5 August 2008, a Panavia Tornado of the Royal Air Force overshot the runway while making an emergency landing following a bird strike.

LIVERPOOL JOHN LENNON (SPEKE): LPL

Speke, Liverpool, England, UK

Owner and operator: Liverpool Airport plc
Runways: 09/27, 2,286m (7,500ft)
Terminals: One
Airlines using airport as base or hub: easyJet, Ryanair
Annual passengers: 5,520,283

Annual cargo: 3,744 tonnes
Annual aircraft movements: 84,880

Background

Situated 12km (7½ miles) south-east of Liverpool, the airport was built partly in the grounds of Speke Hall and was for many years known locally as 'Speke' and formally as Liverpool (Speke) Airport. Scheduled flights began with a service by Imperial Airways via Manchester and Birmingham to Croydon Airport, south of London, in 1930. The airport was officially opened in summer 1933, and was used extensively by Railway Air Services, who pioneered many domestic routes as well as those to the Isle of Man, Belfast, and Dublin. Within a few years, a passenger terminal, control tower, and hangars were built, with the Irish Sea traffic being especially important for the airport.

The airport was taken over by the Royal Air Force on the outbreak of the Second World War in Europe in 1939, but it continued to have some commercial flights from Dublin as the Irish Republic was neutral. Under RAF control, the airport was home to the Merchant Ship Fighter Unit, which had fighter aircraft catapulted off merchant ships to protect ships in convoys, and the Rootes car manufacturer ran a 'shadow factory' building combat aircraft and assembling aircraft from the United States imported through Liverpool in crates.

Commercial air services started to return to normal after the end of the war in Europe, so that in 1945 some 50,000 passengers used the airport, but by 1948, this had risen to 75,000. The airport was owned during this period by the Ministry of Civil Aviation, and local authority-owned Manchester, then as now its main rival, became the more important airport in the northwest of England. The airport was passed to the local authority, Liverpool Corporation, in 1961, and ambitious development plans were prepared. A new runway was opened to the southeast of the original airfield in 1966. When a new local authority, Merseyside, was created in the 1970s, the airport passed into its ownership, but when Merseyside was in turn the victim of local

government reform in the 1980s, ownership passed to a consortium of five local councils.

In 1986 the original 1933 terminal was replaced by a new passenger terminal, while the original terminal lay derelict for some years before being converted into a hotel, while the apron outside now accommodates a number of preserved aircraft. In 1990, the airport was privatised and the aircraft manufacturer British Aerospace took a 76 per cent interest, but the airport has since been taken over as a wholly-owned subsidiary of Peel Holdings. A new passenger terminal opened in 2002, and has been extended since, with growth driven by a conscious decision to encourage low-cost airlines such as easyJet and Ryanair. The current name was adopted in 2002 in memory of John Lennon, a member of the pop band 'The Beatles'.

The runway and taxiways have been reconstructed and upgraded in recent years, with new lighting allowing Category III ILS operations.

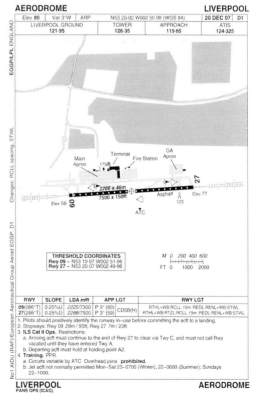

One of the first accidents at the airport after civilian services restarted after the Second World War was to a Consolidated Liberator, a converted bomber being used for air cargo by Scottish Airlines, which landed short of the runway on 13 October 1948 and struck two street lights, with the aircraft damaged beyond repair, although the crew of four were unhurt. Another cargo flight also suffered a landing mishap at the airport on 3 January 1997, when a Titan Airways Short 330, on a flight from Exeter to East Midlands, was diverted to Liverpool because of poor visibility, and landed heavily, causing the undercarriage to collapse. The aircraft was too badly damaged to be repaired, but the three crew members survived. On 10 May 2001 a Spanair McDonnell Douglas MD-83, landing from Palma de Mallorca, suffered a failure of the right main landing gear on touchdown and skidded to a halt, with considerable damage to the aircraft, although the 6 crew and 45 passengers were uninjured.

EAST MIDLANDS AIRPORT: NOTTINGHAM, LEICESTER, DERBY: EMA

Castle Donington, Leicestershire

Owner and operator: Manchester Airports Group
Runways: 09/27, 2,893m (9,491ft)
Terminals: One
Airlines using airport as base or hub: bmi (maintenance only), bmi regional, bmibaby, DHL, easyJet
Annual passengers: 5,422,198
Annual cargo: 304,460 tonnes
Annual aircraft movements: 87,858

There is a shuttle bus between the terminal and East Midlands Parkway Station, some 7km (4 miles) away, with trains to Nottingham, Derby and Leicester.

Background
Known at various times as Nottingham/Derby (despite being in Leicestershire), East Midlands,

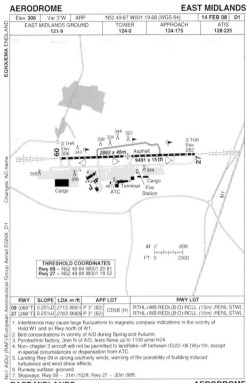

Nottingham International, and briefly in 2004 as Nottingham East Midlands, the current title of 'East Midlands Airport: Nottingham, Leicester, Derby' was formally adopted in 2006. The airport is within 32km (20 miles) of all three, but closest to Derby at 13km (8 miles).

There was a small airfield near Derby at Burnaston, used as a flying school by Derby Aviation, the predecessor of today's bmi group of airlines, but this airfield has been given over to industrial development. The present airport started as a Second World War Royal Air Force station, RAF Castle Donington, which opened in 1943, was used mainly by RAF Transport Command, and was decommissioned in 1946. It was bought by the neighbouring local authorities in 1964 and developed as an airport for the area, known initially as East Midlands Airport, which opened in April 1965. Derby Airways, the successor to Derby Aviation which had developed into a mainly charter airline and was renaming itself British Midland Airways, moved to the new airport that same year, establishing a small network of scheduled services.

The new airport was slow to gain acceptance amongst passengers, but quickly established itself as a centre for air cargo, and in 1970 a cargo terminal was created and the runway extended. Before the end of the decade, the runway was extended further and the passenger terminal enlarged and renovated. In 1987, legislation changed the means of ownership into a limited company, although still owned by the three local authorities (Nottinghamshire, Derbyshire, and Leicestershire) and in 1993, to assure funds for development, it was sold to the National Express Group, at that time mainly an operator of long-distance coach services. The runway was extended by 600m (1,950ft) for long-haul flights, and the UK's second highest control tower was constructed. In 2000, DHL opened a new cargo terminal at the airport and a business park was built next to the airport, but the following year National Express abandoned airport operation and sold its three airports, including East Midlands, to the Manchester Airports Group. This was the period when Britain's low-cost airlines were developing, and in 2002 the new airline Go established a hub at the airport, with passenger numbers that year rising by 36 per cent. Later, the company was bought by easyJet, who continued to use the airport as a hub, but the resident airline, British Midland, which had changed its name to bmi, turned over most of its operations at the airport to a low-cost subsidiary, bmibaby.

Despite this rapid growth, the airport still has passengers walking or being taken by bus between aircraft and terminal, although this is the preferred means for low-cost airlines. The growth, nevertheless, has sparked environmental protests. The terminal building is being extended and a new pier is being built to reduce the distance passengers have to walk.

The airport has seen a number of serious accidents. One of these was on 20 February 1969 when a British Midland Airways (now bmi) Vickers Viscount 700 was landing from Glasgow in a snow storm and at the second attempt undershot the runway, with the undercarriage collapsing and the fuselage badly damaged, although the 5 crew and 48 passengers survived. Bad weather also contributed to an accident on 31 January 1986 when an Aer Lingus Short 360 was landing from Dublin, but the crew lost control because of icing and landed in a field some distance short of the runway after striking several electricity cables in its descent, but while the aircraft was written off, the 3 crew and 33 passengers survived. Almost a year later, on 18 January 1987, a British Midland Fokker F-27 Friendship was on a training flight with one engine shut down when the aircraft slipped below decision level and hit the ground, being damaged beyond repair, although the three pilots aboard survived. The worst accident at the airport was on the evening of 8 January 1989, when a British Midland Boeing 737-400 flying from London to Belfast suffered engine problems after taking off, and the captain opted to fly to East Midlands, but shut down the engine that was working perfectly and instead nursed the aircraft on a failing engine, which finally stopped working as the aircraft was approaching the airport over the M1 Motorway and undershot the runway hitting the embankment between the motorway and the airport. The aircraft broke up in the accident, killing 47 of the 118 passengers, and although all 8 crew survived, the 2 pilots were badly injured.

BELFAST INTERNATIONAL (BELFAST ALDERGROVE): BFS
Aldergrove, County Antrim, Northern Ireland, UK

Owner and operator: Belfast International Airport Ltd
Runways: 07/25, 2,780m (9,121ft); 17/35, 1,891m (6,204ft)
Terminals: One
Airlines using airport as base or hub: Aer Lingus, easyJet
Annual passengers: 5,230,280
Annual cargo: 50,019 tonnes
Annual aircraft movements: 76,799

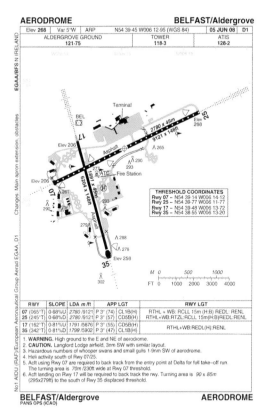

AERODROME				BELFAST/Aldergrove
Elev **268**	Var 5°W	ARP	N54 39·45 W006 12·95 (WGS 84)	**05 JUN 08** D1
ALDERGROVE GROUND 121·75			TOWER 118·3	ATIS 128·2

THRESHOLD COORDINATES
Rwy 07 – N54 39·14 W006 14·12
Rwy 25 – N54 39·77 W006 11·77
Rwy 17 – N54 39·48 W006 13·72
Rwy 35 – N54 38·55 W006 13·20

RWY	SLOPE	LDA m/ft	APP LGT		RWY LGT
07 (065°T)	0·68%U	2780 /9121	P 3° (74)	CL1B(H)	RTHL + WB: RCLL 15m (H:B) REDL: RENL
25 (245°T)	0·68%D	2780 /9121	P 3° (57)	CD5B(H)	RTHL+WB:RTZL:RCLL 15m(H:B)REDL:RENL
17 (162°T)	0·81%U	1791 /5876	P 3° (55)	CD5B(H)	RTHL+WB:REDL(H):RENL
35 (342°T)	0·81%U	1799 /5902	P 3° (47)	CL1B(H)	

1. **WARNING**. High ground to the E and NE of aerodrome.
2. **CAUTION**. Langford Lodge airfield, 3nm SW with similar layout.
3. Hazardous numbers of whooper swans and small gulls 1·9nm SW of aerodrome.
4. Heli activity south of Rwy 07/25.
5. Acft using Rwy 07 are required to back track from the entry point at Delta for full take–off run. The turning area is 70m /230ft wide at Rwy 07 threshold.
6. Acft landing on Rwy 17 will be required to back track the rwy. Turning area is 90 x 85m (295x279ft) to the south of Rwy 35 displaced threshold.

BELFAST/Aldergrove
PANS OPS (ICAO)

AERODROME

Background

Situated 21km (13 miles) north-west of Belfast, the airport first opened in 1917 as a flying school for the Royal Flying Corps during the First World War, and after the war it became a base for the newly-formed Royal Air Force. In 1922, newspaper flights started from Chester, but the first passenger flights did not follow until 1933 with a service from Glasgow by Midland & Scottish Air Ferries. Flights to the Isle of Man, Liverpool, and London Croydon then followed, some of them by Railway Air Services. The airport was developed considerably during the Second World War, when it was used by RAF Coastal Command, and two long-paved runways suitable for heavy maritime-reconnaissance aircraft replaced the original four short grass runways.

During the war years two rival airfields emerged – at Belfast Harbour, where Shorts, the aircraft manufacturer, had moved production,

and at Nutts Corner, just 4.8km (3 miles) away from Aldergrove. It was the latter that was chosen to be Belfast's airport after the war, despite being smaller than Aldergrove. It was used throughout the 1950s but, in poor weather, aircraft were often diverted to Aldergrove.

In October 1963 Belfast Aldergrove opened as the 'new' airport for the city, with a new terminal and apron. The main operator out of the new airport was BEA (British European Airways) whose main service was to London Heathrow, but who also operated to Glasgow and Manchester, while two of its associated companies, Cambrian and BKS, operated to Liverpool, Bristol and Cardiff, and Newcastle. Initially, services were mainly by turboprop aircraft, including Vickers Viscounts and Vanguards, but by 1966 the then British United Airways launched a service to London Gatwick using BAC One-Eleven jet airliners, as competition started gradually on the United Kingdom's 'domestic trunk' services. In 1968 Aer Lingus inaugurated a service to New York via Shannon, and the British Overseas Airways Corporation started a service to New York via Prestwick. Both services were short-lived.

Northern Ireland Airports was formed in 1971 and embarked on a major redevelopment programme, including a new pier for international flights. The new British Airways, which included BEA, BOAC, BKS and Cambrian, launched Europe's first 'no booking' shuttle services on the domestic trunk routes, and NLM Cityhopper, now part of KLM Royal Dutch Airlines, introduced a service to Amsterdam. The airport was renamed Belfast International in 1983 and the terminal was further extended, while a new terminal for business aircraft opened in 1987, and one for cargo in 1991. The airport was privatised in 1994 and was sold to TBI in 1996. Throughout this period, civil unrest and terrorism in Northern Ireland meant that the airport had to apply strict security measures to passengers and their luggage. There was a Royal Air Force section to the airport (RAF Aldergrove) used for flying troops into and out of the province, while also acting as a base for

RAF helicopters, with security provided by the RAF Regiment.

The return of peace to Northern Ireland saw new operators appear, with easyJet introducing low-cost services to London Luton and, later, to Liverpool. These have grown to a total of 9 domestic and 15 European services, so that the airline is now the airport's main user. British Airways pulled out of its service to London Heathrow and was replaced in 2007 by the Irish airline, Aer Lingus, which is now expanding the number of destinations served from Belfast. In 2005, Continental Airlines introduced a non-stop service from New York Newark, and briefly there was a service to Vancouver by the Canadian airline Zoom, which collapsed in 2008.

Despite these changes, passenger growth has slowed, largely because of growing competition from what was Belfast City (now called Belfast George Best), which has a growing range of services, including one by bmi to London Heathrow, which was transferred from International.

Starting in 2006, a programme of expansion and improvements is under way and will continue to 2015, including improved access and parking both for aircraft and for cars, while the terminal is being expanded. In the longer term, to 2030, a railway link is amongst a number of improvements planned.

Despite the problems of terrorism, the airport has had a relatively uneventful history and has also suffered few serious accidents. An Air Bridge Carriers Armstrong-Whitworth Argosy freighter had an undercarriage collapse on landing on 17 April 1982, damaging the aircraft beyond repair, but the crew of two were unharmed. Also damaged beyond repair was a British World Airways Vickers Viscount 800 on a training flight on 24 March 1996, which also had an undercarriage collapse, but the two pilots, the only occupants, were unharmed.

ABERDEEN DYCE: ABZ
Dyce, Aberdeen, Scotland, UK

Owner and operator: Ferrovial (BAA)
Runways: 16/34, 1,829m (6,001ft)
Terminals: Five – a main passenger terminal, three helicopter terminals, and one for oil company charter flights and corporate shuttles
Airlines using airport as base or hub: bmi Regional, Brintel Helicopters, City Star Airlines, Eastern Airways
Annual passengers: 3,434,493
Annual cargo: 5,479 tonnes
Annual aircraft movements: 121,947

Bus link to Dyce Station with trains to Aberdeen.

Background

The airport is at the village of Dyce, just over 9km (almost 6 miles) from the centre of Aberdeen. It is Europe's busiest commercial helicopter airport, with several companies serving the offshore oil industry.

It originally opened in 1934 as Dyce Airport. On the outbreak of the Second World War it was taken over by the RAF, although initially some passenger flights to the northern Isles (Orkney and Shetland) continued. After the war the airport reverted to commercial use under the control of the Ministry of Civil Aviation, with Aberdeen being an important domestic airport because of the distance from the major cities of the south. The discovery of substantial oil fields in the North Sea resulted in the first offshore helicopter flight from a Scottish airport by Bristow Helicopters to an exploration platform in 1967.

The airport passed to the British Airports Authority in 1975, which was privatised in July 1987, and later the Spanish consortium, Ferrovial, purchased the BAA airports in June 2006, operating them through a subsidiary, Airport Development and Investment Limited (ADI). Meanwhile, a new passenger terminal was completed and opened in 1992, and later extended. Currently, runway lengthening is planned, but the airport offers flights to a large number of destinations within the UK and Europe, especially Norway.

The airport has been the departure point or the destination for a number of helicopters suffering en route accidents, but there have been relatively few accidents at Dyce itself. One of these was on 13 June 2001 when a Beech King Air, on a charter flight to Humberside, returned with an undercarriage problem. The undercarriage collapsed on landing, but without casualties amongst the two crew and four passengers. A North Flying Swearingen Metroliner III went down after taking off on 24 December 2002 for a positioning flight to Aalborg. The loss of power in the right engine caused it to crash into a field and on to a road, hitting a moving car. One crew member suffered minor injuries but the other pilot and the car driver were unharmed. On 22 June 2006 a City Star Dornier 328, landing from Stavanger, overshot the end of the runway, but none of those aboard (16 passengers and 3 crew) was injured.

LONDON CITY: LCY

London Docklands, England, UK

Owner: GIP
Operator: London City Airport Ltd
Runways: 10/28, 1,508m (4,984ft)
Terminals: One
Airlines using airport as base or hub: Cityjet, BA
  CityFlyer
Annual passengers: 2,928,920
Annual aircraft movements: 91,489

Docklands Light Railway provides direct link to City of London and to Canary Wharf.

Background

A modern airport deliberately built in the centre of a business district, London City Airport is 11km (almost 7 miles) east of the City of London and is in two former docks. It cannot provide either a second runway or expand its area.

Then idea of a city airport for London originated around 1981 as the London Docklands Development Corporation tackled the task of

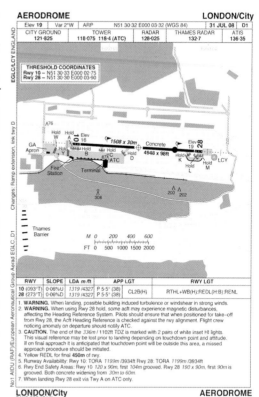

regenerating an area which largely consisted of abandoned docks and warehouses as shipping had moved downstream following the introduction of containers. To prove the concept, a de Havilland Dash 7 STOL (short take-off and landing) airliner of Brymon Airways was landed on an improvised airstrip at Heron Quays in the West India Docks. It took until 1986 to obtain planning permission, but on 26 October 1987 the first commercial air services started. The challenges to be overcome included a new air traffic control area, Thames Radar, to handle flights using the airport, which is under one of the main flight paths to London Heathrow.

When the airport opened, the initial services linked it with Amsterdam, Paris, and Rotterdam, operated by two airlines, one of which was London City Airways, owned by the same group as today's bmi and Brymon. The airport was essentially suitable for nothing larger than a de Havilland Dash 7 as the runway was at first just 1,080m (3,543ft) long and required a glidescope of 7.5°. In 1993 the runway was lengthened and the glidescope reduced to 5.5°, allowing jet aircraft such as the BAe 146/Avro RJ to use it. The airport was sold in 1985 by the builders, the Mowlem construction group, to an Irish entrepreneur, Dermot Desmond, who sold it to a consortium in 2006. That same year, the Docklands Light Railway opened a station on a branch line running into the airport. In 2008, an extended apron with additional aircraft parking stands was opened.

The largest aircraft now able to use the airport, after successful trials, are the Embraer E-190 and the Airbus A318, with British Airways introducing a service to New York using this aircraft in all-premium configuration in late 2009, although this requires a refuelling stop at Shannon. Most of the main British and European airports are served from London City, with Luxair having transferred its flights from Heathrow to the airport, while the Air France subsidiary Cityjet and BA Cityflyer are the two main airlines.

Helicopters are not allowed to use the airport because of noise restrictions, and operational hours are limited from 6.30am to 10pm Monday to Friday, 6.30am to 12.30pm on Saturdays, and 12.30pm to 10pm on Sundays. Up to 38 flights an hour can be handled, which is an achievement as aircraft preparing to take-off have to backtrack along the runway. There are no hangars.

Despite the steep approach and the short runway, the airport has shown itself to be safe, and pilots are specially trained before flying into or out of the airport. The one serious accident was on 18 August 2007 when a Swiss European Air Lines Avro RJ100, from Geneva, was flying slightly too slowly and then suffered the loss of headwind, landing heavily and damaging the tail, although the aircraft was able to be repaired and the 5 crew and 88 passengers were unharmed.

LEEDS BRADFORD INTERNATIONAL: LBA
Yeadon, Leeds, West Yorkshire, UK

Owner: Bridgepoint Capital
Operator: Leeds Bradford International Airport Ltd
Runways: 14/32, 2,250m (7,382ft)
Terminals: One
Airlines using airport as base or hub: Jet2.com
Annual passengers: 2,906,464
Annual aircraft movements: 66,355

Background

Often still known to locals as Yeadon, after the nearby village, Leeds Bradford International Airport is Britain's highest.

The airport's history dates back to its opening on 17 October 1931 as the Leeds and Bradford Municipal Aerodrome, which was operated by the Yorkshire Aeroplane Club on behalf of the two city corporations. It was enlarged slightly in 1935, and in April that year a service was started by North Eastern Airways between London Heston and Newcastle-upon-Tyne Cramlington, later extended to Edinburgh Turnhouse, which called at Leeds Bradford. In June 1935 Blackpool and West Coast Air Services started a service to the Isle of Man. In 1936 the Royal Auxiliary Air Force formed its No. 609 (West Riding) Squadron at Yeadon, while for civil use work began on a terminal building, but this stopped when it was far from complete.

On the outbreak of the Second World War in Europe in September 1939, most civil aviation within the United Kingdom stopped. Avro built a shadow factory (a factory intended to replicate the production of existing factories) just north of the aerodrome with a taxiway linking it to the aerodrome. During the years that followed, the factory produced 250 Bristol Blenheims, as well as Avro's own Lancaster (695), Anson (4,500), York (45), and Lincoln (25). The aerodrome was used for testing military aircraft, and for this two paved runways and extra hangars were built.

The airport returned to its owners in 1947, and Yeadon Aviation was formed in 1953 to run both the aerodrome and the associated aero club. In 1955 there were air services to Belfast, Dusseldorf, the Isle of Wight, Jersey, Ostend, and Southend. With the formation of BKS Air Transport, later absorbed by British Airways, there were flights from 1960 to London Heathrow and then to Dublin. A new runway opened in 1965, but that year the terminal was destroyed by fire and it was not until 1968 that a replacement opened. In the years that followed, inclusive tour package holidays became an important part of Europe's air transport, and from 1976 there were charter flights from the airport to Spain. Leeds Bradford became a regional airport in 1978, and in November 1984 work was completed on an extension to the runway over the A658 road, for which an underpass was built. The following year, the first stage of an extension to the terminal opened. For a while, starting in 1984, the Canadian airline, Wardair, operated transatlantic charter flights to Toronto, but these did not become a permanent feature of the airport's operations. In the years that followed there were occasional Concorde supersonic airliner charters from the airport. From 1994 the airport started to operate 24 hours a day, which was important for charter flights.

Further work on developing the airport began in 1997, and in October 2005 the original runway, 09/27, closed to provide an extra taxiway and additional aircraft parking space. Passenger numbers doubled between 1997 and 2007, due in no small part to the low-cost airline Jet2.com using the airport as its base. The airport also became the base for the Yorkshire Air Ambulance in 2000. In 2008 long-haul scheduled flights to Islamabad were introduced by Shaheen Air, but these were suspended after four months and have since been replaced by a service provided by Pakistan International Airlines.

Plans are being implemented for the development of the airport, with an extension to the terminal and the addition of airbridges, improvements to the taxiway, additional hangars, and a new fuel farm, as well as a railway branch line into the airport.

The airport is owned by Bridgepoint Capital, which acquired it in 2007.

At one time there were a number of incidents of aircraft aquaplaning on landing at Leeds Bradford, involving Vickers Viscount aircraft of British Midland, but it was not until 27 May 1985 that a serious accident resulted. This was when a British Airtours Lockheed TriStar, landing from Palma de Mallorca after it had been raining, overshot the runway. However, all 14 crew and 398 passengers survived with only minor injuries. This was followed by a Jordanian Airbus A320, operating on behalf of a Spanish company, landing from Fuerteventura on 18 May 2005, which touched down too far along the runway and then suffered a failure of its braking system, and was turned off the runway on to grass by the captain, without injuries to any of the passengers or crew.

GLASGOW PRESTWICK: PIK
Prestwick, Ayrshire, Scotland, UK

Owner: Infratil
Operator: Glasgow Prestwick Airport Ltd
Runways: 13/31, 2,987m (9,799ft); 03/21, 1,829m (6,000ft)
Terminals: One
Airlines using airport as base or hub: Ryanair
Annual passengers: 2,423,460
Annual cargo: 31,562 tonnes
Annual aircraft movements: 48,143

Glasgow Prestwick Airport railway station has frequent trains to Glasgow Central.

Background
More usually known as Prestwick, Glasgow Prestwick is just outside Prestwick and 46km (almost 29 miles) from Glasgow.

The airport was first used in 1934 for training, and was owned by the proprietor of Scottish Aviation, which later founded an aircraft factory on the site. A passenger terminal was opened in 1938, and the airport became firmly established during the Second World War when it was used as the main point of landfall for transports flying across the North Atlantic, for which long, surfaced runways were built. Before this, transatlantic air transport had been the preserve of flying boats. After the war, before blind landing equipment had been invented, it became a diversionary airport when fog closed London Heathrow, which it frequently did. In 1952 the United States Air Force opened a base for transport aircraft at the airport, although it was formally an RAF station, and this closed in 1966, although part of it remains as RNAS Prestwick, also known as HMS *Gannet*, which for many years had a large squadron of Westland Sea King anti-submarine helicopters based there to protect British and US nuclear submarines based on the Clyde, and it still has a naval search-and-rescue squadron today.

In 1964 a completely new terminal, runway extension, and parallel taxiway opened, with the runway extension being crossed by a main road, controlled by traffic lights when aircraft were operating, until a new perimeter road could be completed. The runway extension was nothing compared to an early post-war plan for a 4-mile runway and facilities for flying boats (only the main road and railway line separate the airport from the sea), but this was abandoned largely because the day of the flying boat was over. Scottish Aviation, which had built a number of aircraft, including the Pioneer and later the Bulldog trainer, after Beagle (its original manufacturer) collapsed, was taken over by the British Aircraft Corporation (later British Aerospace, or BAe) and production of the Jetstream range of small airliners and business aircraft was moved there after the collapse of the original manufacturer, Handley Page. There is still aircraft manufacturing activity on the site, with Spirit Aerosystems producing components for both Airbus and Boeing.

From 1967 to 1992 the airport also hosted a bi-annual airshow.

The airport was put under the management of the British Airports Authority and became Scotland's transatlantic airport, while also being used for airline pilot training. After BAA was privatised, the portfolio of airports included

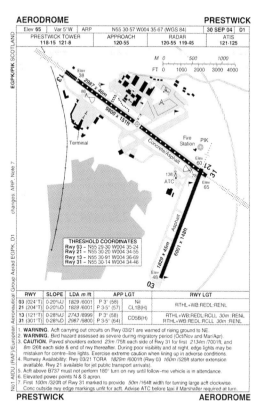

both Glasgow, at one time owned by the City of Glasgow, and Prestwick, and it was decided to sell Prestwick and concentrate transatlantic flights on Glasgow Airport. From 1991 onwards, passenger traffic at Prestwick virtually disappeared and the airport was used mainly for air freight, although Royal Navy helicopters remained. In 1994 the new owners built a railway station, which they still own, for the airport, with covered pedestrian access from the terminal. Real recovery came with the arrival of the low-cost airline, Ryanair, which first opened a route to Dublin and then followed with a route to London Stansted. The airline now has a maintenance base at the airport and almost 30 destinations are served direct from it. Throughout this time, and to the present, the airport continues to be used by British, Canadian, and US military aircraft, and still handles transatlantic air cargo. A major renovation of the terminal was completed in April 2005.

It is owned by Infratil, a New Zealand Company, which owns Wellington and Manston airports. For the future, there is a plan to double the size of the existing terminal.

The airport shares with Stansted the role of being the designated landing site for flights that are at risk, which means flights with hijackers or explosives on board. Earlier, during the immediate post-war period, the airport was the first landfall for aircraft having flown across the Atlantic and the last before a transatlantic crossing from Europe.

In bad weather on 20 October 1948 a KLM Royal Dutch Airlines Lockheed Constellation aborted the first landing attempt and then tried from a different direction, hitting power cables because of an incorrect altimeter setting, crashing with the loss of 30 passengers and 4 crew. Early on 25 December 1954 a BOAC (British Overseas Airways Corporation) Boeing Stratocruiser, landing while en route from London to New York, crashed short off the runway, killing 28 out of the 36 passengers and crew. The accident was due in part to the landing lights being out of action and the pilots being fatigued as they were over their duty limits because their departure from London had been delayed. The airport was also popular for crew training before simulators became more advanced, and on 17 March 1977 a British Airtours Boeing 707-420 crashed following a simulated engine failure during take-off, with the undercarriage collapsing and the engines ripped off, but the four crew were uninjured. This was followed by another accident during a simulated engine failure on 6 October 1992 during a test flight for a BAe Jestream 31, when the aircraft rolled and hit the ground killing both pilots.

GEORGE BEST BELFAST CITY: BHD

Queen's Island, Belfast, Northern Ireland, UK

Owner: Ferrovial
Operator: Belfast City Airport Ltd
Runways: 04/22, 1,829m (6,001ft)
Terminals: One

Airlines using airport as base or hub: Flybe, Ryanair
Annual passengers: 2,186,993
Annual aircraft movements: 43,022

Belfast Sydenham railway station is close to the airport, across the road from the old terminal, while a courtesy bus links the new terminal with the railway station.

Background

Still usually known as Belfast City, or as Sydenham Airport, because of its location, the airport is just 3.2km (2 miles) from the city centre.

The airfield was originally built by Short Brothers for their new aircraft factory at Belfast in 1937, and this was used by commercial flights as well, for which it was known as Sydenham Airport. It is beside the harbour, which was important for the manufacturer as at the time its main business was the production of large flying boats for Imperial Airways and the Royal Air Force. During the Second World War it became a Fleet Air Arm base.

After the war it was used by the FAA and RAF, as well as Shorts, and it was not until 1983 that it reopened again for commercial flights as Belfast Harbour Airport, later becoming Belfast City to stress its proximity to the centre. The approaches and take-off paths are over a densely-populated urban area, so the airport is controversial and there are restrictions on operations, especially on the number of airline seats that can be sold. As the factory no longer produces completed aircraft but instead manufactures airframe sections, there are no aircraft deliveries from the site. After Shorts was acquired by Bombardier, the Canadian aircraft manufacturer, there was considerable investment in the airport before it was sold to the Spanish civil engineering and airport company, Ferrovial, which is reportedly planning to sell it. In 2006 it was given the current name in memory of a footballer.

There have been no serious accidents at the airport at the time of writing, but before it opened, on two occasions Shorts aircraft awaiting delivery to customers were destroyed by terrorist bombs.

CARDIFF INTERNATIONAL: CWL

Rhoose, Glamorgan, Wales, UK

Owner: TBI plc
Operator: Cardiff Airport Ltd
Runways: 12/30, 2,392m (7,848ft)
Terminals: One
Airlines using airport as base or hub: bmibaby,
   Highland Airways, and a maintenance base for
   British Airways
Annual passengers: 2,116,685
Annual aircraft movements: 43,973

A shuttle bus links the terminal to Rhoose Cardiff
International Airport station, with trains to Cardiff
and Bridgend.

Background
The airport is 19km (almost 12 miles) west of Cardiff and is effectively the only airport in Wales, as Anglesey Airport is situated at RAF Valley and its sole scheduled service is to Cardiff.

Although Great Western Airways, a subsidiary of the Great Western Railway, introduced a service from Cardiff to Plymouth before the Second World War, the present airport was built by the Air Ministry during the war and opened on 7 April 1942 as RAF Rhoose, an operational training unit for fighter pilots. After the war Cambrian Airways made the airport its base, claiming the first post-war civil flight in Great Britain on 1 January 1946, when a three-seat Auster light aircraft flew to Bristol with a reel of wire rope and a prototype aircraft seat as cargo. A service started shortly afterwards to Weston-super-Mare, followed by the Channel Islands in 1949, and later the company became an associate of British European Airways (BEA), and began operating scheduled services to Liverpool. In 1952 Aer Lingus started a service to Dublin. A new terminal building was provided and the airport also began to attract inclusive tour holiday charter

flights. Throughout this period the airport was known simply as Rhoose Airport, but this was changed during the 1970s to Glamorgan Rhoose Airport, and in the following decade to Cardiff-Wales Airport.

The original airline, Cambrian, eventually became part of British Airways. The airport has not had great success with Welsh-based airlines, with the charter airlines Paramount and Airways International Cymru (Welsh for Wales) not surviving for long, while a scheduled operator, Air Wales, suspended operations in 2006. The service to Anglesey, supported for three years from 2007 by the Welsh Assembly, is provided by a Scottish airline, Highland Airways. A runway extension in 1986 enabled British Airways to select the airport as its heavy maintenance base as it can handle a lightly-loaded Boeing 747.

The airport was privatised in 1995, being sold to TBI, which is itself now a subsidiary of Abertis Airports. An upgrade of the terminal started in 2006. The launch of low-cost airlines has provided renewed growth for the airport, which is a base for bmibaby, the low-cost subsidiary of bmi, the former British Midland Airways, and both Ryanair and Flybe are expanding their operations. Transatlantic charter flights use the airport.

SOUTHAMPTON INTERNATIONAL: SOU

Southampton, Hampshire, England, UK

Owner and operator: BAA
Runways: 02/20, 1,723m (5,653ft)
Terminals: One
Airlines using airport as base or hub: Flybe,
   Aurigny, Blue Islands
Annual passengers: 1,966,774
Annual cargo: 2,496 tonnes
Annual aircraft movements: 54,182

Airport station for trains to Southampton and
London Waterloo.

Background

Southampton can trace its history back to 1910 when a local man, Eric Rowland Moon, built and tested his Moonbeam 2 aircraft, flying from the meadows at North Stoneham Farm. The site clearly became associated with flying for it was chosen by Gustav Hamel for a public flying display of his Morane Saulnier monoplane in 1914, watched by a crowd supposed to be 10,000 strong. It was not until 1917 that the military showed an interest, with the airfield purchased by the War Office as an aircraft acceptance park for the Royal Flying Corps, but it was not used as such before being passed to the United States Navy as an assembly area. With the return of peace, it was licensed as a civil aerodrome; soon renamed Atlantic Park, and eventually direct flights were available to Plymouth, London, France, Bristol, and Bournemouth via the Isle of Wight, and later to the Channel Islands.

Atlantic Park was purchased by Southampton Corporation in 1932 and renamed Southampton Municipal Airport. The following year it became the base for the Hampshire Flying Club, whose members included Reginald Mitchell, Chief Designer for the aircraft manufacturer, Supermarine, whose works were just a few miles away on the River Hamble. The prototype of the Supermarine Spitfire fighter was brought to the airport, assembled and tested and made its first flight on 5 March 1936.

On the outbreak of the Second World War in 1939, the airfield was requisitioned by the Admiralty and commissioned as HMS *Raven* (all Royal Naval Air Stations were given ships' names), which German propaganda later claimed to have been sunk! The Royal Navy's Fleet Air Arm used *Raven* for training and communications flights. As the war in Europe ended, the airfield was returned to Southampton Corporation and flights to the Channel Islands resumed. Nevertheless, the airport did not prosper, and it was threatened with closure until a private owner acquired it during the early 1960s and began a programme of improvements, including the building of the current 1,723m runway, which contributed to a fourfold increase in passengers within a year. Later, a new air traffic control tower was built and radar installed and, in due course, an airport station was added making the most of its position next to the main line between London and Southampton. In 1984, a subsidiary of the British Airports Authority was appointed to manage the airfield, which passed to a new owner in 1988 before being acquired by BAA in 1990.

Under BAA ownership, complete redevelopment took place with a new passenger terminal, which opened in 1994, the same year that the name Southampton International Airport was adopted. BAA was privatised in July 1987, and later the Spanish consortium, Ferrovial, purchased the BAA airports in June 2006, operating them through a subsidiary, Airport Development and Investments Limited (ADI). More recently, in June 2008, check-in and baggage facilities were nearly doubled to allow for continued expansion. In recent years the airport has developed from primarily handling flights to and from the Channel Islands of Jersey, Guernsey, and Alderney to also supporting a wider range of UK domestic and European flights.

The airport was the scene of an emergency landing by a BAe One-Eleven 500 en route from Birmingham to Malaga on 10 June 1990, when an explosive decompression saw the aircraft's captain half-sucked out of the aircraft, and with the cabin crew hanging on to the unfortunate pilot, the co-pilot landed the aircraft safely. Potentially very serious was the landing by a Cessna Citation II on 26 May 1993 with a tailwind 5 knots higher than the 10 knots limit for this aircraft, which resulted in the runway being overshot and the aircraft crashing on to the M27 Motorway before hitting two cars and bursting into flames. The two crew and three people in the two cars suffered only minor injuries.

JERSEY: JER

St Peter, Jersey, Channel Islands

Owner and operator: States of Jersey
Runways: 09/27, 1,706m (5,597ft)
Terminals: One
Annual passengers: 1,596,757
Annual cargo: 7,406 tonnes
Annual aircraft movements: 72,366

Background

Jersey Airport is the only one on the island and the largest airport in the Channel Islands, which are associated territories of, but not part of, the United Kingdom. It is 7.5km (4.7 miles) north-west of the island capital, St Helier.

Air services to Jersey began after the Second World War, with flying boats operated by British Marine Air Navigation from Southampton, which remains an important departure point for air services to all three Channel Islands. In the years that followed, airliners used the beach at St Aubin's Bay to the west of the island, and the island developed a substantial airline of its own, Jersey Airways. The beach was unsatisfactory as aircraft movements were dependent on tide and weather conditions. The present airport opened on 10 March 1937, built by the island's government, the States, with a passenger terminal and four grass runways.

During the Second World War the airport was used initially by the Fleet Air Arm and the Royal Air Force, but as defeat in France became inevitable, the Channel Islands were demilitarised and the British armed services left, while the aircraft and aircrew of Jersey Airways became a Fleet Air Arm transport and communications squadron. Despite the lack of any defences, the airport was one of the areas of the island bombed before the Germans landed. The Luftwaffe used the airport during the occupation, which lasted until German surrender in May 1945, and built hangars and concrete taxiways. The airport was seldom, if ever, used for offensive operations, as better airfields were available in France.

After the war the airport returned to civilian control, and commercial flights resumed, using the 1937 terminal, with the appearance of Jersey Airlines, later absorbed into British United Airways, and flights by BEA (British European Airways). A tarmac runway was opened in 1952, and the grass strips were closed. Aircraft being moved to and from a hangar had to cross a public highway, which was closed by traffic lights during aircraft movements. The runway was extended several times over the years, reaching its present length in 1976, but scope for further extension is limited as the land falls away sharply at the western end. The 1937 terminal was also extended in 1976, and a completely new terminal opened in 1997.

The airport can take aircraft up to Boeing 757 size, but for normal operations the Boeing 737 or Airbus A320 series is the usual maximum. The most frequent service is to Guernsey by Aurigny Air Services, with flights at half-hourly intervals at peak periods.

The worst accident at the airport was on 14 April 1965 when a British United Airways (later British Caledonian before being absorbed by British Airways) Douglas C-47 was attempting to land from Paris in poor visibility. Despite approach minima being below those in the company manual, the pilot aborted the first landing and made a second attempt, striking a lighting pole and crashing into a field where the aircraft caught fire, killing all 23 passengers and leaving just one survivor from the crew of 4. All aboard survived the next accident, which was on 24 December 1974 when a British Island Airways Handley Page Herald, on a flight from Southampton to Guernsey, suffered an engine failure and diverted to Jersey because of the longer runway, but on approach the aircraft yawed because of asymmetric drag, and confusion between the captain and co-pilot over whether or not the aircraft should go-around resulted in it damaging the right wing and engine and swinging off the runway, writing off the aircraft, but all 4 crew and 49 passengers survived. The daily early morning newspaper flight from Bournemouth was the next casualty when, on 6 May 1997, a Channel Express Fokker F-27 Friendship, with the co-pilot handling the aircraft, landed nose first and drove the nose wheel into the fuselage, causing substantial damage to the aircraft, but the two pilots survived. Another Channel Express F-27 suffered an engine fire after taking-off for Bournemouth on a positioning flight on 5 June 2001, but the aircraft returned to land safely at Jersey, and the three crew were unharmed.

BOURNEMOUTH: BOH
Hurn, Christchurch, Dorset, England, UK

Owner and operator: Manchester Airports Group
Runways: 08/26, 2,271m (7,451ft)
Terminals: One
Airlines using airport as base or hub: Ryanair, Palmair, Thomsonfly
Annual passengers: 1,092,785
Annual cargo: 10,747 tonnes
Annual aircraft movements: 74,675

Background
Known at different times as Hurn and Bournemouth International, Bournemouth Airport is 6.5km (4 miles) north-east of Bournemouth. It is actually located at Hurn, which is part of Christchurch.

The airport was originally opened during the Second World War as RAF Hurn on 1 August 1941. It was used by Army Co-operation Command and for training paratroopers and glider pilots. A Hurn-based squadron, No. 570, landed agents in France and dropped supplies to the French Resistance. Before the war ended, commercial flights started with the British Overseas Airways Corporation operating flights across the Atlantic and to Canada. After the war, until London Heathrow opened, Hurn was the main long-haul airport for the United Kingdom, and it was from the airport that the first landplane service between England and Australia started, using Avro Lancastrians (modified Lancaster bombers). Pre war, the service had been by flying boats operating from Hythe, at the mouth of Southampton Water.

After the war the airport was much quieter, but Vickers-Armstrong took over the ex-BOAC

hangars in 1951 and started to produce the Vickers Varsity, the military navigational training variant of the Viking airliner and Valetta military transport. Later the Vickers Viscount turboprop airliner and the BAC One-Eleven short-haul jet airliner, were produced at Hurn. In 1958 a locally-based airline, Palmair, started to operate charter flights to Mediterranean resorts.

In 1960 the airport was purchased by Bournemouth Corporation and Dorset County Council, and became Bournemouth Airport, before later adding 'international' to the name. Redevelopment of the airport began with the construction of a new terminal, and charter traffic began to grow. In 1993 the airport was sold to the National Express Group, and then in 2001 to the Manchester Airports Group, the largest UK-owned airport operator. A new runway extension was completed in 1996, and Ryanair began a regular low-cost service to Dublin. There are also infrequent long-haul charter flights to North America and the Caribbean.

In 2007 the new owners announced that they intended to build a new international arrivals terminal, while the number of aircraft stands would treble, but in granting permission the local authority has stipulated road improvements and a maximum of 3 million passengers annually, as well as the use of quieter aircraft. The work should be completed during 2010.

During the period when the airport handled transatlantic flights, a BOAC (British Overseas Airways Corporation) Avro Lancastrian (a converted Lancaster bomber) suffered a take-off accident on 15 August 1946 when the undercarriage collapsed, but the only occupants, the four crew, were unharmed. An Airwork Services Vickers Viscount 800 was written off during a delivery flight from Germany on 28 January 1972, but again without any casualties amongst the crew of two aboard. An Air UK Handley Page Herald was written off after being struck by a lorry while parked at the airport on 11 June 1984, while on 8 April 1997 a Channel Express Herald was also written off after taxiing into airport lighting.

ROBIN HOOD – DONCASTER SHEFFIELD: DSA

Finningley, Doncaster, South Yorkshire

Owner and operator: Peel Airports
Runways: 02/20, 2,893m (9,491ft)
Terminals: One
Annual passengers: 1,078,374

Background

The airport for Doncaster and Sheffield is just under 6km (3½ miles) south-east of Doncaster and 29km (18 miles) east of Sheffield.

The airport dates from 1915 when the Royal Flying Corps opened an airfield at Finningley, which was a base for fighters to prevent German Zeppelin airships from attacking northern industrial cities. It closed after the First World War, but was reopened in 1936. Although an RAF Bomber Command station during the Second World War, it mainly served as an operational training unit for heavy bomber crews. It remained open, and during the Cold War was a base for the Avro Vulcan bombers carrying Britain's nuclear deterrent, before becoming a training station throughout the 1970s and 1980s. It was decommissioned in 1995, but reopened as an airport in 2005. The first commercial flight was to Majorca on 28 April. The airport has become popular with charter operators and low-cost airlines, mainly operating to destinations in Europe, but the Scottish low-cost airline, fly-globespan, operates to Canada, and Thomsonfly to Florida, the Dominican Republic, and Mexico, while Flybe operates domestic services.

UNITED STATES OF AMERICA
(And Associated Territories)

As the country that made the first aeroplane flights, the United States also saw many of the early experiments in the practical application of aviation. Development of the hydro-aeroplane,

later to evolve into seaplanes and flying boats, was largely conducted in the United States. There was also an early experiment with airmail on 23 October 1911, when Earle Ovington flew from Garden City, New York, to Mineola, Long Island, in a Blériot monoplane. As with the British air cargo operation earlier that year, the distance was short, in this case just six miles.

As elsewhere, serious and sustained development of air transport had to await the period between the two world wars, although a regular airmail service was started in the United States before the First World War was over. The US Post Office inaugurated a regular airmail service between New York City and Washington, DC on 12 August 1918, and was later to use the United States Air Corps (part of the US Army) for its mail flights until a spate of accidents (probably because of the military pilots' more ambitious approach to flying) cast doubt on safety levels, and it was decided to put the task out to tender. Before this decision, however, the Hubbard Air Service, one of the first American airlines, operated the first North American international airmail service, which began on 3 March 1919 when a Boeing Type C flew between Seattle, Washington, and Victoria, British Columbia. The US Post Office must have been pleased with the service, as a contract was awarded to Hubbard on 14 October 1920.

At the opposite end of the United States, an international air service was inaugurated on 1 November 1920 by Aeromarine West Indies Airways, linking Key West in Florida with Havana in Cuba, a distance of 90 miles. The Caribbean, and especially links with Cuba, featured prominently in the history of US air transport.

The early aeroplane was unreliable, frail, slow, and short on range, and for the United States to have inaugurated a transcontinental airmail service as early as 1 July 1924 was no mean achievement. It should not come as a surprise, though, that this service required no fewer than 14 stops between New York and San Francisco.

The development of air transport in the United States, notwithstanding the similarities between the achievements of Pan American and Imperial Airways, differed widely from that of the United Kingdom, and indeed of mainland Europe. Given the size of the country, internal air services had a far higher priority than in Europe. Because air transport was seen as something for the mass of the people in the United States, it soon lost the sophisticated image that prevailed in Europe. Air fares were lower in America than in Europe, partly because of competition, although at first this was tightly controlled, and it was not until 1978 that deregulation occurred in the US. As elsewhere, deregulation encouraged growth. Small towns that had received a, sometimes subsidised, daily service with a Boeing 737, soon found themselves with a more frequent service using much smaller aircraft. The age of the feeder airline and of hub and spoke operations had dawned, but as traffic volumes increased, so too did the number of direct services. Given lower air fares, Americans did not have to resort to inclusive tour charters to obtain value in air transport, and so it was that in the US, charter (or, in American terminology, supplemental carriers) accounted for just 10 per cent of the market, much of it under contract to the armed forces or to sports clubs, against more than 40 per cent in Europe.

However, the US did have a strong supplemental (or charter) airline industry. Some, such as Saturn Airways, did concentrate mainly on moving US service personnel and their families to overseas postings in Europe and the Far East, while others, such as World Airways, tended to look towards the consumer market and eventually became low-cost carriers.

It was, after all, the United States that invented the low-cost airline, with South-West Airlines being the first. As the 'new' Pan Am experience showed, low-cost has not always meant success, but there have been many airlines that have grown rapidly and profitably as a result, while, as in Europe, many of the established airlines have struggled.

An interesting feature of many United States airports is the importance of general aviation, mainly private fliers, which means that many airports have less than 25 per cent of their total aircraft movements provided by airlines and that (as Appendix III shows) many are very high in the aircraft movements tables even if they are much further down in terms of passengers handled. Most US airports are in municipal ownership, often through a stand-alone authority, which also has responsibility for seaports, and there is some competition over which was the first US municipal airport.

HARTSFIELD-JACKSON ATLANTA INTERNATIONAL: ATL
Atlanta, Georgia, USA

Owner and operator: City of Atlanta Department of Aviation
Runways (all parallel running east-west):
9R/27L, 2,743m (9,000ft); 9L/27R, 3,624m (11,889ft); 8R/26L, 3,048m (10,000ft); 8L/26R, 2,743m (9,000ft); 10/28, 2,743m (9,000ft)
Terminals: One, with six airside concourses
Airlines using airport as base or hub: Delta, World Airways
Annual passengers: 89,379,287
Annual cargo: 720,209 tonnes
Annual aircraft movements: 994,346

The Metropolitan Atlanta Rapid Transit Authority (MARTA) is located on the west end of the terminal between the North and South terminal baggage claim areas.

Background
Situated 16km (10 miles) from the centre of Atlanta, Hartsfield-Jackson is the world's busiest airport, both in the number of passengers handled annually and the number of aircraft movements. There is a single terminal complex, but with no fewer than six concourses, linked by a frequent people mover, with a total of 151 domestic and 28 international gates. One unusual statistic about the airport is that it is the eighth largest consumer of water in the state of Georgia.

Hartsfield-Jackson Atlanta dates from 1925 when the city took a five-year lease on a former motor racing circuit to create an airport, known as Candler Field after the former owners of the site. The first commercial flight was when a Florida Airways mail flight landed from Tampa and Jacksonville on 15 September 1926. Pitcairn Aviation, a predecessor of Eastern Airlines, started a regular airmail service on 1 May 1928. The following year, the city bought the site and the name was changed to Atlanta Municipal Airport. Delta Air Service, the predecessor of today's Delta Air Lines, which is based at the airport, started regular services in June 1930, linking Atlanta with Birmingham, Alabama, and before the end of the year Eastern started a regular passenger service to New York. The airport's first control tower opened in March 1939.

The US government declared the airport an air station in 1940, and in the same year Delta moved its headquarters from Monroe, Louisiana, to Atlanta. During the Second World War the airport doubled in size, and by 1942, with as many as 1,700 aircraft movements in a single day, it was already the nation's busiest.

After the war full-scale commercial operations resumed, using a disused hangar as a temporary terminal, and development continued, so that by 1957 it was the world's busiest. In 1961 a new terminal was opened to cater for 6 million passengers annually, but was used by 9.5 million. One of the founding fathers of the airport, William B. Hartsfield, died in 1971, and the airport was named after him that year. At the same time Eastern introduced the airport's first international services, to Mexico City and Montego Bay. In 1978 the first regular service by a foreign airline began with the launch of flights from Brussels by the Belgian airline, Sabena. The world's largest passenger terminal, capable of handling 55 million passengers annually, opened in 1980. A fourth runway came into operation in 1984, and another was extended to 3,624m (11,889ft) ready for the largest commercial aircraft under development, and in 1988 the airport was linked to the Atlanta rapid transit system. From 1992 facilities for handling horses and perishable food were provided. Four years later, the airport handled the heavy traffic generated by

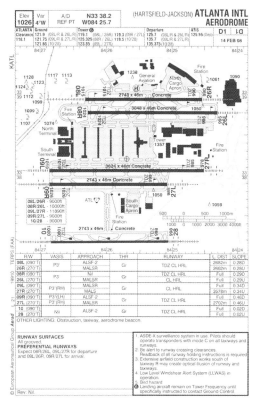

the Olympic Games.

The present name was adopted in 2003 to honour Maynard Jackson, a former mayor of Atlanta. The fifth runway, Georgia's largest construction project, opened in 2006.

The weather can provide major problems for the airport, the most recent instance being the evening of 23 April 2009 when the control tower was struck by lightning during a severe thunderstorm. All movements were already on hold, a 'ground stop', because of dangerous windshear. Four minutes after the lightning strike, smoke was detected and the control tower was evacuated. Although staff returned after 20 minutes, ten minutes later the mains electricity supply failed. Lightning continued, with estimates of up to a thousand strikes an hour, and there was heavy hail. Power was restored, but further cuts followed over the next hour, and even when the airport reopened shortly before midnight, only three runways were operational.

Atlanta has suffered a number of accidents. A Delta Air Lines flight crashed shortly after take-off on 23 May 1960 with the loss of four people. More recently, on 8 June 1995, a ValuJet flight had an engine failure during take-off, which had to be aborted, while on 29 November 2000, an AirTran flight had to return shortly after take-off because of an electrical fire aboard the aircraft. There was also a near miss on 11 January 2008 when an Atlantic Southeast Airlines Bombardier CRJ-200 and a Delta Air Lines Boeing 757 came within 380m (1,250ft) of collision. Before this, on 12 January 2007, a stowaway was found dead in the undercarriage compartment of a Delta Air Lines aircraft that had landed from Dakar, Senegal.

CHICAGO O'HARE: ORD

Chicago, Illinois, USA

Owner: City of Chicago
Operator: Chicago Airport System
Runways: 4L/22R, 2,286m (7,500ft); 4R/22L, 2,461m (8,075ft); 9L/27R, 2,286m (7,500ft); 9R/27L, 2,428m (7,967ft); 10L/28R, 3,962m (13,000ft); 14L/32R, 3,050m (10,005ft); 14R/32L, 3,962m (13,000ft); there is also a large helipad. *(Under a plan approved in 2005, four runways will be added and two decommissioned in order to give the airfield an eight-runway parallel 6+2 configuration, including a new north runway, designated 9L/27R, which will initially serve as a foul weather arrival runway, addressing one of O'Hare's primary causes of delay.)*
Terminals: 1 to 5, with 1 exclusively for United Airlines, and 5 for international flights
Airlines using airport as base or hub: American Airlines, United Airlines, plus a major cargo terminal
Annual passengers: 76,177,855
Annual cargo: 1,533,606 tonnes
Annual aircraft movements: 926,973

Chicago Transit Authority's Blue Line serves an underground station at the airport, and there are bus shuttle feeds to the O'Hare Transfer Station for the Metra North Central Service.

Background

O'Hare's origins lie in an airfield constructed during 1942–3 for the Douglas Aircraft Company to build its C-54 Skymaster (military DC-4) transports for the USAAF during the Second World War. The site was chosen because of Chicago's large population (it was the second largest US city at the time) and the city's excellent railway links, a legacy of its connection with the cattle trade. Because of its proximity to an existing community, Orchard Place, the airfield was known at the time as Orchard Place/Douglas Field, and this led to the ORD designator. The USAAF also based its 803 Special Depot at Orchard Place for the storage of special and experimental aircraft, including a number of captured German and Japanese types retained for evaluation.

After the war the airfield was selected by the City of Chicago as the site for its future main airport, and in 1949 the airport received its present name after a Second World War USN fighter ace, Lieutenant Commander Edward 'Butch' O'Hare. It had become clear that the existing Chicago airport, Midway, which had been the city airport since 1931 and was already congested, would not have room for the projected first generation of jet airliners. Together, the City and the Federal Aviation Administration developed O'Hare as Chicago's main airport. The airport had to be annexed to Chicago by a narrow strip of land so that it fell within the city limits. Commercial passenger flights started in 1955 and an international terminal was built in 1958, but most domestic flights remained at Midway until expansion at O'Hare, completed in 1962, saw domestic flights transferred from Midway, making O'Hare the world's busiest airport, with 10 million passengers annually; within two years this figure had doubled.

The Chicago Transit Authority extended its Blue Line subway system to the airport in 1984.

O'Hare's success created the inevitable problems of congestion in the air and on the ground, despite American Airlines and United Airlines cooperating to avoid congestion at peak periods. While Midway once again became a major air-

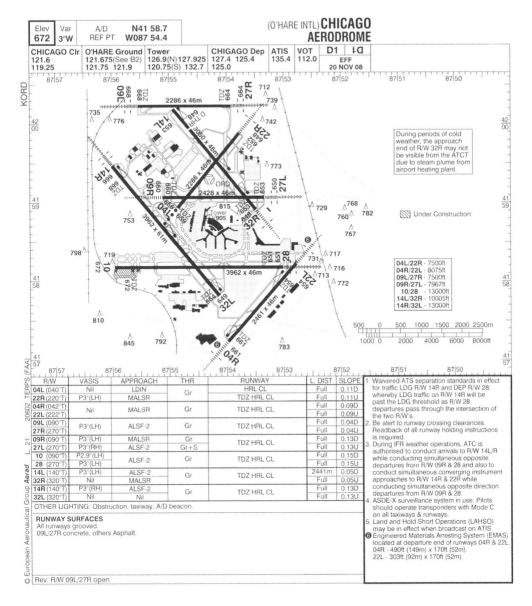

port with growing traffic, an expansion programme for O'Hare was approved in 2005 intended to increase capacity by 60 per cent, with the airport reconfigured with four new runways and two older runways decommissioned to give eight parallel runways and extra terminal space. The first results of this programme are already apparent, with an additional runway available now, and a new air traffic control tower that was commissioned on 20 November 2008.

The airport set the record for the worst single aircraft accident to-date in the US, when, on 25 May 1979, an American Airlines McDonnell Douglas DC-10 bound for Los Angeles crashed on take-off killing all 271 passengers and crew and another 2 people on the ground. There have been a number of other accidents at the airport over the years, as well as a number of incidents. On 17 September 1961, a Northwest Orient (now simply Northwest Airlines) struck overhead power lines shortly after take-off and crashed killing all 37 passengers and crew. This was followed on 27 December 1968 by an aircraft crashing in to a hangar at the airport, killing all 27 passengers and crew and one person on the ground. A North Central Airlines flight crashed after take-off on 20 December 1972, killing ten passengers. A United States Air Force Boeing KC-135 crashed on approach to O'Hare on 19 March 1982, with the loss of all 27 USAF personnel aboard the aircraft. An American Trans Air aircraft exploded into flames on the tarmac on 10 August 1986, and the plane was burnt out, although everyone aboard was evacuated. On 31 October 1994 an American Eagle flight crashed on approach with all 68 passengers and crew killed. An American Airlines flight landing from Kansas City on 9 February 1998 crashed, with 22 passengers injured.

The airport also saw the end of an incident on 8 October 2001, when an American Airlines flight, approaching from Los Angeles, had a psychotic passenger storm the flight deck, but he was subdued by other passengers and flight attendants, while the USAF scrambled two Lockheed Martin F-16 Fighting Falcon interceptors to escort the aircraft to the airport.

LOS ANGELES: LAX

Los Angeles, California, USA

Owner: City of Los Angeles
Operator: Los Angeles World Airports
Runways: 6L/24R, 2,720m (8,925ft); 6R/24L, 3,135m (10,285ft); 7L/25R, 3,685m (12,091ft); 7R/25L, 3,382m (11,096ft); there is also a helipad
Terminals: 1 to 9, plus the Tom Bradley International terminal
Airlines using airport as base or hub: American Eagle, Delta
Annual passengers: 61,896,075
Annual cargo: 1,884,317 tonnes
Annual aircraft movements: 680,954

A shuttle bus provides a free connection to the Aviation/LAX station on the Metro Green Line, and an extension into the airport is seen as a priority for the future.

Background

The main airport for Los Angeles was originally Grand Central Airport in Glendale, but Los Angeles International can trace its long history back to 1928, when the City selected 640 acres in the southern part of the suburb of Westchester as the site of a new airport. At the time, the area was in agricultural use, and the airfield consisted of dirt landing strips without terminal buildings, and was named Mines Field after William W. Mines, the estate agent who handled the sale of the land. The following year the airport received its first building, Hangar No. 1, which was later listed on the US National Register of Historic Places. Nevertheless, the airport was still in private ownership at the time and did not become the official airport for the city until 1930, and was not purchased by the city until 1937. It became Los Angeles Airport in 1941 and Los Angeles International in 1949.

Before the 1930s, existing airports used a two-letter designator based on the weather station at the airports. So, at that time, LA served for Los Angeles International Airport. But, with the rapid growth in the aviation industry, the designators expanded to three letters, and LA became LAX, but the letter X does not have any specific meaning.

As the airport began to expand westwards towards the Pacific, the western perimeter road, Sepulveda Boulevard, was relocated into a tunnel. This was done in 1953, and it is believed that LA was the first airport in the world to allow expansion by such means. In 1958, with the jet age already starting on long haul flights, a master plan was prepared for redevelopment of the airport and expansion, involving a series of terminal buildings linked to a central dome, but the full plan was never completed and the dome was not built. Instead its site was taken by the Theme Building, completed in 1961, which appears like a flying saucer on four legs. Meanwhile, the first

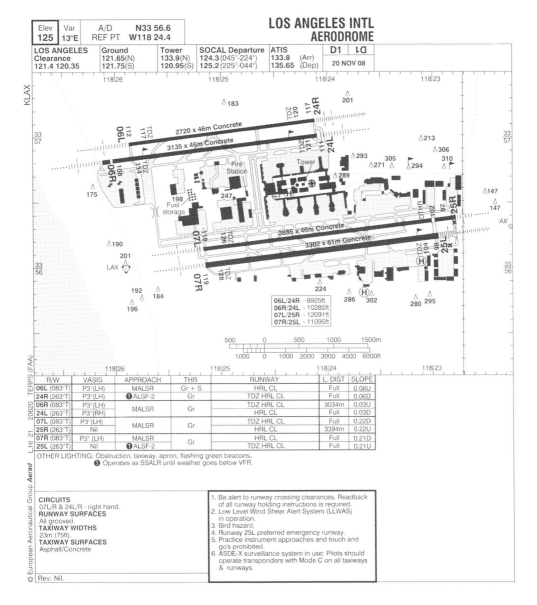

Elev 125	Var 13°E	A/D REF PT	N33 56.6 W118 24.4			LOS ANGELES INTL AERODROME		

LOS ANGELES Clearance 121.4 120.35	Ground 121.65(N) 121.75(S)	Tower 133.9(N) 120.95(S)	SOCAL Departure 124.3(045°-224°) 125.2(225°-044°)	ATIS 133.8 (Arr) 135.65 (Dep)	D1 LD 20 NOV 08

Runway distances:
06L/24R - 8925ft
06R/24L - 10285ft
07L/25R - 12091ft
07R/25L - 11095ft

Runway dimensions:
2720 x 46m Concrete
3135 x 46m Concrete
3685 x 46m Concrete
3382 x 61m Concrete

R/W	VASIS	APPROACH	THR	RUNWAY	L. DIST	SLOPE
06L (083°T)	P3°(LH)	MALSR	Gr + S	HRL CL	Full	0.06U
24R (263°T)	P3°(LH)	❶ALSF-2	Gr	TDZ HRL CL	Full	0.06D
06R (083°T)	P3°(LH)	MALSR	Gr	TDZ HRL CL	3034m	0.03U
24L (263°T)	P3°(RH)			HRL CL	Full	0.03D
07L (083°T)	P3°(LH)	MALSR	Gr	TDZ HRL CL	Full	0.22D
25R (263°T)	Nil			HRL CL	3394m	0.22U
07R (083°T)	P3° (LH)	MALSR	Gr	HRL CL	Full	0.21D
25L (263°T)	Nil	❶ALSF-2		TDZ HRL CL	Full	0.21U

OTHER LIGHTING: Obstruction, taxiway, apron, flashing green beacons.
❶ Operates as SSALR until weather goes below VFR.

CIRCUITS
07L/R & 24L/R - right hand.
RUNWAY SURFACES
All grooved.
TAXIWAY WIDTHS
23m (75ft).
TAXIWAY SURFACES
Asphalt/Concrete

1. Be alert to runway crossing clearances. Readback of all runway holding instructions is required.
2. Low Level Wind Shear Alert System (LLWAS) in operation.
3. Bird hazard.
4. Runway 25L preferred emergency runway.
5. Practice instrument approaches and touch and go's prohibited.
6. ASDE-X surveillance system in use; Pilots should operate transponders with Mode C on all taxiways & runways.

Rev: Nil.

jet service into the airport came in 1959, linking Los Angeles with New York.

In 1981 the airport began a substantial $700 million expansion in preparation for the 1984 Summer Olympics, and to improve traffic flow and ease congestion, the U-shaped roadway leading to the terminal entrances was rebuilt on two levels, with the lower level for picking up arriving passengers and the upper level dedicated to dropping off departing passengers. Two

new terminals (Terminal 1 and the International Terminal) were constructed, and Terminal 2, then two decades old, was rebuilt. A new international terminal was completed on 11 June 1984 and named after a former major, Tom Bradley. In 1996, a new 84m (277ft) tall air traffic control tower was completed.

In common with many major airports, plans for expansion and modernisation have been thwarted by objections from residents and environmental groups. Nevertheless, a compromise has emerged that has led to runway improvements, with Runway 7R/25L moved and rebuilt 55ft south to prevent runway incursions and prepare it for the Airbus A380. The new runway also has storm drains, and enhanced runway lighting. A major facelift of the Tom Bradley International Terminal has also been taking place, recognising that many airlines have been making greater use of other airports, such as San Francisco, because of the terminal's dated appearance.

The United States Coast Guard, USCG, has an air station at the airport, providing air support for its Eleventh District, including search-and-rescue and law enforcement. It also provides helicopters for USCG cutters, in addition to the three helicopters which are permanently assigned to the station.

There have been a number of serious accidents at the airport, or to aircraft in the vicinity of the airport. On 13 January 1969 an SAS (Scandinavian Airlines System) Douglas DC-8-62, approaching from Seattle, crashed into the sea 11km (almost 7 miles) west of the airport, and it appears that everyone aboard survived the accident, but 3 of the 9 crew and 12 of the 36 passengers drowned afterwards. Just a few days later, on 18 January, a United Airlines Boeing 727-100 also crashed into the sea 18km (just over 11 miles) west of the airport killing all 6 crew and all 32 passengers. An accident after take-off occurred on 6 June 1971 to an Airwest Douglas DC-9 bound for Salt Lake City when it was struck by a United States Marine Corps McDonnell F-4 Phantom just nine minutes into the flight, with the loss of all 5 crew and 44 passengers aboard the flight, and 1 of the 2 crew in the fighter. A Continental Airlines McDonnell Douglas DC-10, taking off for Honolulu, suffered a series of tyre bursts on 1 March 1978, with the left main landing gear collapsing and rupturing a fuel tank. The take-off was aborted, but the aircraft was enveloped in flames by the wings, and two people died when they used the over-wing emergency exit and fell into the flames, and another two died of their burns later, while 74 passengers and crew were injured, as

were 11 airport firemen. Another accident occurred to a Swift Aire Nord 262 after it had taken off for Santa Monica on 10 March 1979, when engine problems forced it to ditch, with the loss of both pilots and a passenger, while a cabin attendant and three other passengers escaped. There was a ground collision on 1 February 1991 as a USAir (now US Airways) Boeing 737 landed and collided with a Skywest Fairchild Metroliner about to take off for Palmdale. All 12 passengers and crew on the Metroliner were killed along with 22 aboard the USAir flight.

A JetBlue Airbus A320 with an undercarriage problem made an emergency landing at Los Angeles on 21 September 2005, after circling for three hours to burn off fuel, with the nose wheel collapsing as the aircraft landed without any casualties. It was later repaired and returned to service.

The airport also suffered a terrorist attack, when a bomb exploded in Terminal 2 on 6 August 1974, killing three people and wounding another 35. Nevertheless, an Al-Qaeda attack in 2000 was foiled when the would-be bomber was caught as he attempted to enter the United States with explosives in the boot of his car. A gunman killed two Israelis at the El Al ticket counter at the airport on 4 July 2002.

DALLAS/FORT WORTH: DFW
Dallas and Fort Worth, Texas, USA

Owner: City of Dallas & City of Fort Worth

Operator: DFW Airport Board

Runways: 17L/35R, 2,590m (8,500ft); 17C/35C, 4,085m (13,400ft); 17R/35L, 4,085m (13,400ft); 18L/36R, 4,085m (13,400ft); 18R/36L, 4,085m (13,400ft); 13L/31R, 3,425m (11,240ft); 13R/31L, 2,835m (9,300ft); plus one helipad

Terminals: Five, with A, B, C, and E for domestic passengers, and D for international passengers (a high speed 'Skylink' train connects all terminals)

Airlines using airport as base or hub: American Airlines

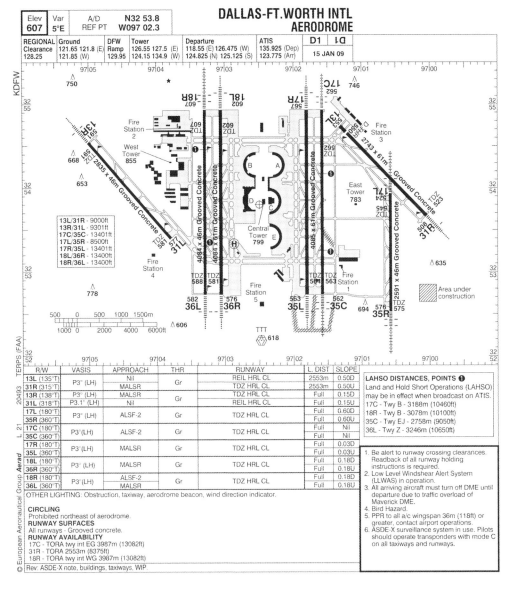

Annual passengers: 59,786,476
Annual cargo: 724,140 tonnes
Annual aircraft movements: 685,491

The only airport in the world with three control towers.

Background

In 1927 a joint airport to serve both Dallas and Fort Worth was suggested, but Fort Worth decided that it wanted its own airport so both cities opened their own airports, Dallas at Love Field, Fort Worth at Meacham Field. Despite their close proximity, both airports attracted scheduled services. It was not until 1940 that the Civil Aviation Administration offered US $1.9 million for the construction of a joint airport, but despite a site being proposed by both American Airlines and Braniff Airways, the two cities continued to disagree and, with the involvement of the United States in the Second World War, the project was abandoned. It was not until after the war ended that Fort Worth selected the site and developed it with American Airlines as Amon Carter Field, and in 1953 flights were transferred to the new airport from Meacham Field.

Fort Worth purchased Amon Carter Field in 1960 and renamed it Greater Southwest International Airport (GSWI), but the new airport suffered in competition with that of Dallas Love Field, just 19km (12 miles) away. By the middle of the decade, Dallas was attracting 49 per cent of all Texas air traffic, and Fort Worth just one per cent. Meanwhile, the Federal Aviation Administration (FAA) refused to invest further in separate airports for the two cities. While GSWI was abandoned, Dallas Love Field was congested and could not expand. Eventually, under FAA pressure, the two cities agreed on a site just north of GSWI and equidistant from the two city centres. A joint purchase of the land was made in 1966 and construction started in 1969, with completion in 1973 marked by a visit by the Anglo-French Concorde supersonic airliner. For a short time, until Braniff pulled out, there was a collaborative agreement between Braniff, British Airways, and Air France.

Dallas/Fort Worth (DFW) opened finally on 13 January 1974, becoming Dallas/Fort Worth International in 1985, by which time Love Field was closed to longer distance flights. In 1979 American Airlines moved its headquarters to the old GSWI and established its first hub at DFW in 1981, with transatlantic flights to London following in 1982, and transpacific flights to Tokyo in 1987. Delta Air Lines also established a hub at DFW around this time, but this closed in 2004 as part of a restructuring. Continued development saw the airport open a seventh runway in 1996, while the existing runways were extended, making DFW the only airport in the world to have four runways in excess of 4,000m (13,000ft).

The new terminal D, solely for international flights, opened in July 2005. In May of that year, Skylink, the world's largest rapid airport railway system, opened, with fully-automated trains running between the terminals every few minutes at speeds of around 35–40mph, replacing an earlier, much slower TrAAin system.

There have been a number of serious accidents at the airport. One of these was caused by severe windshear on 2 August 1985, which was encountered by a Delta Air Lines Lockheed TriStar landing from Fort Lauderdale, which crashed killing 8 of the 11 crew and 128 of the 152 passengers, as well as one person on the ground. A take-off accident involved another Delta flight, bound for Salt Lake City, when the Boeing 727 crashed killing 2 out of the 7 crew and 12 of the 101 passengers. More fortunate were those aboard an American Airlines McDonnell Douglas MD-80 which took off for Orlando and had to return after an engine failure, but landed successfully.

DENVER INTERNATIONAL: DEN
Denver, Colorado, USA

Owner and operator: City and County of Denver Department of Aviation
Runways: 7/25, 3,658m (12,000ft); 8/26, 3,658m (12,000ft); 16L/34R, 3,658m (12,000ft); 16R/34L, 4,877m (16,000ft); 17L/35R, 3,658m (12,000ft); 17R/35L, 3,658m (12,000ft)
Terminals: One, known as the Jeppesen
Airlines using airport as base or hub: Frontier Airlines, Great Lakes Airlines, and the second hub for United Airlines
Annual passengers: 49,863,352
Annual cargo: 267,294 tonnes
Annual aircraft movements: 614,065

Railway link to Denver city centre planned for 2015.

Background
Built to replace the congested Stapleton International, Denver opened on 28 February 1995, some 16 months late, and the final cost of US $4.8 billion was some $2 billion over the original estimate. All of the runways were completed before the airport opened, and a temporary des-

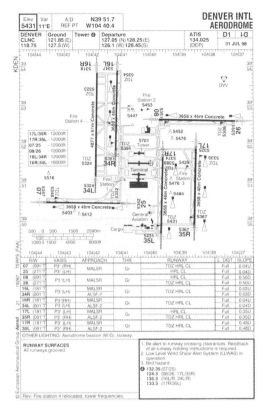

Elev	Var	A/D	N39 51.7	DENVER INTL
5431	11°E	REF PT	W104 40.4	AERODROME

DENVER	Ground	Tower ☉	Departure	ATIS	D1	LD
CLNC	121.85 (E)		127.05 (N) 128.25 (E)	134.025		
118.75	127.5 (W)		126.1 (W) 128.45(S)	(DEP)		31 JUL 08

17L/35R - 12000ft
17R/35L - 12000ft
07/25 - 12000ft
08/26 - 12000ft
16L/34R - 12000ft
16R/34L - 16000ft

R/W	VASIS	APPROACH	THR	RUNWAY	L. DIST	SLOPE
07	(091)	P3' (RH)	MALSR	Gr	TDZ HRL CL	Full	0.04U
25	(271)	P3' (LH)			HRL CL	Full	0.04D
08	(091)	P3'(LH)	MALSR	Gr	HRL CL	Full	0.50D
26	(271)				TDZ HRL CL	Full	0.50U
16L	(181)	P3' (LH)	MALSR	Gr		Full	0.03U
34R	(001)		ALSF-2		TDZ HRL CL	Full	0.03D
16R	(181)	P3'(RH)	MALSR	Gr		Full	0.04U
34L	(001)	P3' (LH)	ALSF-2		TDZ HRL CL	Full	0.04D
17L	(181)	P3' (LH)	MALSR	Gr	HRL CL	Full	0.35U
35R	(001)	P3' (RH)	ALSF-2		TDZ HRL CL	Full	0.35D
17R	(181)	P3' (LH)	MALSR	Gr		Full	0.48U
35L	(001)	P3' (RH)	ALSF-2		TDZ HRL CL	Full	0.48D

OTHER LIGHTING: Aerodrome beacon (W/G), taxiway.

RUNWAY SURFACES
All runways grooved.

1. Be alert to runway crossing clearances. Readback of all runway holding instructions is required.
2. Low Level Wind Shear Alert System (LLWAS) in operation.
3. Bird hazard.
4. **132.35** (07/25)
   124.3 (08/26, 17L/35R)
   135.3 (16L/R, 34L/R)
   133.3 (17R/35L)

© European Aeronautical Group Aerad

© Rev: Fire station 4 relocated, tower frequencies.

NEW YORK
JOHN F. KENNEDY: JFK
New York, New York State, USA

Owner and operator: Port Authority of New York & New Jersey

Runways: 4L/22R, 3,460m (11,351ft); 4R/22L, 2,560m (8,400ft); 13L/31R, 3,048m (10,000ft); 13R/31L, 4,442m (14,572ft); there are also four helipads

Terminals: Eight, Nos. 1 to 8, arranged in a U-shape around a central area

Airlines using airport as base or hub: JetBlue, North American Airlines, and Polar Air Cargo, but also used as a hub by American Airlines and Delta

Annual passengers: 47,716,941

Annual cargo: 1,607,050 tonnes

Annual aircraft movements: 446,348

AirTrain JFK links all terminals and also connects with the New York City Subway and the Long Island Railroad to provide access to the centre of New York.

Background

Construction started in 1943 on the Idlewild golf course and for many years the airport was known unofficially as Idlewild, but officially as the Major General Alexander E. Anderson Airport, after a local National Guard (effectively the US Army's locally-raised reserve force) commander who died in 1942. Even after the airport opened on 1 July 1948, and was officially named New York International Airport, it was generally known as Idlewild, and its designator was IDL. At the time, two US airlines were designated as national flag carriers for the North Atlantic routes, Pan American (Pan Am) and Trans World Airlines (TWA). In 1962, with the jet age already started on transatlantic services, Pan Am opened its own terminal, the Worldport (now Terminal 3), one of the first to have jetways so that passengers could walk straight from the terminal to the aircraft without using air stairs, and TWA opened the TWA Flight Center (now Terminal 5). Neither airline exists today.

ignation was provided until the airport opened and took DEN from the old Denver Stapleton.

Denver is 40km (25 miles) from the city centre, so is more remote than Stapleton. The airport has a single massive terminal, Jeppesen, and has six runways, including the longest in the United States, 16R/34L, which at 4,877m (16,000ft) is the second longest in the world. The airport is the largest by area in the United States.

Despite being hot in summer, severe winter weather can be a problem in Colorado, and the airport has not escaped the worst of this. On 31 October 2002, freezing fog and rain resulted in a number of aircraft engines being damaged by ice during take-off. A heavy blizzard in March 2003 tore a hole in the white fabric roof of the Jeppesen terminal and closed the airport for two days, with up to 2ft of snow on runways.

Continued expansion saw JFK become New York's leading airport during the mid-1980s. Between 1977 and 2003, JFK was the US destination for the Concorde supersonic airliner services of both British Airways and Air France, which gave it the distinction of turning round more supersonic airliner flights than any airport in the world, even though no US airline operated the aircraft.

Today, JFK handles more international travellers than any other US airport.

Given the heavy traffic handled and the long time the airport has been open, it is inevitable that there have been a number of serious accidents. One of the earliest on record was on 18 December 1954, when a Linee Aeree Italiane (later absorbed into Alitalia) Douglas DC-6 crashed on its fourth approach after circling for 150 minutes, killing 26 of the 32 passengers. Another even more serious accident was on 16 December 1960 when a United Airlines Douglas DC-8 and a TWA Lockheed Super Constellation collided on approach, with the DC-8 crashing in Brooklyn and the Super Constellation on Staten Island, with the loss of all 127 people on board and another 5 on the ground. On 1 March 1962, an American Airlines Boeing 707 crashed after taking off when the rudder separated from the tail, killing all 12 crew and 95 passengers. Two accidents in succession involved Eastern Air Lines and two of its Douglas DC-7s, one of which crashed during a missed approach on 30 November 1962 and the other off Jones Beach following take-off when the pilots tried to avoid a Pan Am Boeing 707.

Not all of the accidents have involved aircraft on passenger service. One exception was a Trans International Airlines Douglas DC-8-63F freighter on a positioning flight to Washington Dulles on 8 September 1970, which suffered a loss of control during take-off when an elevator jammed, causing it to crash and killing all 11 crew aboard. Another positioning flight saw a Northwest Orient (now Northwest Airlines) Boeing 727 on 1 December 1974, flying to pick up a sports team at Buffalo, crash after the crew failed to turn on the pitot heater – it froze, deny-

When TWA was taken over after some years of contraction, its terminal was abandoned until it was taken over and rebuilt as a completely new terminal by low-cost carrier JetBlue, which opened it in late 2008.

The airport's current title was adopted in 1963, a month after the assassination of President John F. Kennedy, and was given the new IATA code KIA, but this was changed later because, to most Americans, it had connotations of 'Killed in Action' and the war in Vietnam was at its height in the years that followed. The current code, JFK, was adopted in 1968, and once again the airport has an unofficial but widely used title, simply 'JFK' or 'New York JFK'.

In 1970, National Airlines (later acquired by Pan Am to give the airline a domestic network) opened its Sundrome, which is today's Terminal 6, and which was used by JetBlue during the airline's early days.

ing them any airspeed readings. The crew of three were killed.

Windshear during a heavy thunderstorm on 24 June 1975 resulted in an Eastern Air Lines Boeing 727, landing from New Orleans, hitting the runway lights and killing all 112 passengers and crew. On 25 January 1990 an Avianca Boeing 707-320, landing from Bogotá and Medellín, crashed after missing the approach to JFK and then running out of fuel. More fortunate were those aboard a TWA Lockheed TriStar, taking-off for San Francisco, which aborted shortly after lift-off, but while the aircraft was destroyed, all 280 people aboard survived. The worst so far was on 12 November 2001 when an American Airlines Airbus A300, which had just taken-off for Santo Domingo, crashed in Queens after losing most of the fin in severe wake turbulence as the co-pilot applied severe pressure to the rudder. All 260 passengers and crew, and another five people on the ground, were killed.

LAS VEGAS McCARRAN INTERNATIONAL: LAS

Clark County, Las Vegas, Nevada, USA

Owner and operator: Clark County
Runways: 1L/19R, 2,739m (8,985ft); 1R/19L, 2,979m (9,775ft); 7L/25R, 4,423m (14,510ft); 7R/25L, 3,208m (10,526ft)
Terminals: Three, 1 and 2, with Terminal 3 scheduled to open in 2012
Annual passengers: 49,961,011
Annual cargo: 91,205 tonnes
Annual aircraft movements: 609,472

Background

The site of the airport has been in use since 1942, when George Crockett, a descendant of the famous Davy Crockett, opened Alamo Airport. The airport was purchased by the local authority, Clark County, in 1948, and renamed as Clark County Public Airport. It was renamed again in December that year as McCarran Field, after Senator Pat McCarran, the Nevada politician who introduced the Civil Aeronautics Act.

With Las Vegas growing into a major tourist resort, traffic grew considerably after the war, and in March 1963 a new terminal opened at Paradise Road, closing the old terminal in Las Vegas Boulevard South. The new terminal was based on that for Trans World Airlines (TWA) at what was still New York International (today's New York John F. Kennedy). In 1978 Congress passed the Airline Deregulation Act, freeing airlines from government control over their routes, and as a result, the number of airlines serving McCarran doubled from 7 to 14 over a short period. The impact on the airport was such that a development programme, 'McCarran 2000', was adopted in 1978 and funded by a $300 million bond in 1982. The developments included a new central terminal with a nine-storey car park, as well as runway additions and expansions, and a new tunnel and revamped roadways into the airport. The first phase of McCarran 2000 opened in 1985 and was completed by 1987. This

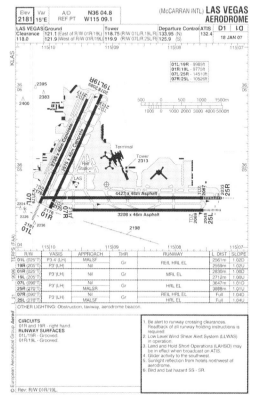

was followed by the construction of a second terminal, Terminal 2, replacing two smaller terminals that had been used by American Airlines and Pacific South West Airlines, and which opened in 1997. In late 2003, the airport introduced SpeedCheck kiosks which enabled passengers to check in quickly regardless of which airline they had booked with – the first airport in the world to offer this facility. That same year the airport was one of the first to introduce a baggage-tracking system using radio frequency identification (RFID) bag tags to improve air safety.

Most flights use Terminal 1, but Terminal 2 also handles scheduled and charter flights, including international services, while the airport's many tourist sight-seeing flights also use this terminal. There are plans to extend the Las Vegas monorail to the airport, serving terminals 1 and 3.

There is no record of a fatal aircraft accident at the airport, but aircraft have been written off in accidents. One of these was on 15 November 1956 when a TWA Martin 404 suffered an engine failure after taking off for Los Angeles, and the captain opted to return to Las Vegas. He landed too fast, and in attempting a go-around lost control and the aircraft skidded to a halt. The 3 crew and 35 passengers were unharmed. A training flight on a Fairchild FH-227 (licence-built Fokker F-27) of Bonanza Airlines on 18 April 1965 resulted in the loss of the aircraft after a full flap landing was followed by a flapless take-off, but in fact the flaps were extended unevenly and the aircraft spun off the runway. The two pilots were unharmed. A piston-engined Lockheed Starliner of Fly by Night Safaris was lost on 9 December 1968 when it was refuelled with kerosene (i.e. jet fuel) and the engines failed shortly after lifting off, with the aircraft wrecked on the runway, but fortunately the 8 crew and 96 passengers all survived. A TWA Boeing 707-320 parked at the airport was damaged beyond repair when a bomb exploded on the flight deck on 8 March 1972. No one was aboard, but earlier a demand had been made for US $2 million otherwise a bomb would be planted on a TWA aircraft.

HOUSTON GEORGE BUSH INTERCONTINENTAL: IAH
Houston, Texas, USA

Owner and operator: Houston Airport System
Runways: 15L/33R, 3,658m (12,001ft); 15R/33L, 3,048m (10,000ft); 9/27, 3,048m (10,000ft); 8L/26R, 2,743m (9,000ft); 8R/26L, 2,866m (9,402ft)
Terminals: Five, A, B, C, and international D and E
Annual passengers: 42,998,040
Annual cargo: 409,193 tonnes
Annual aircraft movements: 603,656

Background
Originally known as Houston Intercontinental, the airport opened in June 1969, replacing the earlier William P. Hobby Airport, which remained open for general aviation and, in recent years, has also begun to handle low-cost airlines. Opening was in fact two years late because of design changes. Of the original terminals, just A and B remain, while the Lewis W. Cutrer Terminal C opened in 1981 and the Mickey Leland International Airlines Building, Terminal D, opened in May 1990, while the new Terminal E was fully opened on 7 January 2004. Terminal D is the arrival point for all international flights into Houston, except for flights operated by Continental Airlines, which use Terminal E.

The idea of renaming the airport came in the late 1980s, when the proposal was made that it should be named after a local Congressman, Mickey Leland, but after some controversy locally the plan was shelved and it was not until 1997 that it was given the current name, after George H. W. Bush, the 41st President of the United States.

In the USA, Houston George Bush International ranks as the third most important in terms of domestic passengers handled and is the seventh in terms of international passengers. In 2007 it was seventh worldwide in terms of total aircraft movements.

The terminals are linked by a surface train and there is an underground train linking the ter-

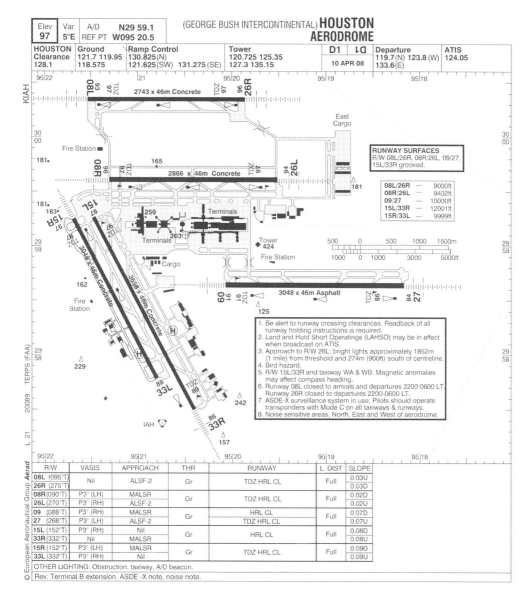

Elev 97	Var 5°E	A/D REF PT	N29 59.1 W095 20.5	(GEORGE BUSH INTERCONTINENTAL) **HOUSTON AERODROME**				
HOUSTON Clearance 128.1	Ground 121.7 119.95 118.575	Ramp Control 130.825(N) 121.625(SW) 131.275(SE)		Tower 120.725 125.35 127.3 135.15	D1 ⌐◻ 10 APR 08	Departure 119.7(N) 123.8(W) 133.6(E)	ATIS 124.05	

RUNWAY SURFACES
R/W 08L/26R, 08R/26L, 09/27, 15L/33R grooved.

08L/26R	—	9000ft
08R/26L	—	9402ft
09/27	—	10000ft
15L/33R	—	12001ft
15R/33L	—	9999ft

East Cargo

2743 x 46m Concrete
2866 x 46m Concrete
3048 x 46m Asphalt
3048 x 46m Concrete
3658 x 46m Concrete

Fire Station
Terminals
Terminals
Cargo
Tower 424
Fire Station
Fire Station

1. Be alert to runway crossing clearances. Readback of all runway holding instructions is required.
2. Land and Hold Short Operatings (LAHSO) may be in effect when broadcast on ATIS.
3. Approach to R/W 26L: bright lights approximately 1852m (1 mile) from threshold and 274m (900ft) south of centreline.
4. Bird hazard.
5. R/W 15L/33R and taxiway WA & WB: Magnetic anomalies may affect compass heading.
6. Runway 08L closed to arrivals and departures 2200-0600 LT. Runway 26R closed to departures 2200-0600 LT.
7. ASDE-X surveillance system in use: Pilots should operate transponders with Mode C on all taxiways & runways.
8. Noise sensitive areas, North, East and West of aerodrome.

R/W	VASIS	APPROACH	THR	RUNWAY	L. DIST	SLOPE
08L (095°T)	Nil	ALSF-2	Gr	TDZ HRL CL	Full	0.03U
26R (275°T)						0.03D
08R(090°T)	P3° (LH)	MALSR	Gr	TDZ HRL CL	Full	0.02D
26L (270°T)	P3° (RH)	ALSF-2				0.02U
09 (088°T)	P3° (RH)	MALSR	Gr	HRL CL	Full	0.07D
27 (268°T)	P3° (LH)	ALSF-2		TDZ HRL CL		0.07U
15L (152°T)	P3° (RH)	Nil	Gr	HRL CL	Full	0.08D
33R (332°T)	Nil	MALSR				0.08U
15R (152°T)	P3° (LH)	MALSR	Gr	TDZ HRL CL	Full	0.09D
33L (332°T)	P3° (RH)	Nil				0.09U

OTHER LIGHTING: Obstruction, taxiway, A/D beacon.
Rev: Terminal B extension, ASDE -X note, noise note.

© European Aeronautical Group **Aerad**

minals, albeit at some distance from them, but there is no railway link into the airport.

There have been a couple of serious accidents in recent years. One of these was on 19 February 1996 when a Continental Airlines Douglas DC-9, coming in from Washington, landed with its undercarriage up and slid along the runway, but there were only minor injuries amongst the passengers and crew. Another Continental Airlines aircraft, a Boeing 737-500, landing from Denver on 20 December 2008, overshot the runway and caught fire, with 38 of the passengers and crew injured, some of them seriously.

PHOENIX SKY HARBOR INTERNATIONAL: PHX

Phoenix, Arizona, USA

Owner: City of Phoenix

Operator: Phoenix Airport System

Runways: 7L/25R, 3,139m (10,300ft); 7R/25L, 2,377m (7,800ft); 8/26, 3,502m (11,489ft)

Terminals: Three, Nos. 2, 3, and 4

Airlines using airport as base or hub:

Southwest Airlines is the main operator, but is also used as a hub by US Airways and Great Lakes Airways

Annual passengers: 42,184,515

Annual cargo: 251,925 tonnes

Annual aircraft movements: 539,211

A free shuttle bus service links the terminals with the Metro light railway, and this is due to be replaced soon by the Sky Harbor Airport Automated People Mover.

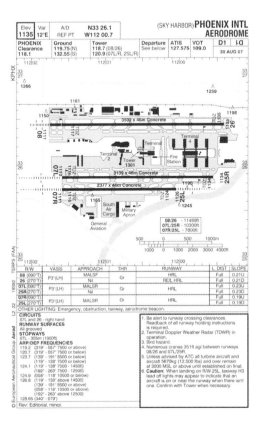

Background

Although one of the major airports in the United States, until recently the only services outside the United States and Canada was that by British Airways to London, although by the time of publication both Emirates and the German airline, Lufthansa, may also be operating into Phoenix. The airport is owned by the local authority and is a joint civil and military operation.

The airport dates from the late 1920s and was purchased by the local authority in 1935, by which time the name Sky Harbor was already in use as was the 'PH' designator, later extended to the present PHX when three-letter designators became necessary. A new terminal was opened in 1952, and until 1990, when this was demolished, this was Terminal 1. Terminal 2 opened in 1962 and Terminal 3 in 1979, while Terminal 4 opened in 1990 and has been named after the 1964 presidential candidate, Senator Barry S. Goldwater. International flights use Terminal 4. Terminal 2 includes a Military and Veterans Hospitality Room, sponsored by the Phoenix Military and Veterans Commission. Rapid growth in recent years has meant that Phoenix-Mesa Gateway is being used as a satellite. For the future, demolition of Terminal 2 is planned, with replacement by a new West Terminal.

The airport is the main base for the Arizona Air National Guard and its 161st Air Refueling Wing (161 ARW), an AANG Air Mobility Command (AMC) unit.

The airport has not suffered any serious accidents to aircraft either landing or taking off.

ORLANDO INTERNATIONAL: MCO

Orlando, Florida, USA

Owner and operator: Orlando Greater Aviation Authority

Runways: 17L/35R, 2,743m (9,000ft); 17R/35L, 3,048m (10,000ft); 18L/36R, 3,659m (12,005ft); 18R/36L, 3,659m (12,005ft)

Terminals: A single central terminal connected to four satellite terminals by an overhead railway

Airlines using airport as base or hub: AirTran
HQ, and hub for AirTran
Annual passengers: 36,480,416
Annual cargo: 183,070 tonnes
Annual aircraft movements: 360,075

Background

Originally opened as McCoy USAF base, Orlando started to handle scheduled commercial flights in 1970 when Delta Airlines, Eastern Airlines, National Airlines (later absorbed by Pan Am, providing that airline with a US domestic network), and Southern Airlines all started services. Four years later, McCoy closed, leaving Orlando as a purely civil airport, with ownership transferred to the city the following year when the Great Orlando Aviation Authority was established. In 1976 the airport was renamed Orlando International. Serving the popular Florida resorts, the airport became the fastest growing in the United States by 1978, when United, TWA, and USAir introduced services, followed by Northwest in 1979, when the FAA designated the airport as a hub. American Airlines and Continental Airlines added Orlando to their networks in 1981, the same year that a second terminal, the north terminal, opened. International operations followed in 1984 when Icelandair introduced a service to Orlando, followed by British Airways, and Bahamasair in 1985. Other airlines followed, including KLM and TransBrasil, so that in 1989, when a third runway opened, international traffic more than doubled. In addition to scheduled and charter services to Latin America, Canada, and Europe, by 1993 the low-cost airline, Valujet, was also serving Orlando, and by 1996 it was the world's fastest growing airport.

To cope with the expansion a fourth runway opened in 2003, a year after what was then the tallest air traffic control tower in the USA had opened at Orlando. Freight facilities had also grown, and FedEx was operating regular services into and out of the airport. JetBlue also established a training facility at Orlando. Nevertheless, the following year, three hurricanes,

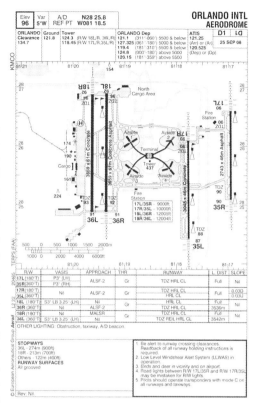

Charley, Frances, and Jeanne stopped operations for a total of six days – a hazard for airports close to the Caribbean.

There have been few of the more usual incidents at the airport since it opened for commercial use. The most notable was on 2 April 1994 when a Continental Airlines Boeing 727-200, en route from Newark to Fort Myers, diverted to Orlando because of undercarriage problems. Having burnt off most of the fuel, the aircraft landed safely without harm to the 9 crew or 141 passengers.

NEWARK LIBERTY INTERNATIONAL/NEW YORK NEWARK: EWR

Newark, New Jersey, USA

Owners: The Port Authority of New York and New Jersey

Runways: 4L/22R, 3,353m (11,000ft); 4R/22L, 3,048m (10,000ft); 11/29, 2,073m (6,800ft); there is also a helipad

Terminals: Three, designated A, B, and C

Airlines using airport as base or hub: Second main hub for Continental Airlines and third for Federal Express (FedEx), which has a major cargo terminal

Annual passengers: 36,367,240

Annual cargo: 963,794 tonnes

Annual aircraft movements: 435,691

A monorail system, AirTrain Newark, connects the terminals with the Newark Liberty International Airport Rail Link Station for connection to Amtrak and New Jersey Transit service, which includes transfers to New York's Penn Central Station.

Background

Although these days viewed as an alternative to the two New York airports at JFK and La Guardia, Newark is itself now a busy and sometimes congested hub. It was the first major airport in the New York area and opened on 1 October 1928, after an area of New Jersey marshland had been reclaimed. In 1935 the pioneering aviatrix Amelia Earhart opened the Newark Airport Administration Building, North America's first commercial airline terminal, and second only to that at Croydon, England. Newark was the busiest airport in the world until La Guardia Airport opened in 1939, dividing New York's air traffic and allowing Chicago Midway International Airport to become the busiest. Initially, the airport had been known simply as Newark Airport, and then Newark International Airport, but after the war it became known as Newark Liberty International Airport, but for many passengers it is simply 'New York Newark'.

During the Second World War, Newark was closed to commercial traffic and became a United States Army Air Force air transport base and logistics centre.

The Port Authority of New York and New Jersey took over the airport in 1948, with airline traffic resumed, while the port authority undertook major improvements, including building new runways and hangars, and updating the airport's terminal. The original Administration Building remained in use as a terminal until the opening of a new terminal, known initially as the North Terminal, in 1953. In 1979 the Administrative Building was added to the US National Register of Historic Places. Plans to relocate the airport and create a new international airport for the entire New York and New Jersey area on what is now the Great Swamp National Wildlife Refuge were defeated by conservationists. This meant that further development and enlargement became necessary, and during the 1970s the

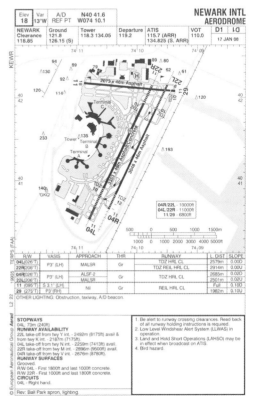

current terminals A, B, and C were built, with the first two opening in 1973, while the North Terminal remained in use mainly for charter and international flights. Despite being almost complete, Terminal C was mothballed and then used only for certain flights until being finally completed and opened in June 1988.

Despite this expansion, Newark was under-used for many years while there was still surplus capacity at the other two airports in the New York area. This persisted throughout the 1970s, and it was not until People Express decided to use the airport as its base and main hub in 1981 that rapid expansion began. When Virgin Atlantic introduced flights from London to Newark in 1984, it once again became an international gateway, and in 1986, Federal Express chose Newark as its second hub. Even after People Express was acquired by Continental in 1987, Newark remained important as a hub for Continental, which today has its 'Global Gateway' at Terminal C, and in 2001 the airport became the US terminus of what was then the world's longest non-stop air service, that by Continental to Hong Kong. This record was broken in 2004 when Singapore Airlines introduced a non-stop 18-hour service from Singapore to Newark, and then later Continental began services to Beijing and Delhi in 2005, when it became the only airline providing a non-stop service to India from North America.

These developments and others meant that Newark soon became congested rather than under-used, and flight caps were introduced in June 2008, limiting the airport to 81 flights an hour, but these were short-term measures that expired in 2009.

Given its size and the number of aircraft movements, the airport has suffered relatively few serious accidents and incidents in recent years. On 31 July 1997 a FedEx McDonnell Douglas MD-11 cargo flight, arriving from Anchorage, landed heavily and the No. 3 engine struck the runway, with the aircraft overturning and being destroyed by fire, but the three crew members and two people riding in the jump seats escaped without harm. On 28 October 2006 a Continental Airlines Boeing 757 landed on Taxiway Z instead of Runway 29, but there were no casualties. Both pilots were dismissed.

On 11 September 2001 a United Airlines flight to San Francisco was amongst the aircraft hijacked by terrorists that day, but the passengers attacked the hijackers and the aircraft dived into a field rather than into the intended terrorist target, believed by many to have been the White House.

DETROIT METROPOLITAN WAYNE COUNTY: DTW
Detroit, Michigan, USA

Owners: Wayne County, Michigan
Operator: Wayne County Airport Authority
Runways: 4R/22L, 3,659m (12,003ft); 4L/22R, 3,048m (10,000ft); 3R/21L, 3,048m (10,000ft); 3L/21R, 2,591m (8,501ft); 9L/27R, 2,654m (8,708ft); 9R/27L, 2,591m (8,501ft)
Terminals: Two, the Edward H. McNamara Terminal and the North Terminal
Airlines using airport as base or hub:
    Northwest, Northwest Airlink (provided by Compass), Pinnacle, and Mesaba Airlines
Annual passengers: 35,983,478
Annual cargo: 233,034 tonnes
Annual aircraft movements: 467,230

Connections to the regional railway system are planned for the longer term.

Background
Wayne County dates from 1930 when Thompson Aeronautical Corporation, later absorbed into American Airlines, began operations from the airport, which had been built by the County on a site that is now part of the north-eastern corner of the current airport, while the original runway is now part of two taxiways, M-4 and P-4. Between 1931 and 1945, the airfield was shared with the Michigan Air National Guard, the USAAC's reserve force in Michigan.

With the end of the war, expansion of the airport resumed and it grew to become the main airport for Detroit. It was renamed Detroit-

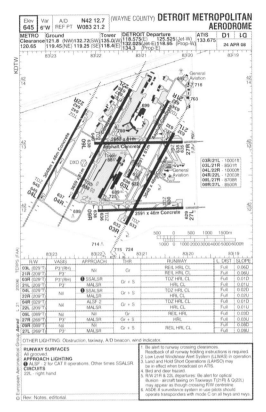

| Elev | Var | A/D | N42 12.7 | (WAYNE COUNTY) **DETROIT METROPOLITAN** |
| 645 | 6°W | REF PT | W083 21.2 | **AERODROME** |

METRO	Ground	Tower	DETROIT Departure	ATIS	D1	LQ
Clearance 121.8 (NW)132.72(SW)135.0(W) 118.575(E) 125.525(Jet-W)	133.675	24 APR 08
120.65	119.45 (NE) 119.25 (SE)118.4(E) 132.025(Jet-E) 118.95 (Prop-W) 134.3 (Prop-E)

03R/21L - 10001ft
03L/21R - 8501ft
04L/22R - 10000ft
04R/22L - 12003ft
09L/27R - 8708ft
09R/27L - 8500ft

R/W	VASIS	APPROACH	THR	RUNWAY	L DIST	SLOPE
03L (029°T)	P3'(RH)	Nil	Gr	REIL HRL CL	Full	0.06D
21R (209°T)	P3'			REIL HRL CL	Full	0.06U
03R (029°T)	P3'(RH)	❶ SSALSR	Gr + S	TDZ HRL CL	Full	0.01D
21L (209°T)	P3'	MALSR		HRL CL	Full	0.01U
04L (029°T)	Nil	❶ SSALSR	Gr + S	TDZ HRL CL	Full	0.02D
22R (209°T)	Nil	MALSR		HRL CL	Full	0.02U
04R (029°T)	Nil	ALSF-2	Gr + S	TDZ HRL CL	Full	0.01D
22L (209°T)	Nil	MALSR		HRL CL	Full	0.01U
09L (089°T)	Nil	Nil	Gr	REIL HRL	Full	0.03D
27R (269°T)	P3'	MALSR	Gr + S	HRL	Full	0.03U
09R (089°T)	Nil	Nil	Gr + S	REIL HRL CL	Full	0.08D
27L (269°T)	P3'	MALSR			Full	0.08U

OTHER LIGHTING: Obstruction, taxiway, A/D beacon, wind indicator.

RUNWAY SURFACES
All grooved.
APPROACH LIGHTING
❶ ALSF - 2 for CAT II operations, Other times SSALSR.
CIRCUITS
22L - right hand

1. Be alert to runway crossing clearances. Readback of all runway holding instructions is required.
2. Low Level Windshear Alert System (LLWAS) in operation.
3. Land and Hold Short Operations (LAHSO) may be in effect when broadcast on ATIS.
4. Bird and deer hazard.
5. R/W 21R & 22L departures: Be alert for optical illusion - aircraft taxiing on Taxiways T(21R) & Q(22L) may appear as though crossing R/W centreline.
6. ASDE-X surveillance system in use pilots should operate transponders with mode C on all twys and rwys.

Rev: Notes, editorial.

Waynes Major Airport in 1947 and trebled in size over the following three years with the addition of three new runways. At the same time, the small Detroit City Airport lost most of its traffic to Detroit Willow Run Airport some 32km (20 miles) west of Detroit and 16km (10 miles) west of Wayne County.

The expansion was followed by the introduction of transatlantic services operated jointly by Pan American Airways and the British Overseas Airways Corporation, (BOAC). In 1958 American Airlines and four other carriers moved their operations from Willow Run to Wayne County, while the US Federal Aviation Administration included the airport amongst those airports designated to receive long-radar equipment ready for the jet age, while the L. C. Smith, or South, Terminal was completed. The current name was also adopted during the year.

As more airlines moved from Willow Run to Wayne County, the North Terminal opened in 1966; this was later renamed the Davey Terminal. A third terminal, the Michael Berry International Terminal, opened in 1974. Republic Airlines began using Wayne County as a hub in 1984 and, after it was absorbed by Northwest Airlines in 1986, traffic grew considerably. Transpacific operations by Northwest to Tokyo began in 1987. The last of three parallel runways opened in 1976 and a crosswind runway, 9R/27L, opened in 1993, while the final runway of the six, 4L/22R, opened in December 2001. The following year, the mile-long McNamara Terminal was completed, with an ExpressTram system running from one end to the other.

Links to the regional railway network are planned for the future.

Accidents at the airport have included a Northwest Airlines McDonnell Douglas MD-82 taking off for Phoenix and Santa Ana on 16 August 1987, which did not have the flaps deployed and struck a bridge over an interstate highway, killing all the passengers and crew apart from a young girl. On 3 December 1990 a Northwest Douglas DC-9, taking-off for Pittsburgh, collided with a Northwest Boeing 727-200Adv bound for Memphis, with the deaths of a flight attendant and 7 passengers on the Pittsburgh flight. A landing accident due to icing followed on 9 January 1997 when a Comair Embraer Brasilia crashed on approach some 29km (just over 18 miles) from the airport, killing all 3 crew and 26 passengers.

SAN FRANCISCO INTERNATIONAL: SFO
San Francisco, California, USA

Owner and operator: San Francisco Airport Commission

Runways: 10L/28R, 3,618m (11,870ft); 10R/28L, 3,231m (10,602ft); 1L/19R, 2,286m (7,500ft); 1R/19L, 2,636m (8,648ft)

Terminals: Four, designated 1, 2 (formerly known as the Central Terminal), 3, and International

Airlines using airport as base or hub: United Airlines

Annual passengers: 35,792,707

Annual cargo: 562,933 tonnes
Annual aircraft movements: 379,500

The Bay Area Rapid Transit system, BART, operates into the airport, with the San Francisco International Airport BART Station situated in Garage G of the International Terminal. There is also an internal inter-terminal AirTrain automatic railway within the airport.

Background

San Francisco International dates from 7 May 1927 when the airport was opened on part of a dairy farm leased from a local landowner, Ogden Mills. It was known as Mills Field until 1931 when it became San Francisco Municipal Airport, and its current title was not adopted until 1955.

During the 1930s, United Airlines used both San Francisco and nearby Oakland for its services. Situated on the shore of San Francisco Bay, the airport was able to act as the terminus for the Pan American World Airways 'China Clipper' transpacific flying boat service from 1935 until the outbreak of the Second World War in the Pacific. Domestic air services using the airport increased dramatically when the United States entered the Second World War in December 1941, because Oakland Municipal Airport was taken over as a military air station and all domestic flights into and out of the Bay area were concentrated on San Francisco.

After the war, Pan Am continued to use San Francisco for its transpacific flights and the airport also became a major hub for United Airlines. The Central Passenger Terminal was opened in 1954, and by the end of the decade the airport was handling United's fleet of new Douglas DC-8 jet airliners, with the first 'jetway' bridge in the United States opened in July 1959.

Planning for expansion started during the late 1980s, and the booming traffic of the 1990s led to the airport becoming the world's sixth busiest by passenger numbers, but it has since dropped out of the top 20. Nevertheless, expansion has continued, and a new International Terminal was opened in 2000, with international traffic

transferred from Terminal 2. A feature of the new terminal is its aviation museum and library. In June 2003 the Bay Area Rapid Transit system was extended into the airport at the same time as the internal AirTrain inter-terminal shuttle system opened, using automatic trains.

Despite, or perhaps because of, its position on San Francisco Bay, expansion of the airport is proving difficult. During bad weather, delays are caused because of the limited separation between the runways. While further expansion into the bay on reclaimed land has been proposed, under local planning laws other space in the bay would have to be restored to compensate, and this is meeting opposition from environmental groups. The result is that the airport has lost the boom in low-cost carriers to other airports, including its old rival, Oakland. Nevertheless, in recent years there has been a revival, with Qantas putting Airbus A380 flights into the airport, Spirit Airlines adding it to its network,

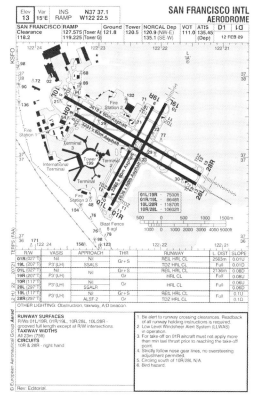

United Airways using it for non-stop services to South Korea and Taiwan, and Air China introducing a service from Shanghai. A world airport survey in 2008 saw the airport cited as the best international airport in North America.

Amongst the serious accidents at the airport was that to a Flying Tiger Line Lockheed Constellation cargo flight bound for New York, which crashed into the hills west of the airport after taking off on 24 December 1964, killing all three crew members. Less serious, but highlighting problems with escape from aircraft, was the accident that followed a Pan Am Boeing 747 which struck navigational aids at the end of the runway as it took off for Tokyo on 30 July 1971, damaging its undercarriage and other systems, as well as seriously injuring two passengers when metal components entered the cabin. The aircraft dumped its fuel over the Pacific before returning to land, but veered off the runway after touchdown and came to rest on its tail, with the forward escape chutes hanging vertically, with passengers evacuating the aircraft using these chutes being injured, in some cases seriously, although there were no fatalities amongst the 218 passengers and crew.

Thanks to a newly-developed ground control and monitoring system at San Francisco an accident was avoided on 26 May 2007 when a Sky-West Airlines aircraft was prevented from crashing into an aircraft belonging to Republic Airlines. However, on 13 January 2008 an empty United Airlines Boeing 757, which was being pushed back towards the maintenance hangar, struck a SkyWest regional jet being pushed back ready for departure. There were no casualties, but both aircraft suffered tailplane damage.

One mysterious incident was to a cargo Boeing 767 of ABX Air, which caught fire as it was departing on 28 June 2008. The aircraft was seriously damaged, but both pilots escaped unharmed.

MINNEAPOLIS-SAINT PAUL INTERNATIONAL: MSP
Minneapolis, Minnesota, USA

Owner and operator: MSC

Runways: 4/22, 3,354m (11,000ft); 12L/30R, 2,499m (8,200ft); 12R/30L, 3,048m (10,000ft); 17/35, 2,438m (8,000ft)

Terminals: Two, named Lindbergh (with seven concourses, one for international passengers) and Humphrey

Airlines using airport as base or hub: Northwest Airlines (through acquisition of Delta Airlines)

Annual passengers: 35,157,322

Annual cargo: 257,394 tonnes

Annual aircraft movements: 452,972

Served by the Hiawatha Line light-railway, with stations at both the Hub Building (Lindbergh Station) and Humphrey Terminal (Humphrey Station), connecting the airport with Minneapolis.

Background

Minneapolis-Saint Paul is the largest and busiest airport in the five states of Minnesota, Iowa, South Dakota, North Dakota, and Wisconsin, which together comprise the Upper Midwest of the United States. The airport is situated across the Mississippi River from Saint Paul.

The airport was originally built on the site of a former speedway track that had gone bankrupt and had been rescued by local businessmen shortly after the end of the First World War. Hence the airport being first called Speedway Field, but in 1921 it was renamed Wold-Chamberlain Field after two wartime pilots, Ernest Wold and Cyrus Chamberlain. This was changed in 1944 to Minneapolis-Saint Paul Metropolitan Airport/Wold-Chamberlain Field, and in 1948 it became Minneapolis-Saint Paul International Airport/Wold-Chamberlain Field. In the meantime, the airport had been one of the stopping places on the round-the-world flight by Howard Hughes.

The larger of today's two terminal buildings, the Charles Lindbergh, after the first man to fly solo across the Atlantic, was completed in 1962, and was joined in 1977 by the Hubert H. Humphrey Terminal, named after the former US vice-president. The Humphrey Terminal originally handled all international flights, but it has been proposed that in future all flights other than those of Northwest Airlines and its SkyTeam Alliance partners will use the Lindbergh Terminal leaving an expanded Humphrey Terminal to handle the rest. This has raised concerns about the dominant position of Northwest at the airport, especially after the acquisition of Delta in 2008.

The airport is the base for the Minneapolis-Saint Paul Joint Air Reserve Station.

Amongst the accidents at the airport was that on 28 August 1958, when a Northwest Orient Airlines (now Northwest Airlines) Douglas DC-6 crashed on taking off for Portland in poor visibility. The aircraft caught fire, but all 5 crew and 58 passengers escaped. What could have been amongst the world's worst air accidents was narrowly avoided on 31 March 1985 when a Northwest McDonnell Douglas DC-10 was taking off for Seattle just as another DC-10 of the same airline was cleared to taxi across the runway. Air traffic controllers had failed to appreciate the conflicting paths of the two aircraft. Disaster was avoided by the captain of the aircraft taking off rotating his aircraft and climbing at a lower speed than usual, clearing the second aircraft by less than 50m (80ft). There were more than 500 passengers and crew in the two aircraft. Being shared with the Air National Guard, the airport has also had accidents with military aircraft, including a Lockheed C-130 Hercules on a training flight on 20 April 2004, which suffered undercarriage problems and, although it landed safely, the right side main gear collapsed as it taxied, causing the right wing to hit the ground. A fire broke out, but this was soon extinguished and the crew of four were unharmed. On 10 May 2005 a Northwest Airlines Airbus A319, taxiing to depart for San Antonio, was damaged when a Douglas DC-9 with engine problems rolled back into it, but there were no casualties.

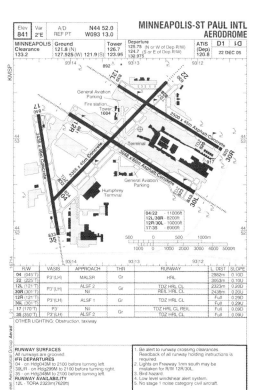

MIAMI INTERNATIONAL: MIA
Miami, Florida, USA

Owner and operator: Miami Dade County Aviation Department

Runways: 8L/26R, 2,621m (8,600ft); 8R/26L, 3,202m (10,506ft); 9/27, 3,962m (13,000ft); 12/30, 2,851m (9,354ft); there is also a heliport within the terminal area

Terminals: One, but with eight pier concourses designated A, C, D, E, F, G, H, and J, plus a substantial air cargo terminal

Airlines using airport as base or hub: American Airlines, American Eagle, Air France, Gulfstream International, Sky King Airlines

Annual passengers: 33,740,416

Annual cargo: 1,992,985 tonnes

Annual aircraft movements: 386,058

It is planned to use a people mover to link the terminals with an inter-modal centre with access to the Miami-Dade Metrorail and the future BayLink light railway, but in the meantime there is a free shuttle bus to Hialeah Market Station on the Tri-Rail suburban line.

Background

Miami's history dates from 1928 when Juan Trippe started his airline, Pan American Airways, and flew from what was then known as Pan American Field to Cuba using a fleet of just two Fokker F.VII/3M trimotors. A solitary hangar doubled up as a terminal. Pan American later switched to using flying boats and acquired the major operator between the United States and South America, the New York, Rio and Buenos Aires Line, and flights were moved to a flying boat station at Dinner Key in Florida. The airfield was then abandoned until Eastern Air Lines started to use it in

1934, and Eastern was later joined by National Airlines in 1937.

The airport remained in Pan American ownership, although renamed 36th Street Airport (the address of its new terminal) until 1945, when the City of Miami established a port authority and purchased it, before combining it with an adjoining USAAF base in 1949 to create Miami International Airport. Further expansion followed in 1951, and in 1959 the original 36th Street terminal was replaced by a new building. Meanwhile, between 1949 and 1959, the USAF used the airport for air transport and search-and-rescue operations. By this time Pan American had become Pan American World Airways, more usually known as Pan Am, and was once again a landplane operator, but remained an operator of international services only. It later acquired National Airways and inherited that company's domestic route network and transatlantic services from Florida to London. After Pan Am's acquisition of National, Pan Am and Eastern became the two major operators at Miami, but both collapsed in 1991. The vacuum was almost immediately filled by United Airlines and American Airlines, but while the latter expanded its operations at Miami, United started to reduce services, and eventually closed its station. American transferred routes, personnel and aircraft from Nashville and Raleigh-Durham, and expanded its services from Miami to Latin America, while air cargo increased dramatically during these years.

Unusually, Miami also became a hub for two European airlines, with Iberia using it as a connecting hub for services to and from Latin America to link with its transatlantic routes, and Air France for services to the French Caribbean. Nevertheless, much tighter security following the attacks of 11 September 2001 led to the loss of the Iberia operations and more direct flights between Latin America and Spain, although Air France's operations continue. Despite this, Miami remains one of the few US airports with direct flights to Cuba, although these have to be booked through travel agents with a special dispensation from the US government.

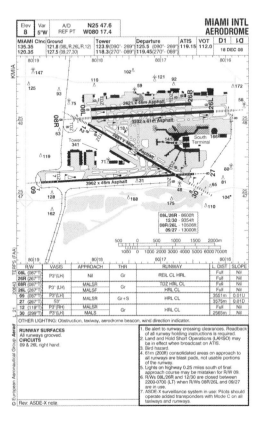

In recent years the airport has grown and developed in line with Florida's popularity as a holiday destination and retirement area for both Americans and Europeans. The main concourses have been routinely up-dated and expanded over recent years.

Because of its location, the airport has been the scene of many aircraft hijackings, especially during the 1960s and 1970s when aircraft seemed almost routinely to be hijacked and flown to Cuba. There have been about 40 accidents and incidents recorded at the airport since 1949, but almost half of these have involved Latin American-operated aircraft, and six of them have been Cuban.

Two accidents involved aircraft that ended up in the Everglades, the huge area of swamp close to the airport. The first of these was on 12 February 1963 when a Northwest Orient Airlines Boeing 720, which had taken off for Chicago, encountered severe up and down drafts in a tropical storm and was torn apart, with the loss of all 8 crew and 35 passengers. The second was to an Eastern Air Lines Lockheed TriStar approaching Miami from New York towards midnight on 29 December 1972. The aircraft suffered problems with its undercarriage, and this distracted the crew from watching their descent, and the plane came down in the Everglades and broke up. Altogether, 5 of the 13 crew and 94 of the 163 passengers were killed, but it is not clear how many died in the accident and how many were killed by alligators as they attempted to leave the wrecked aircraft. Another Eastern TriStar, departing for Nassau on 5 May 1983, suffered first one and then a second engine failure, and eventually managed to make a one-engined landing at Miami without harm to the 10 crew and 162 passengers.

CHARLOTTE DOUGLAS MUNICIPAL: CLT

Charlotte, North Carolina, USA

Owner and operator: City of Charlotte
Runways: 18L/36R, 2,644m (8,674ft); 18C/36C, 3,048m (10,000ft); 18R/36L, 2,743m (9,000ft) opening December 2009; 5/23, 2,287m (7,502ft)

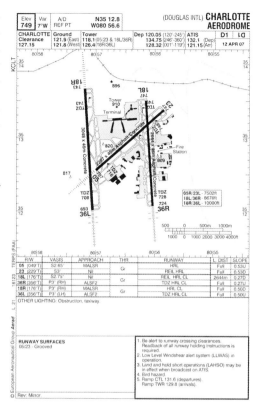

Terminals: One, with five concourses, A, B, C, D, and E
Airlines using airport as base or hub: US Airways
Annual passengers: 33,165,688
Annual cargo: 122,149 tonnes
Annual aircraft movements: 522,541

Background

Charlotte Douglas has its origins in a grant of US $200,000 dollars from the federal government in Washington in 1930 as part of a public works programme to create employment during the years of the Great Depression. Work started in 1935, and the Charlotte Municipal Airport opened in 1936 with a small passenger terminal that survives today as the Carolinas Aviation Museum. The first regular passenger services at the airport started in 1937, operated by Eastern Air Lines. In 1941, with US entry into the Second World War, the USAAF took control and renamed it Morris Air Force Base, and it was used as a training station for the US Third Air Force.

After the war the airport reverted to the City of Charlotte, and Eastern resumed services in 1950. In 1954 a new passenger terminal opened and the airport was renamed Charlotte Douglas after a former mayor of Charlotte, Ben Douglas, Senior. Delta Airlines also introduced services to the airport in 1956. By 1962, when Eastern introduced the first jet air services to the Carolinas, United, Southern, and Piedmont had all added Charlotte to their route networks. Later in the decade, the passenger terminal was expanded considerably, and this continued until early in the next decade as further improvements were made.

Airline deregulation for domestic flights in the United States followed in 1978, and between then and 1980, passengers numbers using Charlotte Douglas almost doubled. This growth was helped when, in 1979, Piedmont adopted the airport as a hub on its route network, and in 1982, with the opening of a new terminal and the conversion of the existing terminal to an air cargo base, the airport was renamed Charlotte Douglas International. In 1987 Piedmont began operations to London, before being taken over by USAir in 1989. In 1990 a new international and commuter airline concourse opened, and the following year the terminal buildings were expanded further. The German airline, Lufthansa, started a service to Charlotte in 1992, but this was soon discontinued, while in 1994 British Airways started a joint service with USAir during a short-lived alliance between the two airlines. By the time USAir became US Airways in 1996, Charlotte was the airline's largest hub. US Airways later merged with America West Airlines, although the US Airways name was retained by the merged company.

Growth is set to continue at Charlotte, with Lufthansa having resumed operations and plans for a service to Beijing by US Airways, albeit with a change at Philadelphia, probably starting in 2010.

There have been a number of accidents at or near the airport. One of these was on 11 September 1974 when an Eastern Air Lines Douglas DC-9, approaching from Charleston in poor visibility (with the pilots discussing 'non-operational topics'), descended into trees, at which point the pilots initiated a go-around, but the aircraft started to break up and caught fire. Of the 82 passengers and crew, 13 survived the accident, but two died within days. A single pilot-operated de Havilland Canada Twin Otter of Mountain Air Cargo also descended below the glide path on approach to the airport on 19 January 1988, and collided with a tree, killing the pilot. Windshear struck a USAir (now US Airways) Douglas DC-9, approaching from Columbia on 2 July 1994, dropping the aircraft into a residential area with a total of 37 dead on the ground and on board the aircraft. Most recently, an Air Midwest aircraft operating as US Airways Express flight crashed at the airport killing the 21 passengers and crew.

PHILADELPHIA INTERNATIONAL: PHL

Philadelphia, Pennsylvania, USA

Owner and operator: City of Philadelphia
Runways: 9R/27L, 3,202m (10,500ft); 9L/27R, 2,896m (9,500ft); 17/35, 1,664m (6,500ft); 8/26, 1,524m (5,000ft)
Terminals: Seven, A-West, A-East, B, C, D, E and F
Airlines using airport as base or hub: US Airways, US Airways Express, Southwest Airlines
Annual passengers: 32,211,439
Annual cargo: 543,357 tonnes
Annual aircraft movements: 499,653

SEPTA's High Speed Rail Line (R1) provides easy connection to AMTRAK at 30th Street Station.

Background
Situated on 2,302 acres today, Philadelphia dates from 1925 when the city provided 125 acres of land, now part of the north-east corner, for train-

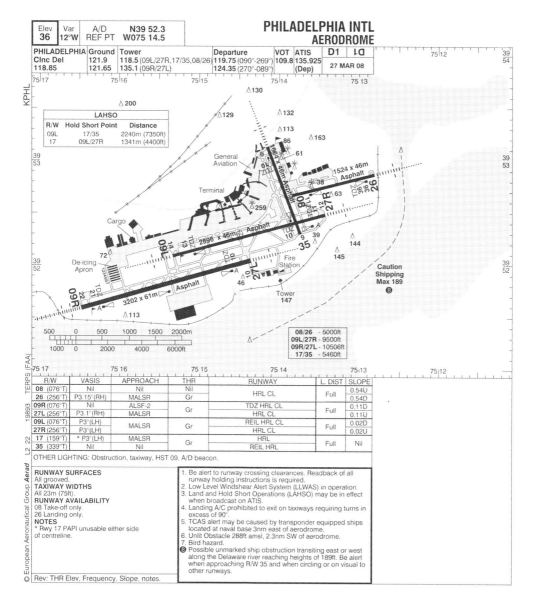

Elev 36	Var 12°W	A/D REF PT	N39 52.3 W075 14.5				**PHILADELPHIA INTL** **AERODROME**

| PHILADELPHIA Clnc Del 118.85 | Ground 121.9 121.65 | Tower 118.5 (09L/27R,17/35,08/26) 135.1 (09R/27L) | Departure 119.75 (090°-269°) 124.35 (270°-089°) | VOT 109.8 | ATIS 135.925 (Dep) | D1 27 MAR 08 | I·D |

LAHSO

R/W	Hold Short Point	Distance
09L	17/35	2240m (7350ft)
17	09L/27R	1341m (4400ft)

General Aviation

Terminal

Cargo

De-icing Apron

1524 x 46m Asphalt

2896 x 46m Asphalt

3202 x 61m

Asphalt

Fire Station

Caution Shipping Max 189

Tower 147

08/26	- 5000ft
09L/27R	- 9500ft
09R/27L	- 10506ft
17/35	- 5460ft

500 0 500 1000 1500 2000m
1000 0 2000 4000 6000ft

R/W	VASIS	APPROACH	THR	RUNWAY	L. DIST	SLOPE
08 (076°T)	Nil	Nil	Nil	HRL CL	Full	0.54U
26 (256°T)	P3.15°(RH)	MALSR	Gr			0.54D
09R (076°T)	Nil	ALSF-2	Gr	TDZ HRL CL	Full	0.11D
27L (256°T)	P3.1°(RH)	MALSR		HRL CL		0.11U
09L (076°T)	P3°(LH)	MALSR	Gr	REIL HRL CL	Full	0.02D
27R (256°T)	P3°(LH)			HRL CL		0.02U
17 (159°T)	* P3°(LH)	MALSR	Gr	HRL	Full	Nil
35 (339°T)	Nil	Nil		REIL HRL		

OTHER LIGHTING: Obstruction, taxiway, HST 09, A/D beacon.

RUNWAY SURFACES
All grooved.
TAXIWAY WIDTHS
All 23m (75ft).
RUNWAY AVAILABILITY
08 Take-off only.
26 Landing only.
NOTES
* Rwy 17 PAPI unusable either side of centreline.

1. Be alert to runway crossing clearances. Readback of all runway holding instructions is required.
2. Low Level Windshear Alert System (LLWAS) in operation.
3. Land and Hold Short Operations (LAHSO) may be in effect when broadcast on ATIS.
4. Landing A/C prohibited to exit on taxiways requiring turns in excess of 90°.
5. TCAS alert may be caused by transponder equipped ships located at naval base 3nm east of aerodrome.
6. Unlit Obstacle 288ft amsl, 2.3nm SW of aerodrome.
7. Bird hazard.
8. Possible unmarked ship obstruction transiting east or west along the Delaware river reaching heights of 189ft. Be alert when approaching R/W 35 and when circling or on visual to other runways.

Rev: THR Elev, Frequency, Slope, notes.

© European Aeronautical Group Aerad

ing aviators of the Pennsylvania National Guard. The following year an agreement with Ludington Exhibition Company, a forerunner of Eastern Airlines, allowed them to manage it as the 'Municipal Aviation Landing Field', one of the many places at which Charles Lindbergh landed during his 1927 tour of the USA with his aircraft *The Spirit of St Louis*. In 1930 a 1,000-acre derelict site (Hog Island) adjoining the airport was purchased for expansion, but, because of the Great

Depression, no work was undertaken until 1937. It opened as Philadelphia Municipal Airport in 1940, and four airlines, including American and United, then transferred their operations to the new airport from the nearby Central Airport in Camden, New Jersey. In its first year, 40,000 passengers used the airport, with the airlines mainly flying twin-engined Douglas DC-3s.

Closed during the Second World War, the airport reopened on 26 June 1945, initially as the

Northeast Philadelphia Airport, but by the end of the year it became Philadelphia International Airport when American Overseas Airlines inaugurated a transatlantic service. Further expansion proved necessary and a new terminal was opened in 1953.

With the dawn of the jet age, further development proved necessary, and a $22 million all-weather runway (9R/27L), including related high-speed taxiways, was opened on 11 December 1972. A new Overseas Terminal came into operation in April 1973, which handled international and charter flights until it was replaced with the new Richardson Dilworth International Terminal A in March 1991. In spring 1977, the $300 million modernisation and development of the domestic terminal area was completed, replacing a single central type terminal with four terminals (B, C, D, and E). In December 1980, a state-of-the-art $6.5 million Federal Aviation Administration air traffic control facility opened. A rail link to the city centre followed in 1985, with a rapid transit line, while terminals B, C, D and E were upgraded. An additional terminal, F, opened in June 2001, followed by international A-West in May 2003. On 3 December 1999 the airport commissioned runway 8/26, a 1,524m (5,000ft) runway for regional and general aviation aircraft.

In recent years, other developments have included a new 11-storey ground control tower between terminals A-East and B, and de-icing facilities that can handle up to three aircraft at once. The new international terminal A-West, which opened in 2003, and the existing A-East, between them handle around 4 million international passengers annually.

The airport has suffered a number of accidents since the Second World War. One of these occurred when a runway was being extended and, on 14 January 1951, during snow with warnings about slippery conditions on the runway, a National Airlines Douglas DC-4 landed too far down the runway, overshot into a ditch, and burst into flames. One of the crew of 4 was killed along with 6 of the 24 passengers. On 3 January 1960 the undercarriage of a Lockheed Constella-

tion of Eastern Air Lines collapsed after landing, and the aircraft was scrapped for spares, but there are no records of casualties. Poor use of the engine controls led to a Douglas DC-7BF of Universal Airlines, landing on a cargo flight, aquaplaning off the runway and being damaged beyond repair, but the three crew members seem to have survived. The first recorded incident to a jet airliner was on 19 July 1970 when a United Air Lines Boeing 737-200 was taking off for Rochester, but as it left the ground there was a loud bang, and with the aircraft not responding to the throttles, the captain put it back on the runway, which it overshot, careering through a fence and into a field before it stopped. The pilots believed that both engines had failed, but only one had done so. The aircraft was written off, but the 6 crew and 55 passengers all survived. Windshear was to blame for an accident to a Douglas DC-9 of Allegheny Airlines on 23 June 1976 as it approached from Windsor Locks, and settled tail first on to the runway. The aircraft was a write-off, but all 4 crew and 102 passengers escaped. Another DC-9, on a cargo flight to Wilmington for Airborne Express, rolled to the left and suffered a double engine failure after lift-off, dropping back on to the runway, with ice on the wings believed to be the cause, but both crew members escaped. On 8 February 2006 a UPS (United Parcel Service) Douglas DC-8-71F landed from Atlanta on fire, but despite confusion over which runway the aircraft was to use, it landed safely and the crew of three escaped before the aircraft was burnt out.

SEATTLE TACOMA INTERNATIONAL: SEA
Seattle, Washington State, USA

Owner and operator: The Port of Seattle
Runways: 16L/34R, 3,627m (11,900ft);
   16C/34C, 2,873m (9,425ft); 16R/34L, 2,591m
   (8,500ft)
Terminals: Three, designated the Central
   Terminal, North Satellite Terminal, and South
   satellite Terminal (the latter handling
   international passengers and flights)

Airlines using airport as base or hub: Alaska
  Airlines, Horizon Air
Annual passengers: 31,296,628
Annual cargo: 319,013 tonnes
Annual aircraft movements: 347,046

Background

Originally the airport for Seattle was Boeing Field, operated as a public airport but owned by the aircraft manufacturer, and Seattle-Tacoma was constructed by the Port of Seattle in 1944 during the Second World War after the USAAF took over Boeing Field. The town of Tacoma contributed US $100,000 towards the cost of building the airport on condition that their involvement was reflected in the airport's name. Nevertheless, the first scheduled services to use the new airport were not until 1947. In 1949 it became Seattle-Tacoma International after Northwest Airlines introduced a service to Tokyo. The main runway was lengthened in 1959 ready for jet airliners, and that same year the current main terminal was completed, while the runway was extended again in 1961 to handle increased traffic for the Century 21 World Fair. In 1967, Scandinavian Airlines System (SAS) launched the first direct flights between Seattle and Europe. Between 1967 and 1973 a second runway was laid and two satellite terminals opened. By this time the airport's growth was challenged by many local residents, and a substantial number of properties had to be purchased and others soundproofed to address the problems. A further objection from local residents followed a proposal in 1983 to rename the airport as the Henry M. Jackson International Airport in honour of a US senator, and the Port of Seattle had to back down in the face of opposition from the residents of Tacoma who resented the removal of their town's name from the airport's title.

Deregulation of domestic air services in the United States in 1978 led to a substantial growth in traffic, and a number of airlines introduced services to Seattle-Tacoma for the first time. By the late 1980s it was clear that the airport would soon need further expansion if it was to manage the growing traffic, but after opposition to a third runway, the Port of Seattle began to look for a site for a completely new airport, but this proved impractical and, after further fuss and an independent report, a third runway was eventually built, and was completed in 2008. The Seattle area not only has Seattle-Tacoma, but also the two Boeing airfields at Renton and Everett. The air traffic control tower was damaged by an earthquake in 2001, but has now been replaced by an earthquake-resistant structure.

The 'Open Skies' Agreement between the United States and the European Union that took effect in 2008 is already encouraging many European airlines to consider including Seattle in their networks, so further development is likely in the future.

Amongst the accidents at Seattle was that on 30 November 1947 to a Douglas C-54 landing from Anchorage, which touched down in heavy fog after attempts to land at the two Boeing air-

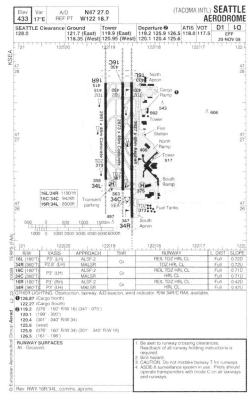

fields had failed. It touched down too far down the runway and overshot on to a road, colliding with a car and killing the occupants before bursting into flames. Altogether nine people were killed in the accident. A take-off accident occurred to a Northwest Orient (now Northwest) Airlines Boeing Stratocruiser flying to Portland on 2 April 1956 which suffered reduced power because of a maintenance failure, and the aircraft was forced to ditch in Puget Sound, where it sank with 5 of the 38 passengers and crew still aboard. A Horizon Air de Havilland Canada Dash-8 taking off for Spokane on 15 April 1988 suffered a loss of power in the No. 2 engine followed by a fire, so that when the aircraft landed it was out of control and veered off the runway, colliding with the terminal before stopping. There were 4 serious injuries amongst the 37 passengers, but no fatalities. On 26 December 2005 an Alaska Airlines McDonnell Douglas MD-83, which had just taken off for Burbank, lost cabin pressure and returned to Seattle safely, where it was discovered that a baggage vehicle had hit the aircraft before take-off and the area of impact became a 30cm (12in) tear in the fuselage once in the air and the aircraft cabin pressurised. There were no casualties.

BOSTON LOGAN INTERNATIONAL: BOS

Boston, Massachusetts, USA

Owner and Operator: Massachusetts Port Authority, Massport
Runways: 4L/22R, 2,396m (7,861ft); 4R/22L, 3,050m (10,005ft); 15L/33R, 779m (2,557ft); 15R/33L, 3,073m (10,083ft); 9/27, 2,134m (7,000ft); 14/32, 1,524m (5,000ft)
Terminals: Four, designated A, B, C, and E (international)
Airlines using airport as base or hub: AirTran Airways, American Airlines, JetBlue, US Airways
Annual passengers: 28,102,455
Annual cargo: 298,536 tonnes
Annual aircraft movements: 399,537

No direct railway connection, but a waterbus service links the airport with the centre of Boston.

Background

Opened on 8 September 1923 as Jeffrey Field, and initially used by the US Army Air Service and the Massachusetts Air Guard, it became known as Boston Airport when Colonial Air Transport opened a route to New York in 1927, the airport's first regular service. The construction of the airport was in response to pressure from the local business community, which feared that Boston could be left behind without an airport. It was also regarded as important that Boston should be served by the fledgling US Airmail service. It is claimed that in 1925 First Lieutenant Donald Duke of the Army Air Service, who was airfield manager, first coined the term 'airport'. In 1928 the State of Massachusetts took over the airport, and the following year it was transferred to the city under a 20-year lease. The local authority gave responsibility for the airport to its parks department, and several improvements were made, including additional buildings and surfaced roads, while land started to be reclaimed from the harbour for airport expansion.

By the late 1930s Boston was being used by American Airlines. In 1939 the Massachusetts Aeronautical Commission was established to develop air transport and airports, including Boston. Shortly before the attack on Pearl Harbor the federal government assumed responsibility for the airport and started a major programme of expansion, laying down new runways and hangars and reclaiming more land from the harbour. The airport became known as Commonwealth Airport. A bond issue was made to finance the expansion, and in 1943 the airport received a new name, General Edward Lawrence Logan Airport, after a local resident who became a hero of the Spanish-American War. Continued expansion of the airport took place via the reclaimed land from the harbour, and this included absorbing Governor's Island and Apple Island.

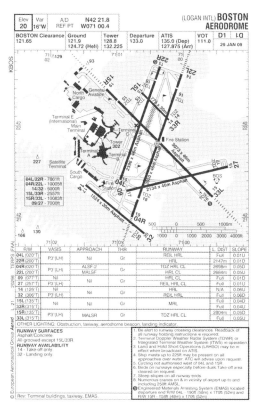

mitigate the impact of aircraft noise. These policies continued when the Logan Modernisation project was initiated in 1994, which saw most of the airport approaches and the terminals revamped, with a new international terminal E.

The airport has had just two serious accidents in the past 50 years. The first of these was on 4 October 1960 when an Eastern Air Lines Lockheed Electra crashed into the sea after taking off, with the loss of 62 of the 71 passengers and crew aboard. The other accident was to a Delta Air Lines Douglas DC-9 which crashed into a sea wall at the airport, killing all 83 passengers and 6 crew.

The two aircraft that were taken over by terrorists and crashed into the World Trade Center in New York on 11 September 2001 both took off from Boston Logan. Later that year, on 22 December, an attempt to blow up an American Airlines aircraft flying from Paris to Miami was foiled and the flight was diverted to Boston after the suicide bomber was overpowered by passengers and crew.

NEW YORK LA GUARDIA: LGA

Long Island, New York, New York State, USA

Owner: City of New York

Operator: New York & New Jersey Ports Authority

Runways: 4/22, 2,134m (7,001ft); 13/31, 2,135m (7,004ft); there are also two helipads

Terminals: Four, being the Central Terminal with four concourses, the Delta Terminal, US Airways Terminal, and the Marine Air Terminal

Airlines using airport as base or hub: Delta; US Airways

Annual passengers: 25,026,267

Annual cargo: 10,596 tonnes

Annual aircraft movements: 391,872

Background

The smallest of the three main airports serving New York and adjoining Newark, New Jersey, La Guardia dates from 1929 when the Gala Amusement Park was converted into an airfield for private flyers. Located on Long Island on the

After the war the airport was returned to the state and continued to expand, and in 1949 the new Boutwell Terminal was opened, approximately where Terminals B and C now stand. In 1953 transcontinental services started linking Boston with Los Angeles, followed in 1959 by transatlantic jet services by Pan American to London. The state of Massachusetts created the Massachusetts Port Authority, Massport, in 1956, and this took control of the airport in 1959. By this time the airport was using the Logan name, and further expansion had seen it with four runways and a north and a south terminal, with the latter eventually becoming Terminal C.

The relationship with the local community first became strained during the 1960s when the port authority acquired a substantial area of residential land, and also expanded into a popular area for anglers. Measures designed to relieve the situation included relocating homes and providing soundproofing and air-conditioning to

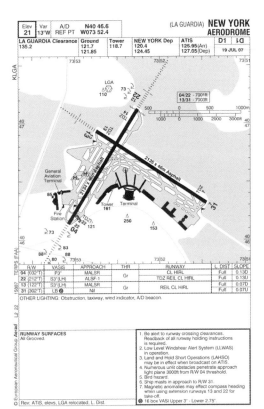

the city paid for American to have four hangars at the airfield as an incentive. The formal opening was on 15 October 1939, when the name was changed to New York Municipal Airport. American started regular services from the airfield on 2 December. The idea was controversial at the time, with many predicting that the airport would fail, but it soon became clear that it was a success, even though one news magazine, *TIME*, called it 'the most pretentious land and seaplane base in the world', which may have helped as this dual role attracted many airlines that were still flying boat operators, and soon another four airlines, including Pan American, United, Eastern and Transcontinental & Western Air, had joined American operating from the new airport and seaplane base.

Not surprisingly, given his involvement, a popular but unofficial name for the airport became La Guardia Field, and this name was adopted officially on 1 June 1947 when the then Port of New York Authority took over the running of the airport under lease from the city.

Nevertheless, the post-war period was a difficult one for the airport, which had become far too small for the traffic on offer. By 1968 the operators were actively seeking to discourage traffic, and make the most of limited take-off and landing slots by charging prohibitively high fees for general aviation aircraft at peak periods. To make the most of the small airport, aircraft such as the Lockheed TriStar and Douglas DC-10 were developed so that high capacity widebodied aircraft could use it. In 1984 the airport's management went further, banning aircraft from using the airport for flights of more than 1,500 miles, and while Western Airlines challenged this in court, the decision was declared to be lawful. The port authority also backed the extension of the AirTrain network to New York JFK and Newark, so that these airports could ease the pressure on La Guardia. The Federal Aviation Authority also imposed limits on the number of flights and the size of aircraft that could use La Guardia. Many have questioned whether the runways are long enough for modern aircraft, but other major airports in the United States

shores of Flushing Bay, it was originally named Glenn H. Curtiss Airport after the celebrated aviation pioneer who came from Long Island and did much to develop seaplanes and flying boats. Commercial services did not start immediately, and it is said that they were a result of an outburst by the mayor of New York from 1934 to 1945, Fiorello La Guardia, incensed at his Transcontinental & Western Air (predecessor of Trans World Airlines) flight landing him at Newark when his ticket was written for New York, so he demanded that the aircraft take off again and land at Floyd Bennett Field in Brooklyn. When American Airlines took up the challenge to fly to Floyd Bennett, the service failed because Newark was more conveniently situated for Manhattan!

After an alternative site was found to be too small, La Guardia had the city and American Airlines develop the site at Curtiss Airport, and

have shorter runways.

A brief respite from the pressure of growing traffic came in the downturn in air travel following the terrorist attacks of 11 September 2001. Later, this was followed by a new control tower, and in 2007 the limitations imposed by the FAA were removed. Improvements to the terminal building and airfield layout have also made the airport more efficient in recent years. Nevertheless, it remains without a railway link into the airport.

A number of serious accidents and a terrorist attack have occurred at the airport. The terrorist attack was on 29 December 1975 when a bomb exploded killing 11 people at the airport and wounding another 74. One of the accidents was on 1 February 1957 when a Northeast Airlines aircraft crashed after take-off into Rikers Island killing 21 of the 101 passengers and crew. An American Airlines flight on approach crashed into the East River on 3 February 1959, killing 65 of the 73 passengers and crew. A USAir, now US Airways, flight to Charlotte crashed after aborting a take-off on 21 September 1989, when it rolled off the runway into the East River, breaking into three sections with three passengers killed. Ice on the wings caused the crash of another USAir flight taking off for Cleveland on 22 March 1992, with the loss of 27 of its 51 passengers and crew. More fortunate was the aborted take-off of a Continental Airlines flight to Denver on 2 March 1994 in a snowstorm, as the aircraft skidded down the runway and into a ditch.

The most spectacular accident at the airport was that to a US Airways Airbus A320 that had taken off for Charlotte on 15 January 2009, and suffered a double engine failure after hitting a large flock of geese, but the captain landed the aircraft amidst the ice on the Hudson River and all 5 crew and 150 passengers were rescued – many of the passengers and crew being taken off the wings of the aircraft before it sank.

WASHINGTON DULLES INTERNATIONAL: IAD
Dulles, Virginia, USA

Owner and operator: Metropolitan Washington Airports Authority
Runways: 1L/19R, 2,865m (9,400ft); 1C/19C, 3,505m (11,500ft); 1R/19L, 3,505m (11,500ft); 12L/30R, 3,200m (10,500ft); 12R/30L, 3,200m (10,500ft) planned
Terminals: Three, with a Main Terminal and two Midfield Terminals, one with concourses A and B, the other with concourses C and D
Airlines using airport as base or hub: United Airlines, United Express
Annual passengers: 24,525,487
Annual cargo: 358,527 tonnes
Annual aircraft movements: 383,939

Bus connection to railway station, with extension of Washington Metro Silver Line planned for 2016.

Background
Situated some 40km (25 miles) west of Washington DC, the airport is named after John Foster Dulles, US Secretary of State under President Dwight D. Eisenhower. It was envisaged as a relief for Washington National as air traffic grew rapidly after the Second World War. Several suggested sites were rejected, and the current one was chosen by President Eisenhower. The new airport was opened by President Kennedy on 17 November 1962 as Dulles International Airport and did not receive its present title until 1986. This was the first airport in the world to be designed for the needs of jet airliners, but one feature that did not find widespread favour was the concept of mobile people lounges which could move more than 100 passengers at a time between terminal and aircraft, and had scissor lifts to reach the level of the airliner cabin. These mobile lounges are currently being retired in favour of an 'AeroTrain' shuttle between the terminals.

Initially the airport's distance from the city and the limited range of destinations offered

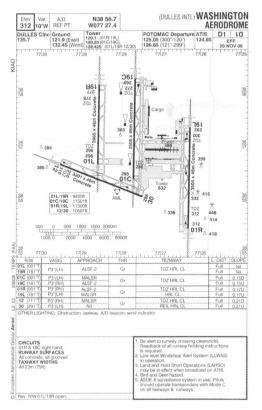

departed from Dulles. There have also been a number of accidents and incidents, including no fewer than four instances of Air France Sud Aviation/BAC Concordes suffering one or more burst tyres, and on two occasions these resulted in further damage to the aircraft. An undercarriage problem also affected a Federal Aviation Administration Douglas DC-7 on 30 July 1974, when the nose wheel collapsed after landing, but the aircraft was repaired and the three crew and five passengers were unharmed. Another landing accident was on 17 December 1987 when a Swearingen Metro II of AVAir, approaching from Newark, touched down in a field short of the runway because of icing, but the two crew and six passengers survived. The one fatal accident actually at the airport was on 20 July 1988 when a corporate de Havilland Twin Otter was making a positioning flight from Dulles to Washington National and the pilot used the flaps incorrectly, so that the aircraft climbed steeply after taking off and then plunged to the ground, killing the sole occupant, the pilot. A Saab 340A of United Express from White Plains on 8 June 2005 with a faulty undercarriage made an emergency landing during which the right undercarriage leg collapsed, damaging the plane beyond economic repair, but the 3 crew and 27 passengers survived. The worst accident of all was to a TWA (Trans World Airlines) Boeing 727 which flew into a hillside on its initial approach to the airport on 1 December 1974, after having been diverted, killing all aboard the aircraft.

gave rise to fears that it might be under-used. Nevertheless, the steady growth in air traffic in the intervening period and the establishment of substantial businesses along the main route between the airport and the city has meant that the airport has grown steadily and is now undergoing a major redevelopment of its terminals and the construction of a fifth runway.

Amongst the unusual features of the airport is that in December 2003, the National Air and Space Museum opened an annex at the Steven F. Udvar-Hazy Center. This houses an Air France Concorde, the *Enola Gay* Boeing B-29 that dropped the first atomic bomb on Hiroshima in August 1945, the space shuttle Enterprise, the Boeing 367-80, the prototype of the Boeing 707, and other aerospace relics that are too large for the main Smithsonian building.

The airport has had at least two hijackings end on its site, and the aircraft that was crashed into the Pentagon on 11 September 2001

FORT LAUDERDALE HOLLYWOOD INTERNATIONAL: FLL

Dania Beach, Broward, Fort Lauderdale, Florida, USA

Owner and operator: Broward County

Runways: 9L/27R, 2,743m (9,000ft); 9R/27L, 1,608m (5,276ft); 13/31, 2,112m (6,930ft)

Terminals: Five, designated Terminal One (or New Terminal), Terminal Two (Delta Terminal), Terminal Three (Main Terminal), Terminal Four

(International Terminal), and a Commuter Terminal

Airlines using airport as base or hub: Amerijet International, JetBlue, Southwest Airlines, Spirit Airlines

Annual passengers: 22,681,903

Annual cargo: 137,219 tonnes

Annual aircraft movements: 307,975

Background

Claimed to be the fastest growing airport in the United States, the airport opened on an abandoned golf course on 1 May 1929, and initially was known as Merle-Fogg Airport. When the United States entered the Second World War it was taken over by the United States Navy as NAS Fort Lauderdale, and initially was an aircraft maintenance and conversion yard as airliners were converted for naval use. Later it became a training station as a satellite of NAS Pensacola. The Naval Air Station closed on 1

October 1946 and the site was handed over to the local authority, becoming Broward County International Airport. Nevertheless, regular commercial flights did not begin until 2 June 1953, with a service to Nassau in the Bahamas. Domestic routes followed in 1958 and the first purpose-built terminal building was opened and the current name adopted in 1959. At this time the airport was used by Eastern Airlines, National Airlines, and Northeast Airlines.

The airport soon began to show rapid growth, passing the million passenger mark in 1969 and ten million in 1994. During the 1990s the airport began to attract the new breed of low-cost carriers, including Southwest Airlines and JetBlue. Plans have been made in recent years for runway extensions, and these are currently subject to approval by the FAA.

There have been few significant incidents at the airport.

SALT LAKE CITY: SLC

Salt Lake City, Utah, USA

Owner and operator: Salt Lake City

Runways: 16L/34R, 3,659m (12,004ft); 16R/34L, 3,658m (12,000ft); 17/35, 2,925m (9,596ft); 14/32, 1,491m (4,892ft); there are also three helipads

Terminals: Three, designated Terminal 1, Terminal 2, and International Terminal

Airlines using airport as base or hub: Delta Air Lines, SkyWest Airlines

Annual passengers: 22,045,333

Annual cargo: 177,710 tonnes

Annual aircraft movements: 422,010

Utah Transit Authority is extending its UTRAX light railway system into the airport.

Background

Salt Lake City's airport dates from 1911 when a small landing strip was built with a cinder runway at the Basque Flats, which had been used by French and Spanish shepherds. This replaced the field at the Utah State Fairpark, which had already been used by aircraft. While air services

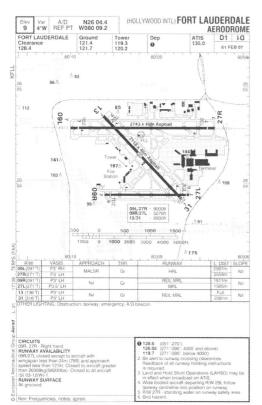

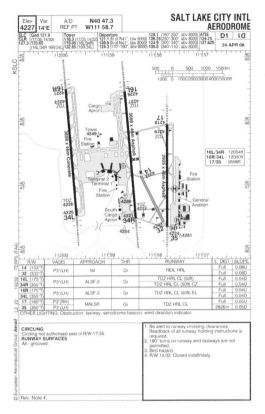

were still some time off, the new airstrip hosted the great International Aviation Carnival in its first year, with teams representing Curtiss and the Wright brothers, while Glenn Curtiss himself brought his new hydro-aeroplane and flew it on to and off the Great Salt Lake. For the next few years the airstrip was used for training and aerobatic displays.

It was not until after the First World War that regular air services began to use the airstrip, with the United States Postal Service providing an airmail service starting in 1920. That year the airstrip was named for the first time as the Woodward Field, after a local aviator, John Woodward. Hangars and other buildings were constructed, and the airfield began to assume a look of permanence. In 1925 the Post Office started to award airmail contracts to the fledgling airlines, and Western Air Express, predecessor of Western Airlines, won the contract to operate from Salt Lake City to Los Angeles via

Las Vegas. The new airfield continued to draw the pioneers, with Charles Lindbergh landing in 1927 on his post-transatlantic tour flying the famous *Spirit of St Louis*. A second runway was built, and in 1930 there was a further change of name to Salt Lake City Municipal Airport. In 1933 United Airlines started to call at Salt Lake City on its New York to San Francisco service, and a terminal and administration building opened.

During the Second World War the United States Army Air Force used the airport as a base, and a third runway was built.

After the war the airport resumed its expansion. In 1960 Terminal 1 was opened, and the airport was renamed again, gaining its current title in 1968. As with other US airports with traffic that is mainly domestic, airline deregulation in 1978 stimulated growth, and Western Airlines chose the airport as one of its hubs, with Terminal 2 being built originally for the airline's exclusive use, and the airport remained a hub when Western was absorbed by Delta Air Lines in 1987. In the meantime, both terminals had been expanded and the runways extended. In 1995 a new runway and the International Terminal were opened, while a new concourse was added to Terminal 1 for SkyWest Airlines. A further boost to traffic followed in 2002 when Salt Lake City became the venue for that year's Winter Olympic Games. The airport's first direct transatlantic flights followed in 2008 when Delta inaugurated a service to Paris, while transpacific services to Tokyo have followed and the airport already has cross-border flights to destinations in Canada and Mexico.

For the future the airport plans to realign runway 17/35 with parallel runways 16L/34R and 16R/34L, and runway extensions for additional transatlantic flights, while a fourth parallel runway is a distinct possibility in the longer term, possibly after 2020. A new terminal is also planned. Extension of the Utah Transit Authority TRAX light railway into the airport is also in hand.

In addition to its commercial role, Salt Lake City International is also a base for the Utah Air

National Guard, located on the airport's eastern side, with the 151st Air Refueling Wing of Air Mobility Command stationed at the base.

There have been a few serious accidents at the airport. One of these was on 11 November 1965 when a United Airlines Boeing 727 crashed short of the runway with the loss of 43 of the 91 passengers and crew. A Fairchild Metro of SkyWest Airlines collided with a Mooney on a pilot training flight while on final approach on 15 January 1987, with the loss of all ten passengers and crew of the Metro and the student pilot and instructor in the Mooney. Perhaps the most embarrassing accident was on 3 December 1974 when a Frontier Airlines flight scheduled to land at the airport accidentally landed at Salt Lake City Municipal Airport, a much smaller airport directly south and with a runway of the same heading as one at the main airport.

BALTIMORE/WASHINGTON THURGOOD MARSHALL INTERNATIONAL: BWI

Baltimore, Maryland, USA

Owner: State of Maryland
Operator: Maryland Aviation Administration
Runways: 15L/33R, 1,524m (5,000ft); 15R/33L, 2,896m (9,501ft); 4/22, 1,829m (6,000ft); 10/28, 3,201m (10,502ft); there is also a helipad
Terminals: One, with five concourses, A, B, C, D, and E
Airlines using airport as base or hub: Southwest Airlines
Annual passengers: 21,498,091
Annual cargo: 115,402 tonnes
Annual aircraft movements: 296,872

A free shuttle bus links the terminal with the BWI Rail Station a mile or so from the airport, which is served by Amtrak and the MARC Penn Line, with trains to Baltimore Penn Station and Washington Union Station.

Background

Planning for a new airport started at the end of the Second World War and the new airport was opened on 24 June 1950 by President Harry Truman. The airport was initially named Friendship International Airport. In 1972 the airport was purchased from the City of Baltimore by the State of Maryland, and in 1973 it was renamed Baltimore/Washington International Airport in an attempt to earn a share of the Washington air travel market. The IATA code was changed from BAL to BWI in 1982, with the latter code having been used by another airport until then. Under new ownership, modernisation and expansion began, with improvements to the runways and the construction of three air cargo terminals, while the passenger terminal more than doubled in size. The process was completed by the opening of the BWI Rail Station in 1980, with trains to Baltimore and Washington. Despite this, the airport has struggled to

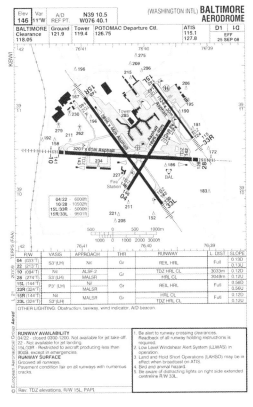

increase its share of transatlantic flights. A further blow was the loss of the US Airways hub in 2000, although at the same time the low-cost carrier, Southwest Airlines, established a strong base and is now the airport's main user, followed by another low-cost airline, AirTran.

In October 2005 the airport was renamed again as Baltimore/Washington International Thurgood Marshall Airport after a US Supreme Court judge who was a native of Baltimore.

There have been few accidents or incidents at the airport, but on 22 February 1974 it was the scene of an attempted hijacking of a Delta Air Lines Douglas DC-9 getting ready to depart for Atlanta. The hijacker shot and killed a security guard before boarding the aircraft, killing the co-pilot and wounding the captain, while the passengers fled. The police surrounded the aircraft and killed the hijacker.

CHICAGO MIDWAY INTERNATIONAL: MDW

Chicago, Illinois, USA

Owner: City of Chicago
Operator: Chicago Airport System
Runways: 4L/22R, 1,679m (5,507ft); 4R/22L, 1,965m (6,446ft); 13L/31R, 1,567m (5,141ft); 13C/31C, 1,988m (6,522ft); 13R/31L, 1,176m (3,859ft)
Terminals: One, with three concourses
Airlines using airport as base or hub:
     Southwest Airlines, AirTran
Annual passengers: 19,378,855
Annual cargo: 13,357 tonnes
Annual aircraft movements: 304,657

Airport terminal has its own station served by Chicago Transit Authority Orange Line trains running to the city centre.

Background

Sometimes referred to as the 'busiest square mile in the world', Chicago Midway is exceptionally neat and square in shape when viewed from above, with the runways running diagonally from the four corners. It is clear that there is no room for expansion. The shape in fact dates from the time when the state of Illinois was created and each community was granted a square mile for educational use, but as communities combined to provide larger schools, much of this land was sold off for other purposes.

The airport came into being when it was opened in 1923 as the Chicago Air Park on Chicago Board of Education land, with a single cinder runway. It was intended initially for airmail services, replacing the landing strip at Grant Park, closed after an accident when an aircraft crashed into a building with the loss of 13 lives. The City leased the land from the Board of Education in 1926 and the following year it was officially named as Chicago Municipal Airport. The airport continued to be owned by the BoE until 1982, when it was finally sold to the city.

In 1928 the airport had 12 hangars and 4 runways, with basic lighting for night operations, and flagmen provided air traffic control from their positions at the end of the runways. A new passenger terminal and administration building opened in 1931, and by the following year it was declared the world's busiest airport with more than 100,000 passengers and almost 61,000 flights. When the airport finally lost this accolade after almost 30 years, it was to Chicago's new airport at O'Hare.

The airport's position during the Second World War meant that it became still more important, especially for military transports crossing the United States. Additional runways were built and neighbouring railway lines were moved to allow expansion.

After the war, in 1949, the airport was renamed Chicago Midway Airport to commemorate the Battle of Midway in June 1942, the turning point in the war in the Pacific when the Imperial Japanese Navy lost four aircraft carriers in a single day. That year also saw phenomenal growth in traffic, with 3.2 million passengers passing through the airport, which handled 223,000 flights. Ten years later, Midway was handling 10 million passengers. This seemed to be the peak of the airport's success, however, as it was having difficulty in handling not just larger and heavier aircraft, but the new jet airliners then coming in to service. It compared unfavourably with O'Hare that had opened in 1955. Traffic dropped by 60 per cent by 1961, and the following year the last major carrier to use the airport, United Airlines, transferred its flights to O'Hare.

This was not the end of the story, for rebuilding started with the support of investment from the city, including the building of a new motorway, the Stevenson Expressway, to make the airport more easily accessible. During 1968 the major airlines began to return to Midway again, with 1.6 million passengers handled. A new generation of smaller jet airliners were able to use Midway's runways comfortably. US airline deregulation in 1978 also helped to boost recovery, with the launch of a new airline, Midway Airlines, in 1979, using the airport as its main base until it ceased operations in 1991. Nevertheless, during its short life, the airline put the airport once more on the map for air travellers, attracting low-cost airlines with the compact airport's lower costs and the convenience of its rapid transit railway line, especially after the airport station opened in October 1993.

Given the renewed growth at the airport, in 1996 the City of Chicago invested in the Midway Airport Terminal Programme. A new passenger terminal was completed on the other side of Cicero Avenue, connecting by a pedestrian bridge to the main concourses, with the new terminal building opening in 2001, and the following year international services resumed. For a number of years Midway was an important hub for ATA Airlines before they ceased operations in 2008.

For the future, with a compact and highly efficient operation, the question of privatisation has emerged, but at the time of writing no firm decision has been made. While privatisation has been widespread in airports around the world, it remains less common in the United States where many airports are owned by the local authority rather than by a national or nationalised concern.

Despite the confined nature of the airport, accidents and incidents have been few, but oddly two of the most serious both occurred on 8 December, but 33 years apart. On 8 December 1972 a United Airlines Boeing 737-200, coming in to land, crashed into a residential area causing the deaths of 43 of the 61 passengers and crew and 2 others on the ground. On 8 December 2005 a Southwest Airlines Boeing 737-700, landing in heavy snow from Baltimore, slid off the runway, through the airport fence, and on to the road outside the airport, hitting a car and killing a young boy who was a passenger in the car.

TAMPA ST PETERSBURG: TPA
Hillsborough, Tampa, Florida, USA

Owner and operator: Hillsborough County Aviation Authority
Runways: 9/27, 2,133m (6,999ft); 18L/36R, 2,530m (8,300ft); there is also a helipad
Terminals: One, with four airside satellites
Annual passengers: 19,154,957
Annual cargo: 98,018 tonnes
Annual aircraft movements: 258,349

A light railway linking the airport with Tampa city centre is being considered.

Background
On 1 January 1914 Tony Jannus started flights by the St Petersburg-Tampa Airboat Line between the two Florida towns across Tampa Bay with a Benoist flying boat, believed to have been the first heavier-than-air air service in the world. However, it was not until 1928 that Tampa opened its first airfield, Drew Field, and in 1935 Peter Knight opened an airport on Davis Island, near the centre of Tampa, and this was used by both Eastern Airlines and National Airlines for the next 11 years. Nevertheless, it was Drew Field that was acquired by the United States Army Air Force during the Second World War, expanding the airfield for the US Third Air Force, which used it as an aircrew combat training centre.

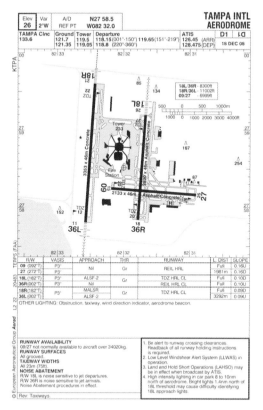

TriStars. The new terminal was the first to use a people mover shuttle to increase the throughput of passengers and reduce walking distances. The following year a 227ft high air traffic control tower was commissioned, and for a while this was the highest in the USA. In 1977 the airport gained its first transatlantic services with National introducing flights to Amsterdam and Paris. Nevertheless, the airside satellite terminal B closed in 1991 with the collapse of Eastern Airlines.

The airport is currently planning a 25 per cent increase in passenger traffic once its current improvements are completed, including a new runway, 17-35, and a second landside air terminal will be built to the north of the existing terminal, which will boost capacity to 50 million passengers annually by 2025. There is also the possibility of a light railway connecting the airport with the centre of Tampa. The completion of these plans may be delayed as there is evidence of a slow-down in traffic following the international credit crisis.

At the time of writing, the airport has not had a major accident or incident.

RONALD REAGAN WASHINGTON NATIONAL: DCA
Arlington County, Virginia, USA

Owner and operator: Metropolitan Washington Airports Authority
Runways: 1/19, 2,094m (6,869ft); 4/22, 1,497m (4,911ft); 15/33, 1,586m (5,204ft)
Terminals: Three, designated A, B, and C
Airlines using airport as base or hub: US Airways is the main operator
Annual passengers: 18,670,924
Annual aircraft movements: 275,433

Yellow and Blue Lines of the Washington Metro share a station between Terminals B and C.

After the war the Davis Island airport was too small for the new four-engined airliners that were entering service and both Eastern and National moved to Drew Field, using the former operations building as a terminal. In 1950 they were joined by Trans Canada Airlines, the predecessor of today's Air Canada, and in the years that followed, Capital, Delta, Northeast, Northwest Orient, and Trans World Airlines all followed as Florida became an increasingly popular holiday and retirement area. An annex was built east of the original terminal to accommodate the new arrivals.

In 1960 National introduced Douglas DC-8 jet airliners and was followed in 1961 by Pan American with Boeing 707s on a service to Mexico City. The original terminal was expanded further, but it was not until 1971 that a new terminal was opened, just in time for the introduction of wide-bodied air services by Boeing 747s, Douglas DC-10s, and Lockheed

Background

Strangely for the nation that invented the aeroplane, before the Second World War Washington was ill-served for airports. The first significant airport in the area was Hoover Field, close to the site of the Pentagon today, with a single runway running across a street, so that motor traffic had to be stopped whenever aircraft were taking off or landing. A site adjoining Hoover Field set up as Washington Airport, but during the Great Depression traffic was so poor that the two merged in 1930 to form Washington-Hoover Airport. The enlarged airport suffered from high-tension electric cables on one approach and a high chimney on the other. Eventually, the need for an airport close to the federal capital was met by the construction of the airport on land recovered from mudflats at Gravelly Point on the Potomac River, south of Washington and just four miles from The Capitol, which opened on 16 June 1941. As it was in Virginia, an Act of Congress in 1945 placed the airport under its jurisdiction.

After the war traffic grew, and runway extensions were completed in 1950 and again in 1955, although the following year an east–west runway was closed and is now used for taxiing and aircraft parking. The original terminal building was joined by a second in 1958, and in 1961 a connection was built between them. The location of the airport makes growth difficult, which led to the opening of a new airport, Washington Dulles, in 1962. The airport was not used by jet aircraft until 1966, and complaints about noise led the Federal Aviation Administration to impose restrictions on landing slots and the approaches in 1969. The airport was one of the first in the United States to have a direct railway link, with a Metro Station opened in 1977, initially separate from the terminals but now connected by pedestrian walkways.

An independent Metropolitan Washington Airports Authority was created in 1987, taking over control of the two airports from the federal government. In 1998 the current name was adopted on the 87th birthday of former President Ronald Reagan. This was a controversial measure requiring an act of Congress, as Reagan was still remembered by air traffic controllers for dismissing more than 11,000 of them during their nationwide strike in 1981.

The airport's proximity to The Capitol and the Pentagon may be an advantage for passengers, but even before the terrorist attacks of 11 September 2001, these important buildings required that aircraft did not come close during the landing approach or after take-off. In fact, central Washington is prohibited airspace below 18,000ft. Aircraft approaching from the north have to follow the course of the Potomac and make a steep turn before landing. This is a visual approach that requires a cloud base of at least 3,500ft and three miles visibility. In fact, the airport was closed for several weeks after the terrorist attacks, one of which ended with an aircraft crashing into the Pentagon and one failed attempt is generally believed to have been intended for the White House. There are lights on several of the bridges across the river to help pilots flying this approach, which is regarded as one of the most demanding in the world, but probably also one of the most satisfying for passengers as those sitting on the left side can see The Capitol and the Washington Monument, and those on the right side can see the Arlington National Cemetery and the Pentagon.

The most serious accident at the airport was on 13 January 1982 during a period of exceptionally cold weather, when an Air Florida Boeing 737 took off after waiting 49 minutes, by which time ice and snow had accumulated on the wings. The aircraft failed to climb after lifting-off and came down on to the 14th Street Bridge, slicing the roofs off vehicles stuck in heavy traffic and then continuing through thick ice on the Potomac River. Only 5 of the 79 passengers and crew survived, while 4 people who had been in cars on the bridge were also killed.

SAN DIEGO INTERNATIONAL AIRPORT/LINDBERGH FIELD: SAN

San Diego, California, USA

Owner and operator: San Diego County
  Regional Airport Authority
Runways: 9/27, 2,865m (9,401ft)
Terminals: Three, designated Terminal 1,
  Terminal 2, and Commuter Terminal
Annual passengers: 18,336,761
Annual cargo: 140,304 tonnes
Annual aircraft movements: 227,329

Background

Also known as Lindbergh Field, San Diego is just three miles north of the city and is close to the border with Mexico. It is the busiest single runway airport in the United States and the entire airport occupies just over a square mile of land.

Opened on 16 August 1928 as San Diego Municipal Airport – Lindbergh Field, because

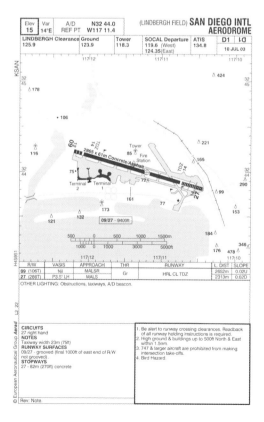

the city was home to the factory where Lindberg's aeroplane, *Spirit of St Louis*, was built, and flown away by the first man to make a solo transatlantic crossing. It was the first airfield to serve seaplanes and landplanes, and used as a testing ground for many early US glider designs, while there was also a glider school at the airfield, run by William Bowlus, the same man who supervised the building of the *Spirit of St Louis*. It was not until 1 June 1930 that an airmail service was started linking San Diego with Los Angeles. International services to Mexico followed in 1934, and the United States Coast Guard established a station next to the airfield in April 1937, with their landplanes making use of the airfield.

During the Second World War the airfield served as a base for the United States Army Air Force, and a number of improvements were made, including extending the runway to 2,670m (8,750ft) for heavy bombers. Post war, commercial air services returned, and the airport's role was enhanced when Pacific Southwest Airlines (PSA) chose San Diego as its headquarters in 1949, flying initially to destinations across California. Jet operations came in 1960 when both American Airlines and United Airlines used Boeing 720s on services to Phoenix and San Francisco.

Throughout this period the airport managed with the original terminal, despite growing passenger volumes and the growth in the size of aircraft, and it was not until 5 March 1967 that what is now Terminal 1 was opened. It was followed by Terminal 2 on 11 July 1979, and by the Commuter (i.e. very short distance frequent flight) Terminal on 23 July 1996, while Terminal 2 was enlarged two years later. Obstructions near one end of the runway mean that aircraft landing from the east do not use the entire runway, but have a displaced threshold, meaning that they touch down part-way down the runway, reducing the landing distance to 2,314m (7,591ft), and for aircraft taking off eastwards there are maximum weight restrictions. Not surprisingly, with these limitations and the steady growth in traffic, attention has been given to relocating the airport, and at one time the US Marine Corps air station at Miramar was considered, despite objections from the USMC, but the plan was defeated when local residents objected. Nevertheless, in the long term a new airport for San Diego will be needed as expansion at the current site would be difficult.

Although originally owned by the city, control of the airfield passed first to the San Diego Unified Port District and then to the current owners and operators in 2001. It is still used occasionally by the USCG for fixed-wing flights, which requires their aircraft to cross a busy six-lane road that separates the base from the airfield, but, fortunately, most aircraft actually based at Coast Guard Air Station San Diego are helicopters!

There has been one serious accident at San Diego in recent years. On 25 September 1978 a PSA Boeing 727-200, approaching from Sacramento via Los Angeles, collided with a Cessna 172 over the city's North Park, with the loss of all 135 passengers and crew in the 727 and both occupants of the 172.

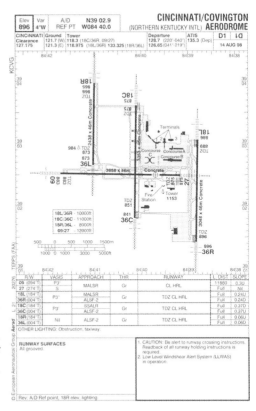

CINCINNATI/NORTHERN KENTUCKY INTERNATIONAL: CVG

Hebron, Kentucky, USA

Owner and operator: Kenton County Aviation Board
Runways: 18L/36R, 3,048m (10,000ft); 18C/36C, 3,353m (11,000ft); 18R/36L, 2,438m (8,000ft); 9/27, 3,658m (12,000ft)
Terminals: Two, designated Terminal 2 and Terminal 3
Annual passengers: 15,736,220
Annual cargo: 39,691 tonnes
Annual aircraft movements: 328,059

Background
Operations began at Cincinnati on 10 January 1947 when an American Airlines Douglas DC-3 landed from Cleveland. The airport continued to develop, but the major factor in modernisation was the arrival of the jet age in 1960, with

Delta Air Lines operating Convair 880 Coronado airliners into the airport. This led to the terminal being enlarged, and the north–south runway was extended to 2,620m (8,600ft), with further expansion of the terminal in 1964, and a new east–west runway in 1971. Passenger traffic fell after Delta filed for bankruptcy protection in 2005, when the number of flights was substantially reduced. Terminal 1 has been closed, although there is the possibility that it may reopen for use by low-cost airlines. Terminal 3 is used by Delta, its Skyteam partners, and both Continental and Northwest, while other airlines, including US Airways, US Airways Express, American and United, use Terminal 2.

There is competition for Cincinnati from Combs Field Airport at Hebron which provides an alternative for regional flights.

A number of accidents have occurred at the airport over the past 50 years or so. One of these was on 12 January 1955 when a TWA Martin

202, taking off for Cleveland, collided with a privately-owned Douglas DC-3, killing 13 aboard the 202 and the crew of 2 on the DC-3. More fortunate were the 2 crew of a Zantop Douglas DC-4 on a cargo flight that crashed into an orchard on 14 November 1961 as they both survived. An American Airlines Boeing 727 crashed on approach on 8 November 1965, killing 5 of the 6 crew and 53 of the 56 passengers. An aborted take-off ended with a TWA Boeing 707 overrunning the runway on 6 November 1967, injuring 11 of the 29 passengers, one of whom died four days later, but the crew of 7 was unhurt. Later that month a TWA Convair 880 crashed on approach killing 5 of the 7 crew and 65 of the 75 passengers. A Comair Piper Navajo crashed shortly after take-off on 8 October 1979, killing the pilot and all 7 passengers. On 2 June 1983 an Air Canada Douglas DC-9 flying from Houston and Dallas to Toronto and Montreal was diverted to Cincinnati with a cabin fire, and although all 5 crew members survived, 23 of the 41 passengers died of smoke inhalation. Fuel starvation and double engine failure brought down an Air Tahoma Convair 580 approaching from Memphis on 13 August 2004 on a cargo flight, killing the first officer and injuring the captain.

ST LOUIS-LAMBERT: STL

St Louis, Missouri, USA

Owner and operator: City of St Louis
Runways: 12L/30R, 2,744m (9,003ft); 12R/30L, 3,359m (11,019ft); 11/29, 2,743m (9,000ft); 06/24, 2,317m (7,602ft)
Terminals: Two, consisting of the Main Terminal with four concourses A–D, and an east Terminal with Concourse E
Airlines using airport as base or hub: American Airlines, American Eagle
Annual passengers: 15,384,557
Annual cargo: 83,251 tonnes
Annual aircraft movements: 254,302

The airport is served by MetroLink Red Line trains which connect it with the city centre.

Background

St Louis can trace its aviation origins to the days before the First World War when the airport site was known as Kinloch Field and, as well as being used by balloons, it was also visited by the Wright brothers and their exhibition team. In 1920 a former US Army officer, Major Albert Lambert, bought Kinloch Field and developed it as an airport, building hangars and a terminal. He had earlier been the first person in St Louis to receive an aviator's certificate, or pilot's licence, and the airport today is named to commemorate his achievements. Another famous aviator connected with the airport was Charles Lindbergh, who flew airmail flights for Robertson Airlines. In 1927 Lambert sold the airport to the city and as a result it rivals Cleveland to be the first municipally-owned airport in the United States. Before the decade was over, it also became the first with an air traffic control system, although this consisted of waving flags to let pilots know if it was safe to take off or land. The airport soon attracted regular air services, with both Eastern Air Lines and Marquette Airlines operating services.

The Second World War saw the airport become a manufacturers' field, with both McDonnell and Curtis-Wright establishing factories. Commercial flights resumed after the war, and in 1956 a new passenger terminal was completed, with what was then regarded as an innovative four-domed design. Nevertheless, continued growth also brought problems, and during the 1970s it was proposed that Lambert be replaced by a new airport across the state line in Illinois, but for once local residents objected to the loss of their airport and a massive expansion programme saw its capacity increased by 50 per cent. In 1982 Trans World Airlines (TWA) relocated its main hub from Kansas City International Airport, and when the airline was acquired by American Airlines in 2001, by which time TWA was a fraction of its peak size, Lambert became a relief airfield for AA's hubs at Chicago O'Hare and Dallas/Fort Worth. In the meantime, the proposed Illinois airport went ahead and was completed in 1997 as MidAmerica

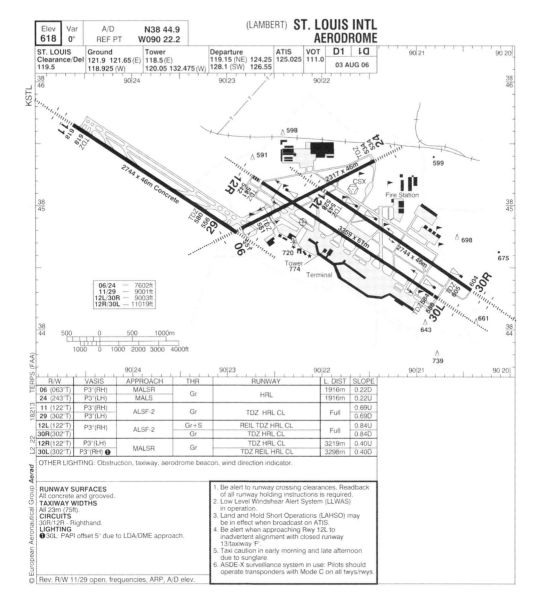

| Elev | Var | A/D | N38 44.9 |
| 618 | 0° | REF PT | W090 22.2 |

(LAMBERT) **ST. LOUIS INTL AERODROME**

ST. LOUIS Clearance/Del 119.5	Ground 121.9 121.65 (E) 118.925 (W)	Tower 118.5 (E) 120.05 132.475 (W)	Departure 119.15 (NE) 124.25 128.1 (SW) 126.55	ATIS 125.025	VOT 111.0	D1	I-O

03 AUG 06

KSTL

06/24	—	7602ft
11/29	—	9001ft
12L/30R	—	9003ft
12R/30L	—	11019ft

TERPS (FAA)

R/W	VASIS	APPROACH	THR	RUNWAY	L. DIST	SLOPE
06 (063°T)	P3°(RH)	MALSR	Gr	HRL	1916m	0.22D
24 (243°T)	P3°(LH)	MALS			1916m	0.22U
11 (122°T)	P3°(RH)	ALSF-2	Gr	TDZ HRL CL	Full	0.69U
29 (302°T)	P3°(LH)					0.69D
12L (122°T)	P3°(RH)	ALSF-2	Gr+S	REIL TDZ HRL CL	Full	0.84U
30R (302°T)			Gr	TDZ HRL CL		0.84D
12R (122°T)	P3°(LH)	MALSR	Gr	TDZ HRL CL	3219m	0.40U
30L (302°T)	P3°(RH) ❶			TDZ REIL HRL CL	3298m	0.40D

18213   L2 22

OTHER LIGHTING: Obstruction, taxiway, aerodrome beacon, wind direction indicator.

RUNWAY SURFACES
All concrete and grooved.
TAXIWAY WIDTHS
All 23m (75ft).
CIRCUITS
30R/12R - Righthand.
LIGHTING
❶ 30L: PAPI offset 5° due to LDA/DME approach.

1. Be alert to runway crossing clearances. Readback of all runway holding instructions is required.
2. Low Level Windshear Alert System (LLWAS) in operation.
3. Land and Hold Short Operations (LAHSO) may be in effect when broadcast on ATIS.
4. Be alert when approaching Rwy 12L to inadvertent alignment with closed runway 13/taxiway 'F'.
5. Taxi caution in early morning and late afternoon due to sunglare.
6. ASDE-X surveillance system in use: Pilots should operate transponders with Mode C on all twys/rwys.

© European Aeronautical Group Aerad

Rev: R/W 11/29 open, frequencies, ARP, A/D elev.

St Louis, near Mascoutah, and is available as a relief airport for Lambert, but it has failed to attract any of the major US domestic airlines. Lambert also lost its transatlantic flights. American announced in late 2006 that it intended to develop its services from Lambert with more direct flights and larger aircraft.

Over the years, Lambert has also been used by the USAF, but the resident squadrons have now been relocated to Montana.

One of the accidents and incidents at the airport over the years had a happy outcome when, on 5 April 1977, an American Airlines Boeing 707 which had taken off for Los Angeles was forced to return when the No. 3 engine broke away from the aircraft, which landed safely. Less fortunate were the three crew of a Fleming International Airways Lockheed Electra which took-off on a cargo flight to Detroit on 6 July 1977 with the No. 2 engine performing badly, and after lift-off the aircraft veered to the left and crashed, killing all aboard. On another cargo flight, on 9 January 1984, a Skycraft Douglas C-47 crashed after take-off for Toronto because it had been refuelled with kerosene rather than avgas; one of the two pilots was killed. A runway incursion by a Cessna 441 on 22 November 1994 ended when it was struck by a TWA McDonnell Douglas MD-82 taking-off for Denver. The MD-82 hit the 441 as it accelerated down the runway, killing both occupants, but the 8 crew and 132 passengers of the MD-82 were unharmed. An American Airlines Douglas DC-9, which had taken off from St Louis on 28 December 2007, was forced to return with an engine fire, but the nose wheel wouldn't extend, so an emergency landing had to be made. All 5 crew and 138 passengers evacuated the aircraft without injury.

OAKLAND: OAK

Oakland, California, USA

Owner and operator: Port of Oakland
Runways: 9L/27R, 1,662m (5,454ft); 9R/27L, 1,893m (6,212ft); 11/29, 3,048m (10,000ft); 15/33, 1,028m (3,372ft)
Terminals: Two, designated Terminal 1 and Terminal 2
Airlines using airport as base or hub: Federal Express (FedEx), Southwest Airlines
Annual passengers: 14,846,832
Annual cargo: 647,594 tonnes
Annual aircraft movements: 342,024

Background

The airport was opened by Charles Lindbergh in late 1927 after his transatlantic solo flight. In 1928 it was an important stopping place for Charles Kingsford Smith's first transpacific flight to Australia, and it also saw Amelia Earhart's fatal final flight in 1937. Before this, it had scheduled flights from late 1927 when Boeing Air Transport, a predecessor of United Airlines, formed when anti-trust legislation prohibited US manufacturers from involvement in air transport, introduced a service, and in 1932 it

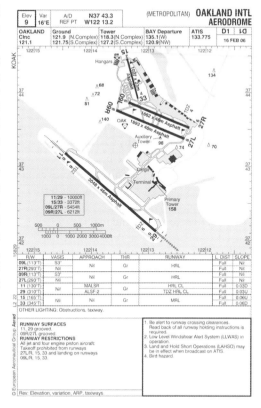

was joined by Transcontinental & Western Air, the predecessor of Trans World Airlines. Like many other airports during the Second World War, it was taken over in 1943 by the US military for transport flights to the Pacific islands, displacing scheduled flights to San Francisco.

The airport reverted to commercial use after the war and, starting in 1946, first Western Airlines, and then American Airlines, TWA, and Pacific Southwest started services from Oakland. The current Terminal 1 was opened in 1962, with the airport's first jetways. A boom came during the Vietnam War, with World Airways, the leading US supplemental (charter) carrier carrying large numbers of military personnel on trooping flights. It was at this time that an international terminal was built. The end of the war in Vietnam saw traffic levels drop, but airline deregulation in the United States in 1973 brought a number of low-fare carriers to the airport and prompted renewed growth. A second terminal was built, also known as the Lionel J. Wilson Terminal 2, for PSA and AirCal. Federal Express (FedEx) opened a cargo base at the airport in 1988 and it has become one of the busiest in the USA. Southwest Airlines has established a base and is now the airport's main carrier. International flights have generally been to Mexico, with occasional and relatively short-lived charter operations by Corsair from France and Martinair from the Netherlands. For many years United Airlines ran a maintenance centre at Oakland, but this has now been transferred to San Francisco International.

Major improvements and renovations started in 2006, but plans for a Terminal 3 have been shelved following the rise in fuel prices in 2008 and the downturn in air traffic as the world economy went into recession. The loss of ATA and Aloha saw the airport's frequent flights to Hawaii reduced.

One of the most serious accidents at the airport was on 24 August 1951, when a United Airlines Douglas DC-6B, approaching from Chicago through low cloud and slightly off course, flew into a hillside killing all 6 crew and all 44 passengers. No one seems to have been injured when an International Aircraft Services Lockheed Constellation was in a ground collision with a Douglas DC-7 on 20 June 1961. Another ground accident on 31 August 1962 wrote off a United States Air Force Lockheed Super Constellation, again without casualties. A Saturn Airways Douglas DC-6 was written off when it landed after a training flight on 24 January 1967 because of mishandling of reverse pitch, but the four crew survived.

PORTLAND INTERNATIONAL: PDX

Portland, Oregon, USA

Owner and operator: Port of Portland
Runways: 10L/28R, 2,438m (8,000ft); 10R/28L, 3,353m (11,000ft); 3/31, 2,134m (7,001ft)
Terminals: One, with five concourses, A, B, C, D (international), and E
Annual passengers: 14,654,222

Annual cargo: 254,754 tonnes
Annual aircraft movements: 264,518

A light railway connects the airport terminal with Portland city centre.

Background

The site of the city's airport (the largest in Oregon) has changed over the years. The original airport was on Swan Island on the Willamette River, which was officially opened by Charles Lindbergh in 1927, although not finally completed until 1930. This airport was soon outgrown by traffic and the increase in aircraft sizes, so that by 1935 it was clear that a new airport was needed, as Swan Island did not offer space for expansion. Despite these limitations, in the meantime Swan Island was officially named as Portland Airport.

The site of the present airport was purchased by the City in 1936, and work proceeded with

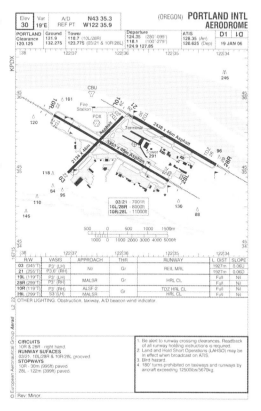

the aid of federal funds, as the construction project provided employment during the years of the Great Depression. When completed in 1940, the new airport was named Portland-Columbia Airport. It was taken over by the United States Army Air Force during the Second World War, but returned to commercial use when the war ended. The airport had been built to a high specification for the day, and was a so-called 'super airport', with a terminal and five runways, all of which proved adequate for increasing traffic until 1952 when a new terminal was opened and a longer east–west runway constructed. The one drawback was that it was too low, and in 1948 the entire site was flooded, and airlines had to divert to Troutdale Airport for several months. A new terminal was completed in 1958, which remains in use today but much extended and renovated, and after these improvements were completed the airport added 'International' to its title. Ten years later it was suggested that a third runway could be provided by reclaiming land from the Columbia River, but this met with strong local opposition. In 1974 the southern runway was extended to permit operations by Boeing 747 'jumbo jets'.

Further major improvements, including a new air traffic control tower, followed during the 1990s, and in 2001 the 'H' shape of the present terminal was completed.

The airport was originally designated PD, with the 'X' added to give a three-letter designation as the number of airports grew.

Portland developed as a gateway to Asia with Delta Air Lines developing a route network based on the airport, but the collapse of stock markets in Asia in 2000 and complaints about the immigration controls at Portland, that led the airport to be nicknamed 'DePortland', also led to a sharp fall in traffic. Delta dropped its last services to Tokyo Narita and Nagoya in March 2001. Lufthansa started direct flights from Frankfurt in March 2003, and Mexicana introduced services to several destinations that year, although these were cut in 2008 as fuel prices escalated, while Northwest took over the service to Tokyo Narita in June 2004. Alaska Airlines

still provides a Mexico service, and Northwest introduced a service to Amsterdam in 2008.

For the future there is a choice between expansion or relocation. The operators prefer the former option, but there are opportunities for relocation to Hillsboro Airport, also owned by the Port of Portland. There are also possibilities at Salem's McNary Field. Portland does suffer from problems with one of the runways, as base material has begun to soften under pressure from aircraft landings, which may lead to an extension of the other runway to 3,353m (11,000ft) to allow operations to continue during repair work.

A Douglas DC-8-61 of United Airlines was forced to crash-land short of the runway on 28 December 1978 when it ran out of fuel, despite having left Denver with the necessary contingency supplies, killing 2 of the 8 crew and 8 of the 181 passengers. On 24 December 2005 an Empire Airlines Cessna Caravan I Super Cargomaster failed to gain height after taking off, and crash-landed beyond the airport on to a golf course, but the sole occupant, the pilot, survived.

KANSAS CITY INTERNATIONAL: MCI
Missouri, USA

Owner and operator: Kansas City
Runways: 1L/19R, 3,292m (10,801ft); 1R/19L, 2,896m (9,500ft); 9/27, 2,896m (9,500ft)
Terminals: Four, designated Terminal A, Terminal B, and Terminal C
Airlines using airport as base or hub: Midwest Airlines, Southwest Airlines
Annual passengers: 12,000,997
Annual cargo: 127,767 tonnes
Annual aircraft movements: 194,969

Background
The area around Kansas City was badly flooded in 1951, and this destroyed the Fairfax Airport where Mid-Continent Airlines and Trans World Airlines both had their regional bases, although the area's main airport, Kansas City Downtown Airport, was not as badly damaged. There was a

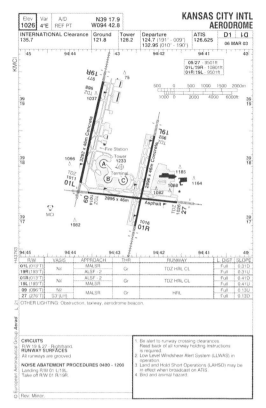

include the airport before further major expenditure on passenger terminals and a control tower was undertaken. It was officially opened in October 1972 and renamed Kansas City International Airport, although retaining its Mid-Continent designation of MCI. The design of the terminals owed much to TWA as the main airline, which wanted to avoid using people-movers because of the cost. Instead, it was decided to have a single-level terminal with the flight gates indicated by signs along the road so that passengers would not have to walk more than 23m (75ft) from the road to the departure gate. The system was sound in theory but flawed in practice, as it was unsuitable for large-capacity, wide-bodied aircraft, and it also meant that each gate had to have its own security rather than a centralised security area, introduced during the 1970s following a spate of hijackings of US airliners. It also made it difficult to provide amenities for passengers. The inevitable happened: even though it was built to their specification, TWA asked for the terminal to be redesigned. Kansas City refused, so TWA moved its hub to St Louis!

Later, three circular terminals were built, each with a short-stay parking area in the middle of the circle and aircraft stands on the outside. Foundations were laid for a fourth such terminal, although it was never built. While people-movers have still not been installed, a free shuttle bus connects the terminals, but this only became free as a result of passenger protests over the original 25 cents charge. There is widespread belief that eventually Kansas City will have to build a central terminal, but there is no date for this or a proposed railway link with the city.

The worst accident in the history of the airport was on 13 April 1987 when a Buffalo Airways cargo flight from Wichita approached in fog and clipped a ridge, killing all four crew members. On 8 September 1989 a USAir (now US Airways) flight, approaching from Pittsburgh, clipped power lines, before diverting to Salina, but none of the 64 passengers and crew was injured. A second attempt at take-off by an Air Transport International Douglas DC-8

third airport, Grandview Airport, in the area, but the city decided to build a completely new one north of the city and as far away as possible from the threat of floods from the Missouri River. Construction began in September 1954 and the runways were ready in 1956. Grandview was donated to the United States Air Force, which established a base there.

The locally-based Mid-Continent Airlines was absorbed by Braniff in 1952, but despite this the city opted to name the airport Mid-Continent International Airport because it served the Mid-Continent Oil Field. The city also built a maintenance base, which it leased to TWA. However, the airport did not have any scheduled services until 1963, as TWA continued to use the Downtown Airport until the Federal Aviation Agency decided that it was unsuitable for large jet aircraft and had no room for expansion. While Mid-Continent was outside the boundaries of Kansas City, these were extended to

departing for Westover on 16 February 1995 ended in a crash after directional control was lost as the tail struck the runway during rotation, and all three occupants were killed.

CLEVELAND HOPKINS INTERNATIONAL: CLE

Cleveland, Ohio, USA

Owner and operator: City of Cleveland
Runways: 06L/24R, 2,743m (9,006ft); 06R/24L, 2,743m (9,006ft); 10/28, 1,834m (6,017ft); 06C/24RC, 2,163m (7,096ft) currently closed
Terminals: One, divided into International Arrivals and Concourses A, B, C, and D
Airlines using airport as base or hub:
   Continental Airlines
Annual passengers: 11,459,390
Annual cargo: 86,690 tonnes
Annual aircraft movements: 244,719

The airport has its own station on the Cleveland Transit Systems Red Line.

Background

Situated just 14km (9 miles) from the centre of Cleveland, Cleveland Harry Hopkins dates from 1925. The airport rivals St Louis as the first municipally-owned airport in the United States, as well as having the first air traffic control tower and ground-to-air radio, and the first airfield lighting system, with these innovations all completed in 1930. Also, in 1968 it was the first American airport to have its own railway station. It was named after the former city manager, Harry Hopkins, in 1951. It is the larger and more important of two airports operated by the city, with the other being Cleveland Burke Lakefront Airport.

Air Canada is the only foreign airline to operate scheduled services into the airport, although it did have a transatlantic service for some years operated by JAT Yugoslav Airlines, and since 1999 Continental has operated to London, initially to Gatwick, switching to London Heathrow in spring 2009. A service to Paris, introduced early in 2008, was withdrawn later in the year. There are charter flights to Mexico by Aeromexico.

There has been one recorded hijacking, an armed confrontation between a man and police at a ticket counter, and one serious accident at the airport in recent years. The accident was on 18 February 2007 when a Delta Connection flight operated by a Shuttle America Embraer E-170, landing from Atlanta, skidded off the runway and crashed through a fence, but none of the 4 crew and 70 passengers was injured.

MEMPHIS INTERNATIONAL AIRPORT: MEM

Memphis, Shelby County, Tennessee, USA

Owner and operator: Memphis-Shelby County
   Airport Authority
Runways: 18L/36R, 2,743m (9,000ft); 18C/36C, 3,389m (11,120ft); 18R/36L, 2,841m (9,320ft); 9/27, 2,727m (8,946ft)

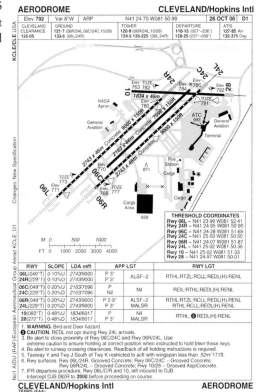

Terminals: One, with three concourses, A, B, and C

Airlines using airport as base or hub: Federal Express, Northwest Airlines

Annual passengers: 11,290,477

Annual cargo: 3,840,491 tonnes

Annual aircraft movements: 374,989

Background

Memphis International is 11km (7 miles) from the centre of Memphis, and became the world's busiest air cargo airport when it was selected as the global freight hub for Federal Express (FedEx) in 1973.

Opened during the early 1930s, the airport was built on farmland, like so many others at the time, and had an unpaved runway and three hangars. The early passenger and airmail flights were provided by American Airlines and Chicago and Southern Airlines, but in 1939 these were joined by Braniff Airways, Capital Airlines, Eastern Air Lines, and Southern Airways. During the Second World War the airport was used by the United States Army Air Force as a base from which to ferry new aircraft to operational units around the world, and during this time paved runways were laid.

The airport opened a new passenger terminal in 1963, and in 1969 the current title was adopted, although there were no direct international routes until the KLM Royal Dutch Airlines began a service to Amsterdam in 1995, and this route is now operated by Northwest Airlines. Before this, Republic Airlines established a hub at the airport in 1985, and this passed to Northwest when it acquired Republic the following year.

The military connection remains, as the airport is also the Memphis Air National Guard Base of the Tennessee Air National Guard, operating Lockheed C-5A/B Galaxy transports of the 164th Airlift Wing, part of Air Mobile Command of the USAF.

One of the potentially most serious incidents at the airport was on 7 April 1994 when a FedEx McDonnell Douglas DC-10-30F, which had taken off for San Jose, suffered an attempted hijacking by a pilot riding in the jump seat. The man had been found to have lied about his flying experience and was about to be dismissed, but planned to seize the aircraft and make a suicide attack on the FedEx headquarters. He attacked the two pilots and flight engineer with hammers, fracturing the skull of the first officer before he could be overcome, and the aircraft landed safely back at Memphis despite being over its landing weight due to the volume of fuel being carried. On 21 December 2001, maintenance failings after a fuel leak had been discovered in an Air National Guard Lockheed C-141 Starlifter resulted in the aircraft being damaged beyond repair while still on the ground. A Mesaba Airlines Avro RJ85 of Northwest Airlink was also damaged beyond repair while being taxied from the maintenance hangar to the terminal on 15 October 2002. The aircraft ran out of control and hit the terminal building, but the two occupants survived. Windshear and

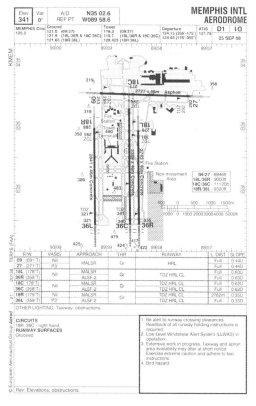

high winds resulted in the loss of a FedEx McDonnell Douglas MD-10-10F landing from Oakland on 18 December 2003, but the seven occupants (higher than normal because of the line check of a pilot) all escaped. Another FedEx MD-10-10F was badly damaged while landing from Seattle on 28 July 2006 when the undercarriage collapsed, but the three crew members escaped unharmed.

SACRAMENTO INTERNATIONAL: SMF

Sacramento, California

Owner and operator: County of Sacramento
Runways: 16L/34R, 2,622m (8,601ft); 16R/34L, 2,621m (8,600ft)
Terminals: Two, designated Terminal A and Terminal B
Airlines using airport as base or hub:
Southwest Airlines is the major carrier

Annual passengers: 10,748,982
Annual cargo: 79,117 tonnes
Annual aircraft movements: 174,946

Background

Situated some 16km (10 miles) north-west of the town, the airport opened on 21 October 1967 when it was called Sacramento Metropolitan Airport. The current name was adopted in 1998, yet it was not until four years later that its first international flights began, operated by Mexicana from Guadalajara.

A new Terminal B is under construction and should be ready for 2012, when the existing Terminal B will be demolished.

The one recorded incident at the airport was to a United Airlines Boeing 727 on 9 September 1980, when a small bomb exploded in a hold as passengers were leaving the aircraft after it had landed from Portland. There were no injuries to crew or passengers, but two baggage handlers were wounded.

SAN JOSE NORMAN Y. MINETA INTERNATIONAL: SJC

San Jose, California, USA

Owner and operator: City of San Jose
Runways: 12L/30R, 3,353m (11,000ft); 12R/30L, 3,353m (11,000ft); 11/29, 1,402m (4,599ft)
Terminals: Two, designated Terminal A and Terminal C (the latter due to be replaced by a new Terminal B in 2010)
Annual passengers: 10,658,389
Annual cargo: 82,927 tonnes
Annual aircraft movements: 187,276

Background

The smallest of the three airports in the San Francisco Bay Area, after San Francisco and Oakland, even though San Jose has the largest population of the three, San Jose airport is centrally placed, but whilst convenient this has also been its downfall as there is no room for expansion.

The airport dates from 1939 when a group of local businessmen acquired an option to pur-

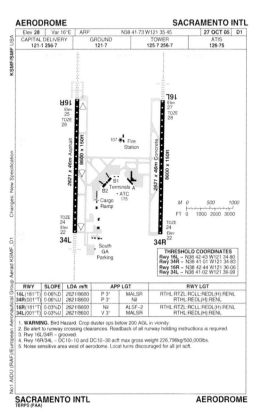

chase land, and the following year one of them, Ernie Renzel, pressed for a bond to raise the cost of buying the land and building an airport. Further progress was prevented by the Second World War, but in 1945 part of the land was leased for the construction of hangars, an office, and a flying school. Over the next two decades the small airfield developed into an airport with three terminals, the last of which, Terminal C, was opened in 1965. The airport was adopted as a hub by Air California and, when this airline was acquired by American Airlines in 1986, American continued operations but not as a hub, although later Reno Air, a Nevada airline, established a hub there.

Further expansion followed in 1990 with the opening of a new Terminal A. In 2001 the airport took its present name to commemorate Norman Yoshio Mineta, a local man who became mayor and congressman, eventually holding the offices of US Secretary of Commerce and then Secretary of Transportation.

Situated close to Silicon Valley, the airport prospered during the 'dot-com' bubble, but when this burst, the sharp fall in demand up to 2004 saw many airlines reduce their flights or drop the airport from their schedules. Air Canada ended its flights from Ottawa and Toronto, and American Airlines dropped its flights to Tokyo, Taipei, Vancouver, and Paris, as well as its domestic services to six major US cities, while the flights within Southern California became American Eagle flights. This sharp fall continued with Alaska Airlines cutting its flights to Mexico.

The local authority instigated a plan to revive the local economy, and tried to encourage airlines to restore transatlantic and transpacific flights. Nevertheless, this initiative was hampered by the sharp rise in oil prices during 2008, and San Jose lost most of what remained of its transcontinental services, even while work continued on a three-phase nine-year expansion plan with a new terminal, the James Nissen (after the test pilot who opened the flying school in 1945), capable of handling almost double the 2007 traffic volume. Included in the plans was a people-mover to link the terminal with a planned Bay Area Rapid Transit station. These ambitious plans were scaled back in late 2005, and called for instead was a new and simplified Terminal B to replace the ageing Terminal C.

The one serious incident at the airport was on 15 September 1975 when a man who had raped a woman took two Continental Airline employees hostage and boarded one of the company's Boeing 727s, from which the two hostages escaped and the would-be hijacker was shot dead by the police.

SAN JUAN LUIS MUÑOZ MARÍN INTERNATIONAL: SJU

Carolina, Puerto Rico

Owner and operator: Puerto Rico Airports Authority
Runways: 08/26, 3,049m (10,002ft); 10/28, 2,443m (8,016ft)
Terminals: One, with five concourses, A, B, C, D, and E
Airlines using airport as base or hub: American, Continental, Delta
Annual passengers: 10,470,357
Annual cargo: 234,427 tonnes
Annual aircraft movements: 189,656

Background

The Caribbean's busiest airport, Luis Muñoz Marín is the main airport for the US territory of Puerto Rico and is 5km (just over 3 miles) southeast of the capital, San Juan, on an island, Isla Verde (Green Island).

The airport opened in 1955 and was at first known as Isla Verde International Airport after the location, and it was not until 1985 that the current title was adopted in memory of the island's first democratically-elected governor. During the early days it became a Caribbean hub for several of the major US airlines, including Pan Am, Caribbean Airways, and Eastern Air Lines, and between 1966 and 1984 it was the main base for Puerto Rico's own airline, Prinair, until it collapsed. In 1986 American Airlines and its feeder carrier, American Eagle, also operated

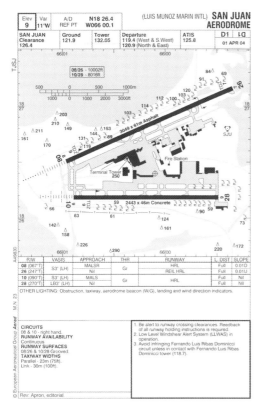

Elev 9	Var 11°W	A/D REF PT	N18 26.4 W066 00.1	(LUIS MUNOZ MARIN INTL)	**SAN JUAN**
					AERODROME

| SAN JUAN Clearance 126.4 | Ground 121.9 | Tower 132.05 | Departure 119.4 (West & S.West) 120.9 (North & East) | ATIS 125.8 | D1 LG |
| | | | | | 01 APR 04 |

R/W	VASIS	APPROACH	THR	RUNWAY	L. DIST	SLOPE
08 (067°T)	S3' (LH)	MALSR		HRL	Full	0.01D
26 (247°T)		Nil	Gr	REIL HRL	Full	0.01U
10 (090°T)	S3' (LH)	MALS			Full	Nil
28 (270°T)	LB3' (LH)	Nil	Gr	HRL	Full	Nil

OTHER LIGHTING: Obstruction, taxiway, aerodrome beacon (W/G), landing and wind direction indicators.

CIRCUITS
08 & 10 - right hand.
RUNWAY AVAILABILITY
Continuous.
RUNWAY SURFACES
08/26 & 10/28 Grooved.
TAXIWAY WIDTHS
Parallel - 23m (75ft).
Link - 30m (100ft).

1. Be alert to runway crossing clearances. Readback of all runway holding instructions is required.
2. Low Level Windshear Alert System (LLWAS) in operation.
3. Avoid infringing Fernando Luis Ribas Dominicci circuit unless in contact with Fernando Luis Ribas Dominicci tower (118.7).

Rev: Apron, editorial.

a hub. There have been difficulties in attracting and retaining long-haul international flights, especially over the past year or so when even American dramatically reduced the number of flights into the island, but there are also flights to several of the more important towns on Puerto Rico.

A second terminal building is being built, and this will have just a single concourse.

The airport is also a base for the United States Coast Guard and for the Puerto Rico Air National Guard.

There have been a number of accidents at the airport, but none of them involved fatalities. An American Airlines McDonnell Douglas DC-10, taking-off for Dallas-Fort Worth in 1985, over-ran the runway and ended up in a lake, but without injuries to the crew or passengers. On 24 September 1998 a Trans-Florida Airlines Convair 240 suffered engine problems after taking off and, in attempting to return, ditched short of the runway in a salt water lagoon, but without injury to the three occupants. An American Eagle ATR-72 punctured its tyres on landing on 9 May 2004, with 17 of the passengers and crew injured, but there were no fatalities.

RALEIGH-DURHAM INTERNATIONAL: RDU

Raleigh-Durham, North Carolina, USA

Owner and operator: Raleigh-Durham Airport Authority

Runways: 05L/23R, 3,048m (10,000ft); 05R/23L, 2,286m (7,500ft); 14/32, 1,088m (3,570ft)

Terminals: Two, designated Terminal 1 and Terminal 2

Annual passengers: 10,219,138

Annual cargo: 107,485 tonnes

Annual aircraft movements: 252,708

Background

A municipal airport for Raleigh was originally opened in 1929 close to the city centre, but as aircraft sizes and traffic increased it became clear that it was not suitable for commercial flights. Encouraged by Eastern Air Lines, which saw the airport as a stop on its route linking New York and Miami, plans were made for a new airport that could be used by both Raleigh and Durham. The present airport opened on 1 May 1943, with flights by Eastern, but before that it was already in use as a military airfield for the United States Army Air Force, which continued to share it, and a small passenger terminal was built from materials left after four USAAF barracks had been built.

After the war, Eastern was joined by Capital Airlines and Piedmont Airlines, and in 1955 the original terminal was replaced by today's Terminal 1. Many years later, in the 1970s, Delta Air Lines and Allegheny Airlines followed, as did Trans World Airlines, American Airlines and, until it ended operations in 2003, Midway Airlines. The terminal was joined by a second terminal in 1981, with the new building becoming Terminal A and the earlier one Terminal B. A transatlantic service started in May 1994 when American launched flights to London Gatwick, later switching this to London Heathrow in March 2008 as it proved more convenient for business travellers, many of whom work in the pharmaceutical industry.

The airport is in the middle of a major expansion programme which should be completed by late 2011. The older Terminal B closed in 1989, and in 2008 Terminal A, much extended, became Terminal 1 and will be extensively renovated starting in 2011, while the present Terminal 2 began life as Terminal C at a time when American Airlines had a hub at the airport. It is being extended as part of the modernisation and expansion programme.

Raleigh-Durham maintains its links with military aviation. The North Carolina National Guard maintains a Boeing AH-64A/D Apache attack helicopter unit at the airport, and there are facilities in Terminal 1 for military families.

Accidents at the airport included that to a United Airlines Vickers Viscount 700 landing on 28 November 1967, which suffered a nose wheel collapse, but although the aircraft was written off, the 4 crew and 39 passengers survived. An Eastern Air Lines Douglas DC-9, landing from Miami on 4 December 1971, collided with a Cessna 206, killing the two occupants of the 206, but the DC-9 suffered only minor damage and the 4 crew and 23 passengers were unharmed. British Aerospace Jetstream 31s featured in another two accidents. The first of these was on 30 January 1991, when a CC Air aircraft, operating a USAir Express flight, was landing from Charlotte-Douglas and touched-down heavily because of icing. The impact was sufficient to cause the aircraft to be written off, but the 19 occupants all survived. The other Jetstream accident was when an American Eagle flight, operated by Flagship Airlines, crashed on 13 December 1994 as it approached from Greensboro. Problems with one of the engines convinced the captain that it had flamed out, and he attempted a go around, but the aircraft stalled and hit some trees, killing both pilots and 13 of the 18 passengers. A de Havilland Canada Twin

Otter, flying from Hinkley to Louisburg on a positioning flight, was diverted to Raleigh-Durham on 31 July 2000 because of fog at the destination, but the pilot was not certified for instrument flying and, in poor visibility and at night, lost his bearings and flew the aircraft into a wooded hillside. The pilot died, but the two passengers survived.

SANTA ANA/JOHN WAYNE: SNA

Santa Ana, Orange County, California, USA

Owner and operator: Orange County
Runways: 01L/19R, 1,738m (5,701ft); 01R/19L, 880m (2,887ft)
Terminals: One (the Thomas F. Riley Terminal) divided into two terminal areas designated A and B
Annual passengers: 9,979,699
Annual cargo: 19,852 tonnes
Annual aircraft movements: 331,452

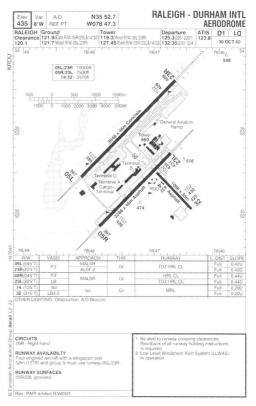

Background

Santa Ana has the unenviable reputation of its longest runway being amongst the shortest of any major airport in the United States, limiting it to aircraft of Boeing 757 size or smaller. Pilots often have to spool up to full power before releasing the brakes for the take-off run. The second runway is used primarily for commuter flights and general aviation. Long-haul commercial flights are not a possibility.

The airport's history dates back to the establishment of a flying school by one Eddie Martin in 1923, and the airfield was purchased in 1939 by the local authority, Orange County. Traffic must have been slow to develop, as even after the Second World War, from 1950 to 1959, a runway was used every Sunday for drag racing, known as the 'Santa Ana Drag'. Eventually, the volume of air traffic forced the drag racing to stop, but it was not until 1967 that a passenger terminal was constructed; this was named after Eddie Martin. In 1979 the airport changed its name to John Wayne, although airline timetables and arrival and departure monitors continued using the locality, Santa Ana. Nevertheless, regardless of the name, Santa Ana was by this time being used more fully, and in 1990 the present terminal, the Thomas F. Riley, opened, and four years' later the abandoned Eddie Martin Terminal was demolished. Traffic growth was sufficient for relocation to be considered around the turn of the century, with the site of the former El Toro Marine Corps Air Station chosen, but this proved controversial and was later dropped, as was a later proposed name change to 'O.C. Airport, John Wayne Field' because of the popularity of the US television series *The O.C.*, presumably for Orange County.

One of the longest routes out of Santa Ana was that to Hawaii started in 2001 by Aloha Airlines, but this was dropped on 31 March 2008 when the airline suspended operations. The airport has also been affected by service reductions by American Airlines, Continental Airlines, and United Airlines. The possibility of other airlines filling the gaps is being pursued, but the state of the economy and uncertainty over longer-term

fuel prices has made airlines hesitate, while Hawaiian Airlines, for example, has a core fleet of Boeing 767 aircraft which the airport cannot handle.

There has been one serious accident at the airport. On 23 November 1968 a Cable Commuter de Havilland Twin Otter, approaching from Los Angeles in fog, crashed into a pole short of the runway, killing both pilots and the seven passengers.

PITTSBURGH: PIT
Findlay, Pittsburgh, Pennsylvania, USA

Owner and operator: Allegheny County Airport Authority
Runways: 10L/28R, 3,201m (10,502ft); 10C/28C, 2,959m (9,708ft); 10R/28L, 3,505m (11,500ft); 14/32, 2,469m (8,101ft); there is also a helipad
Terminals: One, with four concourses designated A, B, C, and D (with E recently demolished)
Annual passengers: 9,822,588
Annual cargo: 84,266 tonnes
Annual aircraft movements: 209,303

Background

The airport was originally developed as a United States Army Air Force base, mainly for training, during the Second World War. Whilst a civil airport (the Allegheny County Airport) had been in existence since 1926, this had become congested and was too small for growth in air travel, and county officials selected the air force base for the new civil airport to serve the area. After the war, work started, and the new airport was opened on 31 May 1952, initially named Greater Pittsburgh Airport, although this became Greater Pittsburgh International Airport in 1972 when an international wing opened. In its early days the new airport was the largest in the United States until New York's Idlewild (now New York JFK) opened in 1958. The first airlines to use the airport were Trans World Airlines (TWA), Capital Airlines (which was later absorbed by United Airlines), Northwest Orient (now simply Northwest), Eastern

Air Lines, and All American (which later became USAir and then was renamed US Airways). By 1959 the terminal was extended by the addition of an 'east dock', while that same year TWA started jet services at the airport with Boeing 707s.

By 1987 USAir was the dominant carrier and was using Pittsburgh as a hub. The airline supported further expansion, and on 1 October 1992 a new Midfield terminal was opened and the old terminal closed, although not demolished until 1999. Nevertheless, by this time traffic growth had fallen and USAir was concentrating on expansion at Charlotte and Philadelphia. The airline, by this time US Airways, decided in 2004 to move its primary hub to Philadelphia, and cut its flights at Pittsburgh by more than two-thirds, including dropping transatlantic flights and the closure of Concourse E, which had been used by the airline. The loss of business resulting from this decision was later mitigated by the opening of a new flight operations centre at Pittsburgh. More recently, the airport has been seeking new airlines and has been successful with new services by the low-cost carriers AirTran Airways, Southwest Airlines, and JetBlue Airways, while USA3000 has started flights to Florida and the Caribbean. American Airlines developed its services at the airport during 2009, and Delta introduced a new service to Paris. There are also plans for a new air cargo centre.

There are other sides to Pittsburgh. The airport hosts an annual air show ('Wings Over Pittsburgh') for two days each year. There is a military area at the airport which may well develop further as a USAF and US Army base exchange, or BX, as a nearby facility has closed. On the south-eastern side of the airport is an Air Force Reserve Command Air Mobility Command unit operating Lockheed C-130H Hercules transports, while on the south-western side is the Pennsylvania Air National Guard, with another Air Mobility Command unit operating Boeing KC-135T Stratotankers for in-flight refuelling. The Federal Aviation Administration also has its regional administration at the airport.

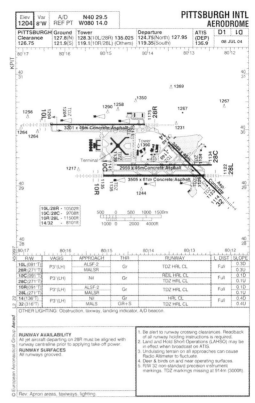

There have been some serious accidents at the airport. One of these was on 1 April 1956 when a TWA flight to Newark crashed shortly after take-off, killing 22 of the 36 passengers and crew, because the pilots had not taken prompt action to deal with an engine malfunction. A USAir Boeing 737-300, arriving from Chicago on 9 September 1994, plunged earthwards from 1,800m (6,000ft) because of a rudder problem that caused control to be lost, and all 132 passengers and crew were killed. Most recently, on 21 November 2001, a corporate Learjet stalled and crashed after take-off, killing all those aboard the aircraft.

AUSTIN-BERGSTROM INTERNATIONAL: AUS

Austin, Texas, USA

Owner and operator: City of Austin
Runways: 17L/35R, 2,743m (9,000ft); 17R/35L, 3,733m (12,248ft); there are also two helipads
Terminals: Two, designated the Barbara Jordan or Main Terminal and the South Terminal
Annual passengers: 8,885,391
Annual cargo: 95,587 tonnes
Annual aircraft movements: 214,440

Background

Austin's first airport was the Robert Mueller Municipal Airport, which opened in October 1930. In 1942, shortly after the United States entered the Second World War, the city bought land and donated it to the federal government for military use on condition that the land would be returned once the need had passed. The United States Army Air Force used the land to build Bergstrom Air Force base. In the immediate post-war period, Mueller continued as the city's airport, but urban growth towards the airport encroached on the flight paths and, as air traffic grew, complaints about noise began, while Mueller's runway proved too short for wide-bodied aircraft. The Federal Aviation Administration recommended that Austin and San Antonio build a regional airport jointly. When, in 1976, Austin sought United States Air Force consent for shared use of Bergstrom AFB, the USAF rejected the idea as being too disruptive. Nevertheless, pressure groups in the areas affected by Mueller continued to call for the airport's closure and a move to a new site, and the city chose a site near Manor, short-listed from a number. While this choice was ratified in a local referendum in 1987, objections started and the situation was only relieved when the Base Alignment and Closure Commission decided to close Bergstrom, leaving it free to become the city's new airport.

Austin-Bergstrom opened for air cargo on 30 June 1997, using the designator BSM until Mueller finally closed. The new South Terminal is being used by low-cost airlines, including the new Mexican operator, Viva Aerobus.

The only serious accident at the airport was to a United States Air Force Globemaster in 1968, but no fatalities were recorded.

HOUSTON WILLIAM P. HOBBY INTERCONTINENTAL: HOU

Houston, Texas, USA

Owner: City of Houston
Operator: Houston Airport System
Runways: 12L/30R, 1,569m (5,148ft); 12R/30L, 2,317m (7,602ft); 04/22, 2,317m (7,602ft); 17/35, 1,829m (6,000ft)
Terminals: One
Annual passengers: 8,819,521
Annual cargo: 409,193 tonnes
Annual aircraft movements: 603,656

Background

Situated 13km (just over 8 miles) from the city centre, Houston Hobby was the original airport for Houston, opened in 1927 as a private airstrip, which was acquired by the city and renamed Houston Municipal Airport in 1937, by which time both Braniff and Eastern Air Lines were using it. The airport was renamed Howard R. Hughes Airport in 1938, as Hughes was responsible for a number of improvements, including its first control tower, but the name was changed back almost as quickly, as Hughes was still alive and federal funds for improvements were not available for any airport named after a person still alive. The city opened a new passenger terminal and hangar in 1940. It saw steady expansion, and in 1950 Pan American Airways provided the first international flight to Mexico City. A new and much larger terminal opened in 1954 and KLM provided the first transatlantic service in 1957 from Amsterdam. Nevertheless, the airport was becoming congested, and construction of a new airport began. This opened as Houston Intercontinental in 1969, and all airline traffic was moved from Hobby to the new airport. In 1971 Hobby reopened to airline traffic, and in the intervening years it has attracted air services to most destinations in the United States and can handle international flights with border pre-clearance, which includes many from Canadian airports.

The current name was adopted in 1967 in memory of a former governor of Texas.

There have been no accidents actually at the airport.

INDIANAPOLIS INTERNATIONAL: IND
Indianapolis, Indiana, USA

Owner and operator: Indianapolis Airport Authority
Runways: 05L/23R, 3,414m (11,200ft); 05R/23L, 3,048m (10,000ft); 14/32, 2,318m (7,605ft)
Terminals: One, with two concourses, A and B
Airlines using airport as base or hub: Federal Express (FedEx)
Annual passengers: 8,271,632
Annual cargo: 998,675 tonnes
Annual aircraft movements: 203,136

Background
Indiana's largest airport, Indianapolis International is 11km (7 miles) south-west of the city. It opened in 1931 as Indianapolis Municipal Airport, and in 1944 it became Weir-Cook Municipal Airport to commemorate Colonel Harvey-Weir Cook, a veteran ace fighter pilot of two world wars who was shot down by the Japanese over New Caledonia whilst flying with the USAAF. The name changed again in 1976 when the Indianapolis Airport Authority, which took the airport over in 1962, adopted the current title.

A new passenger terminal was opened on the eastern side of the airport in 1957, and this was expanded several times, with new concourses in 1968 and again in 1972 and 1987, while an international arrivals terminal was built in 1976, before a completely new terminal was opened mid-field between the two parallel runways on 12 November 2008. The new terminal has been named the Col. H. Weir-Cook Terminal, and

the now redundant terminal will be demolished in due course, although some of it is currently used as office accommodation.

For some years USAir (now US Airways) maintained a secondary hub at Indianapolis, but by the mid-1990s this had ended. Later in that decade ATA Airlines operated a hub. However, after the airline went into Chapter 11 bankruptcy protection in 2004, this was also run down and ended altogether when new owners took over in 2006. Since then, Northwest has developed a hub at the airport, but the future of this is uncertain now that the airline has merged with Delta Air Lines. Meanwhile, Federal Express maintains a cargo hub there.

In 1994 the British airport operator, BAA, was given a ten-year management contract which was later extended by three years before later being cut short at BAA's request, and the airport is now back under Indiana Airport Authority control.

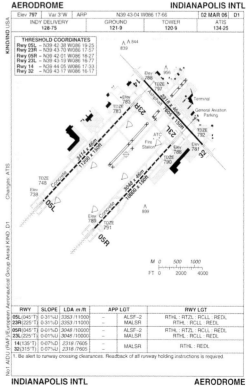

INDIANAPOLIS INTL   AERODROME

For the future, a third parallel runway is planned.

One of the two major accidents near the airport was on 9 September 1969 when an Allegheny Airlines Douglas DC-9, approaching from Cincinnati, was descending and collided with a Piper Cherokee, with both aircraft crashing and killing all 4 crew and 78 passengers in the DC-9 and the student pilot in the Cherokee. The other was on 31 October 1994 when an American Eagle flight, that had just taken off for Chicago, crashed with all 68 passengers and crew killed.

SAN ANTONIO INTERNATIONAL: SAT

San Antonio, Texas, USA

Owner and operator: City of San Antonio
    Aviation Department
Runways: 12L/30R, 1,682m (5,519ft); 12R/30L,
    2,591m (8,502ft); 3/21, 2,288m (7,505ft)
Terminals: Two, designated Terminal 1 and
    Terminal 2, (due to be replaced 2010–2 with
    Terminals A, B and C
Annual passengers: 8,033,314
Annual cargo: 124,390 tonnes
Annual aircraft movements: 219,437

Background

San Antonio International dates from 1941 when land to the north of the city was purchased by the local authority to build San Antonio Municipal Airport, but before it could be finished it was taken over by the United States Army Air Force and opened in July 1942 as Alamo Field AFB, a flying training school. As the war progressed, other units moved in, training aircrew for reconnaissance and air observation post (AOP) duties with frontline army units. An antisubmarine squadron was also posted for patrols over the Gulf of Mexico looking for German U-boats.

With the return of peace, the airfield was handed back to the city, and commercial air services began with just one terminal. A second terminal was opened in 1953, with a new control

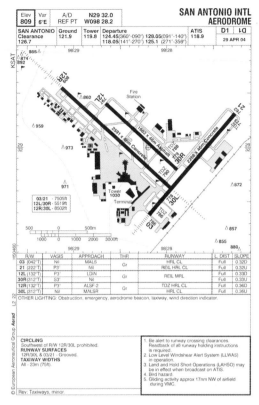

tower. When San Antonio was chosen for the 1968 World Fair, a new satellite terminal with eight jet bridges was built. Traffic began to outstrip the capacity of the two terminals, and a new Terminal 1 was opened in 1984, and in 1986 a new control tower became operational. These were part of an airport master plan, and in 1994 a second master plan was prepared, calling for two new terminals to replace Terminal 2, which will be demolished, while the present Terminal 1 becomes Terminal A, with the new Terminal B opening in 2010 and the new Terminal C following in 2012. Improvements to the airport access roads and car parking are also intended to be completed at the same time.

The airport was used for the test flights of the Swearingen Merlin (an executive turboprop) and for pre-delivery trials and training, which combined have led to a few minor incidents, but no fatalities. The one serious accident was on 31 January 1967 when a Saturn Airways Douglas

DC-6, on a cargo flight to Kelly Air Force Base, diverted to San Antonio, but dropped below the glide slope and crashed into trees, killing the crew of three.

FORT MYERS/SOUTHWEST FLORIDA INTERNATIONAL: RSW
Fort Myers, Florida, USA

Owner and operator: Lee County Port Authority
Runways: 06L/24R, 3,658m (12,000ft) 06/24 until 2010; 06R/24L, 2,774m (9,100ft) opens 2010
Terminals: One, with three concourses, B, C, and D
Annual passengers: 8,029,204
Annual cargo: 18,234 tonnes
Annual aircraft movements: 92,008

Background
Built to replace Page Field, the original airport for Fort Myers, Southwest Florida Regional Airport opened on 14 May 1983. International flights started to use the airport the following year, but 'international' was not added to the title until 1993, by which time the German charter airline, LTU International Airways, was operating from Dusseldorf. By 2004 the airport was handling nearly twice the number of passengers for which it had been designed, and relief came the following year with the opening of a new terminal known as the Midfield Terminal Complex, although strictly-speaking it does not become a 'midfield' terminal until the second runway is opened in 2010.

There has been just one serious accident at the airport since it opened, to a light aircraft in November 2007.

DALLAS LOVE FIELD: DAL
Dallas, Texas, USA

Owner and operator: City of Dallas
Runways: 13L/31R, 2,363m (7,752ft); 13R/31L, 2,682m (8,800ft); 18/36, 1,874m (6,147ft)
Terminals: One

Airlines using airport as base or hub:
    Southwest Airlines
Annual passengers: 7,953,385
Annual aircraft movements: 244,609

Dallas Area Rapid Transit Green Line light railway will serve Dallas Love Field Station from 2010.

Background
Named after a US army officer, Lieutenant Moss Love, who was killed in a flying accident, Love Field was opened for military use on 19 October 1917. Some 9km (almost 6 miles) from the city centre, it did not open for commercial traffic until 1927, quickly becoming the airport for Dallas. Braniff Airways, at one time one of the leading US airlines, chose Love Field as its headquarters in 1936. A new terminal with three concourses was opened in 1958. At the time, the airlines using Love Field included American, Central, Continental, Delta, and Trans Texas (which later became Texas International) as well as Braniff. Continental was the first US airline to operate turboprop aircraft, using the Vickers Viscount, which it introduced to its Dallas routes in April 1959, but in July American Airlines started Boeing 707 operations on its New York route.

It was to Love Field that President John F. Kennedy flew when he made his fateful visit to Dallas in late November 1963, and Love Field had the unique distinction of having a US president sworn in aboard an aircraft on the ground at Love Field when President Lyndon Johnson took office.

By this time Love Field was becoming increasingly congested and it was agreed, with some encouragement from the FAA, that they should build a new joint airport, which at the time was known as Dallas/Fort Worth Regional Airport, and that both cities should close their own airports to commercial flights. Fort Worth's Greater Southwest International Airport was in fact closed and a business park built on the site, but Love Field was allowed to remain open for general aviation and aircraft maintenance. Even before Dallas/Fort Worth opened in 1974, these plans were overturned when Southwest Airlines was founded as the first of the 'low-cost' US carriers, ready for deregulation of domestic air services in the United States, with its headquarters at Love Field. The airline felt that its business model would be ruined by the long drive to Dallas/Forth Worth and took legal action to be allowed to use Love Field. Southwest won its legal battle in 1973, and for a while was the only airline operating out of Love Field as it had been decided that no airline could use the new airport if it also used Love Field. Nevertheless, Love Field had several terminals that had to be decommissioned, leaving just one for Southwest flights.

Initially, Southwest only operated within Texas, but deregulation in 1978 meant that it was able to operate nationwide. However, the US Congress passed an amendment restricting use of Love Field to air services within Texas and to neighbouring states, or to aircraft with no more than 56 passenger seats: this was known as the Wright Amendment after the congressman who introduced it. Nevertheless, not only did Southwest continue to expand within these limitations, but its passengers got round the restrictions by changing planes, and by doing so created mini-hubs at airports such as Houston Hobby. The airline's success also led to imitators appearing, and when Continental tried to launch services from Love Field, a court battle ensued as it was also operating out of DFW. Eventually, Congress passed the Shelby Amendment, which added Alabama, Kansas, and Mississippi to the states that could be reached from Love Field. The result was a succession of lawsuits, with at one time Fort Worth suing Dallas, and it was not until 2000 that the Federal Appeal Court removed many of the restrictions on the use of Love Field, allowing 56-seat jets to fly anywhere, while larger aircraft could operate within Texas and seven other states.

The drop in air travel following the terrorist attacks of 11 September 2001 meant that longer distance services using 56-seat jets were dropped, and by 2003 Southwest and Continental Express were the only two airlines using Love Field. The continuing success of Southwest encouraged the city to carry on developing Love Field, and in 2005 Missouri was added to the list of states that could have a direct air service from the airport. In the meantime, American Airlines and American Eagle had started operations out of Love Field. The following year, not only American and Southwest, but also the two city councils and Dallas/Fort Worth International Airport joined to support the repeal of the Wright Amendment, although with certain conditions including the continuation of the ban on flights outside the Wright zone until 2014. The conditions also include a limit to 20 gates, 16 for Southwest and two each for American and Continental, which in turn provoked protests from JetBlue and Northwest Airlines. Some of these matters have still to be resolved, but Love Field now has one-stop services by both American and Southwest to destinations outside the Wright zone.

Over its long history, the airport has seen many accidents, almost inevitable given the poorer reliability of piston-engined aircraft and the limited navigational aids available in the early days. One of the first was on 23 December 1936 when a Braniff Airways Lockheed Electra (the original aircraft to bear this name, a twin-engined piston as opposed to the later four-engined turboprop) was having a test flight following an engine change, but the engine failed during a touch-and-go circuit, and as the pilot attempted to return to the airport to land, he lost control, the aircraft entered a spin and crashed, killing all six occupants, all employees of the airline. The worst accident at the airport was on 29 November 1949, when an American Airlines Douglas DC-6 touched down and the pilots then lost control, with the aircraft veering off the runway into a parked aircraft, a hangar, and a flying school before leaving the airfield, crossing a road and crashing into a building, when it burst into flames. Of the 41 passengers, 26 were killed, as were the 2 cabin attendants, but the captain, co-pilot, and flight engineer survived. On 28 June 1952 a Temco Swift light aircraft collided with an American Airlines

Douglas DC-6 landing from San Francisco. The Swift was catapulted over the airliner after hitting the propeller of No. 4 engine and it span into a street, killing both occupants, while the DC-6 suffered little damage and the 60 passengers and crew were unharmed. A wet runway led to poor braking action when a Braniff DC-4 slid off the runway and across a busy street before coming to rest against an embankment, but no motor vehicles were hit and the 5 crew and 48 passengers suffered no more than minor injuries. A post-maintenance accident occurred on 14 September 1960, when a Braniff DC-7 was being taxied by a maintenance inspector, who lost control of the aircraft and crashed into a hangar at high speed, killing himself and injuring five of the six mechanics aboard. There was a take-off accident on 10 February 1967 when a Beech 18 lost a propeller and crashed, killing the pilot and both passengers. Another business aircraft accident was to an Aero Commander 560E on 27 September 1967, when a wing spar failed on approach and the aircraft crashed killing the pilot and six passengers.

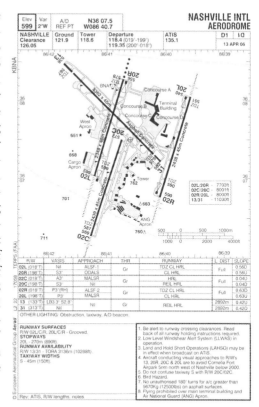

NASHVILLE INTERNATIONAL: BNA

Nashville, Tennessee, USA

Owner and operator: Metropolitan Nashville
  Airport Authority
Runways: 02L/20R, 2,348m (7,702ft); 02C/20C,
  2,438m (8,000ft); 02R/20L, 2,438m (8,000ft);
  13/31, 3,362m (11,030ft)
Terminals: One, with four concourses, A, B, C,
  and D (although D is currently out of use)
Annual passengers: 7,802,454
Annual cargo: 67,917 tonnes
Annual aircraft movements: 213,185

Background

Nashville International originally opened in 1937 as Berry Field, after Harry Berry, who was in charge of the Works Progress Administration, and the designation, BNA, still in use today, derives from 'Berry Field Nashville'. It was taken over by the United States Army Air Force during the Second World War and used for ferrying aircraft to operational units outside the United States. After the war it returned to commercial use, and in 1961 the original passenger terminal was replaced by a much larger building. The current terminal dates from 1987, and later Concourse A had an international wing built when American Airlines started a service to London, which it has since dropped. At one time American Airlines had a hub at Nashville, but this has now closed, although the airline still serves the city, and Southwest Airlines is now the dominant carrier with 47 per cent of all flights.

The airport suffered a number of accidents to United States Army Air Force aircraft during the Second World War and shortly afterwards. The worst accident after the war was to a Grumman Gulfstream I cargo aircraft on 31 May 1985, which crashed after take-off, killing both occupants, because of the incorrect setting of the controls after the engine failed. On 3 February 1988 an American Airlines McDonnell Douglas MD-83 landed from Dallas with a chemical fire in the cargo hold, but all 11 crew and 120 passengers were safely evacuated on a taxiway, and the aircraft was not badly damaged. A Valujet Airlines Douglas DC-9, coming in from Atlanta on 7 January 1996 with pressurisation problems, landed heavily, climbed away again for a go-around, and then landed safely with 5 crew and 88 passengers, but was found to have suffered considerable damage. Another Douglas DC-9, of Trans World Airlines (TWA), made a heavy landing on 9 September 1999, and part of the undercarriage collapsed, causing the aircraft to slew off the runway, but the 5 crew and 41 passengers escaped, although the aircraft was written off.

PORT COLUMBUS INTERNATIONAL: CMH

Columbus, Ohio, USA

Owner and operator: Columbus Regional Airport Authority

Runways: 10L/28R, 2,438m (8,000ft); 10R/28L, 3,086m (10,125ft)

Terminals: One, with three concourses, A, B, and C

Annual passengers: 7,726,421

Annual cargo: 6,135 tonnes

Annual aircraft movements: 173,984

Background

Usually known locally as Port Columbus, the airport is 10km (just over 6 miles) from the city centre. The IATA code for the airfield derives from 'Columbus Municipal Hangar', and it is hardly surprising that the name has long since been changed. The owner and operator, the Columbus Regional Airport Authority, has two other airports in the area, Bolton Field and Rickenbacker International Airport.

The airport has the distinction of having been built on a site chosen by Charles Lindbergh for Transcontinental Air Transport as the eastern terminus of an air–rail route between New York and Los Angeles. The combination of air and

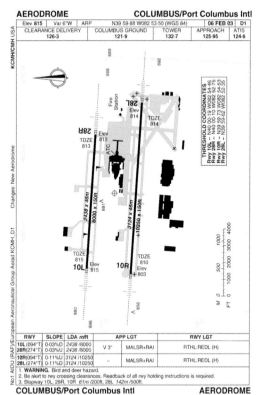

rail was not uncommon at the time, and airlines such as Imperial Airways initially used rail across Europe and then air onwards for its early flights to the Middle East and India. In this case passengers travelled by sleeper train between New York and Columbus, and then by air between Columbus and Waynoka, Oklahoma, and then returned to the railways between Waynoka and Clovis, New Mexico, before flying between Clovis and Los Angeles. The airport opened on 8 July 1929, and the original buildings still remain, with the terminal used as office space, and the hangars still in use for general aviation operators. Traffic grew steadily, but not spectacularly, so that in 1939 there were ten flights daily by Transcontinental & Western Air, which later became Trans World Airlines, and another four by American Airlines. Although the aircraft were small, loadings must have been low as the airport handled an average of just 21 passengers daily.

In more recent years the airport has benefited from substantial investment in new or upgraded facilities. In 1979 it was handling 250 flights daily, and a new terminal could boast fully enclosed airbridges for every gate. In 1989 a second concourse was added to the terminal, mainly for the use of USAir (now US Airways), and a third concourse (now known as Concourse C) opened in 1995. Facilities were provided in 1999 for Net-Jets, the fractional ownership business aircraft operator. This was followed by a new air traffic control tower in 2004. Further development is planned over the next 15 years.

An American Airlines Convair 240, landing from Dayton on 27 June 1954, collided with a United States Navy Beech SNB-2C, and while the 240 recovered and landed, with the nose wheel collapsing after touchdown, the Beech crashed, killing both occupants. An Atlantic Coast Airlines BAe Jetstream 41 on a United Express flight was approaching on 7 January 1994 when the aircraft stalled and crashed into trees before hitting a building and bursting into flames. Two of the crew of three, and five of the nine passengers were killed.

MILWAUKEE GENERAL MITCHELL INTERNATIONAL: MKE

Milwaukee, Wisconsin, USA

Owner and operator: Milwaukee County Airports
Runways: 01L/19R, 2,954m (9,698ft) being extended to 3,256m (10,690ft); 01R/19L, 1,275m (4,183ft); 07L/25R, 1,463m (4,800ft); 07R/25L, 2,442m (8,012ft) being extended to 2,745m (9,012ft); 13/31, 1,789m (5,868ft)
Terminals: One, with three concourses, C, D, and E
Airlines using airport as base or hub: MidWest Airlines, AirTran Airways
Annual passengers: 7,713,144
Annual cargo: 88,237 tonnes
Annual aircraft movements: 200,205

There is a shuttle bus to the Milwaukee Airport Station, which has Amtrak Hiawatha Line service linking Milwaukee and Chicago.

Background

The airport is 8km (5 miles) south of Milwaukee and has been named after a local hero, Brigadier-General Billy Mitchell of the United States Army Air Service, who was court martialled for his strong advocacy of an autonomous air service in the years following the First World War. The location makes the airport convenient for some of Chicago's traffic.

The airfield opened as early as 1920, named Hamilton Airport after the proprietor, and was purchased by Milwaukee County on 19 October 1926. Regular air services did not follow until 31 August 1929, when Kohler Aviation introduced a service across Lake Michigan. The first passenger terminal opened in 1940. It became General Mitchell Field in March 1941, although it was to be some years before the USAAF became the USAF. From January 1945 the airport was leased by the US War Department for use as a prisoner-of-war camp, and at one time held 3,000 POWs.

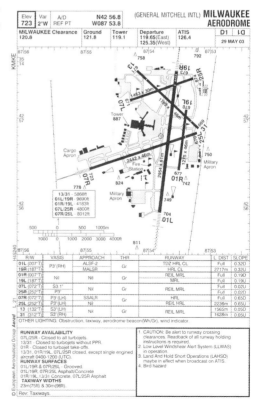

After the war the airport was returned to commercial traffic. The existing terminal was opened in 1955 and underwent considerable expansion in the late 1980s. The current title was adopted in June 1986.

Considerable expansion is planned for the future, with runway extensions and 'buffer zones' that comply with the latest requirements, while the terminal will either be extended, possibly even doubling in size, or a new terminal will be built.

In addition to its commercial and general aviation traffic, the airport also doubles as the General Mitchell Air National Guard Station, home to the Wisconsin Air National Guard, which has a Boeing KC-135R Stratotanker wing stationed there.

Heavy accumulations of insect smears on the windscreen of a North Central Airlines Convair 580 on 4 August 1968 was a contributory factor in a collision with a Cessna 150, whose three occupants were killed, while the 580 was able to make an emergency landing at Milwaukee with the Cessna cabin still attached to the aircraft. On 6 September 1985 a Midwest Express Douglas DC-9 crashed as it took off for Atlanta when the No. 2 engine failed and the handling pilot did not take rapid corrective action, with the loss of all 31 passengers and crew. A Northwest Airlines Douglas DC-9 skidded off the runway in heavy snow after an engine exploded and the pilots aborted a take-off, but of the 104 passengers and crew, just one person was injured. Air Traffic Control was blamed for a taxiway collision between two Freight Runners Express cargo aircraft, a Cessna 402 and Beech 99, on 23 January 2007, leaving both aircraft on fire, but the pilots escaped. A Cessna Citation II, taking off for Detroit with an organ transplant team, crashed on 4 June 2007 after problems with a trim tab, killing the 2 pilots and 4 passengers. An emergency landing was made on 29 December 2008 by a Midwest Connect aircraft after the pilot reported smoke in the cockpit, but there were no injuries amongst the crew or 40 passengers.

NEW ORLEANS LOUIS ARMSTRONG INTERNATIONAL: MSY

Kenner, New Orleans, Louisiana, USA

Owner and operator: City of New Orleans
Runways: 10/28, 3,080m (10,104ft); 01/19, 2,134m (7,001ft); 06/24, 1,088m (3,570ft)
Terminals: One, with four concourses, A, B, C (international arrivals), and D
Annual passengers: 7,525,533
Annual cargo: 44,872 tonnes
Annual aircraft movements: 114,318

Background

Only Amsterdam's Schiphol lies lower than New Orleans, which has an average elevation of just 1.4m (4½ft) above sea level.

New Orleans was originally served by Shushan Airport, but by 1940 it was clear that a new airport was needed. During the Second World War the site was used for a military air station, and it was not until after the war ended that it became a civil airport, with commercial air services starting in May 1946. The new airport had the designation MSY, for Moisant Stock Yards, as the old airport kept the New Orleans designation NEW, and remains to this day as New Orleans Lakefront Airport, handling general aviation. The name Moisant Field was chosen in memory of the pioneering stunt flyer, John Moisant, who was visiting New Orleans with his troupe, the 'Moisant International Aviators' in 1910, when he fell out of his aircraft and was killed on the land that became the airport. The opening was short-lived, as a hurricane on 19 September 1947 forced it to close for a short while because the airport was under 2ft of water.

Despite the setbacks, the airport soon attracted many of the major airlines of the post-war period, including Eastern Air Lines and National Airlines (later absorbed by Pan Am). In 2001 it received its present name to mark the centenary of the birth of jazz musician Louis Armstrong.

The airport suffered from another hurricane in 2005. It was closed on 28 August because of

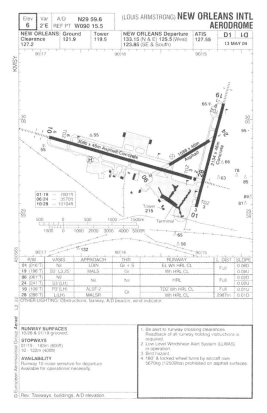

Elev 6 | Var 2°E | A/D REF PT | N29 59.6 W090 15.5 | (LOUIS ARMSTRONG) **NEW ORLEANS INTL AERODROME**

NEW ORLEANS Clearance 127.2 | Ground 121.9 | Tower 119.5 | NEW ORLEANS Departure 133.15 (N & E) 125.5 (West) 123.85 (SE & South) | ATIS 127.55 | D1 LQ 13 MAY 04

R/W	VASIS	APPROACH	THR	RUNWAY	L DIST	SLOPE
01 (016°T)	Nil	LDIN	Gr + S	EL Wh HRL CL	Full	0.06D
19 (196°T)	S3' L3.25°	MALS	Gr	Wh HRL CL		0.06U
06 (061°T)	Nil	Nil	Nil	HRL	Full	0.02D 0.02U
24 (241°T)	S3' (LH)					
10 (106°T)	P3' (LH)	ALSF-2	Gr	TDZ Wh HRL CL	Full	0.01U
28 (286°T)	L(LH)	MALSR		Wh HRL CL	2987m	0.01D

OTHER LIGHTING. Obstructions, taxiway, A/D beacon, wind indicator.

RUNWAY SURFACES
10/28 & 01/19 grooved.
STOPWAYS
01/19 - 183m (600ft)
10 - 122m (400ft)
AVAILABILITY
Runway 10 noise sensitive for departure.
Available for operational necessity.

1. Be alert to runway crossing clearances.
   Readback of all runway holding instructions is required.
2. Low Level Windshear Alert System (LLWAS) in operation.
3. Bird hazard.
4. 180° & locked wheel turns by aircraft over 5670kg (12500lbs) prohibited on asphalt surfaces.

Rev: Taxiways, buildings, A/D elevation.

return, while regular international scheduled services returned in 2009.

The worst accident at the airport was on 25 February 1964 when an Eastern Airlines Douglas DC-8, that had taken-off for Washington with reported problems with its instruments, went out of control in turbulence and windshear, and crashed killing all 7 crew and 51 passengers. There was an attempted hijacking of a Douglas DC-8 of National Airlines on 17 November 1965 by a 16-year-old boy, who fired six revolver rounds into the floor of the aircraft before he was overcome by the passengers. A chartered Avion Airways Douglas DC-3 carrying a team of sportsmen crashed on landing in poor visibility on 20 March 1969, with the aircraft cartwheeling and bursting into flames, killing all 3 crew and 13 of the 24 passengers. An Air New Orleans BAe Jetstream 31 that had taken off for a Continental Express flight on 26 May 1987 appeared to be suffering problems with both engines, and in making an emergency return to the airport the aircraft overshot the runway and was written off, but the two crew and nine passengers were unharmed.

LA/ONTARIO INTERNATIONAL: ONT
Ontario, California, USA

Owner and operator: Los Angeles World Airports
Runways: 26R/8L, 3,718m (12,200ft); 26L/8R, 3,109m (10,200ft)
Terminals: Three, designated Terminal 2, Terminal 4, and International Arrivals
Annual passengers: 7,207,150
Annual cargo: 483,309 tonnes
Annual aircraft movements: 147,678

Background
Ontario, California, had its first airport as early as 1923 when land was leased from the Union Pacific Railroad for an airport named Latimer Field after a nearby orange packing company. This was some 3 miles from the site of the existing airport. In 1929, the local authority pur-

warnings that Hurricane Katrina was approaching, and although the runways and taxiways were not flooded, considerable damage was done to the buildings and, as the city itself was badly flooded, there was little movement. Nevertheless, the airport was reopened in early September for humanitarian flights and military aircraft, and on 13 September for commercial flights, although services were limited at first. A second blow came early in 2006 when a tornado hit the airport in the small hours of 3 February, causing severe damage to Concourse C, used for international arrivals and by AirTran, American, and United. The post-Katrina period has seen the airport offering incentives to airlines operating at more than 85 per cent of pre-Katrina capacity and for those serving an airport not provided with a direct flight from New Orleans for 12 months or more. There are also incentives for passengers. Even so, it was not until 2006 that seasonal international charter flights began to

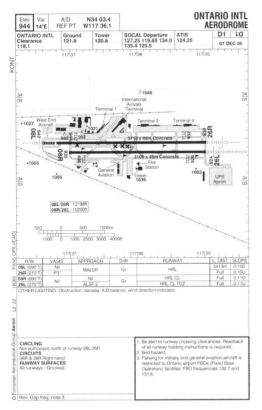

and passed two million in 1978. In 1981 a new runway capable of handling the Boeing 747 was opened. Passenger traffic continued to grow, exceeding five million in 1989 and six million in 1992. Cargo traffic also became important with United Parcels Service (UPS) starting construction of a new West Coast cargo hub building in 1990. Improved facilities for passengers were not neglected, and between 1995 and 1998 a new passenger terminal complex was built. In 2000 Air Canada introduced a daily return service for Toronto, and AeroMexico operated services to Mexico City and other Mexican destinations, while the following year UPS introduced a four-times-a-week service to the People's Republic of China.

In 2005 runway 26R/8L was closed for rebuilding and lengthening, reopening in March 2006. Passenger traffic passed the seven million mark in 2005, and the following year the airport name was changed to LA/Ontario International.

The one serious accident at the airport was on 31 March 1971, when a Western Air Lines Boeing 720, making a three-engined landing on a training flight from Los Angeles, lost control and was written off, but the crew of five survived.

PALM BEACH INTERNATIONAL: PBI
West Palm Beach, Florida, USA

Owner and operator: Department of Airports, Palm Beach County

Runways: 09L/27R, 3,050m (10,008ft); 09R/27L, 979m (3,213ft); 13/31, 2,113m (6,932ft)

Terminals: One, with three concourses, A, B, and C

Airlines using airport as base or hub: JetBlue

Annual passengers: 6,967,277

Annual cargo: 14,699 tonnes

Annual aircraft movements: 186,583

chased a 30-acre plot in what is now the southwest corner of the airport for Ontario Municipal Airport, which was considerably expanded in 1941 when a further 470 acres were purchased and runways laid. During the Second World War Ontario became a USAAF base, mainly used for training, although a fighter unit was also stationed there. By the end of the war it was being used for military cargo flights across the Pacific, and post war it was renamed Ontario International Airport as a result. The USAAF left in 1947 and the airport returned to commercial use, although regular services did not resume until 1949. To encourage commercial flights, a new terminal was completed in 1951.

An agreement between the municipality of Ontario and that of Los Angeles saw the airport become part of the Los Angeles system in 1967, and in 1970 the terminal building was enlarged. The following year the number of passengers using the airport passed the one million mark,

Background

Situated 5km (3 miles) west of West Palm Beach in Florida, the airport was opened in 1936 as Morrison Field, named after Grace Morrison who was one of its founders. It was used almost immediately by scheduled air services, with Douglas DC-2s of Eastern Air Lines being flown on a service to New York. For its first year the airport consisted of an airstrip and a building that doubled as offices and a terminal. The following year the Palm Beach Aero Corporation leased the airfield and built the first terminal for Eastern Air Lines on the airport's south side, as well as some hangars. During the Second World War the United States Army Air Corps (later USAAF) took over the airfield.

The USAAF did not leave the airfield immediately the war ended, and it was not until 1947 that Eastern Air Lines and National Airlines were operating commercial air services. The following year the current name was adopted. Nev-

ertheless, the military, by this time the USAF, were back in 1951 using it as a flying school during the Korean War. The USAF wanted to keep Morrison AFB permanently and it was not until 1959 that the local authority was able to take over the airport, which was soon being served by Delta Air Lines and Eastern Air Lines, joined by Capital Airlines in 1960. In 1966 a new terminal building, designed for the jet age, and a new control tower were opened. The 1966 terminal was replaced in 1988 by a new terminal, named the David McCampbell Terminal after a Second World War USN air ace, and this was designed with the capability of being expanded to double its original size. Despite these developments, strong competition from Fort Lauderdale/Hollywood International meant that there was little growth during the 1990s, and this was further inhibited by the terrorist attacks of 11 September 2001. Nevertheless, as early as 2002, traffic began to grow again, largely because of intensive development, but also helped by the airport being used as a hub by Jet-Blue, the low-cost carrier. Further development is now in hand with a planned Concourse D.

There have been two significant incidents and accidents at the airport. On 12 September 1980 a Florida Commuter Airlines Douglas DC-3, that had taken off for Freeport, crashed into the Atlantic: there were no survivors. Smoke in the cockpit forced an American Airlines Boeing 757, en-route from San Juan to Philadelphia, to make an emergency landing at West Palm Beach on 30 January 2008, where a passenger and 5 members of the crew, including both pilots, had to be taken to hospital, but the other 2 crew members and 136 passengers appear to have been unharmed.

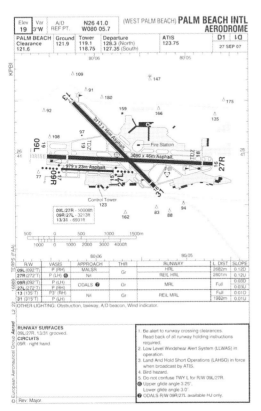

ALBUQUERQUE INTERNATIONAL: ABQ

Albuquerque, New Mexico

Owner and operator: City of Albuquerque
Runways: 3/21, 3,048m (10,000ft); 8/26,
4,204m (13,793ft); 12/30, 1,829m (6,000ft);
17/35, 3,048m (10,000ft)
Terminals: One, with two concourses, A and B,
plus a commuter airline area
Annual passengers: 6,727,384
Annual cargo: 69,598 tonnes
Annual aircraft movements: 191,050

A bus service operates to Bernallilo County/International Sunport Station for the New Mexico Rail Runner with services to Albuquerque and Sante Fe.

Background

Originally, Albuquerque had two airports, West Mesa and Oxnard Field, both private, and it was not until 1935 that the proposal was made that a new airport be built using federal funds provided to alleviate unemployment, and work began on 28 February 1937. When it opened in 1939 it was amongst the better airports of the day, with two paved runways at a time when most just had a grass or earth strip, and a Pueblo-style terminal, while the hangar was designed for the still to fly Boeing 307, the world's first pressurised airliner.

Even before the United States entered the Second World War, the new airport was taken over by the then United States Army Air Corps as Albuquerque Army Air Base, which survives to this day at the airport as Kirtland AFB.

After the war the airport resumed commercial operations, and today's terminal was opened in 1965 just to the east of the 1937 terminal, and has been extended twice, most recently in 1996. The original terminal has been restored and is used by the Transportation Security Administration as offices, and is on the US National Register of Historic Places.

There have been several accidents at or near the airport. Two of the accidents involved mili-

tary aircraft. On 11 September 1958 a Convair F-102 Delta Dagger skidded off a runway in heavy rain and crashed into a car, killing both the occupants, while on 14 September 1977 a Boeing KC-135 crashed into the Manzano Mountains, killing all 20 people aboard. The other accidents have been to commercial aircraft. One of these was on 19 February 1955 when a Trans World Airlines Martin 404, which had taken off for Sante Fe, crashed into the Sandia Mountains, killing all 16 passengers and crew. An uncontained engine failure showered the fuselage of a National Airlines McDonnell Douglas DC-10 with metal on 3 November 1973, blowing a hole in the fuselage, and the explosive decompression sucked a passenger out of the cabin, but the aircraft, en route from Houston to Las Vegas, was able to make an emergency landing at Albuquerque. On 6 July 1997 a Delta Air Lines Boeing 727 suffered a right main undercarriage failure while landing, injuring three of the passengers and causing severe damage to the aircraft.

HARTFORD BRADLEY INTERNATIONAL: BDL

Windsor Locks, Hartford, Connecticut

Owner and operator: Connecticut Department
of Transportation (ConnDOT)
Runways: 06/24, 2,899m (9,510ft); 15/33,
2,087m (6,847ft); 01/19, 1,301m (4,268ft)
Terminals: Two, designated Terminal A (with an
East Concourse and a West Concourse), and
Terminal B (also known as the Murphy
Terminal)
Annual passengers: 6,519,181
Annual cargo: 162,929 tonnes
Annual aircraft movements: 147,720

There are plans for railway services to the airport, but not necessarily into the terminals. Meanwhile, bus links are used to Windsor Locks and Windsor railway stations for Amtrak services.

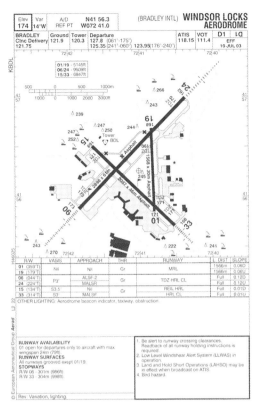

| Elev | Var | A/D | N41 56.3 | (BRADLEY INTL) | **WINDSOR LOCKS** |
| 174 | 14°W | REF PT | W072 41.0 | | **AERODROME** |

BRADLEY	Ground	Tower	Departure		ATIS	VOT	D1	LQ
Clnc Delivery	121.9	120.3	127.8 (061°-175°)		118.15	111.4	EFF	
121.75			125.35 (241°-060°) 123.95 (176°-240°)				10 JUL 03	

01/19 - 5145ft
06/24 - 9509ft
15/33 - 8847ft

Δ266
Δ243
Δ239
Δ247 244Δ
Δ250 Tower
247Δ 252Δ ⊗ BDL

R/W	VASIS	APPROACH	THR	RUNWAY	L DIST	SLOPE
01 (359°T)	Nil	Nil	Gr	MRL	1566m	0.06U
19 (179°T)					1566m	0.06U
06 (044°T)	P3°	ALSF-2	Gr	TDZ HRL CL	Full	0.12D
24 (224°T)		MALSR			Full	0.12U
15 (134°T)	S3.5°	Nil	Gr	REIL HRL	Full	0.01D
33 (314°T)	S3°	MALSF		HRL CL	Full	0.01U

OTHER LIGHTING: Aerodrome beacon indicator, taxiway, obstruction.

RUNWAY AVAILABILITY
01 open for departures only to aircraft with max.
wingspan 24m (79ft).
RUNWAY SURFACES
All runways grooved exept 01/19.
STOPWAYS
R/W 06 - 301m (986ft)
R/W 33 - 304m (998ft).

Rev: Variation, lighting.

1. Be alert to runway crossing clearances.
   Readback of all runway holding instructions is
   required.
2. Low Level Windshear Alert System (LLWAS) in
   operation.
3. Land and Hold Short Operations (LAHSO) may be
   in effect when broadcast on ATIS.
4. Bird hazard.

© European Aeronautical Group Aerad

Background

Although Hartford had a small airport, Hartley Brainard, this was already seen as too small before the Second World War. In 1940 the State of Connecticut bought almost three square miles of land to build an airport, but the land was loaned to the then United States Army Air Corps to build an airfield. On 21 August 1941 a young airman, Lt. Eugene M. Bradley, from Oklahoma, was killed when his aircraft crashed. The air station was renamed Bradley Field Army Air Base the following January. The air station was handed back to the state in 1946, and the following year it opened as Bradley International Airport. Amongst the first airlines to use the airport was Eastern Air Lines, and even during its first year it was handling international air cargo.

A terminal for international arrivals opened in 1971. The airport suffered damage from a tornado in 1979. A new Terminal A and an air cargo

terminal were opened in 1986. The enhanced security measures following the terrorist attacks on 11 September 2001 led to a decision to improve the terminals and centralise passenger screening. Terminal B has a Federal Inspection Area with its own jet bridge for disembarking passengers.

While the airport has suffered a slight fall in passenger numbers recently, largely because of soaring fuel prices and the onset of a recession, it has also attracted a maintenance and repair facility for the business aircraft manufactured by the Brazilian company, Embraer, which opened in late 2008. The airport is also home to the Connecticut Air National Guard, whose 103rd Airlift Wing is nicknamed the 'Flying Yankees', and operates C-21 transports, and the Connecticut National Guard's 126th Aviation Regiment.

For the future there are plans to replace the existing Terminal B with a new building, although there is still some doubt over whether this will be connected to Terminal A.

A Slick Airways Curtiss C-46 Commando, on a cargo flight landing from New York on 4 March 1953, had difficulty finding the runway localiser, and the pilots became disorientated, leaving the aircraft to crash after a wing hit a tree, killing both pilots. Another cargo flight, on 3 May 1991, involved a Ryan Airlines Boeing 727QC that aborted take-off for Boston when No. 3 engine suffered problems, but while the crew of three escaped, the aircraft was burnt out. A Continental Express ATR-42, landing from Newark, suffered an engine fire, but all 3 crew and 36 passengers were evacuated and the fire was put out by the airport fire service. Another landing accident involved a Beech 1900D of Colgan Air, which had arrived from Syracuse on a US Airways Express Service and was hit by a fuel bowser as it taxied to the terminal, but both pilots and the 14 passengers were unharmed.

JACKSONVILLE FLORIDA: JAX

Jacksonville, Duval County, Florida, USA

Owner and operator: Jacksonville Aviation
Authority
Runways: 07/25, 3,048m (10,000ft); 13/31,
2,347m (7,701ft)
Terminals: One, with three concourses, A, B
and C
Annual passengers: 6,319,016
Annual cargo: 75,499 tonnes
Annual aircraft movements: 118,493

Background

Shared with the military, Jacksonville is some
14km (just under 9 miles) north of Jacksonville.
When opened on 31 October 1968 it replaced an
earlier airport at Imeson Field. One innovation
was that arriving and departing passengers were
separated into different sides of the terminal, but
it now conforms to the more usual configuration
of having departing passengers on the upper
level and arriving passengers below. Despite the
number of US naval bases in the area, and the
increasing popularity of Florida as a holiday and
retirement location, traffic at the new airport
grew only slowly to begin with, and by 1982 it
had just 2 million passengers annually. However,
deregulation of domestic air services in the USA
saw more airlines start to serve Jacksonville, and
by 1999 the number of passengers had more than
doubled to five million. Expansion started in
2000 and included rebuilding of much of the terminal. The original concourses A and C have
been demolished and new concourses completed, and the existing Concourse B will be
rebuilt later.

When Imeson Field closed, the Florida Air
National Guard also transferred its resident unit
to Jacksonville, and established Jacksonville Air
National Guard Base at the airport. Features
resulting from this include USAF-pattern aircraft arresting gear on the runways (but not used
by commercial flights) and an enhanced USAF
fire and rescue service in addition to the airport's
own facilities. Most of the usual USAF infrastructure is located away from the airport at
NAS Jacksonville. At the time of writing, the
resident unit is the 125th Fighter Wing, flying F-
15C/D Eagle air superiority fighters.

One of the recorded accidents at the airport is
to a Lockheed Lodestar of Caribbean Atlantic
Airlines on 8 January 1947, which overshot the
runway and crashed into woods on a second
attempt at landing, but the 3 crew and 12 passengers survived. A hijacking attempt on a Delta
Air Lines Douglas DC-9 on 6 January 1970
ended when a passenger subdued the hijacker as
the plane landed from Orlando. One of the
worst accidents at the airport was on 6 December 1984 when an Embraer Bandeirante of PBA,
which had just taken off for Tampa, crashed with
the loss of all 13 passengers and crew. There has
been one military accident at the airport, and
that was when a United States Navy Lockheed
P-3A Orion suffered an undercarriage failure
after landing on 23 February 1978.

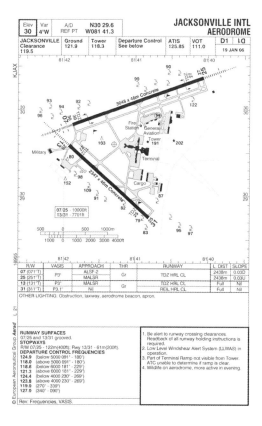

BURBANK BOB HOPE: BUR

Burbank, California, USA

Owner and operator: Burbank-Glendale-
   Pasadena Airport Authority
Runways: 15/33, 2,099m (6,886ft); 8/26,
   1,768m (5,801ft)
Terminals: Two, designated Terminal A and
   Terminal B (linked to operate as one)
Annual passengers: 5,921,336
Annual cargo: 45,818 tonnes
Annual aircraft movements: 123,521

The Ventura County Line of MetroLink runs
directly from the airport to the city centre.

Background

The airport is 5km (3 miles) north-west of Burbank. It opened on 30 May 1930 as United Airport (named after the main user). Although built
and owned by the local authority, the site had
been selected by Boeing Air Transport for its
subsidiary Pacific Air Transport some years earlier but, by the time the airport was ready,
Boeing had been forced to move out of air transport by US Anti-Trust legislation that prevented
aircraft manufacturers running airlines. The airport was the largest in the Los Angeles area at
the time, and remained so until the new Los
Angeles Airport opened in Westchester in 1946.
United Airport was renamed Union Air Terminal in 1934, and the name was changed again in
1940 to Lockheed Air Terminal when it was
bought by the aircraft manufacturer. The need
for Lockheed to have its own airfield for aircraft
deliveries spared the airport from being
taken over by the military during the Second
World War.

After the war, the airport continued to
develop, but a major setback occurred in February 1966 when a fire broke out in a restaurant
and spread throughout the terminal and to the
control tower, but there were no casualties. The
airport reopened the following day, using a
hangar as a temporary terminal, and temporary
air traffic control facilities were also set up with
borrowed equipment. The terminal and air traffic control tower were rebuilt and opened the
following year, when Lockheed renamed the airport once again, this time as Hollywood-Bur-
bank Airport. The airport continued to attract
airlines, and in 1969 Continental inaugurated a
service to Portland and Seattle.

Yet another name change followed in 1978,
when the airport was sold to the present owners
and became the Burbank-Glendale-Pasadena
Airport. This lasted until 2003 when the current
title was adopted in honour of the famous comedian Bob Hope, who had been a local resident
and had kept a private aircraft at the airport for
some years.

As elsewhere, proposals to expand the airport
have run into fierce local opposition from residents and environmental groups, despite the
Federal Aviation Administration recommending
development. Nevertheless, both terminals have
been upgraded and the redundant Lockheed
buildings were demolished during the 1990s to
accommodate commercial development.

Originally built for smaller aircraft, the airport has been described as 'challenging'. Apart
from the fire in the terminal, there have been
two serious incidents at Burbank. Potentially
very serious was that on 5 March 2000 when a
Southwest Airlines Boeing 737, landing from
Las Vegas, overshot the runway, crashed
through a blast barrier and a perimeter fence,
crossed a highway and eventually stopped close
to a petrol station, injuring 43 of the passengers
and crew, for which both pilots were dismissed,
and the petrol station was later closed as a safety
measure. Another overshoot was on 13 October
2006 by a Gulfstream business jet, but the two
crew and five passengers were unharmed.

BUFFALO NIAGARA
INTERNATIONAL: BUF

Cheektowaga, Erie County, New York State,
USA

Owner and operator: Niagara Frontier
   Transportation Authority
Runways: 05/23, 2,690m (8,827ft); 14/32,
   2,183m (7,161ft)

Terminals: One
Annual passengers: 5,308,723
Annual cargo: 44,222 tonnes
Annual aircraft movements: 127,307

Background

The busiest airport in 'upstate' New York, and third busiest in the state as a whole, Buffalo Niagara is so named because of its proximity to the famous falls. In addition to serving Buffalo and bringing tourists to the falls, it also serves many Canadian communities as it is close to the border with Ontario.

The airport was built in 1926 as Buffalo Municipal Airport. Because of its location traffic grew rapidly, and by 1955 it had begun to expand. The name was changed in 1959 to the Greater Buffalo International Airport on being acquired by the Niagara Frontier Port Authority. The terminal was extensively rebuilt in 1961, and a new control tower was opened. The 1961

terminal was renamed the 'East Terminal' in 1971 when a second terminal, the 'West Terminal', was added. The 1971 terminal was meant to last for just ten years but, despite considerable expansion of the East Terminal, the airport struggled to cope with passenger growth, and planning began in 1991 for a new terminal placed between the two earlier terminals. The current name for the airport was adopted when the new terminal opened on 3 November 1997. The two older terminals were demolished shortly afterwards to allow the new terminal to expand. Both runways were resurfaced and extended in 2006.

For many years the 'upstate' airports were accused of high costs, and the airlines serving them of high fares, but this image changed with the arrival of the low-cost carriers, and Southwest Airlines has overtaken US Airways as the main carrier at Buffalo, and another low-cost carrier, the fast-expanding JetBlue Airways, is already third.

There is some pressure in the area to rename the airport after Tim Russert, a popular news commentator and a native of Buffalo.

The worst accident at the airport was on 12 February 2009, but an earlier accident was to a light aircraft, which crashed on to a private house in 1972, killing the three occupants of the plane and three people on the ground. The accident in February 2009 was to a Colgan Air Bombardier Dash 8 Q400 operating a Continental Connection flight as it approached from Newark in poor weather and with ice building up on the wings, leading the aircraft to crash into a house killing all 49 passengers and crew as well as an occupant of the house.

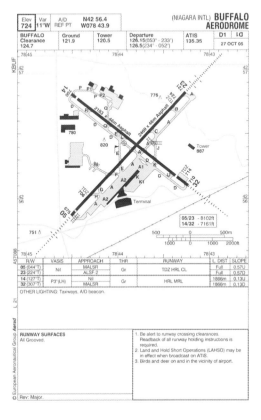

ANCHORAGE TED STEVENS INTERNATIONAL: ANC

Anchorage, Alaska, USA

Owner and operator: State of Alaska Department of Transportation
Runways: 7L/25R, 3,231m (10,600ft); 7R/25L, 3,322m (10,900ft); 14/32, 3,531m (11,584ft)
Terminals: Two, designated South Terminal (for domestic passengers and having three

concourses, A, B, and C) and North Terminal
(for international passengers)

Airlines using airport as hub: Alaskan Airlines,
Federal Express (FedEx), Northwest Cargo,
United Parcel Service (UPS)

Annual passengers: 5,304,145

Annual cargo: 2,825,511 tonnes

Annual aircraft movements: 276,209

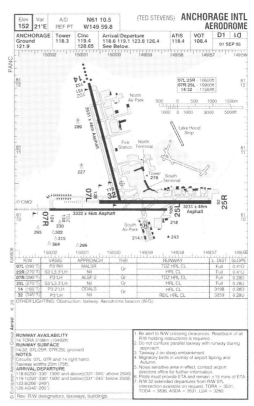

Background

The largest and most important in Alaska, the
airport is 6km (less than 4 miles) from the centre
of Anchorage. It was built in 1951 as Anchorage
International Airport, and for years many of the
aircraft movements were those flying to and
from eastern Asian destinations because aircraft
belonging to airlines in North America, Asia,
and Western Europe were not allowed to use
Soviet airspace, and until the 1980s range was
also a problem. That apart, because of its position the airport has become a major air cargo
hub, with both FedEx and UPS using it, and it is
the third busiest air cargo airport in the world,
after Memphis and Hong Kong. The main passenger carrier is Alaska Airlines with its busy
services to Seattle and Fairbanks.

The current name was adopted in 2000 by the
state legislature to commemorate a US senator.

Passenger traffic has been growing slowly in
recent years, but the airport does act as a hub for
oil industry workers flying on to the oilfields,
and it is hoped that it will also become a hub for
traffic to and from the Russian Far East.

One of the worst losses of aircraft in an accident occurred at Anchorage on 6 November
1974 when three aircraft were destroyed in a fire
believed to have been started by a welder's torch
in a hangar owned by the Federal Aviation
Administration but part of which was leased to
Reeve Aleutian Airways. Reeve lost a Lockheed
Electra and a NAMC YS-11, while the FAA lost
a DC-3, and the airport was closed for several
hours. Other accidents include a Mobil Oil
Canadair CL-44 from West Kuparuk on 1 May
1969 landing heavily, causing its undercarriage
to collapse and resulting in the aircraft being
written off, but the crew of four were unharmed.

A Capitol International Airways Douglas DC-
8-63CF, taking off on a military charter to Cam
Ranh Bay via Tokyo failed to get airborne on 27
November 1970, because the wheel brakes
engaged, and crashed after overshooting the
runway, killing 1 of the 10 crew and 46 of the 219
passengers. A Japan Air Lines Boeing 747-200,
taking off for Tokyo, skidded off the runway in
poor weather on 16 December 1975, causing
substantial damage to the aircraft, but the 20
crew and 101 passengers survived. Another JAL
aircraft, a Douglas DC-8-62 freighter, crashed
on taking off for Tokyo on 13 January 1977, possibly because the captain's blood alcohol level
was almost three times the limit for motorists in
Alaska, and killed all five occupants of the aircraft. Another take-off accident was to a Chase
C-122 Avitruc on 31 January 1977 when the aircraft stalled and crashed, killing one of the crew,
but the two others survived. A McDonnell Douglas DC-10-30 of Korean Air Lines took the

wrong runway during take-off for Los Angeles and crashed into a South Central Piper Navajo, injuring the nine occupants, but the three crew of the DC-10 were unharmed, although the aircraft was a write-off. A ground accident to an Alaska Airlines Boeing 727, which was being taxied, occurred when it hit an airbridge and caught fire after the two technicians handling the aircraft accidentally disengaged the braking system. A Japan Air Lines Boeing 747-100 freighter, which had taken off for Chicago on 31 March 1993, encountered severe turbulence and lost an engine, causing the pilots to return, making a successful landing at Anchorage. An Aeroflot Ilyushin Il-62M, standing at the terminal during a stop on a flight to Los Angeles, was destroyed when an Asiana Boeing 747-400, making a tight turn too fast for the slippery conditions, nearly cut through its tail. The 12 crew aboard the Russian aircraft were unharmed.

RENO-TAHOE INTERNATIONAL: RNO

Reno, Washoe County, Nevada, USA

Owner and operator: Reno-Tahoe Airport Authority
Runways: 16L/34R, 2,743m (9,000ft); 16R/34L, 3,353m (11,002ft); 7/25, 1,860m (6,102ft)
Terminals: One, known as the Howard Cannon Terminal
Annual passengers: 5,043,986
Annual cargo: 58,617 tonnes
Annual aircraft movements: 140,806

Background

Reno-Tahoe is 6km (3¾ miles) from the centre of Reno, and 1,346m (4,415ft) above sea level. It dates from 1929 when it opened as Hubbard Field, named after the head of Boeing Air Transport, Eddie Hubbard, whose company built and owned the airport. It passed to United Airlines when Boeing was forced to dispose of its airline interests following the enactment of anti-trust legislation. The local authority bought the airport in 1953. A new terminal opened in 1960 for

that year's Winter Olympics. Many of the airport's passengers every year are winter sports enthusiasts arriving on holiday. By this time the airport was known as Reno-Cannon International Airport, in honour of Howard Cannon, a former US senator who was also a retired major-general in the USAF Reserve. When the present passenger terminal was opened in 1994 it was named the Howard Cannon Terminal, and the airport name was changed to Reno-Tahoe International Airport.

The west side of the airport accommodates the Reno Air National Guard Base, opened in 1954 when the Nevada Air National Guard transferred units from the now closed Stead AFB. The base accommodates an Air Mobility Command Lockheed C-130H Hercules unit.

There has been just one serious accident at the airport. On 21 January 1985 a Galaxy Airlines aircraft crashed while making an emergency landing after having taken off for Minneapolis. The pilots had become distracted by excessive vibration (found to have been because of a maintenance error) and lost control of the aircraft. Only one of the 71 passengers and crew survived.

TUCSON INTERNATIONAL: TUS

Tucson, Pima County, Arizona, USA

Owner and operator: Tucson Airport Authority
Runways: 11L/29R, 3,352m (10,996ft); 11R/29L, 2,563m (8,408ft); 3/21, 2,134m (7,000ft)
Terminals: One, with two concourses, A and B (international flights handled in A)
Annual passengers: 4,429,905
Annual cargo: 36,634 tonnes
Annual aircraft movements: 257,191

Background

Tucson is a shared military and civil airport some 10km (6 miles) south of the centre of Tucson. It is 806m (2,643ft) above sea level.

The airport dates from 1919 and despite claims that it was the first municipal airport in the United States, regular flights did not begin

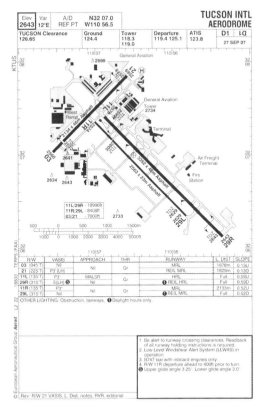

Elev 2643	Var 12°E	A/D REF PT	N32 07.0 W110 56.5						TUCSON INTL AERODROME
TUCSON Clearance 126.65			Ground 124.4		Tower 118.3 119.0	Departure 119.4 125.1	ATIS 123.8	D1	LQ 27 SEP 07

R/W	VASIS	APPROACH	THR	RUNWAY	L. DIST	SLOPE
03 (045˚T)	Nil	Nil	Gr	MRL	1878m	0.13U
21 (225˚T)	P3¹ (LH)			REIL MRL	1829m	0.13D
11L (135˚T)	P3¹	MALSR	Gr	HRL	Full	0.59U
29R (315˚T)	S(LH) ❺	Nil		❶ REIL HRL	Full	0.59D
11R (135˚T)	P3¹	Nil	Gr	MRL	2133m	0.52U
29L (315˚T)	Nil			❶ REIL MRL	Full	0.52D

OTHER LIGHTING: Obstruction, taxiways. ❶ Daylight hours only.

1. Be alert to runway crossing clearances. Readback of all runway holding instructions is required.
2. Low Level Windshear Alert System (LLWAS) in operation.
3. B747 taxi with inboard engines only.
4. R/W 11R departure ahead to 400ft prior to turn.
❺ Upper glide angle 3.25˚. Lower glide angle 3.0˚

© Eurocean Aeronautical Group Aerad L2 22   TERPS (FAA)   KTUS

Rev: R/W 21 VASIS, L. Dist, notes, RVR, editorial

until 1928 when Standard Airlines, a predecessor of American Airlines, introduced a service. In 1930 an airmail service was started. During the Second World War the airport was used by the United States Army Air Force's Air Technical Service Command, and there was also some manufacturing on the site. After the war it was returned to civil use.

In 1948 the Tucson Airport Authority was established as a non-profit-making organisation to operate and develop the airport. The layout was changed, and three hangars, used for manufacturing during the war, became the terminal and administration area. A new terminal opened in 1963, and an international inspection station was added, allowing the airport to adopt its current 'international' title. In March 2008 an extensive remodelling of the terminal was completed, with the old East Concourse becoming Concourse A, and the former West Concourse becoming Concourse B, while international arrivals are now located in Concourse A rather than in a separate terminal.

The airport was the scene of an attempted hijacking and an accident. The hijack incident was on 16 March 1979 on a Continental Airlines Boeing 727, but the plane was stormed, and the hijacker, who had been demanding to be taken to Cuba, was arrested. There are no reports of casualties amongst the 95 passengers and crew. The accident was to an American West Airlines Boeing 737-200, which landed from Pheonix on 30 December 1989 with an electrical fault that had damaged the aircraft's hydraulics, and it overshot the runway, collided with an airport structure, and suffered a collapsed nose wheel. The aircraft was written off, but the 5 crew and 125 passengers all survived.

OMAHA EPPLEY AIRFIELD: OMA
Omaha, Douglas County, Nebraska

Owner and operator: Omaha Airport Authority
Runways: 14L/32R, 2,591m (8,500ft); 14R/32L, 2,896m (9,502ft); 18/36, 2,485m (8,153ft)
Terminals: One, with two concourses, A and B
Annual passengers: 4,421,274
Annual cargo: 85,967 tonnes
Annual aircraft movements: 136,092

Background
The largest airport in Nebraska, Omaha's scheduled flights are all domestic. The airport is a long-established municipal airfield 5km (3 miles) north-east of Omaha, and it takes its name from Eugene Eppley, a hotelier whose estate paid to upgrade the airport to handle jet airliners in 1960.

One accident has occurred near the airport. On 6 August 1966 a Braniff Airways BAE One-Eleven approaching from Kansas City was holding, waiting for bad weather to clear, before starting its landing approach, but violent turbulence broke up the aircraft with the loss of all 42 passengers and crew.

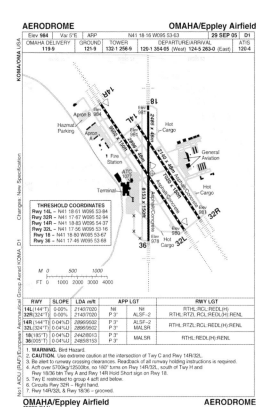

AERODROME   **OMAHA/Eppley Airfield**

Elev 984	Var 5°E	ARP	N41 18·16 W095 53-63	29 SEP 05	D1
OMAHA DELIVERY 119·9	GROUND 121·9	TOWER 132·1 256·9	DEPARTURE/ARRIVAL 120·1 354·05 (West) 124·5 263·0 (East)		ATIS 120·4

KOMA/OMA USA

Changes: New Specification

Not AIDU (RAF)/European Aeronautical Group Aerad KOMA D1

THRESHOLD COORDINATES
Rwy 14L – N41 18·61 W095 53-84
Rwy 32R – N41 17·67 W095 52-94
Rwy 14R – N41 18·83 W095 54-37
Rwy 32L – N41 17·56 W095 53-16
Rwy 18 – N41 18·80 W095 53-67
Rwy 36 – N41 17·46 W095 53-68

M 0   500   1000
FT 0   1000 2000 3000 4000

RWY	SLOPE	LDA m/ft	APP LGT		RWY LGT
14L(144°T)	0·00%	2140/7020	Nil	Nil	RTHL:RCL:REDL(H)
32R(324°T)	0·00%	2140/7020	P 3°	ALSF–2	RTHL:RTZL:RCL:REDL(H):RENL
14R(144°T)	0·04%D	2896/9502	P 3°	ALSF–2	RTHL:RTZL:RCL:REDL(H):RENL
32L(324°T)	0·04%U	2896/9502	P 3°	MALSR	
18(185°T)	0·04%D	2442/8013	P 3°	MALSR	RTHL:REDL(H):RENL
36(005°T)	0·04%U	2485/8153	P 3°		

1. **WARNING.** Bird Hazard.
2. **CAUTION.** Use extreme caution at the intersection of Twy C and Rwy 14R/32L.
3. Be alert to runway crossing clearances. Readback of all runway holding instructions is required.
4. Acft over 5700kg/12500lbs. no 180° turns on Rwy 14R/32L, south of Twy H and Rwy 18/36 btn Twy A and Rwy 14R Hold Short sign on Rwy 18.
5. Twy E restricted to group 4 acft and below.
6. Circuits Rwy 32R – Right hand.
7. Rwy 14R/32L & Rwy 18/36 – grooved.

OMAHA/Eppley Airfield   **AERODROME**
TERPS (FAA)

MANCHESTER-BOSTON REGIONAL: MHT

Manchester, New Hampshire, USA

Owner and operator: City of Manchester, New Hampshire
Runways: 17/35, 2,819m (9,250ft); 6/24, 2,179m (7,150ft)
Terminals: One
Airlines using airport as base or hub: UPS
Annual passengers: 3,892,630
Annual cargo: 87,747 tonnes
Annual aircraft movements: 90,345

The Massachusetts Bay Transportation Authority is proposing to extend one of its lines into the airport, but no firm dates have been announced.

Background

One of the most reliable airports in the United States, the airport is equipped for Category IIIB operations and has never closed because of bad weather. It is 5km (3 miles) from Manchester, New Hampshire.

The airport came into existence in 1927 when in June that year the city's council provided funds for an airfield, and the airport was opened before Christmas with two 550m (1,800ft) runways completed. Northeast Airways was established at the airport in 1933, and this led to the construction of a passenger terminal.

During the Second World War the airport was used by the United States Army Air Force as a bomber base, and also for the Army Air Forces Anti-submarine Command. The USAAF named the airport Grenier Field in February 1942 to commemorate 2nd Lt Jean Grenier, a local man killed in an air accident in 1934. The airport remained as a military base with the formation of the autonomous United States Air Force in 1947, and the name changed slightly to Grenier Air Force Base. It was not until later that it was decided that it should become a joint civil and military operation, and in 1961 commercial flights resumed with the opening of a terminal. In 1966 the USAF left, which made room for further development of the airport, but it was not until 1978 that it was renamed as Manchester Airport, a title that remained until 18 April 2006 when it became Manchester-Boston Regional Airport, to make the most of it being just 80km (50 miles) from Boston.

With the return of commercial flights after the war, the airport resumed its links with Northeast. Delta Air Lines took over the airline in 1972 and continued to serve the airport until it withdrew in 1982. The gap was filled in 1984 when United Airlines introduced a service using Douglas DC-9 jet airliners to Chicago O'Hare. During the early 1990s United briefly operated a service to Washington Dulles. USAir, as it was then known, also introduced services from the airport during the early 1990s. Later, both airlines used the Boeing 757 on services at Manchester, and this remains the largest aircraft to use the airport, which is now served by United Airlines, Northwest Airlines and, now infrequently, by US Airways.

Expansion and modernisation of the airport began in 1992, with a new terminal opened in 1994, while the runways and taxiways were reconstructed and strengthened. In 1998, Metro-Jet, Northwest Airlines, and the low-cost carrier Southwest Airlines all introduced services to Manchester, ushering in a period of rapid growth in passenger numbers.

Just one accident has been recorded at the airport. An AirNow Embraer Bandeirante, which took off on a cargo flight to Bangor on 8 November 2005, crashed in flames into a garden centre just 1.4km (almost 1 mile) from the airport. The pilot, the sole occupant, survived the crash.

LOUISVILLE INTERNATIONAL (STANDIFORD FIELD): SDF
Louisville, Kentucky, USA

Owner and operator: Louisville International
    Airport Authority
Runways: 17L/35R, 2,615m (8,579ft); 17R/35L,
    3,624m (11,890ft); 11/29, 2,210m (7,250ft)
Terminals: One, with two concourses, A and B
Airlines using airport as base or hub: UPS
Annual passengers: 3,819,154
Annual cargo: 2,078,947 tonnes
Annual aircraft movements: 171,573

Background
The US Army built the airport in 1941, in preparation for US involvement in the Second World War, on land that had not been affected by the Ohio River flood in 1937. It was named Standiford Field after a local businessman and politician who had owned part of the land. After the war the United States Army Air Force retained control of the base until it was transferred to the local authority in 1947, which already had a small airport, Bowman Field.

A small terminal was used at Standiford until the 1980s when the airport underwent reconstruction and modernisation, which included a new terminal and parallel runways, which led to United Parcel Services (UPS) selecting the airport as a hub. The airport retains a connection with the military, as it is the base for the Kentucky Air National Guard, which has a unit operating Lockheed C-130 Hercules transports.

The worst accident at the airport was on 28 September 1953 when a Resort Airlines Curtis C-46 Commando was landing from Philadelphia. The aircraft ballooned slightly on levelling-off after the flare, and the captain applied increased power and started to climb, as if for a go-around, but the aircraft stalled and crashed, killing all 3 crew and 22 of the 38 passengers. The next recorded accident was on 8 September 1970 when a Delta Air Lines Douglas DC-9 was landing from Chicago and touched down on a slope short of the runway, bounced, and landed on the runway, where it skidded and overshot, before coming to rest. Parts of the aircraft, including the tailcone, were found on the runway, and the aircraft was damaged beyond repair, but the 5 crew and 89 passengers survived. Another cargo service, operated by a UPS McDonnell Douglas MD-11F landing from Anchorage on 7 June 2005, suffered a nose wheel failure after touchdown and was damaged, but repairable, and the crew of four were unharmed.

OKLAHOMA WILL ROGERS WORLD: OKC
Oklahoma City, Oklahoma, USA

Owner and operator: Oklahoma City Airport
    Trust
Runways: 17L/35R, 2,988m (9,802ft); 17R/35L,
    2,987m (9,800ft); 13/31, 2,377m (7,800ft);
    18/36, 938m (3,078ft)
Terminals: One
Annual passengers: 3,737,135
Annual cargo: 32,708 tonnes
Annual aircraft movements: 121,415

Background
The more important of the two airports in the Oklahoma City area (the other is Oklahoma Wiley Post), it is almost 10km (6 miles) from the city centre. It is named after local hero Will Rodgers, comedian and cowboy actor, who died in an air crash with Wiley Post while they were flying in Alaska in 1935.

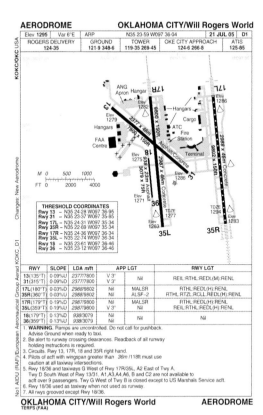

The airport was built before the Second World War, and during wartime was used, as Will Rogers Field, for the initial training of fighter and bomber aircrew by the United States Army Air Force. It reverted to commercial use after the war, and during the 1960s a new terminal was opened with twin concourses. This has since been demolished and replaced with a larger terminal, and at present the terminal is undergoing further expansion.

The airport includes the 'Ninety Nines Museum of Women Pilots', which is an archive of papers and artefacts of noted women pilots, and includes a library and exhibition area.

At the time of writing, the airport has not had any serious accidents recorded.

NORFOLK INTERNATIONAL: ORF
Norfolk, Virginia, USA

Owner and operator: Norfolk Airport Authority
Runways: 5/23, 2,744m (9,001ft); 14/32, 1,486m (4,875ft)
Terminals: One, with two concourses, A and B
Annual passengers: 3,718,399
Annual cargo: 31,772 tonnes
Annual aircraft movements: 135,098

Background

Situated just 5km (3 miles) north-east of Norfolk, the airport also serves the Hampton Roads area of south-east Virginia, and north-east Carolina.

The first air service to serve Norfolk was the 'Mitten Line' to Washington, provided by the Philadelphia Rapid Transit Air Service for a few months in 1926 before it had to be abandoned because of high costs. In 1929 Ben Epstein started an air taxi service from a field, which was also used by the Ludington Line for a scheduled service to Washington, and then joined by Eastern Air Lines flying to Richmond. Air transport in the area suffered a setback in 1932 when the United States Navy opposed the expansion of a local airfield because it interfered with flying at the Norfolk Naval Air Station, and this was followed by the Great Depression, which so affected aviation in this part of the USA that all services to and from Norfolk were abandoned.

The history of the present airport started in 1938, when the city converted the Truxton Manor Golf Course, which it owned, to Norfolk Municipal Airport. The old clubhouse was renovated and converted into a passenger terminal. The first airline to use the new airport was Penn Central Airlines, which was later taken over by United Airlines. A permanent terminal opened in 1940.

During the Second World War, what was then the United States Army Air Corps took over the airport, extending the original runway and building two more to cope with the growth in aircraft sizes. Once the war ended, what had become the United States Air Force surrendered the airport back to the city. Commercial flights were soon resumed, and in 1948 work started on a larger terminal. The airport began to show strong growth in the years that followed, and during the early 1950s was handling more flights daily than New York La Guardia. The airport passed to the Norfolk Port & Industrial Authority in 1950, and the following year the new passenger terminal was completed. The 1960s saw the airport developed, with runways lengthened and strengthened, and taxiways and aprons were also readied for the new jet airliners. This was so successful that in 1968 the airport was renamed Norfolk Regional Airport, and it became the main airport in its area.

A new terminal was opened in 1974 and land was purchased to permit further expansion. The addition of customs facilities in 1976 allowed the airport to adopt its present title. This was followed by improvements to air traffic control and other facilities, as well as a new general aviation terminal and an air freight terminal. The name of the owner and operator was also shortened to Norfolk Airport Authority. In 1991 the passenger terminal was enlarged by the addition of a new concourse and a new federal air traffic control tower.

Despite the 'international' title, the only passenger services going beyond the United States were those operated by Air Canada using Bombardier CRJ regional jets, and these were dropped in the aftermath of the fall in air travel that followed the terrorist attacks of 11 September 2001. The airport does handle international air cargo and is on the networks of the major air cargo operators, as well as the US Mail, and the cargo terminal has warehouse accommodation as part of the facility. New arrivals areas in the terminal were opened in 2002.

There have not been any serious accidents recorded at the airport at the time of writing, but on four occasions in recent years it has been used for emergency landings, all of which were successful, by airliners experiencing in-flight failures, including a fuel leak and a hydraulic problem.

RICHMOND INTERNATIONAL: RIC
Sandston, Virginia, USA

Owner and operator: Capital Region Airports Commission
Runways: 16/34, 2,744m (9,003ft); 2/20, 2,014m (6,607ft); 7/25, 1,623m (5,326ft)
Terminals: One, with two concourses, A and B
Annual passengers: 3,634,302
Annual cargo: 51,071 tonnes
Annual aircraft movements: 121,244

Background
Located 8km (5 miles) east of Richmond, the airport opened as Richard Evelyn Byrd Flying Field in 1927 in honour of the aviator, the first man to fly over the North Pole, pioneer of Arctic and Antarctic flight, and brother of the then Governor of Virginia.

Like many secondary airports, it has been enjoying strong growth in air cargo as the cargo carriers seek to avoid the delays and high costs of the major airports. The two most important airlines are US Airways and Delta Air Lines, each with just under a quarter of the passenger market. In recent years the airport has undergone modernisation and expansion, with the terminal modified to a two-level layout and a new air traffic control tower.

The only significant incident recorded at the airport was in 1996, when an Eastwind Airlines flight landing from Trenton experienced a temporary loss of rudder control, but the aircraft landed safely and no one on board was harmed.

SPOKANE INTERNATIONAL: GEG
Spokane, Washington State, USA

Owner and operator: Spokane City
Runways: 3/21, 2,744m (9,001ft); 7/25, 2,499m (8,199ft)
Terminals: One, with three concourses, A, B, and C
Annual passengers: 3,472,901
Annual cargo: 47,696 tonnes
Annual aircraft movements: 101,634

Background

The second busiest airport in Washington after Seattle-Tacoma, it is 8km (5 miles) west of the centre of Spokane.

Opened before the Second World War, it was originally known as Sunset Field and owned by Spokane County, while at the time Spokane's airport was at Felts Field. It was purchased by the federal government in 1941 for the United States Army Air Force during the Second World War, which renamed it Geiger Air Force Base after the army airman Major Harold Geiger. The USAAF handed the airport back to the city in 1946 and it replaced Felts Field as the local airport. The current title was given in 1960.

The area served by the airport has seen population grow in recent years, and there are plans to increase the number of direct flights to the major international hubs to improve transfers on to transatlantic flights. Meanwhile, the airport is being expanded and a new control tower has recently been added. For the future, expansion of the terminal's Concourse C with additional gates, adding a main runway, and extending the main runway are all possibilities.

There have been just two accidents at the airport. On 18 March 1994 a Salair Douglas DC-3 that had been grounded for an engine change took off for Portland on a cargo flight, but the replacement engine failed, and as the aircraft returned to the airport it struck high ground and burst into flames, killing both pilots, the only occupants. Another Salair aircraft, a Convair 440 landing from Phoenix on 5 January 1996 on a positioning flight, suffered engine problems because of a shortage of fuel and crash-landed in a field, wrecking the aircraft but without harm to the two pilots.

EL PASO INTERNATIONAL: ELP

El Paso, Texas, USA

Owner and operator: City of El Paso
Runways: 8L/26R, 1,674m (5,493ft); 8R/26L,
　2,751m (9,025ft); 4/22, 3,664m (12,020ft)
Terminals: One, with two concourses designated
　A and B

Annual passengers: 3,402,700
Annual cargo: 74,963 tonnes
Annual aircraft movements: 103,990

Background

Situated just 6km (less than 4 miles) from the centre of El Paso, the airport dates from 1929 when it was built by Standard Airlines, a predecessor of American Airlines, as Standard Airport – a stage in their transcontinental airmail service. At the time, the city owned El Paso Municipal Airport close to the Franklin Mountains, and in 1936 American Airlines exchanged Standard Airport for El Paso Municipal, and the present El Paso International became the city's airport. The old municipal airport closed in 1965.

During the Second World War the airport was taken over by the United States Army Air Corps (United States Army Air Force from 1941) for operational training of its heavy bomber squadrons before they were deployed to the European or Pacific theatres. When the war ended, the airport was returned to the city for civil use, much improved with the long runways needed by heavy bombers.

The airport grew strongly in the post-war period and became a major base for Continental Airlines, which offered direct services, latterly with jet aircraft, to the main cities across the West and Mid-West of the United States, although the airport did not have direct flights to the East Coast cities. With deregulation, Continental switched to a 'hub and spoke' system with fewer direct flights, and El Paso was one of the airports that suffered the loss of direct flights between 'city pairs' at this time. Over the years, there have been flights to destinations in Mexico, both by US and Mexican airlines, from El Paso, but many of these were short-lived.

A hijacking occurred to an American Airlines Boeing 727 on 24 November 1979 at the airport, but it lasted just a day, and the culprit was arrested. A Reliant Airlines Dassault Falcon 20, on a cargo flight, was overloaded by the shipper and this contributed to a runway overrun following an aborted take-off. Despite crossing a four-lane highway and hitting several vehicles, no one was killed, but the aircraft was damaged beyond repair.

BOISE AIRPORT (GOWEN FIELD): BOI

Boise, Ada County, Idaho, USA

Owner and operator: City of Boise
Runways: 10L/28R, 3,048m (10,000ft);
    10R/28L, 2,976m (9,763ft)
Terminals: One, with two concourses designated
    A and B
Annual passengers: 3,365,303
Annual cargo: 42,565 tonnes
Annual aircraft movements: 181,945

Background

Boise Airport, also often referred to by its military designation as the Boise Aviation Terminal, Gowen Field, is just 6km (less than 4 miles) from the centre of the town.

The first municipal airport for Boise opened in 1926, and Varney Airlines (later becoming part of United Airlines) started airmail operations in April, followed by a regular passenger service, which began in 1933. It was one of the airports on the post-transatlantic solo flight tour of Charles Lindbergh with his Ryan monoplane *City of St Louis* in September 1927. Work on the present airport started in 1936, and in 1938 the airport opened what, at 2,680m (8,800ft), was the longest runway in the United States at the time. Varney moved to the new airport in 1939. The airport's hangar soon proved inadequate as aircraft grew in size, and it was converted into a passenger terminal.

The United States Army Air Corps (United States Army Air Force from 1941) took over the airport and renamed it Gowen Field after a graduate from the University of Idaho who joined the USAAC, but was killed in a crash in Panama in 1938, flying a B-10 bomber. For the rest of the Second World War, Gowen Field was used for operational training of heavy bomber crews before they were sent to operational theatres.

After the war the airport was returned to the city and commercial operations resumed, but the Idaho Air National Guard (the local reserves for the USAF) started to lease part of the airport, and this continues to this day with a Lockheed C-130 Hercules transport unit stationed at Boise. The airport also provides logistical support for the National Interagency Fire Centre, while the United States Forest Service uses the airport as a base for aerial fire-fighting aircraft during the forest fire season.

The airport underwent extensive modernisation between 2003 and 2005, with a new terminal opened in 2004 to replace the original terminal converted from a hangar. A new air traffic control tower is being built and should open in 2010. The main airlines operating out of Boise are Horizon Air and Southwest.

An accident occurred at the airport on 9 December 1996 when a Desert Air Transport Douglas C-47A took off for Salt Lake City but suffered an engine fire almost immediately afterwards and turned back, but lost control of the aircraft, and it crashed, killing both pilots, the sole occupants on this cargo flight. Another cargo flight, a Dassault Falcon 20 of Smith Air suffered an undercarriage failure when landing from Omaha on 27 November 1999, writing off the aircraft, but both pilots survived.

BIRMINGHAM-SHUTTLESWORTH INTERNATIONAL: BHM

Birmingham, Alabama, USA

Owner and operator: Birmingham International
    Airport Authority
Runways: 06/24, 3,658m (12,002ft); 18/36,
    2,164m (7,100ft)
Terminals: One, with two concourses designated
    A and B
Annual passengers: 3,222,689
Annual cargo: 28,984 tonnes
Annual aircraft movements: 138,975

Background

Birmingham-Shuttlesworth International is 8km (5 miles) north-east of the centre of the city, and is also the 'low-cost' alternative to Atlanta, Georgia.

Birmingham's first air services were introduced in 1928 by St Tammy and Gulf Coast Airways which used Roberts Field to the west of the city en route from Atlanta to New Orleans. The following year they were joined by a Delta Air Service route from Dallas Love Field. Even at this early stage, the city started to miss air services because Roberts Field could not handle aircraft such as the Ford Trimotor, the mainstay of many early airlines. To overcome this difficulty, the present airport was built as Birmingham Municipal Airport and opened on 31 May 1931.

When it opened, Birmingham Municipal had a single runway running east–west and a white two-storey 'Georgian-style' (Georgia, USA, as opposed to British Georgian period) terminal. The new airport immediately attracted American Airlines, and when Eastern Air Lines followed in 1934, a second runway was built.

During the Second World War the airport became a base for the United States Army Air Force, which used it as a fighter station (Birmingham Army Airfield). The USAAF built a new control tower and expanded the airport, while also providing additional paved taxiways. An aircraft modification centre was added and this is used as a maintenance facility today.

The airport returned to commercial use in August 1948, when Southern Airways introduced services. Four runways were operational, including the present 06/24 and 18/36, although much shorter than today. Growth continued throughout the 1950s, and turboprop services were introduced by Capital Airlines, for which one of the runways was lengthened, and when Capital was acquired by United Airlines, jet Sud Aviation Caravelles used the airport. These aircraft were followed during the 1960s by Convair 880 and Douglas DC-8 jet airliners. A second passenger terminal was opened in 1962 when a new air traffic control tower was also commissioned. The current terminal, which is semi-circular, opened in 1973. Following deregulation of domestic air services, many new airlines started to serve Birmingham, of which the most successful and enduring was Southwest Airlines. The introduction of flights to Canada and Mexico

justified renaming the airport as Birmingham International in October 1993.

In recent years, the runways have been lengthened and a new air traffic control tower built, as well as a new air cargo terminal. In June 2008 the airport was renamed as the Fred L. Shuttlesworth International Airport to commemorate the civil rights activist, but this was changed slightly in October to the present title. The airport can handle Category II landings.

Currently the terminal is being enlarged and so is the air cargo terminal.

The airport is shared with the Alabama Air National Guard, with an Air Mobility Command air refuelling unit based there, as well as a Tactical Air Command unit with McDonnell Douglas RF-4C Phantom reconnaissance aircraft. An Army aviation support unit of the Alabama National Guard is also at Birmingham International, as is the Southern Museum of Flight.

In the past 75 years there have been three fatal accidents to commercial transport at the airport. The first was on 6 January 1946 when a Pennsylvania Central Airlines (later absorbed by United Airlines) Douglas DC-3 landed and ran off the runway with three crew members receiving fatal injuries. The worst accident at the airport was to an aircraft of L'Express Airlines on 10 July 1991 in which 13 passengers and crew were killed. There was also another less serious commuter aircraft accident, and there have been several light aircraft accidents since 1962.

TULSA INTERNATIONAL: TUL
Tulsa, Oklahoma, USA

Owner: City of Tulsa
Operator: Tulsa Airport Authority
Runways: 18L/36R, 3,048m (10,000ft); 18R/36L, 1,860m (6,100ft); 8/26, 2,248m (7,375ft)
Terminals: One, with two concourses, A and B
Annual passengers: 3,218,429
Annual cargo: 54,513 tonnes
Annual aircraft movements: 138,975

Background

Built between the two world wars, Tulsa International is 8km (5 miles) north-east of the centre of Tulsa.

During the Second World War an air force manufacturing plant was located on the south-east side of the airport, and Douglas Aircraft used this to build a number of its military aircraft, and although it was used by other aircraft manufacturers after the war, it is now used for building school buses. American Airlines has its largest maintenance centre at Tulsa.

The Oklahoma Air National Guard has a fighter unit based at the airport.

An American Airlines Douglas DC-4, taking off for Los Angeles on 10 March 1948, struck a snowdrift with its nose wheel and diverted to Dallas where it landed safely, but the aircraft was said to be too badly damaged to repair. Another American Airlines flight, a Convair 240 approaching from Joplin on 6 January 1957, crashed into trees at the top of a hill after confusion over altimeter settings, killing one of the seven passengers. The airport was also the scene of the end of a hijacking, after the hijacker allowed the passengers and cabin crew to disembark, and police boarded the Continental Airlines Douglas DC-9 and arrested the man, who was found to be unarmed.

LONG BEACH/DAUGHERTY FIELD: LGB

Long Beach, California, USA

Owner and operator: City of Long Beach
Runways: 7L/25R, 1,887m (6,192ft); 7R/25L, 1,653m (5,423ft); 16L/34R, 1,301m (4,267ft); 16R/34L, 1,362m (4,470ft); 12/30, 3,048m (10,000ft)
Terminals: One
Airlines using airport as base or hub: JetBlue
Annual passengers: 2,906,464
Annual cargo: 47,079 tonnes
Annual aircraft movements: 398,433

Background

One of the world's busiest general aviation airfields, Long Beach is also known as Daugherty Field and has five runways, with the longest (12/30) needed for the Boeing C-17 Globemaster II transports that are built at Long Beach.

The first landing strip at Long Beach was, in fact, the beach! This is where Calbraith Rodgers landed after his 82-day transcontinental flight in 1911, and the beach remained the landing strip until the airport was built after the First World War. One Earl Daugherty leased a field for his barnstorming air shows and pleasure flights and then founded a flying school at what became known as Daugherty Field. In 1923 he convinced the city council that this would make a good municipal airport. The problem was that the airport faced strong competition from other airports in the area serving larger communities. Nevertheless, it attracted other more colourful users, such as Douglas 'Wrong Way' Corrigan, who flew out of Long Beach before making his famous flight to Ireland in 1938 when, officially, he was supposed to have been flying back from Brooklyn to Long Beach!

To increase the use of the airport, the city built a hangar and an administration building, and offered to lease it to the United States Navy for a token dollar a year as a naval reserve station. It worked. On 10 May 1928 the USN commissioned the Naval Reserve Air Base (NRAB) Long Beach. In 1930 the city built another hangar and administration building to attract the United States Army Air Corps, but in vain.

Long Beach Municipal Airport was served by American Airlines and United Airlines at various times, but neither found operations at the airport viable. More lasting success came with the manufacturer, Douglas Aircraft, which put pressure on space at the airport after work started on their new factory in 1940. The city's attitude to the USN then switched completely to one of open hostility, and the USN started to search quietly for a more welcoming and suitable base, while also pressing the city to maintain the runways properly. A suitable base was found and built, and the USN moved out of

Long Beach to what became NAS Los Alamitos in 1942, but instead of returning their part of the airport to the city, as the municipality had hoped, the USN handed it over to the United States Army Air Force!

During the Second World War, Long Beach was used by the USAAF and the USN, in the latter's case as an auxiliary air station for maintenance of carrier-borne aircraft. The USAAF turned it over to its Ferrying Division, which saw C-47 transports flown out of Long Beach to operational units, with 4,239 produced at Long Beach, as well as around 1,000 A-20 Havocs, 1,156 Invaders, and some 3,000 Boeing B-17 Fortress heavy bombers. When peace returned, the USN and USAF abandoned Long Beach, but fortunately Douglas remained, albeit on a much smaller scale. When Boeing acquired what had become McDonnell Douglas, production of the C-17 remained at Long Beach, and there is a maintenance centre for older Douglas aircraft at the airport, while Grumman has a completion centre for its corporate aircraft.

The post-war history of the site as an airport has been mixed. Eventually, as aircraft sizes grew, Long Beach became hemmed in by restrictions intended to curb the noise suffered by local residents, and today has some of the most severe restrictions of any US airport. It has lost traffic to other airports as a result, but the emergence of low-cost carriers has meant that it still has flights to a wide range of destinations, including transcontinental flights by JetBlue.

At the time of writing, there have been no serious accidents at Long Beach.

ALBANY INTERNATIONAL: ALB
Latham, Albany, New York State, USA

Owner and operator: Albany County Airport
  Authority
Runways: 01/19, 2,591m (8,500ft); 10/28,
  2,195m (7,200ft)
Terminals: One
Annual passengers: 2,874,277
Annual cargo: 26,266 tonnes
Annual aircraft movements: 110,775

Background

Albany International Airport is 10km (6¼ miles) north of Albany, the capital of New York State.

Albany had an airstrip as early as 1908, some 5km north of the town, but this was moved to Westerlo Island in 1909. The original airstrip was on local authority land, so the town claims to have been the first municipal airport in the United States, although it would not have been handling scheduled services at the time. The airfield attracted many of the early aviators, including Glen Curtiss, who won $10,000 for a flight between Albany and New York City, while others who followed included Jimmy Doolittle, Charles Lindbergh, and Amelia Earhart.

A new airport was built by Mayor John Thacher in 1928 on a site sold to the city by the Shaker community. The new airport suffered repeated closures in the early years, but a programme of improvements ensured that eventually a reliable airport was available to the town. Ownership passed from the city to the county in 1960, and the Albany County Airport Authority was established in 1993. The most recent development has been the opening of a new terminal in 1998. An unusual feature of the airport is that it is one of just four airports worldwide to use dual airbridges, one for the front of the aircraft and the other for the back, but only Southwest Airlines makes use of the facility.

Despite its international appellation, the only international flights are to Canada. The largest aircraft using the airport are Boeing 737s and Airbus A320s, and the main airline is Southwest Airlines, with most of the airlines using the airport being feeder operators. While CommutAir used the airport as a hub from 2000, the hub was closed in 2005. There are plans to extend the terminal with the addition of a new concourse.

There have been two serious accidents at the airport. The first was on 16 September 1953 when an American Airlines Convair 240 was landing from Windsor Locks after spending time in a holding pattern because of poor visibility. The captain reported that the flaps would not extend, and then on the approach the aircraft hit two radio transmission towers, which damaged both wings, and it crashed, killing all 4 crew and 27 passengers. The second accident was on 3 March 1972 to a Mohawk Airlines Fairchild FH-227 (a licence-built Fokker F-27) landing from New York, which suffered problems with one of its propellers and crashed into a house. Aboard the aircraft 2 of the 3 crew and 14 of the 45 passengers were killed, while there was an additional fatality on the ground.

DAYTON JAMES M. COX INTERNATIONAL: DAY
Vandalia, Ohio, USA

Owner and operator: City of Dayton
Runways: 6L/24R, 3,322m (10,900ft); 6R/24L, 2,134m (7,001ft) currently closed; 18/36, 2,591m (8,502ft)
Terminals: One, with two concourses, B and C
Airlines using airport as base or hub: PSA (US Airways Express operator)
Annual passengers: 2,833,031
Annual cargo: 9,512 tonnes
Annual aircraft movements: 92,461

Background
Usually referred to as Dayton International Airport, it is 14km (just under 9 miles) north of the centre of Dayton. It dates from 1936 when the local authority bought the airstrip on the site from a private owner, and is named after James Cox, a former governor and publisher of the *Dayton Daily News*.

The airport was a hub for Piedmont Airlines until it was acquired by the then USAir (now US Airways), but after the acquisition the number of longer distance flights was reduced, and the terminal's concourse D, originally used by Piedmont, now remains unused. It is still a hub and base for PSA Airlines, one of the US Airways Express carriers, and in recent years has attracted services from the low-cost airlines, including AirTran Airways and Frontier Airlines.

The only accident recorded at the airport was during the Vectren Dayton Air Show on 28 July 2007 when a pilot performing aerobatics was killed when his aircraft crashed into the runway.

GUAM/HAGÅTÑA (AGANA) ANTONIO B. WON PAT INTERNATIONAL: GUM
Tamuning, Guam, Marianas Islands

Owner and operator: A. B. Won Pat Guam International Airport Authority
Runways: 6L/24R, 3,053m (10,015ft); 6R/24L, 3,052m (10,014ft)
Terminals: One
Airlines using airport as base or hub: Asia Pacific Airlines, Continental Micronesia
Annual passengers: 2,391,135

Background
Named after the first member of the US House of Representatives from Guam, a United States territory, but often known simply as Guam or Guam International Airport, it is operated by a government body and is 5km (3 miles) from the capital city of Hagåtña, formerly known as Agana.

Before the Second World War, the only way of reaching Guam was by sea, but a flying-boat station was built in 1935 as a preliminary for Pan American Airways developing transpacific routes from the United States to the Philippines via Hawaii, Wake, and Guam. The through route was opened in 22 November 1935, operated by a Martin M-130 'China Clipper'.

The present airport was built during the Second World War as Guamu Dai Ni (Guam No. 2) by the Japanese Navy Air Force, and is believed to have opened in 1942/3 for the fighter defence of the Marianas. It was captured by US forces in 1944 when they retook the island, and was used by United States Army Air Force bomber squadrons before they moved on to Okinawa as US forces advanced across the Pacific. It was eventually handed over to the United States Navy and became Agana Naval Air Station or Brewer Field. After the war the USN retained the airfield, but civil operations were allowed and put under the management of the territory's Department of Commerce in

1969. It was used again by the United States Air Force for Boeing B-52 bomber operations against North Vietnam during the Vietnam War. The Guam International Airport Authority, the present operator, was established in 1975, and when the naval air station closed in April 1995, GIAA became the sole operator of the airport.

It was not until 1982 that a passenger terminal building was opened, and this was replaced by the current building, which opened in stages between 1996 and 1998. The old terminal is now disused, but was used for commuter flights.

The airport has been the scene of many accidents over the years, even after excluding the fact that it was on the frontline during the Pacific War. Sometimes the weather has been the culprit, and never more so than on 8 December 2002 when Hurricane Pongsona wrote off a Volga-Dnepr Ilyushin Il-76TD and two Freedom Air Short 330s, all three of which were parked, the two smaller aircraft even being inside a hangar. Other accidents have been for the more usual reasons, including that to a Korean Air Boeing 747-300 on 6 August 1997, which flew too low on a night approach from Seoul and crashed into Nimitz Hill, killing 22 of the 23 crew and 206 of the 231 passengers. More fortunate was a PAL (Philippine Air Lines) Airbus A330-300, landing from Manila, which struck electricity cables on the same hill on 17 December 2002, but after executing a missed approach and a go-around, landed safely with 14 crew and 101 passengers aboard. A Northwest Airlines Boeing 747-200, arriving from Tokyo on 19 August 2005, suffered a nose wheel collapse on landing, and while the aircraft was written off, the 16 crew and 318 passengers were unharmed.

SYRACUSE HANCOCK INTERNATIONAL: SYR

Syracuse, Onondaga County, New York State, USA

Owner and operator: City of Syracuse
   Department of Aviation
Runways: 10/28, 2,744m (9,003ft); 15/33,
   2,286m (7,500ft)

Terminals: Two, designated Terminal A and
   Terminal B
Annual passengers: 2,360,878
Annual cargo: 24,972 tonnes
Annual aircraft movements: 107,706

Background

Syracuse Airport is 6km (3¾ miles) east of the centre of Syracuse.

The first airport for Syracuse opened in 1928 as the 'Syracuse City Airport at Amboy', a suburb of Camillus, and was used mainly by air-mail flights. After the end of the Second World War the United States Air Force leased their bomber station near Mattydale to the city, and this opened for commercial flights on 17 September 1949 and replaced the pre-war airfield at Amboy. A former machine shop was converted to a passenger terminal. Of the original four carriers using the new airport, only American Airlines still does so today. A new passenger terminal opened in 1962 on the site of the present terminals, and in 1970 the airport became recognised as international.

As demand grew during the 1970s and 1980s, the airport was enlarged and, after 1976, Empire Airlines made it a hub, and it remained a hub for Piedmont Airlines after it acquired Empire in 1986. By 1987 the airport was second only to Buffalo in upstate New York, and the terminal was extended that year. The rapid expansion came to an abrupt halt in 1989 when Piedmont was taken over by USAir (now US Airways) and the hub was closed. The last terminal expansion was in 1996, which created two terminals, designated A and B. US Airways drastically reduced its flights at the airport following the terrorist attacks of 11 September 2001, but before this Jet-Blue introduced low-cost air services to Syracuse. Between 2003 and 2005, when it became bankrupt, TransMeridian Airlines operated scheduled services to Orlando, a route that was taken over by JetBlue in 2006. The airport also suffered when Independence Air ceased operations, while American Eagle operated to Dallas-Forth Worth between 2005 and 2008. Nevertheless, there are still plans to expand the airport, possibly by extending runway 10/28 and building a parallel runway beside it as 10L/28R.

The airport is the base for the New York Air National Guard which has a fighter unit equipped with Lockheed F-16 Fighting Falcons at Syracuse, and an air support operations squadron.

The airport had not suffered any serious accidents at the time of writing.

CHARLESTON INTERNATIONAL: CHS

North Charleston, South Carolina, USA

Owner and operator: Charleston County
   Aviation Authority and the USAF
Runways: 3/21, 2,135m (7,004ft); 15/33,
   2,744m (9,001ft)
Terminals: One, with two concourses, A and B
Annual passengers: 2,275,541
Annual cargo: 9,375 tonnes
Annual aircraft movements: 112,229

Background

A joint civil and military airport which also doubles as Charleston Air Force Base, it is the busiest airport in South Carolina.

Charleston was originally served by a privately-owned airport that opened on 10 August 1929, in which the city acquired an interest in 1931. The airport was developed throughout the 1930s by federal funds from the Works Projects Administration, intended to ease unemployment during the Great Depression, eventually having three runways, two of which remain in use, much extended, and the third is now a taxiway. The city eventually operated the airport as Charleston Municipal Airport until the United States entered the Second World War.

In 1942 the airport was handed over to the United States Army Air Force, but commercial operations were allowed to continue. During the war years the airport was expanded and land was drained and reclaimed to allow the base to expand further. Charleston Army Air Force base closed in 1946 and was handed back to the city,

much improved. With aid from the federal government, the city built a new passenger terminal, which opened in 1949. The United States Air Force returned to the base in 1952 during the Korean War. The city granted 1,605 acres to the USAF, and initially it was intended that as soon as a site for a new airport could be found and the airport built, the city would relinquish its rights and commercial flights would move to the new airport. The USAF later relaxed these conditions and the airport continued in joint use, with agreements reached in 1956 and again in 1973, with the latter transferring the airport from the city to the Charleston County Aviation Authority, which eventually took control in January 1979. Land was purchased to the south of the airport for a new terminal, which opened in 1985.

There has been just one commercial airline accident at the airport since the Second World War, and that was on 14 March 1947 when a Douglas DC-3 hit trees when coming in to land. The aircraft crashed and caught fire, killing the crew of two, the only occupants.

GREENSBORO PIEDMONT TRIAD INTERNATIONAL: GSO

Greensboro, North Carolina, USA

Owner and operator: Piedmont Triad Airport
   Authority
Runways: 05L/23R, 2,743m (9,000ft); 05R/23L,
   3,048m (10,001ft); 14/32, 1,945m (6,380ft)
Terminals: One, with a North Concourse and a
   South Concourse
Airlines using airport as base or hub: Federal
   Express
Annual passengers: 2,180,974
Annual cargo: 72,194 tonnes
Annual aircraft movements: 107,254

Background

Often known locally simply as 'PTI', it is situated just west of Greensboro, and also serves High Point and Winston-Salem in North Carolina.

Greensboro's first airfield was opened in December 1919, with two intersecting runways and hangar space, and was known as Maynard Field after a local man, Lieutenant Belvin Maynard, who was killed flying during the First World War. Two more airfields opened in the area in 1922, Miller Field and Charles Field. The present airport dates from 1927 when the newly-formed Tri-City Airport Commission planned an airport at Friendship with the intention of it becoming a recognised landing spot on the New York and New Orleans airmail route, but at first this ran into difficulties with one of the communities, Winston-Salem, which opted out of construction, leaving Greensboro and Guildford County to fund the construction of what became known as Lindley Field. The new airport opened in May 1927, and in October that year was one of the airports on Charles Lindbergh's celebratory tour with the *Spirit of St Louis*. The following year, regular airmail services operated by Pitcairn Aviation started at the airport. Passenger services followed in November 1930 with a route to Washington operated by Dixie Flying Service, which was later taken over by Pitcairn's successor, Eastern Air Transport, the predecessor of Eastern Air Lines. The airport was forced to close during the worst years of the Great Depression, but reopened on 17 May 1937 after two all-weather runways had been laid.

In summer 1942 the airport was taken over by the United States Army Air Force, and commercial operations were suspended for the rest of the Second World War. The USAAF lengthened the runways, and the airport was handed back to the local authorities once the war ended, reopening with a new passenger terminal, although it faced competition from Winston-Salem's Smith Reynolds Airport. A new passenger terminal was opened in 1958, with a single pier along which airliners parked, by which time it was being served by Capital, Delta, and Piedmont, as well as Eastern Air Lines.

Growth continued, and planning for a new terminal started in 1975, with the project significantly increased in size when Piedmont decided to concentrate all of it services on Greensboro rather than sharing them with Winston-Salem, only for Piedmont to decide to use Charlotte instead! The airport was renamed Greensboro-High Point Airport, but this was later changed to Greensboro/Winston-Salem/High Point Regional Airport. The new terminal, which remains in use today, was opened in 1982. The name was changed yet again in 1987, when the current title was adopted.

In the years that followed, Continental Airlines selected the airport for its planned Continental Lite low-fare airline, and started to develop a hub at Greensboro, but the low fare project was cancelled and the hub closed. Nevertheless, Comair, a Delta Connection carrier, built a maintenance facility at the airport, which opened in 2005. A couple of new airlines used Greensboro, but failed to survive the strong competition of a deregulated air transport system, and of these the most recent was Skybus, which began operations at Greensboro in January 2008, but collapsed in April. Despite these setbacks, the terminal has been extended in recent years, and in 2009 a third runway, 05L/23R, opened. In 2010, a completion facility for the new HondaJet very light jet should open.

The one serious accident at the airport was on 8 August 2000 when an AirTran Airways Douglas DC-9 took off for Atlanta, and shortly afterwards the cockpit filled with smoke and the pilots decided to return to the airport. Despite dense smoke making it difficult to read the instruments, the aircraft landed safely and the 5 crew and 58 passengers evacuated the aircraft on a taxiway. The aircraft was written off, four of the five crew needed treatment for smoke inhalation, and a passenger was slightly injured during the evacuation.

COLORADO SPRINGS AIRPORT: COS

Colorado Springs, Colorado, USA

Owner and operator: City of Colorado Springs
Runways: 17L/35R, 4,115m (13,501ft); 17R/35L, 3,360m (11,022ft); 12/30, 2,520m (8,269ft)
Terminals: One
Annual passengers: 2,067,410

Annual cargo: 12,222 tonnes
Annual aircraft movements: 155,688

Background

Often referred to locally as the Colorado Springs Municipal Airport, it is effectively a joint civil and military airfield, with Paterson Air Force Base on the north side. The airport is 10km (6½ miles) from the centre of Colorado Springs.

The airport dates from 1927 when it opened with two gravel runways, and was used mainly by private aircraft. It became a landing spot for an air service from El Paso to Denver during the 1930s, and did not have a passenger terminal until 1940. Shortly afterwards, the then United States Army Air Corps requisitioned the airfield and it remained in USAAC, and then USAAF, hands throughout the war. After the war it returned to the city and to commercial use. A new terminal was opened in 1966 on the west side of the runways, and this was not replaced until 1994 when the present terminal opened on the south side of the airfield. This was followed by Western Pacific Airlines moving its hub from the airport to Denver in 1996, which led to a slump in passenger traffic at Colorado Springs. During 2009, Frontier Airlines opened a new maintenance facility at the airport.

Most scheduled air services from Colorado Springs are to the hubs of the major airlines, but it does have a number of direct flights, all within the United States. Scheduled air services account for just 14 per cent of aircraft movements, compared to 11 per cent USAF, and 75 per cent general aviation, including air taxi operations.

The one recorded accident at the airport was on 3 March 1991 when a United Airlines Boeing 737-200, landing from Moline and Denver, suffered an uncommanded rudder movement which caused the aircraft to dive. The crash killed all 25 passengers and crew.

SAVANNAH/HILTON HEAD INTERNATIONAL: SAV
Savannah, Georgia, USA

Owner and operator: Savannah Airport Commission
Runways: 09/27, 2,850m (9,351ft); 18/36, 2,134m (7,002ft)
Terminals: One
Annual passengers: 2,029,449
Annual cargo: 9,780 tonnes
Annual aircraft movements: 100,009

Background

The airport, which has been known as Chatham Field, Travis Field, and Savannah International Airport in the past, is 11km (just over 7 miles) from Savannah, while an estimated 40 per cent of its passengers are travelling to or from Hilton Head Island, South Carolina, which is 61km (38½ miles) away.

The airport was originally opened as Chatham Field, and its first commercial air service was by Eastern Air Transport, which later became Eastern Air Lines, using it as a landing place on its route between New York and Miami from 1931. It was developed later during the decade using federal funds to boost employment. It passed to the United States Army Air Force, which renamed it Travis Field AFB, during the Second World War, and units of the US Third Air Force were based there for anti-submarine patrols and training. Returned to the city in 1948, normal air services were soon resumed. In 1960 a new terminal opened, and the airport was used by jet airliners from 1965 when Delta Air Lines introduced Douglas DC-9s on services to Savannah. The name was changed to Savannah International in 1983.

In 1994 the current passenger terminal opened, and this was extended in 2007. An unusual, possibly unique, feature of the airport is that the main runway, 09, has two gravestones placed in it, because the original owners of the property did not wish to relocate the graves when a runway extension was planned. In 2003 the airport was given its present title, even though there are no international scheduled flights, because it is a foreign trade zone and has US Customs facilities. The main airlines are Delta, plus Delta Connection carriers, and US Airways, while the feeder services of other airlines, including Continental Express, Northwest Airlink, and American Eagle also serve Savannah.

In addition to being the headquarters for Gulfstream Aerospace, the business aircraft manufacturer, the airport is the base for the Georgia Air National Guard's 165th Airlift Wing, doubling as Savannah ANGB, which includes the Combat Readiness Training Center, which provides support functions for the tactical aviation units of all of the US armed forces.

There had been no serious accidents or incidents at the airport at the time of writing.

GRAND RAPIDS GERALD R. FORD INTERNATIONAL: GRR
Grand Rapids, Michigan, USA

Owner and operator: Kent County Department of Aeronautics
Runways: 08L/26R, 1,524m (5,000ft); 08R/26L, 3,048m (10,000ft); 17/35, 2,591m (8,501ft)
Terminals: One, with two concourses, A and B
Annual passengers: 1,990,896
Annual cargo: 41,672 tonnes
Annual aircraft movements: 101,378

Background
Situated south-east of Grand Rapids, the airport was named after a former president of the United States in December 1999. For many years it was known as Kent County Airport after its locality.

The first link between Kent County and aviation was as early as 10 September 1911 when a Wright biplane landed at the Comstock Park State Fairground. It was not until after the First World War that attention turned to the construction of an airport, and this was not opened until 1926, when it was used by an air service between Grand Rapids and Detroit. The airport was

extended in 1948 across a highway, and gates had to be used to close the road to traffic when aircraft were landing or taking off.

The present airport opened on 23 November 1963 as Kent County Airport. On 28 April 1968 it received the first scheduled flight of a United Airlines Boeing 737-200, which landed from Chicago O'Hare. The airport was renamed Kent County International Airport in January 1977 with the opening of a US Customs office. Runway 17/35 was opened in 1997 so that runway 08R/26L could be rebuilt. It reopened in 2001.

There had been no serious accidents or incidents at the airport at the time of writing.

DES MOINES INTERNATIONAL: DSM
Des Moines, Iowa, USA

Owner and operator: City of Des Moines Aviation Department
Runways: 05/23, 2,744m (9,003ft); 13/31, 2,743m (9,001ft)
Terminals: One, with two concourses, designated A and C
Annual passengers: 1,982,633
Annual cargo: 91,391 tonnes
Annual aircraft movements: 100,825

Background
Des Moines International is 5km (3 miles) south-west of the city centre.

In the early years of commercial air services, Des Moines was served by a number of small airfields for private aircraft and airmail services. When in 1929 the state general assembly legislated for communities to sell bonds and raise taxes for airport construction, the city considered more than 80 sites before opting for a 160-acre site to the south. The new airport opened in 1933, and its first passenger terminal opened shortly afterwards. During the Second World War it was used by the United States Army Air Force, which extended the runways.

After the war the airport returned to civilian use, and a new terminal opened in 1950, replacing the original, and it remains in use today, much expanded and modernised over the intervening years. The airport adopted its present title in 1986 when a US Customs office opened at the airport. Mesaba Airlines, a Northwest Airlink operator, opened a maintenance centre at the airport in February 2009. The airport is also served by a number of operators, including Delta Air Lines.

Plans are in hand to extend the runways and expand the facilities at the airport, both for passengers and for cargo. The terminal is also being expanded again, and two additional airbridges are being brought into use.

There have been a couple of incidents at the airport in recent years. On 1 December 2007 a United Express feeder service aircraft slid off a taxiway in severe weather, but none of the 44 passengers was harmed. On 31 July 2008 a Northwest Airlines Boeing 757, flying from Detroit to Los Angeles, made a precautionary landing at the airport because the captain thought he could smell fumes in the cockpit.

KNOXVILLE McGHEE TYSON: TYS

Alcoa, Tennessee, USA

Owner and operator: Metropolitan Knoxville
    Airport Authority
Runways: 5L/23R, 2,745m (9,005ft); 5R/23L,
    2,743m (9,000ft)
Terminals: One
Annual passengers: 1,821,581
Annual cargo: 45,482 tonnes
Annual aircraft movements: 133,734

Background

Named after a First World War United States Navy pilot, the airport is 16km (10 miles) south of the centre of Knoxville and is shared with the Tennessee Air National Guard.

The airport first doubled up as a base for the United States Air Force during the Korean War, with the USAF establishing McGhee Tyson AFB to protect the atomic energy research facilities at Oak Ridge. The USAF remained at the

airport until 1958. Since that time it has become a base for the Tennessee ANG, which has an air-to-air refuelling unit stationed there, and which also includes the I. G. Brown Air National Guard Training and Education Center, and Academy of Military Science, effectively an officer training school, as well as an Army Aviation Support Facility for the Tennessee National Guard.

There have been two accidents at the airport over the past half century, both of which resulted in the aircraft concerned being written off. The first of these was on 6 August 1962 when an American Airlines Lockheed Electra, landing from Memphis in a thunderstorm and high winds, veered off the runway and hit a taxiway before losing part of its undercarriage. The 5 crew and 67 passengers survived. On 12 March 1992 a BAe Jetstream of CCAir, flying as USAir Express, fortunately without passengers, landed with the undercarriage raised and overturned, killing both pilots.

ORLANDO SANFORD INTERNATIONAL: SFB

Sanford, Florida

Owner: Sanford Airport Authority
Operator: TBI Ltd
Runways: 9L/27R, 2,926m (9,600ft); 9C/27C,
    1,091m (3,578ft); 9R/27L, 1,067m (3,500ft);
    18/36, 1,829m (6,002ft)
Terminals: Two, designated Terminal A
    (Domestic) and Terminal B (International)
Annual passengers: 1,788,780
Annual cargo: 6,932 tonnes
Annual aircraft movements: 294,781

Background

Orlando's second airport, it is owned by the local authority but managed by a British company, TBI, which also operates Belfast, Cardiff, and Luton airports. Most of the non-US carriers using the airport are British.

Sanford originally opened as Naval Air Station Sanford on 3 November 1942, initially providing advanced operational training for the crews of land-based maritime-reconnaissance aircraft. It was decommissioned in 1946 and placed on a care and maintenance basis, but recommissioned again in 1950 during the Korean War, at first as Naval Auxiliary Air Station Sanford, but soon upgraded to full NAS Sanford. Its post-war role was as an operational shore station for carrier-borne bombers and heavy attack aircraft when the carrier was in port. It was extensively modernised. In February 1959 it was renamed NAS Ramey Field after Lieutenant Commander Robert Ramey, USN, who lost his life nursing a crippled jet aircraft rather than ejecting and risking the lives of those on the ground. NAS Ramey Field closed in 1968.

The city took over the airport in 1969 and renamed it Sanford Airport. The name changed several times in the years that followed, to Sanford Regional Airport, Central Florida Regional Airport, and Orlando Sanford Regional Airport, until finally settling on the current name. New buildings were erected and former naval buildings demolished. A new passenger terminal was opened in 1995. The airport is home to the Delta Connection Academy, which trains pilots for Delta's regional affiliates, and to the Seminole County Sheriff's Office aviation activities.

The one recorded accident at the airport in recent years occurred when a Continental Airlines Boeing 727-200, en route from Newark to Fort Myers, diverted to Orlando with an undercarriage problem, making a partial gear-up landing, but none of the 9 crew or 141 passengers was injured.

MYRTLE BEACH INTERNATIONAL: MYR

Myrtle Beach, South Carolina, USA

Owner and Operator: Horry County Department of Airports
Runways: 18/36, 2,897m (9,503ft)
Terminals: One
Annual passengers: 1,683,823
Annual aircraft movements: 54,943

Background

The airport is owned by Horry County and it is situated just 5km (3 miles) south-west of the centre of Myrtle Beach. It opened in 1976 after an agreement was reached with the United States Air Force that civil aviation could share Myrtle Beach Air Force Base. The new airport replaced the existing airport for the area, which was renamed Grand Strand Airport and remains open for general aviation. The USAF closed Myrtle Beach AFB base in 1993, and the entire airfield was handed over to the present owner and operator. The airport was a hub for Hooters Air before the airline closed in 2006. The runway is available for space shuttle emergency landings, but has never been needed.

The main airline using the airport is US Airways.

The last recorded accident at Myrtle Beach was in 1950 and involved a United States Air Force aircraft.

PENSACOLA GULF COAST REGIONAL: PNS

Pensacola, Escambia County, Florida, USA

Owner and operator: City of Pensacola
Runways: 8/26, 2,134m (7,000ft); 17/35, 2,135m (7,004ft)
Terminals: One
Annual passengers: 1,669,950
Annual aircraft movements: 110,653

Background

Pensacola Gulf Coast Regional Airport is 5km (just over 3 miles) north-east of the centre of Pensacola. It was originally built by a hotelier, Conner Hagler, and a barnstormer, Harry Blanchard, and was opened to commercial air services on 7 April 1934, at the height of the Great Depression, with just two grass runways and a second-hand hangar. The following year the city council used federal funds, allocated for the relief of unemployment, to build a municipal airport on the site. The work was completed by November 1938, and National Airlines started to operate to Pensacola.

Although the airport was one of the few in the United States to remain open to commercial air services throughout the Second World War, it was taken over by the United States Navy, which expanded the airfield, extended the runways, and built two new runways. Pensacola became the USN's main flying school during the war years and was also used to train pilots for the Royal Navy's Fleet Air Arm. It was commanded by Captain A. C. Read who, as a lieutenant commander, had flown the Curtiss NC-4 flying boat across the Atlantic via the Azores in 1919.

The airport reverted to municipal control at the end of the war and, as with many that had been used by the military, was a far better asset than had been the case before the war. The city provided a new control tower and a larger passenger terminal, and in 1957 added an instrument landing system. The terminal was renovated in 1964, and in August 1965 Eastern Air Lines introduced the airport's first jet service using Boeing 727s.

The airport was transformed from Pensacola Municipal Airport to Pensacola Regional Airport in the years that followed, with the terminal largely rebuilt in 1990 including additional gates and capacity for passengers and baggage, while the runways were extended, and in 1995 a new control tower was opened. Between 1989 and 1995 traffic increased by 52 per cent.

Ignoring the accidents to naval aircraft, there have been a number of commercial accidents at the airport. One of these was on 8 May 1978 to a National Airlines flight which landed in Escambia Bay, partly because of pilot error. A hard landing by an Eastern Air Lines Douglas DC-9 on 27 December 1987 caused the fuselage to split open aft of the wing root, and wrecked the aircraft. A Delta Air Lines McDonnell Douglas MD-88 suffered an uncontained engine failure while taking off on 6 July 1996, with fragments puncturing the fuselage and killing 2 of the 148 passengers and crew, and seriously injuring another.

WHITE PLAINS WESTCHESTER COUNTY: HPN
Harrison, New York State, USA

Owner and operator: County of Westchester
Runways: 16/34, 1,996m (6,548ft); 11/29, 1,357m (4,451ft)
Terminals: One
Annual passengers: 1,655,473
Annual aircraft movements: 176,516

Background
The airport is 14.5km (9 miles) east of the centre of White Plains and is actually on the territory of the communities of Harrison, North Castle, and Rye – all of which are in Westchester County. It is 53km (33 miles) north of Manhattan and claims to be an alternative airport for those wishing to avoid the congestion of the New York city airports. The IATA code is believed to represent the initials of the towns of Harrison, Purchase, and North Castle.

The airport was originally opened in 1942 to provide a base for a New York Air National Guard unit providing fighter cover for New York City. The ANG unit moved to Stewart International Airport in May 1983 to avoid interference with the suburban developments surrounding the airport. After the Second World War the airport started to handle commercial flights, and steady development followed until the Airline Deregulation Act saw greater competition and the emergence of low-cost carriers. The most recent of these to serve the airport is JetBlue, which started operations at Westchester in 2007. Nevertheless, growth has been inhibited by tall trees near the end of the main runway (these are in another state, and to avoid them pilots have to make offset landings), and by the usual problems regarding noise, as urban sprawl has meant that aircraft are now flying over residential areas, for which a voluntary curfew has been introduced. Perhaps more important, it is in the watershed for 85 per cent of the residents of New York City and Westchester County, so that many believe that the airport would not be allowed to be built today.

Westchester is also the base for the United States Civil Air Patrol's New York Wing.

The one serious accident at the airport recorded so far was on 11 February 1981 when a Texasgulf Aviation Lockheed JetStar was approaching at night and in poor weather, with the captain distracted by an on-board electrical failure the aircraft strayed off course and crashed into woodland, killing both pilots and all six passengers.

PALM SPRINGS INTERNATIONAL: PSP

Palm Springs, California, USA

Owner and operator: City of Palm Springs
Runways: 13L/31R, 1,509m (4,952ft); 13R/31L, 3,048m (10,001ft)
Terminals: One
Annual passengers: 1,610,943
Annual aircraft movements: 84,677

Background

Just 3km (less than 2 miles) from the centre of Palm Springs, the airport's traffic is highly seasonal, which is unusual in that most flights do not operate during the summer months.

The airport dates from 1939 when it was built for the then United States Army Air Corps. It was not until 1961 that it was purchased by the city, which then converted it to a commercial airport, opening in 1964, originally as Palm Springs Municipal airport.

A Western Airlines Convair 240 suffered a wing leading edge separation after taking off for San Diego on 13 February 1958, with the aircraft crash-landing in the desert and catching fire, but the 4 crew and 17 passengers all survived. A Learjet 23 crashed on 14 November 1965 shortly after take-off when the pilot lost spatial orientation, killing the crew of two and all six passengers.

WICHITA MID-CONTINENT: ICT

Wichita, Kansas, USA

Owner and operator: Wichita Airport Authority
Runways: 1L/19R, 3,140m (10,301ft); 1R/19L, 2,225m (7,301ft); 14/32, 1,921m (6,301ft)
Terminals: One, with two concourses designated East and West
Annual passengers: 1,596,229
Annual cargo: 32,315 tonnes
Annual aircraft movements: 157,654

Background

Because Kansas City Airport is actually in the neighbouring state of Missouri, Wichita can claim to be the busiest airport in Kansas, and is situated in south-west Wichita.

The airport dates from 31 October 1954 when it opened as Wichita Municipal Airport after the United States Air Force had acquired the city's original airport in 1951. The current name was adopted in 1973 when Kansas City dropped the Mid-Continent title from its name, but IATA insisted that it retain the ICT code rather than adopt the MCT code that remained with Kansas City International Airport.

A new terminal building is under construction and should open by 2011.

There have been no airliner accidents at the airport, but there have been a small number involving business and private aircraft.

MADISON DANE COUNTY REGIONAL: MSN

Madison, Wisconsin, USA

Owner and operator: Dane County Airport Authority
Runways: 18/36, 2,745m (9,006ft); 14/32, 1,782m (5,846ft); 3/21, 2,195m (7,200ft)
Terminals: One
Annual passengers: 1,564,975
Annual cargo: 11,186 tonnes
Annual aircraft movements: 119,760

Background

Also known locally as Truax Field, after its military designation, Dane County Regional Airport is 8km (5 miles) from the centre of Madison.

The airport has its origins in an airfield built for the United States Army Air Force, which opened in June 1942. It was known initially as Madison Army Airfield before being renamed Truax AAF after a local man, Lieutenant Thomas Truax, who was killed flying a P-40 fighter in 1941. During the Second World War the airfield was the site of the Army Air Force Eastern Technical Training Center, which taught radio operators and technicians at first, before developing courses for radar operators and air traffic controllers. It closed on 30 November 1945, shortly after the war ended.

With the war over, the airfield became Madison Municipal Airport, but the military connection was renewed when it was made a base for the Wisconsin Air National Guard; a role that continues to this day with a fighter unit flying Lockheed F-16 Fighting Falcons. Nevertheless, during the Korean War the United States Air Force reactivated the base as Truax AFB, reopening on 1 February 1952. The USAF built additional runways, taxiways, and aprons for fighter units under the control of Air Defence Command. The USAF remained at the airport until early 1968, when it handed back to the local authority all except for that part occupied by the Wisconsin Air National Guard, which has since been joined by units of the Wisconsin National Guard.

The airport has seen considerable development in recent years, including doubling the size of the passenger terminal, completed in 2006.

The only incident of any note at the airport was on 23 November 1978, when there was an attempted hijacking of a North Central Airlines Douglas DC-9, but the hijacker's demands could not be understood, and he was overpowered.

SARASOTA-BRADENTON INTERNATIONAL: SRQ

Sarasota, Florida, USA

Owner and operator: Sarasota-Manatee Airport Authority
Runways: 4/22, 1,527m (5,009ft); 14/32, 2,896m (9,500ft)
Terminals: One
Annual passengers: 1,557,212
Annual aircraft movements: 139,442

Background

The airport is shared by Manatee County, in whose area the airfield lies, and Sarasota County, which has the terminal, and it is the latter name that is normally used for the airport by locals and by airline timetable compilers.

Originally, the airport was developed by the United States Army Air Force during the Second World War and was used by the US Third Air Force as a training station and for anti-submarine patrols. In more recent times, the airport's claim to fame was that Air Force One was at the airport during the terrorist attacks on New York and Washington on 11 September 2001, as the president was visiting Sarasota. The airport suffered considerably in the post '9/11' downturn in air travel, while one of the airlines serving the airport, Canada 3000, went bankrupt and another, Canadian Airlines, was taken over by Air Canada. Recovery started in 2003 when the low-cost carrier AirTran Airways started to operate to the airport as a result of a customer survey. An unusual feature of the airport's traffic is that it is busiest in winter and early spring when the surrounding area is most popular with tourists and ornithologists, with the latter visiting to watch the snowbirds.

There have been few accidents or incidents at the airport. A Canadair Argonaut (licence-built DC-4) of Turks Air took off for Miami but had to abort the landing because of undercarriage problems and returned to Sarasota, and after a couple of bouncing 'touch-and-goes' were tried without the left main gear dropping, it made an emergency landing, which wrote off the aircraft but enabled the two pilots to escape. A hijacking attempt occurred on 30 March 1974 when a gunman arrived with two hostages and boarded an empty Boeing 727 of National Airlines, but was disarmed by an engineer and eventually arrested. A ground fire destroyed a Learjet 23 standing at the airport on 23 May 1982.

JACKSON-EVERS INTERNATIONAL AIRPORT: JAN
Jackson, Rankin County, Mississippi, USA

Owner and operator: City of Jackson
Runways: 16L/34R, 2,591m (8,500ft); 16R/34L, 2,591m (8,500ft)
Terminals: One, with two concourses, designated East and West
Annual passengers: 1,457,181
Annual cargo: 11,628 tonnes
Annual aircraft movements: 74,733

Background
The airport is 9km (just over 5½ miles) east of the centre of Jackson. It is named after Medgar Evers, a prominent local personality.

Jackson's first airport was at Hawkins Field, which opened in 1928 and which was first served by Delta Air Lines from Dallas Love Field the following year. The current airport replaced Hawkins Field when it opened in 1963, with airline flights and the Mississippi Air National Guard both transferring to the new facility, which was named Jackson Municipal Airport Allen C. Thompson Field, after the then mayor of the city. The airport was renamed Jackson International Airport in the early 1990s, as it opened a US Customs office and has since established a foreign trade zone. The current title was adopted in 2005.

The airport handles traffic that is predominantly private and general aviation, with airline services accounting for around 16 per cent of movements. Southwest Airlines started using the airport in 1997, and today is amongst the main carriers at Jackson.

Jackson-Evers remains a base for the Mississippi Air National Guard, and currently has a

heavy transport unit operating Boeing C-17 Globemaster II aircraft.

There are no records of serous accidents or incidents.

BURLINGTON INTERNATIONAL: BTV
Burlington, Vermont, USA

Owner and operator: City of Burlington
Runways: 15/33, 2,536m (8,320ft); 01/19, 1,101m (3,611ft)
Terminals: One
Annual passengers: 1,410,745
Annual aircraft movements: 67,389

Background
Burlington International is 5km (just over 3 miles) east of the centre of Burlington, the largest city in Vermont. It has grown rapidly since 2000, and in 2008 completed a terminal expansion with five new gates, of which four are airbridges. Most of the air services are operated by regional aircraft, although Boeing 737s and Airbus A320s, operated by airlines such as Jet-Blue and United, are also used. Most routes are to cities on the East Coast and in the Midwest.

The airport doubles as the Burlington Air National Guard Base (ANGB), and is shared with the Vermont Air National Guard, which has a Lockheed F-16 Fighting Falcon unit based there, and with the Vermont National Guard, which has an Army Aviation Support Facility including an aviation regiment and an air ambulance company.

There have been just a couple of accidents at the airport over the past 60 years. One of the first, on 20 September 1948, was to a Colonial Airlines Douglas DC-3 from Montreal which came in too fast and touched down too far along the runway with no sign of slowing down, and on attempting a go-around it crashed into trees, but the 3 crew and 14 passengers all survived. Much less fortunate were the occupants of an Airborne Express Cessna Caravan I which attempted to take off for Albany in snow and icing conditions on 29 January 1990 while overloaded with freight, and crashed at the end of the runway, killing both occupants.

AKRON-CANTON REGIONAL: CAK
Green, Summit County, Ohio, USA

Owner and operator: Akron-Canton Regional
  Airport Authority
Runways: 1/19, 2,317m (7,601ft); 5/23, 2,316m
  (7,597ft)
Terminals: One
Airlines using airport as base or hub:
  Maintenance base for PSA Airlines (a US
  Airways Express carrier)
Annual passengers: 1,391,836
Annual aircraft movements: 113,454

Background
The airport serves both Akron and Canton and is 16km (just 10 miles) south-east of Akron, and 19km (some 12 miles) north-west of Canton. The airport authority is owned jointly by Summit County and Stark County, into which part of the runways extend.

It was originally decided to build the airport for the United States Army Air Force during the Second World War, but work was delayed by a debate over whether an airport should be built from defence funds, and it was not opened until 13 October 1946, having eventually been built with private funding. The terminal did not open until 1955.

The airport has enjoyed strong growth overall, with the exception of the sharp fall in air travel that followed the terrorist attacks on 11 September 2001. Modernisation and expansion of the passenger terminal was completed in 2006. However, the airport's most ambitious development programme started in 2008 and is due to be completed in 2018, with priority being given to extending runway 5/23 to 2,500m (8,200ft), as well as improvements to the facilities for general aviation, customs, and immigration facilities, enlarging the terminal and developing an industrial park nearby. The main carrier at the airport is AirTran Airways, while most of the other air-

lines, apart from Frontier, are feeder carriers for the US major airlines.

A United Airlines Vickers Viscount 700 overshot the runway while landing from Detroit on 11 December 1967, but while the aircraft was written off, the 3 crew and 15 passengers were unharmed. Landing from Pittsburgh too fast in light rain and fog with poor visibility, an Eastern Air Lines Douglas DC-9 touched down too far along the runway and overran it on 27 November 1973, damaging the aircraft beyond repair, but again the 5 crew and 21 passengers escaped. A privately-owned Cessna Citation crashed while doing 'touch-and-go' landings on 2 August 1979 after stalling into the ground, killing the pilot, but the other two occupants survived. On 28 November 1991 a Rhodes International Convair 240 taking off on a positioning flight to Columbus crash-landed after an engine burst into flames, but both pilots escaped.

FRESNO YOSEMITE INTERNATIONAL: FAT
Fresno, California, USA

Owner and operator: City of Fresno
Runways: 11L/29R, 2,809m (9,217ft); 11R/29L,
  2,196m (7,205ft)
Terminals: One
Annual passengers: 1,318,483
Annual cargo: 10,194 tonnes
Annual aircraft movements: 150,563

Background
The airport was originally known as Fresno Air Terminal, and is 97km (just over 60 miles) from Yosemite National Park. It dates from June 1944 when it was built for the United States Army Air Force as Hammer Field Air Force Base. It was used by the US Fourth Air Force to train night fighter pilots and navigators, while an Army Air Forces hospital was also established on the site. After the war the airfield was handed over to the local authority and became Fresno Air Terminal, while part of it was retained for what became the California Air National Guard after the

establishment of the United States Air Force in 1947.

The airport was officially designated an international point of entry in 1988, while in 1995 the name was changed to attract visitors to Yosemite National Park. Over the years it has been upgraded and expanded, with most recently a new two-level terminal completed in 2002 and a new Federal Inspection Facility opened in 2006. It has also been the headquarters and main base for two airlines, albeit briefly – for Air 21 between 1996 and 1998, and then Allegiant Air before it transferred its headquarters to Las Vegas. In more recent years there has been a shift away from direct air services to regional aircraft feeding the hubs of the main carriers, but this trend has started to reverse with American Airlines and US Airways providing direct flights as well as cross-border services by Mexicana.

The airport remains the base of a California Air National Guard fighter unit, whose area is known as Fresno Air National Guard Base, and which operates Lockheed F-16 Fighting Falcon fighters, while the California National Guard also has an aviation facility at Fresno.

There has been just one serious accident at the airport to a commercial aircraft. This was on 6 June 1990 when a West Air Cessna Caravan I Cargomaster took off for Oakland from Fresno-Chandler, but when the engine oil warning light showed, air traffic control directed the pilot to Fresno Yosemite as the closest airport. Landing downwind, the aircraft missed the runway and landed beyond the end, crashing through a fence and hitting a pole before finally coming to rest in a residential area, but while the aircraft was destroyed, the pilot survived.

MIDDLETOWN HARRISBURG INTERNATIONAL: MDT

Middletown, Dauphin County, Pennsylvania, USA

Owner and operator: Susquehanna Area
  Regional Airport Authority
Runways: 13/31, 3,048m (10,001ft)
Terminals: One

Annual passengers: 1,298,857
Annual cargo: 46,987 tonnes
Annual aircraft movements: 71,011

Background

Although named Harrisburg International Airport, it is officially known as Middletown, with the IATA code MDT because of its proximity to that community. It is 15km (almost 10 miles) from the centre of Harrisburg.

The airport has a long history through its connection with the military. The area was a base for the United States Army Signal Corps as early as 1898, and by 1918 a military airstrip had been built for the US Army Air Service, which named it Olmsted Field. It remained in military hands, first as a United States Army Air Corps airfield and then as one of its successors, the United States Army Air Force, and then the United States Air Force when it was formed in 1947, by which time it was called Olmsted Air Force Base. The USAF remained at Olmsted AFB until 1969, when it was given to the Commonwealth of Pennsylvania, the state government, which in turn passed ownership to the Susquehanna Area Regional Airport Authority, which is owned and controlled by seven local authorities. The airport developed after the closure of the USAF base, and today is served by US and Canadian feeder airlines.

In common with many US airports, it is also a base for a state air national guard unit, in this case the Pennsylvania Air National Guard, which maintains a special operations unit at the base, flying the Lockheed C-130J Commando Solo, and is the only unit of this kind in the USAF.

There has been just one serious accident at the airport, which involved a Convair 440 Metropolitan of Allegheny Airlines. The 440 crashed on 29 November 1966 when it suffered a complete electrical failure while taking off for Pittsburgh, and while the captain aborted the take-off, the propellers would not provide reverse pitch, leaving the aircraft to overshoot the runway. The aircraft was destroyed, but the 4 crew and 12 passengers survived. A bizarre incident affected a

Pennsylvania Airlines Short 330 which took off for Washington on 28 October 1983 with 3 crew and 27 passengers. During the flight, one of the passengers left his seat, opened the cabin door and stepped outside.

ST THOMAS CYRIL E. KING: STT
St Thomas, US Virgin Islands

Owner and operator: Virgin Islands Port
  Authority
Runways: 10/28, 2,134m (7,000ft)
Terminals: One
Annual passengers: 1,265,491
Annual cargo: 8,624 tonnes
Annual aircraft movements: 43,462

Background
The airport is 3km (just under 2 miles) west from the centre of Charlotte Amalie, the capital on St Thomas, and also serves St John and travellers to and from the British Virgin Islands. It was opened in 1990 and retained the name of an earlier airport, which had been constructed before the Second World War. During the war it was used by the United States Army Air Force Sixth Air Force, which based fighter units there in 1942 and 1943. It resumed commercial operations at the end of the war, when it was renamed Harry S. Truman Airport in honour of the president at the time of victory. It was renamed after Cyril King, the second elected governor of the US Virgin islands, in 1984.

The airport suffered for many years from a runway that was too short and allowed little margin of error. On 28 December 1970 a Trans Caribbean Airways flight made a heavy landing and ran off the side of the runway before catching fire, killing 2 of the 48 passengers. This was followed by another accident on 27 April 1976, when an American Airlines aircraft overshot the runway, killing 37 of the 88 passengers and crew, causing the airline to suspend jet operations to the airport and revert to using turboprop aircraft until the runway was extended to its current length.

HUNTSVILLE INTERNATIONAL/ CARL T. JONES FIELD: HSV
Huntsville, Madison County, Alabama, USA

Owner and operator: Huntsville/Madison County
  Airport Authority
Runways: 18L/36R, 3,050m (10,006ft);
  18R/36L, 3,840m (12,600ft)
Terminals: One
Annual passengers: 1,239,813
Annual cargo: 79,307 tonnes
Annual aircraft movements: 60,223

Background
A modernised airport, sometimes referred to locally as Carl T. Jones Field, or Huntsville-Madison County, Huntsville International is 14km (about 9 miles) south-west of the centre of Huntsville. It is the busiest cargo airport in Alabama, with daily flights to Europe, and also services to Hong Kong. There is a new air traffic control tower (opened in 2008), and a new cargo terminal (opened early in 2009), while the passenger terminal is currently being extended. For the future, an additional runway is a possibility, and the shorter of the two existing runways, 18L/36R, is likely to be extended.

There has been just one serious accident at the airport, on 17 October 1965, when a United Airlines Douglas DC-6 was taking off and the nosewheel suddenly retracted, throwing the aircraft on to its nose and damaging it beyond repair, but the 5 crew and 11 passengers survived.

COLUMBIA METROPOLITAN: CAE
Columbia, Lexington County, South Carolina, USA

Owner and operator: Richland-Lexington Airport
  Commission
Runways: 5/23, 2,439m (8,001ft); 11/29,
  2,622m (8,601ft); there is also a helipad
Terminals: One
Airlines using airport as base or hub: United
  Parcel Service
Annual passengers: 1,234,547
Annual cargo: 105,629 tonnes
Annual aircraft movements: 97,674

Background

Columbia Metropolitan Airport, often known locally as the 'Metro', is 8km (5 miles) south-west of Colombia.

The airport was originally built in 1940 as Lexington County Airport. It was almost immediately taken over by the United States Army Air Corps, or United States Army Air Force from 1941, and was the main operational training centre for the USAAF's North American B-25 Mitchell, including the crews who went on the famous 'Doolittle Raid' on 18 April 1942, taking off from the USS *Hornet* to bomb Tokyo and other targets in Japan. After the war the airport returned to civilian operations, and a new passenger terminal was opened in 1952, replacing the original terminal. While never in the front rank of US airports, it was at one time the hub for the short-lived low-cost carrier Air South, and since August 1996 it has been the South-Eastern Regional Hub for United Parcel Service (UPS), while the air cargo ramp can hold up to 22 aircraft of DC-8 size. The airport is also used by other air freight operators, including FedEx and ABX Air.

A new passenger terminal was opened in 1965 and modernised in 1997. In more recent years the runways have been lengthened. Seven passenger airlines serve the airport, although mainly on feeder services.

Accidents at the airport have usually involved smaller feeder aircraft. One of these was a Volpar E18S, which on 26 February 1971, while landing in fog, crashed during a missed approach, killing the pilot and all 7 passengers. Another accident in poor visibility occurred on 20 December 1973 when a Beech C90 dropped below minimum descent altitude, killing the pilot and one of the two passengers, and leaving the other passenger seriously injured. There has also been an accident more recently involving an executive jet, a Learjet 60, which crashed during take off on 20 September 2008, killing four of the six occupants.

ATLANTIC CITY INTERNATIONAL: ACY
Pomona, New Jersey, USA

Owner and operator: South Jersey Transportation Authority
Runways: 4/22, 1,873m (6,144ft); 13/31, 3,048m (10,000ft)
Terminals: One
Annual passengers: 1,199,362
Annual aircraft movements: 105,994

Background

The airport is 14km (9 miles) north-west of the centre of Atlantic City. It was originally built by the United States Navy, opening in 1942 as Naval Air Station Atlantic City. At first the air station provided operational training for carrier aircrews, covering fighter, bomber, and torpedo-bomber squadrons, but from August 1943 it specialised in training naval fighter pilots. NAS Atlantic City did not close immediately after the Second World War, but instead was retained and not finally decommissioned until June 1958, when it was transferred to the Airways Modernisation Board, but at the same time became a base for the New Jersey Air National Guard. When the Federal Aviation Administration absorbed the AMB, it expanded the airfield and established what eventually became the William J. Hughes Technical Center. The South Jersey Transportation Authority leased parts of the airfield from the FAA to establish an airport, but now owns and operates the airport.

The airport has been served by US Airways and other airlines, but these have been reduced in recent years with the switch to hub and spoke operations using feeder aircraft. Spirit Airlines continues to serve the airport and, for the future, hope is being placed in the growth of AirTran Airways with its low-cost operations, encouraged by a terminal and taxiway extension intended to double the size of the existing facilities.

The New Jersey Air National Guard remains at the airport with a fighter unit operating Lockheed F-16 Fighting Falcon fighters at ANGB

Atlantic City, while it is also home to the United States Coast Guard which designates its area Coast Guard Air Station Atlantic City, and operates Aerospatiale HH-65 Dolphin helicopters.

One of the accidents at the airport was on 26 July 1969 when a Trans World Airlines (TWA) Boeing 707-320 arrived from New York on a training flight, and exercises were conducted with a simulated engine out following a take-off, but control was lost and the aircraft plunged into the ground, breaking up and catching fire, and killing all five crew on the flight deck. A hijacking of a People Express Boeing 737 ended at the airport on 15 October 1983, with the hijacker escaping in a taxi before he was arrested. The most recent accident was on 27 October 2007 to a Cessna Citation III of Northeast Air & Sea Services, which suffered substantial damage after approaching too steeply, but the two crew and two passengers survived.

CEDAR RAPIDS EASTERN IOWA: CID
Cedar Rapids, Iowa, USA

Owner and operator: Cedar Rapids Airport Commission
Runways: 9/27, 2,622m (8,601ft); 13/31, 1,890m (6,200ft)
Terminals: One, with two concourses, designated A and B
Annual passengers: 1,061,052
Annual cargo: 24,789 tonnes
Annual aircraft movements: 63,421

Background
Generally known as The Eastern Iowa Airport, or sometimes as Cedar Rapids, the airport also serves Iowa City.

The original airport to serve Cedar Rapids was Hunter Field, named after the owner, Dan Hunter, which was opened during the 1920s. Although used for airmail flights as well as private flying, it was unusable during bad weather. What became Cedar Rapids Municipal Airport was opened in 1944 for the military, and was operated by the Parks Department until the airport commission was formed in 1945. It did not open for commercial use until 27 April 1947, with flights by United Airlines. It was not until 1957 that Ozark Airlines also served the airport. The current terminal dates from 1986, and in 1997 the airport was renamed The Eastern Iowa Airport.

There are no records of serious accidents at the airport at the time of writing.

URUGUAY

MONTEVIDEO CARRASCO GENERAL CESÁREO L. BERISSO INTERNATIONAL AIRPORT: MVD
Montevideo, Uruguay

Owner and operator: Puerta Del Sur
Runways: 01/19, 2,250m (7,382ft); 06/24, 3,200m (10,499ft); 10/28 (closed)
Terminals: One
Airlines using airport as base or hub: PLUNA
Annual passengers: 1,168,199
Annual cargo: 26,083 tonnes

Background
Uruguay's largest and busiest airport, it lies east of Montevideo, the capital.

The airport dates from the mid-1930s and is named after a former president. It was originally state-owned, but was privatised in 2003 and has since undergone extensive modernisation, including the construction of a new terminal which opened in mid-2009 and which required the closure of the airport's shortest runway. The new terminal has just one airbridge, requiring most flights to make use of buses for transfers between aircraft and terminals.

The airport has two serious accidents on record. The earliest of these was to a PLUNA Douglas C-47A which was being flight-tested to enable it to qualify for its certificate of airworthiness and, as well as the pilots, had inspectors on board, making ten occupants in all. On taking off it failed to climb out and a wing grazed the runway several times, before the handling pilot switched off the engines and the plane crashed, breaking into flames and killing all the occupants. A Canadair CC-106 of ALAS (Atlantida Linea Aerea Sudamerica) was damaged beyond repair when it made a belly landing because of an undercarriage malfunction on 10 October 1979, but the six occupants survived.

UZBEKISTAN

TASHKENT INTERNATIONAL: TAS
Tashkent, Uzbekistan

Owner and operator: Uzbekistan Department of Civil Aviation
Runways: 08L/26R, 4,000m (13,123ft); 08R/26L, 3,905m (12,812ft)
Terminals: One
Airlines using airport as base or hub: Uzbekistan Airways
Annual passengers: 2,101,028
Annual cargo: 21,413 tonnes

Background
A former Soviet-era airport, it is situated 12km (7½ miles) from the centre of Tashkent and has enjoyed considerable investment since the break-up of the Soviet Union.

Given the veil of secrecy that surrounded everything in the former Soviet Union, it is perhaps none too surprising that the date of one of the accidents at Tashkent is uncertain, and could be either 24 April or 24 June 1974. A locally-based Aeroflot Ilyushin Il-18 lost an engine because of a bird strike during take-off, and crashed back on to the runway, killing at least one of the 115 or so occupants. A far worse accident occurred on 13 January 2004 when an Uzbekistan Airways Yakovlev Yak-40 landed from Termez on a domestic flight. In poor visibility, the aircraft descended first above and then below the glidescope, and overshot the runway as an attempt was made to initiate a go-around, eventually hitting a building and crashing into a ditch before catching fire, killing all 5 crew and 32 passengers.

VENEZUELA

It is strange that Venezuela, Colombia's neighbour, has far less air transport activity and has just one major airport, serving the capital Caracas.

CARACAS SIMÓN BOLIVAR INTERNATIONAL: CCS
Maiquetía, Caracas, Venezuela

Owner and operator: Instituto Autónomo del Aeropuerto Internacional de Maiquetía
Runways: 09/27, 3,027m (9,930ft); 10/28, 3,500m (11,483ft)
Terminals: Two, designated International and Domestic
Airlines using airport as base or hub: Aeropostal, Santa Barbara Airlines, Vensecar Internacional
Annual passengers: 8,357,446
Annual cargo: 41,535 tonnes
Annual aircraft movements: 144,110

Background
Some 21km (13 miles) from the city centre, Simón Bolivar is usually known as 'Maiquetía' by local people. It is Venezuela's leading international airport, and between 1960 and 1997 was the home base and main hub for the national airline, VIASA, until it collapsed. Today it is the base and main hub for Santa Barbara Airlines, Vensecar Internacional, and Aeropostal.

The airport has had a considerable number of accidents. On 26 June 1948 a LAV, (Linea Aeropostal Venezolana) Douglas C-47 crashed on landing, killing one of the 3 crew, although the 14 passengers appear to have survived. Another LAV C-47 crashed on 1 December 1959 whilst returning after an engine failure during the climb out, but on this occasion the three crew were all killed. On 6 July 1962 a Canadair Argonaut (licence-built DC-4) of LEBCA (Linea Expresa Bolivar) on a cargo flight ran out of fuel and ditched in the sea, but the three crew were rescued. Another aircraft that crashed into the sea was an Air France Boeing 707-320 on 4

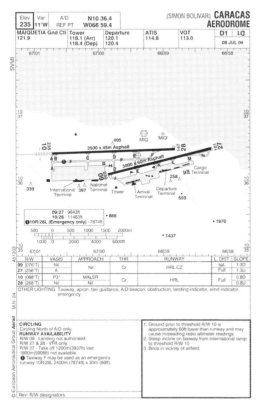

aircraft was an Aserca Airlines Douglas DC-9, which left the hangar on 12 February 2008 and crossed a runway, fortunately without hitting anything, before it eventually came to rest. No one was on board at the time. A Rutaca Boeing 737-200, landing on a domestic flight from Puerto Ordaz on 16 October 2008, swerved left on touchdown and was eventually stopped with its nose against an embankment, but the 7 crew and 47 passengers were unharmed.

VIETNAM

HO CHI MINH CITY TAN SON NHAT INTERNATIONAL: SGN
Ho Chi Minh City, Vietnam

Owner: Government of Vietnam
Operator: Southern Airports Corporation
Runways: 07L/25R, 3,048m (10,000ft);
07R/25L, 3,800m (12,468ft)
Terminals: Two, designated Terminal 1
(Domestic) and Terminal 2 (International)
Airlines using airport as base or hub: Vietnam
Airlines
Annual passengers: 10,286,918
Annual cargo: 254,753 tonnes
Annual aircraft movements: 75,582

Background
Vietnam was originally part of French Indo-China and the airport was first built by the French during the 1930s as Tan Son Nhat Airfield, named after the nearest village, but convenient for the neighbouring city of Saigon. The country was overrun by the Japanese during the Second World War, and after Japanese surrender was used as a base for the French *Armée de l'Air* during the insurgency that followed. Vietnamese independence saw the country divided into two, with Saigon as the capital of South Vietnam. In 1956, aid from the United States paid for a 2,190m (7,200ft) long runway and the airfield became the international airport for South Vietnam. It continued as a commercial airport during the Vietnam War, but also dou-

December 1969, after taking off for Guadaloupe, with the loss of all 63 passengers and crew. A training flight on a Latin Carga Convair 880 resulted in a crash on take-off with all four occupants killed. Two government-owned Short Skyvan aircraft were wrecked when an Aeropostale Boeing 727, being parked, rolled away and crashed into them and a light aircraft on 14 October 1998. A BAE Jetstream of Venezolana crashed into a fire station while landing from El Vigia on a domestic flight on 18 November 2004, killing 4 of the 19 passengers, although both pilots survived. An AeroCaribbean Ilyushin Il-18 failed to take-off for Havana on 28 March 2005, overshot the runway and lost its undercarriage before stopping at a small hill, but the 10 crew and 87 passengers survived. Within a few days, on 31 March, a Transaven Britten-Norman Islander lost a propeller during take-off but the pilot managed to land back on the runway and the aircraft was later repaired. Another runaway

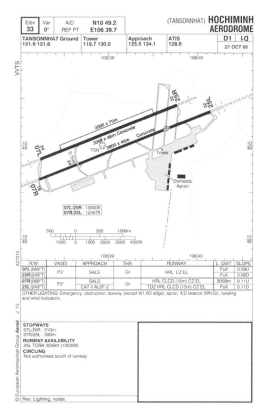

Elev	Var	A/D	N10 49.2	(TANSONNHAT)	**HOCHIMINH**
33	0°	REF PT	E106 39.7		**AERODROME**

TANSONNHAT Ground	Tower	Approach	ATIS	D1	LG
121.9 121.6	118.7 130.0	125.5 134.1	128.0		27 OCT 05

R/W	VASIS	APPROACH	THR	RUNWAY	L. DIST	SLOPE
07L (069°T)	P3°	SALS	Gr	HRL CZ EL	Full	0.08U
25R (249°T)					Full	0.08D
07R (069°T)	P3°	SALS	Gr	HRL CLCD (15m) CZ EL	3059m	0.11U
25L (249°T)		CAT II ALSF-2		TDZ HRL CLCD (15m) CZ EL	Full	0.11D

OTHER LIGHTING: Emergency, obstruction, taxiway (except W1,W2 edge), apron, A/D beacon (Wh/Gr), landing and wind indicators.

STOPWAYS
07L/25R - 310m
07R/25L - 300m
RUNWAY AVAILABILITY
25L TORA 3059m (10036ft)
CIRCLING
Not authorised south of runway

Rev: Lighting, notes.

© European Aeronautical Group Aerad

bled as Tan Son Nhut (sic) Air Force Base, used by the United States Air Force and South Vietnamese Air Force, and at the time one of the world's busiest military air bases.

The fall of Saigon in 1975, and the reunification of Vietnam, saw an end to the US presence, and for some time there was little commercial air traffic into Vietnam, especially the south. Nevertheless, commercial air traffic gradually returned, and by December 2004 United Airlines extended its San Francisco to Hong Kong service to what had become Ho Chi Minh City, named after the victorious North Vietnamese dictator. The return of business and tourist travellers has meant that the airport now handles two-thirds of Vietnam's international traffic. Rapid growth has been accompanied by steady expansion, and a new international terminal (now Terminal 2) was opened in 2007, leaving the old terminal for domestic flights. The continued growth means that a new international airport is planned at Long Thanh for 2015, when Tan Son Nhat will be reserved for domestic flights.

The airport came under attack several times, including during the US evacuation from Vietnam in 1975, when a Lockheed C-5A Galaxy transport, carrying orphans, was shot down. Since then, just two accidents have been recorded. The first was on 28 August 1976 when a Vietnamese man attempted to hijack an Air France Sud Aviation Caravelle airliner, and after releasing the passengers and crew, set off two grenades killing himself as the police moved to seize him. The second was a heavy landing on 19 September 2000 by a Vietnam Airlines Boeing 767-300ER, which resulted in structural damage to the upper fuselage, although the aircraft was repaired.

HANOI NOI BAI INTERNATIONAL: HAN
Hanoi, Vietnam

Owner and operator: Northern Airports Authority
Runways: 11L/29R, 3,200m (10,497ft);
　　　　　11R/29L, 3,800m (12,466ft)
Terminals: One
Airlines using airport as base: Vietnam Airlines
Annual passengers: 6,371,341
Annual cargo: 124,454 tonnes
Annual aircraft movements: 44,353

Background
Originally built by the French before independence, Noi Bai is the largest airport in the north of the country, and is 45km (28 miles) from the centre of Hanoi. Plans have been made for a new airport for Hanoi, as Noi Bai's terminal is too small and the two parallel runways are too close for both to be fully utilised.

There has been just one serious accident in recent years, to a Hang Khong Vietnam Tupolev Tu-134A on 17 February 1988, which was written off on landing. No other details are available of this accident.

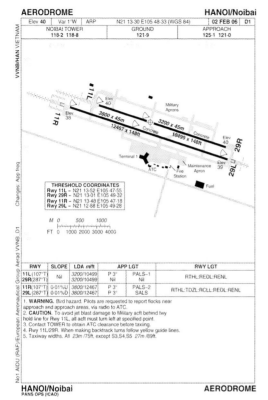

| Elev 40 | Var 1°W | ARP | N21 13·30 E105 48·33 (WGS 84) | 02 FEB 06 | D1 |

| NOIBAI TOWER | GROUND | APPROACH |
| 118·2 118·8 | 121·9 | 125·1 121·0 |

VVNB/HAN VIETNAM

Changes App freq

No1 AIDU (RAF)/European Aeronautical Group Aerad VVNB D1

THRESHOLD COORDINATES
Rwy 11L – N21 13·52 E105 47·55
Rwy 29R – N21 13·01 E105 49·32
Rwy 11R – N21 13·48 E105 47·18
Rwy 29L – N21 12·88 E105 49·28

M 0   500   1000
FT 0   1000 2000 3000 4000

RWY	SLOPE	LDA m/ft	APP LGT		RWY LGT
11L (107°T)	Nil	3200/10499	P 3°	PALS–1	RTHL:REDL:RENL
29R (287°T)		3200/10499	Nil	Nil	
11R (107°T)	0·01%U	3800/12467	P 3°	PALS–2	RTHL:TDZL:RCLL:REDL:RENL
29L (287°T)	0·01%D	3800/12467	P 3°	SALS	

1. **WARNING.** Bird hazard. Pilots are requested to report flocks near
approach and approach areas, via radio to ATC.
2. **CAUTION.** To avoid jet blast damage to Military acft behind twy
hold line for Rwy 11L, all acft must turn left at specified point.
3. Contact TOWER to obtain ATC clearance before taxiing.
4. Rwy 11L/29R. When making backtrack turns follow yellow guide lines.
5. Taxiway widths. All 23m /75ft, except S3,S4,S5 27m /89ft.

HANOI/Noibai   AERODROME
PANS OPS (ICAO)

YEMEN

SANA'A INTERNATIONAL (EL RAHABA): SAH

Sana'a, Yemen

Owner and operator: Government of the Yemen
Runways: 18/36, 3,252m (10,669ft)
Terminals: Two, designated Terminal 1 and
    Terminal 2
Airlines using airport as base or hub: Yemenia
Annual passengers: 1,793,748
Annual cargo: 18,750 tonnes

Background

The airport for the capital of the Yemen. A second terminal opened in 2009.

There have been two recorded accidents at the airport in recent years. The first was to an Air France Airbus A300 taking off for Cairo and Paris on 17 March 1982. As the aircraft accelerated along the runway, the pilots heard a loud bang and assumed that a tyre had burst, but in fact there had been an uncontained failure of the No. 2 engine, which caused a fire. The take-off was aborted and the 13 crew and 111 passengers evacuated. The aircraft was destroyed. A Balkan Bulgarian Airlines Ilyushin Il-18 landed too fast and nose wheel first on 16 June 1984, bouncing four times and overshooting the runway, with the aircraft written off, but the 6 crew and 18 passengers survived.

Appendix I

The world's top 500 airports by passengers handled

Rank	City	Code	Passengers	Rank	City	Code	Passengers
1	ATLANTA GA	ATL	89,379,287	34	SYDNEY	SYD	32,323,380
2	CHICAGO IL	ORD	76,177,855	35	PHILADELPHIA PA	PHL	32,211,439
3	LONDON	LHR	68,068,304	36	TORONTO ON	YYZ	31,452,848
4	TOKYO	HND	66,823,414	37	INCHEON	ICN	31,421,801
5	LOS ANGELES CA	LAX	61,896,075	38	SEATTLE WA	SEA	31,296,628
6	PARIS	CDG	59,922,177	39	GUANGZHOU	CAN	30,958,374
7	DALLAS/FORT WORTH TX	DFW	59,786,476	40	SHANGHAI	PVG	29,083,510
8	FRANKFURT	FRA	54,161,856	41	BOSTON MA	BOS	28,102,455
9	BEIJING	PEK	53,583,664	42	KUALA LUMPUR	KUL	26,453,379
10	MADRID	MAD	52,122,702	43	PARIS	ORY	26,440,736
11	DENVER CO	DEN	49,863,352	44	MEXICO CITY	MEX	25,881,662
12	AMSTERDAM	AMS	47,794,994	45	ISTANBUL	IST	25,561,435
13	NEW YORK NY	JFK	47,716,941	46	MUMBAI	BOM	25,236,400
14	HONG KONG, CHINA	HKG	47,042,419	47	NEW YORK NY	LGA	25,026,267
15	LAS VEGAS NV	LAS	46,961,011	48	WASHINGTON DC	IAD	24,525,487
16	HOUSTON TX	IAH	42,998,040	49	MILAN	MXP	23,885,391
17	PHOENIX AZ	PHX	42,184,515	50	LONDON	STN	23,777,277
18	BANGKOK	BKK	41,210,081	51	TAIPEI	TPE	23,425,794
19	SINGAPORE	SIN	36,701,556	52	NEW DELHI	DEL	23,346,895
20	ORLANDO FL	MCO	36,480,416	53	DUBLIN	DUB	23,287,438
21	NEWARK NJ	EWR	36,367,240	54	PALMA DE MALLORCA	PMI	23,223,970
22	DETROIT MI	DTW	35,983,478	55	MELBOURNE	MEL	23,076,369
23	SAN FRANCISCO CA	SFO	35,792,707	56	FORT LAUDERDALE FL	FLL	22,681,903
24	TOKYO	NRT	35,478,146	57	SHANGHAI	SHA	22,632,962
25	LONDON	LGW	35,218,374	58	MANCHESTER	MAN	22,362,106
26	MINNEAPOLIS MN	MSP	35,157,322	59	SALT LAKE CITY UT	SLC	22,045,333
27	DUBAI	DXB	34,348,110	60	BALTIMORE MD	BWI	21,498,091
28	MUNICH	MUC	33,959,422	61	COPENHAGEN	CPH	21,356,134
29	MIAMI FL	MIA	33,740,416	62	ZURICH	ZRH	20,682,094
30	CHARLOTTE NC	CLT	33,165,688	63	SHENZHEN	SZX	20,619,164
31	ROME	FCO	32,855,542	64	MANILA	MNL	20,467,627
32	BARCELONA	BCN	32,794,575	65	SÃO PAULO	GRU	19,560,963
33	JAKARTA	CGK	32,458,946	66	CHICAGO IL	MDW	19,378,855

Rank	City	Code	Passengers	Rank	City	Code	Passengers
67	TAMPA FL	TPA	19,154,957	113	HANGZHOU	HGH	11,729,983
68	OSLO	OSL	19,043,800	114	BRASILIA	BSB	11,616,097
69	VIENNA	VIE	18,768,468	115	CANCUN	CUN	11,483,741
70	MOSCOW	DME	18,755,098	116	CLEVELAND OH	CLE	11,459,390
71	WASHINGTON DC	DCA	18,670,924	117	XIAN	XIY	11,382,782
72	CHENGDU	CTU	18,586,000	118	MEMPHIS TN	MEM	11,290,477
73	BRISBANE	BNE	18,374,667	119	GENEVA	GVA	10,791,466
74	SAPPORO	CTS	18,361,366	120	RIO DE JANEIRO	GIG	10,782,268
75	SAN DIEGO CA	SAN	18,336,761	121	SACRAMENTO CA	SMF	10,748,982
76	STOCKHOLM	ARN	17,968,023	122	SAN JOSE CA	SJC	10,658,389
77	FUKUOKA	FUK	17,902,563	123	TEL-AVIV	TLV	10,526,445
78	BRUSSELS	BRU	17,838,214	124	COLOGNE	CGN	10,471,660
79	DÜSSELDORF	DUS	17,832,849	125	SAN JUAN (PUERTO RICO)	SJU	10,470,357
80	ANTALYA	AYT	17,795,523	126	MADRAS	MAA	10,424,213
81	JOHANNESBURG	JNB	17,787,673	127	NICE	NCE	10,399,513
82	VANCOUVER BC	YVR	17,710,239	128	CHONGQING	CKG	10,355,730
83	OSAKA	KIX	16,622,853	129	GRAN CANARIA	LPA	10,348,997
84	ATHENS	ATH	16,518,851	130	STUTTGART	STR	10,321,431
85	OSAKA	ITM	15,937,314	131	HO CHI MINH CITY	SGN	10,286,918
86	CINCINNATI OH	CVG	15,736,220	132	RALEIGH-DURHAM NC	RDU	10,219,138
87	KUNMING	KMG	15,729,171	133	SANTA ANA, CA	SNA	9,979,699
88	ST LOUIS MO	STL	15,384,557	134	LONDON	LTN	9,948,959
89	SÃO PAULO	CGH	15,250,058	135	BANGALORE	BLR	9,929,717
90	NAHA	OKA	14,950,970	136	MILAN	LIN	9,926,530
91	OAKLAND CA	OAK	14,846,832	137	PITTSBURGH PA	PIT	9,822,588
92	PORTLAND OR	PDX	14,654,222	138	WARSAW	WAW	9,268,476
93	JEDDAH	JED	14,432,426	139	BIRMINGHAM	BHX	9,232,776
94	MOSCOW	SVO	14,039,843	140	ALICANTE	ALC	9,109,926
95	DOHA	DOH	13,903,320	141	EDINBURGH	EDI	9,049,103
96	SEOUL	GMP	13,811,294	142	AUSTIN TX	AUS	8,885,391
97	MÁLAGA	AGP	13,577,585	143	HOUSTON TX	HOU	8,819,521
98	LISBON	LIS	13,392,059	144	GLASGOW	GLA	8,798,381
99	BERLIN	TXL	13,357,741	145	XIAMEN	XMN	8,684,665
100	HELSINKI	HEL	13,139,044	146	PERTH	PER	8,631,092
101	HAMBURG	HAM	12,780,509	147	TENERIFE	TFS	8,615,757
102	BOGOTA	BOG	12,763,564	148	BUDAPEST	BUD	8,581,071
103	CAIRO	CAI	12,577,451	149	CARACAS	CCS	8,357,446
104	PRAGUE	PRG	12,416,172	150	WUHAN	WUH	8,356,340
105	MONTREAL QC	YUL	12,407,934	151	INDIANAPOLIS IN	IND	8,271,632
106	JEJU	CJU	12,297,159	152	CHANGSHA	CSX	8,069,989
107	CALGARY AB	YYC	12,257,848	153	NANJING	NKG	8,037,189
108	AUCKLAND	AKL	12,222,096	154	SAN ANTONIO TX	SAT	8,033,314
109	RIYADH	RUH	12,134,112	155	FORT MYERS FL	RSW	8,029,204
110	KANSAS CITY MO	MCI	12,000,997	156	DALLAS TX	DAL	7,953,385
111	NAGOYA	NGO	11,862,895	157	QING DAO	TAO	7,867,982
112	TEHRAN	THR	11,782,170	158	NASHVILLE TN	BNA	7,802,454

Rank	City	Code	Passengers	Rank	City	Code	Passengers
159	GUADALAJARA	GDL	7,784,286	205	BUENOS AIRES	AEP	5,665,808
160	COLUMBUS OH	CMH	7,726,421	206	HANNOVER	HAJ	5,644,746
161	MILWAUKEE WI	MKE	7,713,144	207	CHRISTCHURCH	CHC	5,635,166
162	CAPE TOWN	CPT	7,548,735	208	LANZAROTE	ACE	5,625,242
163	NEW ORLEANS LA	MSY	7,525,533	209	KAGOSHIMA	KOJ	5,591,176
164	LIMA	LIM	7,505,832	210	LIVERPOOL	LPL	5,520,283
165	BUENOS AIRES	EZE	7,487,779	211	MACAU, CHINA	MFM	5,498,878
166	BUSAN	PUS	7,410,502	212	FARO	FAO	5,470,472
167	LYON	LYS	7,320,952	213	HERAKLION	HER	5,438,687
168	BAHRAIN	BAH	7,320,039	214	EAST MIDLANDS	EMA	5,422,198
169	DALIAN	DLC	7,281,084	215	LARNACA AIRPORT	LCA	5,387,724
170	HAIKOU	HAK	7,265,349	216	ROME	CIA	5,351,910
171	CALCUTTA	CCU	7,223,537	217	SAYAN	SYX	5,311,622
172	ONTARIO CA	ONT	7,207,150	218	BUFFALO, NY	BUF	5,308,723
173	VENICE	VCE	7,059,141	219	ANCHORAGE AK	ANC	5,304,145
174	WEST PALM BEACH FL	PBI	6,967,277	220	IZMIR	ADB	5,297,986
175	MARSEILLE	MRS	6,962,773	221	BELFAST	BFS	5,230,280
176	KUWAIT	KWI	6,956,550	222	ANKARA/ESENBOGA	ESB	5,062,971
177	MONTERREY	MTY	6,856,100	223	RENO NV	RNO	5,043,986
178	MOSCOW	VKO	6,799,678	224	MEDAN	MES	5,004,398
179	HYDERABAD	HYD	6,777,408	225	BUCHAREST	OTP	4,978,587
180	ALBUQUERQUE NM	ABQ	6,727,384	226	COLOMBO	CMB	4,898,891
181	HARTFORD	BDL	6,519,181	227	NAIROBI	NBO	4,861,706
182	ADELAIDE	ADL	6,498,169	228	BERGEN	BGO	4,852,740
183	SALVADOR	SSA	6,429,990	229	GIRONA	GRO	4,830,047
184	SHARM EL SHEIKH	SSH	6,415,017	230	BANGKOK	DMK	4,805,240
185	HANOI	HAN	6,371,341	231	DURBAN	DUR	4,799,702
186	BERLIN	SXF	6,331,191	232	WELLINGTON	WLG	4,784,294
187	JACKSONVILLE FL	JAX	6,319,016	233	TIJUANA	TIJ	4,760,531
188	TOULOUSE	TLS	6,161,522	234	IBIZA	IBZ	4,750,785
189	ST PETERSBURG	LED	6,138,823	235	RECIFE	REC	4,662,667
190	KARACHI	KHI	6,081,448	236	PORTO ALEGRE	POA	4,606,557
191	CATANIA	CTA	6,079,699	237	FUERTEVENTURA	FUE	4,604,219
192	EDMONTON AB	YEG	6,065,117	238	KOTA KINABALU	BKI	4,536,835
193	HURGHADA	HRG	5,945,254	239	CONFINS	CNF	4,521,711
194	BRISTOL	BRS	5,926,774	240	PALERMO	PMO	4,507,143
195	VALENCIA	VLC	5,924,386	241	SEVILLA	SVQ	4,501,932
196	BURBANK CA	BUR	5,921,336	242	LAGOS	LOS	4,450,726
197	DENPASAR-BALI	DPS	5,888,265	243	CURITIBA	CWB	4,440,731
198	CASABLANCA	CMN	5,858,192	244	TUCSON AZ	TUS	4,429,905
199	NAPLES	NAP	5,775,838	245	QUITO	UIO	4,427,591
200	BERGAMO	BGY	5,737,089	246	OMAHA NE	OMA	4,421,274
201	KAOHSIUNG	KHH	5,717,242	247	GOTHENBURG	GOT	4,385,910
202	PHUKET	HKT	5,704,365	248	BOLOGNA	BLQ	4,354,369
203	NEWCASTLE	NCL	5,701,395	249	CONFINS	CFO	4,340,129
204	KIEV	KBP	5,674,548	250	SHARJAH	SHJ	4,324,313

Rank	City	Code	Passengers	Rank	City	Code	Passengers
251	MONASTIR	MIR	4,282,055	297	KUCHING	KCH	3,236,468
252	BASEL	BSL	4,262,277	298	BIRMINGHAM AL	BHM	3,222,689
253	BILBAO	BIO	4,260,406	299	TULSA OK	TUL	3,218,429
254	NUREMBERG	NUE	4,239,169	300	RIO DE JANEIRO	SDU	3,214,415
255	MUSCAT	MCT	4,218,498	301	CORK	ORK	3,176,365
256	THESSALONIKI	SKG	4,168,557	302	PENANG	PEN	3,174,195
257	DAMMAM	DMM	4,158,261	303	COCHIN	COK	3,162,227
258	TENERIFE	TFN	4,123,554	304	RIGA	RIX	3,160,945
259	MASHHAD	MHD	4,089,282	305	MONTEGO BAY	MBJ	3,136,601
260	OTTAWA ON	YOW	4,088,528	306	PUERTO VALLARTA	PVR	3,134,221
261	HAHN	HHN	4,014,246	307	LAHORE	LHE	3,091,590
262	CAIRNS QLD	CNS	3,997,476	308	KRAKOW	KRK	3,068,199
263	OPORTO	OPO	3,986,748	309	MARRAKECH	RAK	3,050,916
264	TUNIS	TUN	3,946,765	310	AHMEDABAD	AMD	3,037,734
265	ABU DHABI	AUH	3,926,460	311	ISLAMABAD	ISB	3,035,966
266	FORTALEZA	FOR	3,919,820	312	ALAJUELA	SJO	3,031,954
267	GOLD COAST	OOL	3,916,326	313	GUAYAQUIL	GYE	2,996,424
268	MANCHESTER NH	MHT	3,892,630	314	LUQA	MLA	2,980,257
269	AMMAN	AMM	3,850,347	315	MUGLA	DLM	2,959,036
270	DHAKA	DAC	3,820,617	316	SAN JOSÉ DEL CABO	SJD	2,932,345
271	LOUISVILLE KY	SDF	3,819,154	317	LONDON	LCY	2,928,820
272	PANAMA CITY	PTY	3,805,312	318	LONG BEACH CA	LGB	2,906,556
273	ALGIERS	ALG	3,804,731	319	LEEDS	LBA	2,906,464
274	ISTANBUL	SAW	3,791,625	320	ALBANY NY	ALB	2,874,277
275	OKLAHOMA CITY OK	OKC	3,737,135	321	DAYTON OH	DAY	2,833,031
276	PISA	PSA	3,718,608	322	ADDIS ABABA	ADD	2,832,449
277	NORFOLK VA	ORF	3,718,399	323	MENORCA	MAH	2,771,997
278	RICHMOND VA	RIC	3,634,544	324	SANTO DOMINGO	SDQ	2,752,531
279	RODOS	RHO	3,624,302	325	SOFIA	SOF	2,746,330
280	SHANNON	SNN	3,620,623	326	LEIPZIG	LEJ	2,719,256
281	PUNTA CANA	PUJ	3,615,609	327	CAGLIARI	CAG	2,666,957
282	WINNIPEG MB	YWG	3,570,673	328	BODRUM	BJV	2,592,852
283	STAVANGER	SVG	3,528,426	329	MALÉ	MLE	2,591,094
284	VERONA	VRN	3,510,259	330	NANTES	NTE	2,589,890
285	TURIN	TRN	3,500,728	331	PLAINE MAGNIEN	MRU	2,562,830
286	SURABAYA	SUB	3,488,320	332	KATHMANDU	KTM	2,539,488
287	SPOKANE WA	GEG	3,472,901	333	GOA	GOI	2,528,358
288	HALIFAX NS	YHZ	3,469,062	334	BELGRADE	BEG	2,515,968
289	BORDEAUX	BOD	3,463,205	335	LANZHOU	LHW	2,510,903
290	ABERDEEN	ABZ	3,434,493	336	CHARLEROI	CRL	2,458,980
291	BEIRUT	BEY	3,408,834	337	JERBA	DJE	2,449,471
292	TRONDHEIM	TRD	3,406,281	338	GLASGOW	PIK	2,423,460
293	EL PASO TX	ELP	3,402,700	339	FUNCHAL	FNC	2,418,489
294	BOISE ID	BOI	3,365,303	340	CALI	CLO	2,406,823
295	TOLUCA	TLC	3,295,692	341	AGANA	GUM	2,391,135
296	CHIANG MAI	CNX	3,290,856	342	PIARCO	POS	2,388,444

Rank	City	Code	Passengers	Rank	City	Code	Passengers
343	BARI	BRI	2,385,427	389	NOVOSIBIRSK	OVB	1,873,498
344	BELÉM	BEL	2,377,348	390	DRESDEN	DRS	1,849,836
345	SYRACUSE NY	SYR	2,360,878	391	PEKANBARU	PKU	1,839,322
346	EKATERINBURG	SVX	2,345,097	392	ARUBA	AUA	1,837,413
347	MEDELLIN	MDE	2,329,866	393	STOCKHOLM	BMA	1,835,349
348	ADANA	ADA	2,302,535	394	KNOXVILLE TN	TYS	1,821,581
349	CHARLESTON SC	CHS	2,275,541	395	NICOSIA (now Paphos)	PFO	1,819,182
350	BILLUND	BLL	2,262,125	396	XISHUANGBANNA	JHG	1,807,633
351	MANAUS	MAO	2,251,256	397	SANA'A	SAH	1,793,748
352	BREMEN	BRE	2,232,018	398	SANFORD FL	SFB	1,788,780
353	ABUJA	ABV	2,198,674	399	OLBIA	OLB	1,770,665
354	KHARTOUM	KRT	2,190,377	400	PADANG	PDG	1,752,961
355	BELFAST	BHD	2,186,993	401	KINGSTON	KIN	1,735,659
356	KEFLAVIK	KEF	2,182,232	402	SIEM REAP	REP	1,734,308
357	GREENSBORO NC	GSO	2,180,974	403	STRASBOURG	SXB	1,733,050
358	BEAUVAIS	BVA	2,155,633	404	TALLINN	TLL	1,722,653
359	DORTMUND	DTM	2,155,057	405	VILNIUS	VNO	1,717,222
360	SHIRAZ	SYZ	2,154,894	406	FORT-DE-FRANCE	FDF	1,695,741
361	BRIDGETOWN	BGI	2,150,447	407	MYRTLE BEACH SC	MYR	1,683,823
362	CARDIFF	CWL	2,116,685	408	PENSACOLA FL	PNS	1,669,950
363	FLORIANOPOLIS	FLN	2,105,399	409	NATAL	NAT	1,660,285
364	TASHKENT	TAS	2,101,028	410	PALEMBANG	PLM	1,660,013
365	COLORADO SPRINGS CO	COS	2,067,410	411	WHITE PLAINS NY	HPN	1,655,473
366	TRIVANDRUM	TRV	2,054,501	412	ST MAARTEN	SXM	1,651,826
367	SANTIAGO DE COMPOSTE	SCQ	2,048,706	413	LUXEMBOURG	LUX	1,642,848
368	SAVANNAH GA	SAV	2,029,449	414	KOS	KGS	1,641,067
369	MADINAH	MED	2,009,790	415	PALM SPRINGS CA	PSP	1,610,943
370	KERKYRA	CFU	2,009,410	416	TROMSOE	TOS	1,606,226
371	BRATISLAVA	BTS	2,004,541	417	UJUNG PANDANG	UPG	1,600,083
372	MURCIA	MJV	1,994,582	418	PHNOM PENH	PNH	1,598,424
373	STOCKHOLM	NYO	1,994,512	419	JERSEY	JER	1,596,757
374	ZAGREB	ZAG	1,992,455	420	SAN SALVADOR	SAL	1,596,500
375	GRAND RAPIDS MI	GRR	1,990,896	421	WICHITA KS	ICT	1,596,229
376	KATOWICE	KTW	1,985,216	422	SAINT-DENIS	RUN	1,594,805
377	DES MOINES IA	DSM	1,982,633	423	MUENSTER	FMO	1,581,458
378	LUXOR	LXR	1,976,152	424	MADISON WI	MSN	1,564,975
379	SOUTHAMPTON	SOU	1,966,774	425	SARASOTA FL	SRQ	1,557,212
380	POINTE-À-PITRE	PTP	1,960,912	426	ASTURIAS	OVD	1,554,318
381	BOURGAS	BOJ	1,949,197	427	GOIANIA	GYN	1,546,476
382	SALZBURG	SZG	1,946,422	428	EINDHOVEN	EIN	1,544,098
383	MALMÖ-STURUP	MMX	1,911,722	429	JEREZ	XRY	1,537,533
384	LIJIANG	LJG	1,906,317	430	ISFAHAN	IFN	1,535,194
385	FLORENCE	FLR	1,905,143	431	ABHA	AHB	1,525,118
386	VITORIA (BRAZIL)	VIX	1,894,442	432	BODO	BOO	1,519,837
387	CHANIA	CHQ	1,883,278	433	SANDEFJORD	TRF	1,519,305
388	DAKAR-YOFF	DKR	1,875,000	434	ZHANG JIAJIE	DYG	1,516,721

Rank	City	Code	Passengers	Rank	City	Code	Passengers
435	LJUBLJANA	LJU	1,515,839	468	MONTPELLIER	MPL	1,286,877
436	PAPEETE (TAHITI)	PPT	1,511,340	469	LEON/GUANAJUATO	BJX	1,285,859
437	AGADIR	AGA	1,496,875	470	CALICUT	CCJ	1,284,813
438	VARNA	VAR	1,493,267	471	CUIABA	CGB	1,280,002
439	PORT ELIZABETH	PLZ	1,491,800	472	CURAÇAO	CUR	1,274,046
440	TOWNSVILLE	TSV	1,487,580	473	WROCLAW	WRO	1,271,195
441	TRABZON	TZX	1,484,522	474	ST THOMAS	STT	1,265,491
442	VICTORIA BC	YYJ	1,481,600	475	JAIPUR	JAI	1,263,030
443	HERMOSILLO	HMO	1,478,057	476	A CORUÑA	LCG	1,251,606
444	JACKSON MS	JAN	1,457,181	477	HUNTSVILLE AL	HSV	1,239,813
445	MIRI	MYY	1,454,167	478	COLUMBIA SC	CAE	1,234,547
446	DAR ES SALAAM	DAR	1,450,558	479	LA PALMA	SPC	1,207,177
447	GRANADA	GRX	1,448,017	480	CAMPINAS	VCP	1,206,288
448	BANDAR SERI BEGAWAN	BWN	1,447,580	481	ALMERÍA	LEI	1,202,763
449	BURLINGTON VT	BTV	1,410,745	482	ATLANTIC CITY NJ	ACY	1,199,362
450	VIGO	VGO	1,405,786	483	SPLIT	SPU	1,182,387
451	NADI	NAN	1,395,165	484	ACCRA	ACC	1,179,990
452	SAMARA	KUF	1,393,828	485	PUERTO PLATA	POP	1,176,010
453	AKRON OH	CAK	1,391,836	486	ASTANA	TSE	1,170,919
454	HAT YAI	HDY	1,390,145	487	MONTEVIDEO	MVD	1,168,199
455	YEREVAN	EVN	1,382,685	488	BARRANQUILLA	BAQ	1,157,576
456	PONTIANAK	PNK	1,378,529	489	ROTTERDAM	RTM	1,146,144
457	CARTAGENA DE INDIAS	CTG	1,369,784	490	DUBROVNIK	DBV	1,143,168
458	KELOWNA BC	YLW	1,363,391	491	LANGKAWI	LGK	1,122,911
459	MOMBASA	MBA	1,345,786	492	GENOA	GOA	1,116,211
460	GUWAHATI	GAU	1,333,723	493	EILATH	ETH	1,109,472
461	JOHOR BAHRU	JHB	1,324,952	494	TIRANA	TIA	1,107,325
462	FRESNO CA	FAT	1,318,483	495	PRISTINA	PRN	1,093,812
463	CULIACAN	CUL	1,305,255	496	BOURNEMOUTH	BOH	1,092,785
464	ALGHERO	AHO	1,298,950	497	ACAPULCO	ACA	1,090,963
465	MIDDLETOWN PA	MDT	1,298,857	498	DONCASTER	DSA	1,078,374
466	REUS	REU	1,295,612	499	CEDAR RAPIDS IA	CID	1,061,052
467	MERIDA	MID	1,291,575	500	VERACRUZ	VER	1,054,803

Appendix II

The world's top 500 airports by cargo handled

Rank	City	Code	Cargo	Rank	City	Code	Cargo
1	MEMPHIS TN	MEM	3,840,491	34	BOGOTA	BOG	585,578
2	HONG KONG	HKG	3,773,964	35	SAN FRANCISCO CA	SFO	562,933
3	ANCHORAGE AK*	ANC	2,825,511	36	PHILADELPHIA PA	PHL	543,357
4	SHANGHAI	PVG	2,559,310	37	MUMBAI	BOM	536,432
5	INCHEON	ICN	2,555,580	38	TORONTO ON	YYZ	504,608
6	PARIS	CDG	2,297,896	39	LIEGE	LGG	489,746
7	TOKYO	NRT	2,254,421	40	SÃO PAULO	GRU	488,485
8	FRANKFURT	FRA	2,127,646	41	MILAN	MXP	486,667
9	LOUISVILLE KY	SDF	2,078,947	42	ONTARIO CA	ONT	483,309
10	MIAMI FL	MIA	1,922,985	43	JAKARTA	CGK	473,593
11	SINGAPORE	SIN	1,918,159	44	NEW DELHI	DEL	431,623
12	LOS ANGELES CA	LAX	1,884,317	45	MEXICO CITY	MEX	411,383
13	DUBAI	DXB	1,668,505	46	HOUSTON TX	IAH	409,193
14	AMSTERDAM	AMS	1,651,385	47	COPENHAGEN	CPH	395,506
15	NEW YORK NY	JFK	1,607,050	48	SHANGHAI	SHA	388,812
16	TAIPEI	TPE	1,605,681	49	MANILA	MNL	388,551
17	CHICAGO IL	ORD	1,533,606	50	BAHRAIN	BAH	385,278
18	LONDON	LHR	1,395,905	51	DOHA	DOH	365,265
19	BANGKOK	BKK	1,220,001	52	TOLEDO OH	TOL	361,867
20	BEIJING	PEK	1,192,553	53	JOHANNESBURG	JNB	360,831
21	INDIANAPOLIS IN	IND	998,675	54	WASHINGTON, DC	IAD	358,527
22	NEWARK NJ	EWR	963,794	55	MADRID	MAD	356,427
23	LUXEMBOURG	LUX	856,741	56	TEL-AVIV	TLV	350,351
24	TOKYO	HND	852,454	57	ISTANBUL	IST	341,454
25	OSAKA	KIX	845,976	58	CHENGDU	CTU	328,000
26	BRUSSELS	BRU	747,434	59	SEATTLE WA	SEA	319,013
27	DALLAS/FORT WORTH TX	DFW	724,140	60	ABU DHABI	AUH	317,207
28	ATLANTA GA	ATL	720,209	61	SHARJAH	SHJ	312,285
29	COLOGNE	CGN	710,244	62	EAST MIDLANDS	EMA	304,460
30	GUANGZHOU	CAN	694,923	63	BOSTON MA	BOS	298,536
31	KUALA LUMPUR	KUL	652,895	64	FUKUOKA	FUK	292,694
32	OAKLAND CA	OAK	647,594	65	ZURICH	ZRH	289,958
33	SHENZHEN	SZX	616,046	66	NAIROBI	NBO	276,881

Rank	City	Code	Cargo	Rank	City	Code	Cargo
67	NAGOYA	NGO	276,377	113	HELSINKI	HEL	145,481
68	CAIRO	CAI	275,312	114	CHONGQING	CKG	143,523
69	SAPPORO	CTS	274,269	115	TEHRAN	THR	141,500
70	MADRAS	MAA	267,696	116	SAN DIEGO CA	SAN	140,304
71	DENVER CO	DEN	267,294	117	FORT LAUDERDALE FL	FLL	137,219
72	MUNICH	MUC	265,607	118	KHARTOUM	KRT	135,479
73	MINNEAPOLIS MN	MSP	257,394	119	CALGARY AB	YYC	134,250
74	PORTLAND OR	PDX	254,754	120	BERGAMO	BGY	133,932
75	HO CHI MINH CITY	SGN	254,753	121	MOSCOW	DME	133,662
76	PHOENIX AZ	PHX	251,925	122	MEDELLIN	MDE	132,302
77	NAHA	OKA	244,631	123	LAGOS	LOS	130,076
78	FORT WORTH TX	AFW	236,875	124	MOSCOW	SVO	128,152
79	SAN JUAN (PUERTO RICO)	SJU	234,427	125	KANSAS CITY MO	MCI	127,767
80	DHAKA	DAC	233,171	126	HANOI	HAN	124,454
81	DETROIT MI	DTW	233,034	127	SAN ANTONIO TX	SAT	124,390
82	KUNMING	KMG	232,647	128	GUADALAJARA	GDL	124,318
83	CAMPINAS	VCP	229,402	129	STOCKHOLM	ARN	122,922
84	LONDON	STN	228,747	130	CHARLOTTE NC	CLT	122,149
85	VANCOUVER BC	YVR	225,412	131	DALIAN	DLC	121,693
86	LIMA	LIM	225,370	132	ATHENS	ATH	118,237
87	AUCKLAND	AKL	224,774	133	RIO DE JANEIRO	GIG	115,977
88	JEJU	CJU	223,057	134	QING DAO	TAO	115,781
89	RIYADH	RUH	216,469	135	BALTIMORE MD	BWI	115,402
90	JEDDAH	JED	209,118	136	DUBLIN	DUB	114,422
91	PENANG	PEN	208,584	137	XIAN	XIY	112,048
92	VIENNA	VIE	205,024	138	HAHN	HHN	111,689
93	BUENOS AIRES	EZE	204,909	139	PARIS	ORY	109,315
94	HANGZHOU	HGH	195,711	140	RALEIGH-DURHAM NC	RDU	107,485
95	XIAMEN	XMN	193,625	141	COLUMBIA SC	CAE	105,629
96	SEOUL	GMP	186,622	142	BARCELONA	BCN	100,360
97	ORLANDO FL	MCO	183,070	143	COLUMBUS OH	LCK	100,009
98	MACAU, CHINA	MFM	180,955	144	LINCOLN MT	LNK	99,123
99	NANJING	NKG	180,354	145	TAMPA FL	TPA	98,018
100	SALT LAKE CITY UT	SLC	177,710	146	OSLO	OSL	97,311
101	KUWAIT	KWI	177,413	147	AUSTIN TX	AUS	95,587
102	LONDON	LGW	176,822	148	LISBON	LIS	94,515
103	BANGALORE	BLR	176,252	149	CALCUTTA	CCU	93,718
104	KARACHI	KHI	171,330	150	DES MOINES IA	DSM	91,391
105	MANAUS	MAO	170,132	151	LAS VEGAS NV	LAS	91,205
106	MANCHESTER	MAN	166,546	152	WUHAN	WUH	89,596
107	COLOMBO	CMB	164,792	153	MILWAUKEE WI	MKE	88,237
108	HARTFORD	BDL	162,929	154	MANCHESTER NH	MHT	87,747
109	WINNIPEG MB	YWG	155,988	155	KINSHASA	FIH	87,717
110	OSAKA	ITM	154,710	156	CLEVELAND OH	CLE	86,690
111	ROME	FCO	154,441	157	OMAHA NE	OMA	85,967
112	QUITO	UIO	149,719	158	LEIPZIG	LEJ	85,446

Rank	City	Code	Cargo	Rank	City	Code	Cargo
159	AMMAN	AMM	84,900	205	BURBANK CA	BUR	48,818
160	PITTSBURGH PA	PIT	84,266	206	KAGOSHIMA	KOJ	48,805
161	ST LOUIS MO	STL	83,251	207	WARSAW	WAW	48,095
162	SAN JOSE CA	SJC	82,927	208	SPOKANE WA	GEG	47,696
163	PANAMA CITY	PTY	82,462	209	MALMÖ-STURUP	MMX	47,529
164	ALAJUELA	SJO	79,758	210	LONG BEACH CA	LGB	47,079
165	HUNTSVILLE AL	HSV	79,307	211	MIDDLETOWN PA	MDT	46,987
166	SACRAMENTO CA	SMF	79,117	212	ADDIS ABABA	ADD	46,877
167	MUSCAT	MCT	77,392	213	EDINBURGH	EDI	46,747
168	LAHORE	LHE	76,348	214	KNOXVILLE TN	TYS	45,482
169	JACKSONVILLE FL	JAX	75,499	215	NEW ORLEANS LA	MSY	44,872
170	EL PASO TX	ELP	74,963	216	DENPASAR-BALI	DPS	44,861
171	BUSAN	PUS	74,946	217	BUFFALO NY	BUF	44,222
172	SACRAMENTO CA	MHR	74,631	218	BASEL	BSL	44,036
173	FORT WAYNE IN	FWA	74,071	219	MASHHAD	MHD	42,907
174	GUAYAQUIL	GYE	73,473	220	BOISE ID	BOI	42,565
175	GREENSBORO NC	GSO	72,194	221	LARNACA AIRPORT	LCA	41,940
176	SALVADOR	SSA	71,136	222	GRAND RAPIDS MI	GRR	41,672
177	KAOHSIUNG	KHH	70,241	223	CARACAS	CCS	41,535
178	HAIKOU	HAK	69,830	224	MONTERREY	MTY	41,396
179	ALBUQUERQUE NM	ABQ	69,598	225	CALI	CLO	41,176
180	BRASILIA	BSB	69,170	226	GRAN CANARIA	LPA	40,312
181	CHANGSHA	CSX	68,630	227	HAMBURG	HAM	40,234
182	BUDAPEST	BUD	68,144	228	CINCINNATI OH	CVG	39,691
183	NASHVILLE TN	BNA	67,917	229	KOTA KINABALU	BKI	39,682
184	DAMMAM	DMM	66,622	230	LONDON	LTN	38,652
185	ENTEBBE	EBB	64,446	231	PORTO ALEGRE	POA	38,469
186	BEIRUT	BEY	63,845	232	EDMONTON AB	YEG	38,274
187	SUBANG	SZB	63,382	233	FORTALEZA	FOR	38,172
188	BRAZZAVILLE	BZV	63,339	234	VATRY	XCR	37,291
189	GOTHENBURG	GOT	61,790	235	MALÉ	MLE	37,089
190	KEFLAVIK	KEF	61,534	236	LYON	LYS	36,899
191	CASABLANCA	CMN	60,934	237	TUCSON AZ	TUS	36,634
192	RECIFE	REC	60,381	238	GENEVA	GVA	36,599
193	ACCRA	ACC	59,507	239	SÃO PAULO	CGH	34,905
194	RENO NV	RNO	58,617	240	EINDHOVEN	EIN	33,858
195	DÜSSELDORF	DUS	58,026	241	MEDAN	MES	33,649
196	MAASTRICHT	MST	57,754	242	KIEV	KBP	33,541
197	TOULOUSE	TLS	55,225	243	LUXOR	LXR	33,421
198	PRAGUE	PRG	55,179	244	SAINT-DENIS	RUN	33,391
199	ISLAMABAD	ISB	54,530	245	PIARCO	POS	32,828
200	TULSA OK	TUL	54,513	246	OKLAHOMA CITY OK	OKC	32,708
201	MARSEILLE	MRS	51,384	247	OPORTO	OPO	32,585
202	RICHMOND VA	RIC	51,071	248	SURABAYA	SUB	32,475
203	HYDERABAD	HYD	50,853	249	WICHITA KS	ICT	32,315
204	BELFAST	BFS	50,019	250	TRIVANDRUM	TRV	32,091

Rank	City	Code	Cargo	Rank	City	Code	Cargo
251	VITORIA	VIT	32,060	297	ALGIERS	ALG	20,926
252	SIOUX FALLS SD	FSD	31,920	298	BATON ROUGE LA	BTR	20,905
253	FUJAIRAH	FJR	31,907	299	LANZHOU	LHW	20,492
254	TOLUCA	TLC	31,823	300	BERLIN	TXL	20,383
255	NORFOLK VA	ORF	31,772	301	ZARAGOZA	ZAZ	20,151
256	SHREVEPORT LA	SHV	31,602	302	SANTA ANA CA	SNA	19,852
257	GLASGOW	PIK	31,562	303	CONFINS	CNF	19,702
258	BARRANQUILLA	BAQ	31,123	304	ANKARA/ESENBOGA	ESB	19,589
259	HALIFAX NS	YHZ	29,753	305	TABRIZ	TBZ	19,496
260	LANSING MI	LAN	29,665	306	BELÉM	BEL	19,444
261	ST PETERSBURG	LED	29,372	307	NOVOSIBIRSK	OVB	19,001
262	SAN SALVADOR	SAL	29,341	308	SAN LUIS POTOSI	SLP	18,799
263	STUTTGART	STR	29,275	309	SANA'A	SAH	18,750
264	BIRMINGHAM AL	BHM	28,984	310	BOLOGNA	BLQ	18,692
265	SAYAN	SYX	28,634	311	SOUTH BEND IN	SBN	18,632
266	MANSTON	MSE	28,370	312	DAR ES SALAAM	DAR	18,449
267	SHANNON	SNN	27,842	313	ALLENTOWN PA	ABE	18,269
268	TENERIFE	TFN	27,765	314	FORT MYERS FL	RSW	18,234
269	KUCHING	KCH	26,955	315	PAPEETE (TAHITI)	PPT	18,173
270	PHNOM PENH	PNH	26,877	316	LUQA	MLA	18,052
271	ST PETERSBURG FL	PIE	26,833	317	KATHMANDU	KTM	18,051
272	PALMA DE MALLORCA	PMI	26,408	318	PHUKET	HKT	18,005
273	ALBANY NY	ALB	26,266	319	TUNIS	TUN	17,703
274	MONTEVIDEO	MVD	26,083	320	PRISTINA	PRN	17,614
275	IASI	IAS	25,670	321	POINTE-À-PITRE	PTP	17,593
276	CHRISTCHURCH	CHC	25,625	322	CANCUN	CUN	17,585
277	CONFINS	CFO	25,602	323	BUCHAREST	OTP	17,423
278	LIBREVILLE	LBV	25,425	324	SOFIA	SOF	17,389
279	HARARE	HRE	25,289	325	KINGSTON	KIN	17,313
280	COCHIN	COK	25,287	326	UJUNG PANDANG	UPG	17,181
281	SYRACUSE NY	SYR	24,972	327	CURAÇAO	CUR	17,124
282	CEDAR RAPIDS IA	CID	24,789	328	TIJUANA	TIJ	17,104
283	MONCTON NB	YQM	24,527	329	ROANOKE VA	ROA	17,086
284	MOSCOW	VKO	24,402	330	EKATERINBURG	SVX	16,965
285	AHMEDABAD	AMD	24,165	331	ANTANANARIVO	TNR	16,949
286	FAIRBANKS AK	FAI	23,758	332	PEORIA IL	PIA	16,673
287	MILAN	LIN	23,497	333	HANNOVER	HAJ	16,318
288	CURITIBA	CWB	23,322	334	FORT-DE-FRANCE	FDF	16,164
289	SPRINGFIELD MO	SGF	23,034	335	VITORIA (BRAZIL)	VIX	16,104
290	ROME	CIA	22,999	336	MERIDA	MID	16,080
291	CHIANG MAI	CNX	22,869	337	NEW WINDSOR NY	SWF	16,024
292	BANGKOK	DMK	22,753	338	IZMIR	ADB	15,716
293	OTTAWA ON	YOW	22,670	339	LOME	LFW	14,875
294	TALLINN	TLL	22,639	340	WEST PALM BEACH FL	PBI	14,699
295	TASHKENT	TAS	21,413	341	DOUALA	DLA	14,461
296	BANDAR SERI BEGAWAN	BWN	21,150	342	BUENOS AIRES	AEP	14,078

Rank	City	Code	Cargo	Rank	City	Code	Cargo
343	LJUBLJANA	LJU	13,989	389	COVENTRY	CVT	9,173
344	SAINT-NAZAIRE	SNR	13,870	390	DORTMUND	DTM	9,142
345	BIRMINGHAM	BHX	13,533	391	MAPUTO	MPM	9,043
346	VALENCIA	VLC	13,382	392	PONTIANAK	PNK	9,024
347	CHICAGO IL	MDW	13,357	393	PALEMBANG	PLM	9,008
348	TALLAHASSEE FL	TLH	13,163	394	BELGRADE	BEG	8,806
349	PISA	PSA	13,019	395	CATANIA	CTA	8,801
350	VENICE	VCE	12,996	396	NEWCASTLE	NCL	8,728
351	ABIDJAN	ABJ	12,646	397	FUNCHAL	FNC	8,711
352	BORDEAUX	BOD	12,487	398	SHIRAZ	SYZ	8,705
353	COLORADO SPRINGS CO	COS	12,222	399	ST THOMAS	STT	8,624
354	NUREMBERG	NUE	12,146	400	BERLIN	SXF	8,255
355	RENNES	RNS	12,045	401	RIGA	RIX	8,130
356	ELDORET	EDL	11,891	402	DURBAN	DUR	8,126
357	CARTAGENA DE INDIAS	CTG	11,866	403	SEVILLA	SVQ	8,056
358	ISFAHAN	IFN	11,744	404	PONTA DELGADA	PDL	8,017
359	TBILISI	TBS	11,741	405	HOUSTON TX	HOU	7,818
360	PEKANBARU	PKU	11,720	406	WINDHOEK	WDH	7,794
361	NANTES	NTE	11,692	407	KATOWICE	KTW	7,772
362	JACKSON MS	JAN	11,628	408	PORT ELIZABETH	PLZ	7,716
363	NICE	NCE	11,546	409	CUIABA	CGB	7,561
364	MADISON WI	MSN	11,186	410	ADANA	ADA	7,501
365	ISTANBUL	SAW	10,802	411	CHATEROUX	CHR	7,474
366	ZAGREB	ZAG	10,781	412	JERSEY	JER	7,406
367	ZHUHAI CITY	ZUH	10,750	413	GOIANIA	GYN	7,399
368	BOURNEMOUTH	BOH	10,747	414	SAN PEDRO SULA	SAP	7,334
369	SHANTUNG	WEF	10,680	415	MINSK	MSQ	7,290
370	NEW YORK NY	LGA	10,596	416	TERESINA	THE	7,261
371	PADANG	PDG	10,563	417	ÖREBRO	ORB	7,136
372	DJIBOUTI	JIB	10,272	418	SANFORD FL	SFB	6,932
373	FRESNO CA	FAT	10,194	419	MÁLAGA	AGP	6,906
374	YEREVAN	EVN	9,999	420	KAUNAS	KUN	6,816
375	STAVANGER	SVG	9,862	421	HERMOSILLO	HMO	6,793
376	SAO LUIS	SLZ	9,854	422	BLOUNTVILLE TN	TRI	6,784
377	HAT YAI	HDY	9,786	423	BASTIA	BIA	6,683
378	SAVANNAH GA	SAV	9,780	424	TRONDHEIM	TRD	6,672
379	CALICUT	CCJ	9,701	425	BAMAKO	BKO	6,601
380	NATAL	NAT	9,693	426	DIRE DAWA	DIR	6,596
381	RAL AL KHAIMAH	RKT	9,655	427	TONTOUTA	NOU	6,569
382	CIUDAD DEL ESTE	AGT	9,647	428	BLOOMINGTON IL	BMI	6,525
383	CASPER WY	CPR	9,607	429	CHIHUAHA	CUU	6,509
384	TENERIFE	TFS	9,595	430	ANTALYA	AYT	6,480
385	DAYTON OH	DAY	9,512	431	TEGUCIGALPA	TGU	6,366
386	CHARLESTON SC	CHS	9,375	432	UMEÅ	UME	6,252
387	FLORIANOPOLIS	FLN	9,341	433	SANDAKAN	SDK	6,233
388	MOMBASA	MBA	9,296	434	ASUNCION	ASU	6,187

Rank	City	Code	Cargo	Rank	City	Code	Cargo
435	XISHUANGBANNA	JHG	6,148	468	MADINAH	MED	4,806
436	COLUMBUS OH	CMH	6,135	469	ASTANA	TSE	4,677
437	GUERNSEY	GCI	6,122	470	LILONGWE	LLW	4,628
438	BERGEN	BGO	6,103	471	SANTIAGO DE COMPOSTE	SCQ	4,580
439	LANZAROTE	ACE	6,020	472	SAMARA	KUF	4,565
440	MEDELLIN	EOH	6,000	473	CAMPO GRANDE	CGR	4,558
441	SAIPAN	SPN	5,984	474	ALICANTE	ALC	4,540
442	ALEXANDRIA	ALY	5,844	475	POHNPEI	PNI	4,476
443	VILNIUS	VNO	5,780	476	LUSAKA	LUN	4,470
444	COTONOU	COO	5,772	477	HUMBERSIDE	HUY	4,421
445	THESSALONIKI	SKG	5,759	478	KILIMANJARO	JRO	4,392
446	MONTPELLIER	MPL	5,757	479	CULIACAN	CUL	4,379
447	SAN ANDRES	ADZ	5,718	480	IBIZA	IBZ	4,377
448	SANTAREM	STM	5,690	481	GLASGOW	GLA	4,350
449	ST GEORGES	BDA	5,689	482	NAGPUR	NAG	4,335
450	CORK	ORK	5,546	483	ABHA	AHB	4,326
451	EXETER	EXT	5,519	484	LABUAN	LBU	4,319
452	JOHOR BAHRU	JHB	5,508	485	MACEIO	MCZ	4,226
453	ABERDEEN	ABZ	5,479	486	BARI	BRI	4,040
454	MONTEGO BAY	MBJ	5,457	487	ULAANBAATAR	ULN	4,027
455	AJACCIO	AJA	5,451	488	GRAND CAYMAN	GCM	3,876
456	MIRI	MYY	5,370	489	YAOUNDÉ	NSI	3,832
457	MWANZA	MWZ	5,324	490	JAKARTA	HLP	3,808
458	ST CROIX	STX	5,302	491	CORDOBA PAJAS BLANCA	COR	3,745
459	KIGALI	KGL	5,267	492	LIVERPOOL	LPL	3,744
460	OUAGADOUGOU	OUA	5,233	493	ABUJA	ABV	3,737
461	GOA	GOI	5,186	494	MENORCA	MAH	3,721
462	GEORGETOWN	GEO	5,029	495	MACAPÁ	MCP	3,704
463	CONAKRY	CKY	5,022	496	BUCARAMANGA	BGA	3,689
464	CAGLIARI	CAG	5,000	497	KOGALYM	KGP	3,651
465	ST MAARTEN	SXM	4,895	498	HASSI-MESSAOUD	HME	3,562
466	JÖNKÖPING	JKG	4,891	499	SAN JOSE DEL CABO	SJD	3,518
467	NAPLES	NAP	4,880	500	EAST LONDON	ELS	3,487

Appendix III

The world's top 500 airports by aircraft movements

Rank	City	Code	Movements	Rank	City	Code	Movements
1	ATLANTA GA	ATL	994,346	34	ORLANDO FL	MCO	360,075
2	CHICAGO IL	ORD	926,973	35	BARCELONA	BCN	352,489
3	DALLAS/FORT WORTH TX	DFW	685,491	36	SEATTLE WA	SEA	347,046
4	LOS ANGELES CA	LAX	680,954	37	OAKLAND CA	OAK	342,024
5	DENVER CO	DEN	614,065	38	ROME	FCO	334,848
6	LAS VEGAS NV	LAS	609,472	39	TOKYO	HND	331,818
7	HOUSTON TX	IAH	603,656	40	SANTA ANA CA	SNA	331,452
8	PARIS	CDG	552,721	41	VANCOUVER BC	YVR	328,563
9	PHOENIX AZ	PHX	539,211	42	CINCINNATI OH	CVG	328,059
10	CHARLOTTE NC	CLT	522,541	43	FORT LAUDERDALE FL	FLL	307,975
11	PHILADELPHIA PA	PHL	499,653	44	HONG KONG (CHINA)	HKG	305,010
12	FRANKFURT	FRA	492,569	45	CHICAGO IL	MDW	304,657
13	MADRID	MAD	483,284	46	BALTIMORE MD	BWI	296,872
14	LONDON	LHR	481,479	47	PHOENIX AZ	AZA	296,686
15	DETROIT MI	DTW	467,230	48	SANFORD FL	SFB	294,781
16	AMSTERDAM	AMS	454,360	49	SYDNEY	SYD	286,101
17	MINNEAPOLIS MN	MSP	452,972	50	VIENNA	VIE	280,912
18	NEW YORK NY	JFK	446,348	51	ANCHORAGE AK	ANC	276,209
19	NEWARK NJ	EWR	435,691	52	WASHINGTON DC	DCA	275,433
20	MUNICH	MUC	431,815	53	ZURICH	ZRH	268,476
21	TORONTO ON	YYZ	425,500	54	MILAN	MXP	267,941
22	SALT LAKE CITY UT	SLC	422,010	55	LONDON	LGW	266,552
23	BEIJING	PEK	399,697	56	BANGKOK	BKK	265,763
24	BOSTON MA	BOS	399,537	57	PORTLAND OR	PDX	264,518
25	LONG BEACH CA	LGB	398,433	58	BRUSSELS	BRU	264,366
26	NEW YORK NY	LGA	391,872	59	ISTANBUL	IST	262,248
27	MIAMI FL	MIA	386,058	60	GUANGZHOU	CAN	260,835
28	WASHINGTON DC	IAD	382,939	61	DUBAI	DXB	260,530
29	SAN FRANCISCO CA	SFO	379,500	62	TAMPA FL	TPA	258,349
30	PHOENIX AZ	DVT	378,349	63	COPENHAGEN	CPH	257,591
31	MEXICO CITY	MEX	378,161	64	TUCSON AZ	TUS	257,191
32	MEMPHIS TN	MEM	374,989	65	ST LOUIS MO	STL	254,302
33	LOS ANGELES CA	VNY	374,464	66	SHANGHAI	PVG	253,535

Rank City		Code	Movements	Rank City		Code	Movements
67	RALEIGH-DURHAM NC	RDU	252,708	113	MELBOURNE	MEL	184,052
68	CALGARY AB	YYC	250,548	114	BOISE ID	BOI	181,945
69	JAKARTA	CGK	248,482	115	SHENZHEN	SZX	181,450
70	CLEVELAND OH	CLE	244,719	116	MOSCOW	DME	181,141
71	DALLAS TX	DAL	244,609	117	WHITE PLAINS NY	HPN	176,516
72	PARIS	ORY	236,926	118	ABBOTSFORD BC	YXX	175,405
73	MUMBAI	BOM	236,585	119	SACRAMENTO CA	SMF	174,946
74	HOUSTON TX	HOU	232,976	120	PRAGUE	PRG	174,662
75	BOGOTA	BOG	231,947	121	COLUMBUS OH	CMH	173,984
76	DÜSSELDORF	DUS	227,899	122	HAMBURG	HAM	173,499
77	SAN DIEGO CA	SAN	227,329	123	LOUISVILLE KY	SDF	171,573
78	JOHANNESBURG	JNB	226,992	124	BRISBANE	BNE	171,412
79	OSLO	OSL	226,303	125	LANSING MI	LAN	169,485
80	DAYTONA BEACH FL	DAB	225,622	126	SPRINGFIELD MO	SGF	169,081
81	NEW DELHI	DEL	225,510	127	STUTTGART	STR	167,259
82	SINGAPORE	SIN	223,488	128	CHENGDU	CTU	166,382
83	MONTREAL QC	YUL	222,871	129	MOSCOW	SVO	164,664
84	MANCHESTER	MAN	222,778	130	GUADALAJARA	GDL	164,244
85	LAS VEGAS NV	VGT	219,693	131	VICTORIA BC	YYJ	163,936
86	SAN ANTONIO TX	SAT	219,437	132	MELBOURNE FL	MLB	163,869
87	STOCKHOLM	ARN	218,549	133	TAIPEI	TPE	160,120
88	AUSTIN TX	AUS	214,440	134	WICHITA KS	ICT	157,654
89	INCHEON	ICN	213,194	135	COLORADO SPRINGS CO	COS	155,688
90	NASHVILLE TN	BNA	213,185	136	AUCKLAND	AKL	155,662
91	DUBLIN	DUB	211,804	137	WARSAW	WAW	153,480
92	PITTSBURGH PA	PIT	209,303	138	WINNIPEG MB	YWG	151,793
93	LONDON	STN	208,423	139	BERLIN	TXL	151,396
94	SÃO PAULO	CGH	205,564	140	COLOGNE	CGN	151,029
95	ATHENS	ATH	205,295	141	FRESNO CA	FAT	150,563
96	INDIANAPOLIS IN	IND	203,136	142	ORLANDO FL	ORL	149,991
97	MILWAUKEE WI	MKE	200,205	143	KUNMING	KMG	148,185
98	PALMA DE MALLORCA	PMI	197,354	144	HANGZHOU	HGH	148,128
99	TOKYO	NRT	195,074	145	HOUSTON TX	EFD	147,904
100	KANSAS CITY MO	MCI	194,969	146	HARTFORD	BDL	147,720
101	KUALA LUMPUR	KUL	193,688	147	ONTARIO CA	ONT	147,678
102	ALBUQUERQUE NM	ABQ	191,050	148	LISBON	LIS	144,800
103	NICE	NCE	190,078	149	CARACAS	CCS	144,110
104	GENEVA	GVA	190,006	150	RENO NV	RNO	140,806
105	SAN JUAN (PUERTO RICO)	SJU	189,656	151	SARASOTA FL	SRQ	139,442
106	MANILA	MNL	188,797	152	KHARTOUM	KRT	139,426
107	GOODYEAR AZ	GYR	188,015	153	BIRMINGHAM AL	BHM	138,975
108	SÃO PAULO	GRU	187,960	154	OMAHA NE	OMA	136,092
109	SAN JOSE CA	SJC	187,267	155	NORFOLK VA	ORF	135,098
110	SHANGHAI	SHA	187,045	156	CHRISTCHURCH	CHC	134,058
111	WEST PALM BEACH FL	PBI	186,583	157	TULSA OK	TUL	133,739
112	HELSINKI	HEL	184,836	158	KNOXVILLE TN	TYS	133,734

Rank	City	Code	Movements	Rank	City	Code	Movements
159	NAPLES FL	APF	132,739	205	PENSACOLA FL	PNS	110,653
160	LYON	LYS	130,902	206	WELLINGTON	WLG	109,512
161	MONCTON NB	YQM	130,565	207	FAIRBANKS AK	FAI	109,286
162	MILAN	LIN	130,038	208	GLASGOW	GLA	107,959
163	MÁLAGA	AGP	129,693	209	SYRACUSE NY	SYR	107,706
164	OSAKA	ITM	128,628	210	GREENSBORO NC	GSO	107,254
165	EDINBURGH	EDI	128,158	211	ATLANTIC CITY NJ	ACY	105,994
166	BUFFALO NY	BUF	127,307	212	SAN LUIS OBISPO CA	SBP	105,789
167	BRASILIA	BSB	126,853	213	ADELAIDE	ADL	104,514
168	OSAKA	KIX	125,637	214	NAGOYA	NGO	104,033
169	BUDAPEST	BUD	124,298	215	EL PASO TX	ELP	103,990
170	NAHA	OKA	123,596	216	PERTH	PER	102,857
171	BURBANK CA	BUR	123,521	217	SPOKANE WA	GEG	101,634
172	BANGALORE	BLR	123,141	218	GRAND RAPIDS MI	GRR	101,378
173	MOSCOW	VKO	121,977	219	DES MOINES IA	DSM	100,825
174	ABERDEEN	ABZ	121,947	220	COLUMBUS OH	LCK	100,136
175	CAIRO	CAI	121,845	221	SAVANNAH GA	SAV	100,009
176	OKLAHOMA CITY OK	OKC	121,415	222	SACRAMENTO CA	MHR	99,790
177	RICHMOND VA	RIC	121,244	223	LOUISVILLE KY	LOU	99,551
178	MADRAS	MAA	121,224	224	SASKATOON SK	YXE	99,378
179	MARSEILLE	MRS	120,615	225	BERGEN	BGO	99,172
180	LONDON	LTN	120,243	226	SAPPORO	CTS	98,827
181	ALLENTOWN PA	ABE	120,098	227	CAIRNS QLD	CNS	98,538
182	EDMONTON AB	YEG	119,913	228	KANSAS CITY MO	MKC	97,924
183	RIO DE JANEIRO	GIG	119,892	229	COLUMBIA SC	CAE	97,674
184	MADISON WI	MSN	119,760	230	VALENCIA	VLC	96,591
185	QUEBEC QC	YQB	119,441	231	LONDON ON	YXU	96,270
186	XIAN	XIY	119,404	232	THUNDER BAY ON	YQT	95,919
187	CHONGQING	CKG	119,341	233	TOULOUSE	TLS	95,116
188	JACKSONVILLE FL	JAX	118,493	234	TALLAHASSEE FL	TLH	95,074
189	TEHRAN	THR	117,468	235	SÃO PAULO	CBW	93,452
190	MONTERREY	MTY	116,752	236	JEJU	CJU	93,285
191	DOHA	DOH	116,666	237	CAPE TOWN	CPT	93,232
192	JEDDAH	JED	115,819	238	LIMA	LIM	92,880
193	ANTALYA	AYT	115,002	239	YUMA AZ	YUM	92,706
194	BIRMINGHAM	BHX	114,717	240	DAYTON OH	DAY	92,461
195	GRAN CANARIA	LPA	114,351	241	FORT MYERS FL	RSW	92,008
196	NEW ORLEANS LA	MSY	114,318	242	LONDON	LCY	91,489
197	CANCUN	CUN	114,067	243	HYDERABAD	HYD	91,462
198	AKRON OH	CAK	113,454	244	SALVADOR	SSA	90,989
199	OLONGAPO CITY	SFS	112,432	245	KELOWNA BC	YLW	90,544
200	CHARLESTON SC	CHS	112,229	246	MANCHESTER, NH	MHT	90,345
201	RIYADH	RUH	112,210	247	BATON ROUGE LA	BTR	89,408
202	SEOUL	GMP	112,199	248	VENICE	VCE	88,778
203	SANTA BARBARA CA	SBA	111,690	249	HANNOVER	HAJ	88,352
204	ALBANY NY	ALB	110,775	250	MALÉ	MLE	88,308

Rank	City	Code	Movements	Rank	City	Code	Movements
251	MOBILE AL	MOB	88,230	297	KATHMANDU	KTM	77,282
252	EAST MIDLANDS	EMA	87,858	298	LINCOLN MT	LNK	77,042
253	TOLUCA	TLC	87,806	299	EGELSBACH	QEF	76,815
254	SURABAYA	SUB	87,587	300	BELFAST	BFS	76,799
255	BAHRAIN	BAH	87,417	301	BRISTOL	BRS	76,428
256	MONTEREY CA	MRY	87,312	302	HO CHI MINH CITY	SGN	75,582
257	NEW WINDSOR, NY	SWF	87,165	303	CHARLESTON SC	CRW	75,485
258	BANGKOK	DMK	87,064	304	ST MAARTEN	SXM	75,055
259	FORT WORTH TX	AFW	86,910	305	JACKSON MS	JAN	74,733
260	ST PETERSBURG	LED	86,878	306	BOURNEMOUTH	BOH	74,675
261	TORONTO ON	YTZ	86,652	307	PANAMA CITY	PTY	74,438
262	WUHAN	WUH	85,251	308	HELSINKI	HEM	73,657
263	XIAMEN	XMN	85,251	309	NADI	NAN	72,755
264	LIVERPOOL	LPL	84,880	310	CASABLANCA	CMN	72,742
265	PANAMA CITY FL	PFN	84,798	311	NAIROBI	NBO	72,692
266	PALM SPRINGS CA	PSP	84,677	312	JERSEY	JER	72,366
267	GAINESVILLE FL	GNV	84,577	313	OTTAWA ON	YOW	72,342
268	TEL-AVIV	TLV	84,568	314	NAPLES	NAP	72,330
269	KIEV	KBP	83,726	315	FUKUOKA	FUK	71,456
270	KUWAIT	KWI	83,561	316	LAS VEGAS NV	HSH	71,323
271	QING DAO	TAO	82,392	317	GUAYAQUIL	GYE	71,271
272	NANJING	NKG	82,391	318	MIDDLETOWN PA	MDT	71,011
273	DALIAN	DLC	82,367	319	CORK	ORK	70,961
274	ABU DHABI	AUH	82,287	320	CHARLEROI	CRL	70,734
275	LUXEMBOURG	LUX	82,060	321	SAN FERNANDO	SFD	70,715
276	CHANGSHA	CSX	82,041	322	BUCHAREST	OTP	70,588
277	BASEL	BSL	82,025	323	BUENOS AIRES	EZE	70,576
278	ASHEVILLE NC	AVL	81,748	324	ALAJUELA	SJO	70,532
279	BUENOS AIRES	AEP	81,340	325	BRIGHTON	BSH	70,420
280	NUREMBERG	NUE	81,082	326	FORT SMITH AR	FSM	69,177
281	MAROOCHYDORE	MCY	81,000	327	BANGOR ME	BGR	69,148
282	HALIFAX NS	YHZ	80,965	328	PORTO ALEGRE	POA	68,827
283	ABILENE TX	ABI	80,926	329	BORDEAUX	BOD	68,687
284	SIOUX FALLS SD	FSD	80,872	330	MADRID	MCV	67,927
285	LEXINGTON KY	LEX	80,807	331	BURLINGTON VT	BTV	67,389
286	MONTPELLIER	MPL	80,583	332	KAOHSIUNG	KHH	67,149
287	STAVANGER	SVG	79,904	333	BOLOGNA	BLQ	66,698
288	ROANOKE VA	ROA	79,882	334	BERLIN	SXF	66,392
289	ALICANTE	ALC	79,750	335	LEEDS	LBA	66,355
290	NEWCASTLE	NCL	79,484	336	PIARCO	POS	66,309
291	LAGOS	LOS	79,092	337	GOLD COAST	OOL	66,098
292	CALCUTTA	CCU	78,623	338	TENERIFE	TFN	65,836
293	FORT MYERS FL	FMY	77,701	339	RIO DE JANEIRO	SDU	65,689
294	MEDELLIN	EOH	77,633	340	ROME	CIA	65,633
295	MEDELLIN	MDE	77,465	341	FORT WAYNE IN	FWA	65,551
296	QUITO	UIO	77,418	342	ROTTERDAM	RTM	65,529

Rank	City	Code	Movements	Rank	City	Code	Movements
343	TIJUANA	TIJ	65,460	389	PAPEETE (TAHITI)	PPT	55,300
344	SEVILLA	SVQ	65,087	390	CALI	CLO	55,013
345	TENERIFE	TFS	65,036	391	TRONDHEIM	TRD	54,954
346	MALACCA	MKZ	64,936	392	MYRTLE BEACH SC	MYR	54,943
347	PORT ELIZABETH	PLZ	64,593	393	COVENTRY	CVT	54,925
348	PASCO WA	PSC	64,440	394	SHREVEPORT LA	SHV	54,401
349	GOTHENBURG	GOT	64,336	395	SOUTHAMPTON	SOU	54,182
350	BLOUNTVILLE TN	TRI	64,208	396	SHARJAH	SHJ	54,006
351	ANKARA/ESENBOGA	ESB	63,909	397	MEDAN	MES	53,795
352	BUSAN	PUS	63,776	398	NORWICH	NWI	53,566
353	CEDAR RAPIDS IA	CID	63,421	399	OPORTO	OPO	53,410
354	HAIKOU	HAK	63,416	400	MACAU (CHINA)	MFM	53,386
355	CLEVELAND OH	BKL	63,319	401	KARACHI	KHI	52,990
356	BILBAO	BIO	63,079	402	LANZAROTE	ACE	52,968
357	DENPASAR-BALI	DPS	62,689	403	BILLUND	BLL	52,725
358	CURITIBA	CWB	62,563	404	GULFPORT MS	GPT	52,379
359	STOCKHOLM	BMA	62,137	405	PALERMO	PMO	52,152
360	TURIN	TRN	62,136	406	KOTA KINABALU	BKI	52,047
361	GRAZ	GRZ	62,043	407	JACAREPAGUA	JCR	51,949
362	CULIACAN	CUL	61,675	408	TUNIS	TUN	51,944
363	TOPEKA KS	TOP	61,469	409	IZMIR	ADB	51,774
364	BERGAMO	BGY	61,365	410	UJUNG PANDANG	UPG	51,698
365	SABADELL	QSA	61,195	411	ANTWERP	ANR	51,589
366	CATANIA	CTA	60,953	412	BERN	BRN	51,217
367	MACAÉ	MEA	60,938	413	PEORIA IL	PIA	51,047
368	TOLEDO OH	TOL	60,277	414	LEIPZIG	LEJ	50,972
369	HUNTSVILLE AL	HSV	60,223	415	AVIGNON	AVN	50,543
370	RECIFE	REC	59,781	416	PUERTO VALLARTA	PVR	50,501
371	GUERNSEY	GCI	59,774	417	ALEXANDRIA LA	AEX	50,395
372	ROUEN	URO	59,453	418	JEREZ	XRY	50,364
373	SAYAN	SYX	59,284	419	MOLINE IL	MLI	50,294
374	BLACKPOOL	BLK	58,824	420	EXETER	EXT	50,063
375	PAU	PUF	58,380	421	BEIRUT	BEY	49,964
376	IBIZA	IBZ	57,853	422	ALGIERS	ALG	49,724
377	REGINA SK	YQR	57,802	423	TOWNSVILLE	TSV	49,604
378	TEESIDE	MME	57,515	424	BISMARCK ND	BIS	49,483
379	SALZBURG	SZG	57,065	425	KEFLAVIK	KEF	49,352
380	LARNACA AIRPORT	LCA	57,045	426	SOUTHEND	SEN	49,297
381	MEDFORD OR	MFR	56,822	427	PUNTA CANA	PUJ	48,664
382	RENNES	RNS	56,577	428	DAMMAM	DMM	48,653
383	SAULT STE MARIE ON	YAM	56,215	429	SOUTH BEND IN	SBN	48,323
384	DAR ES SALAAM	DAR	55,938	430	HERMOSILLO	HMO	48,297
385	DURBAN	DUR	55,743	431	GLASGOW	PIK	48,143
386	CONFINS	CFO	55,491	432	SHANNON	SNN	48,122
387	CONFINS	CNF	55,491	433	ISLAMABAD	ISB	48,110
388	NANTES	NTE	55,356	434	SHARM EL SHEIKH	SSH	47,699

Rank	City	Code	Movements	Rank	City	Code	Movements
435	MAUN	MUB	47,398	468	BROWNSVILLE TX	BRO	43,105
436	RIGA	RIX	47,347	469	SOFIA	SOF	43,076
437	FRIEDRICHSHAFEN	FDH	47,242	470	VERONA	VRN	43,023
438	FORTALEZA	FOR	47,226	471	BELFAST	BHD	43,022
439	KITCHENER ON	YKF	46,836	472	DHAKA	DAC	42,978
440	LIEGE	LGG	46,557	473	MONACO	MCM	42,916
441	LJUBLJANA	LJU	46,517	474	COLOMBO	CMB	42,878
442	THESSALONIKI	SKG	46,399	475	PISA	PSA	42,691
443	BELGRADE	BEG	45,770	476	INNSBRUCK	INN	42,374
444	FARO	FAO	45,428	477	PHUKET	HKT	41,719
445	SHIRAZ	SYZ	45,424	478	HURGHADA	HRG	41,595
446	GIRONA	GRO	45,282	479	MUSCAT	MCT	41,383
447	BREMEN	BRE	45,213	480	HAHN	HHN	40,980
448	STRASBOURG	SXB	45,046	481	WINDSOR ON	YQG	40,586
449	FUERTEVENTURA	FUE	44,871	482	POINTE-À-PITRE	PTP	40,367
450	ADDIS ABABA	ADD	44,811	483	KRAKOW	KRK	40,269
451	MONTEGO BAY	MBJ	44,762	484	BELÉM	BEL	40,124
452	MILWAUKEE WI	MWC	44,631	485	MALMÖ-STURUP	MMX	40,091
453	SAN JOSE DEL CABO	SJD	44,485	486	HUMBERSIDE	HUY	40,068
454	ISTANBUL	SAW	44,451	487	TROMSOE	TOS	40,063
455	ISLE OF MAN	IOM	44,406	488	VITORIA (BRAZIL)	VIX	39,777
456	HANOI	HAN	44,353	489	HERTZELIYA BETH	HRZ	39,653
457	AMMAN	AMM	44,346	490	DORTMUND	DTM	39,642
458	MANAUS	MAO	44,303	491	PADUCAH KY	PAH	39,629
459	SUBANG	SZB	44,302	492	LAHORE	LHE	39,534
460	BODO	BOO	44,149	493	CUIABA	CGB	39,443
461	LINZ	LNZ	44,118	494	MUENSTER	FMO	39,432
462	CARDIFF	CWL	43,973	495	CASPER WY	CPR	39,430
463	HERAKLION	HER	43,852	496	AHMEDABAD	AMD	39,280
464	GRENOBLE	GNB	43,309	497	PENANG	PEN	39,265
465	ST THOMAS	STT	43,282	498	INVERNESS	INV	39,139
466	ZAGREB	ZAG	43,258	499	SANDEFJORD	TRF	39,076
467	GOIANIA	GYN	43,136	500	TALLINN	TLL	38,844

Glossary

AFB
Air Force Base (USAF and, until 1947, USAAF)

Airbridge
Sometimes also referred to as 'jet bridge', the movable jetty that enables passengers to board or alight from an aircraft without using steps or airstairs.

ANGB
Air National Guard Base

BEA
British European Airways

BOAC
British Overseas Airways Corporation

City pairs
Direct flights between two cities, in contrast to 'hub and spoke' (below)

Engine numbers
Taken from the left as one faces forward, with No. 1 left wing and No. 2 right wing on a twin-engined aircraft; No. 1 left wing, No. 2 centre tail on a tri-jet, and No. 3 right wing; Nos. 1 and 2 left wing and Nos. 3 and 4 right wing on a four-engined aircraft

FAA
Federal Aviation Administration (US)

General aviation
All aviation that is not airline or military, although some exclude private flying as well, and includes police, air ambulance, crop-spraying, flying training, aerial surveys, business aviation

Hub and spoke
A system of airlines operating from hub airports with feeder routes, or spokes, radiating outwards

IATA
International Air Transport Association

Jet bridges
See airbridge above; the term 'jet' is used because, with the exception of the BAe ATP/Jetstream 61, turboprop airliners cannot use these

Mid-field terminal
Normally refers to a terminal between the runways or approach path, and only occasionally actually in the middle of the airport

NAS
Naval Air Station

NASA
National Aeronautics and Space Administration (US)

Positioning flight
A flight in which the aircraft is moved without passengers or cargo to wherever it is needed to start commercial flying. In other modes of transport this would be known as an 'empty working', 'dead mileage' or in some cases 'depot mileage'

RAF
Royal Air Force

RNAS
Royal Naval Air Station

SAS
Scandinavian Airlines System

USAAF
United States Army Air Force

USAF
United States Air Force

USN
United States Navy

Airports:

Listed alphabetically

Aberdeen Dyce: ABZ, 315
Abha: AHB, 215
Abu Dhabi International: AUH, 294
Abuja: ABV, 183
Acapulco: ACA, 171
Accra Kokoka International: ACC, 100
Adana: ADA, 291
Addis Ababa Bole International: ADD, 77
Adelaide: ADL, 20
Agadir: AGA, 173
Agana: GUM, 411
Ahmedabad: AMD, 113
Akron: CAK, 423
Alajuela: SJO, 65
Albany: ALB, 410
Albuquerque: ABQ, 394
Alghero: AHO, 139
Algiers Houari Boumediene: ALG, 13
Alicante: ALC, 260
Almeria: LEI, 270
Amman Queen Alia International: AMM, 149
Amsterdam Schiphol: AMS, 175
Anchorage International: ANC, 398
Ankara/Esenboga: ESB, 289
Antalya: AYT, 288
Aruba: AUA, 178
Astana: TSE, 150
Asturias: OVD, 268
Athens Hellinikon: ATH, 100
Atlanta Hartsfield: ATL, 326
Atlantic City: ACY, 426
Auckland International: AKL, 179
Austin: AUS, 382

Bahrain International: BAH, 25
Baltimore Washington International: BWI, 361

Bandar Seri Bagawan: BWN, 37
Bangalore: BLR, 110
Bangkok: DMK, 283
Bangkok International: BKK, 281
Barcelona: BCN, 257
Bari: BRI, 137
Barranquilla: BAQ, 65
Basle/Mulhouse: BSL, 278
Beauvais: BVA, 85
Beijing: PEK, 51
Beirut International: BEY, 157
Belem: BEL, 35
Belfast City: BHD, 320
Belfast International: BFS, 313
Belgrade Novi Beograd: BEG, 216
Belo Horizonte Confins: CNF (see also Confins
    International), 34
Bergen Flesland: BGO, 185
Berlin Schonefeld: SXF, 95
Berlin Tegel: TXL, 90
Bilbao: BIO, 265
Billund: BLL, 71
Birmingham, Alabama: BHM, 407
Birmingham International (Elmdon): BHX, 304
Bodø: BOO, 188
Bodrum: BJV, 290
Bogota El Dorado International: BOG, 63
Boise: BOI, 407
Bologna: BLQ, 135
Bombay (see Mumbai), 106
Bordeaux Merignac: BOD, 84
Boston Logan International: BOS, 354
Bourgas: BOJ, 39
Bournemouth: BOH, 324
Brasilia: BSB, 31
Bratislava M. R. Stefanik: BTS, 218

Bremen: BRE, 98
Bridgetown: BGI, 27
Brisbane International: BNE, 18
Bristol (Lulsgate): BRS, 308
Brussels National: BRU, 27
Bucharest Henri Coanda: OTP, 203
Budapest Ferihegy: BUD, 104
Buenos Aires Ministro Pistarini: AEP, 14
Buenos Aires Jorge Newbery: EZE, 15
Buffalo: BUF, 397
Burbank: BUR, 397
Burlington: BTV, 422
Busan (see Pusan), 154

Cagliari: CAG, 137
Cairns: CNS, 21
Cairo International: CAI, 74
Calcutta: CCU, 111
Calgary International: YYC, 45
Cali: CLO, 64
Calicut/Kozhikode: CCJ, 115
Campinas: VCP, 37
Cancun: CUN, 167
Cape Town D. F. Malan: CPT, 221
Caracas Simon Bolivar: CCS, 428
Cardiff Wales International: CWL, 321
Cartagena Des Indias: CTG, 65
Casablanca Mohammed V: CMN, 172
Catania: CTA, 131
Cedar Rapids: CID, 427
Changsha: CSX, 59
Chania: CHQ, 102
Charleston: CHS, 413
Charlotte Douglas Municipal: CLT, 349
Charleroi: CRL, 29
Chengdu: CTU, 54
Chiang Mai: CNX, 284
Chicago Midway: MDW, 362
Chicago O'Hare: ORD, 328
Chongqing: CKG, 57
Christchurch: CHC, 180
Cincinnati Greater Cincinnati: CVG, 367
Cleveland: CLE, 374
Cochin: COK, 113
Colorado Springs: COS, 414
Cologne/Bonn: CGN, 92
Colombo Bandaranaike International: CMB, 270

Columbia: CAE, 425
Columbus: CMH, 388
Confins International: CNF (see also Belo Horizonte), 35
Copenhagen: CPH, 70
Cork: ORK, 126
Cuiabá: CGB, 37
Culiacan: CUL, 171
Curaçao: CUR, 179
Curitiba: CWB, 34

Dakar-Yoff: DKR, 215
Dalian: DLC, 59
Dallas: DAL, 385
Dallas/Fort Worth: DFW, 332
Dammam: DMM, 214
Dar-Es-Salaam: DAR, 281
Dayton: DAY, 411
Denpasar-Bali: DPS, 117
Denver: DEN, 334
Des Moines: DSM, 416
Detroit Metropolitan: DTW, 343
Dhaka Zia International: DAC, 26
Djerba (see Jerba), 287
Doha International: DOH, 202
Doncaster/Sheffield Robin Hood: DSA, 325
Dortmund Wickede: DTM, 98
Dresden: DRS, 99
Dubai International: DXB, 292
Dublin International: DUB, 123
Dubrovnik: DBV, 67
Durban Louis Botha: DUR, 221
Dusseldorf: DUS, 94

East Midlands/Nottingham International: EMA, 312
Edinburgh (Turnhouse): EDI, 306
Edmonton International: YEG, 46
Eilat: ETH, 127
Eindhoven: EIN, 177
Ekaterinburg: SVX, 210
El Paso Texas: ELP, 406
El Salvador International: SSA, 321

Faro: FAO, 201
Florence: FLR, 138
Florianopolis: FLN, 36
Fort-de-France: FDF, 86

Fort Lauderdale Hollywood International: FLL, 358
Fort Myers: RSW, 385
Fortaleza: FOR, 35
Frankfurt am Main: FRA, 88
Fresno: FAT, 423
Fukuoka: FUK, 144
Fuerteventura: FUE, 264
Funchal: FNC, 202

Geneva International: GVA, 277
Genoa: GOA, 139
Girona: GRO, 263
Glasgow: GLA, 307
Glasgow Prestwick: PIK, 318
Goa: GOI, 114
Goiania: GYN, 37
Gold Coast: OOL, 22
Gothenburg Landvetter: GOT, 273
Gran Canaria Las Palmas: LPA, 260
Granada: GRX, 268
Grand Rapids: GRR, 416
Greensboro: GSO, 413
Guadalajara: GDL, 167
Guangzhou: CAN, 51
Guayaquil: GYE, 73
Guwahati: GAU, 115

Hahn: HHN, 97
Haikou: HAK, 59
Halifax International: YHZ, 48
Hamburg Fuhlsbuttel: HAM, 91
Hangzhou: HGH, 56
Hanover: HAJ, 96
Hanoi Noi Bai International: HAN, 430
Hartford: BDL, 394
Hat Yai: HDY, 285
Helsinki Vantaa: HEL, 78
Heraklion: HER, 101
Hermosillo: HMO, 170
Ho Chi Minh City: SGN, 429
Hong Kong International: HKG, 61
Houston: IAH, 338
Houston Intercontinental: HOU, 382
Huntsville: HSV, 425
Hurghada: HRG, 75
Hyderabad: HYD, 112

Ibiza: IBZ, 263
Incheon (see Seoul), 152
Indianapolis: IND, 383
Isfahan: IFN, 122
Islamabad Chaklala: ISB, 193
Istanbul Sabiha Gökçen: SAW, 290
Istanbul Ataturk International: IST, 287
Izmir: ADB, 288

Jackson, Mississippi: JAN, 422
Jacksonville Florida: JAX, 396
Jaipur: JAI, 116
Jakarta Soekarno-Hatta Internationa: CGK, 116
Jeddah King Abdul Aziz International: JED, 212
Jeju: CJU, 154
Jerba/Djerba: DJE, 287
Jerez: XRY, 268
Jersey States: JER, 323
Johannesburg International (Jan Smuts): JNB, 219
Johor Bharu: JHB, 162

Kagoshima: KOJ, 149
Kansas: City: MCI, 372
Kaohsiung: KHH, 280
Karachi Quaid-E-Azam International: KHI, 190
Kathmandu Tribhuvan: KTM, 174
Katowice: KTW, 199
Keflavik (see Reyjavik), 105
Kelowna International: YLW, 49
Kerkyra (Kerkira): CFU, 102
Khartoum: KRT, 271
Kiev Borispol International: KBP, 291
Kingston Norman Manley International: KIN, 140
Knoxville: TYS, 417
Kos: KGS, 102
Kota Kinabalu: BKJ, 159
Krakow: KRK, 198
Kuala Lumpur Subang International: KUL, 158
Kuching: KCH, 160
Kunming: KMG, 55
Kuwait International: KWI, 155

La Coruna: LCG, 269
La Palma: SPC, 269
Lagos: LOS, 182
Lahore: LHE, 191
Langkawi: LGK, 162

Lanzarote: ACE, 262
Lanzhou: LHW, 60
Larnaca: LCA, 67
Las Vegas: LAS, 337
Leeds (Leeds/Bradford): LBA, 317
Leipzig: LEJ, 98
Leon/Gaunajuato: BJX, 171
Lijiang: LJG, 60
Lima Jorge Chavez International: LIM, 194
Lisbon: LIS, 200
Liverpool John Lennon: LPL, 310
Ljubljana: LJU, 219
London City: LCY, 316
London Gatwick: LGW, 298
London Heathrow: LHR, 295
London Luton: LTN, 303
London Stansted: STN, 300
Long Beach California: LGB, 409
Los Angeles: LAX, 330
Louisville: SDF, 403
Luqa International: MLA, 163
Luxembourg Findel: LUX, 158
Luxor: LXR, 75
Lyon Satolas: LYS, 82

Macau International: MFM, 62
Madinah: MED, 214
Madison: MSN, 420
Madras: MAA, 109
Madrid Barajas: MAD, 223
Malaga: AGP, 259
Male: MLE, 162
Malmo-Sturup: MMX, 274
Manaus: MAO, 36
Manchester International: MAN, 301
Manchester, New Hampshire: MHT, 402
Manila Ninoy Aquino International: MNL, 195
Marrakech: RAK, 173
Marseilles Provence: MRS, 83
Mashhad (Meshed): MHD, 122
Medellin: MDE, 64
Medan: MES, 118
Melbourne Tullamarine: MEL, 17
Memphis: MEM, 374
Menorca: MAH, 267
Merida: MID, 269
Mexico City Lic Benito Juarez International: MEX, 165

Miami International: MIA, 347
Middletown: MDT, 424
Milan Bergamo: BGY, 133
Milan Linate: LIN, 130
Milan Malpensa: MXP, 129
Milwaukee: MKE, 389
Minneapolis St Paul International: MSP, 346
Miri: MYY, 161
Mombasa: MBA, 151
Monastir Habib Bourguiba: MIR, 286
Montevideo: MVD, 427
Montpellier: MPL, 86
Montego Bay Sangster International: MBJ, 139
Monterrey: MTY, 168
Montreal Mirabel: YUL, 43
Moscow Domodedovo: DME, 205
Moscow Shermetyevo: SVO, 206
Moscow Vnukovo: VKO, 208
Mugla: DLM, 290
Munster: FMO, 99
Munich Riem: MUC, 89
Mumbai (Bombay): BOM, 106
Murcia: MJV, 268
Muscat Seeb: MCT, 173
Myrtle Beach: MYR, 418

Nadi: NAN, 77
Nagoya: NGO, 148
Naha: OKA, 147
Nairobi Jomo Kenyatta International: NBO, 151
Nanjing: NKG, 58
Nantes Chateau Bougon: NTE, 85
Naples Capodichino: NAP, 132
Nashville: BNA, 387
Natal: NAT, 36
New Delhi Indira Ghandi International: DEL, 108
New Orleans: MSY, 390
New York John F. Kennedy: JFK, 335
New York La Guardia: LGA, 355
Newark: EWR, 342
Newcastle International: NCL, 309
Nice Côte d'Azure: NCE, 82
Norfolk, Virginia: ORF, 404
Novosibirsk: OVB, 211
Nuremberg: NUE, 97

Oakland: OAK, 370
Oklahoma City: OKC, 403
Olbia: OLB, 138
Omaha: OMA, 401
Ontario (California): ONT, 391
Oporto/Porto: OPO, 201
Orlando International: MCO, 340
Osaka: ITM, 145
Osaka International: KIX, 146
Oslo Fornebu: OSL, 184
Ottawa Uplands International: YOW, 47

Padang: PDG, 119
Palembang: PLM, 120
Palermo: PMO, 134
Palm Springs: PSP, 420
Palma De Mallorca Son Sant Joan: PMI, 258
Panama City Tocumen International: PTY, 193
Papeete: PPT, 87
Paphos: PFO, 68
Paris Charles de Gaulle: CDG, 79
Paris Orly: ORY, 80
Pekanbaru: PKU, 119
Penang: PEN, 161
Pensacola: PNS, 418
Perth: PER, 19
Philadelphia International: PHL, 350
Phnom Penh: PNH, 40
Phoenix: PHX, 340
Phuket: HKT, 282
Pisa Galileo Galilei: PSA, 136
Pittsburgh Greater Pittsburgh: PIT, 380
Plaine Magnien: MRU, 165
Point-à-Pitre Raizet: PTP, 103
Pontianak: PNK, 121
Port Elizabeth: PLZ, 222
Port of Spain Piarco International: POS, 285
Portland: PDX, 371
Porto Alegre: POA, 33
Prague Ruzyne: PRG, 69
Pristina: PRN, 155
Puerto Plata: POP, 72
Puerto Vallarta: PVR, 170
Punta Cana: PUJ, 71
Pusan: PUS, 154

Qing Dao: TAO, 59
Quito Mariscal Sucre: UIO, 72

Raleigh-Durham: RDU, 378
Recife: REC, 33
Reno: RNO, 400
Reus: REU, 269
Reykjavik Keflavik International: KEF, 105
Richmond, Virginia: RIC, 405
Riga International: RIX, 156
Rio de Janeiro Galeao International: GIG, 31
Rio de Janeiro Santos Dumont: SDU, 35
Riyadh: RUH, 213
Rodos/Rhodes: RHO, 102
Rome Ciampino: CIA, 133
Rome Leonardo da Vinci (Fiumicino): FCO, 128
Rotterdam: RTM, 177

Sacramento: SMF, 376
Saint-Denis: RUN, 87
St Louis: STL, 368
St Maarten: SXM, 178
St Petersburg Pulkovo: LED, 209
St Thomas: STT, 425
Salt Lake City: SLC, 359
Salvador, Brazil: SSA, 32
Salzburg: SZG, 24
Samara (Kuibyshev): KUF, 212
San Antonio: SAT, 384
San Diego: SAN, 368
San Francisco: SFO, 344
San Jose: SJC, 376
San José de Cabo: SJD, 170
San Juan Louis Munoz Marin International: SJU, 377
San Salvador: SAL, 76
Sana'a: SAH, 431
Sandefjord: TRF, 189
Sanford: SFB, 417
Santa Anna: SNA, 379
Santiago de Compostela: SCQ, 267
Santo Domingo Las Americas: SDQ, 72
São Paulo: CGH, 30
São Paulo Guarulhos International: GRU, 30
Sapporo: CTS, 143
Sarasota: SRQ, 421
Savannah: SAV, 415
Sayan: SYX, 60

Seattle Tacoma International: SEA, 352
Seoul Gimpo International: GMP, 153
Seoul Incheon: ICN, 152
Seville: SVQ, 264
Shanghai: SHA, 53
Shanghai: PVG, 52
Shannon: SNN, 124
Sharjah: SHJ, 294
Sharm El Sheikh: SSH, 75
Shenzhen: SZX, 54
Shiraz: SYZ, 122
Siem Reap: REP, 40
Singapore Changi International: SIN, 217
Sofia International: LHE, 38
Southampton International: SOU, 321
Split: SPU, 66
Spokane: GEG, 405
Stavanger Sola: SVG, 186
Stockholm Bromma: BMA, 274
Stockholm Arlanda: ARN, 272
Stockholm Skavsta: NYO, 274
Strasbourg Entzheim: SXB, 86
Stuttgart: STR, 93
Surabaya: SUB, 119
Sydney Kingsford Smith International: SYD, 16
Syracuse, New York: SYR, 412

Taipei Chiang Kai Shek International: TPE, 279
Tallin: TLL, 76
Tampa St Petersburg: TPA, 363
Tashkent Yuzhny: TAS, 428
Tehran Mehrabad: THR, 121
Tel-Aviv Ben Gurion International: TLV, 126
Tenerife North: TFN, 266
Tenerife South: TFS, 261
Thessaloniki: SKG, 102
Tijuana: TIJ, 169
Tirana Nene Teresa: TIA, 13
Tokyo Haneda: HND, 141
Tokyo Narita: NRT, 142
Toluca: TLC, 169
Toronto Lester B. Pearson International: YYZ, 41
Toulouse Blagnac: TLS, 83
Townsville: TSV, 22

Trabzon: TZX, 291
Trivandrum: TRV, 114
Tromsoe: TOS, 188
Trondheim: TRD, 187
Tucson: TUS, 400
Tulsa: TUL, 408
Tunis Carthage: TUN, 286
Turin Citta Di Torino: TRN, 137

Ujung Pandang: UPG, 120

Valencia: VLC, 261
Vancouver International: YVR, 42
Varna: VAR, 39
Venice Marco Polo: VCE, 131
Veracruz: VER, 172
Verona: VRN, 136
Victoria, British Columbia: YYJ, 49
Vienna: VIE, 24
Vigo: VGO, 269
Vilnius: VNO, 158
Vitoria (Brazil): VIX, 36

Warsaw Frederic Chopin: WAW, 197
Washington Dulles International: IAD, 357
Washington National: DCA, 364
Wellington: WLG, 180
West Palm Beach International: PBI, 392
White Plains: HPN, 419
Wichita: ICT, 420
Winnipeg International: YWG, 48
Wroclaw Copernicus: WRO, 199
Wuhan: WUH, 58

Xiamen: XMN, 57
Xi'an: XIY, 56
Xishuangbanna: JHG, 60

Yerevan: EVN, 15

Zagreb: ZAG, 66
Zhang Jiajie: DYG, 61
Zurich: ZRH, 275

IATA codes:

Listed alphabetically

ABQ	Albuquerque, USA, 394		BEG	Belgrade, Serbia, 216
ABV	Abuja, Nigeria, 183		BEL	Belem, Brazil, 35
ABZ	Aberdeen, UK, 315		BEY	Beirut, Lebanon, 157
ACA	Acapulco, Mexico, 171		BFS	Belfast International, UK, 313
ACC	Accra, Ghana, 100		BGI	Bridgetown, Barbados, 27
ACE	Lanzarote, Spain, 262		BGO	Bergen, Norway, 185
ACY	Atlantic City, USA, 426		BGY	Bergamo, Italy, 133
ADA	Adana, Turkey, 291		BHD	Belfast City, UK, 320
ADB	Izmir, Turkey, 288		BHM	Birmingham, USA, 407
ADD	Addis Ababa, Ethiopia, 76		BHX	Birmingham, UK, 304
ADL	Adelaide, Australia, 20		BIO	Bilbao, Spain, 265
AEP	Buenos Aires Ministro Pistarini, Argentina, 15		BJV	Bodrum, Turkey, 290
AGA	Agadir, Morocco, 173		BJX	Leon/Guanajuato, Mexico, 171
AGP	Malaga, Spain, 259		BKI	Kota Kinabalu, Malaysia, 159
AHB	Abha, Saudi Arabia, 215		BKK	Bangkok, Thailand, 281
AHO	Alghero, Italy, 139		BLL	Billund, Denmark, 71
AKL	Auckland, New Zealand, 179		BLQ	Bologna, Italy, 135
ALB	Albany, USA, 410		BLR	Bangalore, India, 110
ALC	Alicante, Spain, 260		BMA	Stockholm Bromma, Sweden, 274
ALG	Algiers, Algeria, 13		BNA	Nashville, USA, 387
AMD	Ahmedabad, India, 113		BNE	Brisbane, Australia, 18
AMM	Amman, Jordan, 149		BOD	Bordeaux, France, 84
AMS	Amsterdam, Netherlands, 175		BOG	Bogota, Colombia, 63
ANC	Anchorage, USA, 398		BOH	Bournemouth, UK, 324
ARN	Stockholm Arlanda, Sweden, 272		BOI	Boise, USA, 407
ATH	Athens, Greece, 100		BOJ	Bourgas, Bulgaria, 39
ATL	Atlanta, USA, 326		BOM	Mumbai (Bombay), India, 106
AUA	Aruba, Netherlands Antilles, 178		BOO	Bodo, Norway, 188
AUH	Abu Dhabi, United Arab Emirates, 294		BOS	Boston, USA, 354
AUS	Austin, USA, 382		BRE	Bremen, Germany, 98
AYT	Anatalya, Turkey, 288		BRI	Bari, Italy, 137
			BRS	Bristol, UK, 308
BAH	Bahrain, 25		BRU	Brussels, Belgium, 27
BAQ	Barranquilla, Colombia, 65		BSB	Brasilia, Brazil, 31
BCN	Barcelona, Spain, 257		BSL	Basel (Basle)/Mulhouse, Switzerland and
BDL	Hartford, USA, 394			France, 278

BTS	Bratislava, Slovakia, 218		CTG	Cartegena de Indias, Colombia, 65
BTV	Burlington, USA, 422		CTS	New Chitose/Sapporo, Japan, 143
BUD	Budapest, Hungary, 104		CTU	Chengdu, People's Republic of China, 54
BUF	Buffalo, USA, 397		CUL	Culiacan, Mexico, 171
BUR	Burbank, USA, 397		CUN	Cancun, Mexico, 167
BVA	Beauvais, France, 85		CUR	Curaçao, Netherlands Antilles, 179
BWI	Baltimore, USA, 361		CVG	Cincinnati, USA, 367
BWN	Bandar Seri Begawan, Brunei, 37		CWB	Curitiba, Brazil, 34
			CWL	Cardiff, UK, 321
CAE	Columbia, USA, 425			
CAG	Cagliari, Italy, 137		DAC	Dhaka, Bangladesh, 26
CAI	Cairo, Egypt, 74		DAL	Dallas Love Field, USA, 385
CAK	Akron, USA, 423		DAR	Dar-es-Salaam, Tanzania, 285
CAN	Guangzhou, Peoples' Republic of China, 51		DAY	Dayton, USA, 411
CCJ	Kozhikode (Calicut), India, 115		DBV	Dubrovnik, Croatia, 67
CCS	Caracas, Venezuela, 428		DCA	Washington National, USA, 364
CCU	Calcutta, India, 111		DEL	New Delhi, India, 108
CDG	Paris Charles de Gaulle, France, 79		DEN	Denver, USA, 334
CFO	Confins Confreza, Brazil, 35		DFW	Dallas Fort Worth, USA, 332
CFU	Corfu, Greece, 102		DJE	Jerba (Djerba), Tunisia, 287
CGB	Cuiabá, Brazil, 37		DKR	Dakar-Yoff, Senegal, 215
CGH	São Paulo, Brazil, 30		DLC	Dalian, People's Republic of China, 59
CGK	Jakarta, Indonesia, 116		DLM	Mugla, Turkey, 290
CGN	Cologne/Bonn, Germany, 92		DME	Moscow Domededovo, Russia, 205
CHC	Christchurch, New Zealand, 180		DMK	Bangkok, Thailand, 283
CHQ	Chania, Greece, 102		DMM	Damman, Saudi Arabia, 214
CHS	Charleston, USA, 413		DOH	Doha, UAE, 202
CIA	Rome Ciampino, Italy, 133		DPS	Denpasar-Bali, Indonesia, 117
CID	Cedar Rapids, USA, 427		DRS	Dresden, Germany, 99
CJU	Jeju, South Korea, 154		DSA	Doncaster-Sheffield, UK, 325
CKG	Chongqing, People's Republic of China, 57		DSM	Des Moines, USA, 416
CLE	Cleveland, USA, 374		DTM	Dortmund, Germany, 98
CLO	Cali, Colombia, 64		DTW	Detroit, USA, 343
CLT	Charlotte, USA, 349		DUB	Dublin, Irish Republic, 123
CMB	Colombo, Sri Lanka, 270		DUR	Durban, South Africa, 221
CMH	Columbus, USA, 388		DUS	Dusseldorf, Germany, 94
CMN	Casablanca, Morocco, 172		DXB	Dubai, UAE, 292
CNF	Belo Horizonte Confins, Brazil, 34		DYG	Zhang Jiajie, People's Republic of
CNS	Cairns, Australia, 21			China, 61
CNX	Chiang Mai, Thailand, 284			
COK	Cochin/Kochi, India, 113		EDI	Edinburgh, UK, 306
COS	Colorado Springs, USA, 412		EIN	Eindhoven, Netherlands, 177
CPH	Copenhagen, Denmark, 70		ELP	El Paso, USA, 406
CPT	Cape Town, South Africa, 221		EMA	East Midlands, UK, 312
CRL	Charleroi, Belgium, 29		ESB	Ankara/Esenboga, Turkey, 289
CSX	Changsha, People's Republic of China, 59		ETH	Eilat, Israel, 127
CTA	Catania, Sicily, Italy, 131		EVN	Yerevan, Armenia, 15

EWR	Newark, USA, 342	
EZE	Buenos Aires Jorge Newbery, Argentina, 14	
FAO	Faro, Portugal, 201	
FAT	Fresno, USA, 423	
FCO	Rome Leonardo Da Vinci (Fiumicino), Italy, 128	
FDF	Fort-de-France, Martinique, 86	
FLL	Fort Lauderdale, USA, 358	
FLN	Florianopolis, Brazil, 36	
FLR	Florence, Italy, 138	
FMO	Munster, Germany, 99	
FNC	Funchal, Portugal, 202	
FOR	Fortaleza, Brazil, 35	
FRA	Frankfurt, Germany, 88	
FUE	Fuerteventura, Spain, 264	
FUK	Fukuoka, Japan, 144	
GAU	Guwahati, India, 115	
GDL	Guadalajara, Mexico, 167	
GEG	Spokane, USA, 405	
GIG	Rio de Janeiro Galeao, Brazil, 31	
GLA	Glasgow, UK, 307	
GMP	Seoul Gimpo, South Korea, 153	
GOA	Genoa, Italy, 139	
GOI	Goa, India, 114	
GOT	Gothenburg, Sweden, 273	
GRO	Girona, Spain, 263	
GRR	Grand Rapids, USA, 416	
GRU	São Paulo, Brazil, 30	
GRX	Granada, Spain, 268	
GSO	Greensboro, USA, 413	
GUM	Agana, Guam, 411	
GVA	Geneva, Switzerland, 277	
GYE	Guayaquil, Ecuador, 73	
GYN	Goiania, Brazil, 37	
HAJ	Hannover, Germany, 96	
HAK	Haikou, People's Republic of China, 59	
HAM	Hamburg, Germany, 91	
HAN	Hanoi, Vietnam, 430	
HDY	Hat Yai, Thailand, 285	
HEL	Helsinki, Finland, 78	
HER	Heraklion, Greece, 101	
HGH	Hangzhou, People's Republic of China, 56	
HHN	Hahn, Germany, 97	
HKG	Hong Kong, 61	

HKT	Phuket, Thailand, 282
HMO	Hermosillo, Mexico, 170
HND	Tokyo Haneda, Japan, 141
HPN	White Plains, USA, 419
HRG	Hurghada, Egypt, 75
HOU	Houston, USA, 382
HSV	Huntsville, USA, 425
HYD	Hyderabad, India, 112
IAD	Washington Dulles, USA, 357
IAH	Houston, USA, 338
IBZ	Ibiza, Spain, 263
ICN	Seoul Incheon, South Korea, 152
ICT	Wichita, USA, 420
IFN	Isfahan (Esfahan), Iran, 122
IND	Indianapolis, USA, 383
ISB	Islamabad, Pakistan, 193
IST	Istanbul Ataturk, Turkey, 287
ITM	Osaka, Japan, 145
JAI	Jaipur, India, 116
JAN	Jackson, USA, 422
JAX	Jacksonville, USA, 396
JED	Jeddah, Saudi Arabia, 212
JER	Jersey, Channel Islands (UK associated territory), 323
JFK	New York John F. Kennedy, USA, 335
JHB	Johor Bahru, Malaysia, 162
JHG	Xishuangbanna, People's Republic of China, 60
JNB	Johannesburg, South Africa, 219
KBP	Kiev, Ukraine, 291
KCH	Kuching, Malaysia, 160
KEF	Keflavik, Iceland, 105
KHH	Kaohsiung, Taiwan, 280
KHI	Karachi, Pakistan, 190
KIN	Kingston, Jamaica, 140
KIX	Osaka Kansai, Japan, 146
KMG	Kunming, People's Republic of China, 55
KOJ	Kagoshima, Japan, 149
KGS	Kos, Greece, 102
KRK	Krakow, Poland, 198
KRT	Khartoum, Sudan, 271
KTM	Kathmandu, Nepal, 174
KTW	Katowice, Poland, 199
KUF	Samara, Russia, 212

KUL   Kuala Lumpur, Malaysia, 158
KWI   Kuwait, 155

LAS   Las Vegas, USA, 337
LAX   Los Angeles, USA, 330
LBA   Leeds/Bradford, UK, 317
LCA   Laranca, Cyprus, 67
LCG   La Coruna, Spain, 269
LCY   London City, UK, 316
LED   St Petersburg, Russia, 209
LEI   Almeria, Spain, 270
LEJ   Leipzig, Germany, 98
LGA   New York La Guardia, USA, 355
LGB   Long Beach, USA, 409
LGK   Langkawi, Malaysia, 162
LGW   London Gatwick, UK, 298
LHE   Lahore, Pakistan, 191
LHR   London Heathrow, UK, 295
LHW   Lanzhou, People's Republic of China, 60
LIM   Lima, Peru, 194
LIN   Milan Linate, Italy, 130
LIS   Lisbon, Portugal, 200
LJG   Lijiang, People's Republic of China, 60
LJU   Ljubljana, Slovenia, 219
LOS   Lagos, Nigeria, 182
LPA   Gran Canaria, Spain, 260
LPL   Liverpool, UK, 310
LTN   London Luton, UK, 303
LUX   Luxembourg, 158
LXR   Luxor, Egypt, 75
LYS   Lyons, France, 82

MAA   Madras, India, 109
MAD   Madrid, Spain, 223
MAH   Menorca, Spain, 267
MAN   Manchester, UK, 301
MAO   Manaus, Brazil, 36
MBA   Mombasa, Kenya, 151
MBJ   Montego Bay, Jamaica, 139
MCI   Kansas City, 372
MCO   Orlando, USA, 340
MCT   Muscat, UAE, 173
MDE   Medellin, Colombia, 64
MDT   Middletown, USA, 424
MDW   Chicago Midway, USA, 362
MEL   Melbourne, Australia, 17
MED   Madinah, Saudi Arabia, 214

MEM   Memphis, USA, 374
MES   Medan, Indonesia, 118
MEX   Mexico City, Mexico, 65
MFM   Macao, 62
MHD   Mashhad, Iran, 122
MHT   Manchester, USA, 402
MIA   Miami, USA, 347
MID   Merida, Mexico, 269
MIR   Monastir, Tunisia, 286
MJV   Murcia, Spain, 268
MKE   Milwaukee, USA, 389
MLA   Luqa, Malta, 163
MLE   Male, Maldives, 162
MMX   Malmo-Sturup, Sweden, 274
MNL   Manila, Philippines, 195
MPL   Montpellier, France, 86
MRS   Marseilles, France, 83
MRU   Plaine Magnien, Mauritius, 165
MSN   Madison, USA, 420
MSP   Minneapolis St Paul, USA, 346
MSY   New Orleans, USA, 390
MTY   Monterrey, Mexico, 168
MUC   Munich, Germany, 89
MVD   Montevideo, Uruguay, 427
MXP   Milan Malpensa, Italy, 129
MYR   Myrtle Beach, USA, 418
MYY   Miri, Malaysia, 161

NAN   Nadi/Nandi, Fiji, 77
NAP   Naples, Italy, 132
NAT   Natal, Brazil, 36
NBO   Nairobi, Kenya, 151
NCE   Nice, France, 82
NCL   Newcastle, UK, 309
NGO   Nagoya, Japan, 148
NKG   Nanjing, People's Republic of China, 58
NRT   Tokyo Narita, Japan, 142
NTE   Nantes, France, 85
NUE   Nuremberg, Germany, 97
NYO   Stockholm Skavasta, Sweden, 274

OAK   Oakland, USA, 370
OKA   Naha, Japan, 147
OKC   Oklahoma City, USA, 403
OLB   Olbia, Italy, 138
OMA   Omaha, USA, 401
ONT   Ontario, USA, 391

OOL	Gold Coast, Australia, 22		RAK	Marrakech, Morocco, 173
OPO	Oporto, Portugal, 201		RDU	Raleigh Durham, 378
ORD	Chicago O'Hare, USA, 328		REC	Recife, Brazil, 33
ORF	Norfolk, USA, 404		REP	Siem Reap, Cambodia, 40
ORK	Cork, Irish Republic, 126		REU	Reus, Spain, 269
ORY	Paris Orly, France, 80		RHO	Rhodes, Greece, 102
OSL	Oslo, Norway, 184		RIC	Richmond, USA, 405
OTP	Bucharest, Romania, 203		RIX	Riga, Latvia, 156
OVB	Novosibirsk, Russia, 211		RNO	Reno, USA, 400
OVD	Asturias, Spain, 268		RSW	Fort Myers, USA, 385
			RTM	Rotterdam, Netherlands, 177
PBI	West Palm Beach, USA, 392		RUH	Riyadh, Saudi Arabia, 213
PDG	Padang, Indonesia, 119		RUN	Saint-Denis, Reunion, 87
PDX	Portland, USA, 371			
PEK	Beijing, People's Republic of China, 51		SAH	Sana'a, Yemen, 431
PEN	Penang, Malaysia, 161		SAL	San Salvador, El Salvador, 76
PER	Perth, Australia, 19		SAN	San Diego, USA, 366
PFO	Paphos, Cyprus, 68		SAT	San Antonio, USA, 384
PHL	Philadelphia, USA, 350		SAV	Savannah, USA, 415
PHX	Phoenix, USA, 340		SAW	Istanbul Sabiha Gökçen, Turkey, 290
PIK	Glasgow Prestwick, UK, 318		SCQ	Santiago de Compostela, Spain, 267
PIT	Pittsburgh, USA, 380		SDF	Louisville, USA, 403
PKU	Pekanbaru, Indonesia, 119		SDQ	Santo Domingo, Dominican Republic, 72
PLM	Palembang, Indonesia, 120		SDU	Rio de Janeiro Santos Dumont, Brazil, 35
PLZ	Port Elizabeth, South Africa, 222		SEA	Seattle Tacoma, USA, 352
PMI	Palma de Mallorca, Spain, 258		SFB	Sanford, USA, 417
PMO	Palermo, Sicily, Italy, 135		SFO	San Francisco, USA, 344
PNH	Phnom Penh, Cambodia, 40		SGN	Ho Chi Minh City, Vietnam, 429
PNK	Pontianak, Indonesia, 121		SHA	Shanghai Hongqiao, People's Republic of China, 53
PNS	Pensacola, USA, 418			
POA	Porto Alegre, Brazil, 33		SHJ	Sharjah, UAE, 294
POP	Puerto Plata, Dominican Republic, 72		SIN	Singapore, 217
POS	Piarco, Trinidad, 285		SJC	San Jose, USA, 376
PRG	Prague, Czech Republic, 69		SJD	San José del Cabo, Mexico, 170
PRN	Pristina, Kosovo, 155		SJO	Alajuela, Costa Rica, 65
PSA	Pisa, Italy, 136		SJU	San Juan, Puerto Rico, 377
PSP	Palm Springs, USA, 420		SKG	Thessalonica, Greece, 102
PPT	Papeete, Tahiti, 87		SLC	Salt Lake City, USA, 359
PTP	Point-à-Pitre, Guadeloupe, 103		SMF	Sacramento, USA, 376
PTY	Panama City, Panama, 193		SNA	Santa Ana, USA, 379
PUJ	Punta Cana, Dominican Republic, 71		SNN	Shannon, Irish Republic, 124
PUS	Busan (Pusan), South Korea, 154		SOF	Sofia, Bulgaria, 38
PVG	Shanghai Pudong, People's Republic of China, 52		SOU	Southampton, UK, 321
			SPC	La Palma, Spain, 269
PVR	Puerto Vallarta, Mexico, 170		SPU	Split, Croatia, 66
			SRQ	Sarasota, USA, 421
			SSA	Salvador, Brazil, 32

SSH	Sharm el Sheikh, Egypt, 75		TUS	Tucson, USA, 400
STL	St Louis, USA, 368		TXL	Berlin Tegel, Germany, 90
STN	London Stansted, UK, 300		TYS	Knoxville, USA, 417
STR	Stuttgart, Germany, 93		TZX	Trabzon, Turkey, 291
STT	St Thomas, US Virgin Islands, 425			
SUB	Surabaya, Indonesia, 119		UIO	Quito, Ecuador, 72
SVG	Stavanger, Norway, 186		UPG	Ujung Pandang, Indonesia, 120
SVO	Moscow Shermetyevo, Russia, 206			
SVQ	Seville, Spain, 264		VAR	Varna, Bulgaria, 39
SVX	Ekaterinburg, Russia, 210		VCE	Venice, Italy, 131
SXB	Strasbourg, France, 86		VCP	Campinas, Brazil, 37
SXF	Berlin Schonefeld, Germany, 95		VER	Veracruz, Mexico, 172
SXM	St Maarten, Netherlands Antilles, 179		VGO	Vigo, Spain, 269
SYD	Sydney, Australia, 16		VIE	Vienna, Austria, 24
SYZ	Shiraz, Iran, 122		VIX	Vitoria, Brazil, 36
SYR	Syracuse, USA, 412		VLC	Valencia, Spain, 261
SYX	Sanya (Sayan), People's Republic of China, 60		VKO	Moscow Vnukovo, Russia, 208
SZG	Salzburg, Austria, 24		VNO	Vilnius, Lithuania, 158
SZX	Shenzen, People's Republic of China, 54		VRN	Verona, Italy, 136
TAO	Qing Dao, People's Republic of China, 59		WAW	Warsaw, 197
TAS	Tashkent, Uzbekistan, 428		WLG	Wellington, New Zealand, 181
TFN	Teneriffe North, Spain, 266		WRO	Wroclaw, Poland, 199
TFS	Teneriffe South, Spain, 261		WUH	Wuhan, People's Republic of China, 58
THR	Tehran, Iran, 121			
TIA	Tirana, Albania, 13		XIY	Xi'an, People's Republic of China, 56
TIJ	Tijuana, Mexico, 169		XMN	Xiamen, People's Republic of China, 57
TLC	Toluca, Mexico, 169		XRY	Jerez, Spain, 268
TLL	Tallinn, Estonia, 76			
TLS	Toulouse, France, 83		YEG	Edmonton, Canada, 46
TLV	Tel Aviv, Israel, 126		YHZ	Halifax, Canada, 48
TOS	Tromso, Norway, 188		YLW	Kelowna, Canada, 49
TPA	Tampa St Petersburg, USA, 363		YOW	Ottawa, Canada, 47
TPE	Taipei, Taiwan, 279		YUL	Montreal, Canada, 43
TRD	Trondheim, Norway, 187		YVR	Vancouver, Canada, 42
TRF	Sandefjord, Norway, 189		YWG	Winnipeg, Canada, 48
TRN	Turin, Italy, 137		YYC	Calgary, Canada, 45
TRV	Thiruvananthapuram (Trivandrum), India, 114		YYJ	Victoria, Canada, 49
TSE	Astana, Kazakhstan, 150		YYZ	Toronto, Canada, 41
TSV	Townsville, Australia, 22			
TUL	Tulsa, USA, 408		ZAG	Zagreb, Croatia, 66
TUN	Tunis, Tunisia, 286		ZRH	Zurich, Switzerland, 275